ROMAN RELIGION

EDINBURGH READINGS ON THE ANCIENT WORLD

GENERAL EDITORS
Michele George, *McMaster University*
Thomas Harrison, *University of St Andrews*

ADVISORY EDITORS
Paul Cartledge, *University of Cambridge*
Richard Saller, *University of Chicago*

This series introduces English-speaking students to central themes in the history of the ancient world and to the range of scholarly approaches to those themes, within and across disciplines. Each volume, edited and introduced by a leading specialist, contains a selection of the most important work, including a significant proportion of translated material. The editor also provides a guide to the history of modern scholarship on the subject. Passages in ancient languages are translated; technical terms, ancient and modern, are explained.

PUBLISHED
Sparta
Edited by Michael Whitby

Greeks and Barbarians
Edited by Thomas Harrison

The Ancient Economy
Edited by Walter Scheidel and Sitta von Reden

Roman Religion
Edited by Clifford Ando

Sex and Difference in Ancient Greece and Rome
Edited by Mark Golden and Peter Toohey

IN PREPARATION
Ancient Slavery
Edited by Keith Bradley

Ancient Myth
Edited by Richard Gordon

Alexander the Great
Edited by Simon Hornblower

Athenian Democracy
Edited by P. J. Rhodes

The 'Dark Ages' of Greece
Edited by Ian Morris

The Age of Augustus
Edited by Jonathan Edmonson

ROMAN RELIGION

Edited by
Clifford Ando

EDINBURGH UNIVERSITY PRESS

© Editorial matter, chapter 10, and selection, Clifford Ando, 2003

Transferred to digital print 2012

Edinburgh University Press Ltd
22 George Square, Edinburgh

Typeset in Sabon
by Norman Tilley Graphics, Northampton
Printed and bound by CPI Group (UK) Ltd, Croydon, CR0 4YY

A CIP record for this book is available from the British Library

ISBN 0 7486 1565 2 (hardback)
ISBN 0 7486 1566 0 (paperback)

The right of the contributors
to be identified as authors of this work
has been asserted in accordance with
the Copyright, Designs and Patents Act 1988.

Contents

Acknowledgments

For permission to reprint the essays and chapters in this volume I thank the following: Jonathan Z. Smith and the University of Chicago Press (Chapter 1); Gregory Woolf (Chapter 2); Richard Gordon (Chapter 3); Denis Feeney and Cambridge University Press (Chapter 5); John Scheid (Chapters 6 and 8); Chicago University Press (Chapter 7); John North (Chapter 9); Sabine MacCormack and the University of Illinois Press (Chapter 11); and Mary Beard (Chapter 12).

Reassembling the images for Chapter 11 – the originals had been lost – required the cooperation of Sabine MacCormack, the aid of John Pollini, and the generosity of the Photothek of the Deutsches Archäologisches Institut in Athens. To the library of the DAI in Rome I owe thanks for assistance of a different kind, namely, aid in reconstructing references to nineteenth-century volumes of that institution's journal.

The maps (pp. xviii–xxi) are drawn from *The World of Rome* with the permission of Peter Jones, Keith Sidwell and Cambridge University Press.

I began to think about this volume at the end of a term of leave financed by the American Council of Learned Societies, while enjoying the hospitality of Wolfson College, Oxford, and the remarkable resources of the Sackler Library. I should like to thank the late John D'Arms, Fergus Millar, John Scheid, and the President of Wolfson College for their contributions in making that period of study both possible and pleasurable.

Many are the friends who gave of their time, energy, and insight during the writing and editing of this volume. Ruth Abbey, Catherine Feeley, and Sabine MacCormack kindly read much of the editorial matter. Christopher Barnes and Philip Purchase provided me with translations of Chapters 6, 8, 13, and 14; I hope that my editing of their work has not done either them, or the authors of those chapters, any disservice. Michele George and Tom Harrison graciously invited me to contribute to their series. Fiona Sewell edited the manuscript with speed and skill; the book is much improved thanks to her care. John Davey of Edinburgh University Press has made work on this volume a pleasure: not only does he correspond with remarkable dispatch, but he seems always to answer in the affirmative.

I delayed completion of this project to spend some time with my father, Albert Ando, during his final illness. For his extraordinary patience and regard in those months I shall remain forever grateful.

Note to the Reader

The articles and excerpts included in this book were originally published in a range of different journals and books. A degree of uniformity has been imposed (for example, in the abbreviations used), but many of the conventions of the original pieces have been preserved. This applies to spelling (UK or US) and to different modes of referencing: chapters using the Harvard (i.e., name and date) system are followed by individual bibliographies; those using 'short titles' usually have footnotes and no bibliography.

The final bibliography contains works referred to by the editor.

Editorial notes and translations of ancient texts are introduced either within square brackets [ ] or in daggered footnotes. Some Greek terms, especially those in use in English, have been transliterated.

All abbreviations of ancient texts, modern collections, books, and journals, used either in the chapters or in the editorial material, are listed and explained on pages xi–xvii.

The chapter translated from Georg Wissowa's *Religion und Kultus der Römer* is an exception to several of the rules stated above. First, in it, as in the chapter by Carl Koch, I have taken the liberty of making further paragraph divisions beyond those in the original publication. Second, Wissowa supplied very minimal bibliographic information for articles and books cited in his notes. I have therefore attempted to complete his references, but Wissowa published before the inauguration of *L'Année Philologique* and it was not possible to track down all the literature he cites.

Abbreviations

1 ANCIENT AUTHORS, TEXTS, AND CORPORA

[Aelius] Arist[ides]	*Or[ationes]* = *Orations*
Anth. Pal.	*Anthologia Palatina*
Apul[eius]	*Apol[ogia], Met[amorphoses]*
Aristotle	*Ath[enaion] Pol[iteia]* = *Constitution of the Athenians*
Arnobius	*Adv[ersus] Nat[iones]* = *Against the Gentiles*
ARS	A. C. Johnson, P. R. Coleman-Norton, and F. C. Bourne, eds, *Ancient Roman Statutes* (Austin, 1961)
Asconius	*[In] Sc[aurianam]* = *Commentary on Cicero's Speech on Behalf of Scaurus*
Aug[ustine]	*[De] Civ[itate Dei]* = *The City of God, En[arrationes in] Ps[almos]* = *Readings on the Psalms, Ep[istulae]* = *Letters*
Aur. Vict.	*[De viris] Ill[ustribus]* = *On Outstanding Men, [De] Caes[aribus]* = *On the Emperors*
Cato	*[De] Agr[icultura]* = *On Agriculture, Orig[ines]* = *Foundation Stories*
Censor[inus]	*De Die Natali* = *On Birthdays*
CFA	J. Scheid, ed., *Commentarii Fratrum Arvalium qui Supersunt* (Rome, 1998)
Cic[ero]	*Acad[emica] Post[eriora]* = *Second Academics, [De Lege] Agr[aria]* = *On the Agrarian Law, [Epistulae ad] Att[icum]* = *Letters to Atticus, [De] Div[inatione]* = *On Divination, [De] Dom[o sua]* = *On his*

	Own House, *[Epistulae ad] Fam[iliares]* = *Letters to his Friends*, *[De] Har[uspicum] Resp[onso]* = *On the Response of the Haruspices*, *Hort[ensius]*, *[De] Leg[ibus]* = *On the Laws*, *[De] Leg[e] Man[ilia]* = *On the Manilian Law*, *[Pro] Mur[eno]* = *In Defense of Murenus*, *[De] Nat[ura] Deor[um]* = *On the Nature of the Gods*, *[De] Off[iciis]* = *On Duties*, *Phil[ippics]*, *[Pro] Planc[io]*, *In Defense of Plancius*, *[De] Rep[ublica]* = *On the Commonwealth*, *Tusc[ulanae Disputationes]* = *Tusculan Disputations*
CIL	*Corpus Inscriptionum Latinarum* (Berlin, 1863–)
Claudian	*[De bello] Gild[onico]* = *The War with Gildo*
Cod. Theod.	T. Mommsen, ed., *Codex Theodosianus*, vol. 1, pars posterior, *Theodosiani Libri XVI cum Constitutionibus Sirmondinis* (Berlin, 1905)
CSEL	*Corpus Scriptorum Ecclesiasticorum Latinorum*
Dig.	T. Mommsen and P. Krueger, eds, *Digesta Iustiniani Augusti* ... (Berlin, 1870)
Diod[orus] Sic[ulus]	
Dionysius	*Ant[iquitates] Rom[anae]* = *Roman Antiquities*
Euripides	*Hippol[ytus]*
Eusebius	*Hist[oria] Eccl[esiastica]* = *Ecclesiastical History*
FGH	F. Jacoby, ed., *Fragmente der griechischen Historiker* (Leiden, 1923–)
Gellius	*N[octes] A[tticae]* = *Attic Nights*
Himerius	*Or[ationes]*
Homer	*Il[iad]*
Hor[ace]	*C[armina]* = *Odes*
IG	*Inscriptiones Graecae* (Berlin, 1873–)
ILCV	E. Diehl, ed., *Inscriptiones Latinae Christianae Veteres* (Berlin, 1925–67)
ILER	J. Vives, ed., *Inscripciones latinas de la España romana* (Barcelona, 1971–2)

ILLRP	A. Degrassi, ed., *Inscriptiones Latinae Liberae Rei Publicae* (Rome, 1963–5)
ILS	H. Dessau, ed., *Inscriptiones Latinae Selectae* (Berlin, 1892–1916)
Iul[ius] Obseq[uens]	*Prod[igia]* = *Prodigies*
Jerome	*Chron[ica]* = *Chronicle*
Josephus	*Bell[um] Iud[aicum]* = *The Jewish War*
Juvenal	*Sat[urae]* = *Satires*
Keil, *Gramm. Lat.*	H. Keil, ed., *Grammatici Latini* (Berlin, 1855–1923)
Lact[antius]	*Inst[itutiones Divinae]* = *Divine Institutes*
Livy	*Epit[omae] Ox[yrhynchi Repertae]* = *The Epitome Discovered at Oxyrhynchus*
Lucian	*Deor[um] Conc[ilium]* = *A Council of the Gods, Icar[omenippus]*
Macrobius	*Sat[urnalia]*
OGIS	W. Dittenberger, ed., *Orientis Graeci Inscriptiones Selectae* (Leipzig, 1903)
ORF	E. Malcovati, ed., *Oratorum Romanorum Fragmenta Liberae Rei Publicae*, 3rd edn (Turin, 1967)
Ovid	*Ars [Amatoria]* = *The Art of Love, [Epistulae ex] Pont[o]* = *Letters from Pontus, Fast[i]* = *Fasti, Met[amorphoses]*
PG	*Patrologia Cursus Completus, Series Graeca*
Philo	*Leg[atio ad Gaium]* = *The Embassy to Gaius*
Phot[ius]	*Bibl[iotheca]*
PL	*Patrologia Cursus Completus, Series Latina*
Plaut[us]	*Amph[itruo], Aul[ularia], Bacch[ides], Cas[ina], Mil[es Gloriosus]*
Pliny	*Nat[uralis Historia]* = *Natural History*
Pliny	*Ep[istulae]* = *Letters, Paneg[yricus]* = *Punegyric*
Plutarch	*Mor[alia]* = *Essays, Q[uaestiones] G[raecae]* = *Greek Questions, Quaest[iones] Rom[anae]* = *Roman Questions*
Procl[us]	*Chr[estomathia]* = *Chrestomathy*
Prop[ertius]	

Prudentius	*[Contra] Symm[achum]* = *Against Symmachus*
RDGE	R. K. Sherk, *Roman Documents from the Greek East* (Baltimore, 1969)
RMR	R. O. Fink, *Roman Military Records on Papyrus* (Cleveland, 1971)
Schol[ia] Bob[iensia]	*[In] Cic[eronis] Planc[ianam]* = *Commentary on Cicero's Speech on Behalf of Plancius*
Seneca	*[Consolatio] Ad Marc[iam]* = *A Consolation Addressed to Marcia*, *Dial[ogi]* = *Dialogues*
Servius	*ad Aen[eidem]* = *Commentary on Vergil's Aeneid, ad Ecl[ogas]* = *Commentary on Vergil's Eclogues*
SIG	W. Dittenberger, ed., *Sylloge Inscriptionum Graecarum*, 3rd edn (Leipzig, 1915–21)
Sophocles	*Antig[one]*
Suet[onius]	*Aug[ustus], Calig[ula], Claud[ius], [De] Dramm[aticis et Rhetoribus]* = *On Grammarians and Orators, Caes[ar]*
Symmachus	*Ep[istulae]* = *Letters*
Tacitus	*Ann[ales]* = *Annals*
Tertullian	*Apol[ogia]* = *Apology, [Adversus] Marc[ionem], Against Marcion, [Ad] Nat[iones]* = *To the Gentiles*
Tib[ullus]	
Val[erius] Max[imus]	
Varro	*Ant[iquitates Rerum] Div[inarum]* = *Divine Antiquities, Ant[iquitates Rerum] Hum[anarum]* = *Human Antiquities, [De] Ling[ua Latina]* = *On the Latin Language*
Virg[il]	*Ecl[ogues], Georg[ics], Aen[eid]*
Xen[ophon]	*Mem[orabilia]*

2 PERIODICALS, MONOGRAPHS, AND WORKS OF REFERENCE

| *AbhMainz* | *Abhandlungen der geistes- und sozialwissenschaftlichen Klasse der Akademie der Wissenschaften und der Literatur in Mainz* |

ACD	*Acta Classica Universitatis Scientiarum Debreceniensis*
AdI	*Annali dell'instituto di corrispondenza archeologica*
AJA	*American Journal of Archaeology*
AJPh	*American Journal of Philology*
ANRW	*Aufstieg und Niedergang der römischen Welt* (Berlin, 1972–)
ARG	*Archiv für Religionsgeschichte*
ARW	*Archiv für Religionswissenschaft*
BCH	*Bulletin de Correspondance Hellénique*
BÉFAR	*Bibliothèque de l'École Française d'Athènes et de Rome*
BICS	*Bulletin of the Institute of Classical Studies, London*
BJRL	*Bulletin of the John Rylands University Library of Manchester*
Bulletino	*Bulletino della commissione archeologica comunale di Roma*
CA	*Classical Antiquity*
CAH²	*The Cambridge Ancient History*, 2nd edn
CÉFR	Collection de l'École Française de Rome
CJ	*Classical Journal*
CQ	*Classical Quarterly*
Crawford, *RRC*	M. Crawford, *Roman Republican Coinage* (Cambridge, 1974)
EPRO	Études préliminaires aux religions orientales dans l'empire romain
HSCP	*Harvard Studies in Classical Philology*
ICS	*Illinois Classical Studies*
JRS	*Journal of Roman Studies*
JThS	*Journal of Theological Studies*
LSJ	H. G. Liddell, R. Scott, and H. S. Jones, eds, *A Greek–English Lexicon*, 9th edn (Oxford, 1968)
MAAR	*Memoirs of the American Academy in Rome*
MDAI[R]	*Mitteilungen des Deutschen Archäologischen Instituts, Römische Abteilung*
MÉFR(A)	*Mélanges de l'École Française de Rome (Antiquité)*

Mommsen, *Ges. Schr.*	T. Mommsen, *Gesammelte Schriften* (Berlin, 1905–13)
MRR	T. R. S. Broughton, *The Magistrates of the Roman Republic* (New York and Atlanta, 1951–86)
NachrGött	*Nachrichten der Akademie der Wissenschaften in Göttingen, Philologisch-Historische Klasse*
OLD	P. G. W. Glare, ed., *Oxford Latin Dictionary* (Oxford, 1968–82)
PBSR	*Papers of the British School at Rome*
PCPhS	*Proceedings of the Cambridge Philological Society*
PP	*Parola del Passato*
PRIA	*Proceedings of the Royal Irish Academy.* Section C, Archaeology, Celtic Studies, History, Linguistics, Literature
RA	*Revue archéologique*
RAC	*Reallexicon für Antike und Christentum* (Stuttgart, 1950–)
RE	*Realencyclopädie der classischen Altertumswissenschaft*
RÉA	*Revue des Études Anciennes*
RÉL	*Revue des Études Latines*
Rev. Ét. Aug.	*Revue des Études Augustiniennes*
RGVV	*Religionsgeschichtliche Versuche und Vorarbeiten*
RhM	*Rheinisches Museum*
RHR	*Revue de l'histoire des religions*
RIC	*Roman Imperial Coinage* (London, 1923–)
Riv. di filol.	*Rivista di filologia classica.* Continued by *Rivista di filologia e di istruzione classica*
RMR	R. O. Fink, ed., *Roman Military Records on Papyrus* (American Philological Association, 1971)
Roscher, *Lex.*	W. H. Roscher, ed. *Ausführliches Lexicon der griechischen und römischen Mythologie* (Leipzig, 1884–1937)
SitzBerlin	*Sitzungsberichte der Deutschen Akademie der Wissenschaften zu Berlin*
StudClas	*Studii Clasice*
TAPA	*Transactions of the American Philological*

	Association
TLL	*Thedaurus Linguae Latinae* (Leipzig, 1900–)
WZ	*Westdeutsche Zeitschrift*
ZPE	*Zeitschrift für Papyrologie und Epigraphik*

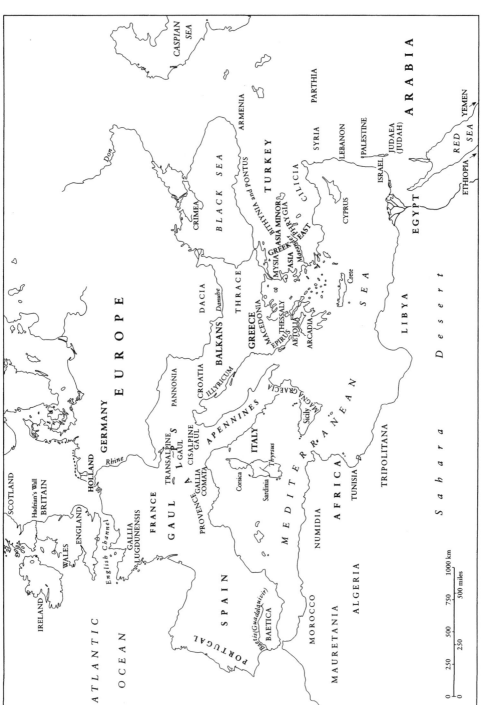

Map 1: The world of Rome

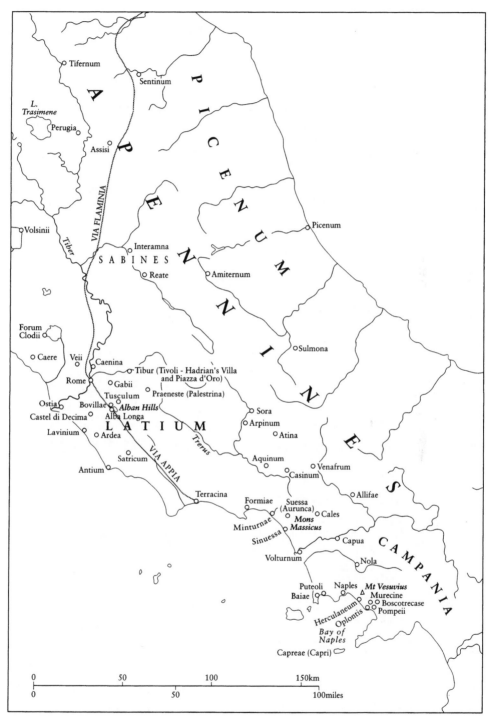

Map 2: Central Italy

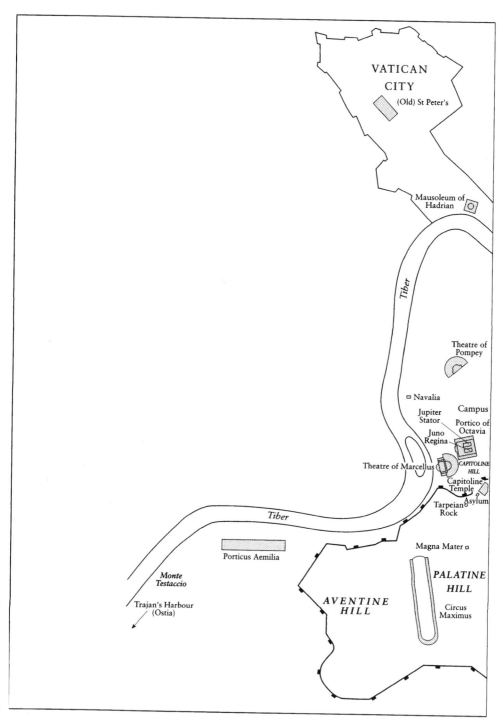

VATICAN
CITY

(Old) St Peter's

Mausoleum of
Hadrian

Tiber

Theatre of
Pompey

Navalia

Campus

Jupiter
Stator

Portico of
Octavia

Juno
Regina

Theatre of Marcellus

CAPITOLINE
HILL

Capitoline
Temple

Asylum

Tarpeian
Rock

Tiber

Magna Mater

Porticus Aemilia

PALATINE
HILL

Monte
Testaccio

AVENTINE
HILL

Circus
Maximus

Trajan's Harbour
(Ostia)

Map 3: The city of Rome

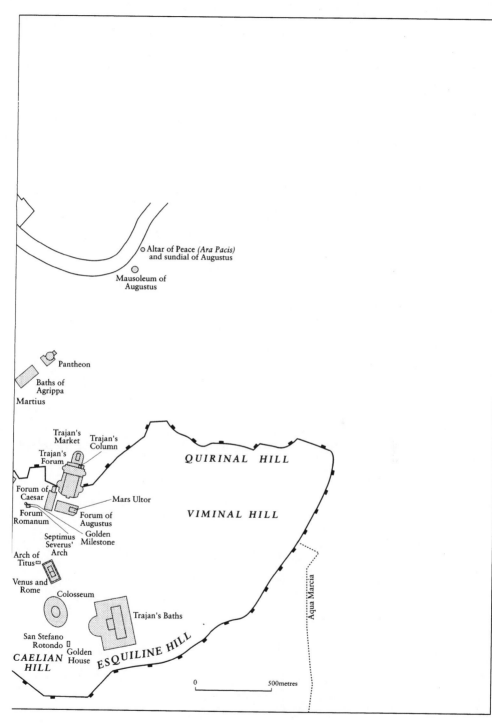

Map 3 continued: The city of Rome

Introduction:
Religion, Law and Knowledge
in Classical Rome

The historian Valerius Maximus, who compiled his nine books of *Memorable Deeds and Sayings* under the emperor Tiberius (AD 14–37), introduced the first section of his first book, "On Religion" (*De Religione*), in the following terms:

> Our ancestors desired that fixed and formal annual ceremonies be regulated by the knowledge of the *pontifices*; that sanction for the good governance of affairs be marshalled by the observations of augurs; that Apollo's prophecies be revealed by the books of the seers; and that the expiation of portents be accomplished in accordance with the Etruscan discipline.
>
> Also, by hallowed practice, observances are paid to divine affairs: by prayer, when something must be entrusted; by vow, when something is demanded; by thanksgiving, when a vow is discharged; by entreaty [for a favorable sign], when an inquiry is made by entrails or lot; and by sacrifice, when something is accomplished through formal ritual, whereby, too, the warnings of prodigies and lightning are expiated.
>
> So great was the desire among the ancients not only for the preservation but also for the expansion of religion (*religio*) that, at a time when the city was flourishing and wealthy, by decree of the Senate, ten sons of leading men were handed over to the peoples of Etruria in order to acquire technical mastery of their sacred rites.[1]

Valerius Maximus possessed neither sharpness of intellect nor clarity of style, and it would be easy to impeach this passage for obscurity

---

[1] Valerius Maximus 1.1.1a–b: *Maiores statas sollemnesque caerimonias pontificum scientia, bene gerendarum rerum auctoritates augurum obseruatione, Apollinis praedictiones uatum libris, portentorum depulsiones Etrusca disciplina explicari uoluerunt. prisco etiam instituto rebus diuinis opera datur, cum aliquid conmendandum est, precatione, cum exposcendum, uoto, cum soluendum, gratulatione, cum inquirendum uel extis uel sortibus, inpetrito, cum sollemni ritu peragendum, sacrificio, quo etiam ostentorum ac fulgurum denuntiationes procurantur. Tantum autem studium antiquis non solum seruandae sed etiam amplificandae religionis fuit, ut florentissima tum et opulentissima ciuitate decem principum filii senatus consulto singulis Etruriae populis percipiendae sacrorum disciplinae gratia traderentur.*

I

of many kinds.[2] But as an ostensive circumscription of Roman religion in a Roman formulation, it can serve as a point of departure, not only in our consideration of what Roman religion was, but also in our reflection upon its study. In this introduction, I concentrate on one specific aspect of that field of inquiry, namely, the epistemological basis of Roman religion; as I shall argue, this basis by its very nature conditions the manner in which Roman religion can be studied. The introductions to the individual sections will consider further problems of theory and practice, and their contents will be flagged here.

We might begin by reflecting on the translation of *religio*.[3] "Religion" is but one possible rendering, and Valerius' lists suggest that it might here be rendered more accurately by "the sum total of current cult practice."[4] It is not that "religion" does not capture the force of *religio* in one of its uses, but that this usage is not primary, and its field proves harder to map onto "religion" than one might expect. Consider the description of the *religio* of the Roman people offered by Gaius Aurelius Cotta, the Academic *pontifex*, in the opening pages of book 3 of Cicero's *On the Nature of the Gods*:

> The entirety of the *religio* of the Roman people is divided into rites and auspices, to which is added a third thing, namely, whatever warnings the interpreters of the Sibylline books or *haruspices* issue for the sake of foreknowledge on the basis of portents and omens. I hold that none of these *religiones* should ever be neglected, and I have persuaded myself that Romulus and Numa laid the foundations of our state by establishing the auspices and rites, respectively, and that our state could never have become so great without the goodwill of the immortal gods. (*Nat. Deor.* 3.5)[5]

The tendency among translators has been to render *harum religionum nullam* with a phrase like "none of these parts of our religion,"[6] in other words to efface entirely Cicero's discomfiting

---

[2] Compare his immediate inspiration for the first paragraph, Cicero *Har. Resp.* 18: "First of all, I regard our ancestors as authorities and guides in the cultivation of religion (*religionum colendarum*) ... they thought that fixed and formal annual ceremonies should be governed by the pontificate, sanction for the good governance of affairs by augury, the ancient prophecies of Apollo by the books of the seers, and the interpretation of portents by the Etruscan discipline."

[3] On *religio* see Pease 1963: 580–3, on Cicero *Div.* 2.148; Michels 1976; Muth 1978; Schilling 1979: 30–93; Sachot 1991; and Bremmer 1998: 10–14.

[4] Compare Cicero *Dom.* 121, translated below p. 5, and see Bremmer 1998: 10.

[5] On this passage see Pease 1955: ad loc. and p. 227, below.

[6] See, for example, the recent Oxford World's Classics translation by P. G. Walsh (Oxford: Oxford University Press, 1997), p. 109 ("I have never regarded any of these constituents of our religion with contempt"); the Penguin Classics translation by H. McGregor (London: Penguin, 1972), p. 195 ("I have never held any of these aspects of our religion in contempt"); or the Loeb translation of H. Rackham (Cambridge, MA: Harvard University Press, 1933), p. 291 ("I have always thought that none of these departments of religion was to be despised").

switch from the singular *religio* to the plural *religiones*. In time, *religio Romanorum* will come to mean something like "Roman religion" or, more accurately, "the religion of the Roman people," for the genitives "of the Roman people" or "of the Romans" signal an essential aspect to the classical Roman conception of religion, namely, that it was of and for a political community or body of citizens, one that included both humans and gods.[7]

During the long opposition of "Roman religion" to the religion of the Christians, the meaning "religion" in a totalizing sense eventually occluded all other meanings of *religio*, and the fractious dialog that required that binarism yields a portrait of Roman religion that the classical term *religio* cannot sustain.[8] So it is, even at the height of pagan–Christian conflict, that Quintus Aurelius Symmachus, prefect of the city of Rome in AD 383, did not think to use *religio* to denominate the cultural systems to which he as a pagan, and the emperor as a Christian, separately adhered: "Of course," he wrote, "it is possible to list emperors *utriusque sectae utriusque sententiae*, of either sect and either conviction."[9] His turn to *secta*, sect, which in classical Latin might refer to a philosophical school or code of conduct, betrays the huge gap that lies between classical *religio* and late antique "religion."[10]

We may likewise learn something from Augustine's dissatisfaction with *religio*. Writing in the decades before and after the sack of Rome in AD 410, Augustine delivered to the west its enduring portrait of Roman religion. Indeed, Augustine's critique of paganism became foundational for almost all Christian theorizing about polytheistic religions, and so has come to influence even those who have not read his work.[11] In the twentieth book of his refutation of Faustus the Manichee, written in the last years of the fourth century, Augustine sought to distinguish Christians' reverence for martyrs and saints from their worship of God. "We do celebrate the memory of the martyrs with religious solemnity," Augustine allowed, "but we neither build altars nor sacrifice to them."

[7] See Cicero *Nat. Deor.* 1.115–16, quoted below, and cf. Scheid 1985a: 69–76, 1985b, 1987/9. This emphasis on the group (and the here-and-now: see p. 20) stands in distinct contrast to Christianity's notional interest in the individual and the hereafter.

[8] See Ando 2000: 392–5, and Bendlin 2001: 200.

[9] Symmachus *Relation* 3.3. To this use of *secta* compare *Acta Cypriani* 4.1. Compare Libanius *Oration* 30.53, viewing Hellenic paganism as a totality in opposition to Christianity.

[10] On "philosophical allegiance," a topic deserving much further study, see Sedley 1989, and cf. Bremmer 1991.

[11] For three quite distinct studies of Augustine's attack on Roman religion, see Mandouze 1958; MacCormack 1998: 132–74; and O'Daly 1999: esp. 74–134.

> But that *cultus*, which is called *latreia* in Greek but which cannot be rendered in Latin by any one word, as it is a sort of servitude owed exclusively to divinity (*cum sit quaedam proprie diuinitati debita seruitu*) – with that *cultus* we neither worship anything, nor teach that anything should be worshipped, other than the one god. Moreover, the offering of sacrifice relates to this *cultus*, whence we name idolatry the practice of those who pay sacrifice to idols.[12] Therefore, we never in any way offer anything of this kind to any martyr, or any holy spirit, or any angel, nor do we teach that such offerings should be made. (Augustine *Against Faustus* 20.21)

If Augustine tacitly rejects *religio* as a signifier for the totality of Christian worship, he at least acknowledges his qualms about *cultus*. His rejection of *cultus* in its traditional meaning in classical Latin we may trace back to Cicero's *On the Nature of the Gods*, a text Augustine knew well. Twice in that work Cicero's characters gloss *religio* as comprising the *cultus deorum*, worship of the gods – a formulation that Augustine would himself embrace later in life.[13] But Augustine presumably came to do so because the field of *cultus* was capacious, and he could in a Christian context avoid the classical implications that had disturbed him a decade earlier.

Those classical implications we can excavate by turning to the speech delivered by Cotta at the end of the first book of *On the Nature of the Gods*. Cotta there refutes the criticism of traditional worship just offered by the Epicurean Velleius, and he concentrates on the network of obligations that bound humans and their gods:

> For why, do you suppose, men should have regard for the gods, if the gods not only do not have regard for men, but neither show concern nor do anything whatsoever for them? ... What *pietas*, what devotion is due to one from whom you receive nothing, or what can be owed to one who does nothing deserving? For devotion is justice toward the gods, but what system of justice can there be for us with them, if there is no community of human with god? *Sanctitas*, piety, is the knowledge of giving the gods their due, but I do not know why they should be so treated, if we have neither received nor expect any good from them. (Cicero *Nat. Deor.* 1.115–16)

The word I translate in the first sentence as "have regard for" is *colere*, a word otherwise well rendered by "worship," for what is at stake in its use normally is what is due the gods, and that is cult. But

---

[12] The compound, first attested in the letters of Paul, derives from Greek εἴδωλον + λατρεία and in Greek (and often in Latin) remained uncontracted: εἰδωλολατρία = *idololatria*. See Waszink and van Winden 1987: 73–9.

[13] Cicero *Nat. Deor.* 2.8: *religione, id est cultu deorum* ("religion, which is to say, the *cultus* of the gods"), and 1.117: *religionem, quae deorum cultu pio continetur* ("*religio*, which is subsumed in the dutiful *cultus* of the gods"). Note Augustine *Civ.* 10.1: *dicere valeamus religionem non esse nisi cultum Dei*, "we can say that *religio* is nothing other than the *cultus* of God."

Cicero through Cotta here emphasizes the asymmetrical reciprocity between humans and gods – they are, after all, members of the same community, albeit ones with very different status and power. Hence Cicero defines "piety" (*sanctitas*) as *scientia colendorum deorum*, as the knowledge of having appropriate regard for the gods, which I render above "the knowledge of giving the gods their due." I will consider the reciprocal nature of Roman religion further in the introduction to parts II and IV, and the citizenship of the gods again in the introductions to parts II and V. At present I want to consider only what it means – more at a foundational level than at the level of practice – for relations between gods and men to be characterized by "justice," and hence to be governed by *ius*, a system of justice or body of law.

We must first recognize that although Romans occasionally referred to "the law" as something that transcended any particular state – speaking in such circumstances of natural law or the law of nations (the *ius gentium* or *ius naturale*)[14] – they also understood that justice is both realized and actualized in particular contingencies and in any given society through statutes and institutions that are locally and historically constructed. The contingent specificity of the *ius* that governed relations between human and divine emerges with particular clarity in an aside in Cicero's speech "On his Own House." Having described in a superficial way the process by which pontiffs consecrated buildings, Cicero allowed that he said *nihil de pontificio iure, nihil de ipsius verbis dedicationis, nihil de religione, caerimoniis,* "nothing regarding pontifical law, nothing regarding the words of the actual dedication, nothing regarding *religio* or rites" (*Dom.* 121).

Laws change (and other priestly colleges have their separate bodies of law); formulae vary; rites develop; religion ... expands? We are returned to the puzzling diction of Valerius Maximus, and to the intellectual challenge presented by a religion that expands.

Roman religion was polytheistic. If the nature of polytheism has been an enduring source of ideological misconstrual, the historical development of Roman polytheism – namely, changes in the identities of the gods worshipped at Rome, and the gradual increase in their number – has been an equally enduring object of historical inquiry.[15] To an outsider, perhaps the most obvious way in which a polytheistic religion can expand is through the incorporation of new

[14] Gaius *Institutes* 1.1, with Zulueta 1946: II, 12–13, and Berger 1953: s.v. "ius gentium" and "ius naturale."
[15] See Scheid 1987, an English version of Scheid 1988.

deities, a problem taken up in the introductions to parts IV and VII.[16] For now, I want to take up two further kinds of "expansion," the mere acknowledgement of the existence of deities previously unknown, and the development of new forms of worship for gods already included in the state pantheon.

To set the stage: north of Athens at the mouth of the Asopus river lies the city of Oropus, famed in antiquity for its Amphiareion, the temple and precinct of Amphiaraus situated within its territory.[17] The Roman general and dictator Sulla had successfully attacked Athens in 87/86 BC, when on his way to war in Asia, and stayed there again in the winter 84/83. The chronology of these events is obscure, but it seems likely that in response to Sulla's victory in 86, the wardens of the Amphiareion expanded the scope of its games to honor both Amphiaraus and Rome.[18] They will have sent a delegation to inform Sulla of their decision, almost undoubtedly before his departure for Asia – the god, known for his prophetic powers, may have forecast a Roman victory. Delighted, Sulla took a vow to honor the god and, upon his return to Athens, Sulla fulfilled his vow by granting to the god ownership of a considerable body of land and a claim on the revenues of the city.[19] That land and those monies, insofar as they belonged to a god, were tax exempt.

Sulla died in 79, and some time thereafter the publicans attempted to collect taxes from Oropus for the valuation of the Amphiareion's land. Oropus sent a delegation to the Roman Senate in 74, in response to which the Senate convened a board of senators to investigate the rival claims and advise the Senate on how to resolve the matter. (The board of senators included the young Cicero, who refers to this case twice in his theological works.) The consuls for 73, advised by the board, called witnesses and considered documents, whose testimony and contents are paraphrased in the Senate's final decree on this matter. The consuls rendered a decision on 14 October, and it formed the bases of a decree of the Senate, which the city of Oropus then inscribed on a stele of white marble. I quote selectively from the 69 lines of that document:

> (ll. 1–5) Marcus Terentius, son of Marcus, Varro Lucullus and Gaius Cassius, son of Lucius, Longinus, consuls, to the magistrates, Council, and People of Oropus, greetings ... We want you to know that we ... have reached

---

[16] See Beard, North, and Price 1998: II sec. 2.6.

[17] On Amphiaraus see Pease 1955: 562 and 1080, 1963: 251–2.

[18] *SIG* 1064, with Dittenberger's n. 4 on that text and n. 43 to *SIG* 747.

[19] On the historical and financial issues at stake in this episode see Kallet-Marx 1995: 272–83.

a decision regarding the dispute between the god Amphiaraus and the publicans.

(ll. 16–19) Whereas Hermodorus, son of Olympichus, priest of Amphiaraus, ... and Alexidemus, son of Theodorus, and Demainetus, son of Theoteles, envoys of Oropus said:

(ll. 19–23) "Since in the law of contract [i.e., the censorial law governing the actions of publicans in the province of Achaea], those lands are exempt that Lucius Sulla set aside for the protection of the immortal gods and their sacred precincts; and since Lucius Sulla gave to the god Amphiaraus the revenues at issue in this dispute; in consequence they should pay to the publican no tax on these lands."

(l. 24) and whereas Lucius Domitius Ahenobarbus on behalf of the publicans said:

(ll. 25–9) "Since in the law of contract those lands are exempt that Lucius Sulla set aside for the protection of the immortal gods and their sacred precincts, but since Amphiaraus, to whom these lands are said to have been granted, is not a god; in consequence it should lie within the power of the publicans to collect taxes on these lands";

(ll. 29–31) In accordance with the decision of our advisory board, we have reached a decision, which we will bring before the Senate. We have also entered it into the record-book of our proceedings.[20]

There is no need to continue: you already know how the case was resolved. For in describing the dispute as lying between "the god Amphiaraus and the publicans," the consuls gave away their decision. What the decree of the Senate, alas, does not clarify are the process and reasoning used to resolve what was, at heart, a theological problem. Hence, in Cicero's recollection, there had been no dispute about the law and, indeed, the speakers before the board did not disagree on the content of the *lex censoria*. Rather, according to Cicero, "the publicans discovered that the *lex censoria* exempted from taxation lands in Boeotia belonging to immortal gods, and so they denied that any were immortal who had once been human" (*Nat. Deor.* 3.49). How many times must the Senate have adjudicated such claims to divinity, put forward by the gods who owned the myriad shrines dotting the landscape of its empire!

What obligation did the Senate incur on behalf of the people of Rome in recognizing Amphiaraus as a god? The answer is, None. The introduction to part V will take up the study of Rome's encounter with foreign gods. Here I wish only to consider the striking authority

---

[20] *SIG* 747; *RDGE* no. 23. English translations include *ARS* no. 70 and Sherk 1984: no. 70. In support of their decision, the consuls then quote (1) the law of contract, (2) the decision of Sulla, insofar as it was later ratified by a decree of the Senate, (3) which is also quoted. The consuls include a reference to an archive of senatorial proceedings: "Present on the advisory board were those same people named in the first book of Senatorial Proceedings, wax tablet 14."

arrogated by the Senate to adjudicate such claims to divinity. I say "arrogated" only because it hardly seems appropriate for a body of mortals to render judgment on the gods. As a matter of law, the Senate had been granted authority in such matters by the Roman people, in whom final authority over such affairs resided.[21] The central question before us might seem to be one of power: who was the Senate, who were the people, to decide who was a god, and who was not? Thus stated, the question seems to lead inexorably to an old-fashioned view of Roman religion as legalistic, as granting power to mortals to dictate to their gods.[22] Should we perhaps subscribe to such a view after all?

Let me attempt to shift our frame of reference and, in so doing, to formulate the question anew. I begin with an ancient question, one asked by the Roman Senate in 216 BC. Not only had Rome recently suffered a sequence of brutal defeats at the hands of Hannibal, but two Vestals were convicted in that year of inchastity.

> Taking place among so many disasters, that impiety was interpreted as a prodigy. The Xviri were ordered to consult the [Sibylline] books and Quintus Fabius Pictor was sent to the oracle at Delphi to learn by what prayers and supplications they might placate the gods and what end there would be to these disasters. Meanwhile, on the authority of the sacred books, several extraordinary sacrifices were performed: among them, a male and female Gaul and a male and female Greek were buried alive in the Forum Boarium, in a place walled by stone, already then stained by human sacrifice – a most un-Roman rite. (Livy 22.57.4–6)

To ask of an oracle how to placate the gods situates the inquirer in a very different position vis-à-vis the gods than did the act of assessing their divinity. One could argue that the Romans humbled themselves in 216 under exceptional circumstances, their confidence shaken;

---

[21] Livy 9.46.6–7: "Licinius Macer dedicated a temple to Concord in the precinct of Vulcan, to the great annoyance of the nobles. Cornelius Barbatus, the *pontifex maximus*, was compelled by the unanimous will of the people to recite the formula of dedication first [for Macer to repeat], although he argued that, by custom of our ancestors, no one other than a consul or general could dedicate a temple. Therefore, on the motion of the senate, a law was passed by the people that no one should dedicate a temple or an altar without the consent of either the Senate or a majority of the tribunes." See also Cicero *Dom.* 136: "You [pontiffs] will find in your records the case of Gaius Cassius the censor: he reported to the pontifical college his desire to dedicate a statue to Concord; Marcus Aemilius, the *pontifex maximus*, responded for the college, saying that unless the Roman people specifically granted him authority, so that he were acting at their command, he did not think that the dedication could properly be performed." On respective roles of the pontifex and the dedicating magistrate, see p. 59. On the authority of the people, see Cicero *Leg.* 2.19 with Dyck 2003: ad loc., as well as below, p. 59.

[22] Warde Fowler 1911: 270–91 offers perhaps the most cogent and historically grounded argument for this view, but it has had many proponents. The Guide to Further Reading discusses some recent histories of the history of Roman religion.

and the period of the war and the quarter century that followed it were without a doubt characterized by unprecedented political, social, cultural, and religious turmoil.[23] But other evidence suggests the Romans acted in similar ways from positions of strength.

In 186 BC the Senate erupted into action and savagely suppressed the private cult of the god Bacchus. For our knowledge of this event we depend principally on two sources, one literary and one documentary, and much toil has been spent in the struggle to reconcile the two, and in particular to explain on their basis why the Senate acted then against a cult that had been present in Italy for some years.[24] What requires emphasis here is the seeming dissonance between Livy's description of the cult, on the one hand, and the actual stipulations of the Senate's decree against the cult, on the other. Livy opens his narrative of the year by announcing that the two consuls were ordered to conduct an investigation *de clandestinis coniurationibus*, "concerning secret conspiracies." For as the Bacchic rites spread and developed – and Livy offers an explanation for that process, too – they became more corrupt and more dangerous:

> To *religio* were added the pleasures of wine and banquets, by which the minds of many were corrupted. When wine inflamed their minds, and night and men mingled with women, and the innocent young with the old, then all power of moral discrimination was extinguished and crimes of every kind began to be practised: ... not merely the shameful violation of freeborn men and women, but perjurious witnesses, false evidence and forged will. (Livy 39.8.3–7)

Speaking before the people, the consul Postumius emphasized not only the criminality of the cult's initiates, but their identity as a political community of suspect allegiance – they constituted "another populace" – as well as the foreignness of the rites.[25] The narrative is remarkable for its sweep and power.

Livy closes the first stage of his account by summarizing the Senate's decree authorizing the consuls to suppress the cult.[26] It is our extraordinary good fortune to possess a copy of the Senate's decree, the one dispatched to the *ager Teuranus*, a territory in Calabria. Its central clauses run as follows:

> (3–6) Let none of them want to host a Bacchanal. If there are any who say that it is necessary for them to host a Bacchanal, let them come before the

---

[23] Toynbee 1965, a monument of classical scholarship, studies the entire period. On its religious history see II, 374–415.
[24] See Chapter 9. For recent bibliography see Cancik-Lindemaier 1996; de Cazanove 2000a, 2000b.
[25] Livy 39.15–16.
[26] Livy 39.18.7–9.

urban praetor at Rome; and concerning that matter, when their words have
been heard, our Senate shall render a decision, provided that not less than
one hundred senators are present when the matter is deliberated.

(7–9) Let no man, whether a Roman citizen or a person of Latin name or one
of our allies, want to be present at a Bacchic rite, unless he approaches the
urban praetor and the urban praetor permits it, in accordance with the will
of the Senate, provided that not less than one hundred senators are present
when the matter is deliberated. Decreed.

(10–14) Let no man be a priest. Let no man or woman be a master. Let none
of them want to have money in common. Let no one want to make either a
man or a woman a master, or make a man or a woman serve in the place of
a master; let no one after this want to swear oaths in common or make vows
in common or pledge things in common or promise in common, nor let
anyone swear loyalty to another among them.

(15–18) Let no one want to perform [Bacchic] rites in secret; let no one want
to perform [Bacchic] rites in public or private or outside the City, unless he
approaches the urban praetor and the urban praetor permits it, in accordance
with the will of the Senate, provided that not less than a hundred senators
are present when the matter is deliberated. Decreed.

(19–22) Let no one want to perform rites with more than five men and
women together, and let not more than two men, nor more than three women
want to be present, except in accordance with the will of the urban praetor
and the Senate, as is written above.

The most remarkable feature of the Senate's decision is not that it
permits the worship of Bacchus to continue. Rather, it is that the
Senate eschews any effort to regulate the forms that Bacchic worship
might take, concentrating instead on the institutionalization of the
cult and the financial and legal relationships amongst its members.
The major exception, the injunction against male priests, can perhaps
be explained by Livy's insistence that that had been a recent innovation, one not authorized by the god.[27] It is loyalty to other
members of the cult, and not loyalty to Bacchus, that is the Senate's
province. To describe the suppression of the Bacchanalia in terms
derived from our study of Amphiaraus and the embassy of Fabius
Pictor: once the Senate had conceded the divinity of Bacchus, it was
no longer the Senate's place to decide "by what prayers and supplications" he wished to be worshipped.[28]

The Senate's question to Delphi returns us, somewhat unexpectedly, to the problem of *religio*. To say that it can often be translated
as "the sum total of current cult practice" is not to denigrate Roman
religion for being legalistic or ritualistic, for lacking a creed, a state-

---

[27] Livy 39.13.8–10.

[28] The introduction to part IV will argue that this question partakes of a peculiarly Roman
view of the divine.

ment of faith to which individuals could adhere.[29] Nor should we be content merely to assert the inappropriateness of these terms: the negative assertion of incommensurate difference marks the start, and not the end, of inquiry. For what we need urgently to understand is what the Romans had, if not faith.[30]

The simple answer is knowledge. For having learned from Delphi how to placate the gods, the Senate will have acted; those instructions, their performance and their results, will have been recorded; and the rites will have been repeated in analogous situations, so long as they were adjudged efficacious.[31] Roman religion was thus founded upon an empiricist epistemology: cult addressed problems in the real world, and the effectiveness of rituals – their tangible results – determined whether they were repeated, modified, or abandoned. Roman religion was in this strict sense an orthopraxy, requiring of its participants *savoir-faire* rather than *savoir-penser*:[32] and knowing what to do – *scientia colendorum deorum*, the knowledge of giving the gods their due – was grounded upon observation.

The Romans' famed rectitude and rigor in the performance of cult should be understood in this context: in light of the terrifying superiority of the gods, and knowing what had worked before, one had an overwhelming obligation scrupulously to recreate precisely that earlier performance.[33] For the gods' part, their willingness to abide by this *ius*, by this body of law, was the highest expression of both their *fides*, their norm-based loyalty to the other members of their community, and their goodwill.[34]

---

[29] On the history of "ritual" as a concept in the study of Greek and Roman religion, see Bremmer 1998. For an indicator of the difference between Roman and Christian valuations of "faith," observe that *religio* (and *peccatum*, sin) are things that cleave to individuals, not things to which one adheres: Cicero *Nat. Deor.* 2.11 and *Div.* 1.30.

[30] For a fuller exposition of a very similar argument, see Linder and Scheid 1993, an exceptionally clear statement of an important theme. See p. 54: "These convictions [actualized in ritual], these beliefs, were never collected in the form of a doctrine for instruction, and above all they did not correspond to an 'act of faith' in the Christian sense. The convictions exposed by the rites did not express a belief in the proper sense – because, for the ancients, belief was an inferior form of knowledge – but a knowing ... The verb 'to believe' and the substantive 'faith' – just like the term 'pious' – were not technical terms in the religious domain."

[31] See Livy 23.11.1–6: "The Senate decreed that the divine matters and supplications should be performed at the first opportunity, with care."

[32] Linder and Scheid 1993: 49–50; on orthopraxy and seemingly related concepts like "formalism" and "invariance" see Bell 1997: 138–69 and cf. 191–7.

[33] See Linder and Scheid 1993: 53, and below, pp. 77, 84–97 passim.

[34] On *fides* see Boyancé 1972: 135–52 and Scheid 1985a: 128–37. On the honouring of prayers as a sign of divine goodwill, Pliny *Nat.* 28.17, discussed below on p. 232. It is perhaps worth emphasizing here that relations between Romans and their gods were *not* governed by any principle such as *do ut des*. The Romans did not give in order that the gods should give. The Romans induced the gods to give by promising themselves to give, so long as the gods did. If the gods did not deliver, Romans simply omitted to fulfill their vows. On this topic see Scheid 1989/90.

Illustrations and reflections of this principle lie near to hand. For example, the consul Marcus Claudius Marcellus was once forbidden by the *pontifices* from consecrating a temple to *Honos* and *Virtus*, "Honor and Virtue," despite his having taken a vow to do so; the pontiffs argued that if some prodigy were then to happen in the temple, they would not be able to determine to which god the expiatory sacrifice should be made.[35] That is to say, an action in this world, once deemed portentous, required a response; and the need to respond precisely drove pontiffs to require, and architects and urban planners alike to produce, cities in which divine messages in the terrestrial landscape would be as clear as possible. Similarly, the correlative to pagan denunciations of Christian credulity (their religion was based on belief!) was pagan confidence that their practice was based on historical evidence.[36]

The study of Roman religion – as a system of embedded symbols and social actions and their institutionalization – must therefore take its epistemological foundation into account. The distribution and diffusion of power and authority in the religious sphere among individuals, offices, colleges, and institutions reflects at every level the basic needs of Roman religion, to acquire, adjudge, and preserve *cognitio deorum*, knowledge of the gods. The expression of this epistemic basis at the level of practice and discourse might occasionally seem paradoxical. For instance, Roman religion was incapable of revivalism: assigning no priority to etiological myths merely because of their antiquity (where they were ancient, of course), Romans could esteem the piety of their ancestors even as they recognized a necessity to act on the basis of more recent evidence. In other words, in matters of religion, their esteem for *mos maiorum* was dispositional and did not extend to practice. What is more, insofar as Romans expected to learn more about the gods over time, Roman etiological myth *was* historical narrative: when a conflict arose, knowledge acquired during the Hannibalic wars, for example, necessarily trumped information of hoary antiquity.[37] It is within this overall

[35] Valerius Maximus 1.1.8.

[36] For a pejorative view of Christian belief see Julian the Apostate quoted by Gregory of Nazianzus *Oration* 4.102. On the evidence supplied by historical events see Symmachus *Relation* 3.8 (and cf. 3.9 and 3.15–16): "For insofar as all reason lies in darkness (where the gods are concerned), whence more properly can knowledge of the gods (*cognitio numinum*) come than from recollection and the evidence supplied by things that turned out well?" This problem might best be studied by careful consideration of the epistemological vocabulary deployed by the various speakers in Cicero's *On the Nature of the Gods*, as well as that used in Augustine's *Against the Academics*, written in no small measure in response to Cicero.

[37] Note the wording used by the praetor Publius Licinius in 209 BC, when he sought to deny the new *flamen Dialis* ex officio membership in the Senate: 'The praetor wanted privileges to

epistemological framework that we should situate the importance of record-keeping among the duties of the priestly colleges and analyze the institutional and political impact of changes in the technologies of knowledge-production.[38]

Finally, the Romans' understanding of the history of religion – as a set of practices developed in response to the gods' immanence and action in the world – lends to their writing on religion an historical awareness deeply at odds with virtually all widely prevalent Christian philosophies of history. The structure and reception of Marcus Terentius Varro's *Human and Divine Antiquities* illustrate this perfectly. Varro's work – written in the final years of the Republic[39] – now exists only in fragments, and the *Divine Antiquities* in particular survive almost exclusively in extracts quoted by Roman paganism's most relentless and influential critic, Augustine, who outlined and analyzed the structure of the *Antiquities* in the sixth book of *The City of God*.[40]

> [Varro] wrote 41 books of *Antiquities*; which he divided into human and divine affairs; to human affairs he apportioned twenty-five books, and to divine sixteen. (Augustine *Civ.* 6.3 = Varro *Ant. Div.* fr. 4)
>
> Varro himself admits that he wrote about human affairs first, and then about divine affairs, because civic societies arose first and subsequently the things established by them. But the true *religio* was not established by any terrestrial society; on the contrary, it was the true religion that established heavenly society. This in truth is revealed and taught by the true god, the giver of eternal life, to his true worshippers. (Augustine *Civ.* 6.4, quoting from Varro *Ant. Div.* fr. 5)

Augustine's critique rests on a presupposition that is, for Christians, axiomatic: God's ontological priority sanctions the authority of his Scripture, and the myths contained therein provide etiologies for Christian rites. Assuming for the sake of argument that Varro wrote under similar beliefs, Augustine construes the organization of Varro's work as surrendering ontological priority to humans. We can rather easily, and perhaps facilely, assert that Augustine was wrong to operate on that assumption, and that we would be wrong to follow him. It is rather more difficult is to pin down the nature of his error.

We might start by identifying two rather paradoxical ruptures

---

rest not upon historical examples of tiresome antiquity, but in each case upon recent practice' (Livy 27.8.9).

[38] Beard 1985, 1991, 1998; North 1998; Scheid 1990b, 1994, 1998c, 1999c. See also pp. 68–75, below.

[39] On this work and its date see Chapter 8, below, and Jocelyn 1982.

[40] Note Linderski 2000: 458: "No student of religion can ultimately avoid or evade choosing between Varro (and Cicero) and Augustine."

between the status of the gods and the truth-content of the information that they provide. They are paradoxical from the perspective of classical metaphysics, and the ruptures exist between Roman and Christian religion, on the one hand, and between Roman religion and classical philosophy, on the other. So, despite's Augustine's mockery, Varro's gods did exist prior to the foundation of Rome, but that (chronological) priority did not translate into a privileged role in the foundation of the city or in the establishment of its religious rites. Again, though the passage of information and instruction from gods to mortals remained enormously indirect – so much so that Roman priests devoted much of their energies to the interpretation of divine communications[41] – the Romans nevertheless construed such information as they did receive as factual in basis, the object of knowledge rather than belief. They presumably did so because communication with the gods took place through physical things in the tangible world. Within an (ancient) empiricist epistemology, that would matter.

Viewed from a Roman perspective, the Christians' insistence that their god had once communicated with them directly and yet they did not so much know as merely believe the basic tenets of their faith betrayed not simply a point of philosophical difference, but one of fundamental error. But then to act – whether in the development of liturgy or in the rejection of traditional rites – on the basis of something less than knowledge! To persist in such behavior required the obstinacy of a depraved mind.[42]

Varro himself offered a justification for treating human before divine affairs, which Augustine, alas, only paraphrases:

> Varro confesses that he wrote about human institutions first, and later about divine ones, because divine institutions are established by humans. This is his reasoning: "As painters are prior to paintings, and builders prior to buildings, so civic communities are prior to the things established by them." (Augustine *Civ.* 6.4)

But Augustine has no sympathy for this argument. Any part of the true nature of the gods would have to be preferred to mortal affairs, and hence treated first. On the basis of the extracts quoted by Augustine – and here we are truly dependent on him – it appears that Varro left himself open to Augustine's attack by slipping between speaking of *res divinae* and *natura deorum*, between speaking of

---

[41] For this view of Roman priests, see esp. Potter 1999 and cf. Potter 1994.
[42] See Pliny *Ep.* 10.96.3.

human institutions established for the worship of the gods and the nature of the gods itself. Augustine seizes on this slippage:

> For, as Varro himself says, if he were writing about the entirety of the nature of the gods, then that nature ought to be preferred in the order of writing. Moreover, as the truth itself declares while Varro falls silent, the nature of the gods certainly ought to be preferred to *res Romanae*, even if it were not all, but merely part of the nature of the gods about which he were writing. And therefore, insofar as the nature of the gods in his treatment is rightly placed after his treatment of human affairs, it is rather none of the nature of the gods that he treats. (Augustine *Civ.* 6.4)

Augustine continues by positing, more or less tacitly, that different kinds of things are the objects of different kinds of knowing. In so doing, Augustine reveals himself as a typical (Platonic) metaphysician. But the cleavage between divine and human presupposed by Augustine then allows no scope either for cultural-historical approaches to the history of religion, or for empiricist approaches to the study of the divine. As gods precede men, so religion precedes human knowing. What follows is a decisive rejection of the fundamental basis of Roman religious practice, a rejection so fundamental that it precludes sympathetic understanding.

> It is not, therefore, that he wished to privilege human affairs over divine ones, but that he did not want to privilege false things over true. For in what he wrote about human affairs, Varro followed the history of actual deeds; but concerning those matters that he calls divine, what did he follow except mere speculation about nonexistent trifles? (Augustine *Civ.* 6.4)

Augustine's mockery cunningly allows for the possibility that Varro agreed with Augustine. That is, pagan readers of Varro in late antiquity could henceforth salvage his respectability only by conceding that he treated "not the truth that belongs to nature, but the falseness that belongs to error". That Varro did not write about "nature', but about practice; that what he wrote was intended to be true only for the moment at which he wrote it; that a theology of practice fundamentally identifies "religion" with "the history of religion" and still seeks "the truth": these possibilities lay beyond Augustine's reckoning. Augustine's legacy to us is a rupture between our conception of religion and the Roman search for *cognitio deorum*, knowledge of the gods, knowledge that was for them as historically specific as the institutions that developed in response to it.

PART I

Historiography and Method

Introduction to Part I:
Historiography and Method

There are no disinterested students of religion. Rather than seek a position of elusive and illusory objectivity, we ought instead to unpack and understand our own frame of reference. What are the terms with which we describe religious experience and whence do they derive? Such historical and theoretical self-consciousness constitutes an important prerequisite for the sort of cultural translation necessary to render ancient experience intelligible today. By intelligible, I mean something other than the accumulation of data positioned only in relation to each other. That kind of antiquarian erudition, with its implicit claim to an insider's knowledge, is itself necessary but not sufficient for the attainment of understanding.[1] Rather, remaining outsiders, we must view Roman religion from a distance both chronological and conceptual, and it is pre-eminently through conscious reflection on that distance, on the precise articulation of its depth and measure, that it might eventually be bridged.[2]

Arthur Darby Nock, one of the greatest scholars of religion in the ancient Mediterranean, famously defined "conversion" as "the reorientation of the soul of an individual, his deliberate turning from indifference or from an earlier form of piety to another, a turning which implies a consciousness that a great change is involved, that the old was wrong and the new is right."[3] Nock developed this definition in order to distinguish local syncretism and adhesion among and between immigrant and native populations – processes he considered characteristic of traditional Graeco-Roman religions – from the "psychological" transformation typical of Christian conversion.

---

[1] Smith 1995: 17–20 discusses five fundamental failings of lexical projects that claim to reveal how "they" understood (in this case) "magic."

[2] Smith 1978a: ix; Bremmer 1998: 12.

[3] Nock 1933: 7.

Proper "reorientation" is thus "seen at its fullest in the positive response of a man to the choice set before him by the prophetic religions."

Nock was a great comparatist, and his work on conversion continues to generate controversy: scholars regularly revisit Nock's test cases (the apostle Paul, the African sophist Apuleius, and Augustine), subjecting his sources and his methods to the latest skepticism.[4] For the present, we need only remark again on the disquieting sense that comparison with "Christianity" provides little more than an impression of what Roman religion was not.[5] Successive arguments of this type ultimately produce a null set: insofar as (Christian) religion's concerns are pre-eminently existential and individual, Roman religion was not a religion at all. Augustine's unabashed polemic – the "truly religious" seek eternal life, which Varro's gods cannot provide – stands somewhat closer to contemporary scholarship than might at first appear.[6]

In fact, Augustine's very own parishioners provide fascinating hints regarding the discrete domains occupied by Christian and pagan religiosity. In a sermon delivered early in the second decade of the fifth century, Augustine deplored the devotion of his flock to traditional cult and imagined their response to his challenge: "These things are necessary for this life. Of course, we are Christians for the sake of eternal life ... But the life that we lead right now, to its concerns Christ does not pertain."[7] Alas, Augustine announced elsewhere, "when their need is of meat, or bread, or water, or wine: these they should seek from God, not from a demon, or an idol, or some unknown power of this age. But there are those who, when they suffer hunger in this age, dismiss God, and ask Mercury or Jupiter, that he should provide for them."[8]

The binarisms and polarities operative in Augustine's screed will no longer do. On the one hand, the dissonance between Augustine and his flock reveals that conversion, for all its fascination as a

---

[4] On Augustine and Apuleius, respectively, see Frederiksen 1986 and Bradley 1998. For attempts to develop new (metaphorical) terms to replace "adhesion" in particular, see North 1992; Bendlin 1997, 2000.

[5] See above p. 11.

[6] Augustine *Civ.* 6.9: "For the present, I think I have shown with sufficient clarity that, according to Varro's division, the urban and poetic theologies belong to a single, civic one. And because both partake equally of shameless absurdity and brazen falsehood, the truly religious should never hope for eternal life from either one." Cf. ibid.: "For all his singular diligence, Varro has neither identified nor named a single god from whom eternal life may be sought, for which thing alone we are Christians."

[7] Augustine *En. Ps.* 40.3.

[8] Augustine *En. Ps.* 62.7.

literary trope, lacks the heuristic power to explain religious change even in the era in which it developed. But the same is true for multitudinous attendant and related phenomena implicated in definitions of religion in which conversion plays a role. Roman formalism, for example, so often taken to reveal a lack of that "sincerity" supposedly expressed by ecstatic emotion, rested on a sense of propriety that rigorously excluded pathos and passion.[9] At the same time, Romans and their dead, their needs and their gods, formed communities "of this time," "of this age," in which were shared "forums and temples, porticoes and roads, statutes and a system of justice."[10] If we are readier now to credit Varro, the consummate insider, with his regard for the contingent nature of institutions of worship, where do we go from there? What should we do with the mass of philological, linguistic, and archaeological data before us?

The essays reprinted in Part I tackle two problems in the study of religion. Jonathan Z. Smith's "On Comparison" offers a devastating look at the impoverished landscape of religious historiography. The book in which this chapter originally appeared, *Drudgery Divine: On the Comparison of Early Christianities and the Religions of Late Antiquity*, considers simultaneously the history, theory, and practice of comparative studies. It is a tour de force of scholarship and style. Its first chapter, "On Origins," argues that scholarship on early Christianity and contemporaneous religions was once implicated in, and continues to be influenced by, early modern ideological warfare between revivalist Protestants and their Catholic opponents.[11] "On Comparison," the second chapter in that book, challenges students of ancient religion to develop models and metaphors whose nuance and sophistication match that of the phenomena under study. It is above all a powerful caution regarding the potential for oversimplification and distortion inherent when we talk uncritically about religion.

Greg Woolf reviews much more recent trends in the study of Roman religion in particular. The contemporary tendency to view religion as a cultural system, one embedded in a political, economic, and cultural context, has unleashed a flood of work on local religions or, perhaps, religious history in very restricted "local" contexts,

---

[9] Linder and Scheid 1993: 52.
[10] Cicero *Off.* 1.53.
[11] Readers of this work should also consult Smith 1978b, which starts as a taxonomic exercise but closes by revealing in earlier scholarship an insupportable shift from putatively logical to purely chronological arguments: in so doing, scholarship has naturalized a set of modern (Christian) prejudices as though they were the result of an inevitable historical evolution.

whether single cities or regions.[12] To a certain extent, this practice harmonizes with ancient theological presuppositions, though these have been rather less well explored.[13] But here as elsewhere, we encounter the risk that we see in localism what the local elites wanted us to see. Religions exist in both space and time, and their maintenance, like their tenets, will have depended on their relationship to other ways of understanding and institutionalizing social power. "*Polis*-religion and its Alternatives" asks what is gained, and what is lost, by conflating religion with "state religion" in the Roman empire.

[12] Outside of Rome, see, e.g., Parker 1996 on classical Athens; Mikalson 1998 on Hellenistic Athens; Rives 1995 on Roman Carthage; and Dirven 1999 on Palmyra. For regional studies, see Mitchell 1993 on Anatolia; Frankfurter 1998 on Egypt, esp. 5–36; Derks 1998 and Woolf 2000 on Gaul; and Belayche 2001 on Judaea. A recent bibliography may be found in Krause, Mylonopoulos, and Cengia 1998: 574–612.

[13] See Smith 1978a: *passim*, 1990: 116–43; Beard, North, and Price 1998: I 167–210; and cf. Chapters 10 and 11 below.

1 *On Comparison*†

JONATHAN Z. SMITH

I

In 1611, when John Donne, in 'An Anatomie of the World', penned, as part of his surprisingly modern description of 'the world's condition now', the poignant well-known lines:

> 'Tis all in peeces, all cohaerence gone;
> All just supply, and all Relation:
> Prince, Subject, Father, Sonne, are things forgot,
> For every man alone thinkes he hath got
> To be a Phoenix, and that then can bee
> None of that kinde, of which he is, but hee.

he described a radical and solitary individualism under the sign of the phoenix, a unique being, *sui generis* in both the popular and technical sense of the term, self-generated and belonging to no wider class. In the words of Isidore of Seville, 'in the entire world, [the phoenix] is *unica et singularis*' (*Etymologies* 12.7.22), so the phoenix became, in Late Antiquity, at one and the same time, a rhetorical topos for the exceptional (e.g. Aristides, *Oration* 45.107; Synesius, *Dio* 9.3) as well as an early figure for the death and resurrection of Jesus (1 Clement 25).

Although the latter will preoccupy us in later chapters, it is with the question of the 'unique' that we are here concerned. Despite Henry J. Todd's view, in his revision of Samuel Johnson's *Dictionary* (1818), that 'unique' was an 'affected and useless term of modern times', it has proved to be both resistent and resilient. The 'unique' is an attribute that must be disposed of, especially when linked to some notion of incomparable value, if progress in thinking through the enterprise of comparison is to be made.

† Originally published in J. Z. Smith, *Drudgery Divine: On the Comparison of Early Christianities and the Religions of Late Antiquity* (Chicago: University of Chicago Press, 1990), pp. 36–53.

Let us be clear at the outset. There is a quite ordinary sense in which the term 'unique' may be applied in disciplinary contexts. When the historian speaks of unique events, the taxonomist of the unique *differentium* that allows the classification of this or that plant or animal species, the geographer of the unique physiognomy of a particular place, or the linguist of each human utterance as unique, he or she is asserting a reciprocal notion which confers no special status, nor does it deny – indeed, it demands – enterprises of classification and interpretation. *A* is unique with respect to *B*, in this sense, requires the assertion that *B* is, likewise, unique with respect to *A*, and so forth. In such formulations 'uniqueness' is generic and commonplace rather than being some odd point of pride. In my language, I would prefer, in such instances, the term 'individual', which permits the affirmation of difference while insisting on the notion of belonging to a class.

It is when the notion of superlative value is conjoined to the unique – an association that the *Oxford English Dictionary* blames on the French (who else!) – that one begins to verge on problematic modes of speech. As William James has reminded us:

> The first thing the intellect does with an object is to classify it along with something else. But any object that is infinitely important to us and awakens our devotion feels to us also as if it must be *sui generis* and unique. Probably a crab would be filled with a sense of personal outrage if it could hear us class it without ado or apology as a crustacean, and thus dispose of it. 'I am no such thing,' it would say, 'I am *myself, myself alone*.'[1]

The irony of this passage, which recognizes the genuineness of the impulse, the affirmation of individuality, but asserts, nevertheless, the probity of class, continues in a host of formulations which merge the notion of the unique and the special, while relativizing the former: a formula of 'unique, but ...'. As irony, the mood has been precisely captured in a fragment of dialogue between Edward Chamberlayne and Sir Henry Harcourt-Reilly in T. S. Eliot's *The Cocktail Party*:

> Edward: Mine is a very unusual case.
> Reilly: All cases are unique, and very similar to others.

Consider two further examples from widely divergent British texts where the ironic 'unique, but ...' appears far less conscious, but is no less present. The first is from the Preface to the *Guinness Book of World Records* (1979 edition):

[1] W. James, *The Varieties of Religious Experience* (New York, 1929): 10.

It should be stressed that unique occurrences and interesting peculiarities are not in themselves necessarily records.

The second is from the epigraph of a science fiction anthology, *England Swings SF* (1968), edited by Judith Merril:

You have never read a book like this before, and the next time you read anything like it, it won't be *much* like it at all.

Such irony is wholly displaced in the typical way in which 'unique' is spoken of in religious studies (and in some other fields within the human sciences). Here the 'unique' is more phoenix-like, it expresses that which is *sui generis, singularis*, and, therefore; *incomparably* valuable. 'Unique' becomes an ontological rather than a taxonomic category; an assertion of a radical difference so absolute that it becomes 'Wholly Other', and the act of comparison is perceived as both an impossibility and an impiety.

While the history of the 'unique' in religious discourse has yet to be written – unlike the history of paradoxography, of singularities and prodigies, within the natural sciences, which is a story well-told – I am willing to hazard the guess that when it is, it will reveal that the 'unique' is a thoroughly modern notion, one no earlier than those same nineteenth century German Protestant discussions which yielded, in reaction to comparative religious data, such diverse innovations as the notion of 'universal Christianity', the World Parliament of Religions ... and the study of religion as an academic pursuit.

The most frequent use of the terminology of the 'unique' within religious studies is in relation to Christianity; the most frequent use of this term within Christianity is in relation to the so-called 'Christ-event'. As one recent New Testament scholar (Burton Mack) has critically observed:

The fundamental persuasion is that Christianity appeared unexpectedly in human history, that it was (is) at core a brand new vision of human existence, and that, since this is so, only a startling moment could account for its emergence at the beginning. The code word serving as a sign for the novelty that appeared is the term unique (meaning singular, incomparable, without analogue). For the originary event the word is transformation (rupture, breakthrough, inversion, reversal, eschatological). For the cognitive effect of this moment the language of paradox is preferred (irony, parable, enigma, the irrational). It is this startling moment that seems to have mesmerized the discipline and determined the application of its critical methods.[2]

---

[2] B. Mack, *A Myth of Innocence: Mark and Christian Origins* (Philadelphia, 1988): 4.

The uniqueness of the 'Christ-event', which usually encodes the death and resurrection of Jesus, is a double claim. On the ontological level, it is a statement of the absolutely alien nature of the divine protagonist (*monogenes*) and the unprecedented (and paradoxical) character of his self-disclosure; on the historical level, it is an assertion of the radical incomparability of the Christian 'proclamation' with respect to the 'environment'. For many scholars of early Christianity, the latter claim is often combined with the former, so as to transfer the (proper, though problematic) theological affirmation of absolute uniqueness to an historical statement that, standing alone, could never assert more than relative uniqueness, that is to say, a quite ordinary postulation of difference. It is this illicit transfer from the ontological to the historical that raises the question of the comparison of early Christianity and the religions of Late Antiquity.

The issue of death and resurrection will be taken up in detail in Chapters Four and Five [*Drudgery Divine*, pp. 85–143]. Here it suffices to recall some parallel instances of the same sort of assertion, for example, the notion that the gospel-genre is unique. In Bultmann's phrasing of the double ontological/historical claim, the gospels 'are a unique phenomenon in the history of literature, and at the same time are symbolic of the distinctive nature of the Christian religion as a whole'.[3]

In its most radical formulations, by K. L. Schmidt and others, the proposition of the uniqueness of the gospel-genre seems to be a variation on the Protestant model of a pristine originary moment followed by corruption, and refers more to the gospel-behind-the-gospels than to the literary products associated with the evangelists. As Schmidt argued, 'Primitive Christianity, in general, did not enter into the World.' Its experiences and its forms of speech are, hence, by definition incomparable. This primitive community was, subsequently, subjected to change, to the 'hellenization, that is to say, the secularization, of the primitive Christian movement'.[4] From that moment on, it used common genres taken from its environment. This is an assertion of absolute originary uniqueness and relies on ontological presuppositions as to the alien nature of the object of Christian discourse. It also, if taken to extremes, would have the

---

[3] R. Bultmann, 'Evangelien', *Religion in Geschichte und Gegenwart*, 2nd edn (1928), 2:419.

[4] I have taken these citations of Schmidt from the important article by J. C. Meagher, 'The Implications for Theology of a Shift from the K. L. Schmidt Hypothesis of the Literary Uniqueness of the Gospels', in B. Corley, ed., *Colloquy on New Testament Studies: A Time for Reappraisal and Fresh Approaches* (Macon, 1983): 203–33; passage quoted, p. 208. (There is also a discussion of Maher's paper, pp. 235–62, and an introduction by Ch. Talbert, 197–202.)

'primordial gospel' fail at communication, unless through some Pentecost-like agency of the Spirit – a not unintended consequence, I fear – consonant with the general Reformers' impulse to shift the locus of inspiration from text to recipient.

Other arguments appear more 'statistical'. Scholarship has related the gospel to many forms of contemporary literature, from biography to aretalogy, but none of them seems precisely the same. However, this is a quite ordinary statement of difference which need not be raised to the language of the 'unique' except when under the influence of a nostalgia for the 'specialness' conceded to early Christianity by the ontological model. Besides, as already observed, such formulations are necessarily relative *and* reciprocal. If the Gospel of Mark is different from Iamblichus's *Life of Pythagoras*, so is Iamblichus different than Mark, so are both different from the Gospel of Matthew, and from Porphyry's *Life of Pythagoras*. Difference abounds. As James Robinson has argued, with respect to our topic, 'in view of the plurality of kerygmatic trends in primitive Christianity ... the view that one distinctive *Gattung* Gospel emerged sui generis from the uniqueness of Christianity seems hardly tenable'.[5]

The use of eschatology as a locus of uniqueness is even more revealing. In the hands of Schweitzer and others, the notion of eschatology was used as a critical tool against the liberal lives of Jesus and the 'perils of modernizing Jesus' (H. J. Cadbury's phrase). That is to say, it was a strongly marked (historical) indicator of difference between the environment of Jesus and that of our time. But in the hands of other New Testament scholars it was transformed into an indicator of absolute (ontological) uniqueness. As Dieter Georgi has shrewdly observed:

> [Bultmann] opposes what he calls the relativism of the history-of-religions school. [In this context] I need to mention the term 'eschatological'. It works for Bultmann and for many New Testament scholars and systematic theologians ever since as a magic wand. Whereas for the history-of-religions school the term 'eschatological' described the foreignness of Jesus and of the early church – together with Jewish apocalypticism and other comparable ancient eschatologies – for Bultmann and many contemporary New Testament scholars and Christian theologians the term 'eschatological' stands for the novelty of Christianity, its incomparable superiority, the uniqueness of the victorious religion ... Wherever a comparison is ventured, wherever analogies lift their head, wherever challenges are heard from other religious

5 J. M. Robinson, 'On the *Gattung* of Mark (and John)', in D. G. Buttrick and J. M. Bald, eds, *Jesus and Man's Hope* (Pittsburgh, 1970), 1:104.

options but the canonical ones, the invocation of the 'eschatological' is made, and the demons, the shadows have to disappear. Historical criticism thus turns into exorcism.[6]

To translate this into my sort of language, what was a relative statement that Jesus is 'alien' or 'strange' with respect to our time has been transformed, by later scholarship, into an absolute statement that Jesus is 'unique' in all respects for all time.

The same sort of critique could be made of the so-called 'criterion of dissimilarity' as a test for the *ipsissima verba* of Jesus.[7] As an ontological notion, it makes impossible the project of communication (leading to odd theories of a parabolic mode of speech which, paradoxically, destroys speech); as an historical project, it is implausible, both practically (by what procedures could we ever hope to gather all instances of contemporary speech?), and in principle (the majority of human utterances, which are nonetheless comprehensible, have never been uttered before).

No, what is required is an end to the imposition of the extra-historical categories of uniqueness and the 'Wholly Other' upon historical data and the tasks of historical understanding. From an historian's viewpoint, to cite Toynbee, 'This word "unique" is a negative term signifying what is mentally incomprehensible.'[8] What is required is the development of a discourse of 'difference', a complex term which invites negotiation, classification and comparison,[9] and, at the same time, avoids too easy a discourse of the 'same'. It is, after all, the attempt to block the latter that gives the Christian apologetic language of the 'unique' its urgency. To offer but one example of the rhetoric of the 'same', [...] Alfred Loisy writing on 'The Christian Mystery' in 1911:

> [Jesus] was a saviour-god, after the manner of an Osiris, an Attis, a Mithra. Like them, he belonged by his origin to the celestial world; like them, he had made his appearance on the earth; like them, he had accomplished a work of universal redemption, efficacious and typical; like Adonis, Osiris, and Attis

---

[6] D. Georgi, 'Rudolf Bultmann's *Theology of the New Testament* Revisited', in E. C. Hobbs, ed., *Bultmann: Retrospect and Prospect* (Philadelphia, 1985): 82, in the series Harvard Theological Studies, 35.

[7] N. Perrin, *The New Testament: An Introduction* (New York, 1971): 281, calls the test of dissimilarity 'the fundamental criterion'.

[8] A. J. Toynbee, *A Study of History* (Oxford, 1961), 12:11.

[9] It is possible, in fact, to make the same argument for theological discourse, although that is not my purpose here. One may note the delicious expression of the difficulty with the notion of utter alterity in H. W. Turner's *Commentary on Otto's 'Idea of the Holy'* (Aberdeen, 1974): 19, 'when Otto describes this experience of the Numen as "Wholly Other", he cannot mean *wholly* "Wholly Other"', as well as the welcoming of the language of 'difference' as opposed to 'otherness' in D. Tracy, *Plurality and Ambiguity* (New York, 1987): 20–21, et passim.

he had died a violent death, and like them he had returned to life; like them, he had prefigured in his lot that of the human beings who should take part in his worship, and commemorate his mystic enterprise; like them, he had predetermined, prepared, and assured the salvation of those who became partners in his passion.[10]

From such a parataxis of 'likeness', little of value can be learned. The reiterated 'like them' has swallowed up the differences that would render such a chain of comparisons interesting.

There is more concerning the matter of 'uniqueness'. If one illicit transfer with respect to the 'unique' shifts an ontological meaning to an historical one with respect to inter-religious comparisons, there has been a second, equally illicit, transfer which centres on an intra-religious comparison. According to this view, if Christianity is 'unique' with respect to other religions, then apostolic (or Pauline) Christianity is 'unique' with respect to other (especially later) modes of Christianity. This is a modulation of the Protestant historiographic myth: a 'uniquely' pristine 'original' Christianity which suffered later 'corruptions'.

In this construction one is not, in fact, comparing early Christianity and the religions of Late Antiquity. The latter have become code-words for Roman Catholicism and it is the Protestant catalogue of the central characteristics of Catholicism, from which it dissents, which provides the categories for comparison with Late Antiquity. [...]

This polemic strategy is often cunningly concealed in more recent writings as if it were merely a matter of chronology. Thus a recent New Testament scholar can assert, as his starting point, in an article concerned with the methodology of comparison:

> First of all, a distinction must be made between the faith and practice of the earliest Christians and that of the Church during subsequent centuries. One cannot deny that post-Constantinian Christianity, both Eastern and Western, adopted not a few pagan rites and practices ... The real difference of opinion, however, arises with regard to the relation of nascent Christianity to its pagan rivals.[11]

Hence the reiterated insistence, by most scholars concerned with the question, on the fact that the bulk of the evidence from the so-called 'mystery' cults is of a third century date, or later. The duplicity of this

---

[10] A. Loisy, 'The Christian Mystery', *The Hibbert Journal*, 10(1911–12): 51.

[11] B. M. Metzger, 'Methodology in the Study of the Mystery Religions and Early Christianity', *Harvard Theological Review*, 48(1955): 1–20, reprinted, with revisions, in Metzger, *Historical and Literary Studies: Pagan, Jewish and Christian* (Grand Rapids, 1968): 1–24, in the series, NTTS, 8. I cite the latter version; passage quoted: pp. 4, 6.

chronological caution is revealed when the same scholars, eager to demonstrate the close relationship of early Christianity to Judaism – the latter imagined to provide an insulation against 'paganism' [...] – recklessly quote alleged rabbinic parallels from Jewish documents no earlier than the same third century, and frequently far later.

Earlier scholars do not trouble with such disguise and state the object of comparison far more bluntly. Take, for example, a characteristic article, from 1924, by John Alfred Faulkner, a professor of New Testament at Drew University, devoted to the question, 'Did Mystery Religions Influence Apostolic Christianity?'[12] His conclusion is the same as the more recent essay in methodology just referred to:

> It has been shown ... that apostolic Christianity did not borrow anything of importance from the mystery religions. But when we come into the third, fourth, and following centuries we are in a different world. (2:266)

But the grounds for insisting on the lack of relationship are far more explicit. It is that 'apostolic Christianity' was essentially 'Protestant', and the 'mystery' religions essentially 'Catholic'. The very first comparison gives the game away. The early Christian communities were small, being only for 'rare spirits' willing to 'wrestle with God' and not, like those with 'untutored souls', distracted by a 'love of ritual'. The 'mystery' cults, by contrast to the Christian, were popular and 'spectacular'.

> Therefore, the Society of Friends is a wee folk, but the Roman Catholic, the Greek Catholic, and the Anglican Catholic Churches are a mighty body. (1:388)

Off-hand polemic comparisons abound: 'Like the Roman Catholic priests and the officers of secret orders today, priests and hierophants of the mystery religions held the keys of the kingdom of light' (1:392); 'the benefit of the initiations [in the "mysteries"] depended on male priests who alone knew the secrets of the Way, as in the Catholic Church of all schools' (1:393); and more extended comparisons insistently reiterate the point.

> So far as we know Christianity of the apostolic age and of the age immediately after, we can impute but little to this [pagan] influence. Christianity did not get the fact of sin from this source, nor her method of dealing with it by repentance and faith in Christ ... She had no secret meetings or initiations ...

---

[12] J. A. Faulkner, 'Did Mystery Religions Influence Apostolic Christianity?' *The Methodist Quarterly Review*, 73(1924): 387–403; Faulkner, 'Did Ancient Christianity Borrow from the Mystery Religions?' *The Methodist Quarterly Review*, 74(1925): 266–78. In citing these articles above, I have distinguished between them by designating them as '1' or '2'.

Nor did she play on the pride of knowledge in general, as did Gnosticism and some of the mysteries. Her first disciples were plain men and not scholastically trained, and she welcomed everybody into her ranks and not simply philosophers and the learned. Nor did Christianity deal in ritual or spectacular display, thus being far removed from the mystery religions. In apostolic times we have a full description of the services in Corinth, and they remind you of a modern prayer meeting or an old-fashioned Methodist class meeting [!]. (1:395)

As Faulkner would have it, apostolic 'Christianity separated itself from all ancient religions by not being magical, no *deus ex machina*, no *ex opere operato*, no repeat-formulae-and-it-is-done, no turn-common-things-into-sacred-by-an-incantation, no priestly-sleight-of-hand' (1:397) until the 'change' to a 'sacramental' doctrine which became characteristic from 'the fourth century to the present in all so-called Catholic Churches. In these the mystery religions still function to-day before our very eyes' (2:269, cf. 2:274).

One can formulate the principle of comparison that has informed the majority of scholarship in this area as follows: 'Apostolic Christianity' and 'Protestantism' are 'unique'; the religions of Late Antiquity, most especially the 'mysteries' and 'Catholicism', are the 'same'.

The model for this defensive strategy is as old as the recorded history of religious comparison. It is the notion of 'autochthony' as present in Herodotus. And this concept of self-generation, in the Herodotean enterprise, is always conjoined to a second topos, the notion of 'borrowing'. Thus the Egyptians are dependent on no one for their customs and borrow no foreign practices (*Histories* 2.79, 91); the Persians, objects of scorn for both the Greeks and the Egyptians, borrow from everyone. 'No people are so ready to adopt foreign ways as are the Persians' (1:135). For secondary cultures, such as Greece, everything depends on pedigree, on borrowing from a prestigious primary centre. Thus, taking up Egyptian propagandistic claims, Herodotus writes that the 'younger' Greeks borrowed freely from the 'older' Egyptians (e.g. 2.4, 43, 49, 50, 57, 58, 81, 82) with no suggestion that this implies a necessarily negative valuation.[13]

In the study of the relations of early Christianity to the religions of Late Antiquity, the names have been altered from Herodotus's

---

[13] See, on the Herodotean enterprise, [J. Z.] Smith, *Map Is Not Territory: Studies in the History of Religion* (Leiden: Brill, 1978): 243–49. On the question of prestigious pedigree in the cultural propaganda of the Hellenistic world, see the suggestive article by E. J. Bickerman, 'Origines Gentium', *Classical Philology*, 47(1952): 65–81.

time, but the relations remain the same. Early Christianity is primarily to be considered as autochthonus. If there is any dependency, it is from a prestigious centre. In this model, Israel appears in the role of the Herodotean Egypt. The Catholic Church, or in more recent treatments, 'Greco-Oriental syncretism', plays the part of Persia. This requires that the enterprise of comparison focus on questions of borrowing and diffusion. The use of comparison as a hermeneutic device, or as a principle of discovery for the construction of theories or generic categories, plays no role. What rules, instead, is an overwhelming concern for assigning value, rather than intellectual significance, to the results of comparison. This may be seen when, in a remarkable moment of candour, the former president of San Francisco Seminary declared in an interview in the *New York Times* (29 May 1966/E:7): 'In his own education, Dr. Gill added, the Jew as opposed to the ancient Greek, the Gnostic or the mystery religionist was the "good guy".' (This common, and duplicitous, use of Judaism as an insulating device for early Christianity will be taken up in Chapter Three [*Drudgery Divine*, pp. 54–84].)

II

Having set aside the issue of the 'unique' in its various forms and questioned the simple discourse of the 'same', we need to think about the enterprise of comparison under the aspect of difference. As I have argued elsewhere:

> It is axiomatic that comparison is never a matter of identity. Comparison requires the acceptance of difference as the grounds of its being interesting, and a methodical manipulation of that difference to achieve some stated cognitive end. The questions of comparison are questions of judgement with respect to difference: What differences are to be maintained in the interests of comparative inquiry? What differences can be defensively relaxed and relativized in light of the intellectual tasks at hand?[14]

That this is *not* the working assumption of many scholars in the field may be seen by noting the poverty of conception that usually characterizes their comparative endeavours, frequently due, as has already been suggested, to apologetic reasons. It is as if the only choices the comparativist has are to assert either identity or uniqueness, and that the only possibilities for utilizing comparisons are to make assertions regarding dependence. In such an enterprise, it would appear, dissimilarity is assumed to be the norm; similarities

---

[14] [J. Z.] Smith, *To Take Place* [(Chicago: University of Chicago Press, 1987)]: 14.

are to be explained as either the result of the 'psychic unity' of humankind, or the result of 'borrowing'.

Within the field of study under review, these options are expressed as the choice between 'analogy' and 'genealogy' (i.e. homology), with the latter used in the sense not only of establishing direct relations (borrowing and dependency), but also prestigious origins (pedigree).[15] The thought appears to be that, from a standpoint of protecting the privileged position of early Christianity, it is only genealogical comparisons that are worthy of note, if only, typically, insistently to be denied. As 'analogies' pose no apparent threat, they are most often

[15] In the above, I appeal to the well-known biological distinction, first formulated in the nineteenth century by Richard Owen, between homology and analogy which replaced the older Aristotelian distinction between substance and accident. As reformulated, after Darwin, in the works of biologists such as E. Haeckel, C. Gegenbaur and E. R. Lankester, a homology is a similarity of form or structure between two species shared from their common ancestor; an analogy is a similarity of form or structure between two species not sharing a common ancestor. To give the textbook illustration, the human hand and the whale's flipper are homologous; the whale's flipper and the fish's fin are analogous. The task of taxonomy, since Darwin, especially in its dominant phylogenetic forms, has been to eliminate analogies (which serve, to use a linguistic term, as 'false friends'), and to construct relationships entirely on the basis of homologies.

Prior to Darwin, analogous relationships were usually explained on the basis of similarity and economy of function (i.e. the whale's flipper and the fish's fin are efficient modes of locomotion); post-Darwin, analogous relations are most often explained by convergent processes of natural selection in terms of environment (i.e. the whale's flipper and the fish's fin are independent and parallel adaptations to an aquatic milieu). Hence, most of the major developments in taxonomy, from the late nineteenth century interest in embryological classification to the contemporary interest in genetic classification, have been attempts to set aside convergent similarities and to base taxonomy entirely on ancestry and descent. The task has been to distinguish 'kinds' (homologies) from 'sets' (analogies), and to privilege the former. Matters are, of course, not quite this simple. The matter of construing the relationship between taxonomic groups remains deeply controversial, most especially when there are different rates of divergence. While numerical taxonomy would insist on a purely phenetic approach, and cladistics on a purely phylogenetic approach, the dominant modes of evolutionary taxonomy have, in fact, compromised the two: all things being equal, phylogenetic classification is to be preferred; however, in cases of relatively rapid development, phenetic classifications are to be employed.

In contradistinction to the taxonomists, contemporary morphologists continue to work successfully with analogies, although the understanding of the phenomenon has clearly changed from the older idealistic postulations of *Urformen* to the notion of the primacy of the environment. Form is no longer a question of pure architecture, of intrinsic relationships and principles of construction, rather, since the 1930s, form is seen as the product of extrinsic environmental selection.

There is one paramount issue which appears to distinguish the biological enterprise of phylogenetic comparison from those within the human sciences. The phylogeneticist strives, at least in theory, for a 'natural' classification; the human scientist must always propose an 'artificial' classification. This is because there is, arguably, nothing comparable to genetic processes within the sphere of human culture. Even here, however, matters are more complex than they first may seem, for in all schools of evolutionary taxonomy, it is *only* at the level of species that the hereditary and reproductive link is key. Hence the fundamental, though far from unproblematic, definition of species in terms of interbreeding. Higher taxa can only be defined by similarity of form and thus represent relatively artificial schema. That is to say, at the level of species (or at lower levels) homology conventionally rules biological comparison; at higher levels, procedures more closely akin to analogy govern classification.

held to be without interest. Thus, in an article entitled 'Methodology in the Study of the Mystery Religions and Early Christianity', which contains the presupposition that 'Christianity is *sui generis*', Bruce M. Metzger writes that:

> Even when parallels are actual and not imaginary, their significance for purposes of comparison will depend on whether they are genealogical and not merely analogical parallels. That is to say, one must inquire as to whether the similarities have arisen from more or less equal religious experience, due to equality of what may be called psychic pitch and equality of outward conditions, or whether they are due to borrowing from one another.[16]

The foundation text for this distinction is that of Adolf Deissmann. About mid-point through his enormous monograph, *Licht vom Östen*, concerned with largely philological parallels, Deissmann pauses to raise a 'methodological problem which has engaged my liveliest interest since the beginning of my studies'. The question is: 'Is it analogy or is it genealogy?' Are the apparent similarities 'parallelisms of more or less equal religious experiences ... or are they dependent upon one another, demonstrable borrowings'? Deissmann's further reflections indicate that he had something more complex in mind than is usually represented in those who cite him.

> Where it is a case of inward emotions and religious experiences and the naive expression of these emotions and experiences in word, symbol, and act, I should always try first to regard the particular fact as 'analogical'. Where it is a case of formula, a professional liturgical usage, or the formulation of some doctrine, I should always try first to regard the particular fact as 'genealogical'.

Unlike later proponents of the distinction (as represented by the Metzger passage), there is no sense in Deissmann that significant parallels are genealogical ones because they threaten the uniqueness of early Christianity, and, hence, the concomitant desire to reduce all parallels to 'mere' analogies. In Deissmann, the significance and utility of both are affirmed. This is because Deissmann has a general theory of religious phenomena which governs the distinction. Whilst there are good reasons to challenge its adequacy, he presumes a dichotomy between spontaneous expressions which reflect 'emotions

---

[16] Metzger, 'Methodology in the Study of the Mystery Religions': 18 and 9. The second sentence of the second citation is an unacknowledged direct quotation from Deissmann, see below, n. 17. The lengths to which Metzger carries this distinction may be illustrated by a characteristic sentence: 'the resemblance between the Lord's Supper and certain Mithraic ceremonies ... may be regarded as either fortuitous or as the result of adaptation by Mithraic priests of an impressive rite in the Christian cultus' (16, n. 2). What an odd choice! For Metzger, the 'resemblance' is either to be classified as analogical, understood as a matter of chance, or it is genealogical and asserted to be of Christian pedigree.

and experiences', and stereotyped second-order expressions, assuming that the generality of the former leads, as an initial hypothesis, to explaining similarities as 'analogical', whilst the specificity of the latter leads, as an initial hypothesis, to explaining similarities as 'genealogical'. He further demonstrates an awareness of the politics of such explanations. 'The apologist, if he ever acknowledges anything, acknowledges as a rule only analogy, and prefers to erect walls and fences around his own little precinct' – an apt description of Metzger! The 'amateur in these subjects thinks only of genealogy'.[17]

Nevertheless, one cannot help but be struck by the paucity of imagination present in even a sophisticated formulation of this apparently self-evident duality. If one opens any dictionary of synonyms, one gains an immediate sense, by contrast, of the rich vocabulary of similarity and difference. While there are terms which suggest the sort of kinship implied by the notion of the 'genealogical' – for example, 'affinity', 'homology', and 'divergent' – the majority of the terms presume *intellectual operations* on the part of the individual making the comparison, as well as the notion that we are comparing *relations and aspects* not things. This observation is reinforced by looking at other comparative endeavours within the field of religion, when the subject is remote from that of early Christianity. One will find, alongside of terms such as 'homology' and 'analogy', 'identity' and 'difference', a vocabulary of 'transformation', 'inversion', 'reversal', 'opposition', 'contrast', 'correspodence', 'congruence', 'isomorphic', 'conjunction', disjunction', and so forth,[18] as well as a more polythetic notion of classification (in opposition to a monothetic one) that employs phrases such as 'family resemblances', 'connotative features', 'fuzzy sets', 'cluster concept', among others.[19]

What this terminology reminds us of is that, like the effort of taxonomy which forms its presupposition, there is nothing 'natural' about the enterprise of comparison. Similarity and difference are not 'given'. They are the result of mental operations. In this sense, *all comparisons are properly analogical*, and fall under J. S. Mill's dictum, 'if we have the slightest reason to suppose any real connec-

---

[17] A. Deissmann, *Lichi vom Östen*, 4th edn (Tubingen, 1923): 226–27; I cite the English translation, *Light from the Ancient East: The New Testament Illustrated by Recently Discovered Texts of the Greco-Roman World* (New York, 1927): 265–66.

[18] While, perhaps, an extreme example, all of these terms can be found in the 'Table of Symbols' in C. Lévi-Strauss, *The Raw and The Cooked* (New York, 1969): xiii.

[19] See the fuller list in the seminal article by F. J. P. Poole, 'Metaphors and Maps: Towards Comparison in the Anthropology of Religion', *Journal of the American Academy of Religion*, 54(1986): 428. The entire article (pp. 411–57) will well repay careful study.

tion between ... A and B, the argument is no longer one of analogy'.[20]

In the case of the study of religion, as in any disciplined inquiry, comparison, in its strongest form, brings differences together within the space of the scholar's mind for the scholar's own intellectual reasons. It is the scholar who makes their cohabitation – their 'sameness' – possible, not 'natural' affinities or processes of history. Taken in this sense, 'genealogy' disguises and obscures the scholar's interests and activities allowing the illusion of passive observation (what Nietzsche has termed [*Zarathustra* 2.15] the 'myth of the immaculate perception').

Without engaging in the intricacies of resemblance theory, it can usefully help us at this point.[21] It is agreed that the statement 'x resembles y' is logically incomplete, for what is being asserted is not a question of the classification of species x and y as instances of a common genus, but rather a suppressed multi-term statement of analogy and difference capable of being properly expressed in formulations such as:

x resembles y more than z with respect to ...;

or

x resembles y more than w resembles z with respect to ...

That is to say, the statement of comparison is never dyadic, but always triadic; there is always an implicit 'more than', and there is always a 'with respect to'. In the case of an academic comparison, the 'with respect to' is most frequently the scholar's interest, be this expressed in a question, a theory, or a model – recalling, in the case of the latter, that a model is useful precisely when it is different from that to which it is being applied.

This is to say, comparison does not necessarily tell us how things 'are' (the far from latent presupposition that lies behind the notion of the 'genealogical' with its quest for 'real' historical connections); like models and metaphors, comparison tells us how things might be conceived, how they might be 'redescribed', in Max Black's useful term.[22] A comparison is a disciplined exaggeration in the service of knowledge. It lifts out and strongly marks certain features within

[20] J. S. Mill, *A System of Logic*, 10th edn (London, 1879), 2:371.
[21] See, among others, D. J. O'Connor, 'On Resemblance', *Proceedings of the Aristotelian Society*, 46(1945–46): 47–77, and P. Butchvarov, *Resemblance and Identity* (Bloomington, 1966), which include the essential bibliography.
[22] M. Black, *Models and Metaphors* (Ithaca, 1962):236–38; cf. M. B. Hesse, *Models and Analogies in Science* (Notre Dame, 1966): 164–65.

difference as being of possible intellectual significance, expressed in the rhetoric of their being 'like' in some stipulated fashion. Comparison provides the means by which *we* 're-vision' phenomena as *our* data in order to solve *our* theoretical problems.

The 'political' implications of this 're-visioning' must be faced as they go to the heart of a widely shared set of assumptions within religious scholarship, nowhere more so than in the study of early Christianity.

In his seminal essay on the sociology of knowledge, Karl Mannheim introduced a valuable distinction which bears directly on the question of the ideological dimension of comparison. Mannheim distinguished between 'right-wing' and 'left-wing' methodologies:

> Early nineteenth century German conservatism ... and contemporary conservatism, too, for that matter, tend to use morphological categories which do not break up the concrete totality of the data of experience, but seek rather to preserve it in all its uniqueness. As opposed to the morphological approach, the analytical approach characteristic of the parties of the left, broke down every concrete totality in order to arrive at smaller, more general, units which might then be recombined ...[23]

Religious studies, with its bias towards the 'unique' and the 'total', expressed methodologically through its deep involvement in morphology, phenomenology and, more recently, a morality of regard for local interpretations, has been a discipline profoundly and not unsurprisingly of the 'right'. The comparative endeavour herein described is relentlessly an affair of the 'left'. To quote the anthropologist, F. J. P. Poole:

> Comparison does not deal with phenomena *in toto* or in the round, but only with an aspectual characteristic of them. Analytical control over the framework of comparison involves theoretically focused selection of significant aspects the phenomena and a bracketing of the endeavor by strategic *ceteris paribus* assumptions ... The comparability of phenomena always depends both on the purpose of comparison and on a theoretically informed analysis. Neither phenomenologically whole entities nor their local meanings are preserved in comparison. What matter in comparison are certain variables that are posited by and cohere in theories and that are aligned with aspects of the phenomena to be compared through some set of correspondence rules.[24]

Comparison, as seen from such a view, is an active, at times even a playful, enterprise of deconstruction and reconstruction which, kaleidoscope-like, gives the scholar a shifting set of characteristics

---

[23] K. Mannheim, *Ideology and Utopia* (New York, n.d.; reprint): 274.
[24] Poole, 'Metaphors and Maps': 414–15.

with which to negotiate the relations between his or her theoretical interests and data stipulated as exemplary. The comparative enterprise provides a set of perspectives which 'serve different analytic purposes by emphasizing varied aspects' of the object of study.[25]

It is the scholar's intellectual purpose – whether explanatory or interpretative, whether generic or specific – which highlights that principled postulation of similarity which is the ground of the methodical comparison of difference being interesting. Lacking a clear articulation of purpose, one may derive arresting anecdotal juxtapositions or self-serving differentiations, but the disciplined constructive work of the academy will not have been advanced, nor will the study of religion have come of age.

[25] Poole, 'Metaphors and Maps': 432.

2 Polis-*Religion and its Alternatives in the Roman Provinces*†

GREGORY WOOLF[1]

1 INTRODUCTION

One of the most striking features of the religious life of the Roman provinces is its sheer complexity: so many gods, so many images, such complex rituals. The search for a rationale that might order that complexity engaged the attention of ancient scholars of religion such as Varro in his *Antiquities*, Plutarch in his monograph *On Isis and Osiris* and (polemically) Augustine in the *City of God*. Modern scholars too are preoccupied by an attempt to find an order in religious practice and belief.

Modern accounts are less ideologically charged than those of ancient writers who were concerned to define collective identities, to impose discipline within citizen bodies and confessional groups, and to reconcile traditional practices and beliefs with other intellectual systems, in particular philosophy.[2] Much ancient writing on religion was prompted by a sense of complexity resulting from contact between very different cultural traditions: Xenophanes and Herodotos, Varro and Cicero, Caesar and Tacitus are cases in point. The use of scholarship as a device for negotiating these cultural transformations was itself a Greek practice, adopted in turn by Romans and others, and used alongside other cultural strategies designed to similar ends, syncretisms of various kinds, the appropriation of new cults and the persecution of groups whose religious practice was regarded as deviant. Ideological concerns are equally evident in

---

† Originally published in H. Cancik and J. Rüpke, eds, *Römische Reichsreligion and Provinzialreligion* (Tübingen: Mohr Siebeck, 1997), pp. 71–84.

[1] This paper represents a revision of that written for the Bad Homburg colloquium and also draws on papers given at the universities of Heidelberg and Göttingen. I am grateful to Jörg Rüpke for comments on an earlier draft of this paper.

[2] For an example of the latter see Beard 1996.

the attempts by writers such as Paul, Philo, Plutarch and Clement to respond to the cognitive challenges posed by philosophical arguments.

The accounts of ancient religion produced since Fustel de Coulanges[3] have a different cultural origin but are equally characterised by attempts to seek order and coherence in the diversity of ancient religion. Naturally, without some attempt at ordering it is impossible to do more than describe and catalogue ancient cults. Yet ordering is never an innocent procedure. Even assigning ancient cults to a series of religions – Athenian religion, Roman religion, Mithraism, Christianity – involves a certain collusion with the disciplinary aims of ancient writers. The best we can hope for is to be aware of the ideological context of the various ordering principles we disengage from our study of ancient cults, to be conscious, in other words, of the interests that were served by various ancient orderings of religion.

2 *POLIS*-RELIGION

It is with these considerations in mind that this paper attempts to examine one ordering principle that has recently become especially prominent in the study of the cults of the Roman provinces, a principle that for convenience I shall refer to as the '*polis*-religion model'. That approach is a powerful one and I should begin by stating clearly that I shall accept that the order it uncovers is not a modern fiction but rather corresponds closely to some ways in which certain ancients understood their religions, even if their understanding was not formulated in quite the same terms and was perhaps manifested more in performance and practice, that is to say in the rituals and routines of cult and in its management, than in explicit statements. But that model of ancient religion itself has an ideological component. The aim of this paper is to consider what difference it makes to our understanding of the cults of the Roman provinces if the *polis*-religion model is regarded not as the key to understanding their organisation, but simply as one among several ordering principles, and an interested one at that.

Let me begin by outlining the main features of the *polis*-religion model. Those who make use of it begin from seeing ancient religion as essentially homologous with the social and political structures of ancient societies. The accounts of Greek religion presented by Bruit

---

[3] Fustel de Coulanges [1864].

[Zaidman] and Schmitt Pantel and by Sourvinou-Inwood (from whom I gratefully borrow the term '*polis*-religion') provide excellent examples of how this is envisaged in practice.[4] The public cults of the city, shared in some sense by all who are citizens of it, occupied a central place in ancient religion. Those cults were controlled and presided over by priests drawn from the civic elite, which collectively also had authority over the entirety of religious action within the *polis* and by its citizens. In this respect (as for Fustel) Greek *poleis* and the Roman Republic are alike. So Beard and Crawford begin their brief survey of Roman Republican religion by stating 'we firmly believe (although we cannot finally prove) that this "official" Roman state cult was the crucial defining element of the religious system as a whole. Here was to be found the "Romanness" of Roman religion; here was the centre around which other elements took a secondary place.'[5]

The *polis*-religion model brings with it a history of ancient religion. The homology of the sacred and the social/political is seen as exemplified in its most perfect form in the archaic and classical *polis* (Rome again included). Its origins have been most fully examined in the case of the Greek *polis*, with de Polignac's argument that as the *polis* emerged in the archaic period so collective *polis* sanctuaries were developed, while others were subordinated to them, linked to them by processions or allocated roles as collective sanctuaries of the constituent entities of the *polis*; demes, tribes, *pagi, vici, komai, compitalia* and the like. Border sanctuaries, federal and international sanctuaries likewise reflected and reinforced the emergent political geography of classical Greece.[6]

The spread of the city state in Greece, through the Mediterranean basin and in Hellenistic and Roman empires, led to the extension of *polis*-religion.[7] Yet as the autonomy and integrity of *poleis* were weakened by those same imperialisms there was a marked growth in alternative forms of religion – Bacchic cult, Judaism, Mithraism, Christianity among others – which paid less respect to *polis* boundaries and the social order. While some see these developments as preserving the homology of the sacred and the social, as an adaptation, in other words, to new patterns of social and political organ-

[4] Bruit Zaidman, Schmitt Pantel 1992, Sourvinou-Inwood 1990; cf. also (more cautiously) Parker 1996.
[5] Beard, Crawford 1985, 25f.
[6] de Polignac 1984, 1994.
[7] Gordon 1990.

isation in which the role of the *polis* was diminished,[8] for North 'the basic story ... is one of development from religion as embedded in the city-state to religion as choice of differentiated groups offering different qualities of religious doctrine, different experiences, insights, or just different myths and stories to make sense of the absurdity of human experience'.[9] Generally, however, the history of ancient religion is inserted into the narrative of the rise and fall of the classical city state.

That brief summary does not do justice to the nuanced and sophisticated arguments of the scholars whose work I have been discussing. All accept the complexity of religion and the extent to which any ordering is incomplete, and to some extent the following discussion develops caveats and qualifications in their accounts. *Polis*-religion, then, in its modern formulation is a heuristic construct. Its strengths may be illustrated from significant advances it has secured in our understanding of several key aspects of ancient religion. Notably it has enabled more convincing accounts to be produced of the interaction of politics and religion in ancient society. The new cults created for the new Cleisthenic tribes and the cult paid to the Roman emperors in the provinces are two cases in point,[10] where previous accounts of insincere 'manipulation' of religion for political ends have been superseded by descriptions of how a religion conceived of as homologous with the political and social might help mediate political and social change. The study of religious innovation more generally, and the roles played in it by civic authorities, has been transformed so that we no longer write of the decline, obsolescence and decay of traditional orders, and rather of religion as a creative and fluid force.[11] The establishment of public cults in the western provinces has been illuminated by a close attention to Roman conceptions of the relationship between the civic and the divine order.[12]

The explanatory power of these accounts derives from the identification of homology as a central structuring or ordering principle of ancient religions, and as one important way in which those religions differed from the religious systems we are familiar with from our own experience. Homology does not, of course, mean identity. Greeks and Romans were perfectly able to conceptualise religion

---

[8] Cf. Rives 1995, 173–249, for a nuanced version of this argument.
[9] North 1992, 178. Gordon 1990 also accords religious change a degree of autonomy from social and political developments.
[10] Kearns 1985, Price 1984 respectively.
[11] E.g. North 1976.
[12] Scheid 1991 followed by van Andringa 1994 and Rives 1995.

as a discrete cognitive domain. All religions are primarily means of making sense of the world, of mankind and of each individual worshipper's place in it, devices that offer a consistent account of the origins and workings of the cosmos and some explanations of and remedies for common misfortunes. What is distinctive is the place that *polis*-religion allocated to society and politics within the cosmos, and the institutionalisation of that relationship in the structures of the classical city state.

It is important to ask not only how ancient religion was ordered but also: Whose order was it? Putting the public cults of the *polis* at the centre of accounts of ancient religion allows us to read some ancient accounts of religion more sympathetically but runs the risk of collusion with just one view of ancient religion, that of those who controlled the *polis*. Gordon's brief account of the religions of the early empire has done most to expose this difficulty.[13]

Gordon's formulation for what I have called *polis*-religion is 'the civic compromise' which he glosses as a 'close nexus between sacrifice, benefaction and domination by the elite'.[14] That model of priesthood and cult he regards as a dominant one, deliberately opposed by Rome to alternative religious systems in Italy and in the provinces alike. It bolstered the power of the elite of the city of Rome over other citizens, and of Romanising elites against their social subordinates and against traditional priesthoods such as the Druids or the Egyptian priesthood. Practices deemed deviant were marginalised as *superstitio* and magic, and from time to time their practitioners were persecuted as well as ridiculed and despised by the powerful and the educated. Naturally the boundary between *religio* and *superstitio* needed constant policing, and practices like astrology appealed to some of the most prominent members of those very elites that legitimated their dominance partly through their public support of 'the right rites'. But in general Gordon sees the proponents of the civic compromise as successful in maintaining their dominance of ancient society and ancient religion. If a few religions, notably Mithraism and Christianity, rejected outright some key features of ancient religion, for the most part the resistance offered by 'oriental cults' and magic came to trace the contours of the hegemonic power of *polis*-religion, strengthening the public cults of the city by tacitly consenting to its cosmology.

[13] Gordon 1990. For a fuller view on similiar lines cf. Beard, North and Price (forthcoming [1998]) volume I, chapter 9. I am grateful to the authors for allowing me to see this work prior to its publication.

[14] Gordon 1990, 235.

Gordon's account has the merit of situating ancient cult in the context of struggles for power within ancient societies. The central tenets of *polis*-religion tell us not how ancient religion was organised but how some groups tried to organise it. That shift in perspective reminds us to read Cicero's religious writings as prescriptive and disciplinary, rather than as disinterested systematisations of norms. The very existence of such works reminds us that at least some of the powerful did not regard the dominance of *polis*-religion as wholly secure. Accepting the interested nature of the religious action need not entail a return to the view of ancient elites as closet rationalists, keeping up the mumbo jumbo for the sake of the gullible and super-stitious masses. Rather we should imagine that a good many of them conceptualised their views in purely religious terms, without being ignorant of their interest in the status quo. The religious sensibilities of those northern European princes who sponsored the Reformation provide a distant parallel, and it is well known that the proponents of any dominant ideology are often those most convinced of its truth.

But if Gordon's view offers a critical approach to *polis*-religion it is inevitable that public cults of the city remain central to his account. In fact all accounts of ancient cult that begin from the public cults have these characteristics; that other cults are relegated to the category of private (defined negatively as cults which were not organ-ised by public authorities); that new cults are seen, as it were, from the perspective of the Capitol, remarkable for their difference from public cults, and most visible at the moment of acceptance (and adaptation) or rejection (and persecution); and that syncretisms and *interpretationes* in the naming and representation of deities tend to be viewed from a political (i.e.: *polis*-centred) perspective, as if Romanisation and Resistance were the only issue at stake when provincials turned to the heavens.

This emphasis is one that the religious and political authorities of ancient cities would have approved of, even if they may have dissented from the critical stance adopted by Gordon's account. It is not simply a product of the evidence, since traces of 'private' cults abound: votive objects and inscriptions are extremely common finds, traces of ritual acts on low status sites are not rare, curse tablets and magical papyri are attested archaeologically and ancient *testimonia* tells us a good deal about how they were used. The emphasis on public cults is a product of the way one ordering principle has been privileged in both ancient and modern studies of ancient religion.

3 SHORTCOMINGS

Some of the strengths of *polis*-religion as a heuristic model have been outlined. It is appropriate now to identify a few areas where it has been less successful.

First, *polis*-religion offers little explanation of the complexity of ancient religion: put bluntly, the profusion of gods, cults and priesthoods seems redundant if the needs of the city are seen as paramount. Even if this complexity is viewed, as it often is, as the result of an accumulation of successive layers of religions (e.g. Indo-European cults on top of mother goddesses, or bronze age rituals overlying. Neolithic survivals and both subordinated to the new religion of the city state) it is difficult to see why redundant cults were preserved and supernumerary deities not simply syncretised into some sort of order by those who ran *polis*-religion.

Second, the emphasis on public rituals leaves little room for some aspects of religion that seem to have been very important to some ancients, myth for example, or even some prominent deities, for example Silvanus or the *Matres*, who never received public cult.[15]

Third, *polis* religion may be good at showing how civic authorities managed change and coped with religious innovation, but not very good at showing why change took place at all. A few cults – the rituals performed by the fetials are usually cited – might seem to have become impractical in changed circumstances, but many public 'innovations' seem in fact to be responses to changes in what might be termed the religious *koine* of the Mediterranean world. If the origins of religious innovation most often came from the world of 'private religion', any perspective that marginalises non-public cult is bound to be handicapped in accounting for change.

Fourth, treating private cult as secondary makes it difficult to account for the continued popularity of paganism in a period when public cults withered away and were abolished. Continuities in ritual from paganism to Christianity – hymns, ritual feasting at graves, votives – are also difficult to examine if such practices are as marginalised by scholars as they were by civic priests and Christian bishops.

This list of 'blind-spots' is not intended to be comprehensive, yet neither does it provide grounds for rejecting the *polis*-religion model and all its strengths. The point of raising them here is to illustrate some of the drawbacks in regarding ancient paganism as structured only or even primarily around the public cults of the *polis*. A more

---

[15] Dorcey 1992.

realistic (if less neat) account might aim to uncover a variety of inter-linked and intersecting ordering principles, some more influential in private cult than in public, some common to both.

4 ALTERNATIVES

A glimpse of the range of possibilities is offered by Glen Bowersock's recent study of late paganism in the east. The post-Constantinian era, when public cults and the religious authority of public bodies steadily diminished, offers a view of what paganism might look like without the *polis*. What emerges is not a formless sea of local superstitions, private cults bereft of the centres around which they had formed, but rather a complex yet structured system of beliefs and practices. Bowersock argues that what linked the pagan cults of Greece, Asia Minor, Syria and Egypt was Hellenism, conceived of as 'language, thought, mythology, and images that constituted an extraordinarily flexible medium of both cultural and religious expression'.[16]

Polis religion had a role to play, of course. To begin with a number of world-famous temples – the Alexandrian Serapeum, the grove of Apollo at Daphne outside Antioch, Syrian Hierapolis, the Temple of Asclepius at Pergamon among others – continued to provide *foci* for pagan cult, as the determination of Christian authorities to destroy and/or appropriate them indicates. These temples had been, at least since the Roman conquest, subordinated to civic authorities and euergetistic priesthoods. But it is equally clear that paganism sur-vived the destruction of its temples, and that even before their destruction those temples drew worshippers from well outside the *poleis* by which they were notionally controlled.

In fact the *polis*-religion model provides only a partial account of the religious life of the Greek east under Roman rule even during the early imperial period. Sacred texts, personal revelation and initiations seem to have gained in prominence since the classical period, as well as the new forms of religious organisation mentioned in the quotation from North cited above. Several alternatives' ordering principles may be discerned, mostly visible through literary texts which reflect and in some senses reproduced a distinct religious sensibility.

Perhaps the most obvious is myth. No canonical account of Greek myths existed, although the Homeric epics provided something similar for writers such as Strabo who were concerned to document

---

[16] Bowersock 1990, 7.

the cultic geography and history of places as well as their political traditions. The importance of Homer and of myth is a reminder that Greek religion pre-dated the *polis*-religion created in the archaic and classical periods. *Polis*-cults had drawn on myth and continued to do so in the Roman period, celebrating them in civic festivals like those at Ephesos connected with the cult of Artemis whose birthplace the city was said to be; on local coinages for which local heroes and deities provided a major source of images; and on the iconography of temples. Hierogamies and syncretisms offered various ways of representing civic identities and relationships like *syngeneia* and *homonoia* between cities. Myth was only able to perform this function of expressing the place of a city in a wider world and a longer tradition because it was already shared by all Greeks. Discrepant traditions did not seem to erode the utility of myth, since no supra-civic religious authorities existed that could rule definitively on these matters.

Closely connected with the use of myth was the ordering of religion by place. If certain gods might be worshipped anywhere, nevertheless some places were more intimately connected with their myths than others, and onto this landscape of myth was grafted a landscape of cult.[17] Places were famous not only for their 'real' history, which might also be celebrated with cult as at Plataea or Actian Nicopolis, but also for the divine deeds that had been performed there. The fact that *poleis* competed to control some sanctuaries, as happened in the case of the long rivalry between Sparta and Messene for the border sanctuary of Artemis Limnatis,[18] demonstrates the religious status some sanctuaries enjoyed independently of their function in *polis*-religion. Other cities owed their own status to the sanctuaries in their territory: Claros and Apollo's oracle, for instance, or Abonoteichos and that of Ion for which the city was renamed Ionopolis.

Oracles provide a good example of a form of cult that co-existed with *polis*-religion but was never wholly subordinated to it. Their popularity during the Roman period is well documented.[19] Other cults too were firmly rooted in one particular place, for example the healing sanctuaries of Asclepius at Epidauros and Pergamon, or the Mysteries at Eleusis. It is notable that in both cases we are dealing primarily with cult paid by individuals. One consequence of this rooting of certain cults in the particular places was the growth of

[17] Alcock 1993, 172–214, for an innovative study case in these terms.
[18] Tac. *ann.* 4.43.
[19] Lane Fox 1986, 168–259, for an evocative account.

pilgrimage, a device that allowed worshippers to use travel as a way of making contact with the divine. Nor was it confined to the very rich. Inscribed footsteps in temples throughout the Roman world attested the fulfilment of pilgrimages. Literary accounts naturally offer a fuller insight into some of the ways religion and place were connected up. Pausanias' account of his journey through Greece is suffused with a religious sensibility,[20] perhaps felt even more acutely by a Greek who was not born in old Greek lands.

Pilgrimage was made much easier by the Roman peace. Its growing popularity provides one example of a general phenomenon, the extent to which Roman rule had begun to undermine the autonomy of the *polis* (and so *polis*-religion). The loosening of the bonds of the classical city is a familiar feature of the Roman period in the Greek east. A general increase in geographical mobility resulted in the growth of immigrant communities in most major coastal cities. Some of these newcomers were doubtless small traders, yet the period also sees the emergence of provincial elites who held land in several *poleis*, while the wealth of some *incolae* and *metoikoi* was significant enough for *polis* authorities to attempt to tap it. The economic growth enabled by better communications, greater security, more unified systems of law, currency and language resulted in the growth of large cities at the expense of small ones, and these large cities with significant immigrant minorities were culturally and so religiously cosmopolitan. When many of a city's citizens lived abroad and many of those resident in the city were not citizens then *polis*-religion was less and less viable as a form of social integration.

Roman rule was not the only threat to the dominance of *polis*-religion. North notes the growth within the Hellenistic and Roman periods of religions whose organisation was not homologous with that of society. Certainly, the larger post-classical *poleis* offered environments well suited to these new cults and freer movement facilitated the travels of Diaspora Jews, Christian and Manichee missionaries, and travelling priests of Cybele of the kind satirised by Apuleius. But it is implausible to account for these cults simply in terms of their capacity to offer a cure for urban anomie. The success of these religions also owed something to their capacity to integrate lower status worshippers into a community more closely than did *polis*-religion, and to the various kinds of salvation and revelation they offered. Although it is now customary to emphasise that so

---

[20] Elsner 1992; cf. Auffarth in this volume ['"Verräter-Übersetzer"? Pausanias, das römische Patrai und die identitat der Griechen in Achaia,' pp. 219–38].

called 'Oriental Cults' like those of Isis, Serapis, Mithras and Christ were largely remodelled and sometimes created in a Mediterranean environment, their alien origin is not irrelevant. Classical Isis did preserve attributes and myths of Egyptian origin, Cybele, even when Romanised as Mater Magna, preserved a 'foreign' character as representations of her priests make clear. If *polis*-religion tried hard to exclude alien cults or else to admit them strictly on its own terms, private worship was clearly much more open to novelty.

One of the main reasons such changes were possible was that, for pragmatic reasons, a huge gap existed between the cults *polis*-religion prescribed and those it proscribed, a space within which citizens were notionally free to worship as they wished in 'private cult'. Those limits were policed and frequently renegotiated by *polis* authorities and religious writers alike, but the gap was never completely closed because *polis* authorities were even less capable than Christian bishops would be to create a totalitarian religious system. It was through this gap that cultural exchanges brought new religious beliefs and rites that would disturb *polis*-religion, especially since some of these new religions rejected the subordination of private cult to public.

It remains to be asked how the *polis*-religion of the Greek east fared in these changed conditions. There, where *polis*-religion owed little to Roman imperialism, it seems likely that the cumulative effect of Roman rule was to loosen the control exercised by the *polis* over cults. New cults and new religious organisations attracted adherents from the citizen body. Although from the perspective of the civic authorities these developments might have been regarded as simply a re-organisation of private cult, in fact the public cults of the *polis* came to be less and less central in the religious lives of the citizens and non-citizen inhabitants, if only because not all those adhering to new religions accepted the official line that these 'private' cults were essentially secondary, and because those adherents included some drawn from the *polis* elites.

This is one context, I suggest, in which we might set the massively increased expenditure by euergetistic elites on public festivals in the second century AD.[21] The great festivals were not, in other words, an expression of the continued importance of *polis*-religion but rather an attempt to bolster it against rival attractions. That attempt did not succeed in restoring to *polis*-religion the dominant position it had enjoyed in the archaic and classical periods. Yet *polis*-religion

---

[21] Spawforth 1988, Mitchell 1993, 217–26, for recent introductory accounts.

remained powerful and through festivals continued to involve many more than just the elite of the city. Civic identity still remained important, after all, not just among those elite members who paid for festivals and public buildings and took on expensive priesthoods, but also among the populations of cities that occasionally rioted against neighbouring cities or against religious minorities within their own. Christian apologists certainly saw *polis*-religion as powerful enough to require a refutation of the charge that Christians were necessarily bad citizens.

One possible response to the argument so far would be to accept that *polis* religion was under pressure in the east but to account for this in terms of a supposed greater degree of resistance to Roman influence on the part of the Greeks.[22] Yet if we turn to the west – and I shall consider the Gallic provinces in particular – some similar patterns can be made out, albeit less distinctly in the absence of many of the categories of evidence available for the Greek world. If the Gauls ordered their religious world with myth it is lost to us now and was perhaps already forgotten in the Roman period. Local coinages did not survive the first half of the first century AD, and neither pre- nor early Roman art in Gaul has any clear narrative element.

Yet pre-Roman religion was not completely obliterated. Syncretism of Roman and local gods – rare in the Greek world – may have served similar ends, and took many forms. Gods might be given double names (Mars Lenus); sometimes Deus or Dea preceded an indigenous name or epithet; hierogamy linked some Roman male deities with some indigenous local ones (Mercury and Rosmerta); gods with Roman names might be represented with local attributes (Sucellu's *sagum* for Silvanus in southern Gaul) or with particular animals (Epona and her horse, Nehalennia and her dog); and occasionally, statuary might combine a series of classical and indigenous deities as happened on the pillar of the nautae at Paris. It is easy to suspect mythic episodes lie behind some common local iconographic motifs, such as Jupiter fighting serpent-footed giants on many of the Jupiter-columns of the north east, or Esus cutting down a tree on the pillar of the nautae. But attempts to interpret these deities and images in terms of a mythology or a pantheon are fraught with difficulty.

But the existence of a landscape of the sacred is much clearer. Deities often had toponymic epithets, like Mercurius Dumias worshipped on the Puy de Dôme in the Auvergne or Dea Bibracte

---

[22] Although the notion that the Greeks did mount a greater resistance to Romanisation might be challenged, cf. Woolf 1994.

worshipped at Autun. It was not only mountain peaks that attracted cult. Early imperial offerings at the source of the Seine and the spring of Chamalières show river-deities too received cult. Earlier cultic geographies contributed to the Gallo-Roman landscape of the sacred. *Fana*, small shrines of hybrid design, are frequent on the sites of abandoned *oppida* and/or overlie iron age sanctuaries as at Gournay-sur-Aronde in Picardy. It has been suggested that pilgrimage was a feature of the pre-conquest period.[23] Whether or not that is the case, pilgrimage certainly developed in the Roman period, for example to the huge oracular shrine at Grand near Toul, some of [the pilgrims being] interested in astrological as well as Apolline predictions.[24] It is irrelevant for present purposes to try to determine which of these cults were new and which old. The point is that Gallo-Roman cult was not ordered solely in terms of *polis*-religion or the civic compromise.

Naturally the Gallo-Roman city did play an important role. The creation of Roman *coloniae* and *municipia* entailed the establishment of a Roman version of *polis*-religion, complete with euergetistic priesthoods, control of cults by the magistrates and decurions, and public festivals at central sanctuaries.[25] But it is difficult to determine how big a part was played by *polis*-religion in the cults of the Gallo-Romans. It certainly mobilised the funds of many of the Gallo-Roman elite in the formative period of Gallo-Roman culture, but whether the absence of great festivals like those of the Greek east in the second and third centuries shows the strength of *polis*-religion or its weakness is difficult to say. Public building of all kinds was rare after 200 AD and in the north after 150 AD, whereas evidence for private cult increases in quantity in the second and third centuries as *fana* and Jupiter-columns were constructed by wealthy landowners on their estates, and as votive practices were adopted from the military in the north east.[26]

Whether or not the decline of *polis*-religion in the west followed the same pattern as in the east, it is clear that the creation of Gallo-Roman religion opened up a similar gap between public cults and the proscribed religions (such as Druidism and human sacrifice), and

---

[23] Goudineau 1991.

[24] Abry *et al.* 1993.

[25] Brunaux 1991 suggests that something akin to *polis*-religion may be discerned in the late iron age when large sanctuaries appeared in some parts of Gaul, but the evidence for social and political change in that period is too slight and its interpretation too controversial to permit certainty.

[26] Derks 1991 on votives; Bauchhenss, Noelke 1981 on Jupiter-columns; Goudineau, Faudet and Coulon 1994 on *fana*.

within this space, conceptualised by Romanised city authorities as
'private religion', a wide range of cultic activity is visible. At the
Altbachtal sanctuary in Trier it included cult to syncretised deities, to
thoroughly Roman gods and to indigenous ones.[27] Cultic practices
attested elsewhere in Gaul included animal sacrifice along traditional
lines in which whole or mutilated corpses were buried in deep pits
surrounded with other objects, including coins, ceramics and metal
ornaments, yet also curse tablets in Latin and in Celtic; votive objects
and (adopted from the military in the north west) the dedication of
votive altars.[28] Naturally Isis, Mithras, Christ and Mater Magna had
their adherents.[29] In short, the cults of the Gallo-Romans seem as
complex and diverse as those of the Romano-Greeks, and those who
controlled *polis*-religion succeeded in organising only a part of them.

5 CONCLUSION

The importance of the *polis*-religion model of Roman provincial
religion is not undermined by the preceding observations. Indeed
the repeated efforts made by the ruling elites of ancient city states to
define proper cult and distinguish it from superstition; to subordinate
religious practice to their vision of civil society; and to retain religious
sanction for their social and political pre-eminence appear all the
more significant when set against the background of the more
complex religious lives of their subjects. Yet an appreciation of
that religious ferment that the term 'private religion' inadequately
describes and deliberately marginalises is equally important, most of
all for understanding the origins of change, both in public cults and
in religious practice as a whole. Myth, landscape and ritual traditions
(in which representational traditions should be included) were only
some of the ways in which that wider religious world might be
ordered and conceived, but give some sense of how others outside
the *polis* elites might have experienced ancient religion, and of what
went on in that crucial gap between the prescribed and the proscribed
cults of the ancient city.

[27] Scheid 1995.
[28] Brunaux 1995 on ritual continuities, Derks 1995 on vows, Lejeune, Marichal 1976/7,
Lejeune 1985 for curses.
[29] Turcan 1986 for an introduction.

BIBLIOGRAPHY

Abry, J. H.; Buisson, A.; Turcan, R. (eds) 1993. *Les tablettes astrologiques de Grand (Vosges): et l'astrologie en Gaule romaine*, Paris.

Alcock, S. 1993 *Graecia Capta*, Cambridge.

Bauchness, G.; Noelke, P. 1981. *Die Jupitersäulen in der germanischen Provinzen*, Beihefte der Bonner Jahrbücher 41, Bonn.

Beard, M. 1996. 'Cicero and divination: the formation of a Latin discourse', *Journal of Roman Studies* 76. 33–46.

Beard, M.; Crawford, M. 1985. *Rome in the Late Republic. Problems and Interpretations*, London.

Beard, M.; North, J. A.; Price, S. R. F. (1998). *Religions of Rome*, 2 vols, Cambridge.

Bowersock, G. W. 1990. *Hellenism in Late Antiquity*, Cambridge.

Bruit Zaidman, L.; Schmitt Pantel, P. 1992. *Religion in the Ancient Greek City*, Cambridge [revised edition of French original 1989].

Brunaux, J.-L. 1991. 'Les sanctuaires celtiques et leurs rapports avec le monde mediterraneen, in: J.-L.Brunaux (ed.), *Les sanctuaires celtiques et le monde méditerranéen*, Dossiers de Protohistoire 3, Paris, 7–13.

Brunaux, J.-L. 1995. 'Religion gauloise et religion romaine. La leçon des sanctuaires de Picardie', *Cahiers du Centre Glotz* 6. 139–161.

Derks, T. 1991. 'The perception of the Roman pantheon by a native élite: the example of votive inscriptions from Lower Germany', in: N. Roymans, F. Theuws (eds), *Images of the Past. Studies on Ancient Societies in Northwestern Europe*, Amsterdam, 235–265.

Derks, T. 1995. 'The ritual of the vow in Gallo-Roman religion', in: J. Metzler et al. (eds), *Integration in the Early Roman West. The role of Culture and Ideology*, Dossiers d'Archaeologie du Musée Histoire et d'Art 4, Luxembourg, 111–127.

Dorcey, P. F. 1992. *The Cult of Silvanus. A Study in Roman Folk Religion*, Leiden.

Elsner, J. 1992, 'Pausanias: a Greek pilgrim in the Roman world', *Past and Present* 135. 3–29

Fustel, de Coulanges, N. D. 1864. *La Cité antique*, Paris.

Gordon, R. 1990. 'Religion in the Roman empire: the civic compromise and its limits', in: M. Beard, J. North (eds), *Pagan Priests. Religion and Power in the Ancient World*, London, 235–255.

Goudineau, C. 1991. 'Les sanctuaires gaulois: relecture d'inscriptions et de textes', in: Brunaux J.-L. (ed.), *Les sanctuaires celtiques et le monde méditerranéen*, Dossiers de Protohistoire 3, Paris, 250–256.

Fauduet, I.; Coulon, G. (eds) 1994. *Les sanctuaires de tradition indigène en Gaule romaine* (Actes du colloque d'Argentomagus), Paris.

Kearns, E. 1985. 'Change and continuity in religious structures after Cleisthenes', in: P. A. Cartledge, F. D. Harvey (eds), *Crux. Essays in Greek History Presented to G. E. M. de Ste. Croix*, London, 189–207.

Lane Fox, R. 1986. *Pagans and Christians in the Mediterranean World from the Second Century* AD *to the Conversion of Constantine*, London.

Lejeune, M. 1985. 'Textes gauloises et gallo-romains en cursive latine: II. Le plomb de Larzac', *Etudes Celtiques 22. 95–177*.

Lejeune, M.; Marichal, R. 1976/7. 'Textes gauloises et gallo-romaines en cursive Latine 1', *Etudes Celtiques 15. 151–157*.

Mitchell, S. 1993. *Anatolia* vol. 1, Oxford.

North, J. A. 1976. 'Conservatism and change in Roman Religion', *Papers of the British School of Rome 44. 1–12*.

North, J. A. 1992. 'The development of religious pluralism', in: J. Lieu, J. A. North, T. Rajak (eds), *The Jews among Pagans and Christians*, London, 174–193.

Parker, R. 1996. *Athenian Religion. A History*, Oxford.

de Polignac, F. 1984. *La naissance de la cité grecque*, Paris.

de Polignac, F. 1994. 'Mediation, competition and sovereignty: the evolution of rural sanctuaries in Geometric Greece', in: S. E. Alcock, R. G. Osborne (eds), *Placing the Gods: Sanctuaries and Sacred Space in Ancient Greece*, Oxford, 3–18.

Price, S. R. F. 1984. *Rituals and Power. The Roman Imperial Cult in Asia Minor*, Cambridge.

Rives, J. B. 1995. *Religion and Authority in Roman Carthage from Augustus to Constantine*, Oxford.

Scheid, J. 1991. 'Sanctuaires et territoire dans la Colonia Augusta Treverorum', in: J.-L. Brunaux (ed.), *Les sanctuaires celtiques et le monde méditerranéen*, Dossiers de Protohistoire 3, Paris, 42–57.

Scheid, J. 1995. 'Der Tempelbezirk im Altbachtal zu Trier: ein "Nationalheiligtum"', in J. Metzler *et al.* (eds), *Integration in the Early Roman West. The Role of Culture and Ideology*, Dossiers d'Archaeologie du Musée d'Histoire et d'Art 4, Luxembourg, 101–110.

Sourvinou-Inwood, C. 1990. 'What is polis religion?', in: O. Murray, S. R. F. Price (eds), *The Greek City from Homer to Alexander*, Oxford, 295–322.

Spawforth, A. J. 1988. 'Agonistic festivals in Roman Greece', in: S. Walker, A. Cameron (eds), *The Greek Renaissance in the Roman Empire. Papers of the 10th British Museum Classical Colloquium*, Bulletin of the Institute of Classical Studies supplement 55, London, 193–7.

Turcan, R. 1986. 'Les religions orientales en Gaule narbonnaise et dans la vallée du Rhône', *ANRW* II.18, 1, 456–518.

van Andringa, W. 1994. 'Cultes publiques et statut juridique de la cité des Helvètes', in: *Roman Religion in Gallia Belgica and the Germaniae, Actes des Quatrièmes Rencontres Scientifiques de Luxembourg*, Bulletin des Antiquités Luxembourgeoises 22, Luxembourg, 170–194.

Woolf, G. D. 1994. 'Becoming Roman, staying Greek. Culture, identity and the civilizing process in the Roman East', *Proceedings of the Cambridge Philological Society n.s. 40. 116–143*.

PART II

Religious Institutions and Religious Authority

Introduction to Part II:
Religious Institutions
and Religious Authority

What we study when we study religion is one mode of constructing worlds of meaning, worlds within which men find themselves and in which they choose to dwell. What we study is the passion and drama of man discovering the truth of what it is to be human. History is the framework within whose perimeter those human expressions, activities and intentionalities that we call "religious" occur. Religion is the quest, within the bounds of the human historical condition, for the power to manipulate and negotiate one's "situation" so as to have space in which meaningfully to dwell. It is the power to relate one's domain to the plurality of environmental and social spheres in such a way as to guarantee the conviction that one's existence "matters." Religion is a distinctive mode of human creativity, a creativity which both limits and creates limits for human existence. What we study when we study religion is the variety of attempts to map, construct and inhabit such positions of power through the use of myths, rituals and experiences of transformation.

Jonathan Z. Smith, Map is Not Territory[1]

Within this quintessential outsider's view of religion, with its jarring, asyndetic list of things that religion "is," lies a view of socialization and social theory profoundly and usefully irreligious.[2] Tacitly setting aside categories contested between religious groups – no gods here, least of all gods who once were mortal – we concentrate instead on problems of autonomy, identity, and power.

To consider for the moment only the last topic, religion as quest for power, we might approach it from two perspectives, one cultural and the other theological. On the one hand, religious beliefs, practices, and institutions mediate the distribution of wealth and power within societies. In doing so, they operate in concert with other cultural systems, each possessing its own modality and register.

---

[1] Smith 1978a: 290–1.
[2] Cf. Versnel 1993: II 1–19.

57

Religious specialists – priests, diviners, prophets, experts in religious law, and magicians – must therefore negotiate a place for themselves within or outside the public sphere, and their claim upon that place, as upon the allegiance of individuals, will stand alongside, as well as occasionally and partially in contradistinction to, those put forward by other authorities. In a literal sense, "religion" must also occupy or control geographic space, whether urban or rural, public or private: to this latter problem we shall return in Part VI.

Religious specialists at Rome were as varied as religious experience itself.[3] Romans writing about priesthoods tended to concentrate on the figures and colleges integrally involved in the religious health of the community as a whole: the Vestal Virgins and *flamines*, the *pontifices*, the augurs and *haruspices*, the *quindecimviri sacris faciundis*, and the *fetiales*.[4] The first set includes the priests of the most important divinities publicly acknowledged and collectively worshipped by the Roman people; the *pontifices* supervised public rituals and the private cult of the dead; the augurs and *haruspices* oversaw different sciences of divination; the *quindecimviri* interpreted foreign prophetic books at the behest of the Senate; and the *fetiales* supervised declarations of war and peace.[5] In so limiting themselves, Cicero, Varro, and Valerius Maximus observed distinctions between public and private, Roman and foreign, that were essential to Roman conceptions of religious practice, distinctions we shall take up in Part V. Excluded from such lists *a priori* were an enormous range of priests and religious authorities, male and female of all social ranks, not least *patresfamiliae*, whose piety was not so much irrelevant as taken for granted.[6]

---

[3] The best English introductions to Roman "priesthood" are Beard 1990; Scheid 1993b; and Potter 1999: 134–41. All three concentrate on priests of the state cult, though all address issues raised by the problem of religious expertise in general.

[4] In addition to Valerius Maximus 1.1.1a–b and Cicero *Nat. Deor.* 3.5, see Cicero *Leg.* 2.20–1 and Varro *Ant. Div.* frr. 4, 51–61.

[5] On these, see the glossary and index.

[6] Cf. Nock 1972: 532: "When Cicero says (*Phil.* 9.14) 'the sanctity of tombs is in the ground itself, which no force can move or destroy; and, while other things are extinguished by old age, tombs only grow more sacred,' he shows a complete absence of fear as to the security of tombs. The dead man *must* be safe there; the assertion that tombs were *religiosa*, 'hallowed,' perhaps made [the legal commandment] *sacer esto*, 'let them be consecrated,' unnecessary. After all, in early Roman times implicit obedience to such definitions could be expected. Consider the analogy of perjury. From the standpoint of religion, it was always serious. But the perjurer needed no special ban; he had brought one on himself. Accordingly, no action was taken against perjury as such (as distinct from false witness): 'slights to the gods are the concerns of the gods.'" Compare Cicero *Leg.* 2.19 and 25: In his "law," Cicero urges that "the god himself" will exact justice if someone does not approach the gods in ritual purity, and allows in his commentary that through this provision "religious scruple seems to be strengthened through fear of imminent punishment."

Defining the sphere of competence even of the major priests and colleges proves rather more complex than one might expect.[7] For example, in his *Laws* Cicero describes the role of the *pontifices* as "presiding over ceremonies and rituals."[8] We might have expected a *pontifex* to *perform* the ceremony. Not so: rather, the *pontifex* possessed specialized knowledge, which he placed at the disposal of elected magistrates in a very precise way. For example, when the consul Decius Mus famously decided to "devote" himself *pro legionibus*, to sacrifice himself to save his legions, he summoned a *pontifex* in the following terms: "We need the help of the gods, Marcus Valerius. Come, *pontifex publicus* of the Roman people, speak before me the words by which I might devote myself for my legions."[9] Cicero and Varro used similar terminology to make it clear that while the pontifex spoke first, it was the magistrate's utterance of exactly the same words that was efficacious.[10] The magistrate's authority in these matters, moreover, derived from the *imperium* and *auspicium* that the Roman people surrendered to him for his term in office.[11] Wherever it was and however it was understood, sacral authority at Rome emphatically did not reside exclusively in its priests.

To speak at a somewhat different level of abstraction, in Roman legal thinking the *ius publicum*, public law, namely, that which respected the condition of the Roman commonwealth, treated *sacra*, *sacerdotes*, and *magistratus*: sacred objects and sacred rites, priesthoods, and magistracies.[12] So, when describing a debate over the legal and religious status of his (illegally) consecrated house, Cicero quoted Marcus Lucullus, then *pontifex maximus*, responding on behalf of his college in the following terms: "the *pontifices* were arbiters of religion, but the Senate was arbiter of the law. Hence he and his colleagues had reached a conclusion insofar as religious scruple was concerned, but they would reach a conclusion in the Senate, with the Senate, where the law was concerned."[13] The supremacy of the Senate flagged by Lucullus in this formulation is

---

On equestrian (see glossary s.v. *eques*) priests see Scheid and Granino Cecere 1999; on women see Richlin 1997 and cf. Boëls-Janssen 1993; on diviners and magicians see MacMullen 1966: 95–162 and Potter 1994.

[7] On the codependency of priests and magistrates, see Scheid 1984.

[8] *Leg.* 2.20.

[9] Livy 8.9.4.

[10] See Varro *Ling.* 6.61 and Cicero *Dom.* 120 and 122, and cf. Historia Augusta *Marcus Aurelius* 4.4, with Nisbet 1939: 209–10.

[11] Mommsen 1887: I 76; Magdelain 1968: 19–20, 1990: 307–11 and 342–56.

[12] Ulpian *Institutes* 1 = Ulpian 1908 at Lenel 1889: II 927 = *Dig.* 1.1.1.2.

[13] Cicero *Att.* 74 (4.2.4).

fundamental, for it was a body as concrete as its judgment was final, and those qualities distinguish it absolutely from the diffusion and confusion characteristic of religious authority in the priestly colleges. There, the sheer multiplicity of religious specialists, combined with the technicality of their secret knowledge, simultaneously suggested that religious know-how was everywhere required, even as it shored up the prestige of the Senate, the very symbol of oligarchic power and aristocratic privilege, by granting it sole authority to act upon the advice of those specialists. Not for naught did the Greek historian Polybius regard δεισιδαιμονία, fear of the gods, as the web holding the Roman social fabric together.[14]

Why fear the gods? Were these not the gods from whom the Romans sought to wrest power? From a theological perspective, one might view religion as mediating the distribution of power not among humans but between god and human. On this topic more than any other the Romans have confounded their students. In the eyes of critics, the legalistic punctiliousness of Roman vows diminishes Roman gods.[15] After all, even a Roman could conclude that "the power of omens is under our control and their influence is conditional upon the way we receive each." But Pliny the Elder, who made that judgment, understood that the reception of omens formed a part of ritual and, as such, was governed by *ius*. It was, furthermore, an essential characteristic of Roman gods that they beneficently submitted themselves to the laws of their community. Indeed, there was in Pliny's opinion "no greater sign of divine indulgence" than that the gods of Rome granted such efficacy to the language of prayer in the proper performance of cult.[16] No greater point of difference between Greek and Roman religion exists.

Richard Gordon and Arthur Darby Nock consider the problems of power and authority in Roman religion from these two perspectives. Gordon's essay was the first of three published together in 1990. As a group, they provide a remarkable, diachronic analysis of religion's position within the changing face of Roman society, first at Rome and subsequently in the municipal landscape of its Mediterranean empire. "From Republic to Principate" studies the city of Rome at the end of the Republic and places religious authorities and institutions amidst crises in politics and alongside developments in the technologies of knowledge production. Nock, for his part,

---

[14]   Polybius 6.56.6–15, with Vaahtera 2000.
[15]   See above p. 11.
[16]   Pliny *Nat.* 28.17, on which see p. 232 below. On the problem of *ius*, see pp. 5–11 above.

studies "a feature of Roman religion," which is to say, he attempts to isolate and describe what is essential and idiosyncratic about the way that Romans addressed their gods. His approach is philological – he concentrates on the language of prayer – and comparative, the point of comparison being Greek religious language of a slightly earlier period.

3 *From Republic to Principate:*[†] *Priesthood, Religion and Ideology*[*]

RICHARD GORDON

PRIESTLY COLLEGES AND THE CREATION OF THE PRINCIPATE

We have no term which accurately represents the institutions and attitudes characteristic of Roman religion. Cicero would have been surprised to discover that we refer to the religion of the late Republic as 'polytheism', thus emphasizing the fact, of interest only in a Christian context, that numerous divinities received worship. By contrast, when C. Aurelius Cotta, the Academic spokesman in Cicero's dialogue *De Natura Deorum* (*On the Nature of the Gods*), describes Roman religion, he does not, in fact, mention gods, whether few or many. He says, 'As a whole, the *religio* of the Roman people is divided into *sacra* and *auspicia* – a third additional heading being the warnings produced concerning the future from portents and prodigies by the interpreters of the Sibyl (that is, the *XVviri sacris faciundis*) and the *haruspices*'. And he goes on – speaking expressly as a priest as well as a philosopher – to lay emphasis on the political character of Roman religion: 'Romulus, by founding the ritual of taking the auspices, and Numa, by founding the *sacra*, laid the foundations of our state, which assuredly would never have been able to become so great without our having taken the greatest care to placate the immortal gods.'[1] What is significant for Cotta about

† Originally published in M. Beard and J. North, eds., *Pagan Priests: Religion and Power in the Ancient World* (Ithaca, NY: Cornell University Press, 1990), pp. 179–98.

* Much of the work on this chapter [...] was done at the British School at Rome; and it was finished at the Fondation Hardt, with financial assistance from the British Academy. I would like to thank all three institutions, and especially Amanda Claridge, for their kindness. The editors [of the original volume], and Robin Cormack, have been over indulgent to a slothful contributor.

1 Cicero, *Nat. D[eor].* 3, 2, 5. This threefold division reappears in Cicero's thinking. See, for example, *Leg.* 2, 8, 20 & 12, 30–1: also *Har. Resp.* 9, 18 (where the *haruspices*, however, appear to form an independent category of a fourfold division of priesthoods). For other

Roman religion is not so much the objects of worship but the institutions which made possible Rome's greatness, among them the two key sacerdotal colleges, the *pontifices*, who supervised the *sacra*, the ensemble of rules and rituals which we loosely group under the word 'religion', and the *augures*, who had responsibility for the *auspicia*, a major axis of communication between men and gods.

This emphasis upon the importance of the priestly colleges to the maintenance of Roman religion and so of the Roman state reappears elsewhere in the late Republic and early Empire. For example, we may instructively compare the organization of the greatest modern book on Roman religion, the second edition of Georg Wissowa's *Religion und Kultus der Römer* (1912), with that of Varro's *Antiquitates Rerum Divinarum* (*Religious Antiquities*) which appeared in 47/46 BC, and of which we have a good general knowledge through its extensive quotation by Augustine in Books 4 to 7 of *De Civitate Dei* (*City of God*).[2] Wissowa, after devoting eighty pages to a historical narrative divided into four periods, chose to describe the gods next, a subject to which he devoted 280 pages, about half his space. The third part, about 200 pages, deals with sacral law, rituals, festivals, games, sacred places and the various priestly colleges. Finally, there are two useful appendices on the calendar and the list of temples officially accorded space by the Roman people. By contrast, Varro omits history almost entirely as a possible means of organizing his knowledge of Roman religion, although some consciousness of historical decay seems clearly to have been central to his purpose in writing the book in the first place.[3] In keeping with his basic assumption that, though a God of some sort truly pre-exists, civic religion is a thoroughly human creation,[4] Varro devotes the three books after the general introduction to an account of the three major sacerdotal colleges.[5] There follow three books on shrines and sacred places, three on festivals and three on rituals public and private. Only then does Varro turn to discuss the divinities of the Roman people.[6] Moreover, there is no evidence that he emphasized

ancient attempts to classify traditional priesthoods, see [...] Beard, ['Priesthood',] 44–7 [...]

[2] See Cardauns (ed.), *Varros Antiquitates RD*, with his more general discussion, 'Varro und die Römische Religion, zur Theologie, Wirkungsgeschichte and Leistung der *Antiquitates Rerum Divinarum*', ANRW II, 16.1, 80–103.

[3] See, for example, [*Ant. Div.*] fr. 2a and 12.

[4] Fr. 20; 22; 35–7; 39.

[5] Cardauns (ed.), *Varros Antiquitates RD*, 39–46. Unfortunately almost nothing survives of these books. Cardauns allows only five, mostly single-sentence, fragments on the pontifical college; the longest surviving fragment, under the *XVviri s.f.*, is really about the Sibylline books and oracles.

[6] For the organization of [*Ant. Div.*], see fr. 4, which establishes the division into four

what is for us one of the most striking features of Roman religious organization, its control by the Senate, for which in a sense the sacerdotal colleges acted as committees.[7] Rather, the scope and minuteness of the authority of the *pontifical* college were stressed, as well as the antiquity of priestly institutions at Rome. For although the historical tradition ascribed the institution of eight sorts of priestly authority to Numa (described in great detail by Dionysius of Halicarnassus), Varro specifically stressed the extraordinary number of 'priests and servants of the gods' appointed by Romulus: 'No one could name any other newly-founded city in which so many priests and servants of gods were appointed from the beginning.'[8]

Although from a modern point of view the various priestly organizations of Rome may be of interest in tracing the historical development of her composite religion, by the late Republic they had mostly become more or less quaint survivals. The massive political and social changes which accompanied Roman imperial expansion led to an effective simplification of religious organization. The chief beneficiaries of these pressures towards simplification were the three major sacerdotal colleges. This is well illustrated by Book 2 of Cicero's *De Legibus* (*On Laws*) in which he attempted a theoretical and systematic description of an ideal religion which is at least convergent with (if not based upon) Varro's analysis of Roman religion.[9] Few of the great variety of Roman priests are mentioned. Greatest stress is laid on the three major colleges, represented as important integrative institutions in the Roman state. The pontiffs not only organize the calendar and the ritual aspects of religion, they provide a crucial bridge between the public world and the private

sections of three books each (omitting Book 1). On the principles of this division (found elsewhere in Varro's work), see J.E. Skydsgaard, *Varro the Scholar* (Analecta Romana, Instituti Danici Suppl. 4, Copenhagen, 1968), 10–37.

[7] See [...] Beard, ['Priesthood',] 31–4 [...]; with Wissowa, *RK*[2] 394–8; Mommsen, *Staatsrecht*[3] 1, 312–13; 2, 20–4; G.J. Szemler, 'Religio, priests and magistrats in the Roman Republic', *Numen* 18 (1971), 103–31.

[8] Dionysius of Halicarnassus, *Ant. Rom.* 2, 64–73 and 2, 21, 1 = Cardauns (ed.), *Varros Antiquitates RD* 62, Appendix ad librum XIII, b.

[9] It is commonly argued that Cicero owed no intellectual debt to Varro. See, for example, J.M. André, 'La philosophie religieuse de Cicéron', in A. Michel and R. Verdière (eds.), *Ciceroniana* (*Mélanges Kumaniecki*) (Leiden, 1975), 11–21, esp. 19–20; E. Rawson, 'The interpretation of Cicero's "De Legibus"', *ANRW* I, 4, 334–56, esp. 342–9. But this view is surely untenable. Cicero and Varro had known each other since at least 59 BC and it is positively attested that, while working on *De Republica* (to which *De Legibus* is a companion piece), Cicero obtained some books by Varro (Cicero, *Att.* 4, 14, 1; 16, 2). Note also several striking similarities between Cicero's and Varro's ideas on religion (compare *Leg.* 2, 19 with [*Ant. Div.*] fr. 32 and *Ling.* 5, 86; *Leg.* 2, 22 and [*Ant. Div.*] fr. 32 and *Ling.* 5, 86; *Leg.* 2, 22 and [*Ant. Div.*] fr. 18). Of course, it is not simply a matter of Cicero copying Varro, but rather of his use of Varronian themes.

world through their supervision of funerary and tomb law (to which Cicero devotes a surprising amount of space). The augurs have the task of integrating the public life of Rome with the signs sent by the gods through *signa* and *auspicia*. The *XVviri* (who however hardly feature in Cicero's account) integrate the prophecies of those outside priestly circles who nevertheless may have insight into the will of the gods, the *fatidici* and *vates* [(prophets and seers)], with the public procedures of the state.[10]

If we ask the reason for the late Republican stress upon the priestly colleges, two answers occur. The first arises from the very emergence of theoretical enquiry into the Roman state and its functions. This made necessary an attempt to make explicit the function of institutions hitherto embedded in unselfconscious practice. We may urge that the three major priestly colleges offered a conceptual framework within which the extreme complexity of Roman public religion could be represented both to outsiders and to the élite itself. They could be used to represent Roman religion as divided into three aspects: rituals (*sacra*); the official sacralization of places and moments (augury); exceptional interventions by divine powers (prodigies and portents). Nor is it difficult to understand why it is that, of these, augury, and to a lesser extent the interpretation of prophecies and omens, dominate the historical record, and the iconography of coinage in particular, in the late Republic. Though the Romans liked to think of themselves as concerned with piety for its own sake, the really interesting facts of a religious kind were those which directly affected political careers and success. Augural symbols appear with increasing frequency on late Republican coins because, as Cicero stresses in *De Legibus*, the priesthood offered a degree of personal authority: augurs did not in general act as a college but as individuals.[11] Moreover, the *auctoritas* (prestige) possessed by a member of

---

[10] See, for tomb law, *Leg.* 2, 25, 45–37, 62; for signs 2, 11, 21; 17, 31; for prophecies 10, 20; 16, 30. Cicero is attempting here (as elsewhere) to impose some coherence on the complex organizational structure of Roman priesthoods – an attempt which leads to some strange over-simplifications (such as his notion that the *XVviri* were solely concerned with prophecy) and awkward divisions (such as that between *flamines* as priests of individual gods and *pontifices* as priests of all the gods). For a rather different attempt at organizing and hierarchizing Roman priesthoods, see Livy's account of Numa's priestly organization – culminating (as Cicero) with the college of *pontifices*, but laying most stress on the position of the single *pontifex* (*maximus*) (Livy 1, 20).

[11] For augurs and augural law, see Linderski, 'Augural law' (esp. 2190–225 on the operation of individual augurs). Augural symbolism on coins is discussed by J.R. Fears, *Princeps a diis electus* (*MAAR* 26, Rome, 1977), 99–111 – though he pushes his case much too far. The first coin of the series, that of C. Minucius Augurinus (135 BC) is discussed by M. Crawford, *RRC* no. 242, with pp. 273–5; n.242[2–5]; and by T. Hölscher, 'Die Anfänge römischer Repräsentationskunst', *RhM* 85 (1978), 315–57.

a sacerdotal college helped one to maintain a political presence of an official kind even when one did not enjoy *imperium* (formal magisterial power). The second reason for the stress upon the sacerdotal colleges is aristocratic competition for membership in them.

There were therefore conceptual and pragmatic reasons for the breaking by Julius Caesar of what had, since the death in 180 BC of C. Servilius Geminus (both *pontifex maximus* and *Xvir s.f.*), been one of the rules of the senatorial élite: that even its most prominent members should hold only one priestly office. Caesar, already *pontifex maximus* since 63 BC, was elected *augur* and *XVvir* in 47 BC; and perhaps in compensation, added one member to each of these three colleges and possibly three to the *VIIviri epulonum*.[12] Octavian, as his heir, rapidly accumulated the pontificate, the augurate and the quindecimvirate; and finally, maybe sometime later, became *VIIvir*.[13] And, as all Italy witnessed, on 6 March 12 BC as Augustus he was elected *pontifex maximus* on the death of the aged former triumvir, M. Aemilius Lepidus, who had been elected immediately after Caesar's death in 44 BC.[14] This cumulation of priesthoods, and the associated attention paid to the sacerdotal colleges, is certainly parallel to the familiar, non-Republican cumulation of traditional magistracies and pro-magisterial *imperium* by Augustus and his successors, and at one level simply marks the exceptional success of Octavian in the deadly game of late-Republican competition for power. But it should also be seen as the institutional expression of several other convergent pressures which are my subject in this paper.[15] My question is this: what are the most appropriate contexts for understanding the cumulation of sacerdotal roles by the Roman emperors?

Augustus' assumption of the office of *pontifex maximus* and his involvement in the priestly colleges acted also to underpin and legitimate his 'revival' of Roman public religion. This revival was both eclectic and self-serving, conservative and radical. The first shrines to be restored by the new régime were not, it seems, the most important but some of the oldest – the temples of Jupiter Feretrius, Victoria and

[12] Dio 42, 51, 4 with Hoffmann Lewis, *Official Priests*, 22, and Scheid, 'Prêtres', 621. J.A. North, 'Religion and politics from Republic to Principate', *JRS* 76 (1986), 251–8 (esp. 257–8), rightly stresses these moments.

[13] The office of *pontifex maximus* was decreed in 44 BC to be hereditary in Caesar's family (Dio 44, 5, 3). Octavian become *pontifex* in 47 BC, *augur* in 42, *XVvir* in *c*.37. That he was *VIIvir* by 16 BC may perhaps be inferred from a coin of that year which includes a representation of the emblems of all four major priestly colleges (*RIC* I, 74, no. 150).

[14] Augustus, *Res Gestae* 10, 2; Degrassi, *Inscriptiones Italiae* XIII, 420–1.

[15] See W. Speyer, 'Das Verhältnis des Augustus zur Religion', *ANRW* II, 16 1.3, 1777–805, esp. 1794–5.

Saturnus, among others; if the choice is significant, there are evocations of Romulus and perhaps even earlier heroes.[16] The revival of the priesthood of Jupiter (*flamen Dialis*) in 11 BC, the closure of the temple of Janus on 11 January 29 BC, the foundation of the temple of Mars Ultor in the Forum Augustum, all evoked the religious activity of Numa.[17] And it is in relation to Numa that Livy comments upon the moral and regulatory functions of religion: '[The Romans'] constant preoccupation with the gods … had so imbued all their hearts with piety that it was regard for promises and oaths by which the state was governed in place of fear of the laws and punishment.'[18] In the next sentence the point is made clear: the moral superiority brought about by Numa's religious innovations justifies Rome's authority and universal hegemony.[19] Ideologically, Numa's religious reforms made it possible for Rome to secure the fruits of the military conquests implicit in Romulus' organization of a military society. As Velleius Paterculus observed, fate, 'preserver of the State and the World', provided in Augustus 'a founder and preserver of the name of Rome' at the conclusion of the civil war – a neat blend, in other words, of Romulus and Numa.[20]

The evident calculation in Augustus' 'revival' of Roman religion marks just one step, albeit an important one, in an already old process, the appropriation by the Roman élite of the religious institutions of the Roman people.[21] What should be emphasized here is not the direct dependence of the state upon lavish gifts for the building of temples by individuals victorious in war nor the control by the senate of religious matters so much as the insidious changes which accompanied the expansion of Rome. The first of these changes

---

[16] Gros, *Aurea Templa*, 26 (though I would stress *if* the choice is significant; it would be easy to exaggerate the implication of such facts).

[17] *Flamen Dialis*: Suetonius, *Aug.* 31, 4; Tacitus, *Ann.* 3, 58, 5; Dio 54, 36, 1 (for the foundation by Numa, see, for example, Livy 1, 20, 1 – though a different version is offered by Plutarch, *Numa* 7, who ascribes the *flamen Dialis* to an earlier period). Janus: Livy 1, 19, 2–3, with specific allusion to Octavian's closure of the gates in 29 BC Numa and the cult of Mars: Livy 1, 20, 3.

[18] Livy 1, 21, 1. See K. Gläser, [*RE*] s.v. Numa, col. 1249 and W. Kunkel, 'Über das Wesen des augusteischen Prinzipats', *Gymnasium* 68 (1961), 353–70, esp. 357–8 (= W. Schmitthenner (ed.), *Augustus* (Darmstadt, 1969), 311–35).

[19] Livy 1, 21, 2 says explicitly only that the neighbours of Rome considered it *nefas* (impious) to offer violence to a state entirely devoted to worship of the gods; but this piety lies behind the successful expansion under Tullus Hostilius (the next king). For late Republican religious justifications of imperialism, see P. Brunt, 'Laus imperii', in P. Garnsey and C.R. Whittaker (eds.), *Imperialism in the Ancient World* (Cambridge, 1979), 159–91.

[20] Velleius Paterculus 2, 60, 1. See E. Cizek, 'L'image de renouvellement historique chez Velleius Paterculus', *StudClas* 14 (1972), 85–92, esp. 89–92.

[21] John Scheid has recently addressed this problem in relation to the election of priests and the *Lex Domitia* of 104 BC; see Scheid, 'Prêtre'.

which I propose to discuss here – and one that relates to priestly operations – is the role of writing in the development of Roman religion.

RELIGION AND WRITING

The numerous calendars surviving from the late Republic and early Empire in whole or part are familiar as 'sources' for the historian of Roman religion.[22] But they are also interesting evidence of the degree to which the complexity of Roman religion was linked to the institution of literacy. The form of the list is here crucial. Even more than in a modern diary (which may include such diverse pieces of information as public holidays, phases of the moon and the birthdays of the royal family), we find in these Roman calendars an enormous amount of information, neatly registered under different categories, information which, if it were stored simply in human memories, could never be presented in such a form. A rational and articulate process of selection and allocation of information has taken place. We may note, for example, (1) the letters marking the *nundinae* ('market days'); (2) letters marking the legal status of each day of the year; (3) each of the three fixed days each month, the Kalends, Nones and Ides; (4) the relation of each day to the fixed days; (5) the dates of all the forty-five traditional public holidays; (6) new holidays and anniversaries of the late Republic and Empire; (7) information about holidays, notices of games, feasts and market days, and notes on their significance; (8) notes on the foundation dates of important temples (*dies natales*), their locations and the gods they are dedicated to; (9) some astronomical information; (10) notes on the significance of certain festivals etc.†

Some of the information given in the calendars is certainly 'practical', but it would be a mistake to assume that the rash of late Republican and early imperial examples is due to a new interest in practical information. For in fact a great deal of the information is quite gratuitous, merely 'interesting', as well as highly unsystematic.[23] Rather, Roman calendars are an excellent illustration of one of the consequences of literacy to which Professor Goody has drawn attention. Writing provides not merely the obvious opportunity of

---

[22] For full information on the surviving calendars from Italy (including drawings and photographs), see Degrassi, *Inscriptiones Italiae* XIII; more briefly Wissowa *RK*², 2–4; Latte, *RRG*, 1–3.

† The example provided in the original publication and printed here on pp. 70–1 illustrates the first nine of these categories of information.

[23] A. Kirsopp Michels, *The Calendar of the Roman Republic* (Princeton, 1967), 3–15; 22–30; Bömer (ed.), *Fasten* 1, 33–44.

recording great bodies of material (which can be, and frequently has been, achieved by illiterate societies by use of mnemonic devices or systems) but also of organizing it in many different ways and from many points of view.[24] The very existence of calendars produced in turn a considerable body of commentary and exegesis, by prompting newly obvious questions concerning the meaning of this or that item of information, or the story 'behind' a given fact – questions which frequently required lengthy descriptive answers which consequently appeared together in the same volume without any coherent connection: the only connection lay in the original list, the calendar. Immediate personal involvement in religious acts could hardly compete with the privilege of this new kind of representation of the religious system. The most famous of these commentaries based on calendars is Ovid's *Fasti*, an incomplete long poem probably based on an earlier prose commentary by Verrius Flaccus.[25] But we know also of Varro's work in the *Antiquitates* on festivals (indeed, that work is, in a sense, as a whole a commentary on the calendar), of Suetonius' *De Anno Romanorum* (*On the Year of the Romans*), and of the sources that lie behind Book 4 of Johannes Lydus' compilation *On the Months*.[26] In the case of the calendar, the development of an ingenious instrument for organizing in tabular form large quantities of information in turn prompted the further development of new kinds of information about the religious system, which re-presented that system in unfamiliar and indeed traditionally unthinkable ways.

A second area in which writing was indispensable to the growth of complexity in the Roman religious system is the pontifical rules: a compilation of precedents, explanations and formulae developed within (and known only to) the pontifical college. According to Livy, these had originally been drawn up by Numa; but they had increased to an enormous extent, and unsystematically, in the post-regal period.[27] The significance of this area of writing was twofold. In

[24] Goody, *Domestication of the Savage Mind*; cf. B. Stock, *The Implications of Literacy* (Princeton, 1978). One must, of course, be cautious here: G. Gossen, *Chamulas in the World of the Sun* (Cambridge, Mass., 1974), 27, emphasizes the complex knowledge of their calendars possessed by the peasants of Chainula (Mexico), without recourse to graphic representations.

[25] See W. Fauth, 'Römische Religion im Spiegel der "Fasti" des Ovid', *ANRW* II, 16.1, 104–86, esp. 113–22. For discussion of Ovid's sources, see Bömer (ed.), *Fasten* 1, 22–8.

[26] Varro's eighth book was on festivals (Cardauns (ed.), *Varros Antiquitates RD*, 53–6); for fragments of Suetonius' work, see fr. 113*–123* and pp. 177–92 (Reifferscheid). Note also Th. Köves-Zulauf, 'Plinius d. Ä. und die römische Religion', *ANRW* II, 16.1, 187–288, esp. 230–2.

[27] Livy 1, 20, 5–7. For the general character of these pontifical rules, see G. Rohde, *Die Kultsatzungen der römischen Pontifices* (*RGVV* 25, Berlin, 1936).

THE ROMAN CALENDAR

The conventions of the calendar (see also pp. 68–9):

1. The letters marking the *nundinae* ('market days') are those in the left-hand column – here, B, C, D, E etc.

2. The letters marking the legal status of each day of the year are in the furthest right-hand column.

> N = *nefastus* (a day on which no assembly was permitted and no formal procedures at civil law could be initiated)
>
> F = *fastus* (a day on which procedures at civil law *could* be initiated)
>
> C = *comitialis* (a day on which assemblies could be held or procedures at civil law initiated)
>
> NP = ?*nefastus publicus* (perhaps a day of public festival, as well as one on which the other restrictions of *nefasti* applied)
>
> EN = *endotercisus* (a day which counted as *nefastus* in the morning or evening, but *fastus* in between)

3. The three fixed days each month, the Kalends, Nones and Ides, are marked here as K (1 Oct), NON (7 Oct) and EID (15 Oct) (central column).

4. The relation of each day to the fixed days is marked by the number (VI, V, IV etc) in the central column, indicating the place of each day in relation to the next, Kalends, Nones or Ides.

5. The dates of the traditional public holidays are marked by an abbreviated title of the festival in large capitals (here, for example, MED for Meditrinalia, 11 Oct).

6. New holidays are here marked also by an abbreviated title in large capitals. So, for example, AUG (12 Oct) indicates the Augustalia, a festival founded in 19 BC.

7. Particular information on holidays, games etc is included in small capitals. In the entry on the Augustalia, the calendar notes 'Fer(iae) ex s(enatus) c(onsulto), q(uod) e(o) d(ie) Imp. Caes(ar] Aug(ustus) ex transmarin(is) provinc(iis) Urbem intravit araq(ue) Fort(unae) Reduci constit(uta)' ('Festival established by decree of the senate, because on that day the Emperor Caesar Augustus returned from overseas territory and entered the city, and an altar was set up to Fortuna Redux (Fortune who "leads back")').

8. Notes on the foundation dates and location dates of temples are also given in small capitals. Here, for example, on 18 October, record is made of the anniversary of the temple of Janus near the theatre of Marcellus (refounded by Tiberius in AD 17).

9. Astronomical information is not included in this calendar. Other calendars mark, for example, the entry of the sun into the different astrological signs.

Opposite: The surviving part of the month of October – from the *Fasti, Amiternini*, an inscribed stone calendar (AD 20) from central Italy (adapted from *Inscriptiones Italiae*, XIII²).

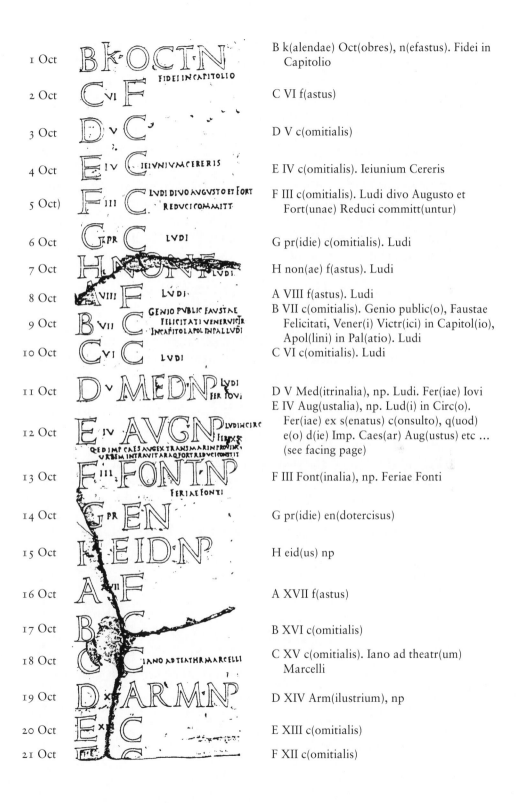

1 Oct		B k(alendae) Oct(obres), n(efastus). Fidei in Capitolio
2 Oct		C VI f(astus)
3 Oct		D V c(omitialis)
4 Oct		E IV c(omitialis). Ieiunium Cereris
5 Oct)		F III c(omitialis). Ludi divo Augusto et Fort(unae) Reduci committ(untur)
6 Oct		G pr(idie) c(omitialis). Ludi
7 Oct		H non(ae) f(astus). Ludi
8 Oct		A VIII f(astus). Ludi
9 Oct		B VII c(omitialis). Genio public(o), Faustae Felicitati, Vener(i) Victr(ici) in Capitol(io), Apol(lini) in Pal(atio). Ludi
10 Oct		C VI c(omitialis). Ludi
11 Oct		D V Med(itrinalia), np. Ludi. Fer(iae) Iovi
12 Oct		E IV Aug(ustalia), np. Lud(i) in Circ(o). Fer(iae) ex s(enatus) c(onsulto), q(uod) e(o) d(ie) Imp. Caes(ar) Aug(ustus) etc … (see facing page)
13 Oct		F III Font(inalia), np. Feriae Fonti
14 Oct		G pr(idie) en(dotercisus)
15 Oct		H eid(us) np
16 Oct		A XVII f(astus)
17 Oct		B XVI c(omitialis)
18 Oct		C XV c(omitialis). Iano ad theatr(um) Marcelli
19 Oct		D XIV Arm(ilustrium), np
20 Oct		E XIII c(omitialis)
21 Oct		F XII c(omitialis)

the first place, just as with Roman law with which it is intimately connected, the writing down of the pontifical rules – particularly the recording of precedents – provided the basis for the growth of a cumulative body of decisions and of a higher system of rules for interpreting them. (The consequence of an objective, and increasing, set of precedents is the need for higher level rules for deciding between competing precedents, just as in law.) The existence of writing both increased the number of precedents that could be discovered and made necessary the formalization of the rules governing the selection and adaptation of precedents. The larger the group of precedents, the more complex these 'secondary' rules; and writing made it more difficult to suppress or forget 'outmoded' precedents, which would have happened more easily in a purely memorized system. Writing here does not so much change the basis of rule-bound argument within the college as allow much greater sophistication and complexity – in short, the elements of a bureaucratic system of religious administration.[28]

Thirdly, writing made it possible to maintain a large mass of what we may term 'obsolescent religious categories', terms for religious institutions, concepts and physical objects which no longer, or perhaps never, had any general acceptance or understanding. In effect, writing offered a sovereign means of institutionalizing unintelligibility. If the *locus classicus* of unintelligible categories in Roman religion is Arnobius' famous chapter in *Adversus Nationes* (*Against the Gentiles*), where he makes such devastating fun of the mumbo-jumbo of the pontifical vocabulary, by the late Republic there were numerous books on various religious topics, of which the earliest known is the commentary on the hymn of the Salii by L. Aelius Stilo Praeconus.[29] What should be stressed is that

---

[28] Latte, *RRG*, 205–6, has a section in his chapter on pontifical religion headed 'Kasuistische Differenzierung', but he does not connect the use of complex argument with any concrete social processes. Search of F.P. Bremer (ed.), *Iurisprudentiae antehadrianiae quae supersunt* (Leipzig, 1896–98), reveals the names of eleven men (prior to the emperor Claudius) who as *pontifices* or even *iurisprudentes* are known to have commented in writing on the pontifical rules – that is, were in some way involved in their systematization; many others must have been involved, but did not write books. In the Principate there was a department of the imperial *familia* with responsibility for such matters (see *CIL* VI, 8878 = *ILS* 1685, with Wissowa *RK*², 497 n.2).

[29] Arnobius, *Adv. Nat.* 7, 24. See Varro's comments on the learnedness of Stilo – *Ling.* 7, 2. In the first century we know of several similar (non-legal) attempts to write on such specifically religious topics. Note, for example, Granius Flaccus, *De Indigitamentis* (*On Religious Formulae*), *De Ritu Sacrorum* (*On Ritual*), *De Sacerdotibus* (*On Priests*); Gavius Bassus, *De Diis* (*On Gods*); Cornificius Longus, *De Etymis Deorum* (*On the Derivation of the Names of the Gods*); C. Iulius Hyginus, *De Diis Penatibus* (*On Household Gods*), *De Proprietatibus Deorum* (*On the Characteristics of the Gods*). For further details, see Rawson, *Intellectual Life*, esp. 298–316.

these commentaries did not remove the unintelligibility of obsolete categories or bizarre rules; they simply compounded it by pseudo-explanations, imaginary etymologies, arbitrary references to 'historical' events and energetic use of all the other weapons in the armoury of obscurantism. As for the significance of such unintelligibility, we may note the comments of Ernest Gellner: 'Unintelligibility leaves the disciple with a secret guilt of not understanding or not avowing it, or both, which binds him to the master who is both responsible for it and seems untainted by it. The belief that the naked emperor is clothed is better social cement than that a naked one is naked – or even that a clothed one is clothed.'[30] As Gellner points out in another essay, we may, by 'excessive indulgence in contextual charity' – that is, by too readily assuming that because it was 'their religion' the Romans necessarily understood it – neglect the possibility of 'social controls through the employment of absurd, ambiguous, inconsistent or unintelligible doctrines' (or, we may add, institutions or practices).[31]

Yet another contribution of literacy to the development of Roman religion can be found in the new possibilities opened up for 'primitive intellectuals'. All so-called traditional societies produce individuals whose self-appointed task it is to think through religious difficulties or to construct their own cosmologies. In the absence of writing, however, their thoughts are doomed to perish except insofar as individual scraps are appropriated into the generally accepted body of religious meaning. But their historical origin in an individual's thought is then lost for ever. In the absence of literacy, this process of absorption of new thinking is unproblematic and unself-conscious, but its long-term effect is to permit a religious system slowly to change, to remain adequate to the cognitive and interpretative demands made upon the system by the members of the society. Literacy provides remarkable opportunities to such people (Hesiod is an excellent example, in Archaic Greece), not only in saving their thoughts from erosion but in permitting a higher degree of systematization and consistency in their thinking.[32] But this advantage for the individuals is more problematic for the system as a whole, and

---

[30] Gellner, 'Is belief really necessary?', 55.

[31] 'Concepts and society', in *Cause and Meaning in the Social Sciences* (London, 1973), 39. I do not intend to imply that there were not other important social pressures involved in the evolution of legal rules; see, especially, R. Bauman, *Lawyers in Roman Republican Politics: a study of the Roman jurists 316–82 BC* (Münchener Beiträger 75, Munich, 1983).

[32] cf. Goody, *Domestication of the Savage Mind*, ch. 5. An example from Rome might be the cosmogony elaborated by M. Valerius Messalla Rufus ([consul] 53 BC), 55 years an augur (see Macrobius, *Sat.* 1, 9, 14).

tends to lead directly to mere reduplication of separate systems of thought which can only be coped with by a process of what we might call 'anarchic syncretism': 'Where all ideas are composible, where anything goes and can be joined with anything else, no exchange, or replacement, no progress will arise: at best, an amorphous accretion, an unselective and uncritical syncretism'.[33] The social production of full-time intellectual specialists which literacy makes possible may be directly contrary to the long-term interests of the religious system even while individual systems of thinking may reach new levels of sophistication (and thus modern approval). The system may be faced with an increasingly large number of unassimilable interpretations, which leads to cognitive despair and hence the demotion of the system as a source of authoritative collective meanings. If it survives, it does so more as cultural quotation, as 'tradition', than as a cognitive system. The intellectual specialists of course imagine they are being helpful: Varro, believing Roman religion to have lost numerous traditional deities 'not by enemy invasion but by the citizens' neglect', actually hoped that his *Antiquitates* would be the contemporary equivalent of Aeneas' saving of the Trojan gods or Caecilius Metellus' rescue in 241 BC of the sacred objects from the temple of Vesta in the Forum.[34] But the erosion of the cognitive adequacy of the system that stems from this intellectual activity encourages rather the growth of specialist, 'pragmatic' cults (especially healing cults), and then the emergence of a sharp gulf between the religious beliefs of the élite and the mass of the illiterate population.

It is of course extremely difficult to separate the effects of literacy from the effects of other social changes which have historically accompanied it. That is certainly the case in the Roman Republic. But we may at least argue that the appropriation by the Roman élite of control over the religious system – not merely the obvious control, which existed from earliest times, over the detailed rules of ritual, but control over the major emphases of the system and over the sorts of meanings it was able to generate – was enormously furthered by the development of literacy among that élite and its application as a technique to aspects of the religious system. In itself, the technique of writing might have led to a greater openness, and indeed to some

---

[33] Gellner, 'Is belief really necessary?', 54. One thinks, in the case of Rome, of Nigidius Figulus; see now D. Liuzzi (ed.), *Nigidio Figulo, astrologo e mago* (Lecce, 1983), esp. the fragments of his *De Diis* (*On Gods*), from at least nineteen books.

[34] See Varro, [*Ant. Div.*] fr. 2a and 12. Cf. C. Koch, [Chapter 13 in this volume, esp. 322–23]; Rawson, *Intellectual Life*, 312–13; Cardauns (ed.), *Varros Antiquitates RD*, 94–6.

extent that did happen;[35] but it also provided the means for further mystification and appropriation. The process can be understood as one which transformed an originally common cognitive project into an essentially arbitrary set of rules whose primary effect was to perpetuate élite control over the system. In short, the growing significance of writing in Roman religion was one of the most important means of turning that religion into ideology, into a means of maintaining the social domination of the élite. But there were other means too of achieving this end.

RELIGION AND IDEOLOGY

The process of Roman expansion under the Republic produced a familiar series of social changes, above all the extraordinary increase in the scale of wealth and power controlled by the élite organized in the Senate and equestrian orders. The unstable competitive ethic of this élite, especially the senatorial élite, led directly to an insatiable demand for additional resources once the critical destabilization of the Hannibalic war (218–202 BC) had taken place. This more or less uncontrolled imperialism led in turn to class, or quasi-class, formation. 'While the social strength of values in simple societies lacking great concentrations of power will usually rest on value commitment, in modern societies, rich in institutions, institutional power, rather than disembodied commitment, becomes of paramount importance.'[36] While of course late Republican or early Imperial Rome was not a 'modern society', it was certainly not 'simple': indeed, one of the theoretical reasons for studying such an empire is the encouragement it offers us to create special 'intermediate' models replacing the insidious bipolarity of the dichotomy 'archaic' versus 'modern'.

---

[35] The classic examples of writing and publication being perceived as a step towards openness are Papirius' publication of the laws of the kings at the time of Tarquinius Superbus, the codification and publication of law in the XII tables in the early years of the Republic and Cn. Flavius' publication in the fourth century both of the correct legal formulae for bringing a case and of the calendar (which marked the days on which an action could be brought) – see H.F. Jolowicz and B. Nicholas, *Historical Introduction to the Study of Roman Law*[3] (Cambridge, 1972) 13; 86 n. 2; 91, and A. Watson, 'Roman private law and the *Leges Regiae*', *JRS* 62 (1972), 100–5, esp. 103–4. But it is a recurrent theme in the record of the early history of Rome – see Livy 1, 32, 2 on the 'publication' by Ancus Marcius (the fourth king of Rome) of Numa's commentaries on religious rites (destroyed, according to the tradition, and later re-copied by Papirius). These stories correspond to the ideal of an integrated society which shares religious and other values. The opposite, 'political' project is legitimated by the famous story of the burning of Numa's secret books by the urban praetor Q. Petillius Spurinus in 181 BC (see, for example, Livy 40, 29, 9–14); religious knowledge is dangerous and must be controlled, especially when written.

[36] Merquior, *Veil and Mask*, 24.

At any rate, one interesting feature of the middle and late Republic is its development of ideological representations whose function was to sublimate the interests of the dominant land-owning élite (above all as organized institutionally in the senate) into a justificatory set of ideals.[37] It was precisely the rapidity and the scale of the transformation of Roman society which created the need for such ideological representations, as the socially-distorting effects of uncontrolled imperialism traced themselves not merely upon the peasantry but upon the élite itself.

The main role of a legitimating ideology is not primarily as a mask consciously employed to deceive social subordinates, even if we can find traces of such an attitude in relation to religion in the Republic.[38] Rather ideology acts as an 'unconscious veil distorting the image of social reality within [a] class and sublimating its interest basis'.[39] The familiar rhetoric of divinely-sanctioned imperialism summarized in Horace's Roman Odes and in Vergil's *Aeneid* Book 8 is an obviously relevant ideological production, since it served to re-present, in the guise of fate and piety, a social fact – that is, imperialism – driven by entirely different social forces. Those real-world forces themselves inexorably threatened the ideological veil which concealed them, when they produced the intestine savagery of the civil wars of the first century BC. But the civil wars themselves were in turn veiled, understood as the punishment of the Romans through their greed for excessive wealth, indifference to natural limitations or boundaries, lack of piety towards the gods. The central cause, the competitive ethic of the élite, could not be admitted.[40] In effect, the response to

---

[37] 'Ideological thinking is always *sectional*; it is to be predicated of groups (mainly classes), not of society as a whole' (Merquior *Veil and Mask*, 34).

[38] e.g. Varro, [*Ant. Div.*] fr. 20; 21; 22; Cicero. *Nat. D[eor]*. fr. 1; *Dom.* 1, 1–2; cf. H.W. Attridge, 'The philosophical critique of religion under the early empire', *ANRW* II, 16.1, 45–78, esp. 46–12.9–11, but it is generally confused with the question of élite belief in the late Republic. For me, the production, both in Greece and in the later Republic, of a two-tiered (at least) religious system, with 'intellectuals' (i.e. self-selected members of the civic élites) distancing themselves from 'normal' practice of civic or traditional religion, is an excellent example of the 'veil' at work. The 'intellectuals' perceive the impossibility of defending 'normal' religion, but produce as an alternative a more sophisticated version of the same basic system, which is much less challengeable (cf. N. Denyer, 'The case against divination: an examination of Cicero's *De Divinatione*', *PCPhS* n.s. 31 (1985), 1–10) – but still perfectly appropriate to their interests as members of an élite. It is also true, and interesting, that the intellectuals generally adopt such critical positions in only one of their roles: 'It is of the essence of social roles that they never demand total involvement by the actors, but only segmental and partial involvement' (A. Gouldner, *For Sociology: renewal and critique in sociology today* (London, 1973), 210).

[39] Merquior, *Veil and Mask*, 24–34.

[40] See P. Jal, 'Las dieux et les guerres civiles dans la Rome de la fin de la République', *RÉL* 40 (1962), 170–200.

the civil war was simply the inverse of the earlier ideological representation of imperial success, and in no sense a breaking through the veil.

One of the characteristic features of the Roman religious system is the effort expended, partly in writing, to fix its forms and usages. The Roman élite came to pride itself on its 'absurd' readiness to repeat ceremonies *ad infinitum* until the performance should be entirely free from fault. Careful record was made of priests forced to quit because they had neglected the rites; one, Q. Sulpicius, because his hat fell off while he was sacrificing.[41] The justification is made clear by Valerius Maximus: 'For our state has always considered that everything should be secondary to *religio*.'[42] Consciousness that the suppliers of sacrificial animals and other 'invisible' interested parties might make thereby untoward profits was not permitted to outweigh the value of sticking rigidly to the rules.[43] This attachment to forms is usually taken as a characteristic of Roman religion from the beginning, and then made into a token of sincerity of belief and commitment. Rather, the attention devoted to formal ritual should be understood as exemplary of a much more extensively operative social good in Roman society, action inspired by pure respect for the customs and conventions recognized by the social group.[44] Even in a period when attention to forms was under threat because of changed life-styles, the appearance of 'greed' and of naked self-interest, one area more than any other could be made to express the attention ideally lavished upon the presentation of social forms. Religious action, and above all sacrifice, could be made into aesthetic action, action for itself, free of self interest. In other words, formulaic religious action represented the pure accumulation of 'symbolic capital'. 'Wealth, the ultimate basis of power, can exert power, and exert it durably, only in the form of symbolic capital; in other words, economic capital can be accumulated only in the form of symbolic capital, the unrecognizable, and hence socially recognizable, form of the other kinds of capital.'[45] The sacerdotal colleges of Rome can be seen as the guardians of the

---

[41] Valerius Maximus 1, 4–5, with various incidents. On the rules, see J. Scheid, 'Le délit religieux dans la Rome tardo-républicaine', in *Le délit religieux dans la cité antique* (CÉFR 48, Rome, 1981), esp. 121–6.

[42] 1, 1, 9.

[43] See, for example, the interesting account of Dio 60, 6, 4–5 (AD 41): fraud and accident meant that even as many as ten repetitions were sometimes necessary, 'generally by those who benefited from these repetitions'. So Claudius had a law passed to shorten the *ludi* to one day only, which in practice prevented repetition.

[44] Bourdieu, *Outline*, 194.

[45] *Outline*, 195. Bourdieu has since ceased to employ the notion of 'symbolic capital', but it serves my purpose here quite adequately.

alchemical transmutation of base wealth into inexhaustible prestige, through the insistence upon the minutely exact performance of forms; and part of the ideological value of the religious system to the élite can be seen as its being the purest case of this 'disinterested' action.

PRIESTHOOD AND MAGISTRACY: THE CIVIC COMPROMISE

There is no reason to halt the analysis here. The notion of symbolic capital can help us to recognize the ideological importance of two other important features of religious action, not merely in the Roman Republic but also more generally in the Hellemstic and Imperial periods. The first feature is the association between priesthood and generosity. Generosity, institutionalized in the various forms of 'voluntary' payments (*summa honoraria*), in practice obligatory for priests on election, should be seen primarily neither as redistribution nor as social insurance.[46] Rather, generosity is one of the most subtle means of maintaining lasting asymmetrical relationships between social unequals. The priest or magistrate, in principle a member of a central or provincial élite group, obtains what is for the most part a symbolic good (the priesthood). In return he (or she) dispossesses him/herself of frequently enormous amounts of real goods, including the provision of games, feasts, monetary distributions and dispensations of oil or wine, help to the poor or orphaned, the construction of useful or prestigious civic buildings.[47] What he or she finally ccumulates, however, is symbolic capital, the most durable form of wealth, in the form of 'obligation, gratitude, prestige, personal loyalty'.[48] The civic magistracy of the Graeco-Roman world, of which priesthood is a sub-class, should be understood as a routinized system for the creation of symbolic capital in a context in which the modern means of institutionalizing such capital, above all through education systems, the art market in all its international forms, and the entertainment industry, were developed to only a very limited

---

[46] Redistribution: Debord, *Aspects sociaux*, 74; 346, n. 205. Social insurance: Broughton, 'Roman Asia Minor', esp. 810–12. In other words I subscribe to a version of P. Veyne's 'political' argument (*Le pain et le cirque* (Paris, 1976), 298–327).

[47] A.R. Hands, *Charities and Social Aid in Greece and Rome* (London 1968), 62–115; cf. Bourdieu, *Outline*, 189: 'The greater the extent to which the task of reproducing the relations of domination is taken over by objective mechanisms, which serve the interest of the dominant group without any conscious effort on the latter's part, the more indirect and, in a sense, impersonal become the strategies objectively oriented towards reproduction.'

[48] Bourdieu, *Outline*, 192.

degree (but nevertheless clearly present). On the other hand, the élites of the Empire did not have to maintain their domination by a constant personal effort of creating or restoring social relations, as they would have had to do in a simpler society. The maintenance of domination could be achieved by discontinuous and routinized means, above all by the holding of public office.

The second feature of Graeco-Roman religious systems of interest in connection with accumulation of symbolic capital is the elusive relationship between civic and religious office. No single formulation of this can be satisfactory; but it can be illustrated by reference to two insignificant but telling mythical incidents. The first concerns the history of Athens under its early kings, and in particular the hero Boutes, the ancestor of the aristocratic family of Eteoboutadae which provided the hereditary priests of Poseidon-Erechtheus. A version known to Hesiod named Boutes as a son of Poseidon; but once the historiographers got to work he was made the son of King Pandion and brother of Erechtheus. Apollodorus continues the story: 'When Pandion died, his sons divided their father's inheritance between them, and Erechtheus got the throne (*basileia*) and Boutes got the priesthood of Athena and Poseidon-Erechtheus.'[49] On the one hand, the elder brother obtains the kingship; but the longer lasting and more prestigious post – surviving for centuries when the kingship was merely a memory of the remote past – turns out to be the priesthood.

The second illustration has already been alluded to: the ambiguous relationship between Romulus and Numa, which with regard to religion is presented now as one of polarity, now as that between a whole entity and its supplement. Livy, in keeping with the first view, makes Romulus the founder of the political system of Rome and the begetter of its military tradition; Numa is the effective organizer of the religious system.[50] Dionysius, however, while insisting that Numa did not alter any of the religious institutions of Romulus, who 'established the principal rites of (Roman) religion', saw his work as one of adding 'whatever he thought had been overlooked by Romulus, consecrating many shrines to gods who had not yet received honours, setting up numerous altars and temples, founding festivals for each of them, appointing priests to take care of them and making rules for rituals and cult, purifications and very many other ceremonies and honours, such as no Greek or barbarian city has, even those who

---

[49] See Plutarch, [*Mor.*] 843 b–c; Hesiod, fr, 223 (Merkelbach–West); Apollodorus 3, 15, 1.
[50] Most explicitly, Livy 1, 21, 6; cf. 1, 10, 1–11, 4; 15, 6–8; 17, 4; 19, 1–2; 21, 1–2.

have now or in the past plumed themselves most upon their piety'.[51] As so often, the supplement bids fair to overwhelm the original; but the point to stress here is the manner in which this uncertainty over the founding facts of Rome replicates a deeper, non-trivial uncertainty over the place of religion, and priesthood, in the Roman scheme of things. Is it religion which is really distinctive of Rome; or its military power?

The crucial point about the Roman (and Greek) distinction between civic magistracy and priesthood is its elusiveness, the sheer impossibility of definitional clarity. The fate of any attempt to impose clarity is illustrated by the following quotation: 'In the senate, just as in all public affairs, separation in priestly and political functions was carefully maintained, although the line of separation was merely a legal technicality if and when the senator or the magistrate was a priest. The fact that most priests were members of the senate by virtue of political magistracies created the conditions in which priestly prestige and senatorial pre-eminence were interwoven.'[52] It has been generally agreed that Roman priests were not magistrates; yet they wore the same robe, the *toga praetexta*, during the performance of their functions; the *pontifices* had extensive powers of interference in private lives; and augurs had the right to cause the discontinuation of public business. Priesthood had, as it were, plagiarized the rules for magistracy.[53] Inversely, it is not difficult to find evidence that priesthoods were conceived in a purely instrumental manner: throughout the Principate, as in the Republic, the Senate, or sometimes the emperor alone, took final decisions with or without the advice of the priestly colleges on matters of religious concern; Pliny the Younger, writing to Trajan in AD 101–2 to ask for preferment to one of the colleges, treats them as though they were exactly like other desirable political fruits; Cicero refers blatantly to the good sense of the *maiores* (ancestors) 'in choosing the most distinguished men for sacerdotal office' to provide ballast for the ship of state.[54] Yet special rules remained to make priests different: they had to be and to remain unmaimed; augurs could not lose their

---

[51] Dionysius of Halicarnassus, *Ant. Rom.* 2, 23, 6; 2, 63, 2. For the emphasis on the role of Romulus in Dionysius, see C.J. Classen, 'Romulus in der römischen Republik', *Philologus* 106 (1962), 174–204, esp. 192–6.

[52] G.J. Szemler, *Priests of the Roman Republic*, 58; cf. Scheid, 'Prêtre', 268–9.

[53] Bleicken, 'Oberpontifex und Pontifikalkollegium'; while Scheid, 'Prêtre', 248–66, re-emphasizes the well-known fact that not all priests on cooptation were even senators.

[54] On decision-making on religious matters in the Principate, see F. Millar, *The Emperor in the Roman World* (London, 1977), 355–61; Pliny's requests, *Ep.* 2, 1, 8; 4, 8; 10, 13; Hoffman Lewis, *Official Priests*, 14–16 (on the practice of election). For the 'good sense' (*consilium*) of the *maiores*, see Cicero, *Dom.* 1, 1, 2.

power of augury, even if they were stripped of membership of the college; Augustus, at the funeral of M. Agrippa, and Tiberius at Drusus' funeral, as *pontifices* were not allowed to see the corpse, and delivered the *elogium* (funeral oration) separated from the corpse by a hanging.[55]

There is a thorough muddle then (and the muddle in the Greek world is even more complete). But it is a muddle with a purpose. The indeterminacy can be linked with the process of ideological domination. On the one hand, the religious system must be represented as an autonomous set of rules, issuing from the past and empirically competent to maintain proper relations with the gods. Neither the set of divinities to whom cult was offered by the state nor the rules under which they were placated could be admitted to be produced directly by a socially-interested dominant group under its own authority. The objectivity, the otherness, of the rules which constitute religion was at least partly guaranteed by the existence of a separate priesthood. At Rome, the type of the priest was the priest of Jupiter, the *flamen Dialis*, who epitomized the ideal separateness of the world of religion from the world of politics and the struggle for power. The more outlandish the rules which separated him, and his wife, from the world (lovingly detailed in the second century AD by Aulus Gellius), the more perfectly the objective existence of the religious rules, and, further back, the divinities they conjure into existence, was confirmed.[56] On the other hand, the ideological benefits of the religious system, above all its exemplification of the purest forms of disinterested action, could not be obtained if there were not close links between the 'executive' (the élite in active politics) and priesthood.

Historically, whether in fact or fiction, what we may call the Graeco-Roman 'civic compromise' – the lack of clear distinction between magistracy and priesthood – derived from the victory in the early Archaic period in Greece and in Rome of the aristocracy over the kings and the absorption by the aristocracy of the kings' religious offices and functions. At the end of a long political evolution, the 'civic compromise' produced its logical culmination, the Roman

[55] Unmaimed: Dionysus of Halicarnassus, *Ant. Rom.* 2, 21, 3; augural powers: Plutarch, *Quaest. Rom.* 99. There is conflicting evidence on the precise details of pontifical purity in relation to corpses. Dio, describing Agrippa's funeral (54, 28, 2–5), cannot understand the presence of a hanging between Augustus and the corpse; presumably the rule did not still apply in his day. It seems most likely that *pontifices* were forbidden to see (Dio 54, 35, 4; Seneca, *Ad Marc.* 15, 3) and so, *a fortiori*, to touch (Dio 56, 31, 3) corpses. A similar rule seems to have applied to augurs (Tacitus, *Ann.* 1,62).

[56] Aulus Gellius, *NA* 10, 15; Plutarch, *Quaest. Rom.* 40. See also Pötscher, 'Flamen Dialis'; Boels, 'Flaminica Dialis'.

emperor. The *princeps* fused permanent multiple magistracy with permanent multiple priesthood. He poured out wealth in return for these symbolic goods. And so he accumulated the kind of symbolic capital that only gods, perpetual givers and perpetual receivers, could aspire to.

*

My argument, then, is that priesthood is by no means as invisible in the late Republic as is normally supposed. The prominence of priesthood (the sacerdotal colleges) can be understood in two complementary contexts, both of which concern the process of transforming Roman religion into a component of a larger ideological structure which directly served the interests of the ruling élite. At the conscious level, it is plain that (1) priesthood was of intellectual value in the process – a lengthy one – of the appropriation of the religious system by the group most interested in perpetuating it; (2) it was understood to be one of the guarantors of the changelessness and permanence of the 'essence' of Rome conceived as fixed right from the early days of the kings; (3) it was represented as a special form of disinterested authority in the factional conflict of the civil war. The cumulation by Octavian/Augustus of membership in all four of the *amplissima collegia* ('most distinguished colleges') should be seen as motivated, in a quite unspecific way, by all these considerations. But there were also less conscious, less 'mask-like', ideological pressures at work. If we place the transition from Republic to Principate in historical context, it becomes plausible to argue that the inclusion among his roles by the *princeps* of membership in the colleges was a logical consequence of a process of 'veiling', whereby the élite concealed from itself the reality of its domination. The crucial consideration is that of symbolic capital, built up both by the particular form of Graeco-Roman priesthood, which involved prestation on a massive scale, and by an increasingly mystified, but of course wholly objective, system of religious rules and practices.

BIBLIOGRAPHY

This bibliography contains full references to those works cited in the notes by abbreviated title only. The exact form of the short title is given in parentheses after the full reference where it seems helpful.

[Beard, M., 'Priesthood in the Roman Republic', in M. Beard and J. North (eds.), *Pagan Priests: Religion and Power in the Ancient World* (Ithaca, 1990), 19–48. ('Priesthood')]

Bleicken, J., 'Oberpontifex und Pontifikalkollegium: eine Studie zur Römischen Sakralverfassung', *Hermes* 85 (1957), 345–66.

Boels, N., 'Le statut religieux de la flaminica Dialis', *RÉL* 51 (1973), 77–100. ('Flaminica Dialis')

Bömer, F. (ed.), *P. Ovidius Naso. Die Fasten* (Heidelberg, 1957–58). (*Fasten*).

Bourdieu, P., *Outline of a Theory of Practice* (Cambridge, 1977).

Broughton, T.R.S., 'Roman Asia Minor', in T. Frank (ed.), *Economic and Social History of Ancient Rome* 4 (Baltimore, 1938), 505–916.

Cardauns, B. (ed.), *M. Terentius Varro Antiquitates Rerum Divinarum* (Wiesbaden, 1976), (*Varros Antiquitates RD*).

[Crawford, M.H., *Roman Republican Coinage* (Cambridge, 1974). (*RRC*)]

Debord, P., *Aspects sociaux et économiques de la vie religieuse dans l'Anatolie gréco-romaine* (EPRO 88, Leiden, 1982). (*Aspects*)

Gellner, E., 'Is belief really necessary?', in I.C. Jarvie and J. Agassi (eds.), *The Devil in Modern Philosophy* (London, 1974), 52–63.

Goody, J. *The Domestication of the Savage Mind* (Cambridge, 1978).

Gros, P., *Aurea Templa: recherches sur l'architecture religieuse à l'époque d'Auguste* (BEFAR 231, Rome, 1976).

Hoffmann Lewis, M.W., *The Official Priests of Rome under the Julio-Claudians: a study of the nobility from 44 BC to 68 AD* (Papers and Mon. of the American Ac. In Rome 16, Rome 1955). (*Official Priests*)

Latte, K. *Römische Religionsgeschichte* (Munich, 1960). (*RRG*)

Linderski, J., 'The augural law', *ANRW* II, 16. 3, 2146–312.

[Merkelbach, R., and West, M.L. (eds.), *Fragmenta Hesiodea* (Oxford, 1967).]

Merquior, J.G., *The Veil and the Mask: essays on culture and ideology* (London, 1979).

Mommsen, Th., *Römisches Straatsrecht* (3rd ed., Leipzig, 1887). (*Staatsrecht³*)

Pötscher, W., 'Flamen Dialis', *Mnemosyne* s. 4, 21 (1961), 215–39.

Rawson, E., *Intellectual Life in the Late Roman Republic* (London, 1985).

[Reifferscheid, A. (ed.), *C. Suetonius Tranquillus. Praeter Caesarum Libros Reliquiae* (Leipzig, 1860).

Scheid, J., 'Le prêtre et le magistrat', in C. Nicolet (ed.), *Des ordres à Rome* (Paris, 1984). ('Prêtre')]

Scheid, J., 'Les prêtres officiels sous les empereurs julio-claudiens', *ANRW* II, 16. 1, 610–54. ('Prêtres')

Szemler, G., *The Priets of the Roman Republic: a study of interactions between priesthoods and magistracies* (Coll. Lat. 127, Brussels, 1972).

Wissowa, G., *Religion and Kultus der Römer* (2nd ed., Munich, 1912. (*RK²*)

4 *A Feature of Roman Religion*†

ARTHUR DARBY NOCK

After the disastrous battle of Lake Trasimene Rome set herself to appease her gods, and by popular vote ordered the performance of a *uer sacrum*, that is, an offering of all the young of animals to be born in spring. Livy records this formula as having been submitted to the people for their approval (22.10.2–6).

[Do you wish and command this to be done? If the commonwealth of the Roman people, that is, of the Quirites, is preserved for the next five years, as I hope and pray, in safety from these wars – namely, the war of the Roman people with the Carthaginians and the wars with the Gauls who are on this side of the Alps – then the Roman people, that is, of the Quirites, vows as a gift to Jupiter whatever that spring shall bear from its flocks of swine, sheep, goats and cattle, whatever shall not already be consecrated, starting from the day that the Senate and people shall command. Let him who performs the sacrifice do so whenever he wants, by whatever rite; however he shall do it, let it be considered to have been done properly. If something intended for sacrifice should die, let it be held profane (*profanum esto**), and let it be understood that no crime has taken place. If someone should unknowingly hurt or kill it, let it not be a crime. If someone should steal it, let no blame attach to the people, nor to that person by whom it was stolen. If the sacrificer should sacrifice on an inappropriate day, let the sacrifice be considered to have been done properly. If by night or by day a slave or a free man should do it, let it be held to have been done properly. If the sacrifice is performed before the day on which the Senate and people order it to be done, let the people be held to be free and released from obligation.]‡

---

† Originally published in *Harvard Theological Review* 32 (1939), 83–96.
* "Profane" is used here to translate Latin *profanum*: objects are *profanum* that have ceased to be dedicated to a god or reserved for religious purposes and are henceforth designated for human use (Macrobius *Sat.* 3.3.2). Latin *profanum* could also be used catachrestically, merely to designate secular or civil things, in opposition to the sacred, or to denominate the uninitiated, and those usages paralleled certain usages of English "profane" (see *OLD* s.v. 1 and 1b).

‡ Uelitis iubeastisne haec fieri? si res publica populi Romani Quiritium ad quinquennium proximum, sicut uelim uoueamque, salua seruata erit hisce duellis, quod duellum populo Romano cum Carthaginiensi est quaeque duella cum Gallis sunt qui cis Alpes sunt, tum donum duit populus Romanus Quiritium, quod uer attulerit ex suillo ouillo caprino bouillo grege quaeque profana erunt Ioui fieri, ex qua die senatus populusque iusserit. qui faciet, quando

This was a most solemn undertaking, to be carried out with minute precision. After it was performed, twenty-one years later, says Livy, in 195 BC, an irregularity was discovered, and the *uer sacrum* was repeated in 194.[1] Nevertheless, the people's vote asserts directly that certain things which might appear irregular were not to count as such: the mode of sacrifice was declared immaterial; any animal dying before it should be sacrificed was to count as human property and not as divine; accidental killing of a victim due to Juppiter involved no guilt, nor did the loss of such a victim through theft, or the offering of a victim on an unlucky day or too early. We might have expected the precise mode of sacrifice to be defined: certainly any one of the other circumstances might have been thought to involve the need for *piacula* [("rites of expiation")] or *instauratio* [("repetition")]. The formula, presumably drawn up by the Pontifex Maximus, asserted that they did not, and made this assertion as with full authority.

Similar explicit phrases occur in many other texts. Livy, quoting an authoritative source, says of *deuotio*: *si is homo qui deuotus est moritur, probe factum uideri* [("if the man who has been devoted dies, it is held to have happened properly")];[2] a later formula of *deuotio* includes *tunc quisquis hoc uotom faxit, ubi faxit, probe factum uideri* [("then whoever shall make this vow, wherever he shall make it, it is held to have been done properly")].[3] We may compare the consul's vow at the beginning of the war with Antiochus, *quisquis magistratus eos ludos quando ubique faxit, hi ludi recte facti donaque data recte sunto* [("Whatever magistrate shall hold these games, whenever and wherever he shall do it, let it be held that the games were properly performed and the gifts duly given")],[4] and the question raised before the second Macedonian War, *consultique fetiales ab consule Sulpicio, bellum quod indiceretur regi Philippo, utrum ipsi utique nuntiari iuberent, an satis esset, in finibus regni quod proximum praesidium esset eo nuntiari, fetiales decreuerunt, utrum eorum fecisset, recte facturum)* [("The fetials were consulted by the consul Sulpicius because war was to be declared against King

---

uolet quaque lege uolet facito; quo modo faxit, probe factum esto. si id moritur quod fieri oportebit, profanum esto, neque scelus esto. si quis rumpet occidetue insciens, ne fraus esto. si quis clepsit, ne populo scelus esto neue cui cleptum erit. si atro die faxit insciens, probe factum esto. si nocte siue luce, si seruus siue liber faxit, probe factum esto. si antidea senatus populusque iusserit fieri ac faxitur, eo populus solutus liber esto.

[1] Livy 33.44.1–2. This paper is indebted to Professor W. S. Ferguson for the notes which appear with his initials, and for other friendly aid.

[2] 8.10.12.

[3] Macrob[ius] *Sat.* 3.9.11; cf. G. Wissowa, *RE* 5.279, 6.1153, and Wessner, ibid. 14.185.

[4] Liv. 36.2.5.

Philip. Did they command that the declaration should be delivered to the king himself, or was it sufficient that the declaration be delivered to the nearest stronghold within the king's territory? The fetials decreed that whichever of the two actions he performed would have been done properly")].[5] Consider further the record of the dedication of the temple of Juppiter Liber at Furfo in 58 BC, a text which has the old local dating *mensi Flusare* [("in the month of Flusaris")] after the Roman date and which is a striking document of Italian religious conservatism before the Augustan restoration, from a time at which some would have us believe that traditional piety was dead or all but dead.[6] This provides directly that iron may be used in work on the building, *fasque esto* [("and let it be religiously proper")], and so dispenses all concerned from a very common taboo: after all, the introduction of any iron into the temple or grove of the Arval Brothers required a *piaculum*. (This dispensation has a parallel in a text of the first half of the third century BC from the temple of Declunus (or Decluna) at Velitrae: *ferom pihom estu*, if we accept the explanation *ferrum pium esto* [("let iron be pious")].[7]) The Furfo text proceeds to enact that any offerings or dedications made in the temple may be sold and thereby cease to be sacred (*ubei uenum datum erit, id profanum esto* [= "whenever something is sold, let it be held to be profane")]: but only the aedile may sell them *sine scelere sine piaculo ... alis ne potesto* [("without guilt or expiation ... but let no one else be able to do so")].

Again, a formula, found both on the altar dedicated in AD 12/13 by the people of Narbo to *numen Caesaris Aug.* [("the godhead of Caesar Augustus")][8] and on an altar to Juppiter Optimus Maximus at Salonae in AD 137,[9] says with reference to a sacrifice lacking one detail *idcirco tamen probe factum esto* [("wherefore, nevertheless, let it be held to have been done properly")]. The Narbo altar has also the formula *si quis tergere ornare reficere uolet, quod beneficii causa fiat, ius fasque esto* [("If anyone should want to clean, decorate or repair [this altar], which would be done for a public service, let it be just and proper to do it")].[10] Both altars have the statement *ceterae leges*

---

[5] Liv. 31.8.3.

[6] *CIL* IX 3513 = I² 756 = *ILS* 4906.

[7] R. S. Conway, *The Italic Dialects* I, 267 f. no. 252: J. Whatmough, *Foundations of Roman Italy* 387. On the other interpretation developed by Fr. Skutsch, *Kleine Schriften* 453 ff., the text states the conditions under which a votive offering may be removed without impiety.

[8] *CIL* XII 4333 = *ILS* 112.

[9] *CIL* III 1933 = *ILS* 4907.

[10] Cf. *CIL* XI 944 (near Carpi = *ILS* 4909) *uti sine scelere sine fraude lic[et] (lic[eat]*,

huic arae titulisque eaedem sunto, quae sunt arae Dianae in Auentino
[("Let the other regulations for this altar and inscriptions be the same
as those for the altar of Diano on the Aventine")],[11] and it is likely
that both follow therefore a precedent of venerable antiquity.

This view is confirmed by comparison with formulas of Italian
cult. A votive offering at Falerii runs thus: *Menerua sacru La. Cotena
La. f. pretod* (= *praetor*) *de zenatuo sententiad uootum dedet*
[("Dedicated to Minerva. Lars Cotena, son of Lars, praetor, dedicated this, in fulfillment of a vow and in accordance with a decree of
the Senate")]: *cuando datu rected cuncaptum*,[12] where Dessau trans-
lates the last phrase as *quocumque tempore dedicatum* [("whenever
it is dedicated, that dedication shall have been properly performed")].[13] Again, in the Iguvine tablets we have phrases which are
translated as *sedens quilibet commolito, sedens commolitis precator.
porrectum erit* [("Let anyone, sitting, grind (the sacrificial cakes);
sitting, let him pray with ground cakes; <the sacrifice> will have been
completed")],[14] *tum arx piata erit* [("then the citadel will have been
purified")].[15] Further, the employment of *ius* where we should expect
fas is found in formulas and is parallel.[16] Again, Cicero preserves
both the idea and its mode of expression in the laws proposed and
discussed in his *De legibus* [(*On the Laws*)].[17]

Skutsch, op. cit. 441 n. 2, probably rightly: but there is a plain *licet* earlier) [("so let it be licit,
without guilt or crime")].

[11] *titulisque* seems to be lacking on the Salonae altar (for the first half of each line of which
we depend on transcripts made before its mutilation). *CIL* XI 4766 (= *ILS* 4911) at Spoleto
provides for cutting timber in a sacred grove on the day of the annual sacrifice; on other days
such an act entails a *piaclum* and, if done in deliberate guilt, a fine as well. They are not strictly
parallel to the dispensation under discussion; for they state a specific annual exception (in fact,
the Spoleto text says *sine dolo* [("without ill intent")], not *sine piaclo* [("without expiation")].
CIL VIII 11796 (= *ILS* 4908) states the conditions of the dedication by an Imperial procurator
of an image of Diana: it may be moved only for cleaning and repair. It is fragmentary, but in
what is preserved there is none of our language of definition from the standpoint of potential
religious guilt.

[12] *CIL* I[2] 365 = *ILS* 3124.

[13] K. Latte, *Die Religion der Römer* (in A. Bertholet, *Religionsgeschichtliches Lesebuch*[2])
6 renders 'Da es geweiht ist, soll es als recht gelobt gelten', and suggests that there may have
been some uncertainty whether there had been an error in the form of the vow. (Mommsen
interpreted as *aliquando*, i.e. *suo tempore, datum*; *recte conceptum* [("<the vow> was fulfilled
in its time; it was properly taken")].)

[14] F. Buecheler, *Umbrica* 79 f. [= VI b 41–2] (cf. 4 [= I b 38–9]): I. Rosenzweig, *Ritual and
Cults of pre-Roman Iguvium* 131 (cf. 145).

[15] Buecheler 81 [= VI b 46–7]: Rosenzweig 132.

[16] Cf. A. Hagerström, *Das magistratische Ius in seinem Zusammenhang mit römischen
Sakralrechte* (*Uppsala Universitets Årsskrift* 1929, 8) 25 n. 1.

[17] So 2.20 *quaeque quoique dino decorae grataeque sint hostiae, prouidento* [("Let them see
to whatever victims are seemly and pleasing to each divinity")]: 2.24 *caste iubet lex adire ad
deos, animo uidelicet, in quo sunt omnia; nec tollit castimoniam corporis* [("The law
commands people to approach the gods in purity, that is, purity of mind, on which all things
depend; not that that excludes purity of body")]: 2.28 *araque uetusta in Palatio Febris et altera*

We have thus statements that a given course of action is right, and commonly the imperative *esto* [("let it be")], used just as in legal texts.[18] Further, the statements are made in direct form, without reference to any supernatural source of authority or to tradition. To be sure, records of public[19] as well as of private *taurobolia*† mention the preliminary taking of omens by the *archigallus* (*ex uaticinatione archigalli* [= "on the inspired instruction of the *archigallus*, the high priest of Cybele")], or a command by the goddess; and again, the preamble to the *Acta* of the celebration of Secular Games under Septimius Severus states that the games were instituted *monitu uetustissimae uatis* [("at the command of ancient Sibyl")],[20] and both these and the *Acta* of the Games celebrated under Augustus refer to the Sibylline books (*uti uobis* (*tibi*) *in ill*(*e*)*is libris scriptum est* [= as was written for you in the books)] in connection with the individual sacrifices prescribed in them.[21] Nevertheless, the authority on which the Games were celebrated was that of the senate,[22] and the details of the ceremony are described as performed in accordance with the decisions of the *quindecimuiri*. The only other official reference which I have found to the Sibylline books as an *aition* [an originary or motivating event; an explanation] is the local title *pater patratus populi Laurentis foederis ex libris Sibullinis percutiendi cum p*(*opulo*) *R*(*omano*) ["*pater patratus* of the Laurentine people, empowered in accordance with the Sibylline books to strike a treaty with the

---

Esquiliis Malae Fortunae detestataque omnia eius modi repudianda sunt [("The ancient altar of Fever on the Palatine and the other of Ill Fortune on the Esquiline are detestable, and all of that kind are to be repudiated")]: 2.28 *recte etiam Spes a Calatino consecrata est* [("hence it was proper for Calatinus to consecrate Hope")]: 58 *statuit enim collegium locum publicum non potuisse priuata religione obligari* [("For the <pontifical> college decided that a public space could not be bound by private religious scruple")].

[18] Cf. G. Appel, *De Romanorum precationibus* (*RGVV* 7.2) 148 f. The fact that *esto* is thus used in religious texts (which are sure to be characterized by conservatism in language) to define the character of a situation, deserves to be set against Fr. Leifer's doubts whether *paricidas esto* [("let it be a parricide")] in lex Numae *ap*. Fest[us] p. 221 M. (p. 247 Lindsay) can be taken to mean *parricida habeatur* [("let it be considered parricide")] (*Studi in onore di G. Riccobono* 2, 1936, 101 ff. I naturally express no opinion on the original meaning of the phrase).

[19] E.g., *CIL* XII 4321, *iussu ipsius* [("by Her command")]. (References in private dedications to commands of Oriental and other deities are not pertinent.)

† A rite practiced in the worship of Cybele, the Great Mother of the Gods, in which the sacrificant is drenched with the blood of the sacrificial bull as it is slain.

[20] *CIL* VI 32326.8 (p. 3249); for another possible reference to the Sibyl in this document cf. ibid., l.20. (The preamble of the account of the Augustan celebration is lost.)

[21] Mommsen, *Ephemeris Epigraphica* 8, 263.

[22] Ibid. 244 f. Under Septimius the senate's rôle seems to be simply that of asking the emperors that the games be celebrated: the *magister*, in purifying the Tarentum, says that he acts *quorum* (sc. *imperatorum*) *iussu mandatuque* [("at the command and instruction of the emperors")] (ibid. 292, *CIL* VI 32328.19).

Roman people"], which may represent a piece of archaizing imagination; the text comes from the principate of Claudius.[23]

On the other hand, in Greek texts some such formula as 'in accordance with the oracle of Delphi (or Dodona)'[24] or 'in accordance with ancestral custom' is frequent. Further, Greek regulations of ritual present another striking difference from those which we have been considering. Whereas Roman regulations give not only prohibitions but also permissions and dispensations, Greek regulations consist mainly of prohibitions and statements imputing the guilt of impiety to this or that action, and give no comparable dispensations. This is the more remarkable in view of the fact that a regular Delphic precept ordered people to perform sacrifices 'according to the law of the city', [*nomôi poleôs*].[25]

The apparent exceptions which I have noted do not invalidate the principle. Thus the benefactors who restored the temple of Apollo at Gythium early in the first century BC were given for themselves and their descendants authority over the temple, ["authority over the temple and the god and all the property of the temple"]; but that means only that the city has ceded to them its power of control, and permits them to preside and care for the temple as they choose.[26] The foundation inscription of Diomedon's family cult on Cos (which does not quote any oracle or other supernatural authority) provides that a forbidden use of a precinct is permitted in time of war:[27] but that is mere necessity, like the Athenian omission of the rites of procession to Eleusis during part of the Peloponnesian War.[28] Of course, texts specifying means of purification can state that after their use a man or a household is pure,[29] and a list of ritual regulations inscribed at

---

[23] *CIL* X 797 = *ILS* 5004; cf. *CIL* XIV, p. 187 n. 2. In the Fasti Praenestini (*ILS* 8744a) we read *Mater magna ex libris Sibullinis arcessita locum mutauit ex Phrygia Romam* [("The Great Mother, in accordance with the Sibylline books, changed her residence from Phrygia to Rome")], but this is one of a series of learned notes in that particular calendar (cf. Varro, *Ling.* 5.15).

[24] Cf. Plato, *Laws* 865B ["Having been purified in accordance with the law of Delphi on these matters, let him be held pure" (*kathartheis kata ton ek Delphôn komisthenta peri toutôn nomon estô*)] (a similar provision in a second century BC law from Lato in Crete, as restored by A. Wilhelm, *Jahresh.* 14, 1911, 203 may lack such a sanction; but the text is mutilated); also the designation of gods whose cult was prescribed by the oracle as ["sanctioned by the Pythian oracle" (*pythochrêstoi*)] (*SIG* 1014). Many sacrifices fell in a different category (n. 60, *infra*).

[25] E.g. Xen[ophon] *Mem.* 1.3.1.

[26] L. Ziehen, *Leges Graecorum sacrae* 163 no. 56.29 ff.

[27] R. Herzog, *Heilige Gesetze von Kos* (*Abh. Berlin* 1927, vi) 28 no. 10 III 86.

[28] Cf. also Thuc[ydides] 2.17, Polyb[ius] 5.106.2–3; for an exception in a civil law Wilamowitz-Moellendorff *SitzB Berlin* 1927, 8.

[29] Ziehen no. 93; *SIG* 982.9 ["Let them be established pure every day" (*katharoi estôsan authêmeron*].

Cyrene during the fourth century BC, in addition to stating what defiles, describes also what is permissible;[30] but the whole text is presented as an oracle of Apollo; thus the god and not a civic authority has decided. [*Hosía* ('divine law')] is here used positively, like *fas* [("religious scruple")]; there is perhaps no verbal parallel in inscriptions, in which the word is rare, and parallels to the sense would be hard to find.[31] A Coan text of about the end of the fifth century forbids any cutting of cypress trees in the precinct, or outside it, under penalty of a fine and the guilt of impiety ["Let him profane the sanctuary" (*to hiaron asebeitô*)], save if the wood is wanted for some public work:[32] but there is nothing like an *assertion* that the conduct is in this case positively correct.

In the *Hercules Furens* of Euripides, when Heracles is sitting with veiled head after recovering his senses and realizing that he has in madness done murder, Theseus removes the veil, saying that a mortal does not defile divine things.[33] We have a parallel in Sophocles, *Antig.* 1043–4 and, although Artemis in Euripides, *Hippol.* 1437 ff. explains that she may not be present at death [("it is not lawful" (*ou themis*))],[34] this is not a very advanced rationalism. On the other

---

[30] A. Vogliano, *Riv. di filol.* N.S. 6, 1928, 262 ff.: G. Oliverio, *La stele dei nuovi comandamenti e dei cereali* (*Docum. ant. della Africa Ital.* 2, 1933) [No. 115, pp. 185 ff. Sokolowski]. The regulation of the funerals of the Labyadae at Delphi, if rightly restored by Blass (Ziehen no. C 19 f.), after forbidding the setting down of the body or the making of lamentation between the house and the tomb, adds 'and let there be no pullution there' (*tênei de mêden agos estô*)] which defines what is permissible and uses as [*està*] Roman assertions of religious propriety do *esto*. Cf. ["lest we be polluted ..."] in the archaic inscription from Cleonae, *IG* IV 1607 (= E. Schwyzer, *Dial. graec. exempla* 129): but, for what is more usual, see the observations of R. Hirzel, *Themis, Dike u. Verwandtes* 49 ff. on [*themis*, "that which is laid down or established"] as often used either with a negative or in a question.

We may note the Babylonian 'sogenannten Sabbathvorschriften', which, after defining what may not be done, state that the king is to sacrifice at night: 'seine Handerhebung ist dann bei Gott angenehm' (H. Gressmann, *Altorientalische Texte zum alten Testament*[2] 329). Translations may be misleading on such a point, but Hittite texts appear to present analogies to the Roman habit of definition: cf. J. Friedrich, *Aus dem hethitischen Schriftum* 2 (*Der Alte Orient* 25, 2, 1925) 13 'Nun essen (und) trinken sie, und sie gehen (dann) fort', and the formalism of other prayers cited in this work and in A. Götze, *Kleinasien* (in *Kulturgesch. d. alten Orients*, ed. W. Otto) 144. The Hittites did not, any more than the Romans (in their official ceremonies), act as though they believed in a magical compulsion of the gods (Götze 142); but they stated with great precision what a rite was intended to secure. If we look further afield, a curse defines exactly what the deity is expected to do, or even pledged to do (cf. the curse of Theseus on Hippolytus, and that of Eshmounazar at Sidon in H. Gressmann, op. cit. 447), but it is essentially a wish, even if it is a wish which implies the expectation that it will be fulfilled.

[31] In *SIG* 47.2 ["to participate in sacred rites"] is more likely than ["to participate in accordance with religious law"]: cf. J. C. Bolkestein, Ὅσιος *en* Εὐσεβής (Diss. Amsterdam, 1936) 70 f.

[32] Herzog, op. cit. 32 no. 11. We may note that in *IG* IX ii 1109, a text of the second century BC, the motive assigned for measures against the cutting of trees in the precinct of Apollo Koropaios is simply 'that the precinct may be magnificent'.

[33] *vv.* 1231 ff.

[34] Cf. *Medea* 1327.

hand, when Heracles proceeds to warn Theseus to flee from the defilement attaching to himself, and Theseus replies that there is no curse from friend to friend, we have an affirmation which is clearly marked as exceptional. While the idea of a transferable pollution by blood guilt did not perhaps take as large a place in men's minds as has sometimes been supposed,[35] we need only look at Plato, *Laws* 871A, to see that it could be treated as axiomatic; and in fact, later in the play (1324) Theseus promises to purify Heracles in Athens: that was at least a social necessity. Euripides is here, as so often, opposing the standards of nature to the standards of convention.[36] He was, moreover, using the traditional heroic pose – like that of Hector, who, when Polydamas urges retreat in view of an evil omen, says that the best omen is to fight for one's country (*Il.* 12.243). Hector can, it is true, quote the counsels of Zeus; but his mood is comparable with that of Theseus.

A Greek city did indeed vote to melt down old votive offerings and use the metal to make new cult objects (even in an emergency to borrow it for the issuing of currency)[37] or to transfer painted tablets dedicated without authority[38] from a shrine to its portico – an action for which modern parallels have been noted in the Catholic Rhineland and in the Greek Church.[39] Yet the body having civil jurisdiction over the place of dedication had to exercise power in these matters, from necessities of space as well as for good appearances: the decrees that a statue of this or that benefactor shall stand in a given temple forever almost imply that an ordinary private dedication had no right to expect as much. Where official dedications were concerned, a propitiatory sacrifice was, sometimes at least, deemed necessary;[40] further, private votives which were removed

---

[35] Cf. the criticisms of R. J. Bonner–G. Smith, *The Administration of Justice from Homer to Aristotle* 2, 192 ff. [W. S. F.]. Their theory that 'The whole matter of pollution in homicide looks like a sort of legalized pollution which was foisted upon homicide procedure by religion for various reasons' (200 f.) is attractive. It is a question (203 ff.) whether a man, who had done what was agreed to be justifiable homicide and who was called ["pure," "holy," or "undefiled" (*katharos, hosios,* or *euagês*)] required a purification. If he did not, that too may have been so determined by the Delphic oracle or by the tradition of the *exegetae*.

[36] Wilamowitz–Moellendorff ad loc. remarks that the line, which we find so striking, is never quoted in antiquity, and suggests that this is due to its wholly exceptional character. – In the *Orestes* 75 f., Helen explains that she is not defiled by talking to Electra *because* she can refer the guilt to Phoebus.

[37] Ziehen 109 no. 38a, 204 no. 67: W. S. Ferguson, *The Treasurers of Athena* 15, 118 ff., also 85 f., 93, 107 f.

[38] Ziehen 113 no. 39; for the need of authorization, cf. A. Rehm, *Milet* 3, 172 no. 32.

[39] Ziehen 114 n. 5, 206 n. 6.

[40] G. Hock, *Griech. Weihgebräuche* 89 f.; on popular susceptibility, cf. Ferguson, op. cit. 107 n. 1.

were not taken from the deity but buried in the precinct.[41] In any case, the Greek decrees in question do not contain any explicit statement like *ius fasque esto* [("let it be held just and religiously proper")].

Let us glance for a moment at two Greek constitutions sketched as ideals. The Athenian in Plato, *Laws* 828A, modestly suggests that it may be the business of the participants in the dialogue to fix when sacrifices are to be offered and how many there are to be, but that what sacrifices are to be offered and to which gods must be fixed with the aid of Delphi: the interlocutor says 'Well, the number'.[42] Aristotle may appear to be approximating to the Roman way when he says (*Politics* 1322 b 25–6) ['such sacrifices ... as the law (*ho nomos*) does not assign to the priests'] (1331a 26–7) ["except those temples which the law (*ho nomos*) or some utterance of the Pythian oracle assigns a place apart"], (1336 b 16–19) ["those gods to whom the law (*ho nomos*) grants even mockery; beyond these, the law (*ho nomos*) permits ... honor to be granted the gods"], but in these quotations ["the law"] is not a civic ordinance: it is, as W. L. Newman says, 'an unwritten law',[43] or, more simply, 'custom', 'usage'.

It is not that the Greeks were more careful than the Romans about the supernatural. There is no Greek parallel for the practice of *instauratio*,[44] the repetition of a whole ceremony because of some formal defect, or for the clause added to all laws *si quid ius non esset rogarier, eius ea lege nihilum rogatum* [('If anything that is not lawful be proposed, then nothing of it has been proposed by this law')].[45]

In fact, we may suspect that the Greeks treated casually some violations of custom, where Romans would have been likely to rationalize the violation. Thus when the Boeotians blamed the Athenians for fortifying the precinct of Delium, doing in it all that men did on unconsecrated ground, and drawing water from a well never used except for lustral purposes, the Athenians, says Thucydides, replied that it was reasonable to suppose that the god

[41] M. P. Nilsson, *A History of Greek Religion* 79: cf., for Rome, Varro *ap.* Gell[ius] 2.10 and I. S. Ryberg, *AJA* 1937, 102.

[42] Cf. *Rep.* 427B: contrast *ILS* 6087, lxiv.

[43] Vol. 3, 492 of his edition. Compare the Athenian reply to the Boeotian complaint about their use of the precinct at Delion (Thuc[ydides] 4. 98.2), ["the law among the Greeks was that conquest of a country brought possession of its temples, along with the obligation to maintain their customary rites, at least as far as possible" (trans. after Crawley)]; and Thuc[ydides] 3.58.3, ["the law among the Greeks is not to kill them"].

[44] Found at Iguvium as well as at Rome.

[45] Cicero *Pro Caecina* 95, *De domo sua* 106, and A. H. Greenidge, *Roman Public Life* 239 (with the form preserved in Probus *si quid sacri sancti* (*sacrosancti* cod. V) *est, quod non iure sit rogatum, eius hac lege nihil rogatur* ["if anything be proposed concerning the sacred which is not lawful, nothing of it is proposed by this law"]: Keil, *Gramm. Lat.* 4.273) [W. S. F.]. The power of definition rested in the *collegia* and in the senate.

would forgive what was done under stress of war and hardship.[46] This argument from what is reasonable, [*eikos*], has a fifth-century ring:[47] but it is likely that other such scruples were at times just disregarded, and nothing was thought of the matter, unless some politician wished to make capital out of it, or a pestilence followed. In any case, the argument from ["what is reasonable" (*to eikos*)] involves Greek anthropomorphism:[48] you could reasonably postulate that the Olympians might act like human beings and show an indulgence which was not to be expected from *numina*. Contrast the Roman principle *cum loca capta sunt ab hostibus, omnia desinunt religiosa uel sacra esse, sicut homines liberi in seruitutem perueniunt: quod si ab hac calamitate fuerint liberata, quasi quodam postliminio reuersa pristino statui restituuntur* ["when places are captured by the enemy, all things cease to be hallowed or sacred, just as free men pass into slavery: but if they are released from this calamity, then they revert to their former condition by a sort of *postliminium*"]:[49] or Cicero's statement about Pompey's abstention from touching anything in the Temple at Jerusalem, *non enim credo religionem et Iudaeorum et hostium impedimento praestantissimo imperatori sed pudorem fuisse* ["For I do not believe that the religious scruples of the Jews and our enemies constrained that excellent commander, but respect for public opinion did"].[50]

Again, after 403 BC Athens seems 'either tacitly or by formal act' to have cancelled its indebtedness to the treasury of Athena.[51] This was a matter of necessity; but let us remember also the way in which the Corcyraean provision against cutting vineprops from the precinct of Zeus and from that of Alcinous had been forgotten.[52]

The Greeks were not less secularist than the Romans. On Greek coins and other works of art commemorating alliances the chief divinity of a city stands for the city; and during the Hellenistic period and later, when a city was suffering from financial stringency, it often made a god a magistrate, i.e. it defrayed from temple funds the

---

[46] Thucydides 4.98.

[47] J. H. Finley, *HSCP* 49, 1938, 54 (cf. ibid. 30, 37 f., 51) [= *Three Essays* 37, 9, 17 f., 34].

[48] As Dr. B. Einarson remarked to me.

[49] Pompon. *ap. Dig.* 11.7.36. Note that the Rhodians, according to Vitruv. 2.8.15, would not remove an insulting trophy set up by Artemisia, *quod nefas est tropaea dedicata remoueri* [("because it is religiously improper for a trophy, once dedicated, to be removed")]. Would not the Romans have found a way out of this?

[50] *Pro Flacco* 68. There was a religious kinship between Athenians and Boeotians which was here lacking (the Romans also drew a line in their acceptance of Italian deities: G. Wissowa, *Religion und Kultus der Römer*[2] 49): but, even so, the contrast is striking.

[51] Ferguson, op. cit. 128.

[52] Thuc[ydides] 3.70. Herzog, *Heil. Gesetze* 33 notes that on Cos it was soon necessary to repeat the prohibition on cutting trees in the sacred grove.

charges to which a magistrate was liable. In fact, to Polybius and to other Greek observers the striking feature of Roman life was the part played in it by [*deisidaimonia*], fear of the gods, and Cicero and Virgil alike accepted this estimate.

The difference lies in the Roman principle of authority and in the systematization which they made on that basis. Consider portents – [*terata*], *prodigia*. They were divagations from the order of nature, eclipses, earthquakes, monstrous births and so forth. Greeks and Romans alike regarded them as indications that, from the standpoint of the city's relations with its gods, all was not well, and took some action to propitiate the supernatural. But only Romans had this formalized as *procuratio prodigiorum* [("attending to/expiation of portents")], a regular proceeding, initiated by the Senate and deemed necessary only when the *prodigium* had been observed on public land.[53] A Greek army, like individual Greeks, observed omens: but there is nothing in Greece which corresponds to *auspicia*[54] as the concomitant of *imperium*, just as in fact there is nothing which corresponds to *imperium*. A Greek may often have thought that the making of a large image magnified a god and that sacrifice not only conciliated the deity to whom it was offered, but also strengthened his power to aid; yet he had nothing corresponding to the Roman phrase *macte hoc sacrificio esto* [("Let him be honored by this sacrifice")].[55]

The control of religion was centralized at Rome in a degree unknown in Greece,[56] and those who controlled it claimed that their decisions were valid in heaven as on earth. Some such claim may appear to be implicit in all systems of ritual; in all of them symbolic action is credited with supernatural validity, in all of them purity and impurity, conformity and failure to conform are defined, in all of them methods of removing impurity and expiating disobedience are prescribed. Yet there is something individual in this Roman attitude. It is not a legal fiction – like the negative confession of the dead man in Egypt, whereby he asserted that he was innocent of a long list of sins and his assertion *ipso facto* had the effects of reality, or the statement that this or that Egyptian king was not dead.[57] It is legal in

[53] Mommsen, *Ges. Schr.* 7, 168.

[54] On which cf. now H. Ericsson, *ARW* 33, 1936, 294 ff.

[55] On which cf. now O. Skutsch–H. J. Rose, *CQ* 32, 1938, 220 ff. (It should be noted that this formula is used not only in sacrifices to the native Roman deities, but also to the Moerae and all the other deities of the Secular Games: *CIL* VI 32323.98, etc.)

[56] M. P. Nilsson, *Röm. Mitt.* 48, 1933, 245 ff. [*Opuscula* 2,504 ff.].

[57] Or, at Rome, the various ways in which a blind eye was turned to unfavourable omens.

form, and it accepts and defines the situation,⁵⁸ and its definition is explicit and not implicit.

The spirit of Roman authority in religion is expressed in words which Livy 39.16.6–7 puts the mouth of the consul who addressed the Roman people in 186 BC about the Bacchanalia:

> [For nothing is more deceitful in appearance than depraved religious scruple. When the divinity of the gods becomes a shield for crimes, then fear enters the soul, lest in punishing the frauds of mortals we should violate something of divine law that has been implicated in it. From that scruple you are freed by innumerable decisions of the *pontifices*, decrees of the Senate, and finally responses of the *haruspices*.]†

The Delphic oracle at its height could have made similar claims for its pronouncements; *haruspicum responsa* [("responses of the *haruspices*")] would have been comprehensible to a Greek, but not *senatus consulta* [('decrees of the Senate')].⁵⁹ We should be hard put to it to find a Greek parallel for the decree of the *pontifices* relieving the *flamen Dialis* of some of the taboos incumbent on his office.⁶⁰

---

⁵⁸ For 'the definition of the situation' as a general phenomenon, cf. W. I. Thomas, *Primitive Behavior* 8.

† nihil enim in speciem fallacius est quam praua religio. ubi deorum numen praetenditur sceleribus, subit animum timor, ne fraudibus humanis uindicandis diuini iuris aliquid inmixtum uiolemus. hac uos religione innumerabilia decreta pontificum, senatus consulta, haruspicum denique responsa liberant.

⁵⁹ On *decreta*, cf. A. S. Pease *ad* Cic. *De diuinatione* 2.73; Fr. Fürst, *Die Bedeutung des auctoritas im privaten u. öffentlichen Leben des röm. Rep.* (Diss. Marb., 1934) 33 f. The Athenian *exegetai* seem to have confined themselves to routine functions: in any case, their supposed function was to interpret traditional rules.

⁶⁰ [Gellius] 10.15.17–8.

Lysias 30.17 ff. (to which Professor W. S. Ferguson drew my attention) accuses Nicomachus, one of the *anagrapheis* [("commissiors")] entrusted with the codification of Athenian laws in 403–1 BC, of adding sacrifices which cost annually six talents and thereby causing ancestral sacrifices costing three talents a year to remain unoffered, [*athuta*], for lack of funds, in the year before the trial. Probably these sacrifices were not omitted from the new calendar, but were neglected simply because there was no cash available (W. S. Ferguson, *Classical Studies presented to Edward Capps* 150 n. 26). Now Lysias, in deploring this, refers to the prosperity enjoyed by the Athenians of old who performed these sacrifices in accordance with the [*kurbeis*] (Solonian laws) and argues that their descendants should perform them, if for no other reason, at least for the good fortune which accrued from them. The basis for the city's provision of funds was the [*kurbeis*] – as in its grant to the sacrifices of the Salaminioi (Ferguson, *Hesperia* 7, 1938, 67) – not an oracle. Was there a distinction between (*a*) sacrifices ordered by an oracle, and offered by the *hieropoioi* [, "the overseers of sacred rites"] (Aristotle, [*Ath. Pol.*] 54.6) and (*b*) other sacrifices, which were offered in accordance with a tradition which enjoyed the prestige of time and civic custom, but which (in spite of the general Delphic sanction for civic law and the fact that law could be regarded as both a divine gift and a human invention: Demosth. 25.16) could be ignored without downright impiety? So far as I am aware, a Greek city made its thankofferings to the gods, and established festivals in perpetuity, without binding itself to such perpetuity by anything like a Roman *uotum*. Accordingly, any omissions in this area are in no sense parallel to relaxations of requirements of ceremonial purity, which were directly the affair of the gods. (When elderly women were substituted for virgins in priesthoods, *ARW* 23, 1925, 30 [...], we do not know the exact form in which it was done: Diod. Sic. 16.26.6 says of the change at Delphi ["They say ... that the citizens of Delphi

Again, there are various traditions asserting that under a variety of circumstances the practice of human sacrifice was replaced here or there by some other rite; but no Hellenistic king forbade it as the Roman senate and Roman emperors did.[61]

In the later Republic and under the Empire the range of Roman worships continued to increase, and the attitudes of Roman worshippers at large to diversify. Neither development was wholly new, and neither destroyed the principle of authority. Aurelian's new college of *pontifices Solis* is in the tradition of the Romanization of Cybele nearly five centuries earlier; his request to the Senate to send a *pontifex* to dedicate the restored temple at Palmyra[62] gave to Rome a primacy exceeding anything which had been seen before; and the centralization of power in the person of the *princeps*, who was also *pontifex maximus*, only confirmed and focussed what had always been characteristic of Rome.

Students of church history have generally recognized that the differences between the Latin Church and the Greek Church turn largely on the legalism of the West. Can we not go further and detect a specific inheritance of this precise tendency to define, not only *de facto*, but *de iure*, what is permissible? As Professor G. La Piana has remarked,[63] in the Orthodox and the other eastern churches the form

made a law" (*phasin ... tous de Delphous nomothetêsai*)]. But was the oracle consulted, on such an occasion, or again when, in Plutarch's time (*QG* 38, p. 300A), the people of Orchomenus transferred the priesthood of Dionysus from the family of Zoilus?)

[61] Cf. again the action of M. Aurelius: ["He separated the rites of Serapis from the indiscriminate commonalty of the Pelusiaca" (*Historia Augusta, Marcus Aurelius* 23.8: *sacra Serapidis a uulgaritate Pelusiaca* [or -*ia*] *summovit*)]. Claudius in AD 41 limited the *instauratio* of horse-races in *ludi* to one day (Cassius Dio 60.6.5: L. R. Taylor, [*TAPA*] 68, 1937, 295) and in 43 abolished many sacrifices and festivals, since 'most of the year was being spent on them and the treasury had no small loss', in addition to making yet other economies (Cassius Dio 60.17.1–2). Two years later he restored the fifth day which Caligula had added to the Saturnalia and which had been discontinued (60.25.8), and it is possible that Claudius mainly abolished innovations of the previous principate and in particular new festivals in honour of members of the Imperial family. According to Aelian fr. 47, after the Delphian oracle had ordained that the Locrians should send two maidens annually to the temple of Athena at Ilion, and had further explained that a pestilence which ensued was due to their failure to replace the original pair, Antigonus (which Antigonus it was, is uncertain: A Wilhelm, *Jahreshefte* 14, 1911, 187) was asked to decide which Locrian city must pay this human tribute, and ordered them to settle the matter by drawing lots: but he was simply acting as arbitrator on a matter of detail. An Attalid letter in C. B. Welles, *Royal Correspondence in the Hellenistic Period* 115 no. 24 determines the privileges of a newly established priesthood; but that side of religion was in the Greek world regularly a matter for civil authority, and anything concerning finance and establishment was or could be a royal interest. Kings and others recognized rights of asylum and also the establishment of new festivals for which privileges were claimed: in this again, they confirmed what was a civic claim and in Welles 197 ff. no. 49, 202 ff. no. 50, Eumenes II makes a similar request of a Carian city and Cos.

[62] [*Historie Augusta, Aurelian*] 31.9. His action in reference to Paul of Samosata (Euseb[ius] *Hist. Eccl.* 7.30.19) is in some ways comparable.

[63] In an unpublished paper, here quoted by the kindness of its writer.

of baptism is 'N. is baptized in the name of the Father, of the Son, and of the Holy Ghost', and the form of absolution is 'May God forgive thy sins; in the name of the Father, of the Son, and of the Holy Ghost', whereas in the Latin Church the forms are not these, but 'I baptize thee in the name of the Father, the Son, and the Holy Ghost', and 'I absolve thee in the name of the Father, the Son, and the Holy Ghost.'

This is a momentous difference, and we may remark that long before forms of absolution in the first person had developed, and even before any belief in the prerogative of the church to absolve from mortal sins was accepted, the Roman bishop Callistus claimed the right to determine that this or that offence was not a mortal sin.[64] Tertullian's quotation of his edict as ["Those who have discharged the requirements of penitence, I absolve of the sins of adultery and fornication"] (*ego et moechiac et fornicationis delicta paenitentia functis dimitto*)[65] may not be literally exact, but it indicates the attitude involved. The power of definition is a necessary part of any religion which bases conduct on a written revelation, and there are both Rabbinic and early Christian precedents. Nevertheless, is it fanciful to see, in this and in much of the later evolution, an offshoot of the Roman tradition of asserting that a given act was free of guilt? *profanum esto.*

---

[64] Contrast the vision of Hermas, which informed him of a special forgiveness for one mortal sin, and compare the whole story of Cyprian and the *lapsi* (H. Lietzmann, *Geschichte der alten Kirche* 2, 231 ff.).

[65] *De pudicitia* 1. The East was not always more rigorous (cf. Dionys. Corinth. *ap.* Euseb[ius] [*Hist. Eccl.*] 4.23.6), but was liable to take a somewhat different view of sins (K. Holl, *Enthusiasmus und Bussgewalt beim griechischen Mönchtum* 226; E. Schwartz, *Bussstufen und Katechumenatsklassen* 11).

On the development of the West, see now the monographs by U. Gmelin, G. Roethe and W. Pewesin in *Geistige Grundlagen römischer Kirchenpolitik* (*Forsch. zur Kirchen-u. Geistesgeschichte* 11, 1937).

PART III

Ritual and Myth

Introduction to Part II:
Ritual and Myth

> Romulus took great care to encourage [the development of these virtues], beginning with the worship of the gods and *genii*. He established temples, precincts, altars; saw to the dedication of cult statues; and determined the forms, symbols, powers and benefactions of the gods ... In all these things he followed the best of the customs of the Greeks. But the traditional myths concerning the gods, those that contained blasphemies or indictments against them, he regarded as shameful and useless and indecent, unworthy not only of gods but of good humans, too. He therefore rejected them and accustomed people to say and think the best concerning the gods and to attribute to them nothing unworthy of their blessed nature.
>
> Dionysius of Halicarnassus *Roman Antiquities* 2.18.2–3[1]

Setting aside his faith in the historicity of Romulus, scholars long echoed the basic tenets of Dionysius's remarks on Roman myth, though no mere list of names could do justice to the range of theories and evidence underpinning their varied judgments.[2] One might summarize their common ground as follows: the Greeks had myths; the Romans didn't. Or, the Romans once had myths, whether Italic and native or Greek and foreign, but forgot them, and later acquired new ones (or reacquired old ones) from the Greeks. That the Romans themselves believed in some originary Greece – where myths were myths, religion was sincere, and gods were savage and immoral – and described their own culture as derivative from it, has proved variously damaging in the history of scholarship. Above all, those claims found a ready audience among Romantic intellectuals: their deep investment in the search for the pure experiences of an

---

[1] Translation after E. Cary, trans., *Dionysius of Halicarnassus, The Roman Antiquities Books I–II* (Cambridge, MA: Harvard University Press, 1937), 363. On this passage see Gabba 1984 and Borgeaud 1993.
[2] Recent historiographical and theoretical essays on the study of Roman myth include Horsfall's introduction to Horsfall and Bremmer 1987; Graf 1993b; Beard 1993; and Feeney 1998: 47–50.

unalloyed race made of Roman culture and Roman studies the poor stepchild of Hellenism.[3]

This privileging of Greek culture is, of course, nonsensical on chronological grounds. Indeed, and ironically, it can only be sustained by subscribing wholeheartedly to the myth of Romulus as it emerges in the Augustan age under the influence of Hellenistic mythopoiesis.[4] Only by insisting that Rome was founded suddenly in the middle of the eighth century BC, from purely Italic stock, can one even begin to explain the astonishing differences in sophistication and complexity scholars once posited between Rome of that period and the equally illiterate villages of Greece.

The myth of a mythless Rome has had an especially pernicious influence on the study of Roman religion, for two reasons. On the one hand, the studies of myth in general, and of myth and religion in particular, have been enormously fruitful areas of research both inside and outside classical studies; but within Classics, Romanists have had to watch with envy as their Hellenist colleagues came to view Greek religion as coterminous with its myths and rituals.[5] That view of archaic religion produced a fatal syllogism: religion lies somewhere at the nexus of myth and ritual; Rome had no native myths; therefore Rome had no religion. In no small measure, scholarship in this vein has sustained a fallacy that originated in an ideologically motivated misconstrual: namely, the insistence that "rites" are merely enactments or performances of "rituals," which in early modern usage designated a written script "directing the order and manner to be observed in performing divine service."[6] That is to say, those dependent on literary descriptions of rites tend to develop theories that privilege discursive interpretations of the rituals over and against cognition-in-performance.[7] And, once invested in

---

[3] See Habinek 1998: 15–23, and cf. Beard 1993: 47–48 and Feeney 1998: 1–8 and 47–50.

[4] On the myth of Romulus see J. Bremmer, "Romulus, Remus and the foundation of Rome," in Horsfell and Bremmer 1987: 25–48; von Ungern-Sternberg 1993; and (on Remus) Wiseman 1995.

[5] For a brief history of theories of "myth and ritual," see Versnel 1993: II, 2:16–48; Bell 1997: 3–8; and cf. Bremmer, "Myth and ritual in ancient Rome: the Nonae Capratinae," in Horsfall and Bremmer 1987: 76–88. On theories of myth and their relationship to the study of Greek and Roman religion, see Burkert 1993. Durand and Scheid 1994 and Bremmer 1998 offer complementary surveys of the history of "religion" and "ritual" as terms and categories in scholarship, with particular emphases on classical studies; for similar reflections on "ritual" as an anthropological category see Bell 1997: 259–66. On the politics of mythology as a field of study see Lincoln 1999.

[6] This definition of "ritual" is from the first edition of the *Encyclopaedia Britannica*; I quote it from Asad 1993: 56. Bell 1992 offers an extremely wide-ranging, concise, and critical survey of theories of ritual.

[7] Boyer 1994: 185–223, and esp. 203–23, seeks to undermine simplistic searches for the

problems of priority, scholars could only set aside literary accounts of rituals by denouncing them as second-order reflections on rites whose original meanings had been lost.

If, then, Rome had no native myths, only native rites, what did its rituals *mean*? If mythological exegesis is necessary to render ritual action intelligible, as many crude theorists once maintained, then, insofar as the Romans did not tell stories about the origin of their rituals, their rituals can have been no more than sequences of gestures and utterances, repeated precisely and endlessly for no reason whatsoever.[8]

Reconstructions of Roman religion along these lines harmonized with several important trends in the study of religion more generally, and it is here that the myth of mythless Rome has worked its second harm upon the study of Roman religion. Above all, such reconstructions depended upon, and seemed in some way to confirm, Protestant valorizations of correct belief over and above correct practice.[9] In propagating historical analyses of this kind, classical scholars joined nineteenth- and early twentieth-century anthropologists in historicizing and secularizing the prejudiced theories of religion popularized by Reformation denunciations of ritual formalism in general and Catholic liturgy in particular. To quote a representative text from this tradition, the *Letter from Rome Shewing an Exact Conformity between Popery and Paganism* of Conyers Middleton (1729), Roman Catholic "ceremonies appear[ed] plainly to have been copied from the ritual of primitive paganism, as if handed down by an uninterrupted succession from the priests of Old to the priests of New Rome."[10]

In spite of the role that Roman religion played in such polemics, serving as the unwitting progenitor of a corrupted Christianity, Roman religion in fact offers several fascinating opportunities to theorists of ritual and some equally fascinating challenges to theorists of myth. I concentrate here on two. First, fate has preserved in or

"meaning" of rituals. To employ terms quite different from his, one might say that he enables a distinction to avoid confusing the so-called "meaning" of a ritual with its logic or, for that matter, with its purpose.

[8] This reasoning obviously depends on two insupportable and, in this case, interrelated assumptions: first, that ritual actions cannot themselves be expressive of beliefs or theological presuppositions and, second, that etiological myth as a literary form should be privileged over all other forms of religious discourse. Put another way, any attempt by participants in a ritual to explain the meaning of the ritual (for them) *must* take the form of an etiological myth, else the ritual has no meaning at all.

[9] On ritual as script and its correspondence with hierarchies of belief and practice, see Asad 1993: 56–62.

[10] I quote this text from Jonathan Z. Smith's brilliant chapter "On the Origin of Origins": Smith 1990: 1–35 at 24.

near Rome two remarkable bodies of texts, records of the ritual actions carried out on the one hand by emperors from Augustus to Severus in celebrating the Secular Games and, on the other, by the Arval Brethren in worshipping Dea Dia.[11] Both groups of texts present considerable challenges; they also grant access to ritual performances without the kinds of mediation seemingly ever-present in literary accounts. This is not to say that the *commentarii*, the records of proceedings, are somehow unmediated or disinterested representations, or that they are "full," whatever that would mean; rather, they present hermeneutic challenges altogether different from those offered by Graeco-Roman literary narratives, with their invest-ment in etiological theories of myth. For what the authors of the *commentarii* did not ever see fit to record were accounts of origins or meaning.

Second, precisely because the Romans told so many myths of such disparate extraction even as they performed "mythless" rituals, Roman religion offers an extraordinary opportunity to study "myth and ritual" as contemporaneous forms of religious experience.

These fields have perhaps shown the most remarkable advances of any in Roman religion in recent years. Scholars had only to overcome their reluctance to see myth-making as an autonomous and creative form of religious discourse, on the one hand, and on the other to shed their unwillingness to see ritual as capable of articulating complex truths even in the absence of their discursive elaboration. As though those tasks were simple![12] The essays reprinted here capture the excitement and display many of the fruits of these developments. Denis Feeney's exploration of the Secular Games under Augustus was first published in his *Literature and Religion at Rome* (1998), at the time of its publication perhaps the most concise and lucid statement in English of the current state of research in Roman religion. What he captures so well in his analysis of the Secular Games is the enor-mous potential for creativity that a devotion to ritual orthopraxy in fact allowed.[13] John Scheid's "Cults, Myths and Politics" explores

[11] The first group must be read in the edition of Pighi 1965; the second has recently been re-edited and published with French translation in Scheid 1998d. The best English intro-ductions to the challenges presented by these texts are probably Beard 1985, 1991, and 1998 (to which add Scheid 1990b: 41–76). They are cited throughout this book: consult the index s.v. Secular Games and Arval Brethren and see pp. 114 and 165.

[12] For the first achievement, much credit belongs to Mary Beard, particularly for her articles on "Romulus' birthday" (1987; reprinted here as Chapter 12) and "Acca Larentia" (1989). For the second, first prize to John Scheid, whose works on the Arval Brethren have marked a watershed in the study of Roman ritual. Many of them are listed in the bibliography.

[13] On creativity in ritual see Bell 1997: 138–69 and 223–42. See also MacCormack 1981, a study of political ceremonial in late antiquity, arguing that political ceremonial gradually

a set of developments in cult and mythography largely contemporaneous with the Secular Games and seeks on their basis to define the tasks of mythography in Roman culture. Scheid argues that mythmaking operated at a level of cognition quite distinct from that of ritual and, therefore, that it will have addressed itself to distinct concerns at a very different level of articulation.

became subject to prescriptions from above rather than manipulation from below and in that way lost its ability to shape and express social consensus.

5 *The* Ludi Saeculares *and the* Carmen Saeculare[†]

DENIS FEENEY

Roman self-consciousness about the Greek component of civic cult did not disappear as time went on, but was always able to be activated. It provides a fascinating example of how self-conscious they could be about the contextual variability of their religious behaviour. As an example of this contextual variability, and as a way of focusing some of the main problems of talking about belief in a Roman context, it is worth looking in some detail at what is perhaps the most spectacular and systematic exploitation of the categories of Greek and Roman in cult, namely, the *ludi saeculares* staged by Augustus in 17 BCE.[1]

The first *ludi saeculares*, in 249 BCE, had been organised to expiate prodigies after the Sibylline books had been consulted by the *decemuiri*, the board of ten priests who supervised the Sibylline oracles and foreign cults in general.[2] Accordingly, in the *ludi* of 249 there was a markedly Greek stamp to the two deities honoured with three successive nocturnal sacrifices performed *Achiuo ritu*, 'according to the Greek rite' – Dis Pater (that is, Dives Pater, 'wealthy father', a calque for the Greek god of the underworld, Pluto, 'Wealth'), and his bride Proserpina (Persephone). Neither of these had cult in the city, and it was the first time that the state had honoured these gods of the underworld. Augustus' *ludi* some 230 years later were organised by the same board of priests responsible for foreign cult (though now fifteen in number, hence *quindecimuiri*). Augustus was himself a member of this panel, and oversaw the production of the Sibylline oracle which prescribed the occasion and the form for the *ludi*;

---

† Originally published in D. Feeney, *Literature and Religion at Rome* (Cambridge: Cambridge University Press, 1998, pp. 28–38.
[1] Pighi (1965) has texts, with discussion, of the *Commentarium* (*CIL* 6. 32323; *ILS* 5050) and of the Sibylline oracle (*FGH* 257 F 37); [Beard, North and Price (1998)], vol. 2, no. 5.7b. On the *ludi saeculares* in general, see Nilsson (1920); on Augustus, see Price in [Beard, North and Price (1998)], vol 1. Ch. 4; Galinsky (1996) 100–6.
[2] Latte (1960), 246–8.

these Greek hexameter texts, traditionally under the care of the *quindecimuiri*, had recently been purged and transferred from the temple of Jupiter Optimus Maximus to the temple of Apollo Palatinus, part of Augustus' residential complex.[3]

Augustus transformed the atmosphere and purpose of the *ludi*, orientating them away from infernal expiation towards future fecundity[4] but the ritual still lay within the purview of the *quindecimuiri*, and Augustus retained the importance of a Greek component, even throwing it into relief with an intricately contrapuntal patterning of night- and day-time activities. There were still three successive night-time sacrifices, beginning with the night of 31 May, at the same site in the Campus Martius as before, performed – *Achiuo ritu* – by Augustus: the emperor probably sacrificed in Greek dress on the first night, and then, at all the succeeding ceremonies, in the toga, but with bare head in the Greek manner.[5] The underworld deities of 249 BCE, Dis Pater and Proserpina, yielded place to three more beneficent honorands, who nonetheless shared with Dis Pater and Proserpina the twin characteristics of being Greek in nomenclature and without cult in the Roman state: Moerae, 'Fates'; Ilithyiae, 'Deities of Childbirth'; and Terra Mater, 'Earth Mother', the [*Gaia*] of the oracle, but sounding like the Greek [*Dêmêtêr*] (and not, be it noted, Tellus, the name of Earth in civic cult).[6] Set against these doubly Greek nocturnal rites were three successive day-time sacrifices, performed by Augustus and Agrippa together, still *Achiuo ritu*, but this time in honour of Jupiter Optimus Maximus, the supreme Roman god and centre of Republican cult (1 June), then Juno Regina, his Capitoline consort (2 June), followed by Apollo and Diana on the Palatine (3 June), inhabitants of the Augustan temple dedicated only ten and a half years previously.

We have here an extraordinarily sharp set of demarcations: night/day, without/with civic cult, Greek/Roman, aniconic/iconic, personifications/individuals, un-Olympian/Olympian, chthonic/heavenly, outside/inside the *pomerium*, plain/hilltop, single/paired sacrificer. The arrangement of the sacrifices shows the *princeps* flaunting the ability of his state, his family, and himself to dominate and control the greatest possible range of religious meaning and power, as he

---

[3] The date of transfer is guaranteed by Tib. 2.5.17–18 and Virg. *Aen.* 6.72: Smith (1913), 444.

[4] Nilsson (1920), 1716.

[5] Turcan (1988), 2.9, on the evidence for Domitian in 88 CE.

[6] Latte (1960), 299, on the absence of these deities from Roman cult. On the strong links in Greece between Moirai and Eileithyiae, see Roscher (1884–1937), 2.2.3091.

draws alien entities of birth and fecundity into the same ring as the
ancient gods of the Roman Capitol, staging a pageant which probes
the boundaries between the Roman state and the *oikoumene*.
Augustus and his colleagues have condensed into one sequence the
dynamic interplay between Greek and Roman categories that had
served the state so well for so long.

These three days must have been among the most significant in
Augustus' life, yet as soon as we start talking about 'personal belief'
the structure that generates that significance falls apart in our hands.
Augustus will have sacrificed to Jupiter Optimus Maximus many
times before, yet he was the first person ever to sacrifice to the
Moerae in the city of Rome, and no other Roman sacrificed to them
again for sixty-three years, when Augustus' great-nephew Claudius
next staged the *ludi saeculares*. Does this mean that Augustus and the
many thousands of spectators believed in what he was doing during
the first day-time rite, because it was Roman and traditional, but not
in what he was doing during the first night-time rite, because it was
Greek and unprecedented? Even to pose the question in these terms
is to reveal its futility. It is precisely the intersection between the
Roman and the Greek, the ancient and the novel, that generates the
cognitive and emotional power of the three days. The rite as a whole
articulates with remarkable economy that theme of rebirth within
a reworked traditional framework which is the hallmark of the
Augustan New Age ideology, and, indeed, of the régime as a whole.[7]
The negotiation between the novel and the traditional is central to
the exercise, and the apparatus is smashed if we concentrate on the
novelty as an inorganic and less meaningful element, or worry away
at which bit of the pageant meant more than the rest.

The rite comes clothed with an aura of tradition, but it is just as
easy to apprehend it as revolutionary.[8] The final recipient of sacrifice,
Apollo, the only Greek-named deity honoured in day-time, is as
interesting a compound of the novel and the traditional as his
protégé, Augustus. He had been established in the city for 400 years,
but now he had a new temple and persona, living within the
pomerium for the first time, and encroaching on the prerogatives of
his father Jupiter. If we look at the distribution of offerings with
Apollo in mind, we see interesting lines of connection being set up

---

[7] Zanker (1988), 49–53, on the new *regnum* of Apollo. As soon as the inscription was
discovered, Mommsen (1905) immediately saw this interstitial character of the rite as crucial;
cf. Nilsson (1920), 1717.

[8] Again, see Mommsen (1905), e.g., 356, on the revolutionary import of praying for the
Roman people and the legions as separate entities.

across the apparently stark dichotomies of the rite. Augustus alone at night sacrificed nine female lambs and nine female kids to the Moerae, and a pregnant sow to Terra Mater, while Augustus and Agrippa together in the day each sacrificed a bull and a cow to Jupiter and Juno respectively. To the Ilithyiae Augustus offered twenty-seven cakes, divided into three categories (two of them transliterated Greek words, *popana* and *phthoes*); most remarkably, since (so far as we know) Apollo had never received bloodless sacrifice in Rome before,[9] Augustus and Agrippa offered the same to Apollo and the same to Diana. The choice of offerings cuts across the gulf of night and day, establishing Apollo and his sister as the mediators between the two categories of the pageant. Apollo's host and protégé, Augustus, like-wise becomes the mediator between the epochs, cults and cultures of the *ludi*. The *quindecimuiri* had oversight of all foreign cults, in particular Apollo and the Magna Mater, the deities whose residences flanked Augustus' own; by Augustus' organisation, Jupiter and Juno have been, as it were, subsumed into the *Graecus ritus* of the whole pageant and of Apollo Palatinus in particular.[10]

THE CARMEN SAECULARE

In the Sibylline oracle's prescriptions for the *ludi* (18–22), following the itemising of the sacrifices are prescriptions for paeans sung in Latin ([*aeidomenoi te Latinoi/paianes*]), performed by youths and maidens, all with their parents still living, in separate choruses. The *Acta* record that a *carmen* was sung twice on the last day, first before Apollo Palatinus and then before Jupiter Optimus Maximus. It was sung by twin choruses of twenty-seven boys and twenty-seven girls with parents still living (one boy for each of the cakes given to Apollo and one girl for each of the cakes given to Diana). The *Acta* further record: *carmen composuit Q. Horatius Flaccus* ('the hymn was composed by Q. Horatius Flaccus'). This *carmen* of course survives in Horace's corpus, as the *Carmen Saeculare*, and in it we may trace a poetic engagement with the ritual categories so carefully built and rebuilt by the *princeps*. If the *ludi* themselves illuminate how self-consciously the Romans could manipulate different contexts and categories in their cult, the distinctive discourse of the *carmen* adds another dimension to that self-examination.

Horace's *carmen* acknowledges the night/day distinctions of the

---

[9] Gagé (1955), 631–2.
[10] Gagé (1955), 635–7.

sacrifices, grouping the three foreign night-time deities in sequence (13–32) and speaking of 'games crowded three times in bright day and as many times in pleasing night' (*ludos | ter die claro totiensque grata | nocte frequentis*, 22–4). From the beginning, however, the hymn concentrates on following up the ritual's use of Apollo and Diana as a bridge across the categories, affirming more openly than the ritual itself their status as the end aimed at by the trajectory of the whole three days.[11] The *carmen* begins with an invocation of the Palatine pair: *Phoebe siluarumque potens Diana, | lucidum caeli decus* ('Phoebus, and Diana with dominion over woods, shining adornment of heaven'). This language already collapses the night/day distinction, for the singular phrase 'shining adornment of heaven' refers jointly to the pair, the brother shining as the sun at day and the sister as the moon at night. The second stanza, referring to the fact that the *carmen* is being sung at the command of the Sibylline verses, glances at the new role of Apollo as the custodian of those verses. The third stanza catches at another new role of Apollo when the choruses turn to Sol, the Sun, saying that he is born 'another and the same', *alius ... et idem* (10). These words allude not only to the physical illusion that the sun is 'another' sun at each new day, but also to the 'otherness and sameness' of Apollo's syncretism with Sol/Helios. In the oracle, Apollo is likewise named as 'the one who is also called Helios' ([*hoste kai Helios kikêsketai*], 17); we must remind ourselves that when the choruses first sang they were facing the temple of Apollo Palatinus, on whose roof stood a representation of the chariot of the Sun, to which the choruses point at the beginning of this stanza, with the words *curru nitido*, 'shining chariot' (9).[12]

After these first three stanzas concerned with the Palatine pair in one manifestation or another, the choruses address Ilithyia, the goddess of childbirth. The movement of the *carmen* uses this ordering to establish the links between Ilithyia and Apollo and Diana that Augustus had established by choice of sacrificial offering. A further connection across these categories is forged when Horace uses 'Lucina' as a possible title for Ilithyia (15), reminding us that Diana herself could be regarded as Lucina, controlling the same sphere as Ilithyia. Prayers to the Fates and Earth follow (25–32), before the choruses once more return to Apollo, mild and calm as in the Palatine cult statue, and Diana (as Luna, 36).

We are now half-way through the *carmen* and there has not yet

[11] Gagé (1955), 635.
[12] Hardie (1993), 125–6.

been any mention of the Roman deities who received sacrifice on the first and second days, Jupiter and Juno; this sense of exclusion is strengthened by the closural force of the address to Apollo and Diana in 33–6, for that address takes us back, by ring-composition, to their initial invocation in the first stanza.[13] Since the discovery of the *Acta* in 1890 it has been clear that Jupiter and Juno must be the gods now addressed as the *carmen* turns at the half-way point (*Roma si uestrum est opus* ..., 'if Rome is your business ...', 37), for the next three stanzas lead up to a description of Augustus sacrificing to these addressees with white oxen (49), and the *Acta* make it plain that Jupiter and Juno were the only gods who received such offerings during the *ludi*.[14] But – in an elision which is practically unthinkable in a hymn, where the proper naming of the invoked deity was considered vital – Jupiter and Juno are not named as they are addressed. Hence the universal assumption amongst commentators before 1890 that this entire section was likewise addressed to Apollo and Diana. The Sibylline oracle, which until 1890 had been the only evidence for the form of the rite, states explicitly that Apollo should receive the same bovine sacrificial offerings as Jupiter and Juno (11–18): only the discovery of the *Acta* revealed that there had been a change of plan, and that Apollo had in fact received the same offerings as the Ilithyiae. With only the misleading evidence of the Sibylline oracle to go by, and without any explicit mention of a change in addressee, the white oxen mentioned by Horace in line 49 would inevitably be taken to refer to Apollo's sacrifices.

Jupiter and Juno are not named, then, although the choruses are now directly addressing them. With this dramatic omission, Horace alludes to and corrects the suppression of the names of Apollo and Diana at the beginning of Virgil's *Georgics,* where Apollo and Diana are invoked anonymously as 'the extremely bright lights of the universe' (*clarissima mundi* | *lumina*, 1.5–6);[15] throughout the hymn, Horace compensates abundantly for that suppression, parading one name after another for Apollo and his sister (Phoebus, Sol, Apollo; Diana, Lucina, Luna). Juno in fact is never named at all in the course of the *carmen*, and Jupiter (apart from brief mention as the sky-god in 32, *Iouis aurae*) finds his way only into the last stanza, where he does no more than approve the favourable response of Apollo and Diana, whose praises close the hymn (*doctus et Phoebi chorus*

---

[13] As Richard Tarrant points out to me.
[14] Mommsen (1905), 357–8.
[15] As Richard Thomas points out to me.

et Dianae | *dicere laudes*, 75–6). It is hard to know whether this suppression of Jupiter and Juno would have been more striking during the first performance of the hymn in front of Apollo Palatinus, or during the second performance in front of Jupiter Capitolinus. The eclipse of the old Capitoline deities by the Palatine gods of the *princeps* is most remarkable, and it has been exposed more nakedly in ten minutes of singing than it had been in three days of ritual action. And as the *carmen* progresses on its career in Horace's lyric corpus, leaving further and further behind the ritual context which makes it possible to glimpse Jupiter and Juno as the addressees here, it paradoxically stresses more and more powerfully the ritual's suppression of the Capitoline deities in favour of the Palatine pair.

The paean is by origin a hymn to Apollo and Artemis,[16] and Horace's hymn, as the paean called for by the Sibylline oracle, is capitalising on this ancient formal feature in order to reinforce the ritual's emphasis on the Palatine pair. If the *carmen* exaggerates this theme of the ritual, however, in other ways it represents not an exaggeration but a departure. In particular, its way of naming the Greek deities who received night-time sacrifice is an interesting variation upon Augustus' emphases.[17]

In line 14, Ilithyia is addressed with her Greek title, for which there was no exact Latin equivalent, but Horace immediately presses the alternative naming style of hymns into novel service when he goes on to say *siue tu Lucina probas uocari* | *seu Genitalis* ('whether you prefer to be called Lucina or Genitalis', 15–16). Here he offers the Greek goddess 'a choice between two Latin cult names, *Lucina* and *Genitalis*: "Ilithyia – shall we (in Latin) call you Lucina or Genitalis?"'[18] The renaming of the alien divinity, hitherto outside the cult of the *res public*, is strongly marked, for her unprecedented function is now to assist the success of Augustus' marriage legislation. It is in order to highlight the stresses of this cultural transference that Horace in the next stanza turns to another world of language altogether, with his notorious evocation of Latin constitutional jargon, so often dismissed as a mere blunder: *patrum ...* | *decreta super iugandis* | *feminis* ('the decrees of the fathers concerning the yoking of women', 17–19). The next Greek deities invoked are the Moerae. They are Latinised as *Parcae* (25), with another

---

[16] Procl. *Chr.* in Phot. *Bibl.* 320a21 (my thanks to A. Barchiesi for this point). In *C.* 4.6.37–8, Horace refers to the *Carmen Saeculare* as a hymn to Apollo and Diana.

[17] McDermott (1981), 1665.

[18] McDermott (1981), 1665, n.71; Bentley's emendation to the Greek *Genetyllis* destroys this point.

Latin equivalent for their Greek name, *fatta*, also placed emphatically as the last word of their stanza (28). Finally, Augustus had sacrificed to 'Earth' under the name *Terra Mater*, deliberately choosing a title which was not part of the state religion, but Horace chooses instead the word *Tellus* (29), which was the name of Earth in civic cult; he reinforces the link with the 'Earth' of civic cult by associating Tellus with Ceres (29–30), for Ceres' statue stood outside the temple of Tellus.[19]

In rewriting the Greek nomenclature used by the *princeps*, the Grecising hymn is more concerned to establish a Latin atmosphere than is the state ritual itself. If we are to read off 'degree of authenticity of belief' against a scale of Latinity or Romanness, we will end up saying that the *carmen* is more 'authentic' than the ritual, at which point we may well conclude that we are not using helpful terminology. Instead, we might see the *carmen* as engaging with the dynamics of the ritual, not replicating them, but setting up a tangentially related set of categories and perspectives for the audience to manipulate as they are challenged to use the *carmen* as a way of looking back over the last three days and forward over the next one hundred and ten years.

Augustus' pageant is a semiotic system of the utmost intricacy, and Horace's *carmen* does not – indeed, can not – reflect or re-embody it. By altering emphases and collapsing distinctions as well as observing them, the *carmen* insistently calls attention to the fact that it is not the rite, that it is not tautologous. It accomplishes this, above all, by marking out a space for poetry as a distinctive discourse. The thorough Latinising of the deities addressed is a sign of this ambition, as is the way the *carmen* looks forward to its reception as a further piece of Horatian lyric.[20] More significant still is the dialogue with the *Aeneid* of Virgil, dead not two years before. Throughout, the *carmen* is acknowledging the fact that the *Aeneid* has already become the cardinal medium for conceptualising the new ideology.[21] Further, Horace depicts the present actions of Augustus as the fulfilment of the text of the *Aeneid*. Augustus is 'superior to the one waging war, gentle to the prostrate enemy' (*bellante prior, iacentem | lenis in hostem*, 51–2), and his empire is world-wide (53–6). Augustus has here become the subject and the addressee of Anchises' prophecy in *Aeneid* 6, which had prophesied world dominion for Augustus

[19] [Pliny *Nat.*] 34.15; cf. Ov[id] *Fast.* 1.671–3.
[20] Barchiesi (1996), 8–9.
[21] Fraenkel (1957), 375.

(6.792–800), and which had itself become a Sibylline oracle at the end. When Anchises turns to the 'Roman', and commands him 'do you, Roman, remember |... to spare the conquered and war down the proud' (*tu ... Romane, memento* | *... parcere subiectis et debellare superbos*, 6.851–3), he is using Sibylline language of the same kind used by the Sibylline oracle for the *ludi saeculares*: 'remember, Roman' ([*memnêsthai, Rhômaie*], 3). The poetic prophecy of a predecessor has here become more than text to be alluded to: its oracular Sibylline power is now reanimated. Horace's chorus makes the Latin hexameters of Virgil collaborate with the Greek hexameters of Augustus' Sibylline oracle, which is an instrument and cause of ritual, but also, after all, a poetic text of a certain kind in its own right. Our categories of poetry and ritual break down as the *carmen* tells us that both Virgil's and Augustus' Sibylline oracles have made this 'happen'.

One of poetry's distinctive powers is its capacity to outstrip time, and Horace's long-standing obsession with this topic is in play here. Horace believes that his poetry can celebrate and preserve memory more powerfully than other media, more powerfully than marble or bronze monuments;[22] the Horatian motif acquires extra power in this ritual context, for the state itself is concerned to preserve the memory of the *ludi*, with seven lines of the inscription devoted to a *senatus consultum* ordering the erection of two monuments, in bronze and marble, for the future memory of the event (*ad futuram rei memoriam*, lines 58–63). In the *carmen*, Horace is celebrating and preserving a particular moment of sacred time (*tempore sacro*, 4), and his characteristic lyric interest in that function is especially charged, for the *ludi* are themselves all about time. Their preservative ritual is designed to create a new cycle of time, a permanence for the state that transcends any individual's lifetime: the *Acta* twice refer to the fact that no one will again see this ritual, that no mortal may see the games twice (lines 54–6). Horace's lyric obsession with transience and permanence is in a novel dialogue with the ritual's obsession with transience and permanence, and with the state's attempts in bronze and marble to preserve the memory of that ritual.[23]

---

[22] Putnam (1986), esp. 300–6; Hardie (1993); Barchiesi (1996), 18–22.

[23] In C. 4.6.44 Horace mentions his name for the only time in the *Odes*; in a poem about the performance of the *carmen saeculare*, this citation clearly alludes to the commemoration of his name on the inscription; but it is significant that he reinscribes that commemoration into the future speech of one of the girls of the chorus, once again stressing the superiority of his own genre.

The *carmen*'s self-consciousness about the fact that it is a poem, and cannot be co-extensive with the rite, is obliquely reflected in the interest modern scholars show in debating whether or not it was 'part of' the rite. In some senses it was (it had been prescribed by the Sibylline verses, and its singing was commemorated on the inscribed *Acta*);[24] in some senses it was not (it was not a *precatio*, 'cult prayer', strictly speaking, and its actual words were not engraved on the marble as were the words of Augustus' and Agrippa's *precationes*).[25] The odd position of the *carmen* within the rite is not a gaffe, but a sophisticated acknowledgment of its nuanced relationship with the rest of the proceedings. As we shall see in Chapter 4, 'Ritual' [*Literature and Religion at Rome*, pp. 127–33], one of the most important contributions from the revisionist studies of Roman religion has been the recognition that exegesis and interpretative dialogue help constitute Roman religious practice, rather than being something extraneous or added on. The *carmen* and the *ludi*, independent yet mutually implicated, are our clearest test case. Interpretation is already explicitly a part of the whole three-day spectacle.

BIBLIOGRAPHY

Barchiesi, A. (1996) 'Poetry, praise and patronage: Simonides in Book 4 of Horace's *Odes*', *CA* 15: 5–47

Beard, M., North, J. and Price, S.R.F. (forthcoming [1998]) *Religions of Rome*. 2 vols., Cambridge

Cairns, F. (1992) 'Theocritus, *Idyll* 26', *PCPhS* 38: 1–38

Fraenkel, E. (1957) *Horace*. Oxford

Gagé, J. (1955) *Apollon romain*. Paris

Galinsky, K. (1996) *Augustan Culture: An Interpretive Introduction*. Princeton

Graf, F. (1993) (ed.) *Mythos in mythenloser Gesellschaft: Das Paradigma Roms*. Stuttgart and Leipzig

Hardie, P. (1993) '*Vt pictura poesis?* 'Horace and the visual arts', in N. Rudd (ed.), 120–39

Latte, K. (1960) *Römische Religionsgeschichte*, Munich

McDermott, E.A. (1981) 'Greek and Roman elements in Horace's lyric program', *ANRW* 2.31.3: 1640–72

Mommsen, T. (1905) 'Die Akten zu dem Säkulargedicht des Horaz', in *Reden und Aufsätze*, 351–9. Berlin

[24] Cairns (1992), 29 n. 92.
[25] Scheid (1993), 113. Interestingly, the words of the new *carmen* for Septimius Severus' games of 204 CE were engraved in the *Acta*: Pighi (1965), 165–6 (fr. Va, 60–71).

Nilsson, M.P. (1920) 'Saeculares Ludi', *RE* 2R.1A.2: 1696–1720

Pighi, G.B. (1965) *De Ludis Saecularibus P. R. Quiritium*, 2nd edn. Amsterdam

Putnam, M.C.J. (1986) *Artifices of Eternity: Horace's Fourth Book of Odes.* Ithaca and London

Roscher, W.H. (1884–1937) *Ausführliches Lexikon der griechischen and römischen Mythologie.* Leipzig

Rudd, N. (1993) (ed.) *Horace 2000: A Celebration. Essays for the Bimillennium.* Bristol

Scheid, J. (1993) 'Cultes, mythes et politique au début de l'Empire', in F. Graff (1993) (ed.), 109–27

Smith, K.F. (1913) (ed.) *The Elegies of Albius Tibullus.* New York

Turcan, R. (1988) *Religion romaine. I: Les Dieux. II: Le Culte.* Leiden

Zanker, P. (1988) *The Power of Images in the Age of Augustus*, trans. A. Shapiro. Ann Arbor

6 Cults, Myths, and Politics at the Beginning of the Empire[†]

JOHN SCHEID

translated by Philip Purchase

In a relatively recent study of Augustus' religious practice,[1] which notably addresses his "religious politics," as the author puts it, we find gathered in one place a set of commonly held beliefs concerning the nature of public cults, myths, politics, and the links between them. According to this line of thought, Caesar and Augustus, cut off from the piety of the people (in the romantic sense of the term), and acting from their aristocratic vantage point, took religion out of the realm of the sacred only to abuse it for political ends. In order to glorify their achievements and their undertakings, they did not hesitate to falsify myths, and in so doing they hastened the decline of myth and belief in the gods.

This article is, to be sure, beginning to look a little dated, but it summarizes a set of opinions that are still quite current. For this reason, the immediate usefulness of the present reflection on Roman mythology will lie in its reaffirmation of truths that we believe – often too hastily – to be universally accepted. I will not linger over the old theme of religious decadence, which has come under such vigorous attack this past decade, nor will I deal with the hazy definition of myth underpinning such studies. For a number of years now, we have tried to demonstrate that public religion was necessarily linked to politics, and even to questions of political advantage, as it expressed the relations of the Roman people (as a juridical entity rather than a group of individuals) with the gods, their divine partners. The language of this religion was that of civic relations, its field of operation the political community of divine and human beings, its

[†] Originally published as "Cultes, mythes et politique au début de l'Empire," in F. Graf, ed., *Mythos in mythenloser Gesellschaft: Das Paradigma Roms* (Stuttgart: Teubner, 1993), pp. 109–27.
[1] W. Speyer, "Das Verhältnis des Augustus zur Religion," *ANRW* 2:16:3 (1984), 1777–1805.

context that of internal and external politics. In other words, the operation of this religion was necessarily marked by a certain coldness, by calculation of advantage and by attention to reality: Roman religion was in good health and held in high esteem *to the extent that* it was linked to politics and the political.[2]

I will not concern myself with demonstrating once again the validity of this assertion, but will rather take as my starting-point the notion that Roman public religion was in its essence political and politicized. There were, no doubt, other facets to the religious experience of the Romans, particularly those that found expression in private life and scholarly reflection. These kinds of religious practice, however, are not under investigation here, and as it has not been demonstrated that they follow any different kind of logic, they scarcely contradict our argument.

What of the second assertion alluded to above, namely that myth was shamelessly manipulated and thus driven into a terminal decline? This assertion is quite as incongruous as the irrevocable condemnation of Roman religious attitudes. There is certainly no question that myth was used for political ends, and that new myths were written in a political climate. Indeed, once the deep bonds between public religion and politics are identified, it would be quite surprising were we not to find such use of myth; at any rate, we surely cannot speak of abuse and decline merely on this account. I am not going to enter into the methodological morass formed by the evaluation in universal terms of the myths recounted or written at Rome. This kind of hierarchy makes no sense from a historical point of view, and in the end it tells us much more about the predilections of the modern western world than about ancient reality. What is more, there is no doubt that many mythological collections dating from the Roman period were greatly valued in antiquity and became classics overnight: this hardly constitutes what the historian would call a decline, especially when this mythographic activity often saved quite ancient mythological traditions from oblivion. Other writers have dealt with this question, and I will not return to it.[3] Rather,

---

[2] E.g. John North, "Conservatism and change in Republican Rome," *PBSR* 44 (1976), 1-12; id., "Religion in Republican Rome," *CAH* 7:2 (1990), 573-624; J. Scheid, *Religion et piété à Rome* (Paris, 1985 [2nd edition, Paris, 2001]). For the prehistory of traditional prejudices, J. Scheid, "L'impossible polythéisme: les raisons d'un vide dans l'histoire de la religion romaine," F. Schmidt (ed.), *L'impensable polythéisme. Etudes d'historiographie religieuse* (Paris, 1988), 424-57 [English translation: J. Scheid, "Polytheism impossible; or, the empty gods: reasons behind a void in the history of Roman religions," *History and Anthropology* 3 (1987), 303-25].

[3] I will merely refer to F. Graf, *Griechische Mythologie. Eine Einführung* (Zürich/München,

I will add weight to their conclusions by examining the articulation of myths and religion, which is to say ritual practice. Were these parallel activities, without immediate connection? Were the relations between them artificial and feigned? Did myth or ritual hold pride of place in the eyes of the Romans when it came to expressing their religious thought? And how could a construction so artificial, and at times so incoherent, express religious thought in the first place? I will try to answer these questions by examining a set of cases dating, for the most part, from the beginning of the Christian era, and by taking the perspective of cult activity.

*

Before going any further, let me make clear that almost all ancient public cults were linked to myth, if only through the decoration of cult sites. So, the introduction of Magna Mater at Rome took place against the backdrop of the Romans' Trojan origins, as was also the case with the installation of Venus Erucina and even of Mens upon the Capitol; the Trojan myth had been self-servingly developed in a large number of Roman tragedies since the third century BC.[4] Our sources for the republican period are sketchy, and so do not allow us to confirm links for this period. At any rate, by the beginning of the Christian era, our documents, even after the disappearance of a huge number of sources, confirm that all-important public cults were linked to myth. So, for example, the month of July saw the celebration of ten public festivals: with the exception of the Furrinalia, which apparently were sinking into oblivion, all were at least furnished with an *aition* [an originary or motivating event; an explanation].[5]

However, this abundance of myths should not lead us to a mistaken conclusion. The recitation of myth – myth as object – does not play a central role in these cults: it develops on the margins of the cult, even outside of any strictly religious context. This is why it is often tempting to treat the myth as a work of art sufficient in itself, a literary or figurative work, even a work of propaganda, which

1991) [English translation by Thomas Marier: *Greek Mythology: An Introduction* (Baltimore, 1993)]; J.N. Bremmer and N.M. Horsfall, *Roman Myth and Mythology* (London, 1987); and C. Calame, "Illusions de la mythologie," *Nouveaux Actes Sémiotiques* 12 (1990), 1–35.

[4] For Venus Erucina and Mens, see R. Schilling, *La religion romaine de Vénus* (Paris, 1982), 242–52; for Magna Mater, see the bibliography in Bremmer-Horsfall (op. cit. n. 3) 105 n.1.

[5] The commentaries of A. Degrassi, *Inscriptiones Italiae*, vol. XII.2: *Fasti anni Numani et Iuliani* (Rome, 1963), 475–89, give a useful first survey of the mythic themes attached to the festivals. – We know from Varro that Furrina no longer inspired the Romans and that she was slipping into oblivion, to the extent that in the second century AD her former sacred wood became home to a new sanctuary.

refers to other myths, but not to the cult in anything more than an artificial manner.

A closer examination reveals that things are far more complicated. In fact, I would argue that it is precisely in the nature of both strong and weak links between these works of art and cult practice that one of the key aspects of Roman mythologizing is revealed. There is no question that the majority of rites did not accord the least place to myth, mythical recitation and mythical characters, and that myth as such was an artistic genre that functioned according to its own rules. Yet many cults also displayed direct and intimate connections with myth. The extended descriptions of rites and festivals that have come down to us reveal precisely the respective places of the two types of discourse.

The rite and particularly the prayers (*precationes*) found in the two extant epigraphic *commentarii* for the *ludi saeculares* do not contain the slightest allusion to the foundation-myth for this festival.[6] This myth appears in the accounts of historians, in books, *bibliothecae*;[7] namely, on the margins of the cult, even if we accept that in the cult's central site in Tarentum, an image, inscription, or even an *aedituus* ["temple-warden"] might have displayed the origin-myth to the inquisitive. In any case, the myth never appears in the words or gestures of the celebrants.

This observation is confirmed by other documents concerning the celebration of the cult. For example, according to Roman poets and historians, priestly offices all dated back to mythic times.[8] Yet one would search in vain the reports on the activities of priests and magistrates for the least confirmation of this point, explicit or implicit. Let us take three examples.

In the hundreds of lines of the *commentarii* of the Arval Brethren, we find no allusion to Romulus, Acca Larentia or the time of origins. The aetiological myth appears in the writings of scholars: Masurius Sabinus, Aulus Gellius and Pliny.[9] The same observation holds for the Laurentes Lavinates, members of the ritual *populi* of the ancient

---

[6] The *commentarii* for the *ludi saeculares* of 17 BC and 204 AD can be consulted in G.B. Pighi, *De ludis saecularibus populi Romani Quiritium libri sex* (Amsterdam, 1965).

[7] The myths are reported in Zosimus 2.1–3 and Valerius Maximus 2.4.5. For the complete sources see Pighi (op. cit. n. 6) 43–72.

[8] M. Beard, "Acca Larentia gains a son. Myths and priesthood at Rome," in Mary M. Mackenzie and Charlotte Roueché, eds., *Images of Authority. Papers Presented to Joyce Reynolds on the Occasion of her Seventieth Birthday*, Proceedings of the Cambridge Philological Society, Suppl. vol. 16 (Cambridge, 1989), 41–61.

[9] See J. Scheid, *Romulus et ses frères. Le collège des frères arvales, modèle du culte public dans la Rome des empereurs*, BÉFAR 275 (Paris, 1990), 17–35, for myths, and 42 for references to epigraphic commentaries.

metropolis of Lavinium. In their (often very precise) inscriptions, there is no trace of the Trojan background to the cult, of Aeneas, Romulus and Titus Tatius: these characters do not have any place in the cult and traditional formulas, but are rather found in works of art.[10] And, finally, we should make mention of the *Sodales Augustales*.† They were created in 14 AD, and Tacitus makes clear that the *Sodales Titii*, companions of the king Titus Tatius, served as a model for this priesthood. Our documentation for the *Augustales* is certainly not abundant, but having said that, up until this day there has never been any question over the presence of this mythic model.[11]

There is no need to go any further, as all the explicit sources confirm the rule: the myth appears on the margins of the canonical ritual process, and is generally relegated to the works of scholars, poets and historians, or to the decoration of sanctuaries and liturgical objects.

However, there are two documents that seem to contradict this observation, as they attest to the intrusion of mythology into the ritual process. They are the *commentarii* for the *ludi saeculares* and the Calendar of Praeneste. The contradiction is only apparent, however, and in fact helps to make even clearer the status of myth in relation to ritual.

While the canonical rites of the *ludi saeculares* contain no allusion to the myth, it nevertheless appeared during the celebration. In the first place, we should note that during the three nights and days of the games, sacrifices were followed by theatrical games.[12] In this way the games made up part of the liturgy, but they were celebrated *sacrificio confecto* ["after the sacrifice was completed"]: they were

---

[10] For the sources and bibliography, see F. Castagnoli, *Lavinium 1: Topografia generale, fonti e storia della ricerche* (Rome, 1972); C. Saulnier, "Laurens Lavinas. Quelques remarques à propos d'un sacerdoce équestre à Rome," *Latomus* 43 (1984), 517–33; A. Dubourdieu, *Les origines et le développement du culte des Penates à Rome*, CÉFR 118 (Rome, 1989), 341–55.

† A college of twenty-five priests, initially comprising twenty-one leading members of state and four members of the imperial house, charged with maintaining the cult of Augustus at Rome. See Hoffman Lewis 1955: 111 and 116–17, and esp. Scheid 1978: 618, 627, 639, 642 and 648–9.

[11] For the mythic models: Tacitus *Ann.* 1.54.1; *Histories* 2.45.3. The rest of the documentation is largely epigraphic, and concerns the *Fasti* of the *sodalitas* or the careers of the *sodales*. The only precise allusion to their function is found in Tacitus *Ann.* 3.64.3, where the author limits himself to reporting the argument used to justify the participation of *sodales* in the celebration of the votive games [for the ailing Livia, widow of Augustus and mother of Tiberius, the reigning emperor]: the argument is that they are *proprium eius domus (= domus Augustae) sacerdotium* ["the priesthood of his house," namely, "the Augustan house"].

[12] For example, Pighi (op. cit. n. 6) 114, Augustan games, line 100: *Ludi noctu, sacrificio [co]nfecto, sunt commissi in scaena quoi theatrum adiectum non fuit, nullis positis sedilibus, etc.* ["The sacrifice completed, games were held at night on a stage, to which no theatre was attached and for which no seats were set out ..."].

separated from the central rite and formed a rite in themselves that was joined to the previous one. Together with the sacrifice, these games formed the *ludi saeculares*. It is a pity that we do not know the program for these games, but I will not be taking too much of a risk in supposing that mythology played a central part,[13] an observation that also holds for all the other "hellenizing" rites linked to theatrical games. Be that as it may, the *ludi saeculares* contained a second rite during which the myth appeared: the performance of the famous *carmen* ["hymn"], written in 17 BC by Horace, and in AD 204 by an unknown poet. On the last day of the games, after the sacrifices to Apollo and to Diana and the theatrical games that concluded them, *pueri patrimi et matrimi* ["boys with fathers and mothers still living"] sang the *carmen saeculare*, which contained mythological elements, to a musical accompaniment.[14] The *carmen* is not a prayer in the strict sense. A *precatio* is strictly traditional, addresses one deity, greets him or her by official names and titles, and addresses him or her with a request, promises, thanks and invocations. The *carmen saeculare* ["the secular hymn," that is to say, the hymn for the Secular Games] is not traditional, is newly composed and addresses all the gods at once (while granting preeminent place to Apollo and Diana). It also introduces explanatory and historical elements, proposing a particular epithet for Diana and making allusion to Augustus' marriage legislation.[15] In 204, the hymn even seems to introduce Bacchus, which is to say one of the poliadic deities of Lepcis Magna, cradle of the Septimii [the family of the emperor, Septimius Severus].[16] Amongst scholarly passages and flattering digressions, Horace's hymn also devotes several verses to the Trojan origins of the descendants of Romulus and the offspring of Venus and Anchises, a subject that no prayer could possibly contain.[17] It should be noted,

---

[13] According to Zosimus 2.5.3, alongside the other spectacles of a sacred character, a "newly composed" hymn was also performed. Pighi (op. cit. n. 6) 54. n. 8, and F. Paschoud, *Zosime, Histoire Nouvelle*, Vol. I, Collection des Universités de France (Paris, 1971), 75 ff. n. 8, have cast doubt on this information. In their eyes, it is due to confusion with the *carmen* of the third day.

[14] The performance of the *Carmen* is described in lines 147 ff. of the Augustan commentary, Pighi (op. cit. n. 6) 117, and in lines Va 58 ff. of the Severan commentary, Pighi (op. cit.) 164 ff. The *carmen* of the Augustan games has come down to us in the corpus of Horace's poetry; the *carmen* of the games of 204 is found in an epigraphic commentary, but is sadly mutilated; see Pighi (op. cit.) 165 ff. (lines Va 60–71), and 222–7 for the restorations.

[15] Epithets and periphrases: Horace *Carmen Saeculare* 2 (Apollo and Diana); 9 (Apollo); 14–16 (Ilithye); 35ff. (Diana). The marriage legislation is invoked in verses 17–20.

[16] See Pighi (op. cit. n. 6) 224, verses 33 ff. Whatever restorations are made, these verses undoubtedly name Bacchus.

[17] Horace *Carmen Saeculare* 37–52. For the opposition *carmen-precatio*, see J. Scheid–J. Svenbro, *Annuaire de l'Ecole Pratique des Hautes Etudes. Section des Sciences Religieuses* 98 (1989–1990) 327–33.

however, that none of this speaks to the cult's origin. The question "why" is never posed.

So myth was directly put to work during the *ludi saeculares*, but in specific rites that gave room for narrative explanation and free inspiration: the hymn, and surely the theatrical games. These rites were part of the liturgy on the same level as the sacrifices and prayers and, like them, they were ordained by Sibylline oracle.[18] What then was the function of these rites? A verse of the *carmen* of 204 explains quite clearly: the children state in their *carmen* that they sing *mulcent[es] inlice cantu / numina pro[—]idum* ["soothing the gods with alluring song"].[19] The *carmen* is not, then, like the prayers, an injunction made to a god in the simple but respectful language of the magistrates and priests, but is rather an aesthetic moment, to quote F. Graf, a sort of poetic *agalma* [a statue in honor of a god], a *monumentum* designed to please and to seduce.[20] We might note in passing that the gods also were supposed to take pleasure in the speculations of the antiquarian, and in the mythological allusions that the hymn contained. This pleasure is of a different sort to the satisfaction rendered by the regulated and codified exchanges of sacrificial rites; it is not a pleasure aroused by worship and respect, but rather an aesthetic enjoyment. We might even speculate that the myth is regulated by the conventions of choral poetry rather than by ritual needs. It is certainly the case that the ritual practice has no need of myth, which belongs to the realm of reflection and almost of *otium* ["leisure"], while the rite finds its place in necessary and effective public action.

So the evidence of the *carmen saeculare* does not contradict our first conclusion, but rather makes it more precise by describing explicitly the status of this decorative rite. What about the second document, the *Fasti* of Praeneste?

The remains of the famous calendar transcribed by Verrius Flaccus contain what are undoubtedly mythological glosses for the rites and festivals of 15 January, 23–24 March, 23 April and 23 December.[21] Do these mythological interpretations, found as they are in a ritual document, invalidate the rule we have proposed? In fact not, because even if the Praeneste calendar was an official document, that is, if it was installed in a public place with the approval of the local senate,[22]

---

[18] Zosimus 2.5.3, verses 19–22.
[19] Pighi (op. cit. n. 6), 224, verse 7, read with the suggestions of Diels.
[20] Graf (op. cit. n. 3), 114.
[21] The most recent edition is that of Degrassi (op. cit. n. 5) 106–45.
[22] The conditions for displaying the calendar are described in Suetonius *Gramm.* 17. As

it played no ritual role whatsoever. It was not this document that laid out the obligations for magistrates, priests and citizens of Praeneste, but, on the contrary, the traditional cult-obligations controlled, announced and carried out by these very magistrates, priests and citizens gave Verrius Flaccus the subject-matter for his *Fasti*. The status of the calendar-monument is close to that of the other monuments that one might find in this forum, or to that of Trajan's column in Rome. The rules in this calendar stand in the same relation to cult-obligations as the images on the famous column to the orders, decrees and provisions of Trajan during the two campaigns against the Dacians.

In other words, the magistrates of Praeneste did not proclaim through this document what should be done and why; all that they authorized was the representation of what was already done, and what was said about it in scholarly circles. It was a reflection of the cult and not a "catechism" designed with practice in mind; it was a monument addressed to public piety, drawn up according to contemporary artistic and scientific criteria, and hence granting a place to mythical exegesis.

The glosses to the Praenestine *Fasti* also lead to a second important piece of information; in fact, this information is essential for a proper evaluation of the status of Augustan mythography. On one hand, these glosses detail the etymology of the name of a month, the reason for the name of a festival, and the details of a rite, while on the other hand, they lay out in the same terms the historic or mythic origin of this or that ancient festival.[23] From the fact that all of these glosses appear in the same place and in the same document (a public one, what is more), it is clear that they are equivalent to each other and interchangeable. In other words, the myth belongs to what we might call the exegesis of the ritual facts. We might note in passing that this equivalence is also attested in all the works of Roman antiquarians and scholars, while also pointing to the fact that in the calendar from Praeneste the exegesis is limited to national history and mythology.

*

Verrius Flaccus had his calendar engraved on the wall of a building situated in the forum of Praeneste, he inevitably obtained the authorization of the local senate. For the problem of calendars, see J. Scheid, "Myth, cult and reality in Ovid's 'Fasti'," *PCPhS* 38 (1993), 118–31.
[23] Etymology of the name of a month: Degrassi (op. cit. n. 6) 121 (March); reason for a festival: Degrassi 111 (1 January), 127 (4 April, Megalensia); ritual detail: Degrassi 127 (1 April, 4 April), 129 (10 April); historical origin of a festival: Degrassi 121 (1 March), 123 (23 March); mythic origin of ancient festivals: Degrassi 123 (24 March, explanation refused but still reproduced by Verrius), 127 (etymology of the month of May), 131 (23 April), 139 (23 December), etc.

So, my first conclusion will be that mythology and religion existed side by side, with the former appearing as an ornament to the latter. But why this juxtaposition that was, it bears repeating, almost systematic? Because it was an old tradition? Such an answer does not seem terribly satisfying. Because religion in truth needed this explicit complement? This is one answer often given, but I do not believe that we should reanimate theories that derive myths from ritual and attribute to them (particularly in the so-called late period) the function of explaining rites that have become incomprehensible. There are several arguments against this procedure, which I will summarize briefly:

- Aetiological myths hardly ever explain the ritual: they transcribe the rite into narrative, move the problem from one context into another, or take advantage of a feature of the cult to produce narratives or speculations that have nothing to do with the rite at hand.
- The proliferation of myths is often so great that it is difficult to talk about any clear explanation of the rites.
- The rite contains, in an implicit state, one or many possible explanations,[24] but for the ancients one explanation was not superior to others.
- Finally, the idea of the rite having a "meaning" is absurd in this type of religion. To celebrate a ritual means to understand it, to seize the primary, literal meaning, those linkages of daily attitudes and gestures known by all, but so complex that they need to be understood in order to be reproduced faultlessly. So, one either knew a cult or one did not, and if one knew it, one understood it in the sense I have indicated. I will pass over the fact that, due to the enormous growth of the civic body and the transformation of Roman religious institutions, many cults were not effectively understood by those who took part in them, at least potentially. But the summaries of these cult traditions recorded by an antiquary like Varro must not be confused with the interpretations that he gave upon the occasion of their performance, as it were. When Varro compiled for the inexperienced consul Pompey a manual *de senatu habendo* ["on senatorial procedure"], he was not explaining the meaning of the institution, but was rather simply teaching him the major customs surrounding a consultation of the senate. The same goes for the rites and "their" aetiological

---

[24] In this regard, see Scheid (op. cit. n. 9), 669–76.

myths: the myths do not unveil the "meaning" of the ritual; they are narrative descriptions of the traditions, or speculations superficially applied to a ritual tradition, or even to one of its elements.

*

It seems, then, that we are still at the same point. By making clear the formal frame of mythography, and thus relegating it to the aesthetic surroundings of the cult, we have confirmed the opinion of those who consider mythography as a simple artistic exercise, or a piece of propaganda, without accounting for the existence of a conventional link between mythography and cult. We still have to make clear the reasons for this link. Let us begin with a prosaic observation.

There is no doubt that the mythical explanations had no direct influence on the logic and system of traditional cults. However, it is no less true that such explanations could well determine religious practice by acting upon the minds of those taking part in the cult and of those who were responsible for it. In this way, if the myths represented in the decoration of a ritual space reflected the explanatory choices of the president of the ritual, they also offered themselves, at least as a suggestion, to the attention of passers-by and celebrants. Even better, we can see that in certain cases, the order of precedence between myth and rite is reversed, and that decisions on the religious plane have been determined and selected according to a mythical tradition. Let us take as an example the Trojan myth. The old gentilician cult of the Iulii at Bovillae allows, according to J.C. Richard,[25] the construction of an etymologico-mythical exegesis from the name Iulius, and in this way reattaches the *gens* to Ascanius and Aeneas. The re-reading of a cult in mythical terms, or the influence of one myth on another, is scarcely surprising. But the opposite effect, which one would expect much less, is also attested. So it is clear that the Trojan legend determined the spectacular development of the city-sanctuary of Lavinium and of its rites from the time of Augustus. On re-reading Livy,[26] one has the impression that the significance of the annual sealing of the treaty with Lavinium was henceforth determined more by the Trojan myth than by the historical reasons behind the pact. A. Dubourdieu has shown that the rites and treaties, first of all renewed by Romulus, then in 338, and from then on annually, were considered to date back to the original alliance between Aeneas and Latinus, a public and private pact concluded by a sacrifice to

[25] J.C. Richard, "Sur une triple étiologie du nom Julus. II," *RÉL* 61 (1983), 108–21.
[26] Livy 8.11.15.

the Penates.[27] This explanatory choice reveals the direct reasons for Augustus' interest in this cult.[28] In the same way, the rite of the *Lusus Troiae* was resuscitated, reformed and celebrated ad nauseam under Sulla, Caesar and Augustus, as it allowed, at the price of an obscure etymology of the term "troia," the games to be represented as the coming together of the descendants of the great Trojan families under the leadership of the latest offspring of the lineage of Aeneas.[29]

This example shows that, even if it does. not belong to the cult-mechanism as such, myth – and other modes of explanation and exegesis – can play a considerable role in the conception and organization of religion. Nevertheless, if this interaction furnishes a new indication of the social and intellectual status of mythology, it does not explain why these narratives were capable of orienting the management of religious traditions, above all at a date when the analysis of myth was no longer to be undertaken. Seemingly reduced to the state of a parasite, myth was still able to inspire action and practice; paradoxically, it was in this futile and decorative annex to cult that one searched for and found suggestions, help, and even answers capable of inspiring religious initiatives and, in the case of the Trojan myth, a whole segment of Caesarian and Augustan politics. If mythology filled this role, we must conclude that it facilitated thought that used a set of traditions as starting-point or subject-matter; in short, that it represented a particular way of conceiving tradition.

*

But this is precisely the point where we run into difficulties. The content of heroic and aetiological myths (as well as that of many other types of explanatory narratives) often strikes modern re-searchers as anodyne, shallow, unspiritual, in fact entirely non-religious. Hence the temptation to speak of decadence, positivism, incoherence, poetic license, expressions of popular spirit and even of obsequious flattery or pure political propaganda.

It is of no use to extract from the shambles of narratives and glosses the most acceptable, the most worthy or simply the "truest." Apparently, all these explanations were worthy in the eyes of the ancients, and all that changed were the social and historical contexts

---

[27] Dubourdieu (op. cit. n. 10) 347 ff.

[28] See N.M. Horsfall in Bremmer–Horsfall (op. cit. n. 3) 23 ff.

[29] N.M. Horsfall in Bremmer–Horsfall (op. cit. n. 3) 23; J. Scheid–J. Svenbro, *Lusus Troiae. Le myth du tissage dans le monde gréco-romain*, forthcoming [see now *The craft of Zeus: Myths of Weaving and Fabric*, trans. Carol Volk (Cambridge: MA, 1996), 40–9].

of their enunciation, or the scientific premises that lay behind them. According to circumstances, a particular explanation would be privileged, created, criticized or silenced; it would never, though, be rejected or excluded. However, to consider the myths from the early years of the Christian era as fanciful, failed or false because they are artificial and biased, because they are attached to both cult and politics, because, in brief, they do not correspond to – or, more precisely, they no longer correspond to – the conception of myth or religious thought entertained by modernity would be a serious misreading, one which overlooks the fundamentals of the matter. I will try to show that the gravity and social efficacy of Augustan mythography derive from the fact that it articulated and examined serious problems in the meaning of things, and that it contributed, like other orders of knowledge, to giving answers. I will choose, to illustrate my thesis, only those myths and cults that were profoundly politicized, at the furthest remove, it would seem, from all speculation of the kind outlined above.

Let us return to the spectacular promotion of Lavinium, particularly in the time of Augustus. What role did Roman mythography play, beyond that of political servant and tool in the re-writing of history? At first glance, the Trojan tradition directly served the political interests of the Iulii, and re-attached the history of Rome to that of the Greek mythic age. However, we should not be content to rest here, although this aspect is undeniably present: there are other, deeper, reasons why the dynamics of the Trojan myth, which find an anchor in Lavinium, were developed.

Two pieces of evidence suggest this. The first might still seem purely utilitarian: it has been demonstrated that the myth of Lavinian origins was accepted at Rome because it legitimized Roman interest in Asia Minor, an interest which found its first expression in the installation of Venus Erucina and of Mens on the Capitol, and above all in the arrival of Magna Mater at Rome.[30] Yet the installation of this divinity, through a kind of "marriage," in the most ancient center of Rome, and the relations set up between her and the figure of Rhea Silvia,[31] signal that more complex links were being forged between Lavinium, Troy and Rome than can be explained by simple diplomatic interest.

---

[30] See n. 4, and the excellent clarification of N.M. Horsfall, in Bremmer–Horsfall (op. cit. n. 3) 20 ff.

[31] E. Will, "Aspects du culte et de la légende de la Grande Mère dans le monde grec," in *Eléments orientaux dans la religion grecque ancienne* (Paris, 1960), 95–111; F. Salviat, "Steles et naïskoi de Cybèle à Thasos," *BCH* 88 (1964), 239–51.

The second piece of evidence comes from cult. If our information is correct, the pact between Rome and Lavinium had been renewed annually since 338; from a diplomatic point of view, this annual renewal is surprising, and it is surely no exaggeration to suppose that, already at this time or a little later (if we are not to put our trust entirely in the annalists), we are in the presence of a ritual commemorating a treaty.[32] Still, such a ritual could hardly fail to surprise, and it was certainly already the object of speculation in antiquity. Whatever its content, this speculation, seemingly called forth by the ritual, can be discerned in the period of the Augustan renaissance.

In a recent article, Yan Thomas has demonstrated that the rites and myths surrounding Lavinium in fact raised the question of Roman identity.[33] They did this in two ways. Lavinium played a role not only in the genealogy of the Romans, but also in their legitimacy: no magistrate with *imperium* could consider himself legitimately installed unless he had first celebrated the *feriae Latinae*, and then given sacrifice before Vesta and the Penates at Lavinium. These rituals expressed not only the links of the Roman people with the Latin environment, but also the people's double origin: Trojan in terms of its lineage, and Italic in terms of its territory. Or, in juridical terms, they expressed the doubleness of birth and local registration, of ancestry and foundation.

To build on Thomas' conclusions: we might suppose that the traditions connected to Lavinium brought to light a central problem in Rome, namely the double origin of the majority of its citizens. The Lavinian rites, as well as the myths that made their content explicit, proclaimed the double personality of the Roman people, born (like most citizens) elsewhere, but settled (juridically speaking) on the banks of the Tiber. However, it is noteworthy that while the Trojan myth played an important role in Rome's diplomatic and hegemonic aspirations from the middle of the third century BC onwards,[34] the traditions linked to Lavinium started to develop only in the time of Augustus. Indeed, the most significant phase of monumentalization at Lavinium does not date to the Julio-Claudian era, but rather to the second century AD. In other words, the site of Lavinium did not share in the monumentalization characteristic of the second century BC, which is attested at all the other major sanctuaries of Latium; hence

---

[32] C. Saulnier (op. cit. n. 10) 533; Dubourdieu (op. cit. n. 10) 339–61.

[33] Y. Thomas, "L'institution de l'origine. Sacra principorum populi Romani," in M. Detienne, ed., *Traces de fondation*, Bibliothèque de l'Ecole des Hautes Etudes de Science religieuse 93 (Louvain/Paris, 1990), 143–70.

[34] N.M. Horsfall in Bremmer–Horsfall (op. cit. n. 3) 19 ff.

it is clear that Lavinium carried no particular significance in the
context of Roman imperialist aspirations in that period. What is
more, the site did not even receive special attention in the period
when the appeal to Trojan origins by the Julio-Claudians was most
insistent: at this time, the theme was largely developed in books or in
the decoration of urban monuments like the forum of Augustus, and
such development took place at Rome in the vicinity of the *princeps*.
We do not know how Lavinium was altered in the Augustan period,
but the facts that we do have give the impression that routine went
largely untouched.[35] At any rate, in the early years of the Christian
era this mythological theme was "reactivated" and received wide
circulation thanks to the *Aeneid*.

According to the documents we have at present, the ritual renaissance of the Lavinian metropolis seemingly hit its stride a half-
century later, in the time of Claudius.[36] The special character of
development in both the institutions and the city-sanctuary suggests
that these traditions and their mythological underpinning, which had
been systematically exploited by a group of Roman families in the
last century of the Republic, engaged, in the consciousness of Rome
as a whole, a theme that was more important than the mere justification of political power. We need only recall the fact that the century
opened by Augustus was marked by the *definitive* integration of a
huge number of new citizens from Italy and elsewhere,[37] and that the
census of Claudius in 48 marked a turning-point in the integration
of local élites, to understand that a problem concerning Roman identity was being worked through. A century and a half later, when
Antoninus celebrated the ninth centenary of the foundation of Rome,

[35] Obviously, the excavations underway at the site are likely to bring new elements to light.
As for the *vicus Augustanus Laurentium*, situated close to Lavinium, the documents do not
sufficiently prove that Augustus was anxious to own a property on the territory of the ancient
metropolis.

[36] The first priests and ritual magistrates that we know of appear under Claudius, *ILS* 5004.
The hypothesis that the Lavinian priesthoods and the annual sealing of the treaty were restored
by Claudius dates back to G. Wissowa, "Die römischen Staatspriestertümer altlatinischer
Gemeindekulte," *Hermes* 50 (1915) 1–33 at 31. I would not connect this restoration, as
Saulnier does (op. cit. n. 10) 524 ff., to the supposed *ludi saeculares* of Claudius, which in fact
took advantage of the celebration of the eighth centenary of the foundation [of the city of
Rome] in order to anticipate the celebration of the "real" *ludi saeculares*; I would instead place
it in the context of his censorship. At any rate, whether it relates to the eighth centenary or to
the censorship, the reference to the ancient metropolis of the Romans takes on its full meaning in either case.

[37] For the integration of the Italic peoples, which started after the Social Wars, and the
developments which followed them, see C. Nicolet, *Rome et la conquête du monde méditerranéen 1. Les structures de l'Italie romaine* (Paris, 1991), 290–7; F. Jacques–J. Scheid, *Rome
et l'intégration de l'Empire (44 av. J.-C.–269 apr. J.-C.). Les structures de l' empire romain*
(Paris, 1990), 214 ff.

he issued coins that represented himself with the features of Aeneas.[38] When we place reference to the Trojan ancestor, interest in the site of Lavinium, and the considerable changes in the composition of the Roman people side by side, a hypothesis emerges. The continual growth of the civic population, along with the ongoing absorption of individuals and communities into one people, made for a quite unprecedented situation, one that could scarcely fail to raise doubts over what constituted a Roman, and what constituted Rome herself. While jurists and statesmen were working to enlarge the city's civic definition and to find a new way for institutions to function, and while the orator Aelius Aristides was proclaiming, in his *Panegyric to Rome*, that "Rome has never rejected anyone; on the contrary, this city receives men from all countries just as the soil of the earth welcomes all men,"[39] others were thinking through this question by reading mythical narratives and by reviving or developing the temporal moorings of these myths. So, according to Thomas, this was the central theme developed by the myth of the double origin of the Romans, as it was constructed around the site of Lavinium. In my opinion, it is the encounter between this myth, made famous above all by Virgil, and the deep-seated problems faced by the Roman state which determined the spectacular growth of this site and its traditions under Augustus, and particularly under Claudius.

We may well ask, however, what role speculation plays in all of this, and where the basic truths about the functioning of the world lie. Can questions of integration and civic status, apparently more suited to the meditations of jurists and functionaries, really be construed as speculation on the order of things? On this point rests the whole problem. For the Romans, the pivotal moment in the history of the universe was neither the creation of Olympus nor of earth, but rather the foundation of the city by men and gods. At Rome, the order of things, or the system of the world, corresponded to the institutions and components of the *res publica*;[40] everything began there, as there was an insoluble continuity between the world and interests of the *res publica* and those of the gods. The central facts concerning the world and the place of the citizen in that world were articulated in the foundation narrative. Now, I have no intention of reducing all Roman mythography to this schema; at the beginning of the Christian era other cosmogonies were known at Rome, and from that point on made up part of the Roman cultural

[38] P.V. Hill, *The Undated Coins of Rome, AD 98–148* (London, 1970), 91.
[39] Arist. *Or.* 26.62.
[40] This aspect has been brought to light systematically by G. Dumézil.

patrimony. But the circulation of these ideas amongst the Roman élite did nothing to suppress other traditions and mythologies, so that at Rome, the myth of foundation remained one of the ways to think through and to examine, in a traditional manner and in public, the relations amongst members of the city; in fact, it was a way to pose the question of the communal identity of the "Romans," whether mortal or immortal, and from there the path was cleared for other types of speculation.

This type of questioning would raise, then, the fundamental problems of the Roman order and its politics on the grandest scale. But is that really the context in which myths are produced? It often seems to be the case that mythology and mythical figures were dragooned into the service of the powerful and into petty political struggles. In the context of Lavinium and the Trojans, we have already referred to the implication of the Iulii and other families in the circulation of these traditions. Is there, then, any way to look at these myths as being anything other than propaganda? I believe that there is. Firstly, because the use of cult and its explanatory mechanisms for immediate political ends does not invalidate their speculative content. Who can point to a religion, or any other system of thought, that has never been manipulated by an earthly master? Secondly, it is important to take on board the evidence that these political statements in fact raised some serious questions. I would go so far as to say that some of these "politicized" myths were used successfully and survived because they linked an immediate political concern with a fundamental fact of the order of things, and that, by striking a fundamental chord of Roman consciousness, they became susceptible to many other kinds of inquiry as well. Associating the Iulii with Aeneas and the events that took place at Lavinium meant inserting them into the problem of Roman legitimacy. The marriage of political interest with myth succeeded because it respected and resuscitated a tradition without doing it any violence, because it corresponded to the opinion of the majority of Romans, and because, beyond immediate political contingencies, it asked a fundamental question that was of interest to every Roman.[41]

Let us take a second case, that of the myth of Romulus, which had a more or less determinant effect on the reign of Augustus, and was

---

[41] The success of an exegesis, a reform or a restoration is explained by its internal coherence and its relevance. The durability of these attempts or themes is the best proof of the Romans' conservatism. The intervention of a great artist surely also plays a role, but we may well ask whether the joy of creation does not also proceed from the liberating encounter of talent with a theme that touches a fundamental structure of consciousness.

even at the root of the newly held prestige of several cults. All of this is already well known. We also know, through Cassius Dio, that in the eyes of the *princeps* and his friends, the *cognomen* Romulus, which the *princeps* considered adopting for a time, was in some way equivalent to the *cognomen* Augustus that he finally adopted in 27 BC: it was intended to demonstrate that Augustus was πλεῖόν τι ἢ κατὰ ἀνθρώπους ὢν ["something more than human"].[42] The *cognomen* Romulus would offer, in a condensed form, a global explanation of the work of the young *princeps*, which was to raise him above the level of other humans. We know that the mythical *cognomen* was abandoned because it risked saying more than was wanted; so Romulus was left to the mythical world, and it was considered sufficient to sketch the outlines of an identification, or rather a parallel, with Augustus on the level of cult.

When we read, on the one hand, the histories of Romulus, and consult, on the other, the cult institutions that were attached to him, we realize that the elevation above other men mentioned by Cassius Dio is not only a glorification of the leader or a metaphorical description of the refoundation of Rome. If Romulus was regarded as the founder of Rome, and notably the founder of sovereign power, of *imperium*, he was also the embodiment of a kind of power quite opposed to that of a traditional Roman magistrate. Although violent, he managed to create the city and guide it towards growth; although the founder of great institutions, he ruled in a mode that, however traditional, scarcely conformed to republican ideals. In a parallel fashion, the religious institutions said to date back to his time were distinct from all republican institutions, as they demonstrated a method of functioning quite alien to community life.[43] So, in a certain way, Romulus was same and other, magistrate and priest, and almost their opposite.

But why this model? Simply in order to raise Augustus above other men, as Cassius Dio states? To reach an answer, we must understand Dio's formula. There was no question of making a god of Augustus while he was still alive. In Rome of this period, such an outcome could not even be imagined. Let us also put to one side the notion that Augustus and his collaborators wanted to express their aspirations for a royal régime by appealing to such a model. In order

---

[42] Cassius Dio 53.16.7.
[43] Bremmer in Bremmer–Horsfall (op. cit. n. 3) 25–48; Scheid (op. cit. n. 9) 669–703, and J. von Ungern-Sternberg, "Romulus-Bilder: Die Begründung der Republik im Mythos," F. Graf, ed., *Mythos in mythenloser Gesellschaft. Das Paradigma Roms* (Stuttgart: Teubner, 1993), 88–108.

to understand their investment in Romulus, we must briefly make a comparison with other aspects of the elevation of Augustus. Augustus' *cognomen* expressed the same thing, in the eyes of Cassius Dio, as that of Romulus, establishing in some way Augustus' otherness. So, on one side we find an aetiological myth reduced to its essentials, on the other an adjective, *augustus*, taken out of its religious context, but on both sides, we find ambiguity. It is the very same ambiguity expressed by what we call the imperial cult, namely, the cult of Augustus' *genius* and that of his *numen*. The former let it be understood that the *genius* of the *princeps* was being honored like the *genius* of a father, that the *genius* of Augustus was being treated as equivalent to the *genius* of every head of family, or indeed to the *genius* of the Roman people.[44] The other cult meanwhile, that of the *numen Augusti*, renders the stakes even clearer: in this cult, it wasn't the divinity of the *princeps* that was in play, but rather that of his extraordinary action.[45] Again, similar ambiguity was expressed when laws and decrees introduced the name of Augustus into prayers and instituted a standard formulation of prayers for his health, as well as a division of power between the people and him.

A comparison of all these elements clarifies the role of the myth of Romulus under the principate of Augustus. The theme broached by this myth corresponded to a major problem faced by Romans, and particularly by the élite, after the civil wars, one caused by the political choices of the winner: how were they to define the position of the *princeps* and of his power in an institutional structure which was supposedly, and in part actually was, restored in its republican form?[46] Augustus' followers decided to deal with this by making his position in every way extraordinary, so that it might express, by all institutional and symbolic means possible, the huge fact of this new power, and so that it might progressively intertwine this fact with people's minds, their traditions, and finally with the order of things itself. In the absence of a traditional Roman concept capable of describing and explaining imperial power, this idea had to be constructed by mobilizing individually all the registers of thought

[44] A. Fraschetti, *Roma e il principe* (Bari, 1990), 331–60.

[45] I use the term *numen* according to the definition given by G. Dumézil, *La religion romaine archaïque, suivi d'un appendice sur la religion des Étrusques* (Paris, 1974), 36–48 [English translation by P. Krapp: *Archaic Roman Religion* (Chicago, 1970; repr. Baltimore, 1996)].

[46] Jacques–Scheid (op. cit. n. 37) 1–21 for the problem and its bibliography; P. Zanker, *Augustus und die Macht der Bilder* (Munich, 1987) [English translation by A. Shapiro: *The Power of Images in the Age of Augustus* (Ann Arbor, MI, 1988)]; and the article of T. Hölscher, "Mythen als Exempel der Geschichte," F. Graf, *Mythos in mythenloser Gesellschaft. Das Paradigma Roms* (Stuttgart, 1993), 67–87.

and practice: literature, mythology, images, cult, along with legis-
lative activity, debates in the senate and strictly political thought. The
myth of Romulus was one of the first acts in this pursuit (ingenuous
or disingenuous) of a new meaning of things. The trial-and-error,
the backtracking, the resistance and the collaboration of all in this
construction, which extends over the whole age of Augustus, demonstrate that this was not merely an artificial ideology, conceived by
political schemers and dictated to artists and scholars as the decorative conclusion of an absolute victory. The development of a final
justification of Augustus' power was a work-in-progress as much as
a glorification, and above all it was a collective endeavor, bringing
together all those who, for one reason or another, wanted to "turn
the page" and regain civic peace.

Once again, then, mythographic activity seems to be integrated
with other thought processes and other social practices that nobody
would dream of questioning. Since laws, decrees and the new "imperial cult" answered a profound need, and attempted to express,
and even to resolve, one of the gravest problems of the age, it is difficult to deny this role to mythography also. Simply put, the ambiguity
and otherness that a law expressed by granting juridical privileges
and exceptional honors to the person of Augustus, or that the cult
of his *genius* and *numen* articulated as divine homage to his force of
action, were expressed in mythography – but also in the cults and
sodalities promoted under his influence – through narrative and
paradigmatic juxtaposition.

*

What role, then, was played by mythology in the life and religious
thinking of the age of Augustus?

By rejecting out of hand the traditional distinctions between myth
and mythology, between Greek and Roman myth, I have not allowed
myself to establish whether Augustan myth played the same role as
myth in archaic Greece (or Rome, for that matter). Rather, I have
tried to determine the status of mythological narrative as a conventional means of expression that was taken up, adapted and developed
by the Romans along with other elements of the symbolic process:
juridical, scientific and philosophical thought.[47]

---

[47] It is obvious that we only know the scholarly versions of mythography, and that popular
exegesis, undertaken by the *vulgus*, largely escapes us, even when, by convention, an author
seems to give it voice. At any rate, we should resist the temptation to ascribe to the domain of
popular thought everything in the exegeses which appears anodyne, flat or imprecise according to modern criteria, as there is no way of demonstrating any popular origin.

Once our aim is no longer defined in terms of reconstituting a myth in its original purity, or of deciphering a proliferation of rites with the help of a supposedly "exact" explanatory tool, things start to take on a relative clarity. To begin with, mythology emerges, in public documents, as an equal of other symbolic practices, while in literary texts, which are largely private, it seems interchangeable with philosophical discourse. We should therefore conclude that mythographical practice is in no way less noble, vital or effective than other intellectual disciplines. Like these, and like myth in the archaic age, yet in a different guise, the mythology of the first years of the Christian era formulates, explains and explores the basic facts in the order of things. It is surely not the case that, because the myth of this period is attached to facts, and because mythographic activity seems to be set in motion through contact with the real rather than developed in a space of unfettered speculation, all intellectual content need be reserved for just a few inward-looking masterpieces. This distinction is not one I have ever understood. To begin with, it is not at all clear that myth ever enjoyed this perfect freedom: either we are entirely ignorant as to the context of a myth's production, or we state that it, too, is already "aetiological." Equally, to the extent that they are reflection and investigation, even the great books of mythology are never entirely detached from concrete reality and can be read as enormous aetiologies, even when we *are* dealing with masterpieces.[48]

There is also no reason to consider Augustan mythography unworthy because it gives a privileged place to explanations of religious or civic institutions. On the contrary, this characteristic, attested in the choice made by the compiler of the *Fasti* of Praeneste, in the numberless myths attached in text and image to public institutions, and even in the public initiatives determined by these myths, reveals both the traces of a conscious will and the scope of effectiveness inherent in mythography. The age of Augustus grants a privileged place in public life, and to a large extent also in the private realm, to the Trojan and Romulean myths of origin of the Roman

---

[48] Next to the *Aeneid*, one would obviously point to the *Metamorphoses* of Ovid, which presents the history of the world from the viewpoint given in its title, particularly in relation to the conclusion of this history, the new Roman system in which apotheosis (that of Caesar) has become a central moment. See in this regard, and for other possible readings, W. Ludwig, *Struktur und Einheit der Metamorphosen Ovids* (Berlin, 1965); G.K. Galinsky, *Ovid's Metamorphoses, An Introduction to the Basic Aspects* (Oxford, 1975), 217–47; M. von Albrecht, "Mythos und römische Realität in Ovids Metamorphosen," *ANRW* 2:31:4 (1981), 2328–42; D. Porte, "L'idée romaine et la métamorphose," J.M. Frécaut and D. Porte, eds., *Journées ovidiennes de Parménie. Actes du Colloque sur Ovide (24–26 juin 1983)* (Brussels, 1985) 175–98; F. Graf, "Ovide, les 'Métamorphoses' et la véracité du mythe," C. Calame, ed., *Métamorphoses du mythe en Grèce ancienne* (Geneva, 1988), 57–70.

people, its institutions and its leaders. Why this preference? In the first place, because this mythological theme allowed a large number of Romans, and particularly Roman citizens, to participate in this process of reflection. Secondly, because this restriction is in accord with that Roman penchant, generally called traditional, for mythography and exegetical literature focused on historical, national and institutional themes. At Rome, the weight of its poliadic heritage was so great that it informed every category of thought, at least up to the beginning of the Christian era. To put it more precisely, as the context of this mythography was that of public life and thought, it was necessarily oriented in the first instance toward such life and thought, and overdetermined by the realm of the political: Augustan mythography thus corresponds (in a slight distortion of the words of Varro) to the *genus civile* ["civic mode"] rather than to the *genus mythicon* ["mythic mode"] of discourse regarding gods and heroes.† It is also worth asking whether this mythographical genre was not also privileged *because* it served to formulate and to explore problems of a constitutional order. As was traditional, and particularly so after a century of civil wars, this type of question overshadowed the problems of the individual among the élite, in the forum, in the *curia* and before the temples; which is to say, that in the settings and the sources of which we are aware, it was inevitable that the problems would be posed in these terms.

Finally – and I have not stressed this aspect – we should not exclude mythological narration from the circle of symbolic operations because the ancients often express doubts over the "truthfulness" of the myths that they tell: from the fact that those who criticize these narratives still go on to transmit them, it is clear that the criticism in fact belonged to mythographical technique, and that "truthfulness," as F. Graf has demonstrated,[49] was not the condition *sine qua non* of effectiveness in the genre.

In other words, it is my opinion that the mythology of the Augustan age fulfilled an active social and intellectual function. It always served to articulate and explain the fundamental problems of the world. It also seems to represent, in its public form, a moment in

---

† Scheid refers to the celebrated "tripartite theology": the division of theological literature into "civic," "natural," and "mythic" branches, appropriate to civic life, philosophical inquiry, and poetics respectively. In the Roman tradition, this system of thought received its most famous exposition in the *Divine Antiquities* of Varro, though the portions of that work devoted to it survive almost exclusively though their citation by Augustine (Varro *Ant. Div.* frr. 6–10). See the index to this volume s.v. "tripartite theology."

[49] Graf (op. cit. n. 48).

the history of Roman mythography that would benefit from a closer analysis, of both its antecedents and its later evolution.

It only remains for me to add a word concerning the relationship between mythography and religion. It has been my intention to demonstrate that Augustan mythology, even if it always concerns gods and heroes, cannot be reduced to a kind of homily capable of revealing religious truths and giving meaning to cult. Cult had no such need and, what is more, myth in no way explained the ritual process. Instead, we are dealing with two parallel practices, both of which treated in their own ways the basic problems that preoccupied the Romans. Very often, their paths crossed, not simply because myth told the stories of gods and heroes, or because rituals implicitly dealt with the same problems, but because these questions had always been raised in public, in public places, in assemblies, banquets and most notably over the course of those festivals that brought together gods, heroes and men.

PART IV

Theology

Introduction to Part IV:
Theology

What is this great benefaction that Varro boasts he has performed for his fellow citizens? He claims not merely to name the gods whom the Romans ought to worship, but even to specify the particularities of each one. For it does no good, he says, to know the name and appearance of a man who happens to be a doctor, if one does not know that he is a doctor. Likewise, he says that it does you no good to know that Aesculapius is a god, if you do not know that he helps the sick and therefore remain ignorant why you should supplicate him ... So, he asserts, no one can doubt but that knowledge of the gods is useful, if it embraces what special strength and ability each god has, and what is that thing over which each has power (*si sciatur quam quisque deus vim et facultatem ac potestatem cuiusque rei habeat*). "For it is from this knowledge," he says, "that we can know which god we ought to summon and invoke for each purpose, lest we should act like some clown on stage and seek water from Liber and wine from the Lymphs."

Augustine *City of God* 4.22 = Varro *Ant. Div.* fr. 3[1]

In the tradition of writing on Roman religion that begins with Augustine, a tradition to which even those who have not read *The City of God* are heir, the gods of Rome present a special problem. To their staggering number and restricted functions – the features of the Roman pantheon that most exercised Augustine – one might add the bewildering multiplicity of their natures: Greek, Italic, Egyptian, Phrygian, native, foreign, anthropomorphic, abstract, impersonal, indeterminate, transcendent, personal, male, female, locative, utopian, and unknown are but a limited number of the ancient and modern categories from which one might construct a taxonomy of

---

[1] Augustine summarizes this passage at *Civ.* 6.1, writing there of gods to each of whom the management of some tiny affair is allotted (*illos deos ... quibus rerum exiguarum singulis singula distribuuntur officia*) and of the men who have written books teaching "why each god ought to be supplicated and what should be sought from each" (*ut sciretur quare cuique deo supplicandum esset, quid a quoque esset petendum*; cf. Augustine *Civ.* 6.9 = Varro *Ant. Div.* fr. 88: Varro shows "what the special task [*munus*] of each god is, and why each ought to be supplicated"). See also Augustine *Civ.* 6.9, where he writes of the gods' spheres of influence, "so usefully and minutely divided," and cf. *Civ.* 4.21.

divine powers in Roman antiquity.[2] What should we make of them?
For that matter, what did Romans make of them?

Varro himself described the topic of his *Divine Antiquities* as
"civic theology," as distinct from "scientific" and "mythic" theology
(the *genera physicon* and *mythicon theologiae*, where "theology" is
an "ordered account that makes sense of the gods" [*theologiae ... id
est rationis, quae de diis explicatur*]). By "scientific" he intended
theology as an intellectual discipline practiced by philosophers; by
"mythic," the theology used by poets; and by "civic," that used by
"the people." "The first is best suited to the natural world; the second
to the theater; and the last to the city."[3] Varro inherited this system
of classification, the so-called "tripartite theology," from Hellenistic
Greece, and he himself subscribed to it.[4] Indeed, Varro continues
to fascinate us precisely because he recognized some divergence
between how one might order the gods and their names *ex formula
naturae*, "according to the rule of nature," and how they were in fact
ordered in Roman practice, and he nevertheless, uniquely in the
ancient world, decided to write a theology of practice.[5]

Although Augustine himself denied the validity of this classification – by identifying connections between the different theologies,
he could use pagan critiques of classical myth against pagan religiosity itself – his *City of God* remains the most important source
of information about it.[6] Paradoxically, Augustine's critique and the
tripartite theology have acted in concert to work untold damage on
the study of Roman religion. For those few scholars who have not
followed Augustine in professing incomprehension before Rome's
"crowd of tiny gods," "whose own worshippers proved unable to
assign different mini-gods to each and every single human good,"
have almost universally followed Varro in separating theology from
cult, to the detriment of both.[7] In other words, scholars throughout
the modern period have essentially taken one or the other of two
interpretive stances toward the gods of Roman religion, either

---

[2] Smith 1978b provides useful deconstruction of the ideological motives of prior attempts
to analyze and classify "demonic powers" in antiquity.

[3] Varro *Ant. Div.* frr. 7–10, all from Augustine *Civ.* 6.5.

[4] On the tripartite theology see esp. Pépin 1956; Lieberg 1973, 1982; together with
Cardauns 1978. Boyancé 1972: 253–82 sets the problems of the tripartite theology to one side
and offers a quite fascinating attempt to understand Varro's "scientific" theology on its own.

[5] Varro *Ant. Div.* fr. 12, and cf. above pp. 13–15.

[6] On Augustine and the tripartite theology see Dihle 1996.

[7] On the *dei minuscularii* see Augustine *Civ.* 7.4 and 11. For the rest, Augustine *Civ.*
4.21.

the bemused condescension or puzzled disdain of the self-declared rationalist, or the scorn of the Christian apologist.[8]

The results of this methodological impasse can be charted along two axes. On the one hand, with a few significant exceptions, scholars have treated Roman cult as an agglomeration of rituals, susceptible perhaps to analysis at the level of their chronological development but not expressive of any other than the most banal truths.[9] Theology, on the other hand, at least the kind of theology that Varro called scientific, was properly a branch of philosophy and hence not part of religion at all.[10] On either view, the only question worth asking about the relationship between "theology" and "religion" was whether the former had harmed the latter.[11] That cult might have a theological basis or that theology, like myth, might constitute an important form of religious experience, albeit at a cognitive level removed from cult, are possibilities that have remained largely unexplored.[12]

It is the great merit of Arnaldo Momigliano's "The Theological Efforts of the Roman Upper Classes in the First Century BC," reproduced here as Chapter 7, that he reads Roman theological writing with sympathetic dispassion. As a result, he sees with uncommon clarity the radical differences that characterize the writings on the gods of Cicero, Varro, and Nigidius Figulus, and he can therefore reject the temptation to classify them all under some easy rubric like "rationalism" or "philosophy." If Cicero's *On the Nature of the Gods* might still be described as an exercise in the translation of Greek philosophy into a Roman context, it is that only in contradistinction to other, kindred works of the same, turbulent era.[13]

---

[8] Ogilvie 1969 is an important exception to this and many other generalizations about the history of scholarship on Roman religion.

[9] See the introducton to Part III and the literature cited there.

[10] To cite only general studies in English, there is no entry for "theology" in the indices to Warde Fowler 1911; MacMullen 1981; Beard, North, and Price 1998; or North 2000. Bailey 1932 is typical in devoting separate chapters to the "spirits," cult, and philosophy (and supersitition).

[11] See, e.g., Brunt 1989 and cf. below pp. 310–26 and 343–46. Scholars writing in this tradition largely and perhaps unwittingly subscribe to a view of civic religion common to both Cicero and Varro. In the former's *On the Nature of the Gods*, Cotta distinguishes what he thinks in his existence as "Cotta the *pontifex*" from what he thinks as Cotta the Academic (*Nat. Deor.* 2.2 and 3.5–6). For his part, Varro not only distinguished civic and natural theology, but regarded the latter as "more than it suits the crowd to examine"; what is "useful" to "civic societies" is that citizens should adhere to traditional beliefs and practices (*Ant. Div.* frr. 11–12 and 20).

[12] Boyer 1994: 185–223 provides an immensely thought-provoking inquiry into the cognitive aspects of ritual behaviors.

[13] For a reasoned portrait of religion and religious thought in the first century, along rather traditional lines, see Liebeschuetz 1979, 1–54. Readers should also consult two detailed

In speaking of the gods, Varro employs a cluster of terms that resonate in many fields, but two in particular. First, he assigns to gods and mortals specific duties in relation to each other and their communities; and, like Cicero, he charges them with cultivating each other, though for that action Varro and Cicero employ quite different terms. In Roman politics and law, this is the language of social relations, and in particular of relations between fellow members of a single political collectivity.[14] To speak of a god's *munera*, for example, is to implicate him or her in a network of social obligations, for *munus* connotes both actions and products of action performed by citizens for their states and, catachrestically, by social superiors for their inferiors.[15]

Cicero argued quite pointedly that gods and mortals should cultivate each other: the term he employs, *colere*, which I rendered in the volume introduction as "giving someone his or her due," can also mean to cultivate a field or inhabit a place (meanings explored in the introduction to Part VI), or to cultivate someone's friendship.[16] It is insistently transitive: hence to employ it of gods in their attitude to mortals amounts to a theological argument of singular radicalism. Varro writes in a more traditional vein when he suggests that the gods bestow gifts and mortals offer supplication, and he writes in a peculiarly Roman vein when he insists that each god is responsible for particular *munera* and no other.

If, on the one hand, this way of conceiving the gods amounts to a theological analog to Quintus Fabius Pictor's question to Delphi ("By what supplications and prayers might the Romans placate the gods?"), it has specific ramifications for the practice of cult.[17] John Scheid's "Hierarchy and Structure in Roman Polytheism" takes up theology at precisely this level. By scrupulous attention to the language of prayer used by the Arval Brethren and preserved in their extant *commentarii*, he discovers a network of logical schemata that

---

attempts at revisionism: Weinstock 1971, an austere and brilliant book, quite simply the most important work on Roman religion of its era, and Jocelyn 1982, in part developing at great length and with much supporting material a portrait of religious life in the late republic first advanced in Jocelyn 1966.

[14] On this way of thinking of about the gods, see the volume introduction, p. ooo, and the introduction to Part V.

[15] See Cicero *Off.* 2.69 with Dyck 1996: 458 on the desire of the rich not to be obligated by receipt of a benefaction. The topic receives extended treatment in Roller 2001: 129–212, esp. 173–210. I have deliberately adopted a rather narrow definition of *munus*. Some apparent exceptions – the female beloved who demands *munera* from her lover at Ovid *Ars* 1.429, for example – are not exceptional at all: Ovid's use of *munus* accords entirely with the inversion in power relations typical of the elegiac lover.

[16] Cicero *Nat. Deor.* 1.115–16, on which see pp. 4–5.

[17] On Pictor's embassy to Delphi see pp. 8–9.

organized both word and action in the performance of worship. Crucial to his project is the recognition that every ritual context is unique, not in its essence, but in respect to historical contingencies that must themselves be respected in performance. Put otherwise, *what* one was asking for, and *where* one did the asking, helped to determine *whom* and *how* one asked.

In some respects, Scheid's attention to the language of prayer continues work performed by Arthur Darby Nock in an essay of 1925.[18] Nock argued three things: first, that "belief in its evolution under the empire" was "directed to divine power rather than divine personalities"; second, that this development offered considerable scope for change in two directions in particular, namely toward non-exclusiveness and syncretism (by investing one deity with the power of others); and third, that it also led to "continued specialization," as the power of gods was "appropriated" by individuals, groups, and towns, largely through the use of epicletics or epithets (so the family of the Valerii might worship Diana Valeriana).

Scheid permits a refinement of Nock's theory of "specialization." What Scheid calls rendering or extrapolation, which yields "the progressive division of divine personalities" (p. 136), looked to Augustine like the senseless division of divine power into bailiwicks that were progressively more precise and more minute, and it might look to us like atomization to the point of incoherence. But Scheid reveals the logic of this practice, which we might call individuation-at-the-level-of-cult. To translate his arguments into the terms employed here and in the volume introduction, any given ritual had to be addressed very specifically to those gods known or thought to be empowered to respond to its concerns, in the time and place in which it was performed.[19] Thus, the Arval Brethren sought to act not only on their knowledge, but also on their ignorance, addressing not simply quite specific named deities, but also quite specific deities whose names they did not know.[20] Hence the "division of divine personality" is, like the cult act itself, contingently specific, and it only looks incoherent when its testimonial (perhaps a dedicatory inscription at the fulfillment of a vow) is robbed of the context in which it made sense.

[18] Nock 1972: 34–45.
[19] Cf. Ogilvie 1969: 30: "Prayer does not presume a favourable result ... it was a good rgument, wherever possible, to advance reasons why a god should consider a request sympathetically. The two most effective reasons were: (a) he had granted it in the past, (b) it was clearly in his competence to grant it on this occasion."
[20] See pp. 182–83 on "the god or goddess who protects this grove and place," and cf. Ogilvie 1969: 24: "Gods, like dogs, will only answer to their names."

The Arval Brethren worshipped Dea Dia at an altar and grove that belonged to her. Scheid's argument also takes account of the specifics of place in the performance of her cult. In this focus his work again shares much with a different essay by Nock, one on the theological implications of housing more than one cult statue in any particular temple.[21] Nock's interest lay in the placement of statues of rulers, Hellenistic and Roman, as cohabitants in the temples of gods. Scheid here reveals the impact of place on prayer and action in the construction of hierarchies among the gods. It is a topic he has treated elsewhere, and it finds important analogs in recent attempts to unpack the theological implications of particular aspects of the iconography of cult objects.[22] This is an area where great progress now seems possible.

[21] Nock 1972: 202–51.
[22] On the placement of cult objects see Scheid 1995a, 1996; Estienne 1997; Dubourdieu and Scheid 2000. On theology and iconography, see esp. Cancik 1990; cf. Kantorowicz 1965: 7–24; Price 1984: 133–206; Gladigow 1994.

7 *The Theological Efforts of the Roman Upper Classes in the First Century* BC[†]

ARNALDO MOMIGLIANO

I

There is no doubt about what the Roman upper class had to face in the twenty years or so between 60 and 40 BC: a revolution which perhaps nobody wanted and to which everyone was contributing. An unparalleled series of conquests was at the same time the first stage and the ultimate condition of this revolution. Enormous armies had to be put together to regain – or perhaps gain for the first time – effective control of Spain in the Sertorian war (80–71 BC) and to extend Roman rule in Asia to the Euphrates over the ruins of the Seleucid kingdom and of the recent empire of Mithridates. Gaul was the prize for Caesar; and there was a moment in 54 BC in which even Britain was felt to be within reach. Egypt was forced for all practical purposes into the zone of Roman control. The great generals who engineered the conquests – Pompey and Caesar – also confronted each other in political and military battles. The elimination of Crassus in the only unmitigated disaster of the period – the failure to conquer Parthia – made the rivalry between the two surviving members of the triumvirate even more pressing. There had been other portents of the forthcoming replacement of senatorial government by military dictatorship: for instance, the rebellion of the slaves led by Spartacus, the wars against the pirates, one of the incidental consequences of which was the declaration of Crete as a Roman province, and the mysterious Catilinarian conspiracy, which certainly appealed to discontented peasants.

It was in this revolutionary atmosphere that – perhaps not surprisingly – some of the Roman intellectuals began to think in earnest

† Originally published in *Classical Philology* 79.3 (1984), 199–211.

about religion.[1] These intellectuals were themselves members of the ruling class, although not of the *gentes* ["aristocratic families"] which could claim a natural right to rule the Roman state. The three best known of them – Nigidius Figulus, Terentius Varro, and Tullius Cicero – happened to be senators and followers of Pompeius. But at least Varro and Cicero easily made their peace with Caesar, and, as we shall see, their most important work on religion was in fact written when they were at peace with Caesar, and with an eye toward Caesar. For Caesar turned out to be intensely concerned with questions of reorganizing religion.

This is not the place to discuss at length one of the most important books on Roman religion of the last decades – the *Divus Julius* by Stefan Weinstock, which appeared in 1971 not long after the author's death. Weinstock was convinced that Caesar was "an imaginative and daring religious reformer." He thought that by 44 Caesar had made himself a god – not just another god, but Iuppiter Iulius. As Iuppiter Iulius, Caesar would have become king of the gods just when he was preparing to become king of the Romans: godlike and king-like honors would have coalesced, if he had lived long enough. It has already been objected by J. A. North that both parts of the construction are open to doubt.[2] The only evidence for Caesar's identification with Jupiter is in a passage Dio Cassius (44. 6. 4) which is almost certainly the result of a misunderstanding. The parallel passage in

---

[1] It is the sole purpose of this paper (one of my lectures in the University of Chicago in the spring of 1983) to contribute some points of view to a general reinterpretation of the religious situation of the first century BC. The paper was written before I could read the very valuable article by J. Linderski, "Cicero and Roma Divination," *PP* 36 (1982): 12–38, with which I am glad to find myself often in agreement. It would make no sense to give here any bibliography on Cicero's religious thought. But I must declare some old debts. First, to J. Vogt, *Ciceros Glaube an Rom* (Stuttgart, 1935; repr. Darmstadt, 1963); P. Boyancé, *Étude sur le Songe de Scipion* (Paris, 1936); M. van den Bruwaene, *La théologie de Cicéron* (Louvain, 1937); W. Süss, *Cicero: Eine Einführung in seine philosophischen Schriften*, [*Abh Mainz*] 1965, no. 5; M. Gelzer, *Cicero* (Wiesbaden, 1969); P. Boyancé, *Etudes sur l'humanisme cicéronien* (Brussels, 1970); R. J. Goar, *Cicero and the State Religion* (Amsterdam, 1972); *Cieroniana: Hommages à K. Kumaniecki* (Leyden, 1975), and especially to the two papers in it by J.-M André (pp. 11–21) and J. Kroymann (pp. 116–28); A. Heuss, *Ciceros Theorie vom römischen Staat*, [*NachrGött*] 1975, no. 8; K. Buchner, *Somnium Scipionis*, Hermes Einzelschr, 36 (Wiesbaden, 1976). Among more recent studies, cf. J. Glucker, *Antiochus and the Late Academy* (Göttingen, 1978); E. A. Schmidt, "Die ursprüngliche Gliederung von Ciceros Dialog *De natura deorum*," *Philologus* 122 (1978): 59–67; J.-P. Martin, *Providentia deorum* (Rome, 1982); K. M. Girardet, *Die Ordnung der Welt*, Historia [Einzelschriften] 42 (Wiesbaden, 1983), on the *De legibus*. See also K. Büchner (ed.), *Das neue Cicerobild* (Darmstadt, 1971).

[2] Review of Weinstock, *JRS* 65 (1975): 171–77. Cf. the discussion of Weinstock by A. Alföldi, *Gnomon* 47 (1975): 154–79, and Alföldi's review of *Die Vergottung Caesars* (Kallmünz, 1968), by H. Gesche, *Phoenix* 24 (1970): 166–76; and in general the two recent monographs by Z. Yavetz, *Caesar in der öffentlichen Meinung* (Düsseldorf, 1979; Eng. trans. London, 1983), and Chr. Meier, *Caesar*[2] (Berlin, 1982).

Cicero *Philippics* 2. 110 – a contemporary and hostile witness – makes no mention of the identification with Jupiter: it shows that a cult of Iulius as Divus had been planned either in Caesar's last months or immediately after his death. Even less can we be certain that Caesar intended to be proclaimed king of Rome. All we know is that in the famous scene of the Lupercalia of 44 BC Antony called Caesar king and tried to put a diadem on his head, but Caesar refused the offer and sent the diadem to Jupiter – which he would not have done if he had himself become Jupiter. When, however, the obvious exaggerations of Weinstock's thesis are discounted, we are left with a considerable amount of evidence, for the first time properly examined by Weinstock himself, about Caesar's interest and that of his circle in changes and innovations in the rituals they had inherited. Caesar gave much thought to religious matters, and this explains why Varro after their reconciliation dedicated to him his *Antiquitates divinae* [*"Divine Antiquities"*], his thorough study of Roman religion, in about 47 BC. The following year it was the turn of Cicero to write *De natura deorum* [*"On the Nature of the Gods"*].

Nigidius Figulus remains the most colorful of the three followers of Pompey we have mentioned, although his work is entirely lost: his misfortune in life was matched by the loss of his books in late antiquity.[3] A senator, he had advised Cicero during the Catilinarian crisis, had reached the position of praetor in 58 BC, and had been a legate of Pompey. Unlike Varro and Cicero, he died in exile before he was able to obtain a pardon from Caesar: that he tried at least once to get the pardon through Cicero we know from a rather inept and embarrassed letter which Cicero wrote to him in 46 (*Fam.* 4. 13). Nigidius did not study Roman religion, especially its augural rituals, simply to be informed and to inform. He developed divinatory gifts. He is supposed to have prophesied to the father of the future Augustus that his son would rule the world (Suet. *Aug.* 94). On a more modest level he helped a friend to discover where a small treasure had been buried (Varro ap. Apul. *Apol.* 42). Obviously he did not aim at restoring traditional Roman practice either. Nigidius can have been nothing like a conventional Roman if St. Jerome chose to define him as "Pythagoricus et magus" (*Chron.* p. 156 Helm), that is, a Pythagorean of a modern cast, which would include occultism,

---

[3] On Nigidius Figulus, cf. L. A. El'nickij, "Social'no-Političeskie Aspekty Brontos-kopičeskogo Kalendarja P. Nigidija Figula," *Vestnik* [*Drevnej*] *Istorii* 116 (1971) 107–16; B. Gallotta, "Nuovi Contributi alla conoscenza della cultura romano-italica," *Centro Studi e Documentazione sull'Italia romana* 6 (1974–75): 139–54.

astrology, and Persian doctrines about the ages of the world. He wrote on grammar, on gods, on the interpretation of dreams and *augurium privatum* ["augury about personal affairs," by someone other than a member of the augural college], on animals, men, and land, and on stars and thunders. He seems to have reinterpreted traditional Etruscan doctrines in the light of Greek and Persian theories, if he is the source of Martianus Capella (who does not mention him by name) in the fifth century and of Johannes Lydus who mentions him, but in suspicious circumstances, in the sixth century. Like the hard-boiled Tories who established the "Catholic Apostolic Church" in the neighborhood of University College London in the early nineteenth century and combined the gift of tongues and prophetism with sound business ability, Nigidius Figulus and his friends were men of the world. They expected help from strange religious practices in trying to control what escaped them in the fast-moving world in which they lived. They had left behind the traditional ways of bargaining with the gods and were trying to discover safer rules for the interplay between men and gods. Divination seemed to them to offer the best chances, but it had to be based on a wide-ranging reassessment of the natural order: hence their interest in details from grammar to celestial spheres. Varro would probably have agreed that ultimately a secret doctrine was needed if one wanted to feel safe in personal terms. We are unexpectedly told by Pliny the Elder that Varro arranged for himself by testament a burial in the Pythagorean style ([*Nat.*] 35. 160). He had been educated in Rome at the school of Aelius Stilo, who had commented on the language of the Twelve Tables and was of the Stoic persuasion. He had later been at the school of Antiochus of Ascalon, where the Platonic tradition had taken a definite turn toward skepticism and students were trained to produce arguments in favor of both sides. Yet if anything emerges from what Varro did and wrote it is the need to separate one's religious and philosophic opinions from the role one is expected to play in one's own society. In Varro's time it was commonplace to distinguish three types of theology: the *genus mythicum* ["mythic"], which was appropriate to poets and was generally dismissed as unworthy of thoughtful people, the *genus physicum* ["natural"], which represented the speculations of philosophers about gods, and finally the *genus civile* ["civic"], or political type, which the citizens and especially the priests of a given state were required to know because it indicated the gods of the state itself, as well as the rites and sacrifices appropriate to them. The story of the research on the history of this "theologia tripartita" has been written by G. Lieberg.[4] What seems obvious from the evidence he brings together is that the distinction between the three kinds of theology acquired importance in Rome in the historical circumstances I am describing and in the authors I am dealing with – namely, Varro and Cicero. It was from Varro and Cicero that Tertullian and St. Augustine derived it and made it an important argument against paganism in general. The only other Christian theologian of antiquity who gave attention to this tripartition, Eusebius in the *Praeparatio evangelica* 4. 1, probably had no first-hand knowledge of the Western, Latin developments and merely reported what he had read in anti-Christian polemicists of the East. Although we must try to forget the importance which this tripartition assumed in the context of Christian–pagan polemics of later centuries, we cannot ignore the fact that this distinction first gained political relevance in Rome precisely among those who were concerned with the future of the Roman state in the first century BC. In Rome the poets could be dismissed more easily than in Greece because after all it was known that the best stories about the gods were written in Greek and did not really belong to the original Roman tradition. But the conflict between philosophy and city-religion could not be equally briefly dismissed by turning against the Greek origins of philosophy. If there was something no one with any education would care to deny in Rome, it was the validity of philosophic argument. In the age of Caesar philosophy had become part of Roman education in a more intimate way than Greek myths had become Roman through Greek poetry – or its Latin equivalent. It will be precisely my argument in the last pages of this paper that poetry replaces philosophy in the discussion about religion at the time of Augustus. In the period of Caesar the men who discuss religion are concerned with the choice between the rational approach and the political approach to religion, not with any dubious relation between poetry and city-religion.

Seen against this dilemma Varro's thought is straightforward. Whatever the merits of philosophical theology, cities live because citizens obey the regulations of civic religion. Insofar as civic religion is a series of rituals and obligations considered compulsory by the citizens themselves (and declared to be such in legal terms whatever the details of the regulations), religion is part of the state. Thus, very self-consciously, Varro states that he has on purpose put the

---

[4] "Die Theologia Tripartita in Forschung und Bezeugung," *ANRW* 1. 4 (1973), pp. 63–115; cf. J. Pépin, "La théologie tripartite de Varron," *Rev. Ét. Aug.* 2 (1956): 265–94.

Antiquitates divinae after the *Antiquitates humanae*. The *civitas* must precede the institutions of the *civitas*, even the religious ones: even more daringly, the painter precedes the painting – "prior est pictor quam tabula picta." Here more than ever we must remind ourselves that most of what we know of Varro's *Antiquitates divinae* comes from St. Augustine's *Civitas Dei*, and St. Augustine may well have sharpened some of Varro's formulations to fit his own style and suit his own argument. But I do not know of any instance in which St. Augustine has betrayed Varro's line of thinking. The difficulty which Varro had to face and did face in his interpretation of civic religion was that such religion, being man-made, changed with the times. As Varro was specifically interested in Roman religion, the first change he thought had happened was the introduction of images of gods in the shape of men. I am not sure that for Varro this was equivalent to what we would consider the anthropomorphization of the notion of god. But it certainly occurred to Varro that a religion without human images of gods existed in his own time among the Jews, and it was not a bad thing either (August. [*Civ.*] 4. 31). We even know from Lydus *De mensibus* ["*On the Months*"] 4. 53 – a text published in full for the first time in 1898 – that Varro knew the name of the Jewish God: Iao.[5] Varro was therefore personally in sympathy with a religion which was noniconic. Yet he did not feel he had to change his attitude toward Roman religion. If the Romans had decided in their wisdom to represent their gods in human form, there was nothing left but to comply. The message which the *Antiquitates divinae* intended to convey was that state religion had to be taken as it was found. What mattered was to preserve it. Varro could compare himself in his learned work to Aeneas, who had brought away the Penates from burning Troy, or to the Roman L. Caecilius Metellus, who in 241 BC had saved what could be saved of the sacred objects from the burning temple of Vesta. The danger in the face of which he was undertaking his rescue operation was not that of enemy attack, but of *civium neglegentia*, the neglect by his fellow-citizens of their ancestral cults. Varro was not the man to conceal his preferences and convictions, but one of his convictions was precisely that there are truths which should remain unknown to the ordinary man and there are falsehoods which should be spread among the mob as truths. Civic religion was ultimately not a matter of truth but of civic cohesion: the Romans owed their empire to their own piety. It was even

---

[5] For the details I must refer to the paper by E. Norden who apparently was the first to draw attention to Lydus' passage in 1921, now in *Kleine Schriften* (Berlin, 1966), pp. 282–85.

useful that people should consider themselves descended from gods, however false that might be, if it added to their self-confidence in undertaking great things. Varro was not going to take responsibility for the truth of what he was trying to preserve. His report was subjective, in the double sense that he gave his own impression and that he reported what was known to him: "hominis est enim haec opinari, dei scire" [("it is for humans to conjecture regarding these things, and for God to know them")] (August. [*Civ.*] 7. 17).

Even within the description of the religious system of Rome to which he devoted most of his *Divine Antiquities* Varro would not start from the gods and proceed to their cults. Very coherently he started from the pontiffs, the augurs, the *quindecimviri*, that is, from the men who were responsible for the cult. Next he turned to the buildings for the cult. The third section was on the festivals and rites, including games. This left only three books out of sixteen for the gods as such. St. Augustine inevitably found them the most interesting from his point of view, and therefore we know slightly more about them than about the other books. How far Varro's classification of the Roman gods reflected traditional Roman distinctions is not entirely clear to me. He certainly interspersed his own opinions and philosophical preoccupations with traditional terminology. The main result was a surprisingly long list of gods, in which functional gods for rare occasions loomed large. Cicero testifies in his eulogy of Varro (*Acad. post.* 1. 9) to the surprise which Varro's *Antiquitates* produced among his contemporaries. They discovered a Rome they did not know in his pages. What impressed them was mainly this world of half-forgotten gods, ceremonies, and religious anecdotes. But of course we have to add to it that general reconstruction of the origins of Rome and of the changes in the Roman ways of life which Varro undertook in to other works, *De gente populi Romani* ["On the Race of the Roman People"] and *De vita populi Romani* ["On the Way of Life of the Roman People"]. It was highly unusual to find a man who knew so much about the traditions of Rome and had such genuine respect for them, and yet was a recognizable freethinker with a taste for satire and wit. He may well have inspired some of the religious regulations of Caesar and later of Augustus. He remained up to the sixth century AD the source to which writers would turn for out-of-the-way details about the religious customs of earlier Rome.

Yet the most remarkable part of the story remains the elementary fact that Cicero, notwithstanding his admiration for Varro, never tried to assimilate all that evidence: indeed he bypassed Varro and may never have read the *Antiquitates*, whether human or divine, in

their entirety. Which implies that even the man most suited by intellectual gifts and common experiences to appreciate Varro's efforts to
save the old religious patrimony of Rome could not make sense of
them. The crude question, once asked, remained: How could one
believe in all these divine forces which were vaguely supposed to
surround a Roman at each stage of his life and of his daily activities?
What were all these goddesses – Adeona, Abeona, Interduca,
Domiduca, Bubona, Mellona, Pomona, and so on – on whom St.
Augustine was later to exercise his easy irony?

II

We are now left to decide what Cicero thought of this effort of his
friend Varro apart from the compliments he formulated about his
erudition. The thesis which I want to propose in this part of the paper
is that Cicero basically agreed with Varro in his earlier philosophic
works (*De republica* and *De legibus*), which were probably published before the *Antiquitates divinae* by Varro and may therefore
even have influenced Varro. When, however, Cicero had before him
Varro's works circa 46 BC, he changed his mind and expressed
profound skepticism both about the existence of the gods and about
the validity of Roman divination. Whether Cicero in his later phase
was shocked by Varro's sanctimonious attitudes is a secondary and
not very interesting question. At this stage Cicero certainly worried
about Caesar's religious policy, which Varro was supporting. What
matters is that Cicero became more skeptical when his contemporaries became more credulous or at least more sanctimonious. And
his skepticism is even more surprising and dramatic because in 45
Cicero's daughter Tullia died, and her father wanted to believe in her
immortality.

I must add two points for preliminary clarification. In a remarkable article published in 1962,[6] the Polish scholar K. Kumaniecki
observed from a different angle that Varro and Cicero had less in
common than Cicero's public utterances would imply. Second, I
cannot agree with the thesis, recently developed with interesting
arguments by H. D. Jocelyn, that the *Antiquitates divinae* were written in the fifties rather than in the forties.[7] I still believe that when

[6] "Cicerone e Varrone. Storia di una conoscenza," *Athenaeum* 40 (1962): 221–43.

[7] "Varro's *Antiquitates Rerum Divinarum* and Religious Affairs in the late Roman
Republic," *BJRL* 65 (1982): 148–205. Cf. the papers on Varro by P. Boyancé collected in
Études sur la religion romaine (Rome, 1972); A. Dihle, "Zwei Vermuthungen zu Varro," *RhM*
108 (1965): 170–83; N. Horsfall, "Varro and Caesar," *BICS* 19 (1972): 120–28; P. Boyancé,

Cicero celebrated Varro's work about 46 BC, he alluded to work which had recently appeared. The allusion to the third-century BC Metellus does not seem to me incompatible with this date; and the other passages quoted by Jocelyn admit of different interpretations. In other words, Cicero's most important philosophical work had already been done before Varro published his *Divine Antiquities*. In any case the inspiration was different. The *De republica* was published in 51 BC: Cicero worked on it, at intervals, for about three years. The *De legibus* alludes to events of the same years and seems to have been composed concurrently with *De republica*.[8] *De legibus* was never formally published while Cicero was alive, and probably was never finished, although the text which circulated in antiquity was considerably longer and more complete than that which has reached us. In a letter to Varro of 46 BC (*Fam.* 9. 2. 5) Cicero indicates his intention of doing more work on the subject of laws, but we can only speculate on what he meant. What is obvious is that about 53 Cicero tried to give a Roman version of both the *Republic* and the *Laws* of Plato. He was not obliged to know what some modern scholars have discovered: that the *Republic* and the *Laws* represent two different stages of Plato's thought. In his version of Platonic thought, Cicero never tried to put philosophers in command or to expel poets. He rather accepted the notion of Polybius that the Roman state satisfied the conditions of a mixed constitution. Perhaps the most deeply felt conviction of his work on the Republic is that human virtue never comes so near to the *deorum numen*, to divine power, as in the founding or saving of a city (*Rep.* 1. 12). The religious interpretation of politics reaches its peak in that surprising and altogether mysterious *Somnium Scipionis* which concludes the *Republic*. Scipio Africanus appears to Scipio Aemilianus in a dream. The "grandfather" advises his "grandson" to exercise *iustitia* ["justice"] and *pietas* ["piety"] and promises him not only immortality of the soul but a better life in the celestial spheres. Cicero was never again to be so definite about the immortality of the soul or

---

"Les implications philosophiques des écrits de, Varron sur la religion romaine," *Atti ... Congresso Studi Varroniani* (Rieti, 1976), pp. 137–61. References to the *Antiquitates Rerum Divinarum* are collected in B. Cardauns, *M. T. Varro "Antiquitates Rerum Divinarum" I–II*, [*Abh Mainz*] (Wiesbaden, 1976); cf. idem, "Varro und die römische Religion," *ANRW* 2. 16. 1 (1978), pp. 80–103.

[8] Cf. P. L. Schmidt, *Die Abfassungszeit von Ciceros Schrift über die Gesetze* (Rome, 1965); E. Rawson, "The Interpretation of Cicero's *De Legibus*," *ANRW* 1.4 (1973), pp. 334–56. My views on Cicero can be considered an independent confirmation of ideas put forward by C. Koch in papers posthumously collected in the volume *Religio* (Nürnberg, 1960), esp. pp. 187–204 [see Chapter 13 below].

about the link between politics and salvation. But he was here indulging in a dream, and a careful reader cannot avoid noticing a certain contradiction between his deprecation of earthly life and his overpraise of political activity as conducive to salvation after death. There is the same ambiguity in the unfinished *Laws* which supplement the *Republic*. On the one hand, he argues that reason unites men and gods: ["The first bond between man and god is reason"] (*prima homini cum deo rationis societas*) (1. 23); consequently, law can be founded on nature, which is reason. On the other hand, he is so far from envisaging a universal law that he makes a point of emphasizing in Book 2 of the *Laws* that he is even more a citizen of Arpinum than of Rome: ["For here is the ancient origin of our lineage, here are our rites, here is our family, here are the many traces of our ancestors"] (*hinc enim orti stirpe antiquissima sumus, hic sacra, hic genus, hic maiorum multa vestigia*) (2. 3). This is of course little more than a preparation for saying that the city, that is, Rome, which extended to the citizens of Arpinum the rights of her own citizenship, is now the real "patria," the city to which he, Cicero, owes allegiance. The conclusion of this sentimental outburst is a very practical one: as Rome has the most perfect form of constitution (2. 23), all a legislator has to do is to produce a slightly improved form of the *mos maiorum*, of the tradition of the ancestors (2. 23). Even the archaic language of the Twelve Tables must be preserved (2. 18). When, therefore, in a good Platonic spirit Cicero begins to formulate specific laws about religion, we know that nothing sensationally new will appear. The purpose is to reaffirm that Rome must worship the gods she has always worshipped in the forms she has received from immemorial tradition (2. 26). At the most some rationalization may have to be introduced. One must divinize virtue, not vice (2. 28). Consequently, goddesses like Febris and Mala Fortuna who had their altars, if not their temples, inside Rome must be repudiated. The whole exposition of the sacred law in the second book of *De legibus* is characterized by three preoccupations: to preserve the main lines of Roman cult, to modify details which for personal or environmental reasons are no longer considered acceptable, and finally to avoid any systematic coverage of the subject which might turn out to be embarrassing. As is evident from the long excursus of 2. 47–69 on the interaction between civil and pontifical laws in the matter of family cults, Cicero was aware of contradictions between *ius civile* and *ius pontificium* ["civil" and "pontifical law"]. But he never puts the problem in sufficiently general terms to make it an important argument for reform. He was equally aware of the enormous importance which ordinary people still attributed to funeral rites. Although many of these customs have no appeal for him, he has no intention of interfering with them and speaks about them more to display his competence in comparative law than in the spirit of a reformer.

If one has to make a comparison between what Cicero wrote in the *De republica* and in the *De legibus* and what was the general trend of Varro's *Antiquities*, two differences seem to be evident, but they are not profound. Cicero does not bother to collect the whole of the evidence; at the same time he allows himself a modicum of reform. While he is concerned with the preservation of the tradition, of the *mos maiorum*, he is not obsessed by it, as Varro was.

When about July 45 (*Att.* 13. 38. 1) he began to write *De natura deorum*, he had the whole of Varro's *Antiquitates divinae* before him. He had also accumulated many more sad experiences, not only political, but personal: a few months before, in February 45, his daughter Tullia had died, and he had tried to cope with this as well as he could by reading and writing philosophy, by hopes of the immortality of the soul, and by planning a sort of *apotheosis* for his dead child. It was also the time of the sudden end of his second marriage to Publilia. We therefore expect to find in the *De natura deorum* an increased respect for theism in general and for Roman traditional religion in particular. The surprise is that there is no noticeable trace of all that in *De natura deorum*. The *De natura deorum* is very different from Varro in every respect.

De natura deorum is, as we all know, a discussion between an Epicurean, a Stoic, and an Academic about the nature of the gods. It does not matter who represents the three philosophies – except for the representative of the Academy, C. Aurelius Cotta, the consul of 75 BC and *pontifex* who on his death in 73 BC had been replaced by Caesar. Since Cotta as an Academic and as the final speaker represented Cicero, the choice is pointed. Cicero himself is supposed to have listened to the discussion, but not to have taken part in it, as he was too young at the time when the imaginary encounter took place, during the *Feriae Latinae*† of a year between 75 and 73 BC. It does not matter much either where Cicero picked up his arguments for the three schools. He had plenty of Epicurean and Stoic acquaintances. Lucretius had been one of the Epicureans he knew well, and another, Philodemus, was still alive. For the Stoics, Cicero certainly knew

---

† "The Latin festival," held in honor of Jupiter Latiaris and celebrated annually, on no fixed date, by the members of the Latin League, at the Alban Mount.

his Panaetius and Posidonius, but may have used them indirectly through some more scholastic summary of Stoic tenets. As we know much less about contemporary Academics, it would be idle to mention names: in any case some of their arguments went back to Carneades, who had lived a hundred years earlier. The essential point is that Cotta, as an Academic, finds himself in greater sympathy with the Epicureans than with the Stoics when it comes to deciding whether gods intervene in human life Cotta is really as uncertain about the existence of the gods as he is about the immortality of the soul. To be sure, before arguing against the proofs of the existence of the gods, Cotta takes the precaution of declaring that in ordinary life he, the ex-consul and pontiff, does not care about Zenon, Cleanthes, and Chrysippus, but about the welfare of Rome. There is one thing he knows about Rome: that Romulus and Numa founded her greatness on the observance of the rituals. *Sine summa placatione deorum* [("Without the great goodwill of the gods")] Rome could never have become as powerful as she is (3.5). This is good enough, but very short and followed by a close argument for the impossibility of proving the existence of gods, to which there is no reply. The inescapable conclusion a reader was bound to draw from the end of the *De natura deorum* was that Cicero, with all due precautions (for which cf. 3. 95), intended to be negative. It was not the impression one would have derived a few years before from a reading of the *De republica* and *De legibus*.

The impression that from circa 51 to circa 45 Cicero has shifted his ground in the matter of religion cannot simply be contradicted by pointing to the mystical crisis he had experienced in 45 because of his daughter's death. As the *De consolatione* [*"On Consolation"*], the treatise he wrote to console himself after her death, is lost, we have no clear idea of what he was saying in it. Nor do we know how closely the idea of immortality was bound up with his belief in gods. The skepticism which unexpectedly emerges from the *De natura deorum* becomes even more conspicuous in the work which followed it, *De divinatione*. This work belongs to the end of 45 and early 44. It was probably drafted before the death of Caesar and revised immediately after the Ides of March. The proem to the second of the two books is certainly later than Caesar's murder and provides an invaluable summary of Cicero's intellectual activities in the previous year. In facing the question whether one had to believe in divination, Cicero was doing something more than supplementing his previous argument in the *De natura deorum*. Auspices were an essential part of Roman official religion. He was himself an augur, and in earlier days (so it appears) he had written a book *De auguriis* ["*On Augury*"], of a technical character, which has not come down to us, but may be alluded to in one of his letters (*Fam.* 3. 9. 3) and in *De divinatione* 2. 75–76. He had of course taken a positive view of Roman divination in his book *De legibus*. At least in the past (he had argued in the *De legibus*) the Roman augurs had been authentic diviners (2. 32). The personal, almost intimate, character of the *De divinatione* is immediately made clear by the fact that it is a dialogue between Cicero and his brother Quintus in Cicero's villa at Tusculum, with nobody else present. The brother plays the part of the Stoic who defends the authenticity and legitimacy of divination: he seems to derive many of his arguments in favor of divination from Posidonius. Cicero plays his role of the skeptic from the point of view of the Academy. He has the final word. He ends by declaring that his denial of any value in divination is meant to save religion from a dubious and dangerous ally: religion must be separated from superstition. But the impossibility of defending religion from a serious philosophic point of view had already been demonstrated in the *De natura deorum*, to which Cicero pointedly refers in this final passage of *De divinatione* (2. 148). No attentive reader could take this escape clause too seriously. What on the contrary is striking is that Cicero so fiercely attacks all forms of divination – Roman or foreign – with the same two basic arguments, namely, the small proportion of verified prognostics in comparison with the multitude of prophecies, and the intrinsic improbability that the entrails of certain animals or the position of remote stars could tell us something specific about what was going to happen to single individuals at a given date. Cicero does not hesitate to use Roman examples and even his own personal experiences (such as one of his dreams, 2. 136) to show the inanity of divination. And it is, as I have said, a denunciation in very personal terms, with the clear intention of assuming full responsibility for what is being said. He repudiates explicitly the arguments in favor of divination of his fellow augur Ap. Claudius Pulcher, who had dedicated a book on the subject to him (2. 75).

We are therefore brought back to my main point. In 51 BC or so we had found another Cicero – a man with ambitions to reform the Roman state on a religious basis. The *Somnium Scipionis* was a remarkable attempt to link the political program with religious aspirations: the good Roman leader was promised immortality in this precise sense. At the same time the book on *Laws* modified, but substantially defended, the traditional Roman attitude to sacred laws, to *auspicia*, and to the ancestral cults. Six or seven years later very little of that was left. The *De natura deorum* had paid lip service to the traditional values of Roman religious tradition, including *auspicia*, but had been a rigorous denial of the possibility of demonstrating the existence of the gods. In the *De divinatione* the game was inverted: lip service was paid to religion, but any form of divination, including the traditional forms of Roman religion, was denied any merit and probability.[9]

The cleavage, as we have seen, was made more remarkable by two circumstances. Most probably between 51 BC and 45 BC Varro had published his *Divine Antiquities*, which Cicero himself greeted enthusiastically as a revelation. They provided a uniquely authoritative picture of Roman traditional religion. They invited a restoration of obsolete cults and in any case provided the evidence for a precise discussion of Roman cults. Cicero did not take any of this new material into account when he wrote *De natura deorum* and *De divinatione*. The other circumstance was that when he came to write these two works Cicero refused, only shortly after his daughter's death, to be carried away by his personal emotions and anxieties.

There is no safe interpretation of this change in Cicero's religious attitudes between 51 and 45–44 BC. But it is impossible to avoid noticing that while Cicero was becoming more skeptical, Caesar and his direct entourage were becoming more religious or at least more concerned with religious questions. These are the years in which Victoria, Fortuna, and Felicitas were much broadcast in obvious connection with Caesar. In 45 a public sacrifice was decreed for Caesar's birthday, if we can trust Dio Cassius (44. 4. 4). On the other hand, as Cicero prominently records in *De divinatione*, Caesar had more than once refused to pay attention to prodigies and showed up their vanity: for instance, in 46 he had sailed to Africa in spite of the warning of the haruspices (Cic. *Div.* 2. 52; Suet. *Caes.* 59). Caesar had been *pontifex maximus* since 63. As such he was apparently entitled to a *domus publica* on the *Sacra Via* (Suet. *Caes.* 46). In the last years of his life the senate decreed that a pediment should be placed

---

[9] It will be enough to refer to the three commentaries on *De natura deorum* by A. S. Pease (1955–58), M. van den Bruwaene (1970–81), and W. Gerlach and K. Bayer (1978); for *De divinatione* see Pease's commentary (1920–23). I am aware that W. Jaeger took the appeal to the authority of tradition at the beginning of Book 3 as the essential section of *De natura deorum* and considered it an anticipation of the Christian argument from authority; but the Christian basis for authority was revelation Cf .W. Jaeger, "The Problem of Authority and the Crisis of the Greek Spirit," *Authority and the Individual*, Harvard Tercentenary Conference (Cambridge, Mass., 1937), pp. 240–50, summarized by Jaeger himself in *Early Christianity and Greek Paideia* (Cambridge, Mass., 1962), pp. 42 and 122.

on this house as if it were a temple (Cic. *Phil.* 12. 110; Suet. *Caes.* 81. 3; Iul. Obseq. *Prod.* 67 and elsewhere). On the night of the Ides of March Caesar's wife dreamed that the pediment had collapsed. The dream must soon have become known and opened up interesting questions about the relation between the validity of the dream and Caesar's ambitions in provoking the decree of the senate. Finally, there were the various, and by no means clear, steps toward the personal deification of Caesar. His statue was often exhibited among those of gods, and there may have been some decree to create a cult of Divus Iulius before Caesar's death. Let us add that Varro had not been the only one to dedicate a book on prayers and rituals to Caesar: a certain Granius Flaccus dedicated to him his *De indigitamentis*† ([Lact. *Inst.*] 1. 6. 7; Censor. 3. 2). Caesar, who had added to his dignity of *pontifex maximus* that of an *augur* in 47, clearly took pleasure in religious details. He passed a *lex Iulia de sacerdotiis* ["Julian law concerning priesthoods"] and (later?) increased the number of *pontifices*, *augures*, and *quinquennales* [municipal magistrates holding office every five years, to conduct a census and perform a *lustratio*]. May we suspect that Cicero was not amused? He had reconciled himself to Caesar's regime as long as it lasted, and was bound to Caesar by intellectual ties which he was the last to underrate. But he was never with him at heart. The more Caesar was involved in religion, the more Cicero tried to escape it.

There was a sequel to the story in Augustus' time. Augustus was of course the great restorer of temples and rites. Like Caesar he became *pontifex maximus* and paraded his dignity as the son of Divus Iulius: *Divi filius*. He had learned people to advise him on religious matters, such as the great lawyer Ateius Capito, who was officially entrusted with the interpretation of the Sibylline Books in 17 BC. No doubt Varro's doctrine was gratefully used in Augustus' circles, although we know far less about this than we should like. But a difference between the Caesarean and the Augustan age is immediately apparent. The men who represented the new age were neither scholars like Varro nor philosophers like Cicero: they were poets – Horace, Virgil, Propertius, Ovid, Manilius. It was a poet, Ovid, who undertook and did not quite complete the task of col-

---

† The meaning of *indigetes* remains disputed; it was controversial in antiquity. One meaning, popular among late antique exegetes of Vergil, was that *di indigetes* were those gods who started out as mortals (see, e.g., Servius on Vergil *Georg.* 1.498). Georg Wissowa (1904: 175–91) advanced the dominant modern theory that the *di indigetes* were the original gods of Rome, in contrast to the *di novensiles*, who were more recently arrived.

lecting the stories attached to the various festivals of the Roman calendar.[10]

Next there were the historians, among whom Strabo should not be underrated. The lawyers (I shall add the name of Antistius Labeo) come third, the pure antiquarians (such as Verrius Flaccus) are fourth: philosophy in Latin, especially on religious matters, does not seem to have been conspicuous under Augustus. When a poet was encouraged to announce ["Your own Apollo now reigns" (Vergil *Ecl.* 4.8: *tuus iam regnat Apollo*),] there was less room for philosophers. There was perhaps less astrological speculation about Augustus than J. Gage has repeatedly suggested,[11] but there was enough to offend the *dii manes* of Cicero (although, as we know, Octavian, as early as 30 BC when he was not yet Augustus, had made Cicero's son his ally as *consul suffectus* [a consul chosen to fill out the term of a consul who has left office] in order to demonstrate that he had had no share in Cicero's murder). But what would Cicero have said on hearing that a comet, the *sidus Iulium* ["the Julian star"], had become both the proof of Caesar's apotheosis and the confirmation of Augustus' power (Pliny [*Nat.*] 2. 94, from Augustus' autobiography)? Indeed the very title of Augustus alluded to *auguria* and more precisely to the *augusta auguria* which had accompanied the foundation of Rome. Even at their lowest number there were too many horoscopes and other portents around Augustus. We can understand why Minucius Felix (by implication) and Arnobius (explicitly) thought the *De natura deorum* to be a refutation of paganism. Arnobius added that Cicero had taken the risk of appearing impious (3. 6). Lactantius, for all his admiration for Cicero (or because of it), declared: ["Taken as a whole, the third book of his *On the Nature of the Gods* overturns and utterly demolishes all religious sentiment"] (*totus liber tertius de natura deorum omnes funditus religiones evertit ac delet*) (*Div. inst.* 1. 17. 4) In a different context

[10] On Ovid. cf. R. Schilling, "Ovide interprète de la religion romaine," *RÉL* 46 (1968): 222–35 (= *Rites, cultes, dieux de Rome* [Paris, 1979], pp. 11–22; cf. also pp. 1–10); W. R. Johnson, "The Desolation of the Fasti," *CJ* 74 (1978): 7–18. For the background, see G. P. Goold, "The Cause of Ovid's Exile," *ICS* 8 (1982): 94–107. Cf. W. Fauth, "Römische Religion in Spiegel der *Fasti* des Ovid," *ANRW* 2. 16. 1 (1978), pp. 104–86, esp. for the bibliography, and T. Gesztelyi, "Ianus bei Ovid: Bemerkungen zur Komposition der *Fasti*," *ACD* 16 (1980): 53–59.
[11] In A. Guarino (ed.), *La rivoluzione romana* (Naples, 1982), pp. 222–35. Cf. P. Jal, "Les dieux et les guerres civiles," *REL* 40 (1962): 170–200; H. Pavis d'Escurac, "La pratique augurale romaine à la fin de la république," in *Religion et culture dans la cité italienne* (Strasbourg, 1981), pp. 27–35.

and in a different religious situation St. Augustine was more severe ([*Civ.*] 5. 9: notice ["faux philosopher"] *philosophaster* in 2. 27).

What Petrarch thought of *De natura deorum* is no longer ancient history.[12]

[12] It is worth mentioning C. B. Schmitt, *Cicero Scepticus: A Study of the Influence of the "Academica" in the Renaissance* (The Hague, 1972). For *De natura deorum* in the Renaissance, cf. D. P. Walker, *The Ancient Theology* (London, 1972).

8 Hierarchy and Structure in Roman Polytheism: Roman Methods of Conceiving Action [†]

JOHN SCHEID

translated by Philip Purchase

Si Deus unus et quae esse beata solitudo queat?

Cicero, *Hortensius*, fr. 47[‡]

Since the publication of *Götternamen* by Hermann Usener, the question of how the Romans understood the divine has primarily exercised students of the archaic period and of so-called Indo-European societies. In the context of research in these areas, Roman theology is seen as a strong argument in favor of Roman cultural underdevelopment. So, the well-known litanies of "functional" deities, those "Sondergötter" dear to the heart of Usener, are treated as fossils of the most primitive Roman piety, the presence of which in the religious practice of the Republic and Empire speaks volumes on the decadence of Roman religious feeling.

However, such thinking fails to take account of historical context, as these lists did not survive *only* in ancient books or in nearly forgotten rites. As we will see below, they were still under construction, both in public cult and private rites, up until the third century CE, and not only amongst the old cults, rooted as they were in Roman prehistory. I will try to show that these litanies and their "Sondergötter" were in fact an active and entirely characteristic element of Roman

---

[†] Originally published as "Hiérarchie et structure dans le polythéisme romain: façons romaines de penser l'action," *ARG* 1.2 (1999), 184–203.

[‡] Translated in n. 63 below.

polytheism. This is not an argument which I can advance by pointing to a book in which Roman religious authorities described, defined and justified this theology; given the fact that such a religious code never existed in this Book-less religion, I will have to imitate Roman antiquarians and philosophers, and extract the implicit theological underpinning from cult practice itself. The evidence from ritual indicates that the traditional Roman gods in imperial Rome were neither merely remnants of the most distant past, nor merely a throng as large as it was incoherent. In fact, they emerge as highly organized groupings in which each divinity should be evaluated according to ritual context, and in relation to the other divinities on any given list. So analysis reveals a divine hierarchy, at once conscious and logical, which the officials (whether they were priests or not) constructed according to the demands of each particular case. It is this *savoir-faire* that we will term the implicit theology of Roman ritualism.

I will begin with one of the only archives of documentary texts that contains continuous and relatively precise evidence for Roman religious services, namely the *commentarii* of the Arval Brethren. The lists that I will be analysing are drawn from epigraphic copies of these priests' annual reports.

The most interesting lists are found in the descriptions of expiatory rites linked to incidents in the sacred grove of the goddess Dia, which was under the management and maintenance of the Arval Brethren.[1] The ritual unfolded as follows: every time an incident such as a fire, a snowstorm or any other event damaged the *lucus* ["grove"], the presiding magistrate of the Arval Brethren, their *magister*, would call a meeting of the Brethren and would announce to them, through an official report (a *relatio*), what had happened and would propose a remedy, namely that they should repair the damages and, above all, because repairs were a given, that they should hold *piacula* at the beginning and end of the work. The report later made clear that the expiatory sacrifices had been undertaken on the chosen day. The most complete example dates from the year 105:

> Under the same consuls, [– the Arval Brethren met] in the temple of Concordia. When [the *magister* Marcus Valerius Trebicius Decianus] informed his colleagues about [the laurels in the sacred grove of dea Dia, which had been burnt as a result of inclement weather, it was decided] that they should be felled after holding [an expiatory sacrifice]. Present in the

---

[1] For the sacred grove of the goddess Dia, see Scheid 1990, 95–132.

college were [Marcus Valerius Trebicius] Decianus, Quintus Fulvius Gillo [Bittius Proculus, Tiberius Iulius] Candidus Marius Celsus, Tiberius [Iulius Candidus, Publius Metilius] Sabinus Nepos. Under the same consuls, on the kalends of [–], an expiatory sacrifice was offered in the sacred grove of dea Dia [due to] the need for felling the laurels that had been burnt as a result of inclement weather, by the president] Marcus Valerius Trebicius Decianus, accompanied by public slaves, of sows, lambs, cakes and pastries.[2]

Until 183, the *commentarii* of the Arval Brethren only record short versions of expiations (such as we see in 105) at the time of the inscription of copies of the reports on the walls of a building situated in the sacred grove.[3] Between 183 and 240, on the other hand, the Brethren constructed complex rites to expiate interventions made necessary by the destruction of various goods belonging to the goddess. In 183, the roof of the temple, where a fig tree had grown, had to be repaired; in 218, the reasons for the *piaculum* are unknown; in 224, repairs were needed after a fire caused by a lightning-

---

[2] CFA no. 64, col. I, ll. 28–41: *Isdem c[o(n)s(ulibus) –] | in aedem Conco[rdiae fratres aruales conuenerunt] | ibique referen[te M.Valerio Trebicio Deciano mag(istro) ad] | collegas de arbor[ibus lauribus in luco deae Diae, quod] | a tempestatibus per[ustae essent, placuit piaculo fac]lto caedi. Adferunt in co[llegio Valerius Trebicius De]lcianus, Q. Fuluius Gillo [Bittius Proculus, Ti. Iulius] | Candidus Marius Celsus, Ti. [Iulius Candidus, P. Metilius] | Sabinus Nepos.* (vacat) | (vacat) *Isdem co(n)s(ulibus) k(alendis) – (vacat)] | in luco deae Diae piaculum factum [ob arbores lau]lrus caedendas, quod tempestatibus perust[e erant,] | porcis et agnis, struibus fertisque per M. Valeri[um] | Trebicium Decianum [mag(istrum)] ministrantibus public[is].*

[3] For example CFA no. 58 (91 CE, inscription of the report for the year 90), ll. 64–66: *[M'. Acilio Glabrione, M. Vl]pio Traiano co(n)s(ulibus) (ante diem tertium) k(alendas) | Maias* (vacat) | *[piaculum factum in luco deae Diae per calatorem et publicos ob ferrum in]latum, ut acta | insculperentur magisteri P. Sallusti Blaesi (alterius).* (vacat) | *[Isdem co(n)s(ulibus) – piaculum factum in luco deae Diae per ca]llatorem et publicos | ob ferrum elatum* ("In the year when Manlius Acilius Glabrio and Marcus Ulpius Traianus were consuls, on the third day before the kalends of May, a *piaculum* was performed in the grove of dea Dia by the *calator* and the public slaves, because iron had been brought <into the grove>, when the *acta* of the *magister* P. Sallustius Blaesus were being inscribed." "Under the same consuls … a *piaculum* was performed in the grove of *dea Dia* by the *calator* and the public slaves, because iron had been removed"). These expiations do not seem to have concerned any divinities other than dea Dia, as is shown by the more detailed text of 225 (CFA no. 105b, ll. 21–25): *Fusco (iterum) et Dextro co(n)s (ulibus) X[I]Iii k(alendas) | Maias in luco deae Diae | [p(iaculum)] f(actum) mag(isteri) (primi) Porci Prisci ob | ferri inlationem sciptur(ae) et scalptur(ae) marmor(is) causa, immol(ante) ipso mag(istro) | porcam et agnam, struib(us) e[t f] ertis et extas (!) reddid(it) ad aram, ministrant\libus public(is) et pr<a>e[s]entibus a sacr(is) d(omini) n(ostri) Aug(usti).* (vacat) *Item immolauit ob ferri | elationem scripturae et scal[p]tur(ae) et operis perfecti* (vacat) *(ante diem tertium) non(as) Mai(as) | per Porc(ium) P[h]ilologo (!) calat(orem) et per public(os) fratr(um) arualium* ("In the year when Fuscus – for the second time – and Dester were consuls, fourteen days before the kalends of May, the *piaculum* of the first presidency of Porcius Priscus was performed in the grove of dea Dia, because of the bringing-in of iron for writing on and carving marble; that same *magister* burned a pig and a kid, along with cakes and pastries, and offered the entrails on the altar, with public slaves attending and in the presence of the minister for cult of our Lord Augustus. He likewise burned, because of the carrying-out of the iron <used> for writing on and carving, and for work completed, on the third day before the nones of May, through Porcius Philologus, the *calator*, and through the public slaves of the Arval Brethren").

strike; in 237(?), a dead tree had to be replaced; and, finally, in 240, work was undertaken to maintain the grove itself.[4] In 183, the report records the *piacula* offered at the beginning and end of repairs, while the other *commentarii* are content with merely describing the beginning.

Before proceeding any further, it would be as well to describe the performance of the sacrifices. The most detailed document is found in the protocol for expiations in February and March 183:

Under the consulship of Lucius Tutilius Pontianus Gentianus, on the sixth day before the Ides of February (the 8th), the *magister* Quintus Licinius Nepos sacrificed adult *suovetaurilia*, in order to begin the work of digging out a fig tree that had grown on the roof of the temple of dea Dia, and in order to repair the temple; he also sacrificed, close to the sanctuary, two female cattle to dea Dia, two rams to father Janus, two sheep with abundant wool to Jupiter, (*Column II*) two rams with abundant wool to Mars, two ewes to the Juno of dea Dia; two ewes to the God-or-Goddess, two ewes to the divine Virgins, two sheep to the divine Servants, two sheep to the Lares, two ewes to the Mother of the Lares, two ewes to the God-or-Goddess who protects this sacred grove and place, two sheep to Fons, two ewes to Flora, two ewes to Vesta, two ewes to mother Vesta; he also sacrificed two ewes to *Adolenda Conmolanda* <sic> *Deferunda*. Also, (he sacrificed) before the Caesareum sixteen sheep to the sixteen *divi*.

Under the consulship of Marcus Herennius Secundus and of Marcus Egnatius Postumus, on the third day before the Ides of May (the 13th) the *magister* Quintus Licinius Nepos sacrificed adult *suovetaurilia* in the sacred grove of dea Dia, on the occasion of the end of work as the tree (had been) dug out and the sanctuary repaired; he also (sacrificed), near the sanctuary, two female cattle to dea Dia, two rams to father Janus, two sheep with abundant wool to Jupiter, two rams with abundant wool to Mars, two ewes to the Juno of dea Dia; two ewes to the God-or-Goddess, two ewes to the divine Virgins, two sheep to the divine Servants, two sheep to the Lares, two ewes to the Mother of the Lares, two ewes to the God-or-Goddess who protects this sacred grove and place, two sheep to Fons, two ewes to Flora, two ewes to Vesta, two ewes to mother Vesta; also (he sacrificed) two ewes to *Adolenda Conmolenda Deferunda*. Also, (he sacrificed) before the Caesareum sixteen sheep to the sixteen *divi*.[5]

---

[4] See the table on p. 169 for references.

[5] *CFA* no. 94, col. I, l. 20–col. II, l. 14: (col. I) [20]*L. Tutilio Pontianus* (vacat) *Gentiano co(n)s(ule) (ante diem sextum) id(us) Februar(ias)* (vacat) | *in luco deae Diae Q. Licinus Nepos mag(ister) operis inchuandi causa, quod* | *in fastigio aedis deae Diae ficus innata esset, eruendam et aedem reficilendam, immolauit suouetaurilibus maioribus; item ad aedem deae* | *Diae boues feminas (duas), Iano patri arietes (duos), Ioui berbeces (duos) altilaneos,* | (col. II) *Marti arietes altilaneos (duos), Iunoni deae Diae oues (duas), Siue deo siue deae oues (duas),* | *Virginibus diuis oues (duas), Fonti uerbeces (duos), Florae oues (duas), Vestae oues (duas), Vestae matri oues (duas); ite[m]* | [5]*Adolendae Conmolandae (!) Deferundae oues (duas), item ante Caesareum Diuis n(umero) (sedecim) uerbec(es)* | *immolauit n(umero) (sedecim).* (vacat) *M. Herennio Secundo, M. Egnatiio Postumo co(n)s(ulibus) (ante diem tertium) id(us) Mai(as)*

The first protocol describes the *piaculum* offered at the beginning of repairs to the roof of the temple of dea Dia, which had been damaged by the growth of a fig tree. The workers had to dig out this fig tree, bring it down from the roof, burn it[6] and then repair the temple. The expiatory rites would begin with a sacrifice of adult *suovetaurilia* – a bull, a ram and a boar in that order – to the god Mars. The link between Mars and *suovetaurilia* was so self-evident that generally the name of the god was not mentioned.[7] The document from 224 (see the table on p. 169) tells of a procession around the sacred grove before the sacrifice: the accounts given describe this procession with the words *lustrum mittere* – *mittere* here functioning analagously to πέμπειν ["to conduct" or "to take part in a procession": see *LSJ* s.v. πέμπω III.2]. As to H. S. Versnel and Jörg Rüpke have shown,[8] the function of this *lustrum*, and more generally of the *lustratio*, was not to purify the object or the persons in question, but rather to call on the god Mars to protect those within the line drawn by the procession: the *lustratio* defines and constitutes a thing or group.

After the *suovetaurilia* sacrifice, which takes place in front of the sacred grove, the head of the Arval Brethren enters the grove and sacrifices two cows to dea Dia before her temple. The goddess receives two cows because there is a need to expiate at least two intrusions, namely the removal of the tree and the subsequent repairs. It should be noted that the new material that follows is preceded by the adverb *item* ("also," "likewise"). There then follows a list, again introduced by *item*, which contains fourteen gods and goddesses. Before examining this in detail, we should briefly explain the spheres of action and influence ascribed to the various deities on the list.

Janus *pater* ("Father Janus"), the god of beginnings, opens the list. He is followed by the sovereign god, Jupiter, and by Mars, the god of war. Jupiter is invoked for honorific reasons; first among Roman

---

| *in luco deae Diae Q. Licinius Nepos mag(ister) operis perfecti causa, quod arboris* | *eruendae et aedis refectae (!), immolauit suouetaurilibus maioribus; item ad aedem* | *deae Diae boues feminas (duas), Iano patri arietes (duos), Ioui uerbeces (duos) altilaneos, Marti* | [10]*ariet(es) altilan(eos) (duos), Iunoni deae Diae oues (duas), Siue deo siue deae oues (duas), Virginibus* | *diuis oues (duas), Famulis diuis uerbeces (duos) {S II}, Laribus uerbeces (duos), Matri Larum oues (duas),* | *Siue deo siue d*e*ae, in cuius tutela hic lucus locusue est, oues (duas), Fonti uerbeces (duos),* | *Florae oues (duas), Vestae oues (duas), Vestae matri oues (duas), item Adolendae Conmolendae De(l)ferundae oues (duas); item ante Caesareum Diuis n(umero) (sedecim) uerbeces immolauit (sedecim).*

[6] For the treatment of dead wood, see *CFA* no. 2, col. I, ll. 1–6, no. 12 c, ll. 21–23, and no. 12d, ll. 1–4 (which will be corrected in *CFA* p. 35, d, l. 4 (commentary); cf. fragm. c, ll. 21–23).

[7] See Scheid 1990, 446 n. 10; Rüpke 1990, 144–146.

[8] Versnel 1975; Rüpke 1990, 144–146.

The *piacula* performed by the Arval Brethren between 183 and 240 of this era

	CFA no. 94, col. I, ll. 20–col. II, l. 6. 183 CE (a)	CFA no. 94, col. II, ll. 6-14. 183 CE (b)	CFA no. 100a, ll. 1-1. 218 CE	CFA no. 105b, col. II, ll. 1-20. 224 CE	CFA no. 107, col. II, ll. 1-9. 237(?) CE	CFA no. 114, col. I, ll. 7-17. 240 CE
Reason	For the sake of starting work, because a fig tree had grown on the roof of the temple of dea Dia, which must be removed and the temple repaired	For the sake of work completed, namely the removal of a tree and repair of the roof	[– – – –]	Because by the force of a storm and blow of lightning … the need to uproot trees, strike them with iron, and burn and dispose of them	[– – – –] another tree of the sacred grove …	For the sake of starting work, that of pruning the grove, digging up the roots of some trees and replacing others
	He burned adult *suovetaurilia*	He burned adult *suovetaurilia*	[– – – –] adult *suovetaurilia*	A lustral procession was performed, together with adult *suovetaurilia*	A lustral procession was performed, together with adult *suovetaurilia*	A lustral procession was performed, together with adult *suovetaurilia*
	At the temple: To *dea Dia*	At the temple: To *dea Dia*	To *dea Dia*	Before the temple: To *dea Dia*	[– – – –] white female … To the Juno of *Dea Dia*	Before the temple: To *dea Dia*
				On temporary altars:	On temporary altars:	
	To *Janus pater*	To *Janus pater*	[– – –]	To *Janus pater*	To *Janus pater*	To *Janus pater*
	Jupiter	Jupiter	[– – –]	Jupiter	Jupiter	Jupiter
	Mars	Mars		Mars	Mars	
	The Juno of *dea Dia*	The Juno of *dea Dia*	The Juno of *dea Dia*	The Juno of *dea Dia*		
	God-or-Goddess	God-or-Goddess	God-or-Goddess	God-or-Goddess	God-or-Goddess	God-or-Goddess
	Virgines divae	*Virgines divae*	[– – –]	*Virgines divae*	*Virgines divae*	*Virgines divae*
	Di famuli	*Di famuli*	[– – –]	*Di famuli*	*Di famuli*	*Di famuli*
	Lares	Lares	[– – –]	Lares	Lares	Lares
	The Mother of the Lares "The God-or-Goddess who protects this grove and place"	The Mother of the Lares "The God-or-Goddess who protects this grove and place"	The Mother of the Lares	The Mother of the Lares	The Mother of the Lares	The Mother of the Lares
	Fons	Fons	Fons	Fons	Fons	
	Flora	Flora	Flora	Flora	Flora	Flora
				Summanus pater	[*Summanus pater*?]	
	Vesta	Vesta	[– – –]	Vesta	Vesta	
	Vesta mater	*Vesta mater*	[– – –]	*Vesta mater*	Vesta of the gods and goddesses	*Vesta mater*
	Adolenda Conmolenda Deferunda	Adolenda Conmolenda Deferunda	[– – – –]	Adolenda Coinquenda	[– – – –]	
	Before the Caesareum:	Before the Caesareum:	Before the Caesareum:	Before the Caesareum: To the *Genius* of our Lord Augustus;	In the tetrastylum: To the *Genius* of our Lord Augustus;	Before the Caesareum: To the *Genius* of our Lord Augustus
	To the sixteen *divi*	To the sixteen *divi*	To the sixteen *divi*	To the twenty *divi*	To the twenty *divi*	

gods, he is associated with appeased deities, but it is also possible to imagine a closer link with dea Dia herself, the goddess of the shining sky.[9] Mars is the protector of the sacred grove and of Roman territory, who was also invoked in the Arval Hymn, declaimed at the end of the annual sacrifice to dea Dia.[10] *Iuno deae Diae* ("Juno of dea Dia") is a special kind of deity. The Juno of a woman, equivalent to the *genius* of a man, represents the abilities and faculties of a being at the moment of its birth: just as gods have a *genius*, so dea Dia has a Juno.[11] The following deity is well known: God-or-Goddess (*Siue deus siue dea*). He or she is not an indication, as previously believed, of the primitive state of Roman religion; we are not dealing with a vague expression of the divine, but rather with the name of a precise deity.[12] While it was understood that he or she was one of the occupants of the sacred grove, he had not yet made himself known, like his colleagues, to the Arval Brethren with his correct name; in this way, they were uncertain as to whether they were dealing with a god or a goddess. The *Virgines diuae* are generally identified with the Nymphs, patrons of running water. We will return later to the divine Servants, after whom come the Lares, earth deities of the soil on which human activities take place. The Mother of the Lares is a mysterious figure who also receives a share in the annual sacrifice to dea Dia; we know little else about her.[13] It is unnecessary for us in this context to be more specific about her potential links with Acca Larentia.[14]

Now, once more, the head of the Arval Brethren addresses an anonymous deity who has not made himself known, but whose presence is either certain or presumed: God-or-Goddess who guards this sacred grove and its surroundings. Next Fons, the patron of fountains, Flora, goddess of flowers, and Vesta, goddess of the public hearth, are all honored. Vesta is invoked twice, and the second time she is called *mater*, "venerable." This strange fact is explained by the parallel document of 224, in which the goddess is first called Vesta *mater*, then Vesta of gods and goddesses: on the one hand we are dealing with the patron goddess of the public hearth, on the other

[9] Schilling 1969.
[10] See Scheid 1990, 616–623.
[11] Goddesses may have *Genii* (*CIL* VI.422 *Genius Forrinarum*) or *Junones*, for example *CIL* II, 2407 = *ILER* 365 (Victoria).
[12] Wissowa 1912, 37–8; Brelich 1949, 11ff., Dumézil 1987, 5–6, 61.
[13] Scheid 1900, 587–598.
[14] [The goddess celebrated at the Larentalia on 23 December. For a review of theories connecting her with the Mother of the Lares, see Scheid 1990, 590–592.]

with the Vesta who is the patron of the sacrificial fire of every deity, of every altar in the sacred grove.

Following Vesta, a new section begins, introduced by *item*, which contains the famous goddess Adolenda Conmolenda Deferunda. The realm of action of this deity is linked to the work of the slaves who remove the fig tree from the roof of the temple, cut it up and burn it, but it should be noted that the tasks are listed in alphabetical order rather than in logical order (which would be Deferunda Conmolenda Adolenda). In the protocol of 224, she is called Adolenda Coinquenda, again in alphabetical order.[15] We will return later to this goddess. All of these deities receive two victims, male or female according to their sex. In 183, God-or-Goddess is honored with female victims, in 224 and 240 by males, the uncertainty over victims mirroring the uncertainty over his or her sex.[16]

The list closes with a final category, the *diui*, resident in the Caesareum on the outskirts of the sacred grove.[17] In 183, there are sixteen *diui*; from 218 onwards, twenty, which indicates that the list necessarily included deified empresses and princesses.[18] From 224 to 240, the *genius* of the reigning emperor was also honored. The *genius* and the *diui* receive one sole victim.

These lists are constructed according to a threefold hierarchy that reveals very clearly the way in which the Romans conceived of their gods.

1   A first level of hierarchy is seen in the rank of victims and in the order of *piacula*.

Inside the sacred grove,[19] dea Dia receives two major victims, both cows, while the other divinities receive two sheep victims, which is to say that they are minor sacrifices. In front of the Caesareum, the imperial *genius* is honored by a major victim (a bull), and the *diui* by

---

[15] For interpretations of her name, and for bibliography, see R. Peter, in Roscher *Lex.* s. v. Indigitamenta, 2:188–190, and Radke 1965, 55 ff.

[16] Brelich 1949, 11.

[17] For the sacred grove, see Scheid 1990, 102–172.

[18] The sixteen *diui* are Augustus, Iulia Augusta, Claudius, Poppaeus, Vespasian, Titus, Nerva, Trajan, Plotinus, Hadrian, Sabinus, Faustinus I, Antoninus Pius, Lucius Verus, Faustinus II, Marcus Aurelius. In 218 Commodus, Pertinax, Septimius Severus and Caracalla were added: see Marini 1795, 387; Henzen 1874, 148 ff. It should be noted that the victims are male even though there are also *diuae*. This is no doubt an excessively elliptical summary. Among others, the Caesareum in the barracks of the *vigiles* ["night-watchmen" charged principally with fire-fighting: Suetonius *Aug.* 30.1] at Ostia proves that these chapels also contained empresses: see Scheid 1990, 161 ff.

[19] Mars of *suovetaurilia* is excluded from this hierarchy, as his field of action is located outside the sacred grove; but we will see that he could still be honored inside the grove itself.

minor victims (sheep). Dea Dia and the imperial *genius* are invoked
in first place in the two cult locations of the site, the sacred grove and
the Caesareum; as such, they are superior to the deities who follow
them in the order of the *piacula*, while the first list, which concerns
the deities of the sacred grove, is superior in *dignitas*, in social standing, to the following list of *divi* and *divae*.

This hierarchy has a straightforward explanation, although we
should be prepared for a surprise in the case of the *diui*. Dea Dia
occupies first place and receives major victims because the sacred
grove is hers; she is the only deity to possess a temple in the sacred
grove (which is called, moreover, *aedes deae Diae*, "the temple of dea
Dia") and a permanent altar, an *ara*. The other gods and goddesses
only enjoy a temporary (*temporalis*)[20] altar made of wood,[21] thus
indicating that their rank is inferior to the titular goddess. All of the
divinities whose names figure between Janus and Vesta are guests of
dea Dia, there either due to their prestige, as with Jupiter, or rather
due to the help they give dea Dia in accomplishing her duties and in
managing the cult site. Dia appears to be linked to nurturing and
mild light during the first stage in the ripening of cereals.[22] The execution of this function benefits from the assistance of Mars, protector
of fields, of Flora, and perhaps also of Jupiter, the heavenly king. The
other deities assist dea Dia in managing the cult site, and in a way
they make up a part of the disposition of the site: the *Virgines divae*,
Fons, Vesta, Adolenda Conmolenda Deferunda, etc.

All of these deities are inferior to dea Dia because she is the owner
of the site. When he receives the *suovetaurilia* Mars occupies a special
place, but in the list of *piacula* he is held to be an assistant to dea Dia.
Yet his presence amongst the guests and assistants is not necessary,
as in 240 he no longer figures on the list. Outside the sacred grove,
at the boundary, he is in the position of *dominus* in a space that
is functionally his: there he, too, receives special victims, amongst
which figures a major victim.   ·

This association of deities, in a role as guests or assistants, with
the principal deity of a cult site or festival recalls an old Italic
and Roman tradition: the naming of an assistant deity through an
epiclesis or a genitive that refers to the owner of the site or the pro-
prietor of the festival. Well known are Hondo Iouio, Çerfo Martio,

---

[20] *CFA* no. 105b, ll. 6, 8 and 17 (224 CE), and no. 107, col. II, l. 5 (237 CE).
[21] Since they were destroyed during the fire of 224 (*CFA* 105b, ll. 4–7). The *commentarius*
["recorded proceedings"] of the secular games of 204 also attests to the existence of temporary
(*temporales*) altars made of wood (Pighi 1965, III l. 69; V[a] l. 47, 53).
[22] Schilling 1969.

Torsa Çerfia, Tefro Iouio of the Eugubine Tables,[23] or the guests of Ceres in her *hurz* at Agnone (Nutrix Cerealis, Lymphae Cereales etc.).[24] Less familiar are the companions of Mefitis in her sanctuary at Rossano di Vaglio in Lucania: Venus Mefitana, Numulus Mefitanus, who is also related to Mamertios, and is worshipped in the company of one Oina Numuli.[25] All of these documents can be dated from the fourth to the first centuries BCE. At Rome herself we find Lua Saturni, Salacia Neptunis, Nerio Martis, etc., who surely show vestiges of the same habit. Yet even if the tradition of adding affixes disappeared over the second century CE, that does not mean that the ritual practice disappeared along with it. Our texts attest to this tradition in the second and third centuries CE, but it no longer appears in the name of the deities concerned: in order to uncover its traces, we must analyse the precedence amongst the gods and the quality of victims offered them.

When applied to the last category of *piacula*, the strict hierarchy that orders the gods on the list reveals an extremely interesting fact. In the lists that mention the imperial *genius* next to the *divi*, which is to say those of 224 and 237, the imperial *genius* occupies first place. According to the document of 224, with its use of the adverb *item*, it is even separated from the *diui*, just as dea Dia is distinguished from deities figuring between Janus and Vesta. This observation is corroborated by the fact that the *genius* receives a bull, the *diui* sheep (*uerueces*). All of these observations force us to consider the *genius* of the emperor as "master" of the Caesareum. How can we explain this surprising hierarchy? Why are the *diui* inferior to the *genius* of a living man?

In order to understand the reasons behind this paradoxical situation, it is important to define briefly what we call, in a very superficial manner, "imperial cult." For us, for example, the *sodales Augustales* celebrate the cult of the *diui*. This is not exactly wrong, but things are rather more complicated. Let us look at Tacitus: the *pontifex maximus* Tiberius considered (at least in the historian's rendition) the *sodales Augustales* to be *proprium eius domus sacerdotium*, which is to say, the priesthood attached to the *domus Augustae* ["the Augustan house"].[26] So above all they were concerned with the Augustan family, with the *genii* and *Junones* of the living members of the family as well as with the *diui*. What is more,

---

[23] Dumézil 1987, 255 ff.; Prosdocimi 1996, 579–585.
[24] Prodocimi 1996, 446.
[25] Lejeune 1990, 15–18.
[26] Tacitus *Ann.* 3.64.5.

the Caesareum of the site *ad deam Diam* and that of the barracks of
the *vigiles* at Ostia contained both statues of *diui* and statues of living
principes: this mixture is attested in the dedications found on the
bases of the statues, which generally date back to the first years of
their respective reigns. In this way the imperial cult should be seen as
the cult tied to the *domus Augusta*, to the imperial family. However,
authority in every family was held by its *paterfamilias*. If we consider
the Caesareum of the Arval Brethren as being a sanctuary of the
domus Augusta, who is entitled to play the role of *paterfamilias*
there? The first Augustus? Our documents provide a different
answer: authority is exercised by the ruling emperor, head of house
for the imperial household, both for the living and for those who
have been deified. It is for this reason that his *genius* occupies first
place in the sequence of *piacula*.

I do not want to claim that things are always so simple.
Hierarchies depend upon their context. The example we have studied
is a sanctuary of the Caesars, a Caesareum,[27] and here our reasoning
makes sense, but in other contexts such reasoning cannot be applied.
Under Claudius, Nero or Otho, the votive sacrifices offered by the
Arval Brethren on the 3rd of January included sacrifices to the Divine
Augustus, the Divine Claudius and the *genius* of the emperor, in that
order.[28] The reason for this hierarchy, the reverse of that of the
Caesareum, is that these votive sacrifices were offered in the temple
of the Divine Augustus, which had been shared with the Divine
Claudius since the year 54. In this temple Augustus and his companion Claudius were the *domini*, the imperial *genius* a guest, and
for this reason the hierarchy was the reverse of a sanctuary common
to all the Caesars. So the hierarchy among deities depended upon
context.

2   We have seen that, in the list of *piacula*, hierarchy is articulated
by the adverb *item*. If we base our inquiry on this piece of evidence,
the hierarchy contains, in descending order after Mars and Dia:
(1) the deities found between Janus and Vesta; (2) Adolenda
Conmolenda Deferunda; (3) the Imperial *genius*; and (4) the deified
emperors.

The fourteen deities placed between Janus and Vesta make up a
group, as we know that Janus and Vesta traditionally framed groups

[27] Scheid 1990, 109–132.
[28] For example *CFA* no. 17, ll. 3–9 (44 CE); no. 26a–lr, ll. 6–9; no. 27, ll. 9–12 (58 CE); or
no. 40, col. I, ll. 47–52 (69 CE); etc. I will return to this group elsewhere.

of deities. In *De Natura Deorum*, Cicero writes: "Since the beginning and the end are the most important parts of any business, Janus is generally considered first in a sacrifice."[29] A little later, he concludes: "The power of Vesta extends to altars and hearths, and for this reason all prayers and sacrifices end with Vesta."[30] Whatever the case might be, this group of deities is superior in rank to Adolenda Conmolenda Deferunda, and thus also to the Imperial *genius* and the *diui*. The superiority of the fourteen gods to Adolenda Conmolenda Deferunda will surprise no one. Adolenda is one of those *di minuti* ("tiny gods") Augustine took pleasure in mocking,[31] so there is nothing strange in this goddess ceding precedence to Jupiter, Mars, Fons or Vesta. But why does this "slave" goddess receive higher billing than the *genius* of the emperor and the *diui*?

This is not an isolated case. The *equites singulares* ["the select cavalry," a mounted cohort of the imperial guard] would normally fulfill a vow during their demobilization, evidence for which is preserved in a certain number of inscriptions.[32] These lists are very tightly constructed, an observation already made by the editors of the *Corpus Inscriptionum Latinarum*.[33] In the majority of these lists, the Capitoline Triad comes first, preceding Mars, Victoria, Hercules, Fortuna, Mercury, Felicitas, Salus, the Fata, the Campestres, Silvanus, Apollo, Diana, Epona, the Matres, the Sulleuiae, and finally, sometimes after the mention of *di omnes* ("all the gods") or *ceteri d(i) i(mmortales)* ("the other immortal gods"), the *genius* of the emperor and the *genius* of the *singulares*. In this way, the *genius* of the emperor figures toward the end of the list, just before the *genius* of the *singulares*, after several minor deities such as the Fata and the Campestres, and even after goddesses of Italic and provincial origin like the Matres and the Sulleuiae. The only explanation for this inferiority lies in the special nature of the *genius*. Born on the day of an individual's birth or a thing's creation, the *genius* perishes upon the death of the individual or the destruction of the thing: its nature

---

[29] Cicero, *Nat. Deor.* 2.27.67.

[30] Cicero, *Nat. Deor.* 2.27.67. We should not wonder at the fact that these rules were not systematically followed. To judge from a passage of Cato, *Agr.* 132.2 (*Vestae, si uoles, dato* ["Give to Vesta, if you wish"]), the formula was not obligatory; one could act this way if one wanted, but there was no obligation. It was an enrichment of the rite rather than a necessary part.

[31] Aug. *Civ.* 4.1; cf. Aug. *Civ.* 7.11: *di minuscularii* ("trifling gods"). For the representation of pagan gods, particularly *Sondergötter*, in Augustine, see Lindemann 1930; Stempel 1964, 165–174.

[32] *CIL* VI, p. 31118; 31139–31146; 31148–31149; 31171; 31174–31175.

[33] See *CIL* VI, p. 3069, for a comparative table.

is clearly different from that of an immortal deity, however minor that deity might be. The *diui* also have a particular divine nature, one that is recent, infinitely more recent than that of immortal deities, and so their place at the bottom of the list is in accordance with logic. I have attempted to demonstrate elsewhere that this implicit theology also controls the hierarchy of architectural spaces in sanctuaries.[34] At any rate, these observations should give pause for thought to those who claim a universally preeminent role for the "imperial cult" under the Empire.

3   The list of deities framed by Janus and Vesta that forms, as we have seen, a sealed group conceals within itself yet another structure, one which Georges Dumézil pointed out fifty years ago. He demonstrated convincingly that such lists, framed by Janus and Vesta, were trifunctional. They contained, in the following order: (1) Jupiter, god of sovereignty, first function; (2) Mars, god of war, second function; and finally (3) a series of deities belonging to the third function, various and linked to generation.[35]

Whatever one's opinion of Indo-European theories may be, Dumézil's analysis here should be welcomed as one of the most elegant examples counting in favor of trifunctionalism as he has defined it. No violence is committed in reconstructing the trifunctional hierarchy of these deities, and, in accordance with the rules of the theory, all of the gods of the third function fall into that category without difficulty. In fact, the list is more coherent than Dumézil himself saw. The first problem he was able to resolve concerned Summanus, attested only in 224. This god of nocturnal lightning was also called Jupiter Summanus, and one might well be tempted to link him with the first rather than with the third function. But Dumézil was able to deal with this without difficulty, as Summanus figures in Roman tradition amongst the deities introduced by Ancus Marcius, mythical king of the third function.[36] From the Dumézilian point of view, then, Summanus is at exactly the right place in the list. Yet Dumézil pointed to a second difficulty that he was unable to resolve, namely the presence of Juno at the head of the third-function deities rather than at the head of the list, where she should figure according to trifunctional theories.[37] This problem, however, does not lie in the

---

[34]   Scheid 1995.
[35]   These observations partially saw the light of day during a colloquium in Strasburg in 1996; see Scheid [and Svenbro] 997, 297–302.
[36]   See Dumézil 1947, 102 ff.
[37]   See Dumézil 1947, 102.

list, but rather in Georges Dumézil's reading, as we are not dealing with Juno, but rather with *the* Juno of dea Dia who, as a deified double of a goddess of the third function, should be placed in the same category as her.

So, the lists in question convincingly bear witness to the theory of Dumézil, as they conform at every point to his strict rules. Unless we are to reject these rules out of hand, we must admit that a tri-functional order exists in these lists. But before making use of this example as an excuse to immerse ourselves in sweeping theories and succumb to the charms of "metahistory," we should analyze as extensively as possible the structure in question. Simply put, we must engage with details. It is then that very grave problems appear.

The first problem concerns chronology. The trifunctional structure is supposed to be vestigial, a fragment of archaic Roman culture. In fact, we find this example, worthy of a place in a trifunctionalist manual, not at the beginnings of Roman history, but right in the middle of the third century CE. This problem cannot be sidestepped by appealing to the supposedly archaic character of the Arval Brethren. Even though the Brethren practiced an agrarian cult and used, among several hymns, one dating to the end of the fourth century BCE at the latest, it is not the case that the Brotherhood necessarily dates back much beyond the fourth century, nor that all the elements of the cult – such as our *piacula* – date back to the origins of the *collegium*. In fact, their sacrifices and lists are above all wonderful witnesses to Roman public cult in the time of Commodus and Severus Alexander. For us, the trifunctional list found in the expiatory sacrifices of the Arval Brethren is above all else a puzzle generated by the imperial age. Let us admit, though, for the sake of discussion, that it is an example of the resurgence of ancient practices.

We will then come across a second, more serious, problem. The list of divinities to be appeased is constructed with great care and in a conscious manner. The preceding pages demonstrate this, and we will be able to confirm this observation when we examine several aspects and details neglected by Dumézil. In fact, for some unknown reason, in his analysis Dumézil did not use the other three contemporaneous documents from the Arval Brethren that contain the same rite or the same list: those of the expiatory rites of 218 CE, 237 CE and above all 240 CE.[38] A comparison of all of the lists reveals another aspect of their construction: it becomes clear that, for

---

[38] See the table on p. 169 for references.

reasons that remain obscure, the Arval Brethren put together the same list of deities in several different ways. Between 183 and 224, the list remained substantially the same, with two changes attested in 224: the insertion of Summanus and the omission of *Siue deus siue dea in cuius tutela hic lucus locusue est*. Also in the list of 224, the name of the deity Adolenda Conmolenda Deferunda is reduced to Adolenda Coinquenda, and the *genius* of Augustus is added to those receiving sacrifices at the Caesareum. Although it is mutilated, the text of 237 shows that the *magister* of the sacrifices had on this occasion extracted the *Iuno deae Diae* from the trifunctional list in order to place her next to dea Dia herself, the goddess who was appeased first of all, at the head of all the *piacula*, in her role as owner of the cult site. This modification was logical and thus necessarily conscious: in 183, when the priests chose to place the Juno of dea Dia amongst the deities associated with the titular goddess of the sacred grove, they did so according to reasoning that conformed to Dumézilian theories, and thus placed her among third-function deities; there, they put her at the head of the group, since dea Dia was the most important deity in the sacred grove. In 240 the situation again changed. *Siue deus siue dea in cuius tutela hic lucus locusue est* is definitively missing, along with the Juno of dea Dia, Fons, Summanus *pater*, one of the two Vestas, Adolenda Coinquenda, the deified emperors and – Mars. According to the evidence, the list of 240 represents a short version of the list of deities associated with dea Dia, just like the examples of *piacula operis faciundi* ("*piacula* for work to be performed") prior to 183, which only evoked the *piacula* offered to dea Dia. We do not know why the Arval Brethren decided to construct the list of 183, or at least make it explicit in the report,[39] and then shorten this list in 240. On the other hand, we can reconstruct the principles according to which the alterations were made.

The rules of Dumézil's comparative method are, as we have already stressed, very strict and precise. In order to be able to speak of a trifunctional structure, five conditions must be met: all of the data in question must be mentioned in the same document; they must be deployed at the same level (three men, three gods, three objects, etc.) and be related one to the other; they must be clear and, of course, there must be at least three of them; finally, there must be

---

[39] Because nothing stops us from thinking that they had always associated a certain number of deities with dea Dia in the context of the *piacula*. The fact that the reports later than 183 do not reproduce the sequence of *piacula* linked to the end of the work confirms this hypothesis. The problem in part hinges on the technique of recording the protocols.

"nothing left over."[40] In the documents of 183 and 224, these conditions are respected to the letter. The lists figure in a rubric of reports describing the same religious service, the elements of the list are deities organized in three clearly hierarchical groups and collected together with the goal of celebrating expiatory sacrifices. The trifunctional structure embraces all of the deities framed by Janus and Vesta, and all are prefectly evident. By all appearances, then, a model trifunctional list.

In 240, however, an essential element is missing. The god Mars, sole representative of the second function, is no longer mentioned, and so one of the major rules that govern trifunctional groupings is violated. According to Dumézilian grammar, the absence of Mars destroys the structure. We could certainly try to come up with a dodge to remedy the gap in the source: for example, we could suppose that the copyist simply forgot Mars. As with all of the reports of the Arval Brethren in the third century, the example from 240 is certainly characterized by a careless style, yet it does not contain such major errors.[41] In fact, all other aspects of these lists, which I do not have to space to detail here, demonstrate that they are constructed in a careful manner and show no signs of negligence. If it were necessary to point to an omission, I would rather choose the omission of a certain number of other deities in the same list: and these omissions, we can be sure, are all consciously and logically motivated. We might also suggest that Mars was removed from the abbreviated list because he had already received the sacrifice of *suovetaurilia* at the beginning of the ceremony. Maybe so, but then what happens to the Dumézilian rules? Can we take that many liberties with them?

Before concluding that trifunctional structures constituted a general and permanent element of Roman religion, it remains to be explained how it is possible for a trifunctional structure to appear and disappear in the same religious service at a distance of just a few years. The structure is sufficiently complex and the attestations sufficiently numerous for us to be able to exclude chance, while if we attribute the anomalies to the lack of understanding of archaic theological logic among a "late" priesthood, the lists of 183 and 224 must also be removed from the body of trifunctional documents. We cannot simultaneously consider certain lists to be well-preserved vestiges and reject other evidence as potentially the result of some

---

[40] Dubuisson 1993, 92.
[41] For the quality of the copies, see Scheid, *CFA*, pp. viii–ix.

misunderstanding. As we have already said, the construction of these lists was not a chance occurrence; all aspects of these lists are perfectly conscious and intentional.

The difficulty arises from the fact that the comparatist doctrine constrains us to find this structure at all times and in every place, at any rate in groups where it is attested once. It is supposed to constitute an inheritance, which is to say an element of a preexisting culture that is transmitted without serious modification and that the researcher is able to identify in documents dating from the historical era. This prejudice is an obstacle to research, taking as the point of arrival what is in fact only a point of departure. Without calling into question the Dumézilian rules, we can use this evidence as a base from which to interrogate trifunctional logic more profoundly, and to ask whether it is something more than a passive heritage. So, the structure may well be potential rather than permanent: like so many other cult regulations, it would not have to be in existence everywhere and always, it would not have to be an omnipresent, all-encompassing system, but might rather be considered the highest point on a scale of possibilities. It would be seen as the last stage in the construction of a complete group that achieved its perfect form, at least at Rome, under the Empire.

I do not know if this conclusion is acceptable. Applications of Dumézil's theories are seductive precisely because of the rigor of the rules that govern the definition of complex structures and their comparison. Is it possible to consider such a structure merely as an element in the process of constructing complete groups? Whatever the case may be, it is clear that if one is content to accept the dogma of inheritance, and one simply searches for a new proof of archetypal structure, these kinds of questions will necessarily be ignored because they are susceptible to no answer.

The lists of deities constructed by the Arval Brethren not only reveal that the priests managed this group of deities according to a finished system of logic and with great precision, but also show how the construction of these lists was undertaken through the creation of deities according to context. They furnish several fascinating insights into the way in which the Romans conceived of gods and of divine action.

Let us begin in 183 with the famous goddess known as Adolenda Conmolenda Deferunda, in the context of repairs that included the removal of a fig tree and the reconstruction of a temple (*quod in fastigio aedis deae Diae ficus innata esset, eruendam et aedem*

reficiendam, "because a fig tree had grown on the roof of the temple
of dea Dia, which must be removed and the temple repaired"). The
name of the goddess details, in alphabetical order, work done on the
tree, but it does not mention the reconstruction of the temple. In
224, despite the detailing of important repairs, notably including the
digging up, sawing up and burning of trees (*earumque arborum
eruendarum, ferro fendendarum adolendarum commolendarum*
["the digging-up, striking-with-iron, burning and disposal of trees"]),
the name of the goddess is not enlarged (for example into Adolenda
Conmolenda Eruenda Fendenda), but is rather given in a synthetic
form: Adolenda Coinquenda. Finally, in 240, the goddess no longer
figures in the list.

These modifications demonstrate the flexibility of priestly
theology and the skillfulness of the priests themselves. In order to
understand the rank of this goddess and the reasons behind her
disappearance, we should return to the fourteen deities contained
between Janus and Vesta, particularly the *di famuli*, who are unique.
Gaetano Marini[42] had already realized in 1795 that these *di famuli*
must belong to the same divine category as the *di anculi* or *deae
anculae* mentioned by Paul the Deacon,[43] whose function was to
serve. A well-known passage of the *Aeneid* calls a snake that comes
out of the tomb of Anchises a *famulus*, a servant: Servius adds in his
commentary that "Vergil shows thereby that Anchises had become a
god through apotheosis: whence he gives to him a *famulus*, as a sort
of servant; for individual gods have inferior powers like servants,
as Venus has Adonis or Diana Virbius."[44] Patristic literature also
recognizes these servant-deities.[45]

In any case, there is no doubt that these *famuli* or *anculi* gods
correspond to Ovid's *di plebei* ("plebeian gods"),[46] and should be
understood as the *familia* of *di nobiles*, which is the way Dumézil

[42] Marini 1795, 372 ff.

[43] Paul s.v. *Ancillae* 18L: *Ancillae dictae ab Anco Martio rege, quod in bello magnum
feminarum numerum ceperit. Siue ideo appellantur, quod antiqui anculare dicebant pro
ministrare, ex quo di quoque ac deae feruntur coli, quibus nomina sunt Anculi et Anculae*
("*Ancillae* are named after King Ancus Martius, because he seized a large number of women
in war. Or they are so called, because the ancients said *anculare* for 'to serve,' whence gods and
goddesses, too, are said to be worshipped by those whose names are *Anculi* and *Anculae*").
According to a scholiast on Juvenal 6.249, *Flora erat apud antiquos ministra Cereris* ("Among
the ancients, Flora was an attendant of Ceres").

[44] Servius *Aen.* 5.95: *aut per apotheosin deum ostendit effectum: unde ei famulum dat,
quasi ministrum; singula enim numina habent inferiores potestates quasi ministras, ut Venus
Adonim, Diana Virbium.*

[45] See Lact. *Inst.* 1.7.5, quoting Seneca; see Stempel 1964, 167–174.

[46] Ovid *Met.* 1.172–176; see Müller 1987.

takes them.[47] What is more, we should note that our Adolenda
Conmolenda Deferunda is separated from the gods who precede her
by *item*, a fact which places her in a subordinate position in relation
to the preceding deities. She is inferior to them not only because
she leads a merely ephemeral existence in the sacred grove, but
also because she is linked to the repairs that are being expiated.
Nevertheless, she has a place, at that particular moment, amongst the
deites present in the sacred grove, and as such, it is fitting that she
should be won over with *piacula*. However, the fact that she can
disappear several years later, from the same religious service, shows
that her presence is not essential. Upon what does her appearance
depend? Amongst the fourteen preceding gods, we find the *di famuli*
or servant gods, but the relationship between these gods and the *dea
ministra* is very interesting. When the priests deem it necessary, they
pull out from the collective category of *di famuli* one or another
specific deity, Adolenda Conmolenda Deferunda or Adolenda
Coinquenda. As with the *di famuli*, the name and function of this
deity coincide,[48] but her function is still more precise than that of the
di famuli: it corresponds to the explanation of the actions of servant
gods in the processes of labor. When it is necessary to abbreviate the
list of *piacula*, the priests limit themselves to the general category.
The same procedure is attested in this list for the *Virgines divae*
and Fons: each of these deities represents an aspect of the presence
of water in the sacred grove, but when brevity is required, only
the deities of running water remain. In respect to these deities, Fons
functions as a more explicit form of their function.

Another example is furnished by Vesta and *Siue deus siue dea*. This
latter deity refers in a certain manner to all those gods or goddesses
whose presence is known, but whose name is unknown, and who
might also be offended by any damage inflicted on the sacred grove
in the course of the repairs. So we are dealing with a kind of un-
organized collectivity, invoked under the divine figure of God-or-
Goddess. Moreover, we should note that again in this case the name
of the deity corresponds to its function: being present, but remaining
(at that moment) unknown to the Romans. When the Arval Brethren
wanted to be exhaustive, they extracted from this deity a secondary
form, adding to his name a phrase that clarified this potential deity's
function: *in cuius tutela hic lucus locusue est* ["who protects this

---

[47] Dumézil 1987, 53 ff.
[48] Prosdocimi 1996, 510–513, speaks of "Nome-Atto" ["Name-Act"].

sacred grove and place"].[49] I have already explained the relationship between Vesta *mater* and Vesta *deorum dearumque*, which follows the same logic, but in all these cases, counter to that of Adolenda Conmolenda Deferunda, the deities belong to the same list. The reason no doubt belongs to the "modesty" of these goddesses, explicity linked as they are to manual labor, to "sordid" activities.

Whatever the case may be, this procedure offers vivid testimony to the multiple hierarchies that structured the band of the immortals, as well as to priestly *savoir-faire* in the middle of the third century CE. The conscious and logical manipulations of these litanies and creations of new and temporary deities are not, as the primitivists and the great Usener believed, prehistoric vestiges. Usener interpreted these lists, along with the list of minor deities invoked during the course of the *sacrum Cereale*, and others as well, in an evolutionary sense:[50] the "gods of the moment" (*Augenblicksgötter*) are succeeded by "individual gods" (*Sondergötter*), whose names still carry transparent meanings. According to this theory, at a precise moment, certain of these "individual gods" transform into "personal gods," with the divine figure correspondingly elaborated in terms of narrative and image. For Usener, the logic of this transformation was essentially linguistic: when the name of the "individual god" becomes incomprehensible and opaque, it can set out on its career as a "personal god" with its own name.

Usener derived the name and notion of the *Sondergötter* both from the facts as he saw them, and from Roman antiquarians.[51] From 1904 onwards, Georg Wissowa[52] criticized the outmoded conception of *indigitamenta* upon which Usener's argument was based, along with the overinterpretation of the passage in Varro concerning *di certi*. Indeed, the dispute between Wissowa and Ernst Bickel over the passage concerning *di certi* only served to reinforce Wissowa's 1904 critique.[53] However, the criticisms leveled at Usener do not diminish the value of his analysis. While there is certainly some speculation that is outmoded by today's standards, the important insight we retain is that the notion of a specialized god is not so much an initial

---

[49] They could just as well have addressed a Tutelanda or Tutelina, in accordance with the formation of the name of these deities. Also see Henzen 1874, 146; Brelich 1949, 11.

[50] Usener 1896. See also Cassirer 1925. For Usener, see Arrighetti *et al.* 1982; for the *Sondergötter*, Piccaluga 1982.

[51] See, notably, Usener 1896, 75–79, inspired by the *di proprii* of Servius *Aen.* 2.141. Usener did not employ the evidence from our lists; compare R. Peter in Roscher *Lex.* 2: 12ff. For other lists of *Sondergötter*, see Bayet 1950.

[52] Wissowa 1904.

[53] Wissowa 1921, with the response of Bickel 1921a; also see Bickel 1921b.

form of deity but rather an ongoing practice in polytheism. The meticulous precision found in litanies of deities, amongst whom the *Sondergötter* appear, is explained by the Roman notion that prayer can only be answered if the deity invoked and the services expected are defined precisely and without potential confusion. In cases of uncertainty, the Roman was faced with two options: either he could invoke an unknown deity charged with a particular function, such as *Siue deus siue dea, in cuius tutela hic lucus locusue est*, or he could transform the object of his prayer into a particular deity whose name was formed from the desired action. In order to formulate exhaustively the object of the appeal, two options were once again available to him: either he could unpack the expected action into its principal moments (as in the *piacula* of the Arval Brethren and in the *sacrum Cereale*), or he could express the essence of the action in a polar fashion by designating the points of departure and arrival (Anna Perenna ["The-Year-Who-Survived-a-Year"], Prorsa Postuerta ["Forward-Backwards"], Nona Decima ["Nine-Ten"], Patulcius Clusiuus ["Open-Closed"], etc.). Several of these deities remained attached to "major" deities like Carmenta (Prorsa Postuerta) or Janus (Patulcius Clusiuus), while others received their own cult (Genita Mana ["Born-Died"], Anna Perenna). Yet others merely existed in prayer formulae in the form of impersonal invocations. So the *Sondergötter* appear in order to complete and make precise the mode of action of a given deity, and help to adapt invocations to the infinite realm of possible appeals and objects. With Georg Wissowa, I do not believe that there was ever a period when the Romans only invoked *Sondergötter* – Vervactor and Inporcitor in the place of Tellus and Ceres: after all, there are so many names designating the object and action under consideration (Janus, Vesta, Tellus, Ops, Fons, Terminus) that we have to ask if it is possible that one could ever have worshipped a force extracted from things before the thing itself, the action before the agent.

Thus, the lists we have examined emerge as rich sources for understanding Roman polytheism and its implicit theology, allowing us to trace religion and theology in broad outline.

We should note in the first place that Roman priests based the construction of these lists on presumption, or better: the understanding that gods were present everywhere, in the form of deities known and unknown (like God-or-Goddess). Even if they are unknown, the gods and goddesses are not imprecise and vague figures, nor are they seen as parts of one all-encompassing deity. They are always precise divine figures, even if the only certain aspect of their personality is that they are not known. We can understand how this type of representation continues by reference to demonology.[54] To speak the language of Ovid: among gods there are always hierarchies, linked either to context, or to their "noble" or "plebeian" nature.

This divine community is continually liable to be enlarged or diminished. The state of our sources does not allow us to understand why, at any particular moment, the priests decided now to construct complex lists, now simplified ones. Perhaps the decision was due to ritual constraints we are unaware of, just as we are unaware of the spirit of the age; or perhaps, more prosaically, it was just a question of the mood of the Arval Brethren's secretary. Whatever the case may be, the process by which groups of deities are transformed should be considered one of the most important facets of Roman polytheism. As I have already indicated, this was scarcely limited to the lists of the Arval Brethren: it comprehends all of Roman history. Seven centuries before the *di minuscularii* of Augustine, Aius Loquens, "Saying-Speaking," was extracted from the collective group of the Fauni.[55] Over the span of Roman history, the relationship between a general category or a deity and the exercise of its precise function is analogous to the relationship that exists between a deity and its epiclesis, its *numen* ("power") or an abstraction linked to it. A report of the Arval Brethren from the year 101,[56] which describes the formulation of vows when Trajan set off to war, employs the same procedure: next to Mars *pater*, we find Mars *uictor* and Victoria.[57] There is a dynamic relationship between these three deities: Mars *pater* is the god of war and of those who make war, Mars *uictor* is the same god in a different guise, considered from the viewpoint of his action and the results of that action, namely victory, a result which is then, in a final step, deified as Victoria. In the same list we also find, next to Jupiter Optimus Maximus, a Jupiter *victor*, the latter an expression of the victorious action of the former. Also present is the traditional Salus who expresses divinely, in vows made for the health of the state and the emperor, the result of the action of the Capitoline triad. This progression is always made in descending hierarchical order.

---

[54] For bibliography, see Brenk 1986; for authors, see, for example, the relationship with traditional gods in Lact. *Inst.* 1.7.8–10; Mandouze 1958, 212 ff.; Pépin 1998. For comparison, see Assayag 1992, 68.

[55] Cic. *Div.* 1.101.

[56] *CFA* no. 62a, ll. 23–70.

[57] *CFA* no. 62a, ll. 48–58.

The process of progressive division of divine personalities turns a spotlight on the prominent place occupied in Roman theology by the problem of action and the relationship between function, ability and effect. When the Romans analyzed the intervention of a deity, they extrapolated from its personality or, rather, from its action and from other divine figures: this extrapolation might involve a more precise rendering of the name of the deity through an epiclesis, or it might involve a "functional" deity (Adolenda, Veruactor) or the action itself (Mens, Fides, Virtus). The same process also governs the figure of the *genius* of a deity or its *numen*, which are its deified capacity for action and deified power, respectively. And as Usener already suggested,[58] imperial powers are also declined according to this grammar, as the *genius* deifies the capacities for action of a mortal. In this context, we should also ask ourselves about the relationships between the collective category of *di manes* and the *di manes* of any given Roman.

All of these divine figures were far from being the evanescent *Augenblicks-* or *Sondergötter* of the primitive world, overtaken little by little by "personified" gods and then drawn up among their clients, as Hermann Usener's evolutionary scheme would have it. The sources I have been reading here demonstrate that these figures need to be understood as aspects of the action of a deity to whom they are linked according to need or context. They are the result of a desire to capture all the moments of an active process, while subordinating them to divine power and protection. Consequently, all of these divine figures and all of these polytheistic structures work together to express, within a given context, one sole concept and one sole action. They represent a ritual method for analyzing a divine principle. Other peoples, and indeed the Romans themselves on other occasions, would carry out this analysis by recounting a myth or by organizing a philosophical debate; in certain cult situations, nevertheless, they carried out their analysis by following traditional rituals.

This reflection on divine presence, power and action, achieved through the dispersal of a divine personality amongst several deities who must represent all the moments of the exercise of that deity's power, cannot be separated from Greco-Roman technical thought. Such thought was in effect incapable of elaborating a unified and global concept of action, of labor, of work. Jean-Pierre Vernant has shown that the ancients did not possess the concept of work, and

---

[58] Usener 1896, 30 ff.

expressed, among other things, the process of production as a multitude of limited activities.[59] In the process of constructing divine clients, they proceeded in the same fashion. They conceived of the function of a deity not only from the viewpoint of a unique agent (from which they were distanced by the ideology of the city, perhaps, eager as it was to avoid concentrations of power), but with reference to need and to custom, and through the lens of an accumulation of limited actions. This dispersal of a god's personality amongst several partners also had the effect of differentiating these divine figures one from another.

Augustine perfectly understood this traditional conception of the gods. By strenuously mocking the *strepitus innumerabilium daemoniorum* ("the din of those innumerable demons")[60] and the *turba quasi plebeiorum deorum* ("that throng of quasi-plebeian gods")[61] with their *officia*, their ridiculous functions, the bishop from Madaura underlined that the real problem for his contemporaries was their inability to imagine what he called the universality of God:[62] "What would they lose," he writes, "if they agreed, through a wise piece of expediency, to worship one sole God?" I imagine that his polytheist adversaries would have replied to him in the words of Cicero's Hortensius: "If God is one, what happiness can he find in his solitude?"[63]

WORKS CITED

Arrighetti, G. *et al.* 1982. *Aspetti di Hermann Usener filologo della religione*. Pisa.

Assayag, J. 1992. *La colère de la déesse décapitée. Traditions, cultes et pouvoir dans le Sud de l'Inde*. Paris.

Bayet, J. 1950. "Les Feriae Sementiuae et les indigitations dans le culte de Cérès et de Tellus." Bayet 1971, 175–205.

Bayet, J. 1971. *Croyances et rites dans la religion romaine antique*. Paris.

Bickel, E. 1921a. "Varros di certi und incerti." *Philologische Wochenschrift* 41, 832–838.

Bickel, E. 1921b. *Der altrömische Gottesbegriff, eine Studie zur antiken*

---

[59] Vernant 1955, 1956, 1957.

[60] Aug. *Civ.* 4.25.177.

[61] Aug. *Civ.* 4.11.160.

[62] Aug. *Civ.* 4.8.156.

[63] Lact. *Inst.* 1.7.4. (Cic. *Hort.* frg. 40 (Müller)): *Sed fortasse quaerat aliquis a nobis id quod apud Ciceronem quaerit Hortensius:* "*Si Deus unus est, quae esse beata solitudo queat?*" ("Perchance someone will complain to us as Hortensius did in Cicero's dialogue, "If God is one, what happiness can he find in his solitude?").

Religionsgeschichte. Leipzig-Berlin. Reviewed by G. Wissowa in *Philologische Wochenschrift* 41 (1921) 990–995.

Brelich, A. 1949. *Die geheime Schutzgottheit von Rom.* Zürich.

Brenk, F. 1986. "In the light of the moon: demonology in the Early Imperial Period." *ANRW* 2.16.3, 2068–2145.

Cassirer, E. 1925. *Langage et mythe. À propos des noms des dieux.* French translation, Paris: 1973.

Dubuisson, D. 1993. *Mythologiques du XXe siècle (Dumézil, Lévi-Strauss, Eliade).* Lille.

Dumézil, G. 1947. *Tarpeia: Essais de philologie comparative indo-européenne.* Paris.

Dumézil, G. 1987. *Religion romaine archaïque.* Paris.

Henzen, W. 1874. *Acta fratrum arvalium quae supersunt.* Berlin.

Lejeune, M. 1990. *Méfitis d'après les inscriptions lucaniennes de Rossano di Vaglio.* Louvain-la-Neuve.

Lindemann, H. 1930. *Die Sondergötter in der Apologetik der Civitas Dei Augustins.* Dissertation, Munich.

Mandouze, A. 1958. "Saint Augustin et la religion romaine." *Recherches Augustiniennes* 1, 187–223.

Marini, G. 1795. *Gli atti e monumenti de' Fratelli Arvali scolpti già in tavole di marmo de ora raccolti, diciferati e commentati.* Rome.

Müller, D. 1987. "Ovid, Jupiter und Augustus." *Philologus* 131, 270–288.

Pépin, J. 1998. "Falsi mediatores duo. Aspects de la médiation dans le sermon d'Augustin Contra paganos (S. Dolbeau 26)." G. Madec, ed. *Augustin prédicateur (395–411).* Études Augustiniennes, Antiquité, vol. 159. Paris, 395–417.

Piccaluga, G. 1982. "Attualità dei 'Sondergötter'? 'Divinità funzionali' e funzionalità divina nella religione romana arcaica." Arrighetti *et al.* 1982, 147–160.

Pighi, G.B. 1965. *De ludis saecularibus populi Romani Quiritium ...* Amsterdam.

Prosdocimi, A. 1996. "La tavola di Agnone. Una interpretazione." L. Del Tutto Palma, ed. *La tavola di Agnone nel contesto italico.* Florence, 435–630.

Radke, G. 1965. *Die Götter Altitaliens.* Reprinted 1979, Münster.

Rüpke, J. 1990. *Domi militiae. Die religiöse Konstruktion des Kreiges in Rom.* Stuttgart.

Scheid, J. 1990. *Romulus et ses frères. Le collège des frères arvales, modèle du culte public dans la Rome des empereurs.* BÉFAR vol. 275. Rome.

Scheid, J. 1995. "Les espaces cultuels et leur interprétation." *Klio* 77, 424–432.

Scheid, J. and J. Svenbro. 1997. "Le comparatisme, point de départ ou point d'arrivée?" F. Boespflug and F. Dunant, eds. *Le comparatisme en histoire des religion.* Paris, 295–312.

Schilling, R. 1969. "Dea Dia dans la liturgie des frères arvales." R. Schilling.

Rites, cultes, dieux de Rome. Paris, 366–370.

Stempel, H.-A. 1964. *Die heidnische Religion in der Theologie Augustins*. Dissertation, Heidelberg.

Usener, H. 1896. *Götternamen. Versuch einer lehre von der religiösen begriffsbildung*. Reprinted 1948, Frankfurt-am-Main.

Vernant, J.P. 1955. "Travail et nature dans la Grèce ancienne." Vernant 1985, 274–294.

Vernant, J.P. 1956. "Aspects psychologiques du travail dans la Grèce ancienne." Vernant 1985, 295–301.

Vernant, J.P. 1957. "Remarques sur les formes et les limites de la pensée technique chez les Grecs." Vernant 1985, 302–322.

Vernant, J.P. 1985. *Mythe et pensée chez les Grecs*. Paris.

Versnel, H. 1975. "Sacrificium lustrale: the death of Mettius Fufetius (Livy 1.28): Studies in Roman lustration-ritual." *Mededelingen van het Nederlands Instituut te Rome* 7, 97–115.

Wissowa, G. 1904. "Echte und falsche 'Sondergötter' in der römischen Religion." G. Wissowa, *Gesammelte Abhandlungen zur romischen Religions- und Stadtgeschichte*. Munch, 304–326.

Wissowa, G. 1912. Religion und Kultus der Römer. 2nd edition. Munich.

Wissowa, G. 1921. "Die varronischen di certi und incerti." *Hermes* 56, 113–120.

PART V

Roman and Alien

Introduction to Part V:
Roman and Alien

Like many other cultural systems, Roman religion possessed mechanisms for regulating contact with foreign ideas and practices, and these were mobilized by, and themselves constrained, the historical dynamics of Roman interaction with foreign peoples, whether conducted through immigration, trade, tourism, or war. Scholars have been only too happy to follow Roman polemicists in reducing this problem to a set of simplistic binarisms, susceptible of purely lexical analysis: *religio*, for example, is good; *superstitio* is bad.[1] Jonathan Z. Smith has shown that the principles underlying such structuralist taxonomies are rarely logical, to say nothing of their utility. Rather, though based on evidence that was itself collected ahistorically, the taxonomies themselves have been constructed in historical terms: Roman religion therefore devolved from cult to superstition, from aniconism to anthropomorphism, from religion to magic, and from sincerity to legalism. In this way, scholars have mapped a whole set of modern prejudices onto a set of ancient polarities, and redeployed them to historicize ideological and sentimental claims on behalf of Christianity triumphant.[2]

In light of these dangers, we would do well to attend more closely to the chronological and geographic specificity of our evidence. This would force us to examine in detail the associative network of ideas and practices in which the simple polarities of religious discourse were embedded. Let us take as an example two laws proposed for Rome by Cicero in his *On the Laws*:

---

[1] On *religio/superstitio* see, e.g., Varro *Ant. Div.* fr. 47. On the history of the terms and their modern study, see esp. Sachot 1991; cf. Gordon 1987 and Smith 1995: 13–18 on religion and magic. On *religio/superstitio* see also Beard, North, and Price 1998: 214–19, and cf. the bibliography cited in p. 2 n. 3.

[2] Smith 1978b.

Let no one have gods separately, either new or foreign, unless they have been recognized publicly.

Let them worship in private those whose worship has been duly handed down by their ancestors. (Cicero *Leg.* 2.19)[3]

The "poles" of the first sentence are the adverbs "separately" and "publicly."[4] They might seem to speak to a division between public and private worship. But "private" religion is precisely the focus of the second clause, which orders people to maintain the cults of their families. Latent in these clauses are potential ruptures at two levels. First, Cicero does not explain the difference between "having a god separately (*separatim*)" and "having a god privately (*privatim*)," but it is clear that he recognized the potential for individual (as opposed to private) action to affect state cult. It is precisely that possibility that he seeks to foreclose. At the same time, the public recognition of a deity might seem to hold out the possibility of obligating or affecting individuals in their private practices. To offer but one illustration: the city of Rome regularly acquired new citizens and resident aliens, and immigrants of either legal status tended to travel with their gods.[5] What happened when that which was duly handed down was foreign or new?

The complexity of our project deepens if we attempt to encompass the actualization of these principles and polarities in forms of social action. Consider the expulsion of the Jews from Rome in 139 BC, by the praetor Cornelius Hispalus. In the diction of Valerius Maximus, as imperfectly preserved by a later epitomator, the praetor expelled the Jews beyond the borders of the city and removed "their private altars from public spaces."[6] At first sight, the praetor's division of the landscape into "public" and "private" accords with Cicero's concern to divide religion into public and private spheres, and there is no doubt but that Romans generally recognized such a division at the

---

[3] Cicero *Leg.* 2.19: *Separatim nemo habessit deos, neve novos neve advenus, nisi publice adscitos. Privatim colunto quos rite a patribus <cultos acceperint.>*

[4] The term is A. R. Dyck's, who made his splendid commentary on *De Legibus* available to me in draft.

[5] See, e.g., Juvenal 3.62–5, translated below on p. 223.

[6] Valerius Maximus 1.3.3, in the epitome of Nepotianus: *Iudeos quoque, qui Romanis tradere sacra sua conati erant, idem Hispalus urbe exterminavit arasque privatas e publicis locis abiecit.* Compare Livy 25.1.6–12, describing events in Rome in 212 BC. His report opens with the announcement that the longer the war went on, "the more *religio*, and in large measure foreign *religio*, attacked the state," and he goes on to describe the failure of an initial attempt by the aediles to remove *sacrificuli*, petty sacrificers and their equipment from the forum. In the end, the Senate took action and forbade anyone from "sacrificing according to a new or foreign rite in a public or consecrated space" (*neu quis in publico sacrove loco novo aut externo ritu sacrificaret*). On this topic see Wissowa 1904: 184–90.

level of cult.[7] According to the second-century AD lexicographer Sextus Pompeius Festus, who relied heavily on the Augustan polymath Verrius Flaccus, "public rites are those performed at public expense on behalf of the people, which take place before mountains, villages, consecrated meeting houses, and sanctuaries; private rites are those performed on behalf of individuals, families, and clans."[8]

Festus supplies a list, presumably not exhaustive, of places where public rites are performed. Where is private space? A later author, the third-century jurist Ulpian, recognized a distinction between public and private places in pontifical law, but this was by no means the only way of categorizing land.[9] We learn from Varro, for example, that augurs divided the land into five categories: "Roman, Gabine, hostile, peregrine, and indeterminate."[10] Regarding the category "peregrine," namely, "legally alien," Festus remarks that "peregrine land is that which is neither Roman nor hostile."[11] These different taxonomies were active in different cultural and political contexts. As with the bodies of experts who supervised them, their overlapping rather than consistent categories were both produced by, and helped in turn to sustain, the diffusion of power and knowledge across and within the Roman elite.

The introduction to Part VI will take up the problem of place in Roman religion. For now, we may observe that there were also "peregrine rites." Were these the rites performed by aliens on alien land? "Those rites are called alien which are performed either for gods called forth to Rome from besieged cities, or for the sake of certain cults sought in peacetime. These include, for example, the cult of Magna Mater, sought from Phrygia, or that of Ceres, sought from Greece, or that of Aesculapius, sought from Epidauros: these are worshipped after the fashion of those from whom the cults were received."[12] It is perhaps worth pointing out that, like *evocatio* itself, that is, "the summoning-forth" of the tutelary deities from cities under siege, the category of "alien rites" gives every sign of being an

---

[7] Cf. Cicero *Leg.* 2.58, discussing the removal of some tombs from a spot that was discovered to be consecrated to Honor: "the pontifical college decided that a public place could not be placed under the constraint of private religious observances" (*statuit enim collegium locum publicum non potuisse privata religione obligari*).

[8] Festus s.v. publica sacra (284L).

[9] Ulpian *Ad Edictum* 68 fr. 1483 (Lenel 1889: II, 806) = *Dig.* 1.8.9.pr-2.

[10] Varro *Ling.* 5.33, on which see below p. 000.

[11] Festus s.v. peregrinus ager (284L).

[12] Festus s.v. peregrina sacra (268L): *Peregrina sacra appellantur, quae aut evocatis dis in oppugnandis urbibus Romam sunt †conata†, aut quae ob quasdam religiones per pacem sunt petita, ut ex Phrygia Matris Magnae, ex Graecia Cereris, Epidauro Aesculapi: quae coluntur eorum more, a quibus sunt accepta.*

ad hoc classification invented to render intelligible the very ancient and variegated religious landscape of late Republican Rome.[13] For the present, let us simply take cognizance of the placement of these "alien rites" in the city of Rome.

In their location "alien rites" stand in distinct contrast to "municipal rites," which Festus, who gave us that definition of "alien rites," defines as follows: "Those rites are called 'municipal' which a population practiced before receiving Roman citizenship and which the *pontifices* desire the people to observe and perform in the same fashion in which they were accustomed to perform them from antiquity."[14] If the different fates of these cults might be explained by saying that some gods established new residences at Rome while others remained in their former homes, the supervisory role arrogated by the *pontifices*, over cults Roman in neither law nor geography, betrays the difficulty of situating such cults in relation to any easy set of dualisms such as Roman or alien, public or private.[15]

Festus cited the cult of Cybele at Rome as an example of an alien rite. Her worship was everywhere odd; at Rome, it was hybrid. The Augustan historian and literary critic Dionysius of Halicarnassus observed its performance in his day:

> The praetors perform sacrifices and celebrate games in her honor every year according to Roman custom, but the priest and priestess of the goddess are Phrygians, and it is they who carry her image in procession through the city, begging alms in her name according to their custom, wearing figures upon their breasts, striking their timbrels while their followers play tunes upon their flutes in honor of the Mother of the Gods. But by a law and decree of the Senate no native Roman walks in procession through the city arrayed in a multi-colored robe, begging alms or escorting flute-players, or worships the goddess with the Phrygian ceremonies. So cautious are the Romans about admitting any foreign religious customs and so great is their aversion to all pompous display that is wanting in decorum. (Dionysius of Halicarnassus *Ant. Rom.* 2.19.4–5[16])

Dionysius does not cite further examples of such balkanization in the performance of cult, but at some level the splicing of Roman and

---

[13] I shall be treating the history of *evocatio* at length elsewhere.

[14] Festus s.v. municipalia sacra (146L). For the text, see below p. 237. Cf. Livy 26.34.12, describing the capture of Capua in 211. A plebiscite fixed the terms of capitulation, specifying the status of persons and profane things. As far as statues of gods and honorific statues were concerned, the college of pontiffs was to decide which were sacred, and which profane (*sacra ac profana*). On this passage see de Cazanove 2000a; cf. Estienne 1997.

[15] Beard, North and Price 1998: I, 211–60; Frateantonio 1997: 85–97; cf. Rüpke 1997, 2001b.

[16] Translation after that of Ernest Cary, itself a revision of that by Edward Spelman: *Dionysius of Halicarnassus: The Roman Antiquities Books I–II* (Cambridge, MA: Harvard University Press, 1937), ad loc.

Phrygian elements in the cult of Cybele parallels the use at Rome, by Roman priests, of rites, customs and formulae consciously labelled and maintained as foreign: the so-called Achaean rite used in the celebration of the Secular Games, the Greek rite, and the tying of one's cloak in Gabine fashion.[17] And insofar as the Romans continued such practices in notionally foreign forms, they represented in the classical period not so much intrusions by foreign elements *into* Roman religion as privileged sites *within* Roman religion for the negotiation of boundaries between Roman and alien.[18] It is also true, to take up the argument of the volume introduction, that the Romans will have justified their habits in this regard by reference to the desires of the gods themselves.

For on their understanding, the Romans dealt not with foreign cults, but with foreign gods.[19] Naturally, the Romans had a college whose bailiwick it was to deal with communications from foreign gods, namely, the *quindecimviri sacris faciundis*. That in practice they largely restricted themselves to reading books of Sibylline prophecy is beside the point, as those books were themselves foreign in origin and language.[20] Haruspicy, too, was of foreign extraction, and it remained the province of Etruscan experts.[21] Likewise foreign, but Greek, was the Delphic oracle, consulted by Fabius Pictor in the midst of the Second Punic War.[22] In point of fact, gods seem rather rarely to have communicated in Latin, Aius Locutius being a notable exception.[23] Such patterns in divine communication at Rome should perhaps not surprise us: in our terms, contact with foreign cultures must have been a principal impulse to innovation in Roman culture generally, to say nothing of religion. The mediation provided by Etruscan specialists and expert readers of prophetic texts ideally allowed the energies of cross-cultural contact to be channeled and controlled. What is characteristically Roman, then, is precisely the

---

[17] On the Achaean rite see above pp. 106–107. On the "Greek rite," see Scheid 1995b, 1998c; on being girt in Gabine fashion (*cinctus Gabinus*), see Wissowa 1912: 417 n. 3. Cf. Livy 25.1.7, on the "Roman rite." Elsewhere Roman authors speak of a "barbarian rite" and an ancestral one (*ritu barbaro*; *ritu patrio*).

[18] For just such an interpretation of Cybele's presence in Augustan Rome see Beard 1994b.

[19] For example, narratives of the transfer of Juno from Veii, or of Cybele from Pessinus, stress the assent of the goddesses themselves: see Livy 5.22.5–6 and Ovid *Fasti* 4.267–70.

[20] On the Sibylline books at Rome see Parke 1988: 136–51 and 190–215, or Potter 1990: 95–140.

[21] On haruspicy as a form of expert knowledge see now North 2000; on the place of haruspicy and particularly *haruspices* in first-century politics and thought see Rawson 1991: 289–323, esp. 300–12.

[22] See above p. 8.

[23] On Aius Locutius see Livy 5.32.6 and 5.50.5, translated with commentary in Beard, North, and Price 1998: II, 42–3.

institutionalization of a mechanism for adjudging, preserving, and ultimately domesticating the foreign, as well as the situation of that mechanism, in an interstitial space between the gods who speak and the Senate that makes decisions.

The essays in this section study very different problems in Roman contact with notionally foreign peoples and religions. John North's "Religious Toleration in Republican Rome" studies the suppression of the Bacchanalia in 186 BC, an obvious test case – and a difficult one, at that – for those who wish to regard polytheistic religions as inherently tolerant, a view of polytheism in general and Roman polytheism in particular popularized in the Enlightenment.[24] What drives North's inquiry is his realization that our major literary source for this episode, the *History* of Livy, must be wrong on one crucial point, namely, that the cult was in some sense "new" and hence that it was suppressed as soon as it became known to the authorities of the state. And in this case – unlike, say, the case of Christianity – we possess a documentary source truly contemporaneous with the decision to outlaw the cult. What it reveals, both about the Senate and about Livy, as about the episode in general, cannot fail to intrigue.

Much writing on this topic concentrates on the arrival of new religions at Rome. "A Religion for the Empire" takes a very different perspective and asks why Roman state cult failed to spread throughout the empire. Its response to that questions proceeds from the observation that a religion in which *evocatio* made sense – that is, in which it made sense to bring gods to Rome in order to worship them – was in a poor position then to export cults to the empire at large. It connects recent studies of Roman myth, as narratives that seek to "place the gods," with related work in the study of so-called mystery cults and in the excavation of Roman religious law. In doing so, it seeks to connect a strictly antiquarian argument about Roman conceptions of immanence and the sacralization of landscape with a set of second-order comparative categories, especially Jonathan Z. Smith's distinction between locative and utopian cults. The essay concludes by seeking to clarify one fundamental difference between Christian and non-Christian imperialism and empire-building in the ancient and late-antique Mediterannean.

---

[24] On "polytheism and pluralism" see now Rüpke 2001a.

9 Religious Toleration in Republican Rome †

JOHN NORTH

It is a familiar fact that the religious tradition of Republican Rome did not depend on overt coercion of the citizen to maintain itself and its rituals. The censor did have powers to discipline those he found wanting in dutifulness towards the *sacra*; Cato once removed the public horse from one Veturius partly on religious grounds, though partly because he was too fat to ride it.[1] In the courts, irreligion on the defendant's part was one of the most familiar themes of abuse; Cicero[2] never underestimated the emotional impact of religious prejudice in his day. But the only formal charge of irreligion we hear of is that of *incestum* ["impious unchastity"] with a Vestal Virgin and, with that uncommon exception,[3] there is nothing at Rome which corresponds even to the Greek *asebeia* ["impiety, sacrilege"] proceedings, let alone to the persecutions or inquisitions of later Christian Europe. This does not prove that religious obligations were not felt or imposed through other forms of social pressure, but the apparatus of the State and the State's religious authorities seem not to have been directly concerned.

The situation cannot, however, properly be called one of religious toleration. Toleration today seems to pre-suppose (*a*) that a choice of religious commitments is available to the individual; (*b*) that the authorities disapprove of possible choices which the individual might make; and (*c*) that a deliberate restraint is imposed for moral reasons

---

† Originally published in *Proceedings of the Cambridge Philological Society* 25 (1979), 85–103.
[1] Cato, *ORF*[3] fr. 72; cf. H.H. Scullard, *Roman Politics*[2] 160, 261; A. Astin, *Cato the Censor* (1978) 81–2.
[2] The accusation of irreligion is made against virtually all his enemies, e.g. Verres (*in Verrem* 2.4.1–7 and *passim*), Clodius (*de Domo Sua* 104–9), Vatinius (*in Vatinium* 14), Antonius (*Philippic* 2.78–84).
[3] The only occasions in the late Republic are the trials of 114/3 BC (Asconius 45–6C; Cicero, *de Natura Deorum* 3.74; cf. Broughton, *MRR* II.114) and that of 73 BC (Cicero, *in Toga Candida*, and Asconius 91C; Plutarch, *Cato Minor* 19.3; *Crassus* 1.2; *MRR* II.114).

on the action to which that disapproval would naturally give rise.[4]
If this is the right kind of definition, then the whole complex is in-
applicable to the republican religious situation, in which there are no
such fundamental choices for the individual to make. You might, of
course, choose to make your vow to one deity rather than another,
but you could not make an act of commitment to a new cult, which
would cut you off from the old ones; there are no alternative religious
systems available. Despite this, there are good reasons for sticking
to 'toleration': there is no other word available and the problem is to
decide how far this avowedly modern terminology can be applied in
the cases where the senate does act as a 'persecutor'.

For there are indeed circumstances in which the Roman State acts
against religious aberrations within its authority. It can ban religious
practices of which it disapproves (as the banning of human sacrifice
in 97 BC[5] and, later, in certain provinces);[6] or it can expel the priests
and practitioners of foreign cults of which it disapproves (as the
Chaldaeans in 139[7] and the Isis cult later on);[8] or it can forbid
Roman citizens to take part in particular, even official, rituals (as
the ban on participation in the Magna Mater cult shows);[9] or it can
forbid particular acts (such as ritual self-castration).[10] If none of these
actions led in practice to a campaign of persecution, so far as we
know, this was not through the senate's inhibitions about banning
the practices or, presumably, enforcing their ban. We certainly do
not know at any period of any theoretical principle of allowing
plurality of worship or belief. The toleration, if that is what it was,
was a function of situation not theory.

It is for this reason that the limits of the senate's toleration take on

---

[4] For an analysis of the modern usage, see Bernard Crick, *Journal of Comparative Politics*
6 (1971) 144–71; especially 156–7; for an overall discussion of tolerance and intolerance in
the Ancient World, A.D. Momigliano, in S.C. Humphreys, *Anthropology and the Greeks*
(1978) 179–92.

[5] Pliny, [*Nat.*] 30.12 '... senatus consultum factum est ne homo immolaretur ...' [("a decree
of the Senate was passed, forbidding humans from being sacrificed"), i.e. sprinkled with meal,
so as to be rendered sacred, then killed, and finally selectively burnt]. Both the context in Pliny
– the discussion of magic – and the use of the technical term *immolare* suggests that it was
magical sacrifices which were forbidden rather than the State's official burial of pairs of
Greeks and Gauls; this was not technically *immolatio* and had taken place in Rome less than
twenty years before with full priestly approval (Plutarch, *Quaestiones Romanae* 83). But cf.
C. Cichorius, *Römische Studien* (1922) 6–12.

[6] F. Schwenn, *Die Menschopfer bei den Griechen und Römern* (1915) 185–7 (= RGVV XV,
3).

[7] Val. Max. 1.3.3; Livy [*Epit. Ox.*] 191; Servius *ad Aen.* 8.187; cf. K. Latte, *Römische
Religionsgeschichte* 275.

[8] Latte (n. 7) 282–3; Cichorius (n. 5) 198.

[9] Dion[ysius of Halicarnassus *Ant. Rom.*] 2.19.5; cf. Latte (n. 7) 260.

[10] Val. Max. 7.7.6; Obsequens 44: cf. T. Mommsen, *Römisches Strafrecht* (1899) 637.

a particular interest as definitions of their habitual non-interference. The actions mentioned above are mostly taken against alien forms; but the senate would in any case describe as alien whatever it saw fit to suppress. 'Alienness' by itself explains nothing, because the Romans were willing at almost all stages of their history to accept foreign cults and practices:[11] evidently, something more is needed to provoke action. Our best opportunity of studying their toleration is afforded by the greatest exception to it – the suppression of the Bacchanalia in 186 BC. On that occasion the regime certainly did emphasize the inconsistency between Bacchic practices and the *mos maiorum*, ["ancestral custom"] while Livy's account, though it does not stick to a single version, does attribute the origins of the movement to the activities of an anonymous Greek priest and missionary.[12]

There seems no hope at all that much progress can be made towards understanding the motives of the persecutors. The information we have is simply inadequate to provide the answers we need: we have no access to the plans or calculations of the senators and no accurate information as to membership of the Bacchic groups either in point of numbers or social composition or geographic distribution. If the question asked is why the senate acted as it did, the answer can only be a generalized guess. The question to which this paper is addressed is rather what is new to the Roman experience in the structure and organization of the cult of Bacchus at this date.[13]

The main facts of the story are not in dispute. The consul of 186, Sp. Postumius, reported to the senate about the cult of Bacchus, on the basis of information which he had just received. The senate set up an investigation (*quaestio*) in the hands of the consuls and this was eventually extended to the whole of Italy, Roman and allied alike. Large numbers of those who could be proved to have been initiated into the cult were arrested and some of these put to death. The senate drew up a set of regulations to be imposed in the future,

---

[11] *PBSR* 44 (1976) 1–12.

[12] 'Graecus ignobilis … sacrificulus ac vates [("an ignoble Greek … a priestling and a prophet"], Livy 39.8.3. For the alternative version, which is different though not necessarily irreconcilable, cf. 39.13.8–10.

[13] The religious issues raised by the crisis have attracted a good deal of discussion in the last forty years, building on the more philological debate of the thirties (cf. below n. 17). The most important contributions are: G. Méautis, *RÉA* 42 (1940) 476–85; J. Béquignon, *RA* 17 (1941) 184–98; A. Bruhl, *Liber Pater. Origine et expansion du culte dionysiaque à Rome et dans le monde romain* (1953) 82–116; M.P. Nilsson, *The Dionysiac Mysteries of the Hellenistic and Roman Age* (1957) 14–21; A. Toynbee. *Hannibal's Legacy* II (1965) 387–402; Clara Gallini, *Protesta e integrazione nella Roma antica* (1970); R. Turcan, *RHR* 181 (1972) 3–28: G. Franciosi, *Clan gentilizio e strutture monagamiche* ed. 2 (1978) 37–68. For fuller bibliography, Gallini, *Protesta* 46–7.

which made the Bacchic cult as it had existed illegal; they made it
difficult, if not impossible, for the god to be worshipped except in
very small groups, or in the context of official, well-established
festivals. Resistance on the part of the Bacchists continued in some
parts of Italy for a few years, though the Roman cell seems to have
been rapidly destroyed.[14] The action seems to have been both brutal
and successful, for we hear no more about the cult of Bacchus as a
problem, though it had been allowed to re-establish itself by the
middle of the first century BC.[15]

The cult as Livy describes it is one of orgiastic license, of ecstatic
ritual and of violence:

> At first, initiations were limited to a small number of people, but soon they
> began to spread amongst men and women alike. To the religious rites them-
> selves, drinking and feasting were added so as to widen the appeal. Their
> senses inflamed by wine, their moral scruples eroded by the darkness as well
> as by the mingling of different sexes and ages, they took to every form of
> corruption, each one finding to hand the gratification of his own particular
> desires ... Many atrocious acts were committed by guile, even more by
> violence – a violence easily concealed amongst the shriekings, the beating of
> drums and clashing of cymbals, which overwhelmed the cries of the victims
> in scenes of lust and bloodshed. (Livy 39.8).

Nobody would accuse Livy of taking a detached view of the proceedings. The problem is to discern reliable elements, if there are any.

Livy's account is based on two firm convictions, and his whole
narrative revolves around these convictions. The first is that the cult
was totally unknown to the authorities before 186 BC and that it
was suppressed immediately that its existence became known. The
second conviction is that the root of the senate's objection lay in the
crimes, the immoralities and the excesses of fanaticism consequent

[14] Livy's notices are neither clear nor consistent, but we know at least that there was trouble
in Apulia under three successive praetors in the late 180's – L. Postumius (Livy 39.29.8–9;
41.6–7; *MRR* I.372; 376), L. Pupius (Livy 40.19.10; *MRR* I.379) and L. Duronius (Livy 40.
19.9–10; *MRR* I.384). Although Livy 39.29 does not mention the Bacchanalia, there is good
reason to suppose that all these notices refer to continued Bacchic resistance in the area; it
would, however, be risky to trust the theory of [P. Wuilleumier, *Tarente des origines à la
conquête romaine* (1939)] 497–8, that *pastores* ["shepherds"] (39.29.8) refers to the grade of
boukoloi ["cattle-herd'" and, in context, "worshipper of Dionysus in his bull-form"], rather
than just shepherds. For discussion, Tenney Frank, *CQ* 21 (1927) 130; Toynbee (n. 13) 321–2;
Gallini (n. 13) 40–2.

[15] Though if the text of Valerius Maximus cited above n. 7 implies, as it probably does, that
the worshippers of Sabazius were amongst the groups expelled in 139 BC, this closely related
cult might be seen as affording continuity of Dionysiac worship in Italy. Some degree of continuity at least is indicated by the Bacchic temple or cult-house at S. Abbondio outside Pompeii,
cf. A. Bruhl (n. 13) 121–2; J. Collins-Clinton, *A Late Antique Shrine of Liber Pater at Cosa*
(1976) 22–3. The cult was allegedly re-introduced, or re-legalized, by Caesar: Servius *ad Ecl.*
5.29, the problems of which are fully discussed by Bruhl (n. 13) 124–32.

on the cult's practice. There can be no doubt that Livy's tradition does preserve some valuable elements,[16] but these central convictions must be open to scepticism. At root his tradition is hostile, if only because friendly opinion was rapidly eliminated in the persecution; nothing could be less trustworthy as evidence about a cult than the perceptions of the persecutors, who have to justify their actions before men and gods alike. The result in this case is a mixture of the fears and fantasies provoked by the Bacchists with the hard political necessity to provide legitimation for the very controversial decisions which the senate took. The decree whose text survives eventually provided the legal framework for the suppression, but that was not passed until much of the violent repression had already taken place at least in the *ager Romanus* ["Roman land": the category is both political and religious], if not the rest of Italy.[17] Altogether, Livy gives us a much better chance of understanding contemporary senatorial propaganda than of reconstructing what actually happened.

It is of the greatest importance to decide whether the cult was in fact a sudden arrival from abroad or whether it has any earlier history in Italy. The issue is, of course, complicated by the fact that in one form or another the god has a long pre-history on Italian soil,[18] and it is only the mystery-cult which can possibly be regarded as new. Livy's chapters give a vivid, dramatic picture of the discovery. A step-father, T. Sempronius Rutilus, had squandered the inheritance of his step-son, P. Aebutius, and wanted to find a way of avoiding rendering an account of his guardianship. So, by way of ruining him and getting a hold over him, he tried to have him initiated into the rites of Bacchus. For this purpose, the boy had to avoid sexual intercourse

[16] For a favourable evaluation of Livy's information on the cult at this date, cf. especially R. Festugière, *MÉFR* 66 (1954) 79–99 (= *Études de religion grecque et hellénistique* (1972) 89–110; for new and impressive archaeological support, J.-M. Pailler, *Mélanges Heurgon* II (1977) 731–42, who reports (739, cf. *MÉFR* 83 (1971) 384–92) 'un sanctuaire bachique aménagé entre 220 et 200 av. J.-C. et detruit par le feu 30 à 60 ans plus tard', discovered during the excavations at Bolsena. But there are still formidable difficulties in the way of knowing how far Livy is reflecting the cult of 186 and how far either later knowledge or literary influence. Worse, the destructive analysis by M. Gelzer (*Hermes* 71 (1936) 272–87 = *Kleine Schriften* III (1964) 256–69) of the relationship between the narrative of Livy and the text of the [Senate's decree concerning the Baccharalia] led to negative conclusions which have not yet been fully refuted.

[17] The famous decree *de Bacchanalibus* (hereafter called *SC*) is *ILS* 18 = *ILLRP* 511, in Degrassi, *Imagines* (1965) no. 392 (photograph). The problems of the text and its status were discussed by E. Fraenkel, *Hermes* 67 (1932) 369–96 = *Kleine Beiträge zur klassischen Philologie* II (1964) 447–75: G. Keil, *Hermes* 68 (1933) 306–12; W. Krause, *Hermes* 71 (1936) 214–20; but all three concentrated on the obscure and problematic last few lines, while only J.J. Tierney, *PRIA* 51 sect. C no. 5 (1947) 89–95 gives a detailed consideration of the substantive regulations in ll.3–22.

[18] The best survey is Bruhl (n. 13) 11–45.

for ten days before the ceremony; naturally, he had to explain all this to his mistress, Hispala Faecenia, but she turned out to know all about the cult, had herself been initiated some years before and passionately warned him against getting involved; she told him exactly what his step-father must be up to. Aebutius duly refused to undergo the initiation, whereupon his step-father and his mother threw him out of the house and he fled to his aunt Aebutia, a respectable lady living on the Aventine; on her advice, he went to the consul Postumius and told him the whole story. Thus, the secret came out.

It is difficult to believe at all in the story of sudden discovery. It may even be doubted whether Livy believed it altogether himself. The problem is very clearly seen in the speech which he gives to the consul Postumius: the speech implies that the hearers already know all about the Bacchanalia, not only by report, but because they have actually heard drummings and howlings in the night, though not known for certain what they meant; Postumius claims that what is new about what he is telling them is not the mere existence of the Bacchic groups, but the scale on which they are operating, the huge number of people mentioned by Hispala.[19] Even here he is cautious; he says that the conspiracy has not yet reached a position of strength, he is worried by its rate of increase. This makes the problem worse still, for by Hispala's own account she had not been near the Bacchic group for years;[20] and even if this is to be understood as a lie to cover herself, had the Roman authorities no better method of finding out how many people attended the meetings of a group they knew to be meeting regularly on the Aventine than to ask a freed-woman of dubious character?

Livy himself then is uneasy about the story of a sudden discovery and seems at least half aware that the cult could not have been altogether secret. He even hints that the senators themselves had more idea of what was going on than one might have thought, for their reaction on hearing the consul's news is, amongst other things, fear lest their own relations be involved.[21] As a matter of fact, we can be quite certain that the cult existed and that the senate knew of its existence long before 186. In the first place, Plautus refers to it as

---

[19] Postumius' speech is Livy 39.15–16, see especially 15.10; 16.3. Hispala's evidence to the consul *ib*. 13. 8–14, see especially 14: '... alterum iam populum esse' [("it is already another populace")].

[20] Livy 39.10.5; 12.6.

[21] Livv 39.14.4.

a familiar phenomenon, characterized by violence and secrecy.[22] Secondly, we now have a little evidence about the cult which existed in Etruria at this date, evidence of a kind which implies that it was public and recognized.[23] Finally, as we shall see later, the decree of the senate implies the existence of cult-centres and a group structure over a wide area of Italy; it is hard to see how such an organization could remain unknown for very long. It looks very much as if what happened in 186 was not that the senate discovered something it did not know, but that it decided to act against something it knew all too well.

On closer examination, Livy's narrative contains another element which is discordant with his own central conviction. The deposition which the freed-woman Hispala offers to the consul, and which represents the crucial evidence in provoking action, tells not of a new cult, but of the reform of an old one.[24] The account she gives is rather precise and circumstantial. She mentions four reforms: the frequency of meetings has been increased from three times a year to five times a month; the time of meeting has been changed from day to night; men as well as women have been introduced into the meetings; and initiation has been limited to those under twenty. The first three are attributed to a named priestess, Paculla Annia of Campania; the fourth is dated to the previous two years, but not attributed to Paculla Annia; her work is never in fact dated, but she is not mentioned amongst the leaders arrested in 186, while her son is, so it is possible that her work belongs some time earlier and that she was dead by the time of the persecution. In the case of the third reform, the introduction of men to the group, the fact is amply confirmed by the senate's decree, which plainly and repeatedly implies that both men and women were members of the same group and indeed allows a small, mixed group to continue meeting in the future.[25] This implies a definite change. In the form known to Euripides, the cult seems to have been exclusively feminine. In the Hellenistic period, this is no longer true, but there seem always to be separate male and female groups; we do not hear of a mixed group. On the other hand, in the later Italian cult we have a very clear example of a mixed *thiasos* [a company assembled to worship a god]

[22] Plaut *Mil.* 1016: *Bacch.* 53; *Amph.* 703–4; *Aul.* 408; *Cas.* 979–83. For discussion, Bruhl (n. 13) 111–13.
[23] S. Weinstock, *Glotta* 33 (1954) 309 n. 6; J. Heurgon, *RÉL* 35 (1957) 106–12; A.J. Pfiffig, *Religio Etrusca* (1975) 293–5; J.-M. Pailler (n. 16) 740–1, and n. 50.
[24] Livy 39.13.8–10.
[25] *SC* 19–22.

in the great Bacchic inscription from Torre Nova.[26] Livy's account, then, seems to be confirmed in a crucial particular. It seems very probable that the introduction of men, at least into the same group, was an innovation.

The case with nocturnal orgies is very different; these are characteristic of the cult already for Euripides and Sophocles.[27] There is also some evidence for night-time meetings in the Hellenistic period.[28] It has been argued that Hispala's claim is therefore false.[29] This seems to me to rest on a misconception. Hispala was not interested in presenting Paculla Annia as an innovator in terms of the history of Bacchism, but as a priestess who, under alleged divine instruction,[30] changed the cult as she found it in Italy. If we could hear Paculla Annia's version of the event, she would presumably call herself not an innovator, but a revivalist, seeking under divine guidance to restore the cult to its original vigour and truth. It would not be surprising, therefore, to find parallels in the earlier Greek cult for what were new practices in the tame Hellenistic one, against which she was reacting.

For the initiation of minors, we have no information about earlier times, but here once again Livy is strikingly in line with later Bacchic practice. It is known that the child holds a very important place in the cult and in particular child-initiation is shown on a series of works of art of Bacchic inspiration;[31] depictions of adult initiations are rare and even when they occur the initiate could as well be under as over twenty.[32] It should be noticed that this element in the story is not a casual mention; the point is repeated[33] and confirmed by the

---

[26] In Euripides' *Bacchae* 820, Pentheus is warned by Dionysus that the women will kill him if they recognize him as a man invading their orgy; cf. also 730: Nilsson (n. 13) 8–10 gives the epigraphic evidence for the sexually segregated *thiasoi* of the Hellenistic East; an exception is *OGIS* 735, from Thera, where an official and his wife are admitted together to the same thiasos; cf. *Anth. Pal.* 7.485, referring to a male leader at a female orgy, and *IG* 12.2.499 (Lesbos) where a male official keeps order (reading [*gunaikonomos*, "a regulator of women"] with Nilsson, *Griechische Feste* (1906) 282 n. 4). For the Torre Nova inscription, Vogliano and Cumont, *AJA* 37 (1933) 215–70 and below n. 49.

[27] Sophocles, *Antigone* 1151; Euripides, *Bacchae* 485.

[28] Nilsson (n. 13) 8–10.

[29] Bruhi (n. 13) 93–4 treats the whole of Hispala's account of the reforms of Paculla Annia with scepticism; doubt, of course, there must be, but the substantial objections do not stand.

[30] '... tamquam deum monitu' [("as if by admonition of the gods")], Livy 39.13.9

[31] The evidence was collected by Nilsson (n. 13) 78–88; 106–15; F. Matz, *Dionysiake Telete* (1963) (= [*AbhMainz*] 1963 n. 15), gives a detailed catalogue and analysis of the relevant representations: 8–9; 18–19. For other youthful initiates, Himerius, *Or.* 23.7–8; *IG* 2².11674.9–12. Festugière (n. 16) inferred from the fact of child initiation that the Bacchists believed in the afterlife, at risk if the child died uninitiated; other interpretations are likelier.

[32] For examples, Nilsson (n. 13) fig. 8 (p. 89); fig. 19 (p. 90); in the catalogue of Matz (n. 31), these are no. 4 and no. 12 respectively.

[33] Livy 39.10.6 and 13.14 – both times the point is made by Hispala.

initiations when very young both of Hispala and Aebutius;[34] finally, the consul mentions it in his speech.[35] It seems to be an integral part of the story. It is curious too that the rule quoted by Hispala is a rule against adult initiation; she implies that the intention is to catch the young and vulnerable, but this does not in itself explain why adults should be excluded. If the Bacchic groups were in fact trying to expand and proselytise, one would expect exactly the opposite, that new adults would be welcome; the effect of limiting initiations to minors would mean that most new recruits would be from the *familia* of existing members, which would tend to limit expansion, rather than encourage it. The picture of the cult towards which we thus move is very different from Livy's own.

The argument so far has rested on the technique of setting Livy against Livy; there seem to be inconsistencies between different elements of his account and probability suggests that the official story, which I have called his central conviction, ought to be rejected in favour of selected elements which imply a different development. In this particular case, the text of the senate's decree affords a hope of controlling these theories. The decree consists of a series of prohibitions, some of them subject to appeal, some not. It is forbidden for any ally to possess a Bacanal, a shrine to Bacchus; presumably, this means any permanent cult-centre where sacred objects could be kept or meetings held.[36] It is forbidden for any Roman citizen, Latin or ally to go to meetings of the Bacchant women; by inference, slaves and foreigners were permitted to do so.[37] Both these clauses are subject to appeal to the praetor and senate in Rome. There follows a series of regulations which offer no opportunity to seek exceptions; within a Bacchic group, there are to be no secular officials, no male priests, no common funds, no taking of an oath; it is clear, again by inference, that the group as such is allowed to survive and that female priests are allowable.[38] Finally, there are two clauses which make provision for the holding of *sacra* by the group, both subject to the

[34] Livy 39.12.1. (initiation of Hispala); 9.2 (of Aebutius, though it never actually happened).

[35] Livy 39.15.13.

[36] SC 28–30 by itself leaves little doubt that Bacanal in this document means a sacred building not a group or lodge: '... Bacanalia, sei qua sunt, exstrad quam sei quid ibei sacri est. ... faciatis utei dismota sient' [("... you should take care ... to dismantle such *Bachanalia*, such places of Bacchic worship as exist ... except any such as hold anything sacred')]. The best discussion of the problem is E. Fraenkel (n. 17) 369 n. 4 = 447 n. 4.

[37] For the interpretation of the phrase 'Bacas ... adiese' [("to be present at a Bacchic rite")] (SC 7–9), cf. Fraenkel (n. 17) 370–1 = 448–9.

[38] This point is apparently missed by Livy's version (39.18.8–9), otherwise not too inaccurate, but here implying that any priesthood became illegal.

appeal procedure, which probably make it legal for a group of fewer than five people, not including more than two men nor more than three women, to perform their rites without specific permission from the senate.[39]

The legislation limits itself to two main topics: the organization and property of the Bacchic group is one topic; the second is the status and number of those who attend Bacchic rites. Other topics might have been expected: the kind of rites to be allowed or forbidden; the age of initiation; the frequency and time of meetings. There might seem to be significance in the absence of reference to the alleged crimes; but, of course, the concern of the decree is with legislating on points where there had previously been no law; murder, rape and fraud and conspiracy to commit them were crimes already and called for no new legislation. Nor is it perhaps significant that there is no test of adherence to the State gods such as were employed against the early Christians, for no doubt Bacchants would have been willing enough to perform a symbolic sacrifice and there is no sign that they were charged with apostasy.

It is important to try to form an assessment of the senate's real intentions for the future of the Bacchic movement. It is clear that they had no intention of trying to enforce its absolute suppression and that they had no overt objection to individuals maintaining their devotion to the god. They certainly provide machinery whereby it would be possible for any existing *thiasos* to apply to continue its existence; but it is here that we meet the complete inadequacy of our record. Did *thiasoi* really apply to the senate for permission; if they did, did they ever get it? It must have been an expensive and even, in the circumstances, dangerous business to go to Rome, apply to the praetor and have a special decree passed through the senate. It could be argued that the whole procedure was designed precisely to make it impossible for any form of Bacchic worship to continue, while maintaining a pretence that anybody could so worship if they chose to ask for permission.

Whether or not one takes this cynical view about the senate's ultimate intentions, one can be certain about the forms which the senate intended that the cult should *not* take. Male priests are banned; male and female officials other than the priestess are banned; it is forbidden for the group to have a common treasury and it is forbidden

---

[39] These regulations are difficult and full of ambiguities, which arise partly from our uncertainty as to the exact meaning of the various activities forbidden by the different clauses, but partly from imprecise and inexplicit wording in the actual text. The best discussion is still that of Tierney (n. 17) 92–4.

for them to take any oath or vow. This tells us: (*a*) that groups organized on these lines had been part of the cult before this date, and (*b*) that the senate objected to such groups. That the cult should have been organized in these groups or *thiasoi* is exactly what we should expect to find from other Bacchic cults. It is obviously a relevant and important fact that the senate should be so interested in controlling the external form and property of the Bacchic group. But it would be quite wrong to argue that this interest in organization shows that they were indifferent about the religious issue; and indeed the religious issue seems to be quite inseparable from the political issue. Whatever they were afraid of, it made sense to strike at the units of organization on which the cults were based.

This evidence suggests the possibility of reconstructing what a Bacchic group before 186 would have been like, or at least the type which the senate had in mind as it passed the legislation. The group would have contained both men and women, initiated into the mysteries and bound by oaths;[40] it would have contained a mixture of social classes including both slave and free;[41] it would have had its own fund and its own cult-centre or meeting-place;[42] it would have had male or female priests and male or female lay officials, *magistri* or *magistrae*.[43] Caution is necessary here. It cannot be assumed that any particular group contained all the characteristics to which the senatorial legislators took exception. To take an example, the fact that Roman citizens are forbidden to 'go to the Bacchant women' – whatever exactly that means[44] – clearly implies that the senate saw a risk of such a thing happening; it suggests that citizens took some part in the rites at least in some groups, but it would obviously be quite wrong to infer that this was true of all or even of many groups. The senate may only have known of a few cases, but still have legislated to stop it happening again. It might be argued, in the same way, that the typical group specified above is simply a composite of what was happening in different parts of Italy. There is a second problem of method: the decree is in Latin, indeed in the Latin of solemn constitutional forms. The ritual of the Bacchists, though we have no direct evidence, was presumably conducted in Greek; so, for instance, if the

[40] For the oath, *SC* 13–14; for the presence of both sexes, which is not forbidden, *SC* 19–22.

[41] This is a probable, though not necessary, inference from the decree: *SC* 7–9 forbids Roman citizens, Latins and allies to go to the rites, while 19–22 assumes that men of some status will continue to be members of the group.

[42] For the fund, *SC* 11 'pecuniam ... comoinem' [("money in common, common fund")]; for the cult-centre, above n. 36.

[43] *SC* 10; cf. 11–12.

[44] Above n. 37.

decree makes a seemingly careful distinction between *magistratus* and *promagistratus* ["magistracy" and "substitute magistracy"],[45] we have no way of telling whether that corresponds to a real distinction in the groups, or is simply blocking a potential loophole out of legalistic caution.

Whatever the force of these reservations, at least an outline picture of the Bacchic group must survive any but excessive criticism. It seems perfectly safe to say that the religion which the senate faced was widely spread in Italy, that it was characterized by its organization into cells with (*a*) an oath taken by all full members, (*b*) a common fund administered within the group, (*c*) a widely-based membership, and (*d*) at least a simple form of articulated structure. There is one point on which we can be more specific: the regulations make a precise distinction between the office of *sacerdos* and that of *magister*; *magistri* are totally forbidden for the future, but only male *sacerdotes* are forbidden while female ones are not. The precision leaves little doubt that the two terms are distinct and not alternative titles for the same job in different groups. It can only be concluded that the typical group contained both to serve different purposes, that is that there were priests responsible for matters of cult and lay officials responsible for administration.[46] The senate allowed the former to continue and totally banned the latter.

The cell structure of the Bacchists is not, of course, any surprise. As early as the cult reflected in Euripides, the *thiasos* is the characteristic form of organization and Agave is to be seen as the priestess-leader.[47] Evidence from the Hellenistic and Roman periods shows the persistence of group organization, while the structure of the groups tends to become more complex as time goes by.[48] The *thiasos* of Agrippinilla, revealed in the Torre Nova inscription,[49] shows the development at its most florid, with a proliferation of grades of priests and processional functionaries. However, despite this elaboration, there seems to be no sign of a distinction between priests and *magistri*. There is sometimes a treasurer or an official to keep order

---

[45] *SC* 11–12. Since the whole clause is not only distinct from that forbidding *magistri* and *magistrae*, but actually separated from it by the clause dealing with funds, these can only be some category of minor officials corresponding to the very familiar *ministri* [attendents] in other *collegia*. Cf. F. Börner, *Untersuchungen über die Religion der Sklaven in Griechenland und Rom* I (1957) 9–29.

[46] If the order of the clauses can be trusted, it seems that the *magistri* were closely concerned with the common fund, as might be expected.

[47] Euripides, *Bacchae* 680–82.

[48] Nilsson (n. 13) 56–9.

[49] Vogliano and Cumont (n. 26) 237–63; Nilsson (n.13) 46–7; A. Geyer, *Das Problem des Realitätsbezuges in der Dionysischen Bildkunst der Kaiserzeit* (1977) 31–4.

at meetings,[50] but no sign of a structural division between priestly and non-priestly office. The implication seems to be that the Italian cult, banned by the senate in 186 BC, had developed its own characteristics, distinct from those of the Greek cults from which it must ultimately derive. The institution which will have mediated the change must be the *collegium*, the standard form of association in republican Italy.[51] The form of group organization we have postulated shows two points of contact with *collegia*: first, the presence of *magistri*; secondly, the presence of both slaves and freemen in the groups. Since the *collegia* provide the only form of religious group available in the period, there can be no serious question that they would have provided the model for the development. The argument provides further support for the view that Bacchism had been an established evolving system in Italy for a considerable period before the suppression of 186.

It is tempting to take a sharp distinction here and say that Bacchic groups represent the first 'specifically religious' groups in their society with which the Roman authorities had had to deal.[52] 'Specifically religious' seems a fair enough description; the individual joined to worship a specific deity in a specific way. It is not so certain that the description could not fairly be applied to earlier institutions, in particular to the more conventional *collegia*. They are the form of association with which the senate was already familiar and which it was accustomed to accept. If we are to establish why the Bacchist groups in particular offered a threat so menacing that the senate set itself to the destruction of the whole fabric, the question must be asked how these new associations differed from the old ones. There is no question that *collegia* do have a religious aspect and can indeed devote themselves to the worship of one deity; on Delos, at approximately this date, the different *collegia* are actually called after par-

---

[50] The second century AD records of the Athenian Iobacchi (Sokolowski, *Lois sacrées des cités greques* (1969) no. 51 = *IG* II².1368) refer, apart from a range of priestly offices, to a εὔκοσμος [*eukosmos*, "a well-ordered person, an acolyte"] (94–5; 136), a προστάτης [*prostatês*, "leader, presiding officer"] (13) and a ταμίας [*tamias*, "steward <of a god>, master of ceremonies"] (100; 123; 146; 150). The functions of the ταμίας and εὔκοσμος are obvious enough for εὔκοσμος cf. L. Robert, *Études anatoliennes* (1937) 58–9. The προστάτης is presumably more senior and might correspond to a *magister*. On the office, Schaefer, *RE* Supp. 9. (1962) 1298–9; 1303.

[51] J.P. Waltzing, *Étude historique sur les corporations professionelles chez les Romains* I (1895) 161–515; Gallini (n. 13) 81–6; F. Bömer (n. 45) 32–56, cf. 98–109, gives the fullest account of the involvement of slaves and freedmen; F.M. de Robertis, *Storia delle corporazione e del regime associativo nel mondo Romano* (1971) 71–7; J.-M. Flambard, *MÉFR* 89 (1977) 131–40.

[52] For the notion of 'specifically religious' cf. J. Wach, *Sociology of Religion* (1944) 109–30, in general, Gallini (n. [13]) 86–90.

ticular gods.[53] Such groups evidently performed other functions as
well, as burial clubs, professional guilds, social clubs or, at least later,
political clubs.[54] The fact is that not enough is known about them at
this, perhaps at any date to establish their primary purpose. It may
well be that they did exist for worship, though performing multiple
other functions; and, in a sense, the same could be said of Bacchic or
any other groups as well.

The comparison must be made more precise. One [point of differ-
ence] concerns the groups' organization: while *magistri* are common
to both types, the *magistri* of *collegia* perform both religious and
administrative functions;[55] the distinction we have found is a new
and characteristic development. Again, the degree of commitment
asked of the member when he joins is patently far higher; he is bound
by initiation and by oath; above all, he is given access through
mystery and intensified awareness to direct personal experience of
contact with the divine. The new structure corresponds to the inten-
sification of religious life and to the new place which religious experience will occupy in the life of the initiate. Another difference
concerns the basis of recruitment: *collegia* are based either on the
locality (*vici* or *pagi* ["districts or villages"]) or on the trade;[56]
Bacchic groups are joined through an act of free choice by the recruit.
Taken together, these differences transform the social meaning of
the group. By the mere fact that it consists of individuals who have
chosen a particular worship, it evades the normal basis of State
control and supervision of religion at all its levels. What is more the
external escape from State control echoes the internal escape of the
Bacchist in the practice of his religion from the normal regulations
and structure of the life of the city. Nor is this aspect of the situation
unknown to the Livian tradition. The consul's speech elaborates
the theme of how the cult's devotees are rendered unfit to perform
as citizens or soldiers of Rome.[57] The same theme is reflected in the

---

[53] For the gods to whom the various known *collegia* normally devoted their offerings, see
Flambard (n. 51) 134 n. 83; the Delian evidence is collected and briefly discussed by Degrassi
ILLRP 747–62; for full discussion, cf. P. Bruneau, *Recherches sur les cultes de Délos à l'époque
hellénistique et à l'époque impériale* (= *BÉFAR* 217) (1970) 585–620, Flambard (n. 51)
134–40.
[54] See especially A. Lintott, *Violence in Republican Rome* (1968) 78–83.
[55] Very rarely a *collegium* has a priest as well as a *magister*: cf. W. Liebenam, *Zur Geschichte
und Organisation des römischen Vereinswesens* (1890) 319 no. 60; cf. 287.
[56] Flambard (n. 51) 131–3.
[57] Livy 39.15.13 'hoc sacramento initiatos iuvenes milites faciendos censetis, Quirites?'
["Have you considered, Roman citizens, that these young men, after being initiated through
this rite, are to be made into soldiers?"].

allegation – false no doubt – that the Bacchists' oath bound them to perform any acts demanded of them, however criminal.[58]

The obscurities of the situation in general would be greatly diminished if it were possible to make a firm connection between the Bacchists and some particular social class or group, best of all perhaps if it could be shown to be anti-Roman or anti-élite in its inspiration. The attempt to find such a connection has given rise to sharply divergent views. Toynbee,[59] in a remarkable chapter of *Hannibal's Legacy*, sought to place religious development in the context of the social and economic transformations of second-century Italy; he treated the Bacchists fundamentally as an escapist movement, based on other-worldly expectations, and supported by oppressed and uprooted peasants and slaves. Fr. Bömer,[60] on the other hand, argued that as far as the evidence went the cult seemed to be primarily an upper-class preserve, or at least that slaves would not have been allowed to be group members or initiates. Clara Gallini[61] was really the first scholar who appreciated the full complexity of the evidence to be dealt with and offered an analysis of the adherents, despite their divergent social and geographic contexts, as all members of 'marginal' groups.

The fact is that our evidence gives us a dizzying collection of pointers in different directions. In Apulia, the suppression of the cult takes on the form of a slave-war, which continues for some time.[62] In Etruria, as we have seen, the evidence implies a degree of public acceptance and support at a high level.[63] In Rome and Campania, the names of those involved seem to suggest that at least the leadership came from well-off, though not top-ranking families;[64]

---

[58] Livy never quite goes so far as to assert that the oath was a formal undertaking to commit crimes, but he implies so repeatedly (cf. 13.11; 16.5; 18.3). It seems more probable that the oath was, like other known mystery-oaths, primarily intended to secure the secrecy of the mystery; for the surviving evidence on these, R. Reitzenstein, *Die hellenistischen Mysterien-religionen*[3] (1926) 192–7, who elaborates, and perhaps over-elaborates, the parallel between the soldier and the initiate. A modern analogy both to the importance attached to the oath and to the controversy over its significance is provided by the oath of the Mau Mau; cf. Bryan Wilson, *Magic and the Millennium* (1973) 259–68.

[59] *Hannibal's Legacy* II (1965) 387–400.

[60] Bömer (n. 45) III (1961) 132–4.

[61] Gallini (n. 13) 30–44.

[62] Above n. 14

[63] Above n. 23.

[64] The ringleaders, according to Livy's account, are Atinii and Cerrinii, from Rome and Campania respectively. For the origins of the Cerrinii cf. Schulze, *Zur Geschichte lateinischer Eigennamen* (1904) 467–8 (= *Abhandlungen der Kgl. Gesellschaft der Wissenschaften zu Göttingen* 5 no. 5); *RE* 3.2.1985–6 (Münzer). They are best known from Pompeii. The Atinii *de plebe Romana* came to Rome from Aricia (Cic. *Phil.* 3.16), though they also are connected with Pompeii and indeed one of their number (Maras Atiniis) is named on an inscription from the Bacchic chapel near Pompeii (Bruhl (n. 13) 86). The family has a remarkable political

this is also precisely the picture which emerges from Livy's narrative
of the discovery, if that can be trusted at all, since it is placed in a very
specific milieu – a well-off group of families living on the Aventine –
and offers no hint of socially revolutionary ideas.[65] To put it rather
crudely, such information as we have about Bacchic groups cuts
across all the obvious boundaries of Italian life at the time: city/
country; Roman/non-Roman; slave/free; young/old; Latin/Greek;
élite/non-élite. The evidence obstinately resists division across any of
these lines. Of course, the record is far from being adequate for any
firm conclusion; but this only makes it more impressive that the few
adherents we do hear about should come from such varied backgrounds. Perhaps the senate's disquiet might have been caused in
part by the very fact that the movement did not fit into the accepted
categories – it was not just the slaves, or just the women, or just the
young bloods, but an unpredictable mixture.

The position taken up in Gallini's book is to emphasize the apoliti-
cal nature of the movement.[66] Drawn as they are from widely different groups, but all feeling themselves oppressed by the structures
of the contemporary social situation, the devotees of the cult are
brought together by their common need to retreat from realities
too unpleasant to be borne. They have no purpose but escape.
Nevertheless, the movement is seen, as in any kind of Marxist
perspective it must be seen, as the product of contemporary social
developments and in particular the emergence of gross social dis-
parities. Its characteristic is its failure, as compared with the slave-
revolts fifty years later,[67] to develop into direct revolutionary action.

There is at least a paradox here. If it is true that the Bacchists were
in revolt against the structures of contemporary life and saw in the
rituals of possession the hope of a new freedom, how ironical that
they should immediately create a new institution so much in the
mould of city life and so very structured in its organization. We ought
not to underestimate the position which their situation conferred on
the *magistri* or the leaders of the groups; once an individual had
undergone initiation, he must have become vulnerable in relation to

---

history in Rome (cf. *RE* 2.2105–6 (Klebs)): first heard of in 211 (*MRR* 1.270), they attain three
praetorships between 195 and 189 (C. Atinius Labeo, *MRR* I.340; C. Atinius Labeo – 190,
MRR I.356; and C. Atinius – 188–6, *MRR* I.369; 371); but after the death of the third in the
course of 186 (Livy 39.21.4), no office-holding Atinius is known until 131. No doubt the guilty
Atinii were from less distinguished parts of the *gens*, but at least the suggestion is strong that
their activities were a severe electoral handicap in the years which followed.
    [65] Discussed best by Gallini (n. 13) 32–6; cf. A. Merlin, *L'Aventin dans d'antiquité* (1906).
    [66] Gallini (n. 13) 86–90.
    [67] See on this [Gallini (n. 13)] 127–31.

the political authorities of the city and hence increasingly dependent on the group and the group's authorities for support in all aspects of his life. The process by which the leaders of unorthodox groups acquire power over the membership is well understood in other societies and there is no reason to see this situation as in any way different.[68] At this level, the intention of those who joined the groups ceases to matter; their weakness and their social discontent can be exploited in the interest of the leadership. It may be that the movement was fundamentally a movement of women and of lower-class men,[69] without an integrated political purpose, but that the leadership consisted of upper-class men in very small numbers, but with definite political purposes. Or again, it may be that this was not the case, but that the senate feared it might be or feared that it might come to be.

In terms of their own attitudes, therefore, the Senate might be said to be solving a political problem or at least a problem of the control of power. But the distinction of political as against religious action is in this context plainly misleading; and in the perspective of religious history the origin of the trouble is best seen in terms of a change in the nature of religious organization, that is the creation for the first time of groups of specifically religious function. The possibility of religious persecution and the end of the period of 'naive toleration' follow more or less inevitably on the change of organization. The significance of the change has been obscured by Livy's implicit belief that the arrival of the cult of Bacchus was sudden, that it was essentially a foreign invasion shallowly rooted, easily eradicated and hence without any significance in the long-term religious history of Italy. Where any significance has been seen at all, it has been as yet another sympton of the spiritual decline of the State cult, which was laying itself open to such wild, if genuinely religious, opposition.

The implication of the above argument is that the process which leads to the creation of Bacchic groups should be treated as an important step in the development of Italian religious life. It is a step which, as far as our sketchy record goes, has few immediate consequences; the persecution seems to have succeeded and comparable groups are not heard of until decades later.[70] Even if it could be

---

[68] Indeed, Livy's narrative itself shows some awareness of these possibilities, since the whole plot turns on the need to make the young Aebutius vulnerable to pressure, or rather blackmail, from his step-father.

[69] For this social pattern in possession cults outside the control of the central institutions of the society, cf. I.M. Lewis, *Ecstatic Religion* (1971) 100–17.

[70] [cf.] n. 78.

shown that the religious impulses, revealed by the Bacchanalia affair, were diverted into other channels, religious associations seem to play no part; we can say at least that they never again present the republican regime with a major political problem, which would bring them to the notice of our sources. But in terms of a broader view of religious developments from 200 BC to AD 200, the emergence of specifically religious groups must be seen as a central characteristic of the period. They came from outside Italy; they were perhaps supported to start with by foreign communities; but in the end religious life in Italy, as in the rest of the Empire, was transformed. In Christianity, the process reached its fulfilment, with an autonomous institution capable of carrying its own hierarchy, its own value-system and asking the total commitment of its members.

If Bacchism should be seen as a step in this direction, it is only a short step. There was no question of a professional priesthood, no question of the devotee rejecting or subverting the worship of the old gods or abandoning the basic tenets on which the State rested. All the same, taking initiation was making an act of commitment of a different order from any act of choice possible in the traditional system of Rome. With the possibility of such choice, the relationship between religion and society already began a process of change. In the traditional order, all aspects of life, all public and private activities, all kinship groups and families and clubs, had a religious or ritual aspect to them. Both Roman and Greek observers regarded the omnipresence of divination and sacrifice as one of the most marked characteristics of the Roman way of life.[71] While the whole of life was therefore saturated with religious observances and religious rules, there were no major institutions which were religious in their central purpose.

The religious changes of the later republic may be seen as two correlated processes. The first is the retreat of the sacred from areas in which it had previously had its place; the second is the emergence of institutions solely devoted to religion. The first was much noticed by our ancient informants and treated as a symptom of the deterioration of religious life;[72] perhaps the most obvious example was the retreat of the taking of auspices from public life.[73] The second, if noticed at all, was seen essentially as the intrusion of foreign

---

[71] Polybius 6.56.8; [Dionysuis of Halicarnassus *Ant. Rom.*] 2.63; Cic, [*Div.*] 1.28 'nihil fere quondam maioris rei, nisi auspicato, ne privatim quidem, gerebatur' ["Once upon a time, practically nothing of importance was done, not even privately, without taking auspices"].

[72] Varro, [*Ant. Div.* fr. 2a]; Cic [*Div.*] 1.27–8; 2.73–4; [*Leg.*] 2.33; [*Nat. Deor.*] 2.9–10.

[73] Latte (n. 7) 264–5.

practices and therefore yet another symptom of the deterioration of religious life.[74] What is really disguised behind this moralizing language is a transformation of the relationship between religion and society. At other periods, in other places, similar developments are called 'secularization';[75] the term is slippery in meaning and highly emotive in its implications for different writers.[76] It would undoubtedly raise more confusion than light to attempt a comparison between republican Rome and post-medieval Europe, where again the retreat of the sacred sphere can be co-ordinated with the emergence of separate, autonomous spheres of religious and secular activities. But the concept of secularization would serve at least to remind us that we have to think in terms of the emergence of new religious forces as well as the retreat of old ones.

The process can perhaps be understood better in relation to developments in other areas of second-century society, where again we can detect the evolution of autonomous structures and specialised roles for individuals within those structures. The most obvious example in the late republic is the history of the army and of the role of soldiers and commanders within it, as it changes from a militia to a professional army within a few decades.[77] The Bacchic phenomenon, however short-lived, suggests that the same mechanisms are at work in the religious sphere. Bacchism itself with its cells, officials, rituals and rules looks like a step towards the differentiation of religious life; meanwhile, in the internal functioning of the groups, we have found a parallel tendency towards the specialisation of roles for individual group-members; and, at yet a third level – that of ritual – the oath-taking, the initiatory experience and the rituals of possession symbolize the separation and specialisation of the individual's experience. His mystical experience turns him towards a new

---

[74] For Varro's reaction to the cult of Isis, cf. Cichorius (n. 5) 198.

[75] The issue is of course central to much of the religious sociology of the modern world; for recent discussion cf. David Martin, *Archives européennes de sociologie* 10 (1969) 192–201; Peter Berger, *The Social Reality of Religion* (1969) 111–30; Michael Hill, *A Sociology of Religion* (1973) 228–66.

[76] Larry Shiner, *Journal for the Scientific Study of Religion* 6 (1967) 207–20, distinguishes six different usages of the word.

[77] For the application of the conception to the late republican period, Keith Hopkins, *Conquerors and Slaves* (1978) 74–96; he discusses the army, education and the development of law and the profession, the third being much the most difficult to argue. Differentiation in the religious sphere in fact corresponds to the third of Shiner's (n. 76) definitions of secularization. For the use of the concept to provide an evolutionary framework for religious history, cf. R. Bellah, *American Sociological Review* 29 (1964) 358–74 = R. Robertson (ed.), *Sociology of Religion* (1969) 262–92; the situation we are discussing would correspond to the transition from *archaic religion* to *historic religion* in his scheme, though he is not, of course, describing a historical process so much as analysing a sequence of ideal types.

conception of the world and the powers which dominate it, a conception shared with the new group, but a diversion from the integrative effects of the traditional, public rituals of the State and its priests. It is thus of some interest, for Livy's day if not for the second century as well, that the Bacchist's oath of commitment to his religion is seen analogously to the soldier's oath of commitment to his commanders.

I have tried to show that the emergence of persecution as a new possibility depends on the arrival of effective religious choices and that in turn on the emergence of religious associations devoted to religious purposes and bearing a particular religious message. If this is true, if the Bacchic groups are in fact the expression of new and continuing forces towards religious change, it becomes impossible to believe that the senate simply suppressed the process by a few weeks' violence. Again, it is Gallini who has tackled the historical problem of continuity, arguing that the religious forces acting as a medium of protest are diverted into different channels. She sees the essence of the phenomenon in the super-human model which Bacchism affords and argues that it is succeeded in this role by the cult of the charismatic leader as expressed in the tradition about Scipio Africanus and the great dynasts of the late republic.[78]

But should we really believe that Bacchism as such did disappear? and, from the whole of Italy? There is, of course, little or no evidence of its existence after 186, but then there are only shreds of evidence before 186 either.[79] It is the fact of persecution and that alone which makes the cult a sensational object of interest for a year. Just as, in early modern England, the beginning and end of witchcraft trials marked neither the beginning nor end of witchcraft,[80] so it may well be with the Bacchists. Even the decree does not propose the total destruction of the groups and it seems a most insecure assumption (for it can be no more than that) that the regulations were sustained with total rigour throughout Roman Italy from 186 onwards. It seems far likelier that the groups would have gone underground and the senate waited to see whether renewed action would be necessary. If so, then the fact may well be that the passage of years brought a situation in which the senate discovered that the groups did not after

---

[78] Gallini (n. 13) 97–120.

[79] For such evidence as there is, above n. 15. An additional, perhaps suggestive fact, is that the head of Bacchus appears on the coinage of the Italian confederates during the Social War (Sydenham, *The Roman Republican Coinage* nos. 628; 641). If this means anything, it suggests that Bacchus became, at least after 186, associated with the resistance to Roman power and that this association was remembered; but it cannot in any way prove cultic continuity.

[80] Keith Thomas, *Religion and the Decline of Magic* (1971) 540–51.

all constitute a political threat, while the groups themselves learned how to live with the Roman authorities without attracting unwanted notice.

The truth is, of course, that we have only a fragment or two of information by which to judge the religious history of Bacchism and of the general tendency towards forming religious associations. One or two observations may help to put the problem in perspective. First, the assumption that group-cults are generally borne by foreign immigrant communities should be treated with serious reserve. It may be so; but it should be remembered that if our knowledge of the cult of 186 were derived from the notice of an *epitomator* – 'Bacchanalia, sacrum Graecum et nocturnum, omnium scelerum seminarium ...'(Livy, [*Periochae*] 39 [:("the Bacchanalia, a nocturnal, Greek rite, a seedbed of every crime")] – we should certainly assume that this was another cult wholly supported by immigrants. It is only Livy's full account, with its discordant details, which warns us to be more careful. In the case of Sabazius, Attis and Isis, we have no such warning. Secondly, the events of 186 leave little doubt of one thing: there is already in second-century Italy a 'market' for new religious experiences and new forms of religious organization.[81] If this is true, it is not so important whether the sequel be pictured as one of continuity, or rather of total suppression, followed by repeated re-fertilisation from the East. This is a secondary question and one which cannot be answered on the evidence we have available. The really important conclusion is quite secure: 186 established both new religious possibilities and a new pattern of authoritarian response.

---

[81] Cf. Berger (n. 75) 141–52.

10 *A Religion for the Empire*[†]

CLIFFORD ANDO

I INTRODUCTION

The Flavian municipal law has been called remarkable for what it omits: the extant chapters make no allusion to priests and no reference to the concrete actions of the provincial governor or the emperor.[1] It is also remarkable for what it takes for granted. Consider, for example, the oath stipulated for town magistrates. Each was to swear openly "in an assembly by Jupiter, the divine Augustus, the divine Claudius, the divine Vespasian Augustus, the divine Titus Augustus, the *genius* of Imperator Caesar Domitian Augustus and the *dei Penates*" that he would act in accordance with the law and in the best interest of the town (*Lex Irnitana* 26; cf. chapters G, 59, 69, and 73).[2] Similarly, while the law almost undoubtedly allowed decurions to establish their city's official calendar anew each year, it presumes that among the *feriae*, holidays, of each city will be days set aside *propter venerationem domus Augustae*, "for the veneration of the imperial house" (*Lex Irnitana* 31; cf. chapters 79, 90, and 92).[3] These clauses have analogs in earlier municipal legislation, and so they have a place in the history of Roman governance, both in its extension into municipal life and in its acculturative effects.[4] But the presence of Jupiter and the *dei Penates* in Irni, Malaca, and Salpensa also presents a theological problem, for these

---

[†] Originally published in A. J. Boyle and W. J. Dominik, eds, *Flavian Rome: Culture, Image, Text* (Leiden: Brill, 2003), pp. 323–44.
[1] Galsterer 1987: 79–80 and 87.
[2] I cite the *Lex Irnitana* and the *Lex Malacitana* from González 1986. On the relationship of extant laws to a postulated *lex Flavia municipalis* see Galsterer 1987, 1988: 83.
[3] Rüpke 1995: 544–55; Scheid 1999b: 390–3.
[4] For control of the calendar at Urso see *lex coloniae Genetivae* chapters 70–1 and 128; for the oath and the location in which it should be administered see *lex coloniae Genetivae* 81 and *Tabula Bantina* ll. 17–18 and 24, and cf. Thomas 1990: 146 n. 19. On the social- and religious-historical importance of municipal legislation see Galsterer 1987, 1988; Scheid 1999b; Ando, forthcoming a.

were cities of Latin status, and if the Romans knew anything about the *dei Penates*, it was that they were worshipped at Lavinium, where they themselves had chosen to reside.[5]

The list of gods charged with superintending the magistrates of Flavian municipalities should surprise us at least as much as the presence of the Capitoline triad at Urso. And, to be sure, the spread of peculiarly Roman cults has long been studied as one part of the formation of Roman *Reichsreligion*, but scholars have generally assumed that it was not Jupiter or the Penates but the emperor who provided the Empire with its only shared deity.[6] This assumption has historically rested on one or both of two subsidiary claims. First, Roman cult of the late Republic was devoid of true – read "personal" – religious significance and its effective domain was that of politics. Hence Roman paganism survived and flourished under the Empire *as* imperial cult only because it had long since abandoned its agricultural, domestic roots and become a formal, secular *Loyalitäts-religion*.[7] Second, Graeco-Roman religion was properly the religion of the *polis*, and the structures and concerns of any particular religion – its priesthoods, participants, and liturgies – were homologous with the social and political structures of its city-state.[8] The application of this model to the Roman Empire is doubly problematic. On the one hand, the binarisms inherent in it, between public and private and center and periphery, necessarily situate diaspora cults and imperial cult in competition with or in opposition to traditional religion.[9] And

---

[5] Valerius Maximus 1.8.7: *Referam nunc quod suo saeculo cognitum manauit ad posteros, penetrales deos Aeneam Troia aduectos Lauini conlocasse: inde ab Ascanio filio eius Albam, quam ipse condiderat, translatos pristinum sacrarium repetisse, et quia id humana manu factum existimari poterat, relatos Albam voluntatem suam altero transitu significasse* ("I will now relate something known in its own time, which has been passed down the generations: Aeneas settled at Lavinium the *deos penetrales* that he had brought from Troy; then, when they had been moved to Alba by Ascanius his son, who founded that city, they sought out their ancient repository; since it was considered possible that this had been the work of human hands, they were carried back to Alba and displayed their will by a second return"). For the connection of the *dei penerales* to the *dei Penates* see Dionysius of Halicarnassus 1.67.1–3, the scholia vetustiora on Juvenal 4.60 and cf. on 12.70; Servius on *Aeneid* 1.270 and 3.12, and *Origo gentis Romanae* 17.2–3. On the Penates in general see Dubourdieu 1989; on their worship at Lavinium see ibid. 219–29 and 319–61, and esp. Thomas 1990.

[6] Fears 1981 is an important exception; Goodman 1994: 20–37 is one of the few attempts to explain this in religious – albeit Christianizing religious – terms.

[7] Warde Fowler 1911; Beaujeu 1955: 28–9; Latte 1967: 25–6 and 31–2. Scheid 1985: 95–127 is perhaps the most sophisticated essay of this kind.

[8] Sourvinou-Inwood 2000; Frankfurter 1998: 33–6 and cf. 97–144; Woolf 1997: 71–7 [see now above, pp. 40–4].

[9] North 1992 and Rives 1995: 173–249 attempt to explain the gradual demise of *polis*-religion in the larger community of the empire: religious identity became less politically charged just as increasingly cosmopolitan societies atomized individuals and presented them with more choices to which to adhere. The argument, both in North's model and in Rives' application, begs serious questions. Gordon 1990 provides a powerful argument for the continued vitality

on the other, its relevance to the new political and religious reality of a united Mediterranean is far from obvious, not least because the nature and function of cities and conduct of municipal life under a universal Empire were hotly contested issues already in antiquity.[10]

The tension between Roman center and peripheral municipalities at the level of patriotism and political philosophy had analogs in religious thought and practice, and it is at this point of rupture that the explanatory power of *polis*-religion might best be tested.[11] In devising such a test, we would do well to consult ancient theorists of *polis*-religion and to consider the challenges that confronted their theoretical and theological presuppositions as the social and political structures of the Graeco-Roman city-state evolved in the larger, ecumenical community of the early Empire. Romans at Rome had long developed sophisticated and self-conscious mechanisms both for importing and naturalizing foreign cults and for sanctioning and controlling the religious life of subject populations.[12] In situating gods in time and place, this body of theory and law may have facilitated and explained the removal of cults and cult-objects to Rome; it may likewise have rendered it difficult or impossible to export any particular Roman cult to the Empire at large.

2 THE ROMAN PEACE AND THE DIASPORA CULTS

The Mediterranean world in the Flavian period was integrated as never before.[13] This can be studied in a number of ways: trade, migration, communication, and, as a special example of the latter two, the spread of diaspora cults. In each of these areas we must observe and

of civic religion under the empire and, therefore, for the continuing usefulness of the *polis*-religion model.

[10] There are, of course, other ways to unpack the history of histories of Roman religion: Smith 1990: 1–53 concentrates on the Protestant, Christian roots of religious studies; Scheid 1987 traces the interdependence of hostility to polytheism and charges of formalism; while Durand and Scheid 1994 and Bremmer 1998 discuss the influence of late nineteenth-century anthropology on twentieth-century studies of Graeco-Roman paganism. There have been few studies of Roman religion, and fewer still of imperial cult, that have not been loosely functionalist.

[11] Cities in political life and thought under the empire: Ando 1999, 2000: 406–12, summarizing a long argument. For a very different view of the effectiveness of ancient communicative practice see Bendlin 1997: 38–44. On Roman interference in local religious life see Bendlin 1997: 54–63; Frateantonio 1997; Beard, North, and Price 1998: 211–44; de Casanove 2000.

[12] On Roman interaction with foreign religions see Wissowa 1912: 38–60 (who perhaps overestimates the historical value of late Republican theological taxonomies that were even then inscribed in religious-historical narratives) 1916/19; Scheid 1995, 1998; Cancik 1999.

[13] Shaw 2000, whose investigation presupposes a notionally unified empire; cf. Ando 2000: 131–74 and 303–35.

attempt to control the bias of our literary sources. Aelius Aristides, for example, praised Rome for its receipt of all the goods of the world, as though all trade passed to the capitol like the spokes of a wheel (*Oration* 26.11). The elder Pliny, on the other hand, considered the Empire-wide trade in medicinal plants one of the crowning glories of the Roman achievement: thanks to the *immensa Romanae pacis maiestate*, the "immense majesty of Roman peace," such plants are transported *ultro citroque humanae saluti in toto orbe*, "here and there throughout the world, for the health of humankind." "Thus do the gods seem to have given the Romans to human affairs, like a second sun" (Pliny *Nat.* 27.2–3: *adeo Romanos velut alteram lucem dedisse rebus humanis videtur*).[14] The actual dynamics of early imperial trade were far more complex.[15]

The same bias bedevils the study of migration, travel, and tourism.[16] Not only do most testimonia concern the flow of eastern migrants into Rome, they deplore it. Juvenal's famous lament that "the Syrian Orontes flows into the Tiber and dumps therein its language and customs, its badly-strung harps, horns and foreign drums, and the girls who sell themselves by the Circus" is but one voice in a chorus that grew more shrill as the tide rose and won (*Sat.* 3.62–5; cf. Seneca *Dial.* 6.2–4, also employing a compound of *fluo* metaphorically, and Tacitus *Ann.* 15.44.3, writing of Rome that in it *cuncta undique atrocia aut pudenda confluunt celebranturque*, "every sort of crime and disgraceful activity flows from everywhere else into the city and is practiced there"). Athenaeus is almost alone is celebrating the capital as "an encapsulation of the world" (τὴν Ῥώμην πόλιν ἐπιτομὴν τῆς οἰκουμένης) precisely because one could count so many individual cities within the οὐρανόπολις, the "heavenly city," of Rome, where ὅλα ἔθνη, "entire nations," settle, each in its own place (Athenaeus 1.20c–d).[17] But we would do well to remember that not all migrants were voluntary, and they did not all

---

[14] See also *Nat.* 14.2. On this aspect of the Roman achievement in ancient thought see Ando 2000: 54, 347–8, and 389.

[15] Harris 2000: 710–31 and Andreau 2000: 784–6, both citing earlier work.

[16] On migration see Cracco Ruggini 1980; Frier 2000: 808–11; Noy 2000; on tourism see Foertmeyer 1989.

[17] Cf. Dionysius of Halicarnassus 2.18.2–19.3: καίπερ μυρίων ὅσων εἰς τὴν πόλιν ἐληλυθότων ἐθνῶν, οἷς πολλὴ ἀνάγκη σέβειν τοὺς πατρίουις θεοὺς τοῖς οἴκοθεν νομίμοις, οὐδενὸς εἰς ζῆλον ἐλήλυθε τῶν ξενικῶν ἐπιτηδευμάτων ἡ πόλις δημοσίᾳ ("Although innumerable races have immigrated to the city, each of which must worship its ancestral gods according to the customs of their native lands, the city itself has avoided adopting publicly any of these foreign rites"). On immigrant communities in early imperial Rome see MacMullen 1993.

travel to Rome.[18] The resolution of the Jewish War produced ninety-seven thousand slaves (Josephus *Bell. Iud.* 6.420); already under Tiberius the Senate had sent to Sardinia some four thousand slaves "infected" with Jewish and Egyptian superstitions, and two generations later under Nero, Cassius Longinus would claim that Roman households contained *nationes in familiis ..., in quibus diuersi ritus, externa sacra aut nulla sunt*, "entire nations of slaves, practicing diverse cults and foreign rites, or none at all" (Tacitus *Ann.* 2.85.4 and 14.44.3).

The political stability and social order that allowed migration and trade to reach new heights also supported the spread of cults, most famously those of eastern origin: Cybele, Isis, Atargatis, Mithras, Jupiter Dolichenus, and Christ. This, too, became a topos of imperial literature. Lucian's Menippus, for example, flew to heaven, only to find himself seated next to Pan, the Corybantes, Attis, and Sabazius, "foreign and dubious gods" (*Icar.* 27), while his Momus found the council of the gods attended by Attis, Corybas, Sabazius, Mithras, Anubis, and Apis (*Deor. Conc.* 9–10). Their astonishment was matched only by their dismay. Christians took a more positive view: Christ had appeared in the reign of Augustus so that his worship might spread more rapidly through a unified world.[19]

The importance of the diaspora cults in the Flavian period would be easy to overestimate. They once loomed large in histories of imperial religion. Looking for precursors to Christianity, scholars postulated a category of "oriental" or "mystery" cults that commingled soteriological messages with private, personal initiations.[20] As scholars have studied them in greater detail, the similarities of these cults have faded and their significance as a category has correspondingly diminished.[21] What is more, these cults traveled with immigrants and so moved mainly through shipping lanes; their worship was largely confined to cities and was far more common in Italy than elsewhere in the west.[22] But their dispersion, however quantitatively or geographically limited, nevertheless makes them the other to the locative cults of Graeco-Roman city-states. We need not be surprised that the diffusion of the mystery cults exhibits a pattern;

---

[18] Harris 1980; Andreau 2000: 721–2.

[19] Ando 2000: 48 n. 148.

[20] Burkert 1987: 1–3; Smith 1990: 31–3, 43–5, and esp. 55–84.

[21] Smith 1990: 116–43; Turcan 1996: 3–9; cf. Burkert 1987: 30–53.

[22] See Malaise 1972: 159–70 and 255–354, and id. 1984, on Egyptian cults in Italy and the western provinces; Stark 1996: 129–45 on Christianity. Turcan 1996 discusses the spread of each cult he surveys, relying (as do all) on the data collected and published in M. J. Versmaseren (ed.), *Études préliminaires aux religions orientales dans l'empire romain*.

nor is the pattern itself unexpected. It is the mere fact of their diffusion, in a world of *poleis* and *polis*-religions, that requires explanation.

For a cult to spread, several factors must converge.[23] First, the relationship between its god or goddess and material reality, in the form of both landscape and cult-object, must be of a kind that permits him or her to be in many places at once. In other words, a cult needs to presuppose theories of materiality, representation, and immanence that allowed worship to have meaning even for practitioners aware of the potential and perhaps of the real, simultaneous replication of their liturgy in multiple locations.[24] Extant narratives of the arrival of Cybele in Rome, for example, stress that the Romans brought from Pessinus "the stone that the natives said *was* the goddess" (Livy 29.11.7). If the *baitulos* that arrived in Rome in 204 BC in some irreducible and exclusive way was the goddess, Cybele's precinct at Pessinus should have closed or, at least, diminished in importance. It did neither. Recognizing further hypostases beyond or between the divine and the corporeal, worshippers of Cybele at Rome and Pessinus might well have understood that Cybele somehow was, and yet was not coextensive with, their black stone; and, in the same way, she might also have been, but not been identical with, other black stones.[25]

Second, the god or goddess must be willing to be known and worshipped by individuals, either without mediation or through the intervention of individuals chosen by the god or goddess himself or herself.[26] The institutional structures of such cults need not be heterologous with the social and political structures of the *poleis* in which they are practiced, but their epistemological basis will be quite different from that underpinning *polis*-religions. At Rome, the selec-

---

[23] I set aside two problems. First, there is that of "choice," which has been central to much recent English-language literature on imperial religion, as though the only precondition for the spread of a cult were the appeal of its practices and doctrines. This seems to me conceptually at best a secondary concern. Then, of far greater theoretical interest, there is the willingness of gods to accept new worshippers: the ancient world knew cults whose members dispersed but whose god did not desire new worshippers.

[24] For two different approaches to this problem, see Ando 2002a, forthcoming b.

[25] Ando forthcoming b.

[26] Consider Apuleius *Met.* 11.1–5: Lucius prays in ignorance of the identity of the *regina caeli*, and it is Isis who chooses to reveal herself, to offer instruction, and to accept Lucius as an acolyte. In the words of the priest, Lucius should henceforth "devote himself to the obedience of our *religio* and subordinate his will to the yoke of priestly office" (*Met.* 11.15: *teque iam nunc obsequio religionis nostrae dedica et ministerii iugum subi uoluntarium*). In contrast to most literature on this passage, which considers the perspective of the human and asks whether he "converted" (e.g. Bradley 1998, citing much earlier work), I would emphasize the agency of Isis.

tion of priests by an electorate composed of citizens, the authority of those priests within their bailiwick, and the power of the Senate in religious life presume the gods' willingness that humans and the institutions humans establish should determine, for well or ill, the shape and structure of their worship. Varro thus did not subordinate gods to men – he did not subscribe to the sort of ontological inversion that Augustine accused him of (Augustine *Civ.* 6.4; Varro *Ant. Div.* fr. 2a).[27] Rather, as a participant in, and theorist of, one particular *polis*-religion, he understood its institutions to be the product of Romans, past, present, and future, striving after *cognitio deorum*, "knowledge of the gods" (*Ant. Div.* fr. 3).[28] The sources of knowledge and lines of authority between god, goddess, priest, and initiate in any religion that had a mystery – and the diaspora cults of the Hellenistic and Roman worlds share this feature, at least – were fundamentally different.[29] If it is true that Christianity as an "organization" ultimately came "to overthrow and eliminate" the "*polis* system," that process must be explained not simply in social and political terms.[30] The one religion's "organization" and the other's "system" expressed something fundamental about the way their gods existed in the world, and it is to the gods in Rome that we now turn.

3 ROMAN THEORISTS OF ROMAN RELIGION

Before expressing surprise that the imperial city did not impose or export its religion on or to its provinces, we would do well to ask

[27] Augustine's deliberate misreading of Varro's ontology is paralleled by his distortion through selective quotation of the epistemological concerns voiced by Varro at the outset of books 14 and 15 of the *Antiquitates Rerum Divinarum* (frr. 204 and 228).

[28] Of course, Varro seeks such knowledge because one cannot obtain any particular benefit if one does not know which god can supply it. That should not obscure the importance of his emphasis on knowledge, a concern matched or surpassed by the terminological precision observed by Cicero when establishing the epistemological basis of each speaker in *De Natura Deorum*. What Balbus and Cotta in that dialogue appreciate is not simply that knowledge of the gods is acquired historically and incrementally, or that increasing knowledge affects the performance of cult, but that historical events become paradigmatic – are read as the actions of the divine in the world – only through the authoritative, interpretive powers of the Senate. Consider, too, Valerius Maximus 1.1.1b: the zeal of "our ancestors" not simply for preserving but also for expanding efficacious cult (*non solum servandae sed etiam amplificandae religionis*) was so great that the then-flourishing city officially sent the scions of ten leading families to Etruria in order to learn the science of their rites (*percipiendae sacrorum disciplinae gratia*).

[29] On the mysteries of mystery cults, see esp. Burkert 1987: 2–3 and 66–88, arguing that their similarities derive not from their putative, "oriental" origins, but from Greece. See also Smith 1990: 121–5, distinguishing between locative and utopian mystery religions: Eleusis is an example of the former, and Cybele, always ideologically foreign, an example of the latter.

[30] Burkert 1987: 51.

what its religion was. According to Cotta the pontiff, speaking in Cicero's third book on the nature of the gods:[31]

> Cumque omnis populi Romani religio in sacra et in auspicia divisa sit, tertium adiunctum sit si quid praedictionis causa ex portentis et monstris Sibyllae interpretes haruspicesve monuerunt, harum ego religionum nullam umquam contemnendam putavi mihique ita persuasi Romulum auspiciis, Numam sacris constitutis fundamenta iecisse nostra civitatis, quae numquam profecto sine summa placatione deorum inmortalium tanta esse potuisset. (*Nat. Deor.* 3.5)

> The entirety of the *religio* of the Roman people is divided into rites and auspices, to which is added a third thing, namely, whatever warnings the interpreters of the Sibylline books or *haruspices* issue for the sake of fore-knowledge on the basis of portents and omens. I hold that none of these *religiones* should ever be neglected, and I have persuaded myself that Romulus and Numa laid the foundations of our state by establishing the auspices and rites, respectively, and that our state could never have become so great without the goodwill of the immortal gods.

Dividing his *Divine Antiquities* into five triads, Varro devoted the first triad *ad homines*, "to men," and employed within it a threefold division similar to that advocated by Cotta: one book treated the pontifices, another the augurs, and the last the *quindecimviri sacrorum* (Varro *Ant. Div.* fr. 4).[32] In adopting this definition of *religio*, Cotta the pontiff – and Cicero the augur – decisively rejected the premise from which Velleius the Epicurean and Lucilius the Stoic began, namely, that religion originates with the impression left by the gods in the minds of all humans (Cicero *Nat. Deor.* 1.43 and 2.5), and he did so for the same reason as Varro treated human matters before divine ones: *quod prius extiterint civitates, deinde ab eis haec instituta sint*, "because communities arise first, and then the things instituted by them." And since Varro was not inquiring into "the entirety of the nature of gods and humans," he investigated human and divine affairs *non quantum ad orbem terrarum, sed quantum ad solam Romam pertinet*, "not with reference to the entire world, but only as far as pertained to Rome alone" (*Ant. Div.* fr. 5). Varro and Cicero thus divorced the *religio* of the city, both in its praxis and its theology, from the naturalist theologies then in vogue in philosophical discourse.[33]

---

[31] On this passage see Pease 1958: 984–6.

[32] The odd man out in this tradition is Valerius Maximus 1.1.1a.

[33] See, for example, *Nat. Deor.* 1.1: the *quaestio de natura deorum* is necessary *ad moderandam religionem*, "for the regulation of religion," but it is not itself *religio*. The most famous and influential way of distinguishing types of religion and religious discourse was Scaevola's "tripartite theology" (Augustine *Civ.* 4.27); note Varro's insistence that the third kind of theology, the "civic," *accommodata est ad urbem*, "is appropriate for civic life" (*Ant. Div.* frr.

The separation between *religio* as praxis, even praxis with attendant theological presuppositions, and theological speculation, what
Cicero calls the *quaestio de natura deorum*, the "inquiry into the
nature of the gods," found expression elsewhere in the regulation of
religion, not least in the boundary drawn between public, private,
and foreign cults.[34] To label something private or foreign did not
necessarily stigmatize it: the Bacchanalia may have been *peregrina
sacra*, but they were abolished only when their conduct *ad per-
niciosam uaesaniam iret*, "passed into pernicious madness" (Valerius
Maximus 1.3.1; trans. Shackleton Bailey). Likewise, the Senate did
not impugn *Fortuna* of Praeneste when it forbade Lutatius Cerco to
consult her: it simply decided *auspiciis patriis, non aliengenis rem
publicam administrari … oportere*, "that the *res publica* should be
administed under national and not foreign auspices" (Valerius
Maximus 1.3.2). And the banishing of the Jews by Cornelius
Hispalus found its most characteristically Roman expression in the
removal of their *aras privatas e publicis locis*, "of their private altars
from public spaces" (Valerius Maximus 1.3.3; see also Livy 25.1.12
but cf. Cicero *Leg.* 2.25). Dionysius of Halicarnassus thus observed
a Roman habit of mind when he separated the *religio* of the state and
the religions of Rome's immigrants and confessed τὴν Ῥωμαίων
μᾶλλον ἀποδέχομαι θεολογίαν, "I prefer to accept the theology of
the Romans" (2.20.2; cf. 2.19.3).

Dionysius praised the Senate for policing the moral boundaries
of the religion of the Roman people (2.19.5; cf. 2.19.2–3). But the
spread of Roman religion will have depended on the maintaining
of boundaries of a different kind, on the situation of the gods in the

---

7–10). On the tripartite theology see Pépin 1956; Lieberg 1973, 1982. On the development of
a Roman theological discourse see Beard 1986; for attempts to situate Varro and Cicero in an
era of rampant religious speculation see Jocelyn 1982; Momigliano 1987: 58–73 [reprinted as
Chapter 7, above]; for a fascinating attempt to situate that religious speculation in its political, imperialist context, see Cancik 1999.

[34] See also Festus s.v. *sacrum* p. 424L: *Gallus Aelius ait sacrum esse, quocumque modo
atque instituto civitatis consecratum sit, sive aedis, sive ara, sive signum, sive locus, sive pecu-
nia, sive quid aliud, quod dis dedicatum atque consecratum sit; quod autem privatis suae religionis causa aliquid earum rerum deo dedicent, id pontifices Romanos non existimare sacrum.
At si sua qua sacra privata succepta sunt, quae ex instituto pontificum stato die aut certo loco
facienda sint, ea sacra appellari, tamquam sacrificium; ille locus, ubi ea sacra privata facienda
sunt, vix videtur sacer esse* ("Aelius Gallus says that those things are sacred which are consecrated according to the custom and law of the city, whether a building or altar or statue or site
or money or anything else which is dedicated and consecrated to the gods; whatever private
individuals dedicate to a god out of religious scruple, that the Roman *pontifices* do not consider
sacred. But any private rite that must be performed on a particular day or at a particular site
in accordance with pontifical law is nevertheless called sacred, like an offering; the site, where
those private rites must be performed, scarcely seems to be sacred"). Cf. Gaius 2.5 and Ulpian
at *Dig.* 1.8.9, both quoted below.

Roman landscape and on the consequent parsing of that landscape along several axes: temporal, political, juridical, and ontological. This feature of Roman religion is at some level well known and much researched.[35] But the principles underlying this system of mapping the world placed enormous obstacles before any attempt to export the *sacra populi Romani*. Put in different terms, Roman religion and theology lagged far behind the political and cultural developments engendered by the imperialist project. Between the polarities of importing gods through *evocatio* and sanctioning the continuation of a city's particular cults lay an enormous range of possibilities for which the *ius pontificale*, "pontifical law," could not account and of which it could not conceive.

4 THE PENATES AT LAVINIUM

According to an oft-related myth, Aeneas settled in Lavinium the gods that he had brought from Troy. When Ascanius subsequently founded Alba, he moved his ancestral gods to the new city of his people. The very next day, the gods were discovered back in their former *sacrarium*. "Since it was considered possible that this had been the work of human hands," the gods were moved again. "They made their will apparent by removing themselves a second time."[36] This tradition existed alongside the presence on the Velia in Rome of a residence for the Penates, attested already in Varro's list of the *Sacraria Argeiorum* and known to Dionysius and Livy (Varro *Ling.* 5.54; Dionysius 1.68.1–2; Livy 3.7.11, 5.30.6, and 45.6.5; but cf. Varro *Ling.* 5.144 and *Ant. Div.* XVab, as well as Livy 5.52.8 and Macrobius *Sat.* 3.4.11).[37] The myth does not recognize that temple. Within its narrative, the Romans accede to the *voluntas*, the "will," of the gods, and so continue throughout their history to travel to Lavinium to worship their ancestral gods in the city where they had chosen to reside (see, e.g., Asconius *Sc.* 19 (p. 21 Clark); Livy 5.52.8;

---

[35] Catalano 1978; Linderski 1986; Scheid 1995, 1996, 1999a.

[36] See n. 5. Compare CIL X 797: Sp. Turranius Proculus Gellianus was *praefectus pro praetore iure dicundo in urbe Lavinio, pater patratus populi Laurentis foederis ex libris Sibullinis percutiendi cum populo Romano, sacrorum principiorum populi Romani Quiritium nominis Latini, quai apud Laurentis coluntur* ("praetorian prefect for the administration of justice in the city of Lavinium, *pater patratus* of the Laurentine people, empowered in accordance with the Sibylline books to strike a treaty with the Roman people, and priest of the rites of the origins of the Roman people, the Quirites of the Latin name, which are celebrated among the Laurentines"). On the treaty and *pater patratus* see Livy 1.24 and Servius *ad Aen.* 9.52, together with Ogilvie 1965: 110–11 and 127–9; Thomas 1990.

[37] On the coexistence of Penates at Lavinium and Rome see Thomas 1990; see pp. 147–8 and 150 on their association with Vesta.

ILS 5004 and *CIL* X 797; Servius on *Aeneid* 2.296 and 3.12; and Macrobius 3.4.11).[38]

Lavinium was one among several sites at which "the thirty peoples of the Latin name" came together for common rites (Livy 2.18.3; Dionysius 5.12.3; cf. Festus s.v. *prisci Latini* 253L and Pliny *Nat.* 3.69, listing the *populi Albenses*), and scholars have long explained the existence of these multiple sites by suggesting that as hegemony over the cities of Latium passed from one city to another, so did the locus of its common festivals.[39] Yet the underlying assumption that the sacred and political topographies of Latium should be homologous fails, not least because it cannot explain why cults and rites were not moved as social, political, and economic energy shifted from city to city. The Roman explanation for the location of the Penates, on the other hand, centered on the *voluntas* of the gods themselves, and on the expression of that will through their presence-in-the-world. Of course, the myth may have evolved to explain a seeming anachronism; if so, we should confess that the myth was current and effective in the early Empire and beyond. Indeed, the anachronism must appear all the more violent if we accept the force of Yan Thomas' demonstration that the centrality of Lavinium in Roman myth and cult was a late development, and that "Lavinium" existed under the Empire as an elaborate fiction: it was no more and no less than a *religiosa civitas* with magistrates and priests but no citizens, a constructed and complex ancestor and double for Rome itself.[40]

The Penates' immanence in Lavinium was not transitory; rather, it was expressed through an identity with their images so complete that the narratives of this episode paradoxically employ the gods in metonymy for their idols. But to analyze the language in these terms is to evade a profound ontological and metaphysical problem by labelling it one of representation.[41] As Greeks and Romans knew of races that worshipped aniconic objects, so they knew of races whose gods did not live in their cities. Citing Xerxes' famous complaint that the Greeks trapped their gods within walls, Cicero affirmed Greek

---

[38] On the sacrifice of magistrates at Lavinium see also Scheid 1981: 168–71, esp. 171; Dubourdieu 1989: 339–61.

[39] Momigliano 1989: 65 and 85; Cornell 1989: 264–9 (discussing earlier work), 1995: 71–2. Oakley 1998: 538–71 surveys settlement of Latin relations with Rome after the Latin war. On Lavinium in particular and the history of its interactions with Rome in the late Republic and Empire see esp. Wissowa 1915: 21–33; Oakley 1998: 506–8, 513, and 560–1; Cooley 2000b.

[40] Thomas 1990; *religiosa civitas*: Symmachus *Ep.* 1.71.

[41] Gordon 1979: 7–8; Ando forthcoming b.

and Roman practice: wishing to increase piety toward the gods, the Greeks and Romans *easdem illos urbis quas nos incolere voluerunt,* "desired that the gods should inhabit the same cities that they did" (Cicero *Leg.* 2.26). To that end, the Romans consecrated *aedes sacrae,* sacred buildings, for the gods, whose actual *sedes* ("residences") were the inner rooms (Varro *Ant. Div.* fr. 70: *delubrum esse ... aut in quo loco dei dicatum sit simulacrum, ut, <sicut> in quo figunt candelam, candelabrum appellat, sic in quo deum ponunt, delubrum dicant* ("a *delubrum,* shrine, ... is a place in which an image of a god has been dedicated: so, just as the object to which people attach *candela,* candles, is called a *candelabrum,* a candelabrum, they call a *delubrum* that place in which they put a *deum,* a god"); cf. id. *Ling.* 5.160 and Festus s.v. *aedis* p. 12L).[42]

The Romans acknowledged and negotiated the place of the gods in the landscape through religious laws, which oversaw the use and management of space, the organization of time, and the performance of ritual. The intimate connection between these categories emerges with particular clarity in the speech of Camillus that closes Livy's fifth book:[43]

> Urbem auspicato inauguratoque conditam habemus; nullus locus in ea non religionum deorumque est plenus; sacrificiis sollemnibus non dies magis stati quam loca sunt in quibus fiant. (5.52.2)

> We inhabit a city founded after auspices were taken and rites of inauguration were performed; no place in it is not full of religious associations and of gods; as many days are fixed for solemn rites as there are places in which they are performed.

Camillus' argument against the Romans' decamping to Veii suggests that Rome is not "full of gods" merely because the Romans invited them to dwell there. On the contrary, the gods act both in the world and in time, and Roman myth merely concretizes in narrative a concern for topography, for the timely and timeless presence of the divine in the material world, that finds expression elsewhere in Roman thought in the use of *sacra* ("things consecrated to a god, and so belonging to or performed for that god") as a substantive to designate both objects and actions.[44]

This apparent blurring within religious thought of ontological

---

[42] Cf. Dubourdieu and Scheid 2000.

[43] On the founding of cities, see Servius on *Aeneid* 1.466 and 4.212.

[44] Roman myths as myths of place: MacCormack 1990: 9–13; Woolf 1997: 78 [p. 47, above]. *Sacra:* see Livy 5.51.9, where they are buried in the earth, and 5.52.4, where Camillus urges that *gentilicia* and *publica sacra* ["private, familial and public, state rites"] not interrupted by war not be interrupted in peace.

distinctions that contemporaneous philosophers would have dogmatically maintained is paralleled in Roman law on the sacralization
of space. According to Livy, the *pontifices* fleeing the Gauls buried
some sacred objects on the Capitol (5.40.7–8, and see Plutarch
Camillus 20.3–6); this legend is likely to be connected to the presence
on the Capitol of chambers and underground cisterns in which
ancient consecrated objects were stored when they were no longer to
be displayed or, in the case of decorative statuary, when they had
fallen from the temple that they once adorned (Varro *Ant. Div.* VIIb
= Gellius 2.10).[45] The sacrality of these objects required that their
disposal be conducted with due reverence, and their presence even
when buried sacralized the land. Yet these objects had been consecrated through human ritual action; they were not gifts of a god,
like Vesta's fire or the Salian shields. About the latter category of
objects, Camillus argued that a god's act of giving in itself sacralized
the site in which it took place (Livy 5.54.7: *hic Vestae ignes, hic
ancilia caelo demissa, hic omnes propitii manentibus vobis di,* "here
is Vesta's fire, here the sacred shields fell from the sky, here all the
gods are favorably disposed to you, so long as you remain"). On this
theory, myth narrates the history of the presence of the gods in the
world, and that presence, however transitory in its impression on
the sense-perception of contemporaries, revealed the gods' abiding
interest in, or attachment to, particular landscapes.[46]

The continued power of Varro's *signa vetera* implies a still more
profound and nuanced appreciation for the relationship between
gods and objects. It reflects, among other things, Roman belief that
humans should take cognizance of gods' attachments, and that man's
primary vehicle for doing so was ritual action, properly performed
(cf. Varro *Ling.* 7.88). In this context, what is worth emphasizing
is not the scruple with which Romans performed their rites and
observed procedure (for Roman reflections on this topic, see, e.g.,
Livy 5.52.5–12; Pliny *Nat.* 28.10). Rather, we should heed Pliny's
confession that the efficacy of prayers, correctly recited in a ritual
context, is much more than evidence merely that "the power of
omens is under our control." On the contrary: there exists "no
greater evidence of divine indulgence" than that the gods allow our
words and actions such authority (Pliny *Nat.* 28.17). Roman law on
the consecration of space, and on the limits of priestly power in that

---

[45] Cf. Thomas 1990: 150; on the continued reverence accorded sacred objects see Bouma
1993, treating Etruscan terracottas, and Glinister 2000.
[46] Cf. Lane Fox 1987: 102–67, a wide-ranging treatment of epiphany, esp. 127–41, on
place.

arena, reflects a similar respect for the ontological and metaphysical hierarchies inherent in the world:

> Sacra loca ea sunt, quae publice sunt dedicata, sive in civitate sint sive in agro. (1) Sciendum est locum publicum tunc sacrum fieri posse, cum princeps eum dedicavit vel dedicandi dedit potestatem. (2) Illud notandum est aliud esse sacrum locum, aliud sacrarium. sacer locus est locus consecratus, sacrarium est locus, in quo sacra reponuntur, quod etiam in aedificio privato esse potest, et solent, qui liberare eum locum religione volunt, sacra inde evocare. (*Ulpian at* Dig. *1.8.9.pr.-2*)

> Sacred places are those that have been publicly dedicated, whether in the city or in the country. (1) It must be understood that a public place can only become sacred if the emperor has dedicated it or has granted the power of dedicating it. (2) It should also be observed that a sacred place is one thing, a *sacrarium* another. A sacred place is a place that has been consecrated, but a *sacrarium* is a place in which *sacra* have been deposited. This could even be in a˙private building, and it is customary for those who wish to free such a place from its religious scruple to call forth the *sacra*.

The terminological precision inherited and maintained by Ulpian, and devised to honor the polarity of public and private so central to Roman religion, was understood to reflect, and perhaps to be, a human institution, one which must yield before the possible presence of a god in unconsecrated sacred objects.[47] It must have been, furthermore, the potential identity of object and god, however conceptualized, that justified the implied attempt to address a religious formula to an inanimate object.

The use of *evocatio* to desacralize a *sacrarium* in itself breaks down the boundary between public and private, not least because the power of sacralizing or desacralizing belonged to the domain of the *pontifices*. *Evocatio* is surely most famous for its use in "calling forth" the gods of besieged cities and inviting them to dwell in Rome.[48] The success of that ritual depended on two crucial things: the god or goddess had to be willing to move, and the Romans seemingly had to transport the cult statue of the god in question from its native city to its new home in Rome. To transfer the statue was to transfer the god: Livy, for example, believed not simply that Camillus promised a new temple to Juno, and that the Veientines failed to understand that Rome had promised new *sedes*, homes, to their other gods (5.21); his narrative of Juno's actual removal elides entirely the fact that the soldiers were (presumably) carrying not the goddess but

---

[47] Cf. Gaius 2.5–7 (quoted below), allowing that provincial soil not properly *religiosus* or *sacer* is nevertheless *pro religioso* or *pro sacro habetur*; cf. Livy 1.55.4, quoted below.

[48] On *evocatio* see Wissowa 1912: 43–50 and Blomart 1997.

her statue (Livy 5.22.5–7; a similar pattern is visible at Dionysius of Halicarnassus 13.3). And the emphasis laid on Juno's assenting to the move, with both gesture and voice, is correlative to the *voluntas* of the Penates: if *evocatio* looks for all the world like an antiquarian, theological justification for imperialism, the decision of the Penates to remain in Lavinium suggests the limitations on human agency and human will inherent in the epistemological framework and meta-physics of power in Roman religion.[49]

5 ROME, ITALY, AND EMPIRE

Evocatio helped to explain the centrality of Rome in the sacred topography of its Empire, and it did so by placing the gods in Rome, in accordance with their express desire.[50] But the need to situate the gods within the landscapes of Rome, Latium, and Italy, which *evocatio* satisfied, scarcely permitted the exportation of gods to Italy and the provinces; nor, indeed, is it obvious how or why a Roman committed to a theology of presence would have explained or justi-fied interfering in the conduct of cults outside the locus of Rome itself. As we have seen, the colonial and municipal charters of the Julio-Claudian and Flavian periods negotiate this problem with a brevity that bespeaks a common understanding. Whence might it have arisen, and how would it have been expressed?

The city of Rome had its own Latin temple and cult, correspond-ing to those of the Penates at Lavinium and of Jupiter Latiaris at Alba. According to Roman legend, Servius Tullius established the temple of Diana on the Aventine *commune Latinorum*, "for the Latin people to have in common" (Varro *Ling.* 5.43; see also Cato *Origines* fr. 58 Peter, Dionysius 4.26.4–5 and 4.49, and Livy 1.45.2). Servius reportedly himself wrote the law of the temple, which listed the cities it encompassed, their mutual rights, and the regulations of the cult. Dionysius of Halicarnassus saw an ancient copy of this law, and it

---

[49] Compare the tradition that develops around Tarquin's effort to *exaugurare* ("to desacral-ize") the Capitol: Festus s.v. *nequitum* (160L) (Cato *Originum lib.* 1 "*Fana in eo loco conpluria fuere: ea exauguravit, praeterquam quod Termino fanum fuit; id nequitum exaugurari*", "there were many shrines in that area; he desacralized them, except the shrine of Terminos; that could not be desacralized"); Livy 1.55.4 (the refusal of Terminus to move even when summoned forth, *evocari*, was taken as an omen), Dionysius 3.69.3–6 (the augurs were supposed to find out ἐὰν παραχωρῶσιν οἱ θεοί, "whether the gods would move"); see also Ovid *Fasti* 2.667–70 and Servius on *Aen.* 9.446: when it was discovered that the Tarpeian hill was littered with the houses of the gods, it was decided to summon the gods forth (*evocare*) to new temples; Terminus alone did not want to move (*discedere noluit*) and so remained. On a similar prob-lem in Roman religious epistemology, namely the formula *sive deus sive dea, in cuius tutela hic lucus locusve est*, see Scheid 1999a: 198–200 [above, pp. 182–84].

[50] Ando 2002b, cf. 2002a: 141–42.

subsequently served as a paradigm for the regulation of Romanizing cults in provincial colonies (Dionysius 4.26.5; cf. Festus s.v. *nesi* p. 164L).[51] At Narbo in AD 12, for example, the people of the Gallia Narbonensis dedicated an altar to Augustus. Having listed a few specific regulations, they allowed that *ceterae leges huic arae eaedem sunto, quae sunt arae Dianae in Aventino*, "the other laws for this altar shall be the same as those for the altar of Diana on the Aventine" (*ILS* 112, side B, ll. 20–2; identical wording is used on *ILS* 4907 and *CIL* 11.361).[52] The paradigmatic value of this law no doubt derived from its status as an ancient text governing a shared cult. About the original foundation we could ask: why Diana?[53] We should also ask: why the Aventine? The answer undoubtedly is that the Aventine lay outside the *pomerium*, the boundary established by the augurs that marked the limit of the urban auspices (Gellius 13.14.1–4 and Varro *Ling.* 5.143). The importance of the *pomerium* as a ritually established boundary would be impossible to overstate: implicated in it were a host of binarisms central to the conduct of Roman public life – urban and rural, civil and military, Roman and foreign – whose divisions were precisely drawn and rigidly observed, for all the difficulty of their reconstruction.[54] The temple to Diana, founded as a site of inter-city cult, had been deliberately situated outside the city of Rome as it was ritually and religiously defined, and it was its placement in that space that endowed its *lex* with continuing relevance.

The expansion of Rome and extension of the franchise taxed this metaphysical geography in a variety of ways, and the Romans devised a number of ways to accommodate these pressures. As Livy understood, even if through antiquarian reconstruction, the ritual of the *fetiales* originated in a period when Rome fought wars of purely local significance (1.32.6–14; cf. Servius on *Aen.* 9.52).[55] Polybius implies that the *fetiales* played little role in declaring war in the mid-second century (13.3.7); their importance had been revived by the time Octavian declared war on Cleopatra, if not before (Dio 50.4.4–5). According to a tradition first attested only obliquely under

[51] Wissowa 1912: 39.

[52] On the *leges* of altars see Wissowa 1912: 473–5.

[53] Romans cited the paradigm of the *fanum Dianae* at Ephesus: Livy 1.45.2 and *De Viris Illustribus* 7.9.

[54] Catalano 1978: 479–82, and Beard *et al.* 1998: 177–81 offer brief surveys of the issues involved; on the role of the augurs in maintaining the *pomerium* see esp. Linderski 1986: 2156–7.

[55] On the evolution and import of the ritual, see Wissowa 1912: 550–4; Ogilvie 1965: 127–36; Rüpke 1990: 97–117.

Augustus, the war against Pyrrhus forced the Romans to adapt the
ritual to the realities of transmarine warfare. "The Romans could not
find a place where they could perform through the *fetiales* this ritual
of declaring war" (*nec invenirent locum, ubi hanc sollemnitatem per
fetiales indicendi belli celebrarent*), so they forced a captured soldier
to buy a plot in the Circus Flaminius adjacent to the temple of
Bellona, outside the *pomerium*, and satisfied the law of declaring war
quasi in hostili loco, "as if in hostile territory" (Servius on *Aen.* 9.52;
cf. Ovid *Fasti* 6.203–8, Suetonius *Claudius* 25.5, and Festus s.v.
Vellona p. 30L).[56] This ritual had an essential correlative in the
Romans' symbolic seizure of some piece of an enemy's land on which
to place their camp and take the auspices (Varro *Calenus* [*Logistorici*
fr. 2 Semi = Servius *ad Aen.* 9.52]: *Varro in Caleno ita ait duces cum
primum hostilem agrum introituri erant, ominis causa prius hastam
in eum agrum mittebant, ut castris locum caperent*, "Varro in his
Calenus says that generals, when about to enter an enemy's territory,
out of religious scruple would first throw a spear into that territory,
in order to seize a place for a camp").

The distinction between Roman and hostile territory formed part
of a sacred topography determined by augural law and developed,
like the ritual of the *fetiales*, in an early stage of Rome's expansion.
"According to our *augures publici*," wrote Varro, "there are five
kinds of land: Roman, Gabine, peregrine, hostile, and indeterminate" (Varro *Ling.* 5.33: *Ut nostri augures publici disserunt,
agrorum sunt genera quinque: Romanus, Gabinus, peregrinus,
hosticus, incertus*).[57] In ossifying a taxonomy relevant to the earliest
stages of Roman history, these categories obviously reveal an inherent conservatism; they also concretize, once again, an essential
recognition of man's epistemological limitations. This mapping
within augural law was paralleled in pontifical law by a distinction
between Roman and provincial *solum*, soil. When Pliny wrote to
Trajan asking whether he could safely move a temple of the Great
Mother in Nicomedia, he attributed his hesitation to the lack of
a *lex* for the temple, "as the method of consecration" (*morem
dedicationis*) practiced in Nicomedia was *alium apud nos*, "different
from that practiced among us." Trajan responded that Pliny could
be *sine sollicitudine religionis*, "without fear of violating religious
scruple," as the *solum peregrinae civitatis capax non sit dedicationis*,

---

[56] The Senate met with returning, victorious generals and foreign embassies in the temple
of Bellona, precisely because it lay outside the *pomerium*: see, e.g., Livy 26.21.1, 28.9.5,
30.21.12.
[57] On these categories see Catalano 1978: 491–8.

quae fit nostro iure, "as the soil of a peregrine city cannot receive consecration as it is performed according to our law" (*Ep.* 10.49–50).[58]

Roman law was not static, and Rome's priestly colleges did not speak with a single voice. The interdependence of the sacred and political emerges with particular clarity in the definition of *municipalia sacra* preserved by Festus: "Those *sacra* are called *municipalia* which a people had from its origin, before receiving Roman citizenship, and which the *pontifices* wanted them to continue to observe and perform in the way in which they had been accustomed to perform them from antiquity" (Festus s.v. *municipalia sacra* p. 146L: *Municipalia sacra vocantur, quae ab initio habuerunt ante civitatem Romanam acceptam; quae observare eos voluerunt pontifices, et eo more facere, quo adsuessent antiquitus*).[59] The extension of the franchise necessarily extended and fundamentally altered the *pontifices*' domain. So, under Tiberius, the *equites Romani* wished to dedicate a statue to *Fortuna equestris* but were unable to find a temple to that goddess in Rome; they did find one in Antium. *Repertum est,* "it was discovered," that all the rites, temples, and idols of the gods in the towns of Italy were *iuris atque imperii Romani,* "under the law and power of Rome" (Tacitus *Ann.* 3.71.1). This assertion harmonizes so naturally with developments in politics, law, and culture that its rupture with the sacred topographies and theological bases of Roman Republican religion easily go unnoticed. It seems thus both intelligible and striking that it was the antiquarian emperor Claudius who enclosed the Aventine within the *pomerium* (Gellius 13.14.7).

---

[58] Cf. Gaius *Inst.* 2.5–7: *(5) Sed sacrum quidem hoc solum existimatur, quod ex auctoritate populi Romani consecratum est, ueluti lege de ea re lata aut senatusconsulto facto. (6) Religiosum vero nostra voluntate facimus mortuum inferentes in locum nostrum* ("That alone is thought to be sacred, which is consecrated on the authority of the Roman people, either by law or by decree of the Senate. We make things *religiosum* in private actions by bearing our dead to particular sites"). *(7) Sed in prouinciali solo placet plerisque solum religiosum non fieri, quia in eo solo dominium populi Romani est uel Caesaris, nos autem possessionem tantum vel usumfructum habere uidemur. utique tamen, etiamsi non sit religiosum, pro religioso habetur. (7a) Item quod in prouinciis non ex auctoritate populi Romani consecratum est, proprie sacrum non est, tamen pro sacro habetur* ("But on provincial soil it is generally agreed that the soil cannot be *religiosum*, since there ownership rests with the Roman people or with Caesar, while we seem to have only possession or use. Nevertheless, even if it is not *religiosum*, it is treated as though it were *religiosum*. Similarly, whatever in the provinces is not consecrated on authority of the Roman people is properly not sacred, but it is nevertheless treated as though it were sacred").

[59] Cf. Livy 26.34.12, from the plebiscite passed before the capture of Capua: the *pontifices* were ordered to adjudicate which of the idols and statues captured from the enemy were sacred and which profane.

6 THE MOST MANIFEST GOD

The emergent realities of political culture in the early Empire did more than bring the Penates to Irni. The continued creation of colonies of Latin status, like the imposition of the *lex Flavia municipalis* on pre-existing towns, testifies to a gradual development whose nodal points can be plotted in the ideology of colonization itself. Domitian did not found Irni *contra suspicionem periculi … ut propugnaculum imperii*, "against the suspicion of danger, as a bulwark of empire" (Cicero *Agr.* 2.73). The juridical status of its citizens, on the other hand, suggests that Domitian did not envision Irni as an *effigies parva simulacrumque quoddam*, "a small representation and kind of reflection," of Rome itself (Gellius 16.13.9). But the anachronistic use of juridical categories devised in a very different geographic reality, however idiosyncratically Roman, raised religious and legal issues whose contours have hopefully now been clarified.

After the death of Augustus, the colony of Tarraco built a temple for him and so provided an example for all the provinces (Tacitus *Ann.* 1.78.1). Other cities presumably learned of Tarraco's action in the same way as they learned of Mytilene's festival for Augustus: Tarraco told them about it.[60] What made it possible for these cities to share the emperor, and for the cult of the emperor to endure longer and spread further than those of the Penates or the Capitoline triad?[61]

Let us return to the Penates in Lavinium. A long and complicated tradition identified them with the Great Gods (Dionysius 1.67.3–4, citing Timaeus *FGH* 566 F59; Cassius Hemina fr. 6 Peter; Varro *Ling.* 5.58, *Curio de cultu deorum* fr. 1, *Ant. Hum.* fr. VIII Mirsch and *Ant. Div.* fr. XVab; Macrobius 3.4.6–10). Why were they called "Great?" "Because, having been moved from Lavinium to Rome, they twice returned to their place; because generals about to go to the provinces sacrifice first before them;[62] because no one knows their names; because they are felt to be *praesentissimi*, most present" (Servius on *Aen.* 3.12: *quod de Lavinio translati Romam bis in locum suum redierint: quod imperatores in provincias ituri apud eos primum immolarint: quod eorum nomina nemo sciat: quod praesentissimi sentiantur*). This last quality, that of immanence, of being present, is one the Penates seem to share with Isis: her first words to

---

[60] On Mytilene's publication of the decree establishing the festival see Ando 2000: 173–4; on similar advertising campaigns in the Hellenistic world, see Edmondson 1999: 78 and 85–6.

[61] On Capitolia outside of Rome see Barton 1982; Ando 2000: 208.

[62] Cf. Wissowa 1912: 164 n. 6.

Lucius were *En adsum,* "Behold! I am present" (Apuleius *Met.* 11.5). But the Penates were present only in Lavinium, while Isis revealed herself to Lucius where he was. The failure of any Roman cult to become a religion for and of the Empire should therefore not surprise us. The gods of the capital made their homes there, and they became attached to its soil.[63] In the end, Rome gave to the Empire as a whole two very different gods, who shared one essential quality. So long as his power endured, the emperor's immanence in his ubiquitous portraits made him ἐπιφανέστατος, "the most manifest," of the numinous powers of this world.[64] His chief rival, who became his chief patron, was likewise present everywhere in potentiality and promise: *Ubi enim sunt duo vel tres congregati in nomine meo, ibi sum in medio eorum,* "Wherever two or three of you are gathered in my name, there I am in their midst" (Matthew 18:20).[65]

REFERENCES

Ando, C. 1999. "Was Rome a *polis?*," *Classical Antiquity* 18.1:5–34.

Ando, C. 2000. *Imperial Ideology and Provincial Loyalty in the Roman Empire.* Berkeley.

Ando, C. 2002a. "Vergil's Italy: ethnography and politics in first-century Rome," in Levene and Nelis 2001:123–42.

Ando, C. 2002b. "The Palladium and the Pentateuch: towards a sacred topography of the later Roman empire," *Phoenix* 55.3–4:369–410.

Ando, C. forthcoming a. "Administration and acculturation in the Roman west."

Ando, C. forthcoming b. "Idols and their critics," in J. B. White (forthcoming).

Andreau, J. 2000. "Commerce and finance," *CAH*[2] XI:769–86.

Barton, I. M. 1982. "Capitoline temples in Italy and the provinces (especially Africa)," *ANRW* 2.12.1:259–342.

Beard, M. 1986. "Cicero and divination: the formation of a Latin discourse," *JRS* 76:33–46.

Beard, M. and J. North (eds) 1990. *Pagan Priests.* London.

Beard, M., J. North, and S. Price 1998. *Religions of Rome. Vol. 1: A History.* Cambridge.

Beaujeu, J. 1955. *La religion romaine à l'apogée de l'Empire.* Paris.

---

[63] Wissowa 1912: 86–7 and cf. 408.

[64] Mitthof 1993; Ando 2000: 232–53, 268–9, 295–6, 394–5 and 407.

[65] I conducted the research for this essay with the support of a fellowship from the American Council of Learned Societies and completed it while visiting Wolfson College, Oxford. I am grateful to those two institutions for their support. For comments and questions my thanks to Sabine MacCormack.

Bendlin, A. 1997. "Peripheral centres – central peripheries: religious communication in the Roman empire," in Cancik and Rüpke 1997:35–68.

Bergmann, B. and C. Kondoleon (eds) 1999. *The Art of Ancient Spectacle.* Washington DC.

Bispham, E. and C. Smith (eds) 2000. *Religion in Archaic and Republican Rome and Italy.* Edinburgh.

Blomart, A. 1997. "Die *evocatio* und der Transfer fremder Götter von der Peripherie nach Rom," in Cancik and Rüpke 1997:99–111.

Bouma, J. W. 1993. "Architectural terracottas unearthed in a votive deposit in Borgo le Ferriere ('Satricum'), 6th–3rd centuries BC," in Rystedt, Wikander, and Wikander (1993):291–7.

Bradley, K. 1998. "Contending with conversion: reflections on the reformation of Lucius the ass," *Phoenix* 52:315–34.

Bremmer, J. 1998. "'Religion,' 'ritual' and the opposition 'sacred vs. profane': notes towards a terminological genealogy," in Graf 1998:9–32.

Burkert, W. 1987. *Ancient Mystery Cults.* Cambridge, MA.

Buxton, R. (ed.) 2000. *Oxford Readings in Greek Religion.* Oxford.

Cancik, H. 1999. "The reception of Greek cults in Rome," *Archiv für Religionsgeschichte* 1.2:161–73.

Cancik, H. and J. Rüpke (eds) 1997. *Römische Reichsreligion und Provinzialreligion.* Tübingen.

de Casanove, O. 2000. "Some thoughts on the 'religious Romanization' of Italy before the Social War," in Bispham and Smith 2000:71–6.

Catalano, P. 1978. "Aspetti spaziali del sistema giuridico-reliigioso romano: mundus, templum, urbs, ager, Latium, Italia," *ANRW* 2.16.1:440–553.

Chastagnol, A., S. Demougin, and C. Lepelley (eds) 1996. *Splendidissima civitas: études d'histoire romaine en hommage à François Jacques.* Paris.

Cohen, S. J. D. and E. S. Frerichs (eds) 1993. *Diasporas in Antiquity.* Providence.

Cooley, A. (ed.) 2000a. *The Epigraphic Landscape of Roman Italy.* London.

Cooley, A. 2000b. "Politics and religion in the *ager Laurens*," in Cooley 2000a:173–91.

Cornell, T. J. 1989. "Rome and Latium to 390 BC," *CAH*² VIII.2:243–308.

Cornell, T. J. 1995. *The Beginnings of Rome: Italy and Rome from the Bronze Age to the Punic Wars (c.1000–264 BC).* London.

Cracco Ruggini, L. 1980. "Nuclei immigrati e forze indigene in tre grandi centri commerciali dell'impero," in D'Arms and Kopf 1980:55–76.

D'Arms, J. and E. C. Kopf (eds) 1980. *The Seaborne Commerce of Ancient Rome.* Rome.

Detienne, M. (ed.) 1990. *Tracés de fondation.* Louvain.

Dondin-Payre, M. and M.-T. Raepsaet-Charlier (eds) 1999. *Cités, municipes, colonies: les processus de municipalisation en Gaule et en Germanie sous le Haut Empire romain.* Paris.

Dubourdieu, A. 1989. *Les origines et le développement du culte des Pénates à Rome.* CÉFR 118. Rome.

Dubourdieu, A. and J. Scheid. 2000. "Lieux de culte, lieux sacrés: les usages de la langue. L'Italie romaine," in Vauchez 2000:59–80.

Durand, J.-L. and J. Scheid 1994. " 'Rites' et 'religion': remarques sur certains préjugés des historiens de la religion des grecs et des romains," *Archives de sciences sociales des religions* 85:23–43.

Edmondson, J. C. 1999. "The cultural politics of public spectacle in Rome and the Greek East, 167–166 BCE," in Bergmann and Kondoleon 1999:77–95.

Fears, J. R. 1981. "The cult of Jupiter and Roman imperial ideology," *ANRW* 2.17.1:3–141.

Foertmeyer, V. A. 1989. *Tourism in Graeco-Roman Egypt*. Dissertation, Princeton University.

Frankfurter, D. 1998. *Religion in Roman Egypt: Assimilation and Resistance*. Princeton.

Frateantonio, C. 1997. "Autonomie in der Kaiserzeit und Spätantike," in Cancik and Rüpke 1997:85–97.

Frier, B. 2000. "Demography," *CAH²* XI:787–816.

Galsterer, H. 1987. "La loi municipale des Romains: chimère ou réalité?," *Revue historiques de droit français et étranger* 65.2:181–203.

Galsterer, H. 1988. "Municipium Flavium Irnitanum: a Latin town in Spain," *JRS* 78:78–90.

Glinister, F. 2000. "Sacred rubbish," in Bispham and Smith 2000:54–70.

González, J. 1986. "The *Lex Irnitana*: a new Flavian municipal law," *JRS* 76:147–243.

Goodman, M. 1994. *Mission and Conversion: Proselytizing in the Religious History of the Roman Empire*. Oxford.

Gordon, R. 1979. "Production and religion in the Graeco-Roman world," *Art History* 2:5–34.

Gordon, R. 1990. "Religion in the Roman empire: the civic compromise and its limits," in Beard and North 1990:235–55.

Graf, F. (ed.) 1998. *Ansichten griechischer Rituale*. Stuttgart.

Harris, W. V. 1980. "Towards a study of the Roman slave trade," in D'Arms and Kopf 1980: 117–140.

Harris, W. V. 2000. "Trade," *CAH²* XI:710–40.

Jocelyn, H. D. 1982. "Varro's *Antiquitates Rerum Divinarum* and religious affairs in the late Roman republic," *Bulletin of the John Rylands University Library of Manchester* 65:148–205.

Lane Fox, R. 1987. *Pagans and Christians*. New York.

Latte, K. 1960. *Römische Religionsgeschichte*. Munich.

Levene, D. S. and D. Nelis (eds) 2002. *Clio and the Poets: Augustan Poetry and the Traditions of Ancient Historiography*. Leiden.

Lieberg, G. 1973. "Die Theologia Tripartita in Forschung und Bezeugnung," *ANRW* 1.4:63–115.

Lieberg, G. 1982. "Die Theologia tripertita als Formprinzip antiken Denkens," *RhM* 126:25–53.

Lieu, J., J. North, and T. Rajak (eds) 1992. *The Jews among Pagans and Christians in the Roman Empire*. London.

Linderski, J. 1986. "The augural law," *ANRW* 2.16.3:2146–312.

MacCormack, S. 1990. "*Loca sancta*: the organization of sacred topography in late antiquity," in Ousterhout 1990:7–40.

MacMullen, R. 1993. "The unromanized in Rome," in Cohen and Frerichs 1993:47–64.

Malaise, M. 1972. *Les conditions de pénétration et de diffusion des cultes Égyptiens en Italie*. Leiden.

Malaise, M. 1984. "La diffusion des cultes égyptiens dans les provinces européennes de l'empire romain," *ANRW* 2.17.3:1615–91.

Mirsch, P. 1888. "De M. Terenti Varronis Antiquitatum rerum humanarum libris XXV," *Leipziger Studien zur classischen Philologie* 15:1–144.

Mitthof, F. 1993. "Vom ἱερώτατος Καῖσαρ zum ἐπιφανέστατος Καῖσαρ: die Ehrenprädikate in der Titulatur der Thronfolger des 3. Jh. n. Chr. nach den Papyri," *ZPE* 99:97–111.

Momigliano, A. 1987. *On Pagans, Jews, and Christians*. Middletown, CT.

Momigliano, A. 1989. "The origins of Rome," *CAH*² VIII.2:52–112.

North, J. 1992. "The development of religious pluralism," in Lieu *et al.* 1992:174–93.

Noy, D. 2000. *Foreigners at Rome: Citizens and Strangers*. London.

Oakley, S. 1998. *A Commentary on Livy Books VI–X, Vol. II: Books VII–VIII*. Oxford.

Ogilvie, R. M. 1965. *A Commentary on Livy, Books 1–5*. Oxford.

Ousterhout, R. (ed.) 1990. *The Blessings of Pilgrimage*. Urbana.

Pease, A. S. 1958. *M. Tulli Ciceronis De Natura Deorum libri secundus et tertius*. Cambridge, MA.

Pépin, J. 1956. "La théologie tripartite de Varron," *Rev. Ét. Aug.* 2:265–94.

Rives, J. B. 1995. *Religion and Authority in Roman Carthage*. Oxford.

Rüpke, J. 1990. *Domi militiae: die religiöse Konstruktion des Krieges in Rom*. Stuttgart.

Rüpke, J. 1995. *Kalendar und Öffentlichkeit: die Geschichte der Repräsentation und religiösen Qualifikation von Zeit in Rom*. Berlin.

Rystedt, E., C. Wikander, and Ö. Wikander (eds) 1993. *Deliciae fictiles*. Stockholm.

Scheid, J. 1981. "Le délit religieux dans la Rome tardo-républicaine," in *Le délit religieux dans la cité antique*. CÉFR 48. Rome. 117–69.

Scheid, J. 1985. *Religion et piété à Rome*. Paris.

Scheid, J. 1987. "Polytheism impossible; or, the empty gods: reasons behind a void in the history of Roman religions," *History and Anthropology* 3:303–25.

Scheid, J. 1995. "Les espaces culturels et leur interprétation," *Klio* 77:424–32.

Scheid, J. 1996. "Pline le jeune et les sanctuaires d'Italie: observations sur les lettres IV, 1, VII, 8 et IX, 39," in Chastagnol *et al.* 1996:241–58.

Scheid, J. 1998. "Nouveau rite et nouvelle piété: réflexions sur le ritus Graecus," in Graf 1998:168–82.

Scheid, J. 1999a. "Hiérarchie et structure dans le polythéisme romain: façons romaines de penser l'action," *Archiv für Religionsgeschichte* 1.2:184–203.

Scheid, J. 1999b. "Aspects religieux de la municipalisation: quelques réflexions générales," in Dondin-Payre and Raepsaet-Charlier 1999:381–423.

Shaw, B. 2000. "Rebels and outsiders," *CAH*² XI: 361–403.

Smith, J. Z. 1990. *Drudgery Divine: On the Comparison of Early Christianities and the Religions of Late Antiquity*. Chicago.

Sourvinou-Inwood, C. 2000. "What is *polis* religion?" and "Further aspects of *polis* religion," in Buxton 2000:13–37 and 38–55.

Stark, R. 1996. *The Rise of Christianity*. Princeton.

Thomas, Y. 1990. "L'institution de l'origine: sacra principiorum populi romani," in Detienne 1990:143–70.

Turcan, R. (trans. A. Nevill) 1996. *The Cults of the Roman Empire*. Oxford.

Vauchez, A. (ed.) 2000. *Lieux sacrés, lieux de culte, sanctuaires: approches terminologiques, méthodologiques, historiques et monographiques*. CÉFR 273. Rome.

Warde Fowler, W. 1911. *The Religious Experience of the Roman People, from the Earliest Times to the Age of Augustus*. London.

White, J. B. (ed.) forthcoming. *How to Talk about Religion*. Notre Dame, IN.

Wissowa, G. 1912. *Religion und Kultus der Römer*. 2nd edition. Munich.

Wissowa, G. 1915. "Die römische Staatspriestertümer altlateinischer Gemeindekulte," *Hermes* 50:1–33.

Wissowa, G. 1916/19. "Interpretatio Romana. Römische Götter im Barbarenlande," *Archiv für Religionswissenschaft* 19:1–49.

Woolf, G. 1997. "*Polis*-religion and its alternatives in the Roman provinces," in Cancik and Rüpke 1997:71–84.

PART VI

Space and Time

Introduction to Part VI:
Space and Time

The Praetor says: "I forbid doing anything in a sacred place or introducing anything into one."

Sacred places (*sacra loca*) are those that have been publicly dedicated, whether in the city or in the country. It must be understood that a public place can only become sacred if the emperor has dedicated it or has granted the power of dedicating it.

This interdict concerning sacred places does not apply to *sacraria*.

It should also be observed that a sacred place is one thing, a *sacrarium* another. A sacred place is a place that has been consecrated, but a *sacrarium* is a place in which *sacra* have been deposited. This could even be in a private building, and it is customary for those who wish to free such a place from its religious scruple to call forth (*evocare*) the *sacra*.

Ulpian *On the Edict* bk 68 frr. 1482–3[1]

Ulpian was a lawyer and high-ranking agent of the imperial government in the early third century AD, the author of more than two hundred books on civil, criminal, and constitutional law. We might have expected him to view the sacralization of space as a problem of the *ius publicum*, of public law: as he wrote in his *Institutes*, "the *ius publicum* consists in the *ius* of *sacra*, the *ius* of priesthoods, and the *ius* of magistracies."[2] His inability so to view the issue reflects underlying presuppositions, even anxieties, about the limits of human agency and the nature of divine immanence that lie at the heart of ancient religion. How, when, and where do the gods exist in the world, and how should humans respond to and commemorate their presence?

---

[1] Translations after those by D. N. MacCormick and Tom Braun, published in A. Watson (ed.), *The Digest of Justinian* (Philadelphia: University of Pennsylvania Press, 1985), 1:25–6 and 4:573. I order Ulpian's text as reconstructed by Lenel 1889: II 805.

[2] Ulpian *Institutes* frg. 1908 (Lenel 1889: II 926–7) = *Dig.* 1.1.1.2.

The tension in Ulpian's remarks arises from the potential for conflict between the desires of state priests, on the one hand, whose theory and actions conditioned the use of space in Roman society, and those of the gods, to the historical pattern of whose actions priestly law notionally conformed. To these two, private individuals fulfilling vows and establishing shrines are added as a third variable, one lamentably underdetermined. But the principal source of tension in Ulpian's meditation is divine: the gods have wills of their own, which are subject to external and internal impulses other than priestly and magisterial action. Plutarch, the imperial Greek scholar and biographer, reflected at length on Roman anxieties over just this problem:

> Why is it forbidden to mention or to inquire after or to call by name that deity, whether it be male or female, whose especial province it is to preserve and watch over Rome? ... Is it because, as some Roman writers have recorded, there are certain evocations and enchantments affecting the gods, by which the Romans believed that certain gods had been called forth from their enemies and had come to dwell among themselves, and they were afraid of having the same thing done to them by others? Accordingly, as the Tyrians are said to have put chains upon their images, and certain other people are said to demand sureties when they send forth their images for bathing or for some other rite of purification, so the Romans believed that not to mention and not to know the name of the god was the safest and surest way of shielding it.[3]

Plutarch's analogy between the power of words and power of objects speaks very precisely to our problem. For if the "calling forth" of tutelary deities through ritual invocation of their names seems emphatically to assign power to human agents, the binding of cult images presumes an identity of some kind between god and statue considerably more alien to modern sensibilities.[4]

We can measure the distance between a Roman perspective and a modern (Platonizing Christian) one by turning to the second book of *On the Laws*. There Cicero reflected on the value of maintaining shrines in cities:

> I believe there should be sanctuaries in cities, and I do not follow the view of the Persian magi under whose persuasion Xerxes is said to have burned the temples of Greece, because they enclosed within walls gods for whom everything ought to be open and free and whose temple and home is this entire universe. The view of the Greeks and our own people is better, who wanted

---

[3] Plutarch *Quaest. Rom.* 61 (*Mor.* 278F).
[4] For two quite different attempts to theorize and historicize this problem see Ando 2002, and Ando, forthcoming.

the gods to dwell in the same cities as we do, in order to increase piety towards the gods.[5]

For Cicero, the question is not one of theology; he does not ask, for example, whether Persians believe in transcendent deities. It is rather one of politics: the gods are in the world, and the Romans are better off having them as fellow citizens. But his unwillingness, when discussing matters of law, at least, to imagine alternative theologies and the cult actions that might reify them reveals again an insistent belief that the gods must be somewhere.

Gods who are in one place at one time, and in another at another, leave traces in the landscape and historical record. The Romans accounted for that fact in ways that reflected, on the one hand, the very different pragmatic problems raised by chronological and topographic commemoration and, on the other, the essentially singular metaphysical position that this view of divine immanence requires. The fragmentary and fascinating definition of *religiosus*[6] offered by the second-century lexicographer Festus opens a window onto a Roman perspective on this problem:

> To be *religiosus* means not only placing great value on the holiness of the gods, but also being dutiful toward humans. Days are *religiosi*, on which it is held illegal to perform actions beyond what is necessary. Such are the thirty-six days called "black days," as well as the Alliensis ... A great many bitter arguments have been fought over the difference between "sacred" (*sacrum*), "sanctified" (*sanctum*), and *religiosus*. A sacred building is one consecrated to a god. A wall is sanctified if it lies around a city; a *religiosus* grave is one where a dead person is interred or buried.[7]

Alliensis refers both to a place and a time: the Allia was a river north of Rome, on a plain near which the Romans suffered a terrible defeat at the hands of the Gauls.[8] Festus draws an implicit analogy between that spectacular historical intervention and the historically contingent processes – public, private, human, and divine – that sacralize space.

Scholars have tended to study the problems of space and time in Roman religion from decidedly irreligious and often antiquarian perspectives. Picking up on the skepticism that Romans often expressed about the sincerity and piety behind particular religious actions – was Clodius really motivated by piety when he consecrated

---

[5] Cicero *Leg.* 2.26 (trans. Zetzel).
[6] In English it might be rendered by a range of words, including "religious," "marked by religious scruple," "sacred," and "devout."
[7] Festus s.v. *religiosus* 348–50L.
[8] For a narrative of this event, see Livy 5.37–9.

Cicero's confiscated house as a shrine to Liberty? Did Caesar's fellow-consul in 59, Marcus Calpurnius Bibulus, really spend several months of that year at home, assiduously watching the skies for omens? – as well as on the functional-rationalist remarks that Romans and others delivered about the origins of religious institutions, many have regarded the state religion as a system widely and cynically manipulated for political ends.[9] At the same time, ancient references to bodies of "law," whether pontifical or augural, have inspired heroic and sometimes quixotic attempts at historical reconstruction, one of the most famous of which deals precisely with augural law, and so with the control of space.[10]

Recent years have witnessed a change in focus in both these fields. In part, this has been motivated not by dissatisfaction with earlier work, but by its quality. Barring the discovery of new evidence, neither new editions nor synoptic treatments of "the" Roman calendar, for example, seemed to be required.[11] On the other hand, it is precisely the existence of multiple Roman calendars – official, private, literary, and inscribed – that has provoked scholars to view them, and the acts of commemoration they record, as creative acts of cultural memory in the broadest sense. Mary Beard's "A Complex of Times," reproduced here as Chapter 12, has achieved classic status in this field. She treats four texts about the Parilia, the so-called birthday of Rome, a festival celebrated on 21 April. Naming it an historical pageant, Beard treats Roman etiologies of that festival not as bits of fossilized or fictive knowledge, but as products of an idiosyncratically Roman mythopoiesis, with profound contemporary relevance.

Myth also lies at the heart of much recent work on space and place in Roman religion. In hindsight, Sabine MacCormack's "*Loca Sancta*" appears to have been an early statement of a now widespread interest in patterns of social action intended to commemorate the presence and actions of the divine. If such commemoration tends to take one of two forms, namely, ritual or pilgrimage, those forms are joined in their concern to respect the intervention or immanence

---

[9] Among the most distinguished of essays along these lines is Taylor 1949: 76–97. On Cicero's house, see Nisbet 1939. On Bibulus, see Beard in *CAH*² IX, 739–42, the whole of which chapter merits careful study.

[10] Linderski 1986, which includes a wide-ranging, lightly annotated bibliography. See also Rohde 1936 and Norden 1939.

[11] The standard edition of Italian calendars is Degrassi 1963. The most important Roman calendar found outside Italy is that discovered at the Roman garrison at Dura, the so-called Feriale Duranum. The first edition of that text remains a publication of the highest importance: Fink, Hoey, and Snyder 1940; cf. *RMR* no. 117.

of the gods in this world and the traces they leave in the landscape. MacCormack brings to this material a wide-ranging expertise in the history of religion, which endows this essay with a felicitous precision in formulation and judgment.

11 Loca Sancta[†]

SABINE MACCORMACK

Balance sheets of change and continuity in late antique religious life have been drawn up in very different ways. In late antiquity itself historians stressed what was new about Christianity, and their opinion carried conviction for centuries. Until the Reformation and beyond, Christianity's *raison d'etre* was thought to be its novelty. But more recently, ideas and modes of behavior which Christians shared with pagans have also seemed important.[1] In the present inquiry, which focuses on change and continuity in late antique perceptions of holy places and on what made these places holy in the eyes of worshippers, I will begin with an issue that occupied the Reformers and still hovers in scholarly consciousness, although less prominently than formerly. For the discovery either of change or of continuity in the late antique transition from paganism to Christianity depends on how and why questions are addressed to the evidence.

† Originally published as "*Loca sancta*: the organization of sacred topography in late antiquity," in R. Ousterhout, ed., *The Blessings of Pilgrimage* (Urbana: University of Illinois Press, 1990), pp. 7–40.

I am grateful to Kenneth Holum and the late John d'Amico for their comments on an earlier draft of this essay. And I dedicate it, with affectionate recollection of her wise words and lovely smiles, to Lynn Hayes.

[1] On the novelty of Christianity as perceived in antiquity, see R. L. Wilken, *The Christians as the Romans Saw Them* (New Haven, 1984); E. Gibbon, *The Decline and Fall of the Roman Empire*, chs. 15–16, stresses what was new about Christianity. Recently R. L. Fox, *Pagans and Christians* (New York, 1987), has carefully differentiated pagan from Christian conviction and action. Similarly, and closer to this article's themes, Peter Brown, *The Cult of the Saints. Its Rise and Function in Latin Christianity* (Chicago, 1981), focuses on the novelty of Christian attitudes. J. Geffcken, *The Last Days of Greco-Roman Paganism* (Amsterdam, 1978), by contrast, saw much common ground between pagans and Christians; further, A. Momigliano, ed., *The Conflict between Paganism and Christianity in the Fourth Century* (Oxford, 1963). M. Simon, *Hercule et le Christianisme* (Strasbourg, 1955), is one of the earliest studies of Christian redeployment of pagan theology. The study of architecture and iconography likewise has revealed what Christians learnt from pagans; a classic and still important treatment of pagan and Christian changes and continuities in funerary architecture and cult is A. Grabar, *Martyrium. Recherches sur le culte des reliques et l'art chrétien antique* (Paris, 1943–46). On the history of Christian archaeology, see J. Engemann, "Altes und Neues zu Beispielen heidnischer und christlicher Katakombenbilder im spätantiken Rom," *Jahrbuch für Antike und Christentum*, 26 (1983), 128–51.

In 16th-century debates, holy places figured as only one part of a wider concern with the role of ritual, images, pilgrimages and the cult of saints in Christian worship. Catholic scholars tended to anchor their investigation of Christian religious observance in ancient tradition. It was the study of this tradition that inspired the monumental and often reprinted *Annales Ecclesiastici* and the work on the Roman martyrs by Cesare Baronio, as well as Bosio's *Roma sotterranea*, the first major archaeological account of the Roman catacombs.[2]

On the other hand, when Protestants discussed the practice of Christian piety, they most often appealed to reason and to theological and philosophical principles. Against the cult of saints and images, they argued that the true likeness of divinity resided, not in images, artifacts, or places, but in man.[3] In the words of John Calvin, a Christian should have "no use [for] place apart from the doctrine of godliness," which could be taught anywhere at all.[4] Protestants therefore considered Catholic emphasis on particular sites of worship to be continuous with paganism.

A trenchant statement of the Protestant case against the Catholic church defined as the Kingdom of Darkness occurs in Thomas Hobbes's *Leviathan*, published in 1651. Hobbes's argument – aspects

[2] Cesare Baronio, *Annales Ecciesiastici ... novissima editio, postremum ab auctore aucta et recognita* (Antwerp, 1604–7); *idem*, *Martyrologium Romanum Gregorii XIII iussu editum et Urbani VIII auctoritate recognitum* (Venice, 1661); A. Bosio, *Roma sotterranea*, ed. G. Severani (Rome, 1632). For the reprints, translations and expanded edition of this influential work, see Giovanni Gaetano Bottari, *Sculture e pitture sagre estratte dai cimiteri di Roma, pubblicate gia dagli autori della Roma Sotterranea ed ora nuovamente date in luce colle spiegazione per ordine de N.S. Clemente XII*, 3 vols. (Rome, 1737–54), I, i–viii.

[3] John Calvin, *Institutes of the Christian Religion*, tr. F. L. Battles (Philadelphia, 1960), 3.20.22–27 on the cult of saints; 1.11.4–14 on religious images, with 4.9.7–4.10.2 on tradition; 1.15.1–4 the image of God in man.

[4] *Ibid.*, 4.1.5. Martin Luther, *Lectures on Genesis*, tr. G. V. Schick and P. D. Pahl (St. Louis, 1968), *ad* 28.16–19 [MacCormack studies the late antique exegesis of this passage in a part of this essay not included in this volume: see pp. 23ff. of the original publication], had already made this same point, but much more cautiously. On the one hand, Jacob found God far from his father's house (*ad* 28.16) and "God does not dwell in human traditions" (*ad* 28.17), but on the other hand, God had joined "the earth with heaven, and heaven with the earth" (*ad* 28.17) in the place where Jacob saw his vision. Throughout, the exegesis is applied to criticize Catholic ritual and worship. Gregory of Nyssa's *Letter* 2, condemning pilgrimages, figured prominently in Protestant argument. For a key passage see *PG* 46, 1012C, with the commentary of J. Gretscher, S.J., stating the Catholic viewpoint; modern edition by G. Pasquali, *Gregorii Nysseni Epistulae* (Leiden, 1959), 15–16. Further, F. E. Cranz and P. O. Kristeller, eds., *Catalogus translationum et commentariorum: Medieval and Renaissance Latin Translations and Commentaries*, V (Washington, D.C., 1984), 27–30; 47–53; Pasquali, *Epistulae*, lxxxiii f. A Latin translation of Gregory's letter was printed and discussed in the *Quarta centuria ecclesiasticae historiae ...* (Basel, 1560), cols. 930 ff. Baronius in the *Annales*, a.a. 386, tried to control the damage. See P. Maraval, "Une querelle sur les pèlerinages autour d'un texte patristique" (Grégoire de Nysse, Lettre 2), *Revue d'histoire et de philosophie réligieuses*, 66 (1986), 131–46.

of which already occur in Calvin's *Institutes* – is threefold. He maintained in the first instance that God, who is infinite, cannot be contained in any place or image. Second, therefore, he argued that holiness is not inherent in any place, so that no place is more suited for worship than any other. Thus, "holy ... implies no new quality in that place ... but only a new relation by appropriation to God." The site of the burning bush, accordingly, was "holy ground not by inherent sanctity but by separation to God's use." Third, to worship God in a place set apart by "private authority and not by the authority of them that are our sovereign pastors, is idolatry." Since Hobbes did not recognize the authority of Catholic bishops as tantamount to that of "our sovereign pastors," he defined Catholic worship as a simple continuation of pagan idolatry. Concrete examples substantiated this assertion. Holy water, Hobbes argued, was the pagan *aqua lustralis* under another name, to canonize saints was to perpetuate the rituals whereby Romulus had been consecrated, and above all, "to worship God as inanimating or inhabiting ... an image or place, that is to say an infinite substance in a finite place, is idolatry."[5]

These arguments, directed against Catholic holy places and pilgrimages, could equally have been applied to Roman pagans, because certain Roman holy places were thought to possess precisely that "inherent sanctity" which Hobbes describes and which did not arise from human action but was merely confirmed by it.

In his poem on the civil war between Caesar and Pompey, Lucan told how Caesar visited the site of Troy. In that venerable place, redolent with mythic memories of Roman origins, "every stone has its story": *nullum est sine nomine saxum.*[6] Not only in Troy but throughout the ancient Mediterranean world, places were imbued with memories going back to a sacred antiquity or with the aura of some divine pressence. Nameless divinity inherent in place moved Roman farmers to invoke the holy presences of the countryside before encroaching on the boundary between the cultivated and the wild land.[7] Indeed, many Roman rituals formulated and defined man's relationship with a fundamentally alien and therefore holy

---

[5] Thomas Hobbes, *Leviathan*, ch. 45.

[6] Lucan, *Pharsalia*, 9.973.

[7] [Cato, *Agr.*], 139; see also, K. Latte, *Römische Religionsgeschichte* (München, 1967), 36 ff., 50 ff.; on the mode of address (*si deus si dea es*), see E. Norden, *Agnostos Theos. Untersuchungen zur Formengeschichte religiöser Rede* (Stuttgart, 1974), 143 ff.; also A. D. Nock, "Mana in Roman Religion," in his *Essays on Religion and the Ancient World*, ed. Z. Stewart (Oxford, 1972), II, 603–5.

environment.[8] As Frontinus observed of the Roman wells which in earlier times had provided the city's water supply, "The memory along with the sanctity of the wells still endures and is tended: they are thought to bring health to diseased bodies, as for instance the wells of the Camenae, of Apollo and of Iuturna."[9] Awareness of holiness inherent in certain places was expressed in truly lapidary simplicity in inscriptions informing the passerby that the site was dedicated "to the genius of this place."

Other places were regarded as holy because they had witnessed some divine action recorded in myth or history. Myth and history humanized the awesome and nameless divine presences who dwelt in holy places of primeval antiquity by attributing to them a concrete identity. Romans of the late republic and early empire tended to conceptualize this identity as Greek, because so often the myths were Greek. A graphic statement of what was at stake comes from Vergil: when Evander showed Aeneas the site of Rome, he

> led Aeneas to the place of Tarpeia and the Capitol, which is now golden but then was dark with forest undergrowth. Even then a fearful dread of the place pressed on the timid countryfolk, even then they trembled at the forest and the rock. "This grove," Evander said, "this hill with its wooded peak is inhabited by a god, but what god is unknown. The Arcadians believe that they have often seen Jupiter himself shaking the darkening aegis in his right hand as he stirred up the stormclouds."[10]

As Vergil described it, there was initially no story and no event attached to the site of the Capitol that made it holy. Rather the stories, the sacred tales of Jupiter, the king of the gods, were brought by newcomers from Greek Arcadia. The reader is left to conclude that it was thanks to their perception of the venerable site that one of the deities who was in due course worshipped on the Capitol was Jupiter. But originally the holiness had been impersonal and inherent in the place, in nature.

---

[8] R. Otto, *The Idea of the Holy. An Inquiry into the Non-rational Factor in the Idea of the Divine and Its Relation to the Rational* (Oxford, 1925); A. Dihie in *Reallexikon für Antike und Christentum*, 8 (1972), s.v. Furcht.

[9] Frontinus, *Aqueducts*, 9.

[10] Vergil, *Aeneid*, 8.347–54:

> hinc ad Tarpeiam sedem et Capitolia ducit
> aurea nunc, olim silvestribus horrida dumis.
> iam turn religio pavidos terrebat agrestis
> diri loci, iam tum silvam saxumque tremebant.
> "hoc nemus, hunc" inquit, "frondoso vertice collem
> (quis deus incertum est) habitat deus; Arcades ipsum
> credunt se vidisse Iovem, cum saepe nigrantem
> aegida concuteret dextra nirnbosque cieret."

The passage is discussed by Norden; see below, n. 16.

If in the eyes of Vergil's contemporaries myth made available one method of rendering intelligible the holy in nature, another and more incisive method came from philosophy. The tripartite theology expounded by the antiquarian Varro in his *Divine Antiquities* correlated religious concepts arising from nature with those arising from myth and civic life.[11] He was thus able to explain how the elements – water, earth, air, fire – had been conceptualized as deities.[12] Varro's ideas appear to have circulated beyond the confines of his study. For an example of the earth being divinized in the way he had envisioned comes from a Roman epitaph: "I lived beloved by my family and died a virgin; here I lie dead and am ashes and the ashes are earth. But if the earth is divine, I also am divine and am not dead. I beg you stranger, do not violate my bones."[13] The tomb is thus a holy place because the earth itself is divine and holy. However, most epitaphs contemplate the divinization of the departed not in the earth, in a terrestial place imbued with holiness, but in the divine stars. While the body rests in the grave, the soul returns to its point of origin in the celestial spheres.[14] Plotinus was thinking in this same age-old idiom when he said that in preparing for death he was "striving to give back the divine in himself to the divine in the All."[15]

In early imperial Rome, such philosophical perceptions of the holy in nature and in the cosmos converged with established religious terminology. The Capitoline Hill covered in the primeval forest that Vergil's Evander showed to Aeneas was imbued with a "fearful

---

[11] M. Terentius Varro, *Antiquitates Rerum Divinarum* [(*Ant. Div.*)] ed. and comm. B. Cardauns (Wiesbaden, 1976), fr. 6–7, see the commentary. P. Boyancé, "Sur la théologie de Varron," *Revue des études anciennes*, 57 (1955), 57–84, at 62 ff., 67 ff.; G. Lieberg, "Die 'theologia tripertita' in Forschung und Bezeugung," *Aufstieg und Niedergang der römischen Welt* [hereafter *ANRW*], ed. H. Temporini and W. Haase (Berlin, 1973), I, iv, 63–115. On Varro and Vergil, P. Boyancé, *La religion de Vergile* (Paris, 1963), 17–38. A. Momigliano, "The Theological Efforts of the Roman Upper Classes in the First Century BC," *Classical Philology*, 79 (1984), 199–211 [reprinted above, Chapter 7]. See further below, n. 14.

[12] Thus on the earth as divine, see Varro, [*Ant. Div.*] ed. Cardauns, e.g. frr. 23, 24, 26, 226, 227, 263, 270 (cf. Servius, *ad Aen.* 1.171), 281.

[13] *ILS* 8168:

> cara meis vixi virgo vitam reddidi
> mortua heic ego sum et sum cinis is cinis terrast
> sein est terra dea ego sum et dea mortua non sum
> rogo te hospes noli ossa mea violare.

[14] Plato, *Timaeus*, 41 d and e, 42b; on the impact of philosophy and mystery religions on widely held beliefs, see A. D. Nock, "Cremation and Burial in the Roman Empire," *Essays*, I, 277–307, at 286 ff., 296 ff.; also F. Cumont, *Lux perpetua* (Paris, 1949), 142–88. On depictions of philosophical ideas, P. Courcelle, "Quelques symboles funéraires du Neoplatonisme latin," *Revue des études anciennes*, 46 (1944), 65–93, at 65–73, but note also the more recent critical evaluation of funerary symbolism and its meaning by R. Turcan, "Les sarcophages romains et le probleme du symbolisme funeraire," in *ANRW* II, xvi, 2 (Berlin, 1978), 1700–35.

[15] Porphyry, *Life of Plotinus*, 2.

dread": *religio dira loci. Religio* defining place denotes a place set apart from regular use. Such places were marked either by temples, the dwellings of the gods, or by tombs,[16] graphically referred to in legislation as "houses of the dead."[17] Both temples and tombs were removed from secular use by the formal juridical procedure of *dedicatio*† and *consecratio*.†[18] However, the consecration of tombs differed from that of temples in being a private, not a public, transaction,[19] so that violations of tombs could only be rectified by representatives of the founder acting as private individuals.[20] Temples by contrast were public property. In addition, temples and tombs were situated in different locations and followed different festal calendars. At the tomb people celebrated the family festivals of the dead, as well as the anniversaries in the life of the deceased which are regularly mentioned in inscriptions, while those who frequented the temples did so to join in public celebrations which included the entire commumty.[21]

Nonetheless temples and tombs shared certain features because both usually consisted of a holy area, marked by a building and surrounded by an enclosure. The entire complex could be described as *lucus* or "grove."[22] The similarity between temple and tomb was

---

[16] Eduard Norden, *Aus altrömischen Priesterbüchern* (Leipzig, 1936, reprint New York, 1975), 16–31, esp. 24–27; Kobbert, in *Pauly's Realencyclopaedie der klassischen Altertumswissenschaft* (Stuttgart, 1920), II, i, 575–80, s.v. Religio.

[17] *Cod. Theod.*, 9.17.4 (356/7 CE): *aedificia manium, domus ut ita dixerim defunctorum* [("the habitations of the shades, the houses, one might say, of the dead")].

† The terms "dedication" and "consecration" are often used together and seem at times to be exchanged for the sake of variation. The processes to which they refer were clearly related. Strictly speaking, "dedication" was the surrender of all claim for the possession or use of something, from a person in favor of a divinity; "consecration" transferred adjudication over that objection from "human" to "divine" law. In the case of public property, both acts were properly performed by a magistrate with *imperium*, prompted by a *pontifex* (Varro *Ling.* 6.61; Cicero *Dom.* 120, 122). See Nisbet 1939: 209–12 or Ogilvie 1965: 254.

[18] M. Kaser, "Zum römischen Grabrecht," *Zeitschrift der Savignystiftung für Rechtsgeschichte, Romanistische Abteilung*, 95 (1978), 15–92, at 32, with works there cited; Wissowa in *Pauly's Realencyclopaedie*, iv, 897–902 and 2356–59; cf. Servius, *ad Aen.*, 1.446. W. Seston, "Les murs, les portes et les tours des enceintes urbaines et le probleme des res sanctae en droit romain," *Mélanges d'archeologie et d'histoire offerts à André Piganiol* (Paris, 1966), III, 1489–98.

[19] Kaser, "Grabrecht," 23–26.

[20] Although the pontifices could also be called upon, see *ibid.*, 26–28, 88, 91; and the state prosecuted major offences against tombs, *ibid.*, 33–4; for the later period, see 90. On potential conflicts between civil and pontifical law regarding tombs, see further, Cicero, [*Leg.*], II.47 ff.

[21] A. Stuiber, "Heidnische und christliche Gedächtniskalender," *Jahrbuch für Antike und Christentum*, 3 (1960), 24–33; on other aspects of the Roman domestic (as distinct from public) cult, see D. G. Orr, "Roman Domestic Religion: The Evidence of the Household Shrines," *ANRW*, II, xvi, 2, 1557–91. The iconography of household deities in their shrines was parallel to that of the gods of the community at large, see 1575 ff. with figs. 2, 3, 20.

[22] Servius, *ad Aen.*, 3.302; cf. Cicero, [*Leg.*], II.19 and 26, distinguishing between *delubrum* in cities and *lucus* in the countryside. A countryside *lucus*, or sacred place mentioned by

also expressed in visual art. Funerary stelai regularly depict the deceased seated or standing in a small temple (Figs. 1–2).[23] A certain Gallus from Langres carefully described the arrangements that could give rise to such an image in his will.[24] He had built a small shrine for himself where his seated statue was to be displayed. The shrine had a door that was to be opened on festal days. Finally, just as altars for sacrifice were raised outside the temples of the gods, so Gallus laid down that there should be an altar containing his ashes in front of his funerary shrine.[25] Similar although less elaborate arrangements were made by many other individuals who were concerned for their continued presence and remembrance among the living.[26]

Like the dead, so the gods were visualized as inhabiting – that is, standing or sitting in – their temples. As Ovid said of the primitive image of Jupiter in its ancient temple in early Rome: "Jupiter was hardly able to stand upright in his narrow shrine."[27] In this same idiom Aeneas is shown on the Ara Pacis making sacrifice in the presence of the Di Penates from Troy, who are seated in a woodland temple (Fig. 3).[28] Similarly some three centuries later the emperor Galerius appeared on his triumphal arch being greeted by citizens and by a goddess who is waving from her shrine (Fig. 4). The imperial coinage regularly showed a god or goddess in a temple (Fig. 5).[29]

These texts and images depict the same practice which Hobbes, taking his cue from the early Christian apologists, decried as idolatrous and as being perpetuated in Catholicism. The apologists also had accused their pagan opponents of attempting to contain the

Tacitus, *Annals*, 12.47. On the enclosure see Varro, [*Ling.*], VII.13: *quod omne templum esse debet continuo septum nec plus unum introitum habere* [("because every temple ought to be enclosed all around and should not have more than one entrance")].

[23] The iconography was empirewide: A. Garcia y Belindo, *Esculturas romanas de España y Portugal* (Madrid, 1949), no. 344; J. M. C. Toynbee, *Art in Britain under the Romans* (Oxford, 1964), pls. 47a, 48a, 48b, 49; R. Bianchi Bandinelli, *Rome. The Late Empire: Roman Art AD 200–400* (New York, 1971), figs. 65, 105, 108, 124, 144.

[24] *ILS* 8379.

[25] Grabar, *Martyrium*, I, 100–102, figs. 95, 99.

[26] E.g., Walters Art Gallery, Baltimore, funerary stele of Miunius.

[27] Ovid, *Fasti*, ed. and tr. J. C. Frazer (Cambridge, Mass., 1959), 1, 201: *Iuppiter angusta vix stabat in aede.*

[28] See A. Grenier, *The Roman Spirit in Religion, Thought and Art* (New York, 1926), 354 f. For similar iconographies, see Toynbee, *Art in Britain*, pls. 40, 43–44; Bianchi Bandinelli, *Late Empire*, figs. 148, 200.

[29] H. P. Laubscher, *Der Reliefschmuck des Galeriusbogens in Thessaloniki* (Berlin, 1975), 61–64, pls. 45–50; I. Scott Ryberg, *Rites of the State Religion in Roman Art*, American Academy in Rome, Memoirs, 22 (1955), fig. 115, with pp. 187–89. On Tertullian's polemic about the similarity between the cult of the dead and the cult of the gods among pagans see V. Saxer, *Morts, martyrs, reliques en Afrique chrétienne aux premiers siècles. Les temoinages de Tertullien, Cyprien et Augustin à la lumière de l'archéologie africaine* (Paris, 1980), 37 ff. and 47 ff.; see also 99 ff.

Fig. 1 (left). Stone relief from Gloucester, England. Mercury and a goddess standing in a temple. *Fig. 2 (right).* Stone tomb relief from Cirencester, England. Philus standing in a house or house-tomb

infinite deity in a finite place, a building. Thus in the later 2nd or early 3rd century, Minucius Felix set down a theological conversation between two friends, Caecilius the pagan and Marcus the Christian. Caecilius opened the discussion by outlining the dignity and universality of Roman imperial religion:

> People in all empires, provinces and cities have their particular holy rites and worship their local gods … all of whom are also worshipped by the Romans. Their power and authority has spread over the entire world and their empire extends beyond the path of the sun and the limit of the ocean because in war they practice reverence and they fortify their city with holy rituals, chaste virgins, with the many honors and titles of priests … and because everywhere they seek out foreign gods whom they make their own and raise altars even to unknown deities and to the spirits of the dead.[30]

Marcus rejected this eclectic religion of outward ceremony: "What temple can I build for God seeing that the whole universe, which is

---

[30] Minucius Felix, *Octavius*, 6.1–3.

Fig. 3. Ara Pacis Augustae, Rome. Aeneas prepares to sacrifice a pig,
overlooked by the Di Penates in their temple

his creation, cannot hold him? And shall I ... enclose within one
small building a power of such majesty? Should God not rather be
worshipped in our mind and consecrated in our innermost heart?"[31]

Marcus thus saw a sharp difference between his own convictions
and those of his pagan friend, and that same difference was later
perceived by Hobbes. This is why Hobbes, like other early modern
students of pagan and Christian late antiquity, endeavored to differ-
entiate true Christianity in as clear-cut a fashion as possible both
from pagan religions and from Catholic "idolatry." Yet the late
antique evidence tells a much more complicated story, in which
absolute and fundamental differences between pagan religions and
Christianity cannot be drawn so easily. For inevitably, late antique
Christians shared their vocabulary and many of their religious
concepts with pagan contemporaries, however much they claimed to
aspire after different goals.

[31] *Ibid.*, 32.1 f.; for man as the temple of God, see also Tertullian, *De Corona*, 9.2.

Fig. 4. Arch of Galerius, Thessaloniki. Solemn arrival of the emperor Galerius
in a city, welcomed by the citizens emerging from the city gate (*right*)
and a goddess in her shrine (*top right*) (photo courtesy of German
Archaeological Institute)

For instance, the terms Marcus used for worshipping and consecrating God in mind and heart, *deus ... in nostra dedicandus ...
mente, in nostro consecrandus pectore* [("God should be worshipped
in our mind, consecrated in our heart")]; are the same terms
as pagans applied to dedicating and consecrating temples.[32] Yet
Marcus's argument implied that the presence of God both in the
heart and universally in the world obviated the need for such ritual
language. Another example involving a Christian redeployment of
the pagan terminology of holy places was recorded by Eusebius.
During his trial the martyr Pamphilus insisted that his city was the
free Jerusalem on high, a city situated "in the East toward the rising
sun." Because the pagan interrogator had in mind an actual city holy
to Christians, he was misled into supposing that the martyr's
Jerusalem was a terrestrial city situated on the Persian frontier,
in territory often at war with Rome, and was thus a military threat
to the Roman empire.[33] Eusebius's more learned readers, however,
will have caught the philosophical and theological meaning of
Pamphilus's statement. For the image of "the city on high" also
evoked the vision by Plato's Socrates of the city that is built in the

[32] Kaser, "Zum römischen Grabrecht," 15–92; Wissowa in *Pauly's Realencyctopaedie*, iv,
897–902 and 2356–59; Seston, "Les murs, les portes," 1489–98.
[33] Eusebius, *The Martyrs of Palestine*, 11, PG 20, 1504; another reason why the interrogator could be assumed to know nothing of Jerusalem is that the city was then known as Aelia
Capitolina – see F. E. Peters, *Jerusalem. The Holy City in the Eyes of Chroniclers, Visitors,
Pilgrims and Prophets from the Days of Abraham to the Beginnings of Modern Times*
(Princeton, 1985), 129–30.

Fig. 5. Coin of Diocletian. Imperial sacrifice before a temple inhabited by a deity

human mind or in heaven.[34] Like other Christian apologists Eusebius reformulated ancient philosophical arguments which were deeply familiar to cultured pagans on behalf of the Christian cause. As a result pagan reflection and self-evaluation of earlier periods came to provide the wherewithal for confrontation and combat between paganism and Christianity.[35]

Augustine's *City of God* is a Roman case in point. His principal source for Roman religion was Varro's *Divine Antiquities*. When discussing holy places Varro had mentioned the Roman Capitol; he noted that before the temple of Jupiter, Juno, and Minerva was constructed there, the site had been occupied by the ancient deity Terminus, a boundary stone, who refused to make room for the new building and therefore had to be accommodated within it.[36] In Augustine's eyes the story was proof of chaos in the pagan supernatural universe. For Varro, on the other hand, it described a venerable and ancient Roman holy site, where from time immemorial Roman worship and history had converged with a certain holiness inherent in place.[37]

However, it was one thing for the Christians to combat and deride the ideas that underlay the institutional fabric of pagan religions. It

[34] Plato, *Republic*, 592 b.

[35] F. M. Young, "The God of the Greeks and the Nature of Religious Language," *Early Christian Literature and the Classical Intellectual Tradition in honorem Robert M. Grant*, ed. W. R. Schoedel and R. L. Wilken (Paris, 1979), 45–74.

[36] Augustine, *City of God*, 4.23; Varro, [*Ant. Div.*], fr. 40–41, ed. Cardauns.

[37] As above, n. 11. For the differences between Ausonius and Paulinus of Nola on how divinity might be perceptible in nature, see J. Fontaine, "Valeurs antiques et valeurs chrétiennes dans la spiritualité des grandes propriétaires terriens à la fin du IVe siècle occidental," *Epektasis. Mélanges patristiques offerts au Cardinal Jean Danielou*, ed. J. Fontaine and C. Kannengiesser (Beauchesne, 1972), 571–95.

Fig. 6. Coin of Bar Kochba. The Temple of Jerusalem displaying the
Ark of the Covenant as an indication of the divine presence

was quite another thing to construct such a fabric in their own right,
for the religious aspirations of ordinary Christians undermined those
clear-cut distinctions that apologists liked to make when arguing
with their pagan opponents. This becomes apparent when we
examine visual images of pagan and Christian holy places and the
ideas which inspired these images.

Pagans had created a variety of visual representations of both the
gods and the dead standing or sitting in their shrines by way of showing how a holy place was inhabited by its occupant (Figs. 1–5). These
images, simple as most of them are, were nonetheless conscious and
deliberate statements that could be adjusted to fit differing circumstances and ideas. An example occurs on the coinage of Bar Kochba:
the front of a temple is shown, but without the customary divine
figure inside. For the image refers to the Temple of Jerusalem, which
did not contain a sacred image but the Ark of the Covenant (Fig. 6).[38]
The God of Israel could not be represented in human form; moreover, although the presence, the glory of this God filled the Temple
of Jerusalem like a cloud, he nonetheless dwelt "in heaven."[39] Bar
Kochba's image represents this tension. When Jerusalem was re-
ounded as Roman Aelia Capitolina with its own mint, the new

---

[38] P. Schäfer, *Der Bar Kokhba Aufstand. Studien zum zweiten jüdischen Krieg gegen Rom*
(Tübingen, 1981), 85–88; A. Kindler, "The Coinage of the Bar-Kokhba War," *Numismatic
Studies and Researches, II. The Dating of Ancient Jewish Coins and Symbols* (Jerusalem,
1958), 62–80, at 64 ff.; on the design visible in the central opening, F. Rickert, review of *L'arche
d'alliance*, by E. Revel-Neher, in *Jahrbuch für Antike und Christentum*, 29 (1986), 218–22
with pl. 32.
[39] II Chronicles 5.13–14, 6.18–21, 7.1–3.

Fig. 7. Coin of Constantine. Imperial sacrifice before an empty temple

coinage was adorned with the image of a temple, but this time in-habited by anthropomorphic deities.[40] However, Bar Kochba's empty temple did have an iconographic descendant. After Constantine had seen his monotheistic vision in 312, his coinage, carrying a legend proclaiming the felicity of the times, displayed an empty temple before which a sacrifice is being offered (Fig. 7).[41]

This Constantinian image with its Jewish antecedent shows both continuity and discontinuity with the pagan past. On the one hand the image states that God does not inhabit any given place or temple in the way that the traditional iconography had suggested. On the other hand the viewer learns that God is indeed worshipped in build-ings and places set aside for the purpose. And in due course, just as pagan gods had dwelt in their shrines and temples, so Christian dedi-catory inscriptions described some churches as "the house of Christ," the "hall of God," or the "hail of the Trinity,"[42] while other churches became the dwelling places of the bodies of martyrs and saints.[43]

Indeed, the continuity between pagan and Christian supernatural beings inhabiting their dwellings extends beyond verbal imagery to a concrete continuity of place. Throughout the Mediterranean world pagan temples were supplanted by – and at times rededicated as – Christian churches.[44] The gods were forcibly expelled from their

---

[40] Leo Kadman, *The Coins of Aelia Capitolina. Corpus Nummorum Palaetinensium* (Jerusalem, 1956), e.g. no. 3, Hadrian; no. 10, Antoninus Pius.

[41] See also Ryberg, *Rites of the State Religion*, 187–89.

[42] *ILCV* 1783, 1784, 1786 B; see also 1800–1801, Nazarius and Christ.

[43] *ILCV* 1761–62, 1765, 1768, 1770, 1774, 1777: *ut dignam meritus habeas sedemque decoram* [("so though you might have a deservedly worthy and decorous seat")], 1785–88, 1791, 1817, 1819–20.

[44] See F. W. Deichmann, "Frühchristliche Kirchen in antiken Heiligtümern," *Jahrbuch*

dwellings to make room for the Christian God and the martyrs. Thus the *Acts of John* describes with all the graphic detail of a novel the relentless solemnity of encounters and confrontations between the apostle and the people of Ephesus which led to the overthrow of the city's patron goddess Artemis. "Where is the power of the demon?" asked John in a public address on the verge of his God's victory, "Where are the sacrifices? Where are [the goddess'] birthday celebrations and where the festivals? Where are her honors? Where is all her magic and her poisoning spells?"[45] Similarly at Daphne, near Antioch, the oracle of Apollo fell silent precisely because the cult of the martyr Babylas, in vain challenged by the emperor Julian, had intruded on the site.[46] The Christian practice of confiscating and rededicating pagan sanctuaries was canonized by Pope Gregory the Great, who wrote to Augustine of Canterbury that the pagan buildings should not be destroyed.[47] Instead the idols should be removed, and the building should be purified with holy water and consecrated by the deposition of Christian relics. In this way, the pope thought, instead of celebrating the festivals of demons the people could gather in the accustomed holy places to honor the anniversaries of the rededication and the commemoration of the martyrs whose remains were sheltered in those former temples.

In the Mediterranean the continuity that resulted from the conversion of temples into churches was accompanied by a continuity ritual regarding the commemoration of the dead. The pagan dead were attended with food, drink, and company by their living kinsfolk. "We have placed a stone table next to [our mother's grave]," wrote

des Instituts, 54 (1939), 103–36; P. Nautin, "La conversion du temple de Philae en église chrétienne," *Cahiers archéologiques*, 17 (1967), 1–43; A. Frantz, "From Paganism to Christianity in the Temples of Athens," *Dumbarton Oaks Papers*, 19 (1965), 187–205. For a discussion of these transitions in a wider context, see P.-A. Février, "Permanence et heritages de l'antiquite dans la topographie des villes de l'occident durant le haut moyen âge," *Topografia urbana e vita cittadina nell'alto medioevo en occidente. Settimane di studio*, 21, Spoleto (1974), 41–138, at 115 ff.; as well as T. Gregory, "The Survival of Paganism in Christian Greece: A Critical Essay," *American Journal of Philology*, 107 (1986), 229–43.

[45] *Acta Apostolorum Apocrypha*, ed. R. A. Lipsius and M. Bonnet (Leipzig, 1898), II, xliii, 172; on the historical background, see R. Oster, "The Ephesian Artemis as an Opponent of Christianity," *Jahrbuch für Antike und Christentum*, 19 (1976), 24–44. For the cult of St. John at Ephesus, see M. Duncan-Flowers, ["A pilgrim's ampulla from the shrine of St. John the Evangelist at Ephesus," in R. Ousterhout, ed., *The Blessings of Pilgrimage* (Urbana: University of Illinois Press, 1990), 125–39].

[46] Socrates, *Ecclesiastical History*, 3.18; the same story in greater detail, Sozomen, *Ecclesiastical History*, 4.19–20. The situation at Troy, where the local bishop extended a sympathetic tolerance to the cult of Hector as analogous to the cult of the martyrs, seems to have been somewhat unusual; see Julian, *Letter 79*, J. Bidez, *L'empereur Julien. Oeuvres complètes*, I, 2, *Lettres et fragments* (Paris, 1960). Further, C. Fowden, "Bishops and Temples in the Eastern Roman Empire, AD 320–435," *Journal of Theological Studies*, 29 (1978), 53–78.

[47] Bede, *History of the English Church and People*, 1.30.

the sons of Aelia Secundula from Satafi, "where we remember her many fine deeds while the food and the drinking cups stand ready ... so that the wound gnawing in our heart should be healed."[48] Similarly, during the 3rd century and later, many Christian martyrs had tables or plates for food next to their graves and were attended regularly by the Christian faithful.[49] The pagan dead were thus visualized as being actually present in the tomb, and so were their Christian fellows.[50]

In other respects also Christian practice continued to reveal ambiguities both theological and practical. The Christian poet Prudentius righteously reproved pagan Romans for honoring sullen Orcus with inscriptions dedicated to the Di Manes, yet some Christians saw no contradiction in invoking the Di Manes along with Christ in their own epitaphs.[51] Pagans had called down curses on those who violated their graves;[52] and Christians, not entirely confident of the ability of bishops and saints to protect their remains, did the same, albeit in their own vocabulary: "I ask you in the name of the almighty Lord and Jesus Christ of Nazareth, that you should not touch me or violate my tomb. For [if you do] I will plead a case against you before the tribunal of the eternal judge."[53] Another

[48] *ILCV* 1570; cf. J. M. Dentzer, *Le motif du banquet couché dans le proch-orient et le monde grec du VIIe au IVe siècle avant J.-C.* (Rome, 1982), 532 ff.

[49] P.-A. Février, "Le culte des morts dans les communautés chrétiennes durant le IIIe siècle," *Atti del IX Congresso Internazionale di Archeologia Cristiana, Roma 1975*, I. *Monumenti Cristiani pre-Constantiani* (Vatican, 1978), 211–74, at 250 ff., 256 ff., 261–62; for Rome during the 3rd and later centuries, see also L. Reekmans, "Les cryptes des martyrs romains. État de la recherche," with discussion, in the same volume, 275–329. H. I. Marrou, "Survivances paiennes dans les rites funéraires des Donatistes," *Hommages à Joseph Bidez et à Franz Cumont* (Brussels, n.d.), 193–203.

[50] A. Stuiber, *Refrigerium interim. Die Vorstellungen vom Zwischenzustand und die frühchristliche Grabeskunst* (Bonn, 1957), to be consulted with P.-A. Février, "La tombe chrétienne et l'au delà," no. 604, *Le temps chrétien de la fin de l'antiquité au moyen âge. IIIe–XIIIe siècles*, Colloques internationaux du CNRS, 64 (Paris, 1984), 163–83.

[51] Prudentius, *Contra Symmachum*, 1.379 ff. For example, *ILCV* 3889–90, 3904, 3911; see also 2378 and the set 3884–3957; see also K. L. Noethlichs, "Spätantike Jenseitsvorstellungen im Spiegel des staatlichen Gräberschutzes. Zur Novelle 23 Kaiser Valentinians III," *Jenseitsvorstellungen in Antike und Christentum. Gedenkschrift für A. Stuiber* (Münster, 1982), 47–54; and Février, "Tombe chrétienne," 168 ff.

[52] *ILS* 8172–8249; A. D. Nock, "Tomb Violations and Pontifical Law," *Essays on Religion and the Ancient World*, II, 527–33. On averting the evil eye, see J. Engemann, "Magische Übelabwehr in der Spätantike," *Jahrbuch für Antike und Christentum*, 18 (1975), 23–48, at 29–30,35–36. There was good reason for wanting to protect one's grave: see K. Hopkins, *Death and Renewal. Sociological Studies in Roman History* (Cambridge, 1983), II, 207–17; R. Lantier, "Coutumes funéraires dans le cimetière wisigothique d'Estagel," *Hommages à Joseph Bidez et à Franz Cumont*, 177–82.

[53] *ILCV* 3864; Christian graves were not exempt from intruders, see A. Ferrua, ed., *Epigrammata Damasiana* (Vatican, 1942), no. 41: Pope Vigilius restored a titulus [commemorative inscription] of Pope Damasus which, along with adjacent graves, had been destroyed by the Goths; see also no. 45.

Christian funerary inscription read: "If anyone violates this tomb may he perish miserably, lie unburied, may he not be resurrected, and may he share the fate of Judas."[54]

The epitaph of Guntelda and her sons Basilius and Guntio from the basilica of St. Julian in Como spells out the rationale of such concerns: "I adjure you, all Christians and you, the guardian blessed Julian, in the name of God and by the fearful day of judgment, that this tomb should never at any time be violated but should endure to the end of the world so that I can return to life without impediment when he comes who is to judge the living and the dead."[55] The author of this epitaph thus believed – quite contrary to official Christian theology – that the dead would be resurrected in exactly the same bodies, the same flesh and bones, as had rested in the grave. The question of the resurrection aside, many other Christian epitaphs – like their pagan antecedents – hint at a belief in some continuing awareness of self in the grave.[56]

Pagan philosophy had counseled the wise to be content with the astral destiny of the soul and not to grieve over the death of the body, while the less philosophically inclined were consoled by the idea of a continuing life in the tomb.[57] By contrast, inscriptions marking the tombs of martyrs and saints regularly associate these two themes – the body resting in the tomb and the soul reigning with God in the stars – with one and the same person.[58] Although Christians changed

---

[54] *ILCV* 3845; also 3844–80, in particular 3859, calling on Sts. Andrew, Donatus, and Justina to punish the violator.

[55] *ILCV* 3863.

[56] Augustine, *De Cura pro Mortuis Gerenda* ["*On the Case to be Taken for the Dead*"], *PL* 40, 591–610. Belief in an afterlife in the tomb was expressed by survivors, whether pagan or Christian, who brought food and drink to the dead on their feast days; see Février, "Culte des morts," 224 ff., 255 ff., and Brown, *Cult of the Saints, passim*. The humble funerary meals of ordinary people were institutionalized in formal banquets for the martyrs, see, e.g., J. Drescher, *Apa Mena. A Selection of Coptic Texts Relating to St. Menas*, edited, with translation and commentary (Cairo, 1946), 150, 157 ff. See also Nöthlichs, "Spätantike Jenseitsvorstellungen," 47–54. The Christian cult of martyrs thus lent authority to the ancient belief in an afterlife in the tomb, see Marrou, "Survivances paiennes"; H. Buschhausen, *Die spätrömischen Metallskrinia und fruhchristlichen Reliquiare. I. Katalog* (Vienna, 1971), C36. At the same time, however, distinctly Christian concepts do emerge in epigraphy, see G. Sanders, "Le tombe et l'éternité: categories distincts où domains contigus? Le dossier épigraphique latin de la Rome chrétienne," *Le temps chrétien de la fin de l'antiquité au moyen âge. IIIe–XIIIe siècles*, Colloques internationaux du CNRS, 64 (Paris, 1984), 185–218; for the ancient background, cf. Dentzer, *Motif du banquet*, 532 ff.

[57] As above, pp. 256, 258.

[58] Venantius Fortunatus, *Carmina*, 4.1, 5, 8, 12, 14; E. LeBlant, *Inscriptions chrétiennes de la Gaule antérieures au VIIIe siècle* (Paris, 1856), 23; *Epigr. Dam.*, ed. Ferrua, 25, 32. However, in Italy, the double vision of the destiny of the deceased may also constitute a re-emergence of an ancient theme; see A. J. Pfiffig, *Religio Etrusca* (Graz, 1975), 162 ff.; M. Meslin, "Persistances paiennnes en Galicie vers la fin du VIe siècle," *Hommages à Marcel Renard* [Col. Latomus, 102], ed. J. Bibauw (Brussels, 1969), II, 512–24, at 524: "la persistance

Fig. 8. Clay pilgrim ampulla, Louvre Museum, Paris. A saint in his shrine

pagan concepts they also gave them a new lease of life. On the tomb of Martin of Tours the visitor thus read: "Confessor in merits, martyr in suffering, apostle in deed, Martin in heaven here shines forth in the tomb; may he remember [us], and purging the sins of our wretched life may he hide our faults by his merits."[59] Another inscription on the tomb of Martin stressed the power of his presence on earth: "Here lies buried Martin the bishop of holy memory, whose soul is in the hand of God, but he is entirely here, present and manifest in all the grace of his virtues."[60] It was thanks to this physical presence in the body that Martin performed miracles at his tomb, and through miracles he not only favored his devotees but also protected his property and thus showed forth his power. Accordingly, just as pagans had depicted the power of a divinity being revealed in a temple, or the deceased sitting in his shrine, so the Christian imagination saw the saint or martyr looking out to his devotees from the doors of his sanctuary (Figs. 8–9).[61]

d'attitudes collectives religieuses nous fait saisir un sacre qui apparaît reposer sur des réalités naturelles, véritables hiérophanies archaïques dont, pour l'heure, le christianisme ne pouvait donner qu'une explication mythique et deformante."

[59] LeBlant, *Inscriptions chrétiennes*, 180; cf. Sidonius Apollinaris, [*Epistulae*] 4.18.

[60] LeBlant, *Inscriptions chrétiennes*, 178; for miracles performed by the saint "from the tomb" see Drescher, *Apa Mena*, 119, 125.

[61] G. Vikan, *Byzantine Pilgrimage Art* (Washington D.C., 1982), fig. 98; C. Metzger, *Les ampoules à eulogie du Musée du Louvre*, Notes et Documents des Musées de France, 3 (Paris, 1981), figs. 98, 100, cf. 102–3; K. Weitzmann, ed., *Age of Spirituality. Late Antique and Early Christian Art, Third to Seventh Century* (New York, 1979), 564–91, see esp. 575, 578, 580–81.

Fig. 9. Ivory relief, Castello Sforzesco, Milan. St Menas before his church

Yet where now it is possible to see continuity between pagan and Christian religious ideas and rituals, late antique observers saw for the most part differences and conflict. Falsity, so Christians asserted, had been defeated by truth, and this conviction determined their missionary strategy throughout the Mediterranean world and beyond. Thus when Benedict founded his monastery on the site of a still-revered temple of Apollo at Monte Cassino, thereby expelling the demon who lived there, he was following a long-established strategy of deliberate confrontation between one sacred code and another.[62]

Precisely this was the issue. If in Christian eyes holiness was not inherent in a place, it could nonetheless be achieved by Christian ritual and by regular worship. Place might be viewed as indifferent, but human action could never be. Augustine pointed out that it was

[62] Gregory the Great, *Dialogues*, 2.8.

human love that endowed the site of a tomb with significance, rather than significance being derived from qualities inherent in that site: "Love leads the way in choosing the place, and therefore when the body has been buried, that same holy place renews and increases the love that had gone before." [63] In short, for many Christians, space, the physical environment in which one lived, was in itself neutral. What made certain parts of space holy was a human impact: worship, possibly the remains of a holy human being, and the unfolding of sacred history.

The similarities between temple and tomb which are suggested by pagan language and iconograpy became fundamental in Christianity. An entire Christian community, not merely single families, paid homage to the martyrs at their tombs, which accordingly became centers of public worship. [64] Concurrently, the martyrs gradually took over the houses of the gods. The sacred topography of the Mediterranean was accordingly transformed in two respects. On the one hand the Christian martyr succeeded the pagan god. And on the other the twofold network of pagan holy places – one of temples, the other of tombs – became a single network of churches sheltering Christian relics and following one single festal calendar in which the private concerns and memories of families were subsumed in the public memory of the entire community. [65] This new sacred topography spelled out not only the collective memories of Christians but also the functioning and distribution of sacred authority in Christian society.

A letter of Sidonius Apollinaris describes a juncture in mid-5th-century Gaul when this evolution was underway but had not yet been completed. Sidonius wrote to inform his kinsman Secundus that thanks to long neglect, the grave of his grandfather had become almost indistinguishable from surrounding ground. Moreover, it had been disturbed by gravediggers, whom Sidonius discovered red-handed and punished with a beating. In doing this, he felt, he had secured the peace of the dead. However, he was also aware that he had intervened in an affair which perhaps should have been left to

---

[63] Augustine, *De Cura pro Mortuis Gerenda*, 4, *PL* 40, 597; on this text, cf. V. Saxer, *Morts, martyrs, reliques*, 165 ff. As so often with Augustine, the sentiment is Ciceronian, see Cicero, [*Leg.*], 2.4, where Atticus, speaking about Cicero's home of Arpinum, says: *movemur enim nescio quo pacto locis ipsis in quibus eorum quos diligimus aut admiramur adsunt vestigia* [("for we are moved in some unknown way by those places in which there are traces of people whom we love or admire")].

[64] The change is stressed by Brown, *Cult of the Saints*, ch. 2.

[65] B. Kötting, *Der frühchristliche Reliquienkult und die Bestattung im Kirchengebäude* (Cologne, 1965).

the local bishop to settle, and to him Sidonius accordingly addressed a letter of apology. In addition he composed an epitaph for the grave and instructed Secundus to supervise its being carved on a slab, seeing that after himself, Secundus was the deceased's next of kin.[66] Thus, where formerly the care of tombs was unequivocally in the hands of kinsmen, Sidonius describes a situation where the bishop's authority had to be allowed for, although the nature of that authority was as yet unclear.[67]

But bishops did in due course become the unchallenged arbiters of elegance in the creation of Christian sacred space. Their decisions were instrumental in bringing into existence a network of holy places – focal points of sacred energy which reached from a saint's body performing miracles in the tomb directly to heaven, where his soul lived with God. Furthermore bishops were the principal beneficiaries of this new view of the environment in that the control of holy places enhanced their power.[68]

One of the first to describe this new understanding of the environment systematically was Pope Damasus. His epitaphs of the Roman martyrs not only designated specific places as holy but also guided the devout visitor through Rome. And they informed the visitor of the city's Christian topography that had been superimposed on the sacred topography of republic and empire. For the first time the "Roma sotterranea" – which was to impassion antiquarians and archaeologists from the 17th century onwards – came to light. But Pope Damasus was more than a helpful guide to holy places and antiquities. For on the one hand his epitaphs introduced to the reader the Roman martyrs and the places where they rested; on the other hand Damasus regularly mentioned his own activity as architect of funerary monuments, panegyrist of the martyrs, and finally as himself a privileged suppliant of those great presences.[69] It thus fell to his successors to perpetuate the work of this doorkeeper of the

---

[66] Sidonius Apollinaris, [*Epistulae*] 3.12.

[67] For other changes in burial customs in late antique Gaul, see H. Sivan, "Funerary Monuments and Funerary Rites in Late Antique Aquitaine," *Oxford Journal of Archaeology*, 5 (1986), 339–53. For two earlier attempts at enhancing episcopal status through claiming jurisdiction over Christian graves, see Augustine, *Confessions*, 6.2; Augustine, *Ep.* 29, *CSEL* 34 (Vienna, 1895); further, Saxer, *Morts, martyrs, reliques*, 133 ff.

[68] For Ambrose's successful bid for authority, see E. Dassmann, "Ambrosius und die Märtyrer," *Jahrbuch für Antike und Christentum*, 18 (1975), 49–68. More generally, on Christian charity, often supervised by bishops and expressed in civic construction, as an extension of sorts of municipal *euergeia* ["euergetism"], see Février, "Permanence et heritages," 131 ff.

[69] [Damasus *Epigrams*], 3, 7 (architect), 15, 18, 18.1, 20, 21, etc. (panegyrist), 16 (suppliant).

Roman saints, as Pope Vigilius did in restoring the site of holy graves
which had been devastated by the Goths.[70] The emergence of a new
supernatural hierarchy punctuated the emergence of a new hierarchy
of potentates on earth. One sustained the other. By the 7th century,
according to the account of a pilgrim, the entire court of heaven was
accessible through and mirrored in the shrines and churches of the
Eternal City:

> As you enter the portico of St. Andrew, the altar of St. Lawrence and then
> those of Sts. Vitus and Cassian meet you on the left, and then the altar of St.
> Andrew himself in the center of the rotunda. [From there you go on to the
> altars of] Sts. Thomas and Apollinaris, and last that of St. Syxtus. As you
> leave, St. Martin will receive you and lead you to [the church of] St.
> Petronella. There, first the Savior of the World will receive you and assign
> you to St. Anastasia, and she to the most holy Mother of God, who will
> commend you to St. Petronella, and then lead you to her son, the Savior of
> the World, who through the blessed Theodore sends you to St. Michael the
> Archangel, so that through his intercesion you should be led once more to
> his most holy Mother, who will bring you to the twelve Apostles, and they
> through St. Peter, the prince of the Apostles, will again send you to St. Mary.[71]

Space as perceived by Christians was thus no longer neutral in the
way that Minucius Felix had envisaged. Rather, in Rome and elsewhere, space was ordered in a system of focal points of sacred power
– that is, by the saints in their churches, most of whom were in turn
surrounded by hosts of departed Christians awaiting the Last Day
in their graves. Sacred topography had come to express the new
religious and social order of postimperial Rome, where, in Gibbon's
graphic phrase, the popes sat enthroned on the tombs of the Caesars.
More concretely, the saints whom the pilgrims visited stage-managed
an elaborate system of courtly introductions that replicated the
introductions a petitioner would need at the court of a terrestrial
potentate.

---

[70] *Ibid.*, 41.
[71] *Codice Topografice della Città di Roma*, ed. R. Valentini and G. Zucchetti (Rome, 1942),
II, 95 f.

12 *A Complex of Times: No More Sheep on Romulus' Birthday*[†][1]

MARY BEARD

This paper argues that one of the functions of the Roman ritual calendar – the sequence of religious festivals as they occurred throughout the year[2] – was to define and delineate Roman power, Roman history and Roman identity; and that it did this by evoking events from different chronological periods of the Roman past and arranging them in a meaningful sequence of time, but not a sequence defined by linear, narrative, history. I am concerned principally with the practice of Roman ritual during the late Republic and early Empire; and my argument depends on taking seriously the discussions of the various festivals preserved in the writings of contemporary Romans and Greeks – men who practised or observed the rituals. I want to stress that we should take the rituals and the preserved exegesis together – and I emphasize *together* – as an important part of a symbolic, religious discourse that continued to be meaningful in the complex urban society of Rome in the age of Cicero, Augustus, Seneca or Hadrian.

1 GENERAL APPROACH

My approach to Roman festivals is different from that normally adopted. Most work on these rituals has looked for (and found) their

---

† Originally published in *Proceedings of the Cambridge Philological Society* 33 (1987) 1–15.

[1] This is an extended English version of a paper first read in French at the Centenary Colloquium of the Fifth Section of the École Pratique des Hautes Études (Paris, September 1986). Thanks are due to Keith Hopkins for his usual good humoured criticism; and to John Scheid whose invitation to the Colloquium encouraged me to think seriously for the first time about the Roman ritual calendar. Richard Hunter, M. M. Mackenzie and Andrew Wallace-Hadrill substantially improved the final form of the paper.

[2] This is the usual sense of the phrase 'ritual calendar' in this paper. Occasionally I use 'calendar' in the perhaps more familiar, but narrower, sense of the written tabulated version of the cycle of festivals (see below, n. 5); the context always makes it clear where this is the case.

underlying logic – their 'meaning', if you like – in the primitive peasant society of archaic Rome. It has tended to relate each festival to the imagined life of the poor Italian farmer, some sweaty noble savage, who worked away with his crops and herds, while solemnly carrying out all the strange and time-consuming rituals related to sowing and reaping, storing and purifying: so, for example, at the festival of the *Robigalia* in April, he sacrificed a dog at the fifth milestone outside Rome to placate the personified spirit of corn-blight (Robigo or Robigus); at the *Vinalia Rustica* in August he made offerings to Jupiter to protect the growing vines; while at the Purification of Trumpets (the *Tubilustrium*) at the end of March he ceremonially marked the beginning of the summer season of war.[3] Even the work of Dumézil and his followers does not substantially change the picture. Although there is much greater sophistication in their comparative approach, which attempts to relate the pattern of Roman rituals to ritual in other Indo-European societies, the central significance of individual festivals is still seen to reside in the agricultural, political and military concerns of the primitive community.[4]

The problem with interpretations of this type is not that they are simply wrong or even implausible; after all, the ancients themselves are known to have claimed that the *Robigalia* was meant to protect the growing corn from blight.[5] The problem is rather their implication, often unnoticed, for the study of Roman religion as a whole. For by locating the 'meaning' of the rituals in the primitive community of peasant farmers, the traditional approaches make it hard to understand the practice of those rituals in the complex urban society of the historical period, several centuries later.[6]

[3] For the standard view on each of these festivals, see H. H. Scullard, *Festivals and ceremonies of the Roman Republic* (1981) 94–5, 108–10, 177. The image of primitive peasant life comes across clearly in C. Bailey, *CAH* VIII (1930) 435–9 and R. M. Ogilvie, *The Romans and their gods* (1969) 70–99.

[4] Perhaps the most characteristic (and strikingly successful) of Dumézil's studies of Roman ritual is his *Fêtes romaines d'été et d'automne* (1975), which elucidates several particularly ill-documented festivals by placing them in a broader Indo-European context. On this book, see now J. Scheid, 'À propos de certaines fêtes d'été', [Aion (Sezione di archeologica e storia antica)] 2 (1980) 41–53. He picks up the notion of the 'peasant society' underlying Dumézil's explanatory framework and asks – pointedly – 'which society, where and at what time?'.

[5] See, for example, the entry in the Praenestine Calendar (dated 6–9 BC) against the day of the *Robigalia* (25 April): 'Feriae Robigo via Claudia ad milliarium V, ne robigo frumentis noceat' ('Festival to Robigus at the fifth milestone on the Via Claudia, to prevent blight (*robigo*) harming the crops'). For the full inscribed entry, see A. Degrassi, *Inscriptiones Italiae* XIII (1963) 130–1, 448–9.

[6] Dumézil does sometimes attempt to demonstrate the continuing significance into the historical period of the 'original meaning' of a festival. So, for example, he claims that it was not by chance that Mark Antony chose the *Lupercalia* (in Dumézil's view a festival concerned with the primitive kingship of the city) to offer Caesar the royal crown; the political importance of the scene depended on the spectators knowing and understanding the original regal

This disjunction between primitive meaning and historical practice is an important factor in our inability to make sense of Roman festivals – and of Roman religion in general – during the late Republic and early Empire. How can we possibly imagine sophisticated intellectuals like Cicero or sceptical poets like Ovid leaping through bonfires in a ritual concerned with the purification of flocks and herds?[7] Or sacrificing pregnant cows, tearing out and burning their foetuses in order to promote the fertility of the land?[8] We know that these rituals continued to be carried out and that men of the elite continued to officiate as priests – our sources make that quite clear; and indeed Ovid more than once writes as if he had himself participated in or observed particular festivals.[9] But we mostly remain at a complete loss about how to relate the supposed primitive agricultural significance of the rituals to the complex urban concerns of those practising the rituals in the historical period. Of course, it is precisely this sense of bafflement that goes to confirm, in traditional accounts, the emptiness of the Roman religious system during the late Republic and early Empire. It seems to be a system in which people went on performing all the old rituals – when even for the practitioners the significance of those rituals was meaningless, lost in the distant past.[10]

I am taking a very different approach. I do this by looking at what the ancients themselves wrote about various festivals of their ritual calendar – particularly the explanations they offered for the origin of these festivals, so-called 'aetiologies'.[11] The main texts referred to were all written during the last century BC and the first and early second centuries AD: they are, most importantly, Ovid's *Fasti*, the *Roman Antiquities* of Dionysius of Halicarnassus, and various

associations of the rite. Yet, even in this case, Dumézil admits the disjunction between his suggested religious meaning and contemporary life: 'our information dates from an era in which we can no longer hope to obtain a complete and systematic view of rites which had long ceased to correspond to religious and social reality'. See G. Dumézil, *Archaic Roman religion* (1970) 346–50 (quote, p. 350).

[7] This particular ritual element forms part of the festival of the *Parilia* discussed below, pp. 277–78.

[8] I refer here to the festival of the *Fordicidia* (15 April); for a brief account, see Scullard, *Festivals* 102 and Dumézil, *Archaic Roman religion* 371–4.

[9] [Ovid] *Fast.* 4. 725 (*Parilia*); 4. 905–9 (*Robigalia*). It is, of course, quite unknowable whether Ovid 'really' participated in or observed these festivals.

[10] Note, for example, the bafflement of R. M. Ogilvie, who writes in relation to the *Lemuria*, a ritual of the dead which involved the celebrant at midnight spitting out black beans from his mouth: 'At first sight it is difficult to imagine Livy or Horace or Agrippa getting out of bed and solemnly going through this ritual. And yet they probably did – at least in a modified form' (*Romans and their gods* 85).

[11] I refer almost exclusively in this paper to *written* aetiologies. No doubt there was also an active oral tradition; but this is now irrecoverable to us.

antiquarian and biographical works of Plutarch. Also taken into consideration are some rather later texts and various comments on individual festivals incorporated into surviving versions of the official state calendar – normally inscribed on stone, but also sometimes in manuscript form.[12]

I am not, of course, treating these aetioiogical stories as objective commentaries or as 'real' explanations of the festivals or of their origins. It would make no sense to take as literally true claims that Aeneas himself founded the *Vinalia Priora* or that Romulus established the *Consualia* in order to lure the Sabines to Rome and so make off with their womenfolk![13] My argument is rather that these stories are themselves symbolic and as such, are an integral part of Roman religious discourse. In other words ritual actions and the narratives which purport to explain those actions *together* form Roman religious experience and *together* construct Roman religious meanings. Roman aetiology is, in an important sense, like the native exegeses discussed by Sperber in *Rethinking Symbolism*: it 'does not constitute the interpretation of the symbol [in this case symbolic ritual] but one of its extensions, and must itself be symbolically interpreted'.[14] One obvious objection to this procedure is that the written narratives I am using are not 'native exegesis' in the proper sense, but rather intellectualizing 'interpretation'. The contrast is drawn sharply by Detienne: 'Exegesis proliferates from inside; it is a speech which nourishes the tradition of which it is a part, whereas interpretation emerges the moment there is an outside perspective, when some in society begin to question, to criticize the tradition, to distance themselves with regard to the histories of the tribe'.[15] In the case of Roman rituals and their aetiologies, men such as Ovid or (even more so) the Greeks Dionysius and Plutarch might be seen as essentially marginal to Roman culture and religion. As 'intellectuals'

---

[12] For full evidence of the surviving calendars, see Degrassi, *Inscriptiones Italiae*.

[13] For Aeneas and the *Vinalia Priora* (a different festival from the *Vinalia Rustica* mentioned above), see [Ovid] *Fast.* 4. 879–900; Plutarch, *Roman questions* 45 (and other references collected by Degrassi, *Inscriptiones Italiae* 446–7). The story was (in Ovid's version) that, during Aeneas' war with Turnus, Mezentius (the Etruscan leader) promised to help Turnus, if he received a pledge in return for half of the next year's vintage; but Aeneas turned the tables on this offer by vowing the vintage, if *he* won, to Jupiter himself. Aeneas, of course, was victorious and from that day on the Romans offered up the first fruits of the vintage at the *Vinalia* to Jupiter. For the *Consualia* and the plot to steal the Sabine women, see Dionysius of Halicarnassus, *Roman antiquities* 2.31 (though there are many divergent versions, including the story told by Dionysius himself that the festival was founded by Evander: 1. 33. 2).

[14] D. Sperber, *Rethinking symbolism* (1975) 17–50 (quote, p. 48).

[15] See M. Detienne, 'Rethinking mythology' in M. Izard and P. Smith (eds.), *Between belief and transgression* (1982) 43–52 (quote p. 48). Detienne is particularly concerned with intellectuals in the Greek world, but the terms of his analysis could equally well be applied to Rome.

and, in some cases, as 'foreigners' they offered a commentary on Roman ritual from an independent external standpoint; their writing did not form an integral part of traditional symbolic religious discourse.

The force of this objection depends on seeing a clear division between 'traditional' Roman religion and the 'foreign' or 'intellectual', as represented by the literary Greco-Roman culture of the late Republic and early Principate. Such a division is not inherently implausible, but it tends to oversimplify the complex amalgam that constituted Roman religion throughout the historical period. In the history of Roman religion there is no easy distinction to be made between the 'inside' and the 'outside'. It is, in fact, a mark of the religious system of Rome that, from its earliest period, it constantly incorporated Greek and other ostensibly foreign elements; and, in an increasingly Hellenized world, it generated new (often 'intellectual') religious perspectives – most of which have a claim to be seen as internal rather than external to 'native' traditions. In my view, there is no reason necessarily to regard the illiterate (and, for us, mute) peasant as a truer representative of the Romanness of Roman religion than Hellenized Roman intellectuals or Roman Greeks. Moreover, by taking the writing of Ovid, Dionysius and Plutarch on religious festivals as internal religious exegesis, rather than marginal commentary, we can arrive at new and useful results in an area of notorious difficulty.[16]

2 THE *PARILIA*: THE TEXTS

For most of this paper I shall consider just one theme that seems to me particularly important in understanding the practice of Roman ritual: the theme of time and history. I shall approach this theme first by analysing some examples of the written accounts and aetiologies of Roman ritual that I have been referring to. In this section (2), I shall present my chosen texts; in the following sections (3–7) I shall draw out their various implications, offering an analysis of the function and operation of Roman ritual.

All the chosen texts refer to the festival of the *Parilia*, which took place each year on 21 April. There were, no doubt, many variant forms of the ritual – but if we follow the account of Ovid (who had himself, he claims, taken part in the ritual) the festival traditionally

---

[16] For Rome's traditional tendency to incorporate religious forms from outside, see J. A. North, 'Conservatism and change in Roman religion', *PBSR* n.s. 30 (1976) 1–12.

proceeded – at least in the countryside – something like this: the celebrant (let us imagine him – as usual – to be a shepherd!) would first clean out his sheep-pens and decorate them with branches and festoons; he would then light a bonfire and scatter onto it sulphur – so that the smoke fumigated the sheep; offerings of cake and milk were then brought and a prayer was said to the deity Pales – asking for protection for the flocks; the shepherd finally washed himself in dew, drank milk and leapt through the still burning bonfire. The urban form of the festival must have differed in various respects, but it probably contained a number of the same elements, modified for the urban context.[17]

There have been many modern interpretations of this festival. The standard textbook answer is to see the ritual as a festival of purification of flocks and herds – a festival which at some point (as we shall see in the following passages) became identified as the anniversary of the foundation of Rome. In fact to this very day 21 April is still celebrated as the birthday of Rome.[18]

The first passage that concerns us is an extract from Plutarch's *Life of Romulus*. Plutarch is describing the foundation of the city of Rome and discussing the general consensus on the precise date of that foundation. For him, at least in this context, the first association of the festival of the *Parilia* is as a marker of the anniversary of the birthday of the city. It is only in second place that he mentions the *Parilia* as a pastoral festival, associated with a time before the foundation of the city.

Text 1

Now it is agreed that the city was founded on the twenty-first of April, and this day the Romans celebrate with a festival, calling it the birthday of their country. And at first, as it is said, they sacrificed no living creature at that festival, but thought they ought to keep it pure and without stain of blood, since it commemorated the birth of their country. However, even before the founding of the city, they had a pastoral festival on that day, and called it *Parilia*.[19]

The same two elements occur in Dionysius of Halicarnassus' account of the festival. Again, Dionysius is concerned with the foundation of Rome; but for him the relationship between the anniver-

---

[17] See [Ovid] *Fast.* 4. 721–862 (lines 783–806 quoted below). In addition to the major texts reprinted in this article, see the citations on the *Parilia* collected by Degrassi, *Inscriptiones Italiae* 443–5.

[18] See, for example, Scullard, *Festivals* 103–5 and G. Wissowa, *Religion und Kultus der Römer* ed. 2 (1912) 199–201. On the identity of the god (or goddess) Pales, see G. Dumézil, *Idées romaines* (1969) 273–87.

[19] Plutarch, *Romulus* 12. 1–2.

sary celebrations of the city and the festival of flocks and herds is rather more problematic.

Text 2

This day the Romans celebrate every year even down to my own time as one of their greatest festivals and call it the *Parilia*. On this day, which comes in the beginning of Spring, the husbandmen and herdsmen offer up a sacrifice of thanksgiving for the increase of their cattle. But whether they had celebrated this day in even earlier times as a day of rejoicing and for that reason looked upon it as the most suitable for the founding of the city, or whether, because it marked the beginning of the building of the city, they should honour on it the gods who are propitious to shepherds, I cannot say for certain.[20]

Ovid's account of the *Parilia* (*text 3*) is much more complex; after describing the practice of the festival, with its bonfires, shepherds' prayers and flame-leaping, he offers a great variety of explanations for the ritual. He picks out particularly the elements of fire and water – the washing of the hands in dew and the lighting of bonfires – and focusses his explanations first on those opposing elements. Only in second place does he turn to 'mythological' explanations for the origin of the rite; and he alludes finally to the role of the festival as the anniversary of the foundation of Rome (a theme fully developed in the passage immediately following that printed below).

Text 3

I have set forth the custom; it remains for me to tell its origin. The multitude of explanations creates a doubt and thwarts me at the outset. Devouring fire purges all things and melts the dross from out the metals; therefore it purges the shepherd and the sheep. Or are we to suppose that, because all things are composed of opposite principles, fire and water – those two discordant deities – therefore our fathers did conjoin these elements and thought meet to touch the body with fire and sprinkled water? Or did they deem these two important because they contain the source of life, the exile loses them, and by them the bride is made a wife? Some suppose (though I can hardly do so) that the allusion is to Phaethon and Deucalion's flood. Some people also say that when shepherds were knocking stones together, a spark suddenly leaped forth; the first indeed was lost, but the second was caught in straw; is that the reason of the flame at the Parilia? Or is the custom rather based on the piety of Aeneas, whom, even in the hour of defeat, the fire allowed to pass unscathed? Or is it haply nearer the truth that, when Rome was founded, orders were given to transfer the household gods to the new houses and to the cottages they were about to abandon, and that they and their cattle leaped through the flames? Which happens even to the present time on the birthday of Rome.[21]

---

[20] Dionysius of Halicarnassus, *Roman antiquities* 1.88.3.
[21] [Ovid] *Fast.* 4. 783–806. For the complex narrative of the foundation of Rome under Romulus, see 807–62.

The final passage (*text 4*) is much later; it is taken from Athenaeus'
Deipnosophistae – a work of the late second or early third century
AD, which depicted in (originally) thirty books the dinner-time discussion of twenty-nine learned men on a variety of academic and
antiquarian topics. This passage is not an aetiology of the festival,
but simply a passing reference to it: the banqueters are in the middle
of their dinner when suddenly they hear outside the noise of a public
procession, which turns out to be associated with the festival of
21 April. The important point to note is the change in the festival's
name: when the emperor Hadrian chose the day of the festival to
found his temple of the Fortune of Rome, what used to be called the
Parilia became the *Romaia*.

Text 4

It so happened that it was the festival of the *Parilia*, as it used to be called,
though it is now called the Roman Festival, instituted in honour of the
Fortune of Rome, when her temple was erected by that best and most enlightened of emperors, Hadrian. That day is celebrated annually as especially
glorious by all the residents of Rome and by all who happen to be staying in
the city.[22]

3 THE VARIETY OF EXPLANATIONS

My first point is, to some extent, an aside. It represents a first, immediate reaction to the texts as presented. One of the most striking
aspects of these ancient accounts is the sheer variety, the sheer range
of explanations on offer – from the symbolic clash of discordant
elements to the circumstantial events surrounding the foundation
of Rome. Of course, it is precisely this feature – this whole series of
diverse explanations – that has led most people to undervalue these
accounts and to dismiss them as ever more fanciful intellectualizing
speculation. This is, no doubt, partly because the traditional aim
of the historian in writing narrative or political history has been to
provide the single best account of the events under consideration and
to dismiss divergent or conflicting evidence as in some sense inferior.
But other types of history – particularly in the fields of religion or
culture – can incorporate divergence as a positive advantage. In the
case of the *Parilia*, for example, the wide variety of different explanations offered by our ancient sources is an indication of the strongly
evocative power of the festival itself: it had no single meaning; it

[22] Athenaeus 8.361e–f. For the background to the Hadrianic developments reported in this
passage, see J. Beaujeu, *La religion romaine à l'apogée de l'Empire* 1 (1955) 128–36.

constantly generated new and changing stories and interpretations. Indeed, as I shall argue in greater detail below, the continued reson- ance of such festivals in Roman society during the historical period depended on this wide dispersion of their meaning; on the festivals' capacity to be constantly reinterpreted and re-understood.

4 THE ARGUMENT: A SUMMARY

I want now to concentrate on the particular aspect of ritual that relates to time and history (or better *Roman* time and *Roman* history). I shall sketch the main outline of my argument first, before returning to the texts associated with the *Parilia* to develop more fully the different points and to draw out the general implications.

My central thesis is that the Roman ritual calendar together with its exegetical texts (and no doubt also its exegetical oral tradition) offered one important way of 'imaging' Roman history, even imaging Rome itself. By 'imaging Rome' I mean that the festivals of the ritual calendar, together with the aetiological narratives associated with each, offered to the Roman participants, year by year, a series of tableaux, evoking different elements of Roman religion and history. That is, each festival, with all its different associations, presented and represented a picture of Romanness – linking the past with the present, and bringing together apparently diverse aspects of the Roman religious and cultural tradition. In a sense, the ritual calen- dar as a whole can be seen as a conceptual pageant of Rome and of what it was to be Roman.

This pageant did not present a fixed, unchanging view of Roman- ness. Like a modern carnival procession – with its jostling and juxta- position of banners, its changing order and hierarchy, its different appearance from one moment to the next, as people join in or drop out from the main line – it incorporated new, changing, divergent images of what Rome was. It could do this because there was no main narrative thread linking one festival and the next. Unlike the Protestant ritual calendar – which year by year reenacts from one festival to another the narrative of the life of Christ, in a sequence which can hardly admit change – the Roman festal year generated new associations and meanings outside any overriding annual story- line.

The essential opposition here is between a calendar (such as the Protestant) whose meaning is dominated by the syntagmatic links between its various rituals, and a calendar (such as the Roman) in which meaning is largely constructed by paradigmatic association.

Drawn from theories of linguistic analysis, 'syntagmatic meaning' is the sense held by a unit of language in a linear sequence. 'In its place in a syntagma, any unit acquires its value simply in opposition to what precedes or what follows, or both.' 'Paradigmatic meaning', on the other hand, invests linguistic units with significance, not through their position in any particular sequence, but through all the associations of opposition or similarity that they evoke in the mind. So, for example, in the catch-phrase 'the cat sat on the mat', the word 'cat' evokes associations with 'dog', 'tiger', 'bat', 'cab' and many more. As Saussure put it, 'any term acts as the centre of a constellation, from which connected terms radiate *ad infinitum*'. It was precisely the Roman calendar's reliance on building up associations and images on a paradigmatic model outside any determining narrative that gave the individual festival a fluid meaning in relation to the others in the sequence. In short, the stress on the paradigm over the syntagm allowed the incorporation into the calendar of new stories, new aetiologies – and so also new *meanings* – for the festivals.[23]

This brief summary needs some amplification. In the following sections (5 and 6) I present two elaborations on my theme in particular relation to the texts printed above. These elaborations – the first on the idea of the historical pageant, the second on the paradigmatic emphasis of the Roman ritual calendar – are not straightforward proofs of my argument; they are rather developments from it, which add depth and weight to my brief summary.

5 THE HISTORICAL PAGEANT

The first elaboration concerns the historical pageant. We can start here from the texts on the *Parilia*. One striking feature of these texts is their stress on the historical time and historical circumstances of the origin of the festival. The accounts of Plutarch (*text 1*) and of Dionysius of Halicarnassus (*text 2*) illustrate this – and its possible complexity – very clearly. At its most straightforward level, the cel-

---

[23] See F. de Saussure, *Course in general linguistics* (tr. R. Harris, 1983, 121–5 (quotes pp. 121 and 124)). The Roman ritual calendar is not, of course, entirely without syntagmatic meaning. There are for example, clear relationships between festivals following one another at particular intervals in the Roman calendar: pairs of festivals, separated by one day, appear often to be complementary (the *Cerealia* of 19 April concerned with crops, the *Parilia* of 21 April concerned with herds; the *Vestalia* of 9 June concerned with the fire of the hearth, the *Matralia* of 11 June with the light of the dawn); while similarly those separated by three days sometimes suggest the same underlying preoccupation from slightly different points of view (the *Consualia* of 21 August and *Opiconsivia* of 25 August; the *Consualia* of 15 December and *Opalia* of 19 December – all concerned with the use and storage of crops). See further, Wissowa, *Religion und Kultus* 437; Dumézil, *Fêtes* 22.

ebration of the *Parilia* evoked for both writers the moment of the foundation of Rome by Romulus. But there were other associations too, as both writers recognized that the history of the festival extended back beyond Romulus' foundation. The *Parilia*, in other words, evoked not only the traditional Romulean foundation of the city, but also that limbo time before Rome was a city but when (by a mythological paradox) many of Rome's customs already existed.[24]

In several accounts of the *Parilia*, the evocation of the misty early history of the city serves to link present day (Augustan) Rome with its paraded forebears – the honourable, incorruptible men of Rome's Golden Age. That certainly is one reading of Ovid's lengthy description (following *text 3*) of the foundation of Rome and of Tibullus' brief allusions to the *Parilia* in Poem 2.5. By focusing on Pales (along with Pan) as the principal deities of the primitive community of Rome, Tibullus imbues with the primitive virtues of piety and simplicity his *contemporary* celebrants of the *Parilia* – countrymen who, even in the age of Augustus, under happy omens, drank deep of their wine and leapt through the flames of the *Parilia*'s bonfires.[25] But the images of the pageant can offer subversive readings too. The display of the heroes of the early city can also point up the distance (rather than the closeness) between Augustan and Romulean Rome. So, for example, Ovid's readers could find a tension between the practice of their own day and their, perhaps quaint, primitive antecedents – a tension whose comic effects served only to deflate Augustus' paraded links with the Romulean past. The evocation of early history in the exegesis of Roman ritual was not, in other words, simply a means of legitimating contemporary claims to authority; it could also undermine those claims. In that subversive potential, no doubt, part of its strength lay.[26]

Other festivals and their exegesis evoke other times. Some, like the *Parilia*, take us back to the myth-history of earliest Rome.[27] Others

---

[24] This limbo time is clearly evoked by the activities of the Arcadian king Evander in *Aeneid* 8 – a Roman *avant la lettre*, who performed already 'Roman' cult (that of Hercules at the *Ara Maxima*, for example) on the site of Rome before the city's foundation by Romulus. (See also n. 27 on the *Lupercalia*.)

[25] Tib. 2.5.28, 87–90, with F. Cairns, *Tibullus* (1979) 79–86 (though Cairns' suggestion that the poem effectively incorporates two *descriptions* of the *Parilia* seems wrong; we are dealing rather with a reference to the primitive deity Pales (28), followed by a brief description of the contemporary *Parilia* (87–90)).

[26] I am grateful to Andrew Wallace-Hadrill for raising this point.

[27] Note, for example, Ovid's explanations of the *Lupercalia* (*Fast.* 2.267–452) which take the reader back to the time of the mythical king Evander, before the foundation of the city, and to the youthful exploits of Romulus and Remus (cf. Plutarch, *Romulus* 21.4–8; Val. Max. 2.2.9). Similarly the *Consualia* and *Vinalia* (n. 13, above).

present more recent time. So, for example, Ovid's treatment of the *Carmentalia* (unlike the *Parilia*) locates its origin in the third century BC; he tells of the protest of Roman women who refused to bear children until their traditional right to drive in carriages – recently removed from them – was returned; the Senate, whose hand was thus forced, gave them back their rights and instituted a festival of the goddess Carmenta (a deity who protected childbirth) in order to help the birthrate.[28]

More recent time still could be evoked by the days in the calendar which marked the anniversary and the celebration of the foundation of particular temples. We know no details of the rituals which took place on these occasions; but each anniversary must surely have called to mind the narrative history of the temple's foundation. So, for example, the annual celebrations of the Temple of *Fortuna Huiusque Diei* in the Campus Martius must have involved recollection of Rome's victory at the battle of Vercellae in 101 BC and the vow made in the midst of that battle by Q. Lutatius Catulus that he would dedicate such a temple at Rome, if the gods granted victory to the Romans. In fact, one of the commonest circumstances for the foundation of a temple was just such a vow by a Roman general in the midst of battle, fulfilled by the building of a temple – often financed by the spoils – after the victory. It was almost as if the days marking the anniversaries of temples acted as a recurrent public reminder of Rome's past successes – recent or far distant.[29]

By the time of the early Empire, of course, festival days gained a new type of association – in the life, career and successes of the emperor, his family and his predecessors on the throne. Important events in the life of Caesar or of Augustus, say, became incorporated into the calendar both on days without any particular previous ritual significance and also on days of the old traditional festivals. So, for example, the day of the *Parilia* became associated under Caesar with games to commemorate the announcement of Caesar's victory at

---

[28] [Ovid] *Fast.* 1.617–36 (refering to the *Carmentalia* of 15 January); see also, for a similar explanation, Plutarch, *Roman questions* 56. For other aetiologies (including the story that the festival was founded by – perhaps – Romulus, after his capture of Fidenae), see Degrassi, *Inscriptiones Italiae* 394–6, 398. For a brief review of the problems of the interpretation of the festival, see Scullard, *Festivals* 62–4. A similar middle Republican aetiology is found for the *Lesser Quinquatrus* (13 June; Scullard, *Festivals* 152–3) – according to which the festival was established after a strike of flute-players in 311 BC (see [Livy] 9.30.5–10; [Ovid] *Fast.* 6. 649–710).

[29] For Catulus' vow, see Plutarch, *Marius* 26. For a similar example, note the foundation of the Temple of Bellona in the Circus Flaminius, vowed in 296 BC by Appius Claudius Caecus ([Livy] 10.19.17).

Munda;[30] while 17 March, the day of the traditional *Liberalia*, was also marked in the calendars as the anniversary of the victory itself in Spain. This did not necessarily wipe out the previous associations of the day, but it did at least offer an alternative. Performing the *Liberalia*, 'thinking' the *Liberalia*, gained a new layer of historical evocation.[31]

The cumulation of all these different associations throughout the year, developed and elaborated in written and oral exegesis, is what constitutes the pageant of the Roman calendar. As the year progressed a whole series of different images was conjured up from different stages of Rome's history, from the era of myth to the present day, overlapping one with another in 'ritual time'.

6 THE IMPORTANCE OF THE PARADIGM

The second elaboration concerns the generation of new ritual meanings in the ritual calendar and the gradually shifting focus of the evocation of individual festivals. I have already mentioned the Caesarian associations acquired by both the *Parilia* and the *Liberalia*, in addition to their traditional meanings. The *Parilia*, in fact, provides further important illustration of the way individual festivals could shift in their major centre of significance.

I have already suggested that the great list of explanations provided by Ovid (*text 3*) was important for our understanding of how the festival continued to have resonance at Rome through changing historical and social circumstances. In my view, it is the continuing capacity to generate stories and aetiologies that is crucial for the continuance of a festival. Some of these stories will necessarily be marginal and idiosyncratic – one person's way of making the ritual make sense for themselves. But other versions and other stories will gain widespread acceptance; and as new stories take over from old, so the 'meaning' of the ritual changes. It is a complicated process; but it is essentially the way in which apparently static ritual forms

·

[30] See [Cassius] Dio, *Histories* 43.42.3 (although note that these games appear quickly to have fallen out of use; cf. *Histories* 45.6.4). Beaujeu, *La religion romaine* 131 suggests that Caesar, like Hadrian later, was rather attempting to turn the festival into an 'official' festival of the anniversary of Rome.

[31] For the *Liberalia* marked in calendars as the anniversary of Munda, see Degrassi, *Inscriptiones Italiae* 426 with Appian, *Civil war* 2.106.442 and [Cassius] Dio, *Histories* 43.44.6. The traditional associations of the *Liberalia* were as a festival of Liber Pater (who became equated with the Greek Dionysus); it was also the day on which Roman boys traditionally 'came of age'. See, briefly, Scullard, *Festivals* 91–2.

manage to continue to be meaningful when the society within which they are practised has radically changed.

Ovid's list, of course, seems a bit absurd. He gives too many explanations at once; no one individual at Rome could ever have thought all that at the same time, in the way we have to read it. There is, moreover, as they are juxtaposed, a certain tension between the different styles of exegesis – the attempts to delineate a 'physical' explanation (in terms of elemental opposition) lying somewhat uneasily beside the appeals to Greco-Roman myth-history (whether Phaethon and Deucalion, Aeneas or Romulus).[32] But if we keep in mind the theoretical importance of Ovid's profusion of explanations and turn to the other passages cited, it is possible to see a shift of focus in the festival of the *Parilia* taking place through historical time.

There are two main explanations of the festival offered by the texts – on the one hand, that it is a festival of herds and flocks, and on the other that it is a commemoration of the birthday of Rome. Plutarch implies a chronological development here – with an early pastoral festival becoming subsequently associated with the foundation of the city; Dionysius queries the relationship between the two – not knowing which came first. I would like to suggest, at the risk of oversimplification, that Plutarch's symbolic narrative is (no doubt quite fortuitously) historical: that is, an early pastoral festival of the primitive Roman community became actively reinterpreted in the increasingly urban society of Rome into a festival of the city and its origin.[33] By the time of Hadrian (as recorded by Athenaeus) the association of the day with the anniversary of Rome had become so strong that the name of the festival had been changed from *Parilia* to *Romaia*; and new celebrations (connected with Hadrian's foundation of the Temple of Rome) marked the day out definitively as the *Natalis* (birthday) of the city.[34]

---

[32] For 'tension' between different styles of Roman religious discourse, see M. Beard, 'Cicero and divination: the formation of a Latin discourse', *JRS* 76 (1986) 33–46. There is, of course, no reason to assume (as has often been done) that Ovid and his sophisticated contemporaries would have 'really believed' the 'scientific', 'rationalising' explanations, and would have effectively dismissed the 'mythological' exegesis as primitive mumbo-jumbo. The point is that the two forms could, if awkwardly, exist side by side.

[33] I must stress here the *fortuitous* coincidence between Plutarch's symbolic narrative and my 'historical' reconstruction. I am not in any sense going back on my primary contention that these exegeses are an integral part of Roman religious experience, not external explanations of it.

[34] In attempting to reconcile the account of Athenaeus with the archaeological evidence for the new temple, I follow here the narrative of the Hadrianic developments suggested by Beaujeu (*La religion romaine* 128–33): that the first *formal* celebration of Rome's birthday on 21 April (a celebration of a *Romaia* that is, rather than just a *Parilia*) probably took place in

That shift is enormous and must be understood in relation to two particular factors. First, there is an important dynamic towards change in ritual meaning provided by the exegetical texts I have been discussing. The constant story-telling, questioning, interpretation and reinterpretation around Roman festivals prevents the significance of the festival from becoming fixed. Only when the story-telling stopped would the dead hand of orthodoxy lock the meaning of the ritual into the concerns of one moment of Roman history. Second, as I suggested above, such a vast shift depends on the very limited importance of the syntagmatic axis in the Roman ritual calendar. If, as in the Protestant Christian church, the calendar incorporated a single narrative story running throughout the year, no one festival could undergo such a vast change – at least not without upsetting the whole story.[35] Because in the Roman calendar meaning is so strongly located in the paradigm, substantial shifts in the focus of individual festivals are possible. New aspects of the present (or the past) can be incorporated (or discarded) at will. The *Parilia* is just one example of this. Right through the calendar the apparently easy incorporation, in the early principate, of new associations with the imperial power – the celebration of the birthday of emperors, the anniversaries of their military successes – provides yet further indication of the adaptability of the Roman ritual year, and hence its astonishing powers of survival.[36]

7 CONCLUSION:
REPRESENTATIONS OF TIME

My main argument in this paper has been that one important aspect of the ritual calendar at Rome (and of the exegesis that went with it)

121 AD; that the decision was taken at that time to found a temple of Venus and Rome (or Fortune of Rome or just Temple of the City, as it is variously called), whose foundation day thus fell on 21 April (although it was not completed till some years later); that in later years the celebrations of 21 April combined the commemoration of the birthday of the city and (as a further symbolic marker) the commemoration of the foundation of the temple. One must remember, of course, that the specific association of the day of the *Parilia* with the birthday of Rome long predated Hadrian; the earliest surviving (Republican) calendar of the city marks the day as '*Parilia*: Roma condita' (*Parilia*: Rome founded); see Degrassi, *Inscriptiones Italiae* 443.

[35] The Protestant church has, of course, other ways of incorporating changes into its festal year. A different political ideology, for example, can be assimilated by providing prominent positions for political leaders in the enactment of ritual or by carrying out rituals in locations normally associated with the political establishment.

[36] The incorporation of 'imperial' festivals into the traditional calendar is not necessarily as 'innocent' a process as my analysis may suggest. In part, we are no doubt dealing with a seamless web, 'naturally' assimilating the new political order; in part, we may imagine a consciously ideological use of existing tradition by Caesar, Augustus and their followers.

was its capacity to project Rome and Roman history, and to adapt the image projected. The calendar was one way (and a changing way) of representing 'Roman time'. It was not, of course, the only way. Consider for a moment the Rome of Augustus – and compare the image of Rome constructed by the calendar with that of the narrative of Livy's history or of the famous map of the Roman empire started by Agrippa, finished by Augustus and publicly displayed in the city.[37] All these cultural forms were about Rome and Romanness – but they operated in different ways. Agrippa's map projected Rome in terms of place and empire. It was principally a synchronic view of Rome – Rome and its empire were there, as if they had been there for ever.[38] Livy's narrative, by contrast, offered a diachronic view of Rome: once upon a time Rome was nothing – but gradually year by year, book by book through Livy's narrative, we see it developing into a splendid imperial power. The ritual calendar and the exegesis that went with it was different from either of these, neither a diachronic nor a synchronic image of Rome. It offered a pageant of what it was to be Roman, which existed in 'ritual time', in time whose sequence had collapsed into an overlapping series of stories. In brief it constituted a perfect image of 'Romanness': to perform the rituals through the year – whether you were a poor peasant or a sophisticated Roman intellectual – was to discover and rediscover that Romanness.[39]

[37] For a full (but dull) account of this exciting document, see O. A. W. Dilke, *Greek and Roman maps* (1985) 41–53. The map is there treated in entirely utilitarian terms; only at the end of the account (p. 53) is there a hint of anything more: 'Also the full extent of the Roman Empire could be seen at a glance'.

[38] I say this image was *principally* synchronic, for of course it also allowed speculation on the (diachronic) narrative history of the growth of the Roman world.

[39] For other discussions of the importance of calendars in cognitive systems, see P. Bourdieu, *Outline of a theory of practice* (1977) 96–109 and the various papers collected in *Systèmes de pensée en Afrique noire* 7 (1984) (special issue on 'Calendriers d'Afrique').

PART VII

Continuity and Change, from Republic to Empire

Introduction to Part VII:
Continuity and Change,
from Republic to Empire

Most historians of Roman religion have been historians of change or difference. Assembling and organizing some body of evidence, they look for, and attempt to explain, patterns in their data indicative of change over time or difference across regions, social strata, sexes, or ethnic groups. To follow Max Black in his analysis of model-building, this process allows us to redescribe things or, perhaps, to reinscribe data within the sphere of our interests, within the stories we wish to tell.[1] The process resembles modeling in others respects, too, not least in requiring historians to emphasize and perhaps exaggerate some patterns at the expense of others. This latter task takes place both explicitly and implicitly, but it is, even when un-acknowledged, an essential component of historical research: for difference – which is often called "interest" or "importance," as though these qualities were intrinsic and adhered to some essence of events – is a relationship *to* something; and change, to be meaning-ful, must be measured *against* something.

Life is messy, and the survival of evidence from the ancient world has been contingent. Although, therefore, ancient literary and material remains exist in outrageous abundance – much, much more, surely, than any one person could control – there may still not be enough of any particular kind, or from any one region or era, to tell the stories that interest us.[2] One challenge facing ancient historians in general, and historians of Roman religion among them, is, there-fore, to frame questions that our data are prepared to answer.

Among the genres of religious historiography practiced by students of Rome, the narration of change presents particular and substantial difficulties. These arise principally from two features of Roman

[1] Black 1962: 219–43.
[2] Cf. MacMullen 1990: 3–12; Millar 2002: 1–22.

culture writ large: first, within our period, Rome grew from a small, iron age village of central Italy into the largest city of the pre-modern world, capital of a vast empire, and in so doing encountered and absorbed gods and ideas on an almost incomprehensible scale; second, Romans domesticated many of the changes attendant on this expansion through professions of adherence to a conservativism of an impossibly high standard. The complex relationship between these cultural-historical phenomena are well captured in a speech Cicero delivered in 66 BC, advocating passage of a law that assigned a province of unprecedented size to Gnaeus Pompey: "I am also urged that nothing new should be done contrary to the precedents and practices of our ancestors. I will not bother to point out here that our ancestors obeyed custom in times of peace, but necessity in times of war, always developing new plans and policies to meet the new crises of the day."[3] In other words, claims Cicero, nothing was so in keeping with the "precedents and practices of our ancestors" as constant innovation.

The enormous energy generated by Roman expansion found expression in Roman religion in three ways that directly impinge upon the historiographic tradition, each implicated in the others. First, often following reductive and interested readings of Roman texts, scholars long posited and sought to describe some original, purely "Roman" religion – the religion of Cicero's "ancestors." Many such projects naturally participated in ideological currents whose parameters developed outside the academy as such, whether Romantic or nationalist. (It would be a grievous mistake, however, to suppose that participation of that kind will have overdetermined the content and worth of its products.) The most obvious and enduring manifestation of the presuppositions underlying this body of research is an insistent focus on decline: from the native spirituality of a simpler era – an aniconic, mythless farmer's religion, according to some – Romans were gradually divorced from their "true" religion, above all through the influence of Greeks, whose myths and philosophical theology shattered the faith of those priests whose sincerity was essential to the functioning of the system.[4]

The second consequence of Roman expansion to concern us here

---

[3] Cicero *Leg. Man.* 60.

[4] Learned, valuable, and yet ultimately distorting histories of this kind include Warde Fowler 1911; Latte 1960; among reviews of the latter, see esp. Weinstock 1961, an important but very difficult text in its own right; Michels 1962. Beard, North, and Price 1998: I 1–18 offers much help by way of historiographic reflection, but the material that follows suffers from a profound uninterest in Italic archaeology.

is the introduction of Hellenistic theology. The introduction to Part IV discusses this problem at some length. In this context we need only observe that we first gain access to Roman theological speculation at a time when sophisticated, self-conscious mechanisms for negotiating between philosophical speculation, civic cult, and poetic mythopoiesis had already developed. Indeed, the Romans must have adopted and adapted these apparatuses simultaneously. Roman advocates of the tripartite theology seem thus to sanction the historiographic impulse toward narratives of decline: that part of Roman religion which was "really" religious, namely, that which was natively Roman, seemed to earn less respect from, and have the lesser claim upon, the intellectuals whose texts have traditionally constituted the bulk of evidence for Roman historical research.

Third, Romans campaigning and trading ever farther afield continually encountered new peoples and new gods. By various routes and under different degrees of compulsion, some of each group will have made their way to Rome. The religious landscape of the city of Rome, and the pantheon of its inhabitants – speaking here inclusively, and not simply of its citizens – became exponentially more variegated and chaotic over time. Even within Roman civic cult, assorted pressures and trends gradually atomized divine power in a way that has struck scholars of monotheist and henotheist backgrounds as, frankly, incomprehensible. The nascent popularity of Christianity was taken by such scholars as the self-evident solution to a system in a baroque state of decay. At times grandiosely setting aside the question of Christianity's truth, these historians then juxtaposed Christianity with other trends toward monotheism in the high and late empire. That these were primarily attested in philosophical literature – the same philosophical literature as was adjudged irrelevant to the study of religion in the classical period – was apparently not an obstacle to the construction of a triumphant and teleological historiography.

The chapters presented here both illustrate and defy these trends. For Carl Koch and Georg Wissowa both focus on the problematic of decline, and yet neither tells a simple story about it. Koch's essay consists of an extended meditation upon the place of state cult in the religious and political lives of the governing class at Rome between the late Republic and early Empire. He begins slowly and proceeds obliquely. At the most basic level, the essay opens by seeking to historicize the Roman elite's evident loss of engagement with civic religion in the first century BC. What was the nature of the religiosity associated with, indeed, required for, the performance of state cult?

Why did it prove so vulnerable to Hellenistic philosophy? Then, weaving back and forth between Republican and Augustan material, Koch asks what resources were available to Augustan Rome, and which were developed in the late Republic, that might have enabled a restoration of state cult, in some newly fashioned ancient guise, in the aftermath of the civil wars.

Georg Wissowa remains Roman religion's greatest student and his *Religion und Kultus* perhaps the field's one touchstone and indispensable reference. I present here selections from the first part of that book, which was an overview of "the historical development of Roman religion." This is perhaps the least consulted portion of the book's three parts, and some words justifying the choice may be in order.

Wissowa devotes part 2 of *Religion und Kultus* to the gods of the Roman state religion, whom he distributes into five categories: "native gods" (*di indigetes*); "new, domesticated gods" (*di novensides*) of Italian origin; "new, domesticated gods" of Greek origin; newly created divinities; and foreign rites. Wissowa's taxonomy largely corresponds to an ancient, Roman one, and I will return shortly to his use of it. Each entry within part 2 studies a god's cult from a number of angles, starting with the date and context of its introduction into the Roman state pantheon. Part 3 then turns to the institutionalization of cult at Rome, studying, inter alia, religious law, ritual forms, the festival calendar, and the priestly colleges. The second and third parts of *Religion und Kultus* thus possess the character of a reference work – the book was, after all, published in a series entitled "A Manual of Classical Studies" – and the constituent entries within those parts certainly reward selective reading.

Yet it might with some justice be said that the awesome quantities of information digested and ordered in the book's latter parts exist in the service of its first, despite the benign neglect with which it has been received. The taxonomy underlying part 2 argues in this direction: although Wissowa had elsewhere to reconstruct the meaning and import of the terms *indigetes* and *novensides*, in *Religion und Kultus* he both defends and employs his reconstruction by juxtaposing it with archaeological and epigraphic evidence for the worship of the gods to whom those labels were attached in antiquity.[5] Though his data are buried in the individual entries that make up part 2, he presents his conclusions in tabular form in his second

---

[5] Wissowa 1904: 175–91.

appendix.[6] And it is that chronology, and the enormous labors that lie behind it, that underpin the authoritative voice of part 1's historical narrative.

Indeed, Wissowa's "Overview" may finally be due for rehabilitation. Recent work on the record-books of Roman priestly colleges has set in motion a reassessment of the quality and reliability of data supposedly transmitted by them.[7] It may well be that this work, in conjunction with the quite remarkable discoveries of contemporary archaeologists, will vindicate in some measure Wissowa's second appendix, and so lend credence to the narrative that he constructs on its basis.[8] What will presumably remain controversial is his investment in "Decline." But Roman religion as it was practiced in the mid-Republic did disappear – it did not merely change – and Wissowa was surely right in his instinct that this failure had its roots in the late Republic, and not in any conflict with Christianity. Roman religion proved incapable of becoming "a world religion" or even "a religion for the Empire," and it is there, he urged, in Roman religion's essential incapacity to meet the changing social and political realities that it had notionally enabled, that historians of religion should focus their energies.[9] He did not discount the importance of the totalizing and hegemonic claims of Christian doctrine, but he believed them to have been chronologically and historically secondary.

Measured against Christianity, Roman religion paradoxically appears both more flexible and more vulnerable. A religion based on knowledge can always change, for knowledge presupposes error. Faith admits no such challenge. In a peculiar, limited but important sense, the history of Christianity *is* the history of doctrine. For that reason, Christians could disdain to acknowledge massive historical events like the sack of Rome in AD 410. Adherents of Roman religion in late antiquity could not, and in the face of disaster on that scale, their faith – their faith in their knowledge – did not so much bend as break.

---

[6] Wissowa 1912: 594–7.
[7] See now Vaahtera 2002, the bibliography cited there, and p. 13 above.
[8] For two quite different surveys of mid-Republican temple-building – both now outpaced by recent work in the Roman Forum and elsewhere – see Ziolkowski 1992; Orlin 1997.
[9] Cf. Wissowa 1912: 95 for the terms "Reichs- und Weltreligion."

13 Roman State Religion in the Mirror of Augustan and Late Republican Apologetics†

CARL KOCH

translated by Christopher Barnes

The *imperium Romanum* should not be separated from its religious *mythos*. The empire included two classes of people, the rulers and the ruled. The political-religious ideology of Rome accordingly alters its appearance and emphases along two axes: according to how it was declared, discussed, and valued in the internal public sphere of Rome, and according to how those in power began to use it in their dealings with enemies or with the conquered. For generations, the Romans maintained in the consciousness of the defeated the symbols characteristic of their first encounter with this ideology. For later subjects of Roman *imperium*, the declaration of war may often have been the act through which they became acquainted with the religious-political thinking of the Romans. To meet the Romans thus was like encountering a behemoth, hard and one-sided, equally disagreeable to an opponent for whom honor constituted the guiding principle of conduct and to those for whom, over time, experienced negotiating, discussion and haggling had become the essential elements of politics.

Indeed, insofar as this religious *mythos* legitimized the naked violence of Roman weapons, the intensity behind any declaration of war largely derived from it and not, one might add, from the importance of what was at stake. It does not matter that the declaration was later read out on Roman soil and no longer, as earlier, on the border of the enemy's land. If we attend rather to the formulation that Livy provides, which may have undergone a period of disuse at the end of

† Originally published as "Die altrömische Staatskult im Spiegel augusteischer und spätre-publikanischer Apologetik," *Religio: Studen zu Kult und Glauben der Römer* (Nürnberg: Verlag Hans Carl), 176–204.

the Republic but which was in any event current again from the time of Augustus' declaration of war against Cleopatra, we encounter the sentence: "Hear, Jupiter, and you, Janus Quirinus, and all you heavenly gods and terrestrial gods and gods of the underworld: I bear witness to you that this nation is unjust and is not making proper restitution."[1]

These words make a huge claim: namely, that right stood only on the side of Rome and that the gods were witnesses to this state of affairs, that Rome acted in league with the gods. The tenor of this declaration of war paralleled a corresponding procedure in conclud- ing war, the *deditio* ['surrender']. Again primarily from Livy we know that nothing short of a strict *confessio culpae* ["admission of guilt"] was demanded from the defeated: in conjunction with *paenitentia* ["contrition"] and *suppliciter veniam petere* ["suppli- antly seeking forgiveness"], the enemy had to admit "that it had been defeated in a pious and just war" (Livy 42.47.9: *se pio et iusto bello superatum esse*). For those who admitted *mea culpa* in this manner it was no extraordinary sacrifice to accept in addition the mythology of Roman superiority: "the glory of the Roman people in war is such that, when it boasts that its author and parent is Mars himself, the races of the world should acquiesce to this claim with the same spirit with which they acquiesce to its rule."[2]

What presented itself to the conquered in this way claimed to be the ancient, vital, world-conquering belief of the Roman people. This impression was underscored by the manner in which foreign policy was conducted: both in earlier times and again during the time of Augustus, many a ceremony developed before the eyes of the world, ceremony which in fact carried with itself the marks of highest antiquity. Among other rituals that were called into service at this subsequent time was, probably, the ritual of the fetial priests, which could now be observed in renditions almost identical to those that were deployed in the wars of Rome against Veii and the Samnites [in the early fourth century BC]. But in a spiritual sense, much had changed during this interval in the world beyond Rome, and this same piece of change conditioned Roman society and even the think- ing of those who wielded power. For long before Augustus, gener-

---

[1] Livy 1.32.9-10: *audi, Juppiter, et tu, Jane Quirine, diique omnes caelestes, vosque terrestres, vosque inferni audite: ego vos testor populum illum iniustum esse neque ius persolvere.*

[2] Livy *praef.* 7: *ea belli gloria est populo Romano, ut, cum suum conditorisque sui parentem Martem potissimum ferat, tam et hoc gentes humanae patiuntur aequo animo, quam imperium patiuntur.*

ations of educated Romans had been influenced by Hellenistic
rationalism, and only a few of them escaped from the danger of
viewing as non-existent everything that they could not control by
means of reason. Were there not already in Lucilius, to name only
one example, verses such as the following:

> As for scarecrows and witches, which our Fauns and Numa Pompiliuses
> instituted: he fears them and thinks them all-important. As babies believe
> that all bronze statues live and are human, so these people think that fictions
> of dreams are true and believe that bronze statues have hearts. Sculptors'
> workshops, nothing real, everything fictive.[3]

It is not our object in the following considerations to delineate the
impact of this rationalism in all its stages, much less to describe the
emergence of a force opposed to it, namely, syncretic superstition. We
want only to consider the extent to which Roman thought was in a
position to develop some kind of reaction.

Let us begin with the secure hypothesis that in the late Republic
and Augustan period no individual priest of the state religion,
coming from the educated class, could carry out his duties with the
credulity of an archaic man. Each perceived the discrepancy between
the extent of his own spiritual freedom and the world of ideas that
he had to reproduce in worship. We want to direct our attention to
whether there were resources – and the Augustan revival of religion
is inconceivable without the existence of such resources, within
apologetic thought, naturally – to which one had recourse, in order
for the sake of the state religion to settle in a sufficiently rational
manner the spiritual rift between the past and the present. What did
a man of the late Republic, of Augustus' lifetime, think about his
traditional state rituals, about their authority and veracity? What can
we suppose about the trains of thought and about the elements of
personal conviction of those men who felt responsible for the state,
who practiced the state cult as serious, thinking men and who,
dogmatically rigid like their ancestors, perhaps even more intense
than those, brought the political-theological claim of Rome before
the world? How do the outward claim and the inner reality relate to
one another?

The state religion for the contemporary Roman was not identical
with the entire complex of religious possibilities that could have

---

[3] Lucilius 524–529 Warmington (trans. after Warmington): *Terriculas Lamias, Fauni quas
Pompiliique / instituere Numae, tremit has hic omnia ponit. / Ut pueri infantes credunt signa
omnia aena / vivere et esse homines, sic isti somnia ficta / vera putant, credunt signis cor inesse
in aenis. / Pergula pictorum, veri nil, omnia ficta.*

occupied him. The question regarding the degree of substance or, more accurately, the decay of substance in belief in the *maiores'* system of rituals constitutes only a partial inquiry into the problematic of late Republican and Augustan religion. This was hardly the most burning question for the average individual if he was not a priest, but it was a serious, pressing concern for the leadership of the state at the beginning of the Principate.

It is, to be sure, in Cicero and Sallust that we first encounter an articulation of the fundamental principle of the Roman political-religious world-view, though it is older than those authors: the people on the Tiber outperformed all other groups in *pietas* and *religio*, were loved by the gods for that reason and received dominion over the world as reward for this devotion and submission. In this way of thinking, moments of tangible success carry special significance and, indeed, cannot be imagined apart from it. According to the Roman point of view – and they were not alone in thinking this way – one can gauge the intensity of love for oneself on a heavenly plane on the basis of one's successes in terrestrial affairs. Cicero presents this view very clearly in a passage in which he, in a reversal of Jewish thought, was able to say: "How dear that race is to the immortal gods may be seen from the fact that they have been conquered" (*Pro Flacco* 69: *quam cara (illa gens) dis immortalibus esset, docuit quod est victa*). Reviewing in hindsight the ups and downs of Roman history, Livy placed in the mouth of the idealized figure of Camillus the frank doctrine: "You will find that all things turn out well for those who follow the gods, and badly for those who spurn them" (5.51.8: *invenietis omnia prospera evenisse sequentibus deos, adversa spernentibus*). We find the same idea expressed in Vergil and need not pursue it further.

We get closer to the state religion when we refer to examples that illustrate the principle of "following the gods." Among these, we find not only formulations of universal religiosity such as "the gods show favor to loyalty and devotion, through which the Roman people arrived at so great a peak" (Livy 44.1.11: *favere enim pietati fideique deos, per quae populus Romanus ad tantum fastigii venerit*), but also indications that these found expression in the performance of the traditional rituals. One of Horace's odes (3.6) allows us to recognize clearly that the disposition of "holding oneself humble before the gods" (*dis minorem se gerere*), which guarantees rule over the world, consisted above all in building temples and not fighting battles "without having taken the auspices" (*inauspicato*). Livy goes into still more detail when he emphasizes that even the smallest of rituals have their worth and their place in the divine order of those accomplishments that bring empire as their reward. Referring to "the oracle of the chickens," he remarked that "these are small things, but our ancestors, by not scorning such small things, made our state the greatest" (Livy 6.41.8: *parva sunt haec; sed parva ista non contemnendo maiores nostri maximam hanc rem fecerunt*). The idea recurs in the boastful formulation of Valerius Maximus: "It is no wonder, then, if the indulgence of the gods has persisted, ever watchful to augment and protect an imperial power that is seen to weigh even minor items of religious significance with such scrupulous care; for our community should never be thought to have averted its eyes from the most exacting requirements of cult."[4]

How far behind these and similar expressions stood something that one can call belief? First, a preliminary remark. Whoever comes from the Christian world and seeks a phenomenon of equal intensity and psychological power in antiquity, such as Christian belief among *homines religiosi* of the West was and can still be, finds little or nothing in this regard. The energy of belief is ultimately not dependent on the degree of resolve with which a belief raises the claim to be true or even *the* truth. In a world in which there were not yet revelations with the binding force of the word of the Christian God, or to go one better, if the people about whom we are speaking had not yet fallen under this power, one can only find shadowy analogies for that which Christianity understands as true belief.

With respect to this issue, let us bring before our eyes this "shortcoming" of the ancient pagan in what will be, in my opinion, an instructive example. I have chosen an event on the heavenly stage in Vergil's *Aeneid*. This is informative not just because it depicts the behaviors of divine personages of wide-ranging, paradigmatic character. Nor is it only because the creator of the scene is Vergil, among the Augustan poets the most thoughtful about the possibilities of religion and the particularity of people's souls. Above all, it is because at stake here is a reaction in the face of a phenomenon that structurally has the character of a divine revelation, corresponding to a certain degree to Christian revelation. I refer to the peculiar behavior of Venus concerning the announcement of the future of Rome by Jupiter, which runs as follows. Thanks to the fate embodied in his person, Aeneas could not perish. On the contrary, he

---

[4] Valerius Maximus 1.1.8 (trans. after Shackleton Bailey): *non mirum igitur, si pro eo imperio augendo custodiendoque pertinax deorum indulgentia semper excubuit, quo tam scrupulosa cura parvula quoque momenta religionis examinari videntur, quia numquam remotos ab exactissimo cultu caerimoniarum oculos habuisse nostra civitas existimanda est.*

would be the founder of a people for whom an "empire without end" (*imperium sine fine*) stood ready in the world. This was revealed to her in the first book, with every emphasis on and indication of infallibility. Nevertheless, in the tenth book, when the battle seemed hopeless and Aeneas on the brink of ruin, she declared to the same Jupiter: "I am no longer moved by thoughts of empire; we hoped for such things, while our fortune held" (42–43: *nil super imperio moveor: speravimus ista, dum fortuna fuit*), and asks him if he might rescue the hero from combat and grant him but a single island. We glimpse here how far removed these people were from a belief contrary to appearances. If Vergil considered such a scene possible on his Olympus, that means that he regarded such a psychological reaction in the human world as normal.

In view of such instability of conviction, we can measure the gap in the ability and will to believe that must have existed between the age of the Social Wars and the early Augustan peace. At the time of the Hannibalic War, it had been possible for a large portion of the people in Rome to accept defeats in a religious sense as the punishment of angry gods. The enlightened people of the Ciceronian age had not uttered such a sentiment for a long time. The educated man experienced bad luck in the moment he suffered it as the confirmation of every doubt and the thousandfold enlightened rationalizations that denied that any gods or providence presided over human fate. On the other hand, a readiness to regard intervention by a higher power as possible, if not probable, caught fire spontaneously with the nascent *pax Augusta*, according to the degree to which individuals or groups experienced the event as a gift contrary to merit and expectations. Before anyone could analyze the situation and circumstances intellectually, a positive mood had already seized the nation and created an atmosphere in which religious matters could receive new life through careful planning. How differently sounded the ideas that the Romans were the most pious of races (*religiossisma gens*) or that empire (*imperium*) was the reward for such a belief, in the mouth of an Augustan Roman rather than in Cicero's around the time of the intrigues of Clodius!

Among a religious people the notion prevails that "necessity teaches prayer." In the Rome of that time, disasters were the signs of a loss of belief, whose reliable corrective, namely, "portents and miracles" (though one should not press this idea too far), offered almost the only way back to the gods. Without a doubt the emperor recognized the opportunity afforded after Actium and knew that it held out the possibility of benefitting not only universal religiosity, but also the renewal, with energy and expense, of traditional cult. Of course, intellectually Augustus' victory could not easily be construed as the reward for faithfully-practiced *pietas*. At the time of Actium, the Roman people were neither more moral nor more religious than shortly before the defeat of Crassus. Their rescue had come un-deserved and the emperor had first to put it in a context that was theologically intelligible. This happened first through the announce-ment of the emperor's transcendental mission. He was sent by the gods in order to lead Rome, within and without, back to the old, divinely-willed order. On this understanding, the victory at Actium created merely the prelude to an event that would first obtain its worth and lasting success on the day when the newly established internal order also came into being. A second factor, psychologically appropriate for bridging the dilemma of the moment, lay in the determined and close juxtaposition of old Rome and the Augustan *imperium*, in the idea that the new era was the accomplishment of what the gods had planned from the outset. In the dazzling gleam of these two, some features got lost that distinguished early Rome perceptibly from Augustan, not least among them the fact that where once the *pietas* of the citizens preceded the fortune and the ascend-ancy of the state, now the rescue resembled an advance gift, for which *pietas* then had to follow in the course of religious renewal. At any rate, the effect was – and on that it depended – that old Roman *pietas* stood before all eyes as the creator of the empire and its great-ness. Actium, too, and the *pax Augusta* presented themselves ulti-mately as divine benefactions earned through *pietas*. There may have been many who assented to this picture and were ready to give credit to a system of divine worship, the practice of which had had such success from the beginning. Once one was on board, so would one – henceforth largely uncritically – have judged even the smallest detail as good and right, in the sense of the aforementioned passage of Livy (6.41.8; see p. 300). And if the particulars of a ritual seemed difficult to understand and appeared to be absurd, nevertheless, the internal workings of the institution had proved their worth. Why shouldn't the gods be allowed to demand a petty and humiliating task from their servants, in order to test the truth whether they did indeed "hold themselves humble before the gods" (*dis se minorem gerere*)! Even historians could frame that question. In this way, the intellect, by necessity, could deal alike with the ritual and its atavism.

Livy's chapter on Numa (1.19) leads us further in the investigation of Augustan religious psychology. From the description of early

Roman history that precedes it, the reader could infer that there was a *fatum* or that there were *di*. Their existence and their works could, among other things, be deduced from the successful foundation of the Roman state and its subsequent growth, at least from the Augustan point of view (cf. 1.4.1). No person had seen the gods face to face, not even Rhea Silvia, who maintained that she had conceived the twin sons of Mars "either because she really thought so" (*seu ita rata*), which means on the grounds of self-deception, "or because it was more respectable that a god be the author of the crime" (*seu quia deus auctor culpae honestior erat*). After Numa's accession to the throne, peace came to the land. Livy recounts the closing of the doors of Janus' temple in order to conclude with the same event in the *pax Augusta*. He could thereby suggest to the reader that the domestic political situation in the past, its advantages and its dangers, were the same as those of the present. Numa had had to overcome the same tasks that fell to the lot of the emperor in the years after Actium. What did Numa do? He knew – it almost seems as though he had read Sallust or his sources – that "fear of the enemy" (*metus hostilis*), "concern for foreign dangers" (*externorum periculorum cura*) and "military discipline" (*disciplina militaris*) are the forces best suited to keep a people in line, but that leisure, *otium*, brings with it the danger that people will fall into licentiousness and luxury. *Ne luxuriarent otio animi*, "lest their spirits grow soft with leisure," he replaced *metus hostilis* abruptly with *metus deorum*, "fear of the gods." This he accomplished by establishing the different cults in ways that suited "the uneducated and boorish multitude of that age" (*multitudo imperita et illis saeculis rudis*), a people who responded only to supposedly supernatural signs. In short, he aroused them to activity with the aid of a pious deception (*pia faus*). He said that he met with the nymph Egeria every night and learned from her "what most pleased the gods" (*quae acceptissima diis essent*).

Various ulterior motives are detectable here. Men of the Augustan age, no longer of primitive disposition, had no need of *miracula* of this kind. Furthermore, they also no longer experienced the religious in the way that Lucretius denounced it, as a form of primitive fear. Instead, they considered cult – and the complete success of Numa's institutions in Livy teaches this – the suitable field of activity for a peaceful nation, in which everyone takes a place at the communal dance and thrives in free morality and with consideration for an imperceptible, omnipresent and venerable partner: "Because heavenly power seemed so involved in human affairs, the continual attention of the gods imbued the hearts of all with such reverence

that loyalty and oath-taking governed the state, instead of an excessive fear of laws and punishments."[5]

If earlier we discovered in the religious stamp of the Augustan
period a motive for "success," namely that the practice of cult draws
down blessings from above, we discover here a new side to this
matter. Cult activity, properly understood, was a means of moral
improvement. One understanding does not exclude the other, in so
far as the gods really only show favor to those who display *pietas*,
fides and the other old Roman virtues in connection with ritual. It is
in this context that we must situate the story of Gaius Valerius
Flaccus (Livy 27.8.4–10). According to Arthur Darby Nock, the
best modern expert on the subject, Livy's narrative of his moral
conversion is without parallel in the whole of ancient literature on
conversions.[6] The *pontifex maximus* Publius Licinius, solidly
convinced that his handiwork would be successful, dared to make
this young man of very wordly behavior *flamen Dialis*, against his
will and precisely because of his "irresponsible and dissipated youth"
(*adulescentia neglegens et luxuriosa*)! The *flamen Dialis* presided
over the most complicated rituals in Rome next to those of the
Vestals. "That man, as soon as responsibility for those rites and
ceremonies seized his attention, suddenly shed his former habits to
such a degree, that no one among the young men of that day was held
in higher esteem or received greater esteem from his elders, those
related to him or those not related alike" (Livy 27.8.6). Flaccus later
arranged for the *flamen Dialis*, as in days of old, to receive again a
seat in the Senate. He had to struggle, but he won: "more through
the sancitity of his lifestyle than by the law of his priesthood."

To summarize the particulars of the passages of Livy we have
examined so far, all have in common that questions of the existence
of the gods, of their form, their number, and their means of manifestation, remain completely undiscussed. It seems therefore quite
clear that the believer and the enlightened, each in his own way, could
hold the business of worshiping the gods to be on the one hand a
means of teaching morality of the very first order and, on the other,
an all-embracing and dignified project for the nation, appropriate
both in war and peace for renewing and maintaining discipline and
order.

---

[5] Livy 1.21.1: *deorum assidua cura, cum interesse rebus humanis caeleste numen videretur,
ea pietate omnium pectora imbuerat, ut fides et ius iurandum pro nimio* – Mss. *proximo* –
legum ac poenarum metu civitatem regerent.
[6] *RAC* 2:111.

But we have not yet fully explored Livy's telling of the story of Numa. This sentence follows the above explanation: "Even as the Romans shaped their habits after those of their king, as if from a unique exemplar, so, too, neighboring peoples ... were induced to such a state of respectfulness that they considered it a crime to attack a city wholy devoted to the worship of the gods."[7] The example of the model king's religious observance and moral purity instructs the people, the *pietas* of the people in turn the environment beyond Rome. With the figure of the ideal king, a new, psychological element enters into the context. Formerly, we were led by purely rational considerations and we saw how the institution of cult in Rome had come about and how this had worked to the advantage of the community. Now there is an appeal to the Roman inclination to *auctoritas*. That which a wise man, in his acknowledged greatness, considers right and does with his own hands, one should not only join confidently, but must follow.

In this context, the irrational, the unverifiable can really happen. As a Roman, one demands from the figure one has chosen as a model no account of the particulars of why he thinks and acts one way and not another. One accepts the whole and lifts it, so to speak, onto the altar. Livy seems to have been sure about the differences in spiritual order that present themselves here. At any rate, it is very remarkable that in the narration of ancient history, the focus is always and exclusively on Rome's future world domination, on an aspect of its greatness that could have been checked *ex eventu* by every contemporary. It is never about the eternity of the city and of the empire, about which no rational statement could have been made. We encounter a statement of the latter kind first in an impressive formulation in a speech of Scipio Africanus Maior (Livy 28.28.11). Livy here consciously innovates and, what is more, he does so through the *persona* of an exemplary individual of the early historical period. He turns the idea into a personal conviction of this greatest model figure of the pre-Augustan age and leaves it as a vision, as a part of Scipio's spiritual essence, rationally removed from every concept in the storehouse of Augustan belief.

Applied to an Augustan context, the doctrine of the Numa chapter suggests that if the emperor, depicted by Vergil and others not only as a new Romulus but equally emphatically as a second Numa,

---

[7] Livy 1.21.2: *et cum ipsi se homines in regis velut unici exempli mores formarent, tum finitimi etiam populi ... in eam verecundiam adducti sunt, ut civitatem totam in cultum versam deorum violare ducerent nefas.*

sets an example for his people through the gestures of a priest carrying out his duties, as we see, among other things, on the reliefs of the Ara Pacis – perhaps precisely there on purpose (*pax!*) – then one has to follow his *auctoritas, nulla ratione reddita,* "without any explanation being given," to use here a phrase of Cicero that will occupy us later in this work. For example, when once the facts of the Eleusinian Mysteries came up in court, Augustus dismissed judge and auditor so as to have a discussion as an initiate alone with the initiated. This conversation compelled the Roman public to respect the institution of the Eleusinian rites simply by virtue of the fact that the emperor took them seriously *coram publico* ["before the public"], something he did not do regarding the worship of oriental divinities, as was well known (Suet. *Aug.* 93). Repeated on countless occasions of solemn and daily involvement with ritual, this seriousness, which like every action of the emperor should be compared with the greatness of the model figures of early Rome and judged accordingly (Suet. *Aug.* 31), inculcated the strongest impulse to a religious revival. This impulse was then realized, to the benefit of state rituals in the Augustan period.

But how far did this renewal extend? To the external observer, ritual events developed with a new intensity, smoothly up to a point, namely to where the festival games ended and real personal sacrifices were demanded. Naturally, there we cannot investigate. Even at the time, caution or ignorance for the most part precluded anyone asking to what extent the cooperation of the individual, educated, social classes derived from true religiosity. In other words, whether this new intensity in the celebration of ritual arose from genuine devotion to ritual itself or from a feeling of loyalty to emperor and empire is a question that no one seems to have asked and for which no answer survives. On the basis of what has been presented thus far, we are inclined to suppose a religiosity of considerable intensity at first, but diminishing among many as they became accustomed to the *pax Augusta*. In the interpretation of cult, many shadings were possible. Stoic thought might have been in the position to help people, urging them to consider the gods at least in part as manifestations of some universal spirit, in other words, as real. Ritual, meanwhile, could be regarded as merely a means of popular instruction, or at best as an allegorical sign language for the learned. Or, the increasing tendency even among those of high rank towards the practice of magic and prophecy of every kind might have aroused a new curiosity even about the traditional rites as such. On the other hand, an attitude such as the emperor probably had in mind – in discussing a passage of Cicero, we will shortly adumbrate further the mode of thought that they seem to have shared – had the potential to shut out the speculative, individual I; instead, it encouraged individuals to believe in the blessing of the matter and thence to submit to the *auctoritas maiorum et Augusti*, the authority of their ancestors and Augustus. Such belief arose among representatives of the upper classes, if at all, only in very few cases, not idly and summarily, but in practice, in the pious exercise of the small, the burdensome, and the absurd. Whether anyone in the circle of the emperor seriously believed, after 200 years of insipid explanation, that one might summon back to life more of the same, we are unable to say. But the restoration of 82 temples and the renewal of vacant priest- and brotherhoods seem to state publicly the objective of the rulers, namely, to reproduce the old true to the letter. It did not succeed, and it also could not succeed.

Sentences like that already cited, "our ancestors, by not scorning such small things ..." (*parva ista non contemnendo maiores ...*), appear in every work of history. Livy also draws attention to the carefulness of the ancients in naming prodigies publicly, in expiating them, and in recording them in historical texts. Today nothing similar happens, and, of course, one must "regard as worthy of record all those things that the wisest men deemed worthy of public action" (Livy 43.13.2: *quae illi prudentissimi viri publice suscipienda censuerint, ea pro dignis habere*). But we do not have – and that is surely no accident – a single example of ground against rationalism being regained in this arena during the Augustan era. In matters of augury, the knowledge of Vergil is so fragmented that we must suppose that likewise here nothing of importance was accomplished. Who is able in the end to show that Augustus took action against someone in the manner that Cato the elder had done in his speech "Against Lucius Veturius, on sacrifice neglected, when he took away his horse": "because you abandoned the established rites incumbent upon you, solemn and consecrated though they were." "It was necessary to bring water from the Anio, [to wash] the repository of the sacred objects. The Anio is distant by not less than fifteen miles."[8] One could no longer demand the humility of plain, troublesome worship far from public view.

No wonder that difficulties appeared when great sacrifice was demanded, whether relating to appointments to the college of the Vestals or to the reoccupation of the office of *flamen Dialis*, vacant

---

[8] Cato p. 47 Jordan, "*In L. Veterium de sacrificio commisso, cum ei equum ademit*": *quod tu, quod in te fuit, sacra stata, sollemnia, capite sancta deseruisti* (frg. 2). *Aquam Anienem in sacrarium inferre oportebat. non minus XV milia Anien abest* (frg. 3).

for seventy-five years. "When it was necessary that another Vestal be chosen in place of the deceased and many campaigned lest they should have to give their daughters to the lot, Augustus swore that he would have so consigned his granddaughters, if either had been of an appropriate age."[9] Behind the resistance of parents to the priest-hood lies, naturally, doubt: to surrender thirty years of life, the most precious in that of a woman, to an existence of rigorous abstinence and a cult of joyless primitiveness, *cui bono*? The emperor's reaction is very telling. We hear not a word from him about the benefits of the institution, no argument that the State needs it. It would be danger-ous to draw from his silence the conclusion that Augustus was a hypocrite, that he had no such beliefs about the institution. We will return to the meaning of his silence. It is certain only that the emperor wanted no discussion. He took a road that at first seems strange to us moderns. Namely, if we may speak thus, he sought to displace discussion by means of a hypothetical example: if I possessed a granddaughter of suitable age, I would not hesitate for a minute to put her forward. The well-disposed and the indifferent might conclude from this assertion that Augustus attributed high worth to the institution of the Vestals. Those concerned perceived only too clearly that the words were equivalent to an order. The reoccupation of the *flamonium Diale*, moreover, was only possible for even an Augustus, after he simplified the ritual of the same office whose severity he had already softened: "Augustus modified to contem-porary inclination some aspects [of the priesthood] that derived from hoary antiquity."[10]

Few additional words are needed to show the gulf that separated reality and ideology in the decisive moment when the reiteration of the values of the past was to be fully and unconditionally realized. Each Augustan man spoke as much of the *maiores* as of *pruden-tissimi viri*, of Numa as the *unicum exemplum*, of the *parva ista* whose fulfillment created the empire and made it great – and we believe that many of these expressions were meant in complete honesty – up to the point that a truly delicate sacrifice should be demanded of him. Then, from the depths of the world of sensation, there awoke what slumbered there, ineradicable, the heirloom of a generation-long, explanation-saturated education, namely the con-viction that the *maiores*, in the final analysis, had been, of course,

---

[9] Suetonius *Augustus* 31.3: *cum in demortuae (virginis Vestalis) locum aliam capi oporteret ambirentque multi, ne filias in sortem darent, adiuravit (Augustus), si cuiusquam neptium suarum competeret aetas, oblaturum se fuisse eam.*

[10] Tacitus *Ann.* 4.16.3: *quaedam ex horrida illa antiquitate ad praesentem usum flexit.*

ignorant, primitive men and their belief in the gods was fundamentally unable to be discussed by advanced, modern people.

The Ciceronian era, on which we will now concentrate, experienced no impulse to the sort of positive mood that could have promoted an inward participation in the worship of the state divinities. Much less was there a man like Augustus, who through the will and strength of his *auctoritas*, his example, and the force of his orders could have been capable of guiding the public in a practical-religious sense. We need not explain external developments in full. What Cicero, altering a word of Cato the elder, says regarding the auspices is valid for the entire system of *sacra*: "By the negligence of the nobility, the discipline of augury was lost, and the truth of the auspices was spurned, while only an appearance was retained" (*neglegentia nobilitatis augurii disciplina omissa, veritas auspiciorum spreta est, species tantum retenta*). Overall, there was often a complete breakdown: the result of a loss of interest, ignorance, and a limited, fragmentary, uninterested, and purely conventional execution of all functions. We are interested in the statements of those who regretted this development. How many more in addition to these witnesses there may have been, who thought in this way or similarly, it is difficult to say. Countless numbers were always talking about the *mos maiorum*. It is unclear whether they included *sacra* in that tradition. Whoever had no burdens to carry, into whose lap only *sine sacris hereditates*, "legacies without rites," had fallen, could easily assert that religious duties were also involved.

We land right in the middle of this time of crisis if we begin with a consideration of the college of augurs. In his books *On the laws*, Cicero, a member of the college at the time, depicts Atticus remarking about it: "But in your college there was a great dispute between Marcellus and Appius, both the best of augurs ... To the former, it seemed that auspices were invented to serve the needs of the state; to the latter, your discipline seemed capable practically of divination."[11] At first sight, we find something suprising: an open exchange between leading men of the colleges of priests about a truly central question. Did the auspices possess an objective, prophetic quality? Or had they nothing to do with religion, at least for the learned, but were to be understood as a useful means of leading the state?

[11] Cicero *Leg.* 2.32: *sed est in collegio vestro inter Marcellum et Appium, optimos augures, magna dissensio ..., cum alteri* (sc. *Marcello*) *placeat auspicia ista ad utilitatem rei publicae esse composita, alteri disciplina vestra quasi divinari videatur posse.*

Of course, the answers reveal only the personal convictions of the augurs meeting in discussion. I doubt that a controversy of this kind was possible in word or print in the Augustan period. An irreligious interpretation opposes the religious.

It is ultimately crucial to understand that both points of view could cloak themselves in an aura of respect for the *mos maiorum*. One could regard the ancients as either religious or political geniuses. Moreover, men who believed personally in a divine world order and led lives of high moral perfection could also subscribe to theories of "utility" (*utilitas*). From the time of Panaetius, Romans had learned from the Stoics to distinguish between three kinds of theology: the "mythic theology" of the poets, the "scientific theology" of the (Stoic) philosophers, and the "civic theology" of the contemporary official state religion (*theologia mythica*, *physica*, and *civilis*). Whosoever agreed with this division was naturally of the conviction that only philosophical religious discourse had a claim to the truth. The other two did not, of course, depict total fictions, since ideas of philosophical truth were always present in them to a certain degree, concealed under a jumble of error or in a world of images that had to be understood allegorically. The more that ancestral religion was understood in a "scientific" sense, the happier contemporary adherents to the tripartite theology were, and the more outraged are religious researchers today. For the learned, such a religious structure possessed no binding force and had to be endured for its importance to the control of the ignorant masses.

It is thus clear how the nobility's "negligence" toward the state cult among others could arise even from reflection based upon a philosophical belief in god. The intellect and perspiration required for the precise execution of received sacred laws would then have been, god knows, unnecessary, had it had as its object anything less than spiritual control of the *vulgus*. That object was itself esteemed according to the tactical-political purposes of the nobility. The accord between the Stoa and *Romanitas*, which grew stronger over time, made this consequence as obvious as it was historically fateful. This was true for two reasons that are themselves causally connected: first, because the traditional worship of the gods, seen as a whole, failed to resonate with this outlook and, second, because religions stand or fall with the unconditional belief and heart-felt zeal of their priests. We will have to resume consideration of this problem below. As concerns the attitude of such individuals, it was a stroke of luck of a particular kind if deep and serious reflection led one to conclude that public morality is a good to which it was worth applying one's own life, but that one could not sufficiently influence the masses with philosophy and autonomous ethics.

In the quest to influence the masses, ritual was more effective than philosophy, even if ritual's representations did not correspond either to the *formula naturae*, to use an expression of Varro, or, above all, to an exemplary *sanctitas vitae*. This noteworthy point of view seems to have been that of Quintus Mucius Scaevola (d. 82 BC), among others. The entire state admired him; the Senate designated him worthy of imitation because he had administered the province of Asia "both bravely and piously" (*tam sancte et fortiter*); he attended scrupulously to his pontifical obligations. Nevertheless, he advocated the opinion, which Varro called his own ("which Varro himself did not hesitate to voice in his *Divine Antiquities*") and which Augustine presented with sarcasm to the pagan public: "it is useful for states to be deceived in matters of religion" (*Civ.* 4.27: *expedire falli in religione civitates*).

These digressions have been necessary to show what Marcellus meant by *utilitas*, "utility." This crucial term covered the whole range of contemporary, enlightened, modern thought, from the cynicism of one who scorned religion because of the multitude's indifference to a Scaevola's Stoic sense of duty. What position within this range Marcellus occupied need not concern us.

What do we find in Appius? A remnant of true belief in the literal worship of the state religion and in an objective, institutional proximity to god? Appius, the father-in-law of Marcus Brutus, the predecessor of Cicero as governor of Cilicia, who as censor yielded to Pompey in 50 BC, whom Sallust thanked for his expulsion from the Senate, is known to us through the light and dark sides of his character. He was not a Mucius Scaevola, neither in his province nor in Rome. His censorship was controversial above all because of his membership in a faction, but matters of religion also played a role. Ateius Capito, for example, tribune in 55 BC, was expelled from the Senate because he held that the auspices were "false." Had those been respected (!), they would have forestalled the expedition of Crassus. In other words, they could have prevented the defeat at Carrhae ...

Be that as it may, his dispute with Marcellus reveals that Appius treated sacred matters seriously not only when they suited his political plans, but above all on principle. We know, furthermore, that Eleusis thanked him for the lesser propylaea of the sanctuary. The oracle of Amphiaraos in Oropos received benefits thanks to him. As the struggle between Caesar and Pompey flared up, Appius went to

Delphi. He received a personal oracle there, which said that the war had nothing to do with him, his "possession" would be the [*Koila tês Euboias*]. He went there and died in that very place, possibly even before Pharsalus. He was a religious man, but oddly so from the standpoint of the Roman aristocrat. We can gauge how odd from two passages of Cicero, which reveal that he was not only an expert in taking auspices, but also concerned himself with necromancy (νεκυομαντεῖα, *psychomantia*) (*Tusc.* 1.37; *Div.* 1.132). Appius was thus no early Roman, but already a man of late antiquity. For him, to all appearances the distinction between *religio* and *superstitio* had evaporated, without which the religiosity of early Rome is unthinkable. Yet Cicero also says of him that he was "as deeply learned in augury as in the public law of our antiquity."[12] We may thus suppose that outside traditional religion, the focal point of his affective, religious world lay in the sphere of prophecy generally and in that superstitious *curiositas* that we encounter in his contemporary Nigidius Figulus, the "follower" of Pythagoras.† Seen from this perspective, his interpretation of the auspices proved paradigmatic: it was an attempt to infuse into an old institution new life from outside, from the spirit of magic and prophetic syncretism. To what extent Appius was conscious of the peculiarity of his position remains unclear. But his theology as established here bore fruit, among other things, in the prodigy, Pythia and necromancy scenes in Lucan.

We suspect it was not possible for Augustus to join with him on this point, although elements of a true devotion to cult existed in a man like Appius. We grasp in the conduct of the emperor as described above, in his "silence," a latent censorship: it functioned to shield the legacy of early Rome not only from the encroachment of enlightened rationalism, but also on the opposite front, from the pressures of syncretic superstition. The best way was in actuality the one he hit upon, namely carrying out whatever was ancient and Roman to the letter, while not allowing himself to get involved in any discussion of principles. Such a conversation would have necessarily been un-Roman and would have led to an immediate falsification of the matter.

We now turn to Cicero himself, the colleague of Appius and Marcellus, and we ask how he stood in relation to the alternatives under discussion. A survey of his remarks about the traditional

---

[12] Cicero *Brut.* 267: *cum auguralis tum omnis publici iuris antiquitatisque nostrae bene peritus.*

† On Nigidius Figulus see pp. 149–50.

worship of the gods reveals a substantial difference between his thought and that of the aforementioned. He offers to the latter a psychological impulse to busy themselves with ritual and a reason to conceive for it an *apologia* according to the logic of their ideological points of view. This was, in the final analysis, the fact that cult really was the legacy of the ancients. But this retrospective consideration does not appear to have been the focal point of their thought and feeling. They searched the institution for a standard of truth or some intrinsic value for their own time. Their willingness to grant cult the right to exist depended on the degree to which they succeeded in convincing themselves of its utility or transcendental nature. In Cicero such contemplations recede behind an inexorable imperative: one has to achieve the *mos maiorum*, regardless whether it is convincing and carries its own contemporary worth or not.

Naturally, Cicero could not avoid a response to the alternatives articulated above, that the science of augury was either truly prophetic or merely useful. While Appius lived, he seems to have recommended a compromise. In an earlier time, he wrote, much in the auspices was made known truly *ad veritatem*: "But it is not to be doubted, that the discipline and skill of augury has now vanished, through age and negligence. Therefore I neither agree with the one, who denies that our college ever possessed this skill, or with the other, who thinks that it still posseses that skill today" (*Leg.* 2.33). In *On divination*, he stands clearly on the side of Marcellus. Romulus certainly believed "that the science of augury was useful for seeing things to come" (*esse in providendis rebus augurandi scientiam*). For Cicero, however, it was not so: "for antiquity erred in many things" (*errabat enim multis in rebus antiquitas*). His wording strongly recalls the phrase "that hoary antiquity" from Tacitus' characterization of the *flamonium Diale*. Cicero continued: "But with an eye toward the beliefs of the masses and their great utility to the state (*et ad opinionem vulgi et ad magnas utilitates rei publicae*), the custom, scruple, skill and law of augury and the authority of the augural college are maintained" (2.70). We need not discuss further the detailed description offer later of the *utilitates rei publicae* (cf. *Leg.* 2.74). In spite of this fully disillusioned point of view, Cicero follows this remark on the errors of antiquity with the remark that, in his opinion, "the consuls Publius Clodius and Lucius Junius fully deserved capital punishment for having set sail contrary to the auspices. For they should have respected religious scruple, nor should they so arrogantly have repudiated ancestral custom" (*parendum enim religioni fuit nec patrius mos tam contumaciter repudiandus*). "It was therefore just that the one was convicted by a vote of the people, while the other took his own life" (*Div.* 2.71).

In general, Cicero, when thinking in a romantic, retrospective vein, avoided discussing "errant antiquity" (*errans antiquitas*). He approaches the topic very differently in *On the laws*: there he admits that the cult and auspices of earliest Rome might well express transcendental religious experiences (2.33). Drawing upon ancient Greek myths that described early humanity as especially proximate to divinity, a tradition newly animated by Posidonius, Cicero described the sacred legacies of ancestors and individual families almost as though they had been handed down by the gods themselves: "we ought to preserve the rites of our families and ancestors. That is to say, because antiquity happened nearest to the gods, we ought to safeguard *religio* as if it were handed down from the gods." [13] His preface to this work, inspired as it was by Plato and others, obscures the fact that here themes are telescoped so as to take tacit account of the people at large. Instead, we find the argument that Ciceronian sacral law, which models traditional Roman conditions, accords wholly with the Platonic and Stoic conviction that the world is governed by superhuman reason. Whoever therefore has confidence in this legislation and its premises "will scarcely shrink from either useful or true belief" (*Leg.* 2.16: *ab utili aut a vera sententia*).

We are thus led to suppose that, up to a point, components of some primary revelation are expressed in cult, and that the spirit of cultic action as a whole accords with what philosophers were able to defend. Beyond this, Cicero ascribes to the leaders of ancient Rome a high degree of psychological understanding of religious phenomena. So, for example, the ancients were able to elevate the piety of the multitude by recourse to such fictive practices as anthropomorphism and the worship of images, and by recourse to the ethically educative force of handling objects of cult. Thus far, Cicero keeps company with Livy, but he goes further, insisting that these actions served not only what was "useful" but also the human posture that arises from a recognition of what is "true." In all of these considerations, the images of "our ancestors" and "the ancient Greeks" meet in that of the primary and original *sapientes* (2.26). In light of the correlation of Pythagoras and the Roman founders of cults, we are thus able to see that the idea that cultic action purifies

---

[13] Cicero *Leg.* 2.27: *ritus familiae patrumque servare (oportet), id est, quoniam antiquitas proxime accedit ad deos, a dis quasi traditam religionem tueri.*

and improves human beings derives from Greek religious philosophy – at any rate, so far as the literary tradition is concerned.

The most important evidence for our topic lies in *On the Nature of the Gods*. Under the critical grasp of Cotta's Academic skepticisim, the structure of Stoic theology breaks down and with it everything that had been naively imported into it from the Roman sphere. Then something happened that a Stoic, completely under the sway of his authoritative reason, could not have accomplished, even if he had been a Roman *pontifex*. Perhaps it was possible only for an Academic, who knew that not everything is true that our reason believes to have been demonstrated, and that there is a reality between heaven and earth that our understanding does not approach. Gaius Aurelius Cotta was such an Academic; about him Cicero remarked retrospectively that "he argued in such a way that he refuted the arguments of the Stoics more than he destroyed the religion of men" (*Div.* 1.8). He was also a *pontifex*, and speaking from that position he explained that in matters of philosophy, and therefore of philosophical religion, a philosophical basis for opinion is an indispensable prerequisite. But in the thought world of Roman cult, the jurisdiction of philosophy had to be rejected. There is authority and there is authority. A philosopher may listen to Zeno, Chrysippus, and their kind. For a *pontifex*, their statements must carry no weight. Here, the authority of the ancestors alone prevails, and above all the authority of past *pontifices*. Nor may belief in that authority be witheld, even if it presents no basis for its doctrine.

> "For you are a philosopher" – Cotta addresses the Stoic Balbus – "and so I ought to receive from you an explanation for your religion (*rationem ... religionis*), but I ought to believe our ancestors without any explanation being given" (*maioribus autem nostris etiam nulla ratione reddita credere*).[14]

> "I am no little moved by your authority, Balbus, and by the plea you delivered in closing your speech, urging that I remember that I am both a Cotta and a *pontifex* [referring to 2.168]. That meant, I suppose, that I should uphold the beliefs concerning the immortal gods that we have received from our ancestors, as well as the rites, ceremonies, and religious duties. Indeed, I will always uphold them, and always have; nor will any learned or ignorant speech dislodge me from the beliefs regarding the worship of the immortal gods that I have inherited from our ancestors. Whenever questions of religion come up, I follow Titus Coruncanius, Publius Scipio, and Publius Scaevola, *pontifices maximi*, not Zeno or Cleanthes or Chrysippus; and I would rather listen to Gaius Laelius, the augur and philosopher, delivering that noble speech of his on religion, rather than any leader of the Stoics ... and I have persuaded myself that Romulus and Numa

14 Cicero *Nat. Deor.* 3.6.

laid the foundations of our state by establishing the auspices and rites, respectively, and that our state could never have become so great without the goodwill of the immortal gods."[15]

Let us consider the advantages of this point of view. Most importantly, traditional religion is freed from the indulgent tutelage of philosophical rationality, which role had commonly been assigned to it, above all by the Stoa. Concomitantly, traditional religion acquired an independent raison d'être, without any diminution in its importance (*sine capitis deminutione*): it stands forth on its own terms, grounded upon an internal authoritarian tradition, alongside the sphere of philosophy. Note, too, a second advantage, one of great psychological importance. Because of a lack of evidence, we do not know what role was played by the provision of explanations (*rationem reddere*) or the absence of reasons in the *commentarii sacrorum*. Just as G. Rohde has delineated for us the cult procedures of the Roman *pontifices*, we may probably suppose that instructions and prayers in them appeared largely without giving a reason for the function.† We incline to the opinion that "the beliefs of the ancestors, no reason being given," was the norm, and that the presentation of an explanation or commentary was more or less the exception. Compared with the Stoic method of insisting everywhere on the assertion of *ratio*, such registers of the names of divinities and cult practices without explanation possessed great advantages. The list allows the individual to make what he will of the matter, and gives practical, unbounded leeway to the ability and desire to believe; at the same time, such a list otherwise gives no scope for an existing inability to believe to be expressed.

The Stoa had dogmatically declared, i.e. in a way that was universally binding, that the religion of the people possessed little if any truth compared with philosophy; consequently, for the sake of the masses, priests should develop popular religion against their own, superior convictions. Such an emphasis on unmasking the irreligious, political *utilitas* of traditional cult, which labeled the entire institution inferior, was the most inappropriate attitude imaginable if a revival of the institution was truly of interest to the state. Above the entry to each priesthood one could read, as if on a placard: "He who enters here has to be illogical his entire life for the preservation of the general morality of the people and has to go through the motions of something that he himself does not completely believe." This is not

---

[15] Cicero *Nat. Deor.* 3.5.
† G. Rohde, *Die Kultsatgungen der römischen Pontifices* (Berlin: Töpelmann, 1936).

to say that one could not lead a meaningful life under such a guise; but men like Scaevola were and remained exceptions.

Under such a theory of religion, a regeneration of traditional cult would have been doomed to failure from the first, solely for the impossible expectations with which it would have burdened its priests, i.e., the Roman nobility. Varro, as we shall see, contemplated just such a possibility. But sentiments like those expressed by him – an enthusiastic patriotism and childlike love for every survival from the past, merely because they derived from the good old days – were able to bring no perceptible relief. Such sentiments can carry the average person only to the point where personal sacrifice begins. I cannot imagine a *flamen Dialis*, together with his family, dedicating many hours of the day and night to his difficult duties and saying of every act that he did it for the sake of the *vulgus* and on grounds of "public utility" (*utilitas publica*). What is more, in view of the realities of Roman political life, the nobility and the priesthood did not form a single caste with a secret doctrine. What for Scaevola had still been possible at the turn of the century, at a time when the majority of the population was still removed from the literary forum, no longer worked after dozens of books had publicized the reality of nonbelief or that of the priests' Stoic "abstaining from intellectual commitment" (*reservatio mentalis*). In view of radical tribunician demagoguery, it is hard to believe that a legal advisor of the plebs, if it fell to his lot, would fail to tell the people how a "a faction of the few" (*factio paucorum*) admitted to forced shamming in the matter of divine worship in order to keep the common man caught up in its self-serving politics. Surely, the gradual diminution of faith among the broader populace with respect to the state religion stems in part from the psychological deficiencies of contemporary, patronizing Stoic theology! And to this the works of Varro were no exception.

In contrast to this, Cotta's point of view possesses advantages for teaching religion. In it, belief derived from *auctoritas* is assimilated to that in a revealed religion. The reproach that Celsus later lays against the Christians, that among them it was said "Don't inquire; just believe!" (μὴ ἐξέταζε, ἀλλὰ πίστευσον), might in large measure have been laid against him. Nevertheless, a basic difference exists. Revealed religions wanted to convey the "truth" in a decisive manner and, naturally, as it derived the *auctoritas auctoritatum*, from God. In the framework of our inquiry, belief derived from *auctoritas* had, in the end, a human basis, even if one derived from a particular kind of person; hence, in the context of such belief, one cannot talk about truth in a narrow sense, but only of "truths mixed with falsehoods" (*vera fictis mixta*). This nature Cotta sought to leave untouched, in that he forbade philosophical *ratio* from unraveling the ins and outs of *vera et ficta*. In this spiritual universe, no subject retains a privileged position. Everything is juxtaposed with equal significance and has an equal chance to be claimed as truth or falsehood by any given individual. When approaching the spiritual, individuals encountered neither a judgment claiming universal validity nor an expression comparable to the common rationale of "utility." Everything was solitary, as we have already indicated, left to individual willingness to believe. Whoever could not soar higher would want to linger on the point of view of *utilitas* and would interpret the thinking of the ancients so that it was consonant. Whoever possessed a feeling for the irrational, whoever could experience the "joyous awe" (*laetus horror*) of a divine presence in an almost physical way – Aemilius Paullus in the presence of Zeus at Olympia "was moved in his spirit as though he looked on Jupiter himself" [16] – was not prevented from devoting himself to the objects that promised to bring about such an experience for him. With such inward variety, whereby individual "enlightenment" existed in potentiality in the highest degree, the external form of the institution remained uniform and venerable, protected from casuistry's claims to a hegemonic truth by the silence of those who believed on faith (*fidele silentium*). Thus, we experience the paradox that from the skeptics' point of view Cotta, a *nobilis*, could enter priestly office without a pain in his heart that he was doomed his entire life to falsehood for the sake of the people. His Stoic colleague, meanwhile, clearly believing in god but dogmatically intransigent, had for the sake of public morality to condemn his priestly colleagues to toil in the arena of a religious system already convicted of error.

We have characterized the attitude of Augustus above – in connection with the selection of Vestals for which particular noble families did not want to make their daughters available – where we noted with astonishment that the emperor spoke not a word about either the blessing or the benefits of the institution, but only let circulate the sworn assertion that if one of his granddaughters had been at the right age, he would not have hesitated to put her on the list of candidates. We now seem to possess the key to this tactic. Augustus was – in the religious-political sphere – more or less a successor of Cotta. He carried out his revivals, without taking notice of the fruitless, rationalistic talk that continually circulated about the worth or

---

[16] Livy 45.28.5: *Iovem velut praesentem intuens motus animo est.*

lack of worth of traditional cult; instead, he proceeded within its framework, solely on the basis of the *auctoritas maiorum* and of his example.

We can now clarify a broader context for this inquiry. Cotta believed that Rome would never have risen to such greatness if the gods had not been won over *summa placatione*. We encountered this idea earlier in such programmatic formulations as we found in Livy (p. 299). We now have a chance to trace back this "theme of Roman success" chronologically. In a passage so deeply resonant with Roman tradition (*Nat. deor* 3.5; p. 315), it is unlikely that Cicero had the *pontifex* express something that was first articulated only in his lifetime. Rather, this apologetic tradition was likely familiar to the authorities cited by Cotta, at least those of the second century BC. To take up an earlier point again, the social power of such a belief in the benefit of the institution always depends ultimately on whether circumstances support such a belief.

That leads to the question whether Cicero thought a revival of the old religion was conceivable in his own lifetime or later. In the political sphere, at least, Cicero believed his entire life in the human example's power to inspire. A few could demoralize a people through their wickedness; on the other hand, even fewer were wanted to raise morality again: "For even a few people – and fewer still if their influence is inflated by office or esteem – can either corrupt the character of the state, or correct it" (*Leg.* 3.32 with reference to *Rep.*). Such a possible *regeneratio morum* ["revival of the national character"] also embraced one of *pietas* ["piety or respect for gods or mortals to whom it is due"] and, in Cicero's thinking, this would only achieve its goal if the men who by their example moved the people to a change in morals also set an example in religion with their seriousness and feelings of responsibility. Did he hope for men like Scaevola or did he have the image of Cotta in mind?

A definite answer is not possible. But we do well to proceed on psychological as well as on historical grounds, and to distinguish between the inspirational power or weakness of an idea in the Ciceronian period and its fate in later epochs. What for Cicero was appealing need not have impressed an Augustan so much and vice versa. We begin with Cotta's point of view. Its historical import – we compose these words on purpose – consisted in this: the figure whom we encounter in Ciceronian writing as the most lively and unrelenting among the philosophically inclined (*in philosophicis*) makes the distinction that philosophy is for philosophers, self-sufficient belief in the authority of the ancestral religion is for those who had to maintain the institution, but a mixture of the two fields is bad. In my opinion, these words later served to give the Augustans formal authority to renew religion without the introduction of modern, philosophical elements.

It seems to me, however, to be highly questionable whether such a "Cotta" in the Ciceronian era could have been a real person and a _pontifex_. The sentences about the _auctoritas maiorum_ sound good on paper, but something about them is comparable to the ostentatious, self-confident way Roman political theology was presented to foreign enemies and those under Roman rule, the phenomenon from which we took our start in this study. The Stoa, to which Cotta addressed himself, was, so to speak, like an enemy coming from outside who threatens the existence, here the spiritual existence, of the nation. The presence of such an opponent spontaneously produced a flare of self-assurance in the Roman speaker – "I, a Cotta and a _pontifex_" – a decisiveness in point of view and a show of a faith that does not correspond to an inner reality. The _auctoritas maiorum_, well known _in religiosis_, among the religious, was in the time of Cicero of no magnitude in serious matters. Certainly it did not have the power to move a person who stood on the heights of reason like Cotta – was there anyone still like him? – such that, for its sake, he would renounce consideration of its opponent, namely, determined, rational argumentation. Out of harm's way, Cicero could naturally condemn every irreligious commander of the First Punic War with the phrase which we quoted above: "For they should have respected religious scruple, nor should they so arrogantly have repudiated ancestral custom." Would he have condemned himself had he been in the situation of Nikias at Syracuse in his own lifetime, had he possessed the religious inhibitions of that unlucky man, which hindered him from following the recognized need of the moment?

In the final analysis, was Cicero's _On the nature of the gods_ anything less than an assassination attempt on the life of the ancestral religion, insofar as it still existed? Cicero wrote that work under the spell of philosophical _ratio_ and industriously served its naturalization at Rome; and that book's gods are emphatically not those of the _maiores_. Is it not shameful how little knowledge of the gods of old Rome that work displays? Nor did Cicero feel any need to redress his ignorance through reading Varro's _Antiquitates_, though that work was already available. In his heart of hearts, he thought and felt like a Stoic and was convinced that he knew what was sufficient for the credulity of the masses (_ad opinionem vulgi_). Indeed, his book offers almost everything that later opponents of the state religion needed to pursue their struggle successfully; moreover, it offered the building blocks of that un-Roman, cosmic religiosity that Christianity then gleefully used to merge its own qualities with the thinking of the national classical authors.

"I know there are many," writes Arnobius [the Christian apologist], "who turn aside from and flee his books on this subject (i.e., *On the nature of the gods*), who do not want to listen to a text that overthrows the presumption of their beliefs ... Others mutter indignantly and say that the senate ought to decree the destruction of these writings, by which the Christian religion is affirmed and the authority of antiquity subverted." [17]

Another factor deserves consideration. Cotta recommended a parallelism of thought without explaining how one could justify this coexistence intellectually. We suggested above that a Stoic *pontifex* could only with daring and difficulty propose a double register of this kind. Furthermore, we opined that Academic skeptics, with their commitment to mere probability, might well have been able to practice tolerance toward traditional systems, insofar as they did not want to convey "truth." Cicero, as it seems, did not make a serious effort to think the problem through completely. At any rate, in lived reality, such a change in thought from "rationality" (*ratio*) to "authority without explanations being given" (*auctoritas sine ratione reddita*) must have encountered obstacles, if it were a movement with real meaning and substance. The more rationalizing the period, the greater the obstacles. Here it came in handy for the Augustans that their representative spirituality, in contrast to that of the Ciceronian era, revolved around poetry and the writing of history and no longer around the philosophical reason that was then in vogue. Thus, in the interaction between *zeitgeist* and conqueror all light fell on the romantic, glorious past and its *auctoritas*, while philosophical uncertainty lost substance and settled largely in the private sphere. There it certainly survived, indeed, tenaciously, and in many ways it undermined much, I don't want to say all, that seemed to have a strong spiritual foundation in official life. In consequence of this shift of emphasis, the parallelism of Cotta's thought no longer presented the contradiction that it must formerly have exhibited to the thinking person – provided that someone in our

---

[17] Arnobius 3.7: (*scio*) *esse non paucos qui aversentur et fugiant libros de hoc eius* (*sc. de natura deorum*) *nec in aurem velint admittere lectionem opinionum suarum praesumpta vincentem, ... alios ... mussitare indignanter et dicere, oportere statui per senatum, oboleantur ut haec scripta quibus Christiana religio comprobetur et vetustatis opprimatur auctoritas.*

area truly was concerned with the relationship between *ratio* and *auctoritas*.

Cotta's ideas experienced a renaissance in the writings of Lactantius. He was, of course, not implicated in the crisis of *auctoritas* with which we have been concerned. Nevertheless, in the assertion that "I could say what it is not more swiftly than I could say what it is,"[18] Lactantius perhaps saw a confession of pagan antiquity. Human reason could not come into possession of truth. Against this background, and fully consistent and plausible with it, the Christian dogma that God had come in person and had brought the truth shone forth as a result whose necessity even human understanding could recognize (*Div. inst.* 1.17.4ff.).

Let us return to the discussion of Cicero. It is perhaps already clear that it was the Stoic view of the world that made his heart race: "When these things had been said, we parted company: Cotta's argument seemed to Velleius the more true, while that of Balbus seemed to me closer to an approximation of the truth."[19] We must therefore return to men like Scaevola, if we want to know what Cicero would have thought, had he allowed himself to ponder the future of Roman theology and the possibility of a renewal of traditional religion on its basis. To entertain this possibility required, naturally, assent to the words of the old *pontifex*: "it is useful for states to be deceived in matters of religion." But for an aristocrat who was not a priest, this position was not so problematic, and great personal advantage accrued to those educated men who could achieve the grandiose universal piety of Stoic philosophy. In view of the traditional religion and its then already ancient debilitation, however, the consequences of Scaevola's position are clear: from Cicero or, at any rate, from the living Cicero, no impulse could proceed that might have realized a restoration of tradition on an autonomous and universally-sustaining foundation. A time that relished the sunny gleam of philosophical thought could bring about nothing that might have maintained its own luminosity over, beside or even in opposition to this brilliance.

The selfsame Scaevola clearly provided a model for his friend Varro, too; indeed, we cited the evidence for this above. Cicero enthusiastically welcomed the Varronian achievement in the *Antiquitates populi Romani* and honored it with emphatic words of praise: "We wandered like foreigners in our own city and your

[18] Cicero *Nat. Deor.* 1.60: *quid non sit citius quam quid sit dixerim.*
[19] Cicero *Nat. Deor.* 3.95: *haec cum essent dicta, ita discessimus, ut Velleio Cottae disputatio verior, mihi Balbi ad veritatis similitudinem videretur esse propensior.*

books, like hosts, led us home, so that we can see now who and where we are. You revealed the age of our homeland, the events of our history, the laws of rites and priesthoods, the customs of war and peace, the sites of temples, districts and place, and the names, types, functions and causes of all matters, divine and human."[20] Varro was himself convinced that in his inventory of Roman sacred antiquities he had produced a work of the highest religious and political significance. Certainly he could not have esteemed himself any higher, as the following fragment makes clear: "Varro says that he is afraid lest the gods perish, not through a hostile attack, but from the indifference of the citizens. From that disaster, he says, the gods are freed by him: through his books they are stored away in the memory of the good, a rather useful chore, as Metullus is said to have rescued the sacred objects of the Vestals from a fire and Aeneas is said to have rescued the Penates from the sack of Troy."[21] The circumstances at that time resemble the burning of Troy or the temple of Vesta in 241 BC, the "indifference of the citizens" resembles the ruinous mass of destroyed homes, the gods resemble the humans who lay buried below. Varro frees them from this condition, as Aeneas and Metellus dragged their *sacra*, their sacred objects, from the conflagration, with only one difference. Varro saved all the gods and had to transplant them into another world, from the reality of "indifference" into the "memory of the good," into that spiritual realm whose objects were commended to the love of patriots. Varro's goal, therefore, really was to introduce a revival of the traditional worship of the gods: "he wrote and researched for this purpose, that the masses might wish to worship rather than despise the gods."[22]

The Stoic tenor of these sentences is obvious. It is necessary to get the masses (*vulgus*) to believe in the old gods. To dedicate themselves to this goal is a *cura utilis* ["a useful duty of case"], for reasons of state. Therefore, it is recommended warmly to the good, the *boni*, the patriots. The gods exist only in the imagination of their worshipers. When through indifference they are no longer noticed, they cease to

---

[20] Cicero *Ac. pr.* 1.3.9: *nam nos in urbe nostra peregrinantes errantesque tamquam hospites tui libri quasi domum deduxerunt, ut possemus aliquando qui et ubi essemus agnoscere. tu aetatem patriae, tu descriptiones temporum, tu sacrorum iura tu sacerdotum, tu domesticam tu bellicam disciplinam, tu sedum regionum locorum tu omnium divinarum humanarumque rerum nomina genera officia causas aperuisti.*

[21] Augustine *Civ.* 6.2: *Varro dicit se timere, ne pereant di, non incursu hostili, sed civium neglegentia, de qua illos velut ruina liberari a se dicit et per eiusmodi libros in memoria bonorum recondi, utiliore cura, quam Metellus de incendio sacra Vestalia et Aeneas de Troiano excidio Penates liberasse praedicatur.*

[22] Augustine *Civ.* 4.31: *ad eum finem se illa scribere ac perscrutari, ut potius (deos) magis colere quam despicere vulgus velit.*

exist (*pereunt*). Varro stands, of course, on the ground of *theologia tripertita*. "Scientific theology" (the *genus physicum*) alone is binding for the educated, diametrically opposed to "mythic theology" as truth is to deceit; "civic theology" takes the middle: "Scientific and mythic theology avoid each other; nevertheless, many notions have been lifted from each of those theologies to form the civic one ... But we ought to have more converse with philosophers than with poets."[23] Varro's close affinity for Stoic philosophy finds further expression in his well-known etymologies. Very often, they impute to old Roman divine names a meaning and a field of reference that have little or nothing to do with what a person of an earlier time once thought about them. In practice, these etymologies, together with allegorical interpretations of every kind, opened for some among the educated a path to the objects of the ancestral religion. Common people with doubts, on the other hand, should have noticed through repeated experience that their beliefs included many elements that the *docti* of the upper class did not dare casually to relinquish. It was thus not the place of the uneducated to despise the gods and not to care for them. And hence one must heed the call to action, which Varro left implicit in his emphatic appeal to "the good," the *boni*, the patriots. His thought can be well paraphrased thus: if you can no longer perform religious duties in large part from personal conviction, then do so at least as a national game, as a demonstration of civic loyalty, as a social form.

In reality, the practice of religion under the empire consisted of a mixture in the widest sense, one as rich in outward forms as in real religiosity. And yet, it was already true of "the good" among Varro's contemporaries that they did not understand the forms of ancient Roman religious practice. Varro therefore instructed them through his work. Indeed, he did so with a diligence and zeal for thoroughness that leads one to ask whether an expansion of antiquarian data at such length was suitable for any purpose other than a renewal of practice. Of course, when one makes many demands, as a rule nothing gets done. On the other hand, Varro is extremely unlikely to have thought that everything that he described would return to life again. When writing, he hardly reckoned on a restoration on the scale he might have experienced under Augustus. At the same time, Varro's achievement – to have excavated everything from the dust of

---

[23] Augustine *Civ.* 6.6: *sic abhorrent (physicum et mythicum), ut tamen ex utroque genere ad civiles rationes adsumpta sint non pauca ... maior societas debet nobis esse cum philosophis quam cum poetis.*

the past, and compiled and thereby "saved" it – was the product of his predisposition. He derived pleasure from research (*perscrutari*): as a result, he did not know to keep his distance from the objects of his passion – distance that would have been necessary to distinguish the worthwhile from the less useful. He may also have felt some unconscious angst, that he and he alone was responsible, for the sake of his people, for making everything as certain as he was able. For all his ostentatious talk of "utility," which might have saved face with the enlightened (and here envision Caesar as recipient and reader of the book), the comparison with Aeneas and Metellus Caecatus is so strikingly drawn that it might well reveal a faint, coy, secretive irrational stirring in his heart.

On the whole, his feelings must have been divided. He could not and might not present the fruits of his ardent and industrious collecting as true, high-quality spiritual food, either to his own intellect or to the educated public. Moreover, he saw clearly that his work had, in practice, to end in compromise. Modern readers see the solutions he crafted, of the most delicate kind; we see how they materialized under the compulsion that some motive like patriotism, of a secondary or foreign nature, be harnessed. Varro proceeded optimistically because he was convinced that Aeneas and Metellus would have thought exactly as he did: they already possessed higher knowledge about the gods and acted as patriots in the service of the citizen body. And yet, within this spiritual, simple, honest man, in the recesses of his mind, won over as he was by Stoic teachings, lingered a suspicion of the tragic truth: the citizen body of an ancient nation, such as the *populus Romanus* was, simply could not grow in respect to "truth." This would remain true so long as such a body lived, because of the numberless, incorrect but essential representations in the domain of its ancestral religion, which were both incommensurate and irreplaceable. "Varro did not hesitate to confess that if he were establishing the state anew, he would have given the gods their names in accordance with the rule of nature. As it was, since he lived among an ancient people, he said that he was obliged to retain the history of their names as it had been received and handed down from antiquity."[24]

Like the Stoic compromise, whose psychological shortcomings

---

[24] Augustine *Civ.* 4.31: *Varro non dubitat confiteri, si eam civitatem novam constitueret, ex naturae potius formula deos nominaque eorum se fuisse dedicaturum. sed iam, quoniam in vetere populo esset, acceptam ab antiquis nominum et cognominum historiam tenere, ut tradita sit, debere se dicit.* Cf. *Civ.* 6.4: Augustine could employ for his own ends not only this idea, but also Scaevola's remark, as well as Varro's lists of primitive, indigenous gods.

we have discussed, Varro's theology had no future. Like Cicero, or perhaps even more than he, Varro thought in too honorable, sincere a manner to be able to confront the victorious, philosophical mode of argument that had so recently taken root at Rome. And Varro was too deeply engaged in modes of thought that focused on the pursuit of truth and understanding to be able to add momentum to any genuine, political "utility" (*utilitas*) such as interested Augustus and his circle. For by means of removing certain themes from discussion, and also by means of the censorship of silence, these men were able to achieve the impossible, at any rate in an external sense: that is, they created the precondition for a renewal of the ancestral religion that could include the entire people, since persons of culture and ordinary people alike were equally called upon to participate. We have shown several times that this was merely a fictive solution. However, it achieved greater success than it would have done, had it been carried out fifty years earlier. As things stood, it harmonized with a general development in spirituality, which gradually distanced itself from the primacy of critical reason, a development documented in another realm by the Academy's choice to follow the path that led to Neoplatonism.

What is true of Varro's Stoic theology need not apply in the same measure to the material that he collected. Without his complete inventory, the scope of the Augustan restoration would have been impossible. Consider only the priest- and brotherhoods, vacant since time immemorial, that again saw the light of day. Varro's relationship to the Augustans might be described figuratively as follows: traditional religion in the late Republic resembled a long-abandoned, long-neglected house. Along came Varro. He entered it, motivated partly by personal interest, and partly by the vague recognition that the future of his country required a cleaning of the house and a new arrangement of its contents. He accomplished this in such a way that all the items stood before the eyes of the people, complete and like new, each in its room, each in its place. Within Varro's work lay a psychological impulse, which proved inviting in the highest degree and which arranged this homecoming more easily than if some Augustan, perhaps one whose love for this had not been characteristic, had led the way and had had to bring the house to order.

We stand at the end of our meditation. To return to the second century BC would shed no new light on our particular question. To be sure, every epoch is important to the one that succeeds it. But we lack the evidence with which to characterize the action undertaken, objectively and forcefully to defend the old worship of the gods against the double threat: namely, the passage of enlightenment from Hellenism to the Roman aristocracy, on the one hand, and the infiltration of the lower classes by the exaggerated piety of the mystery religions, on the other. Indeed, we scarcely have the evidence to describe those threats. If we had the "noble speech" of Laelius, of which Cotta speaks, or could reconstruct its content in its particulars, things would be very different.[25] As things stand, we have nothing but reports about resolutions of the Senate and police actions, which establish fronts in both directions: since they expelled the Epicureans at one time, the philosophers and rhetors at another, and drove actors from the city at another. On the other hand, they took action against "foreign religions" in 213 BC (*religiones externae*), the Bacchanalia in 186, the "testament of Numa" in 181, and the Chaldaeans and Jews in 139 BC. Livy and Varro furnish a restricted view of the action against the books of the pseudo-Numa: "When the quaestor recognized that much of the content of the books was destructive of religion," or "when the leading senators read Numa's explanations why each particular thing among the rites had been instituted," the books were burned "in the *comitium*, ... in the sight of the people. For men of old did not want anything preserved in this community, by which the minds of mortals might be turned away from the worship of the gods."[26] So much for rational, enlightened exegesis.

In the long run, the five republican prohibitions in the first century BC and the early imperial ban on the worship of Isis within the pomerium were as unsuccessful as the earlier actions. With regard to our inquiry, these reports reveal again and again the discrepancy discussed above, between an intolerant animosity on the part of the intervening state authorities, on the one hand, and the success of their actions, on the other. That magistrates took action – the consuls themselves once participated in demolishing a shrine of Isis – suggests that those aristocrats held traditional religion to be a good on which the success and ruin of the nation depended. On the other hand, the success of magisterial action had to remain limited precisely because, in the inner circle of the nobility, contrary to outward appearances,

<hr />

[25] Cic. *Nat. Deor.* 3.43; *Rep.* 6.2.
[26] Livy 40.29.11: *cum animadvertisset (quaestor) pleraque dissolvendarum religionum esse.* Varro, as quoted by Augustine *Civ.* 7.34: *cum primores quasdam causas* – aetiologies! – *legissent, cur quidque in sacris fuerit institutum* ... Valerius Maximus 1.1.12 (translation after Shackleton Bailey): *in comitio ... in conspectu populi: noluerunt enim prisci viri quidquam in hac civitate adservari, quo animi hominum a deorum cultu avocarentur.*

almost no one seriously troubled himself about the old. Quite the opposite: many already took extreme pains about the new.

This observation leads us back to the beginning of our study, to that ostentatious unanimity with which the official Roman ideology overcame opponents and the defeated and to which – to extract the gist of this work – so precious little in the personal "belief" of the ruling class corresponded. We now know that the strongest impulse behind the creation and maintenance of this unanimity was precisely the need to confront an opponent and represent the nation in its honor and its prestige. Between the Ciceronian and Augustan eras, something not unimportant had shifted; and that change helped to endow the public face of this ideology with a new depth and the air of true conviction. At the end of the Republic, every participant in discussion with sufficient insight could identify many widely-available books in which Romans openly allowed that only the ignorant still practiced their ancestral religion. They did not say this openly, of course, but reserved such remarks for their inner circle. But after the Augustan restoration, even this could not easily be done, for the *princeps* had elevated to an undeclared law the principle that one should not discuss details of traditional religion, but accept them "without explanations being given" (*nulla ratione reddita*). The elimination of the much-decried rift between educated and uneducated in Roman public life created on the domestic front a closed façade. Illuminated by the light of Augustan literature, this façade presented itself not simply when an enemy approached, but continually, to the city and the world, to overwhelming effect. An uncommon lot of goodwill and good art entered into the service of the cause.

The development of Europe cannot be conceived without considering the significance of this moment in the history of the world. At this point, a singular process unfolded, that in a spiritual and historical sense is nonetheless thoroughly intelligible. Vergil, who had arrived late on the scene and had set out humbly to explain Numa and his work to a new future, as one among the inalienable achievements of the Roman world, himself initiated a new beginning in the religious thought of the Empire. Augustan apologetics, as we have seen, placed heavy emphasis on the practice of cult, notionally as inspired by Numa. This effort was part and parcel of an imperial project to achieve a common basis for understanding and the possibility of a universal revival. As perceived by Augustan apologists, the form of worship devised by Numa had, by means of rational design, inculcated that stern, old Roman popular morality, whence emerged the *pax deorum* and finally the empire. It was just this understanding that was completely overshadowed by Vergil's ever more timely presentation of prophecy that reached beyond reason and spoke of "empire without end."

14 *The Historical Development of Roman Religion: An Overview*[†]

GEORG WISSOWA

translated by Christopher Barnes

SECOND SECTION: UP TO THE SECOND PUNIC WAR

7 *The foundation of the Capitoline cults and contemporaneous innovations*

If the oldest order of gods was adapted to the interests and needs of a small urban community living in the closest proximity, subsequent religious development was determined by Rome's expansion beyond its own territory and through its gradual absorption of neighboring communities and tribes, whether accomplished through friendly treaties or through violent subjugation, into a steadily-growing state assured of its future. The changed political relations are clearly manifested in the area of religion. The old triad of gods, Juppiter, Mars, and Quirinus, recedes and survives only in the prayer formulae which derived from an older time. In its place came a new group of divinities, Juppiter, Juno, and Minerva, which took its place on the crowning heights of the city.[1] The foundation of this temple, which means the beginning of a new era in more than one respect, is attributed by the ancients unanimously to the Tarquins.[2] Tradition also assigns to the same dynasty a series of important innovations in the area of religion: the construction of a temple of Diana on the Aventine[3]

---

† Originally published as *Religion und Kultus der Römer*, 2nd edn (Munich: Beck, 1912; repr. 1971), pp. 38–47, 70–2, and 78–87.

[1] Invocations of the Capitoline gods in prayers, e.g. Livy 6.20.9; 38.51.9; the meaning is the same when, during the Republic, Roman officials swore an oath to Juppiter Optimus Maximus (and the Penates) when taking office: Mommsen, *Ges. Schr.*, 1:351ff.

[2] *Testimonia* in Jordan, *Topographie*, 1:2, pp. 8 ff.

[3] Dionysius *Ant. Rom.* 4.26. Livy 1.45. Aur. Vict. *Ill.* 7.8 ff., Zonaras 7.9.

and the establishment of the Latin League,[4] the acquisition of the Sybilline books and the appointment of a priesthood that served as guardians of the oracles,[5] the construction of the Circus as well as the introduction of the Roman games,[6] and the ceremony of the triumph.[7] As varying and arbitrary as the attribution of individual accomplishments to the different kings in the house of the Tarquins is in this tradition, nevertheless, the approximate contemporaneity and the internal cohesiveness of all these innovations may be held as assured, not because they have come down to us in this way, but because a test of the indisputable, established facts leads to the same results.

Without a doubt, first, the temple of Diana on the Aventine was a common sanctuary for Rome and the Latin League. Within this temple Dionysius of Halicarnassus (4.26.5) was still able to see the organization of the League and of its festivities marked on a bronze tablet. Since we know that the shrine of Diana at Aricia, of which the Roman version represents a daughter, constituted the religious center of a Latin league of cities,[8] one may confidently assert that the transfer of this cult of Diana to the Aventine simultaneously gave the leadership in the league's *sacra* to Rome (Varro *Ling.* 5.43: "the temple of Diana, common to the Latins" [*commune Latinorum Dianae templum*]). As the increase in the number of Roman divinities always runs parallel to the continuing expansion of Roman rule, the acceptance of the once-foreign Diana into the state cult at this point reflects the beginning of the decline of the Latins in Rome. That this sanctuary was the first to be founded in Rome under new circumstances on the basis of the laws for founding temples is demonstrated by the fact that the *lex arae Dianae in Aventino* ["the law of the altar of Diana on the Aventine"] and only this, even during the Empire, provides the model for universal, recurring laws to which other temple laws refer.[9]

From this shrine of the Roman-Latin federation, one probably should not dissociate the installation or renewal of the festival on the Alban mount and the foundation of the temple of Juppiter Latiaris associated with it. Both installations pursue the same goal: the documentation of Roman leadership in Latium. This is revealed on

---

[4] Dionysius *Ant. Rom.* 4.49.2, 6.95.3. Cf. Aur. Vict. *Ill.* 8.2. *Schol. Bob. Cic. Planc.* 23.

[5] Dionysius *Ant. Rom.* 4.62 and more in Schwegler, *Römische Geschichte*, 1:773ff.

[6] Livy 1.35.8 ff. Dionysius *Ant. Rom.* 3.68.1. Cicero *Rep.* 2.36. Schwegler, *Römische Geschichte*, 1:674. Jordan, *Topographie*, 1.3, p. 120.

[7] Strabo 5.2.2. Plutarch *Romulus* 16. Pliny *Nat.* 33.63 *et al.*

[8] Cato *Orig.* frg. 58 Peter; cf. Nissen, *Landeskunde*, 2:557ff.

[9] *CIL* 3.1933. 11.361. 12.4333.

the one hand by the way that Rome put the sacred focus of the Latin League within its boundary and immediately before the borders of the outskirts of the city. A sort of additional historical legitimation was maintained through the continuation of the Alban festival under Roman direction. One may confidently assert that Alba Longa, which was destroyed early, had stood in the leadership of a league encompassing the entire Latin nation, one which extended considerably further than the Arician League that took its place after Alba's fall. Support for this comes from the festivals that took place on the Alban Mount in the area of this city, through the resumption of which Rome gave expression to its hegemony over the entire *nomen Latinum* ["Latin name"]. The extant passages from the official lists of the communities[10] participating in the celebration of the *Latiar* show that this group comprised the whole area of the *prisci Latini* ("the ancient and originary Latins") and that the renewal of the common festival under Roman leadership, even compared with the transfer of the Arician league's shrine to Rome, still had its own distinctive meaning.

Even disregarding this tradition, the construction of the temple of *Juppiter Latiaris* on the Alban hill should probably be considered simultaneous with the resumption of the *feriae Latinae*, and excavations have in any event established the great antiquity of the site.[11] These scanty remains allow one to recognize at the same time in the plan of the temple and its manner of construction a correspondence with the remains of the Capitolium so remarkable that the supposition that both may belong to the same period probably should not be discounted.[12] This hypothesis finds a meaningful basis in the unmistakably old relationships that existed between the two shrines. The league offering of a white bull[13] is just like the one the Roman consuls sacrificed on the Capitoline on the day on which they took office.[14] The Alban festival produced an effect in Rome itself, since while it took place a chariot race was held on the Capitoline.[15] The temple of Juppiter Latiaris appeared as the end and goal of triumphal

---

[10] Pliny *Nat.* 3.68 ff., Dionysius *Ant. Rom.* 5.61. Cf. Mommsen, *Ges. Schr.*, 5:69ff.

[11] M. St. de Rossi, "Scavi e studii nel tempio di giove laziale sul Monte Albano," *AdI* 48 (1876), 314–333; cf. idem, "Nuove scoperte nella necropoli arcaica albana e l'aes grave fra le rocce vulcaniche laziali," *AdI* 43 (1871), 239–279 and G. B. de Rossi, "Ricerche archeologiche e topografiche nel Monte Albano e nel territorio tusculano," *AdI* 45 (1873), 162–221. Nissen, *Landeskunde*, 2:58off.

[12] Cf. R. Delbrück, *Das Capitolium von Signia: der Apollotempel auf dem Marsfelde in Rom* (Rome: Loescher, 1903), 22.

[13] Arnobius 2.68.

[14] Mommsen, *Staatsrecht* 1:594.

[15] Pliny *Nat.* 28.45.

processions in the same manner as on the Capitoline.[16] These phenomena find an easy explanation only through the supposition that
the temples arose almost simultaneously and under the same historical conditions, one as the focal point of a Latium united at least by
sacra, the other as the seat of the gods of the principal city. In both
cases, it is Juppiter who receives veneration, on the Alban mount
as the tutelary divinity of Latium, on the Capitol as *Optimus* and
Maximus, who surpasses the protecting gods of other communities
just as Rome did its neighbors.

At the side of Juppiter Optimus Maximus stand Juno Regina
and Minerva as companions in cult, and thus a triad of a completely
different sort than the old one of Juppiter, Mars, and Quirinus
becomes important. The origin of this group of gods[17] lies in obscurity. The view that it is based on a general Italic conception of cult has
lost its main support since it has become known that the countless
Capitolia of Italian and other foreign cities are just imitations of the
Roman.[18] The fact, at times overvalued in its meaning, at other times
groundlessly doubted, that there was already a shrine of Juppiter,
Juno and Minerva before the founding of the Capitoline temple[19]
demonstrates nothing further than that this group of divinities had
long found a reception in Rome in discreet form, until it assumed its
commanding position on the Capitol. Since the union of Ζεύς, Ἥρα,
and Ἀθηνᾶ [Zeus, Hera, and Athena] is found in Greece only once
and in a rather remote location (they were the gods of the Phokaian
community of villages, Pausanias 10.5.1),[20] the hypothesis that the
whole triad had been brought from Greece lacks probability; and all
the more so, since we should have expected in that case to find
the Capitoline cult placed under the protection of the *IIviri sacris
faciundis*. However, foreign influence is to be anticipated under any
reconstruction, since neither Juno Regina nor Minerva belong to the
oldest circle of Roman gods.[21] It also probably goes without saying
that the old triad of Juppiter, Mars, and Quirinus was pushed into

---

[16] A. Michaelis, *AdI* 48 (1876), 113 ff. Laqueur, "Triumph," 235.

[17] Varro declares Juppiter, Juno, and Minerva the oldest gods (Tertullian *Nat.* 2.12.).

[18] O. Kuhfeldt, *De Capitoliis imperii Romani* (Berlin: Weidmann, 1882). A. Castan, *Les Capitoles provinciaux du monde Romain* (Besancon: Dodivers et Cie, 1886). G. B. De Rossi, "Miscellanea di notizie bibliografiche ...," *Bulletino* 15 (1887), 61–68 and 67–68. E. Aust in Roscher, *Lex.* 2:793 ff. Wissowa, *RE* 6 (1899) s.v. Capitolium, cols. 1531–1540 at 1538ff. Toutain, *Cultes*, 1:182–193.

[19] Varro *Ling.* 5.158; on the *Capitolium vetus* ["ancient Capitolium"], see Jordan, *Topographie*, 1.3, pp. 411 ff.

[20] H. Usener, "Dreiheit," *RhM* 58 (1903), 1–47, 161–208, and 321–362, at 30.

[21] The detailed discussion concerning the question of the female divinities in the Capitoline triad in M. Zeitlin, *RHR* 17 (1896), 320 ff. contributes nothing new.

the background not by the creation of a new group of divinities who were already worshiped, but through the intrusion of new elements. Since the veneration of Juno Regina as a city goddess outside of Latium is also attested in southern Etruria and the Italic worship of Minerva had its center in Falerii, it is most likely that this group of gods was created in Etruria. From there they were borrowed by the Romans. The "Etruscan discipline" (*Etrusca disciplina*) teaches that three shrines of Juppiter, Juno, and Minerva were planned during the founding of a city,[22] whence it seems that the veneration of Minerva as a city goddess presumes an equivalence with Greek Athena and is suggested by the idea of Ἀθηνᾶ Πολιάς [Athena Polias].[23] Etruscan influence is manifest in the Capitoline temple in the scheme of the ground plan still clearly recognizable from the remains,[24] as well as in the decoration of the building with its terracotta reliefs and ceramic ornaments, and in the temple effigies, produced from the same material. The reports of the ancients, which speak of the assistance of artists summoned from Etruria, from this point of view are shown to be entirely believable.[25] Since, however, the costume of the *triumphator* was created according to that of the effigy and in part is borrowed directly from this,[26] the tradition, which also derives the triumphal insignia from Etruria, takes on special significance. Festival games originally gave rise to a part of the triumphal procession, which first as "great" or "votive games" (*ludi magni* or *votivi*) of an extraordinary nature, then as "Roman games" (*ludi Romani*), were permanently celebrated and were the model for all later celebrations of this kind. Like the triumph, they stood in closest relation to the Capitoline cult and conformed directly, as soon as they became permanent, to the foundation day of the temple. Thus, this institution also became one of the innovations under Etruscan-Greek influence.

---

[22] Serv. *Aen.* 1.422: "Experts in the Etruscan art say that among founders of Etruscan cities, cities were not thought just in which three gates had not been dedicated, with the same number of streets and temples, to Jupiter, Juno, and Minerva" (*prudentes Etruscae disciplinae aiunt apud conditores Etruscarum urbium non putatas iustas urbes, in quibus non tres portae essent dedicatae et tot viae et tot templa, Iovis, Iunonis Minervae*). Cf. Vitruvius 1.7.1. C. Thulin, *Die etruskische Disciplin*, Göteborgs Högskolas Årsskrift 11, 12, and 15 (Göteborg: 1906–1909), 3:43f.

[23] The conjectures of C. Thulin ("Minerva auf dem Capitol und Fortuna in Praeneste," *RhM* 60 (1905), 256–261), who identifies Minerva of the Capitoline Triad with the Praenestine Fortuna and in this sees an Etruscan goddess of fate, lack tenable foundations.

[24] Cf. H. Degering, *Nachrichten der Gesellschaft der Wissenschaften zu Göttingen*, philologisch-historische Klasse, 1897, 153 ff.

[25] Evidence in Jordan, *Topographie*, 1:2, pp. 8ff.; cf. W. Helbig, "Eine Rathsversammlung auf einem italischen Relief," *RhM* 58 (1903), 500–510.

[26] Marquardt, *Staatsverwaltung*, 2:586ff. Laqueur, "Triumph," 222 n. 1.

The Sibylline books were kept in the basement of the Capitoline temple until the reign of Augustus.[27] That collection of Greek oracles, often augmented and altered in their condition over the course of time, provided the basis for the Hellenizing change in the religious belief of the Roman state and in the service of the gods taking place at this time. Its protectors and interpreters, the *IIviri sacris faciundis*, achieved such great importance in this way that they found a place of equal entitlement next to the ancient Roman priesthoods as agents of the *graecus ritus*.† If the Capitoline shrine was furnished with artistic decoration and ceremony that mixed Etruscan influence with strong Greek elements, the Sibylline books are the bearers of Greek points of view advancing directly from the Greek cities of southern Italy, from Cumae most of all. This becomes clear in an apparent matter of secondary importance: as is well attested, Veientine craftsmen created the temple and portraits of the gods in the Capitolium, while in the first temple in Rome built in response to consultations of the Sibylline books, that for Ceres, Liber, and Libera, the Greek artists Damophilos and Gorgasos were active.[28]

The period during which the extremely momentous innovations in the area of religion listed here occurred cannot be defined exactly and chronologically. Only so much is sure, that these happened before the beginning of the keeping of time in the Republic and are so closely related that, if they are not the creations of one and the same person, they belong in any case to the same closely circumscribed period, governed by the same leading ideas. The absolute power of the old *di indigetes* ["native divinities"] is broken. When Servius Tullius created a common constitutional law for both patricians and plebeians, the circle of patrician houses was closed and new *gentes* [notionally, a *gens* was an extended family sharing a common, patrician ancestor] were no longer absorbed.[29] Rather, all new citizens increased the plebs only. At the same time, it was apparently decided that the *pomerium* of the city, which had been expanded more than once, had henceforth to remain fixed, and hence the city's municipal area embraced within its border neither the further expansion of its built-up land nor even the city wall. As a result, this land remained extrapomerial throughout the Republic – until Sulla

---

[27] Dionysius *Ant. Rom.* 4.62.5.

† "The Greek rite," a form of sacrifice that the Romans regarded as Greek in origin, a sort of domesticated or internalized element of foreignness in their ritual repertoire. On this topic see Scheid 1995b, 1998c; introduction to Part V above.

[28] Pliny *Nat.* 35.154; cf. A. Philippi, *Jahrbücher für Philologie* 107, 205 ff. A. Furtwängler, "Von Delos," *Archäologische Zeitung* 40 (1883), 321–368 at 346.

[29] Mommsen, *Staatsrecht*, 3:32; cf. Mommsen, *Röm. Forsch.*, 1:71ff.

– at least from a particular legal perspective.[30] In the same period
of historical development, the circle of native divinities [...], which
up to that time had experienced some growth, was declared complete
and everything that was added later through adoption and invention
was assigned to the notionally foreign but equally important circle
of state divinities, the *di novensides*. This all happened near the end
of the monarchy, and the period of the *di novensides* in the Roman
state religion begins with the Capitoline cult and contemporaneous
sacred innovations. Given the fact that a profound revolution in
the religious conditions of the state had taken place at the end of
the monarchy, the ancients probably retained some memory of it.
History and the individual details of the same were no less dark for
them than for us. However, let there be no mistake that these transformations furnished the only basis for the further development of
Roman religion. Everything that we see carried out to the end of the
third century in the sphere of religion at Rome takes place exclusively
along the paths opened through the reforms attributed to the
Tarquins. The religion of the Tarquins is, in its main features, that of
Republican Rome until the Hannibalic War.

Bibliography

Schwegler, *Römische Geschichte* 1:673ff., 696ff., 706ff., 730ff., 770ff.,
792ff. J. A. Ambrosch, *Studien und Andeutungen im Gebiet des altrömischen Bodens und Cultus* (Breslau, 1839), 196 ff. O. Weise, "Von welchem
Staaten ist Rom in seiner Kultur beeinflusst worden?" *RhM* 38 (1883)
540–566. Concerning Rome and Latium: Mommsen, *Staatsrecht* 3, 607 ff.

8 The expansion of the circle of Roman divinities

As Roman control extended over all of Italy (Sicily included) in the
first three hundred years of the Republic, the circle of Roman gods
expanded too, corresponding to the growth of its external borders
and the multiplication of external relationships from generation to
generation. The tolerance characteristic of all polytheism toward
foreign religion was practiced to an especially great extent by the
Romans, who were intent, always with the most scrupulous care, not
to advance any claim of divine right. This tolerance was naturally
conditioned by a prior understanding that the privileges of the old

---

[30] Richter, *Topographie*, 2:64ff.

gods, based on agreements entered into earlier, should not be diminished. If the Roman at the end of his prayers called upon all the gods of the sky and of the earth, the gods of his own state and those of the enemy which he fought (Livy 8.9.6: *di quibus est potestas nostrorum hostiumque*, "gods whose power extends over us and our enemies"), he stated clearly that he considered the momentary boundary of the circle of the gods of his state temporary and purely the product of fortune and recognized the existence of equally powerful divine beings beyond this border. There were those not yet known to him, but he was ready, as soon as they approached him, for his part, to offer them also a place. Every expansion of Rome's territory and every entry into new political relations brought the state into contact with gods who were previously unknown, whose worship the state was then in a position or was even obligated to adopt.

A duty to accept new gods began for the state as soon as it abolished the political or actual existence of another community. The sacred duties of the latter did not cease to exist, but were transferred in their entirety to their legal successor, the Romans. The gods of the defeated community became divinites of the state of the Roman people:[31] either they kept their cult in its former location through members of the old communities, who now acted in the name of the Roman state and stood under the oversight of the Roman pontifical college,[32] or a temple was dedicated to them in Rome and their service entrusted to the state priests.[33] This obligation the Romans always recognized and expressed also in the form of festivals, since at the siege of an enemy city they invited the gods of those people through *evocatio* to abandon their former homes and to accept the new seats promised to them in Rome.[34]

However, neither conquest nor direct obligation was needed to bring about the acceptance of the gods of other communities into the

---

[31] Mommsen, *Staatsrecht*, 3:579ff.

[32] Festus s.v. *municipalia sacra* (146L): *municipalia sacra vocantur, quae ab initio habuerunt ante civitatem Romanam acceptam, quae observare eos voluerunt pontifices et eo more facere quo adsuessent antiquitus* [translated above p. 196].

[33] Arnobius 3.38: "For the Romans were accustomed to assign maintenance of the cults of conquered cities, some to individual families and some to the state and, lest any god be passed over because of their sheer multiplicity or from ignorance, they were customarily invoked all together under a single name, for completeness and brevity's sake: the *Novensiles*" (*nam solere Romanos religiones urbium superatarum partim privatim per familias spargere partim publice consecrare, ac ne aliqui deorum multitudine aut ignorantia praeteriretur, brevitatis et compendii causa uno pariter nomine cunctos Novensiles invocari*).

[34] Macrobius *Sat.* 3.9; Pliny *Nat.* 28.18; Servius *Aen.* 2.224, 351; Livy 5.21; Plutarch *Quaest. Rom.* 61. Cf. Pernice, "Sakralrechte I," 1157. Wissowa, *RE* 11 (1907) s.v. *evocatio*, cols. 1152–1153. [On *evocatio* see above p. 233.]

state cult.[35] The limited community of *commercium*† that connected Rome with the other Latins and made possible the award of Roman citizenship to Latins must have led often to state recognition of the corresponding Latin divinities. Naturally, the Tusculan or Ardean who moved to Rome and became a Roman citizen was not free of his duties, once undertaken, toward the gods of his home and the Roman state allowed him to put nothing in the way of this obligation.[36] The toleration of this private practice of cults not recognized by the state led in many cases to its official reception. When the number of adherents of a god was small, the worship was kept naturally within the boundaries of cult in the home, and we may assume that pretty well all the gods recognized in the Italian communities connected with Rome found their worship at Rome in the house of one person or another. When immigration from a certain city to Rome was particularly significant and the families, who were the chief practitioners of the cults in question, stood in high repute and prosperity, most often they were accepted into the company of the state gods of Rome. The worship of Hercules at the *Ara Maxima* is an especially instructive example: long a family cult of the Pinarii, who had come previously from Tibur, it was transferred to the state during the censorship of Appius Claudius Caecus.

Naturally, a lot also depended on the character of the gods and cults proposed for adoption, and in the first centuries of the Republic, the Romans decided with great care and acted with discretion. Although in the abstract the bearers of the highest civil authority were authorized to vow a temple to a divinity on behalf of the state and thereby legally to obligate the community,[37] the admission of new gods into the Roman pantheon probably belonged all along to the acts for which a magistrate was bound to consult the Senate and subsequently to submit to its opinion.[38] The Senate, logically, had to have the least hesitation when it dealt with divinities worshiped among the nearest neighbors and relatives and whose cults generally worked in the same ways as the Roman. If these gods belonged to the

---

[35] Through this Tertullian *Apol.* 10 differentiates the *di adoptivi* and *captivi* (i.e. those transferred to Rome through *evocatio*; cf. ibid. 25 and Prudentius *Symm.* 2.347 ff.).

† The right of individuals from different communities to engage in trade with each other, established by treaty between the communities.

[36] Mommsen, *Ges. Schr.*, 3:401ff.

[37] Mommsen, *Staatsrecht*, 2:602 [cf. above p. 194].

[38] Mommsen, *Staatsrecht*, 3:1051. Tertullian *Marc.* 1.18; *Nat.* 1.10; *Apol.* 5.1 (= Eusebius *Hist. Eccl.* 2.2.5) [Varro *Ant. Div.* 44] repeatedly alludes to the dedication of a temple performed or sought without this agreement of an otherwise unknown god *Alburnus* by an M. Aemilius (the name is uncertain, see Wissowa, *RE* 1 (1893) s.v. *Alburnus*, cols. 1337–1338).

class of *di novensides*, one could treat them as indigenous and entrust the practice of their cult to the state priests. Otherwise, one confronted the gods of foreigners, above all those of the Greek cities of southern Italy and Sicily.[39] No one could fail to notice that fundamentally divergent religious viewpoints and practices were at stake, and the Romans sought therefore – certainly in vain – to prevent confusion and damage from being introduced to the old, indigenous religious ideas. The oversight of these cults was therefore not the duty of the *pontifices*, but of the keepers of the oracles. The maintenance of their cult was not carried out by Roman citizens, but through priests who were drawn to Rome from the cult's original home. Until the end of the period under discussion, the temples of these foreign gods, although temples of the state like all others, remained excluded from the city proper, whose border was the holy municipal boundary of the *pomerium*.†

The growth of the Roman pantheon by no means resulted only from immigration, but came about to no lesser extent also from expansion of the Empire. If the ideas of an earlier time, which connected a person with individual gods, remained simple and intact, now the richer form of outward community life and of lively traffic led to the point that the responsibility for individual gods also multiplied and one distinguished the manifestations of power due to each more sharply in different areas. The Romans' inclination toward the specialization of divine functions, this divided view of the different aspects in the existence of one and the same god, emerges not simply in specialized epithets, but the individual differentiations exist as more or less independent entities, so that Juppiter Feretrius and Juppiter Stator, Juno Moneta and Juno Lucina, hardly more than different aspects of the same divine entity, were perceived as individual divinities.[40] What is more, an attribute of a god not infrequently freed itself completely and found its place in cult as its own divine being. In this way, the worship of abstractions and the personifications of ethical powers and characteristics developed: if one

---

[39] These two categories of *sacra peregrina* Verrius Flaccus probabably recognized, whose opinion in Festus s.v. *peregrina sacra* (268L) seems somewhat obscure: *peregrina sacra appellantur, quae aut evocatis dis in oppugnandis urbibus Romam sunt coacta, aut quae ob quasdam religiones per pacem sunt petita, ut ex Phrygia Matris Magnae, ex Graecia Cereris, Epidauro Aesculapi, quae coluntur eorum more, a quibus sunt accepta* [translated on p. 195]. The last clause shows that the second type only included non-Italic divinities.

† For a development of this argument see Wissowa, "De dis Romanorum indigetibus et novensidibus disputatio," *Abhandlungen*, 175–191.

[40] Only thus does the Arval Brethren's sacrifice first to Juppiter Optimus Maximus and then to Juppiter Victor, each receiving its own offering in the same ceremony, make sense, e.g. *CFA* 99a, ll. 26–28, etc. [On the sacrifice of the Arval Brethren see Chapter 8.]

venerated Juppiter first as the protector of loyalty or Mars as the god
of war, from there it was only a small step to the creation of the
specific goddesses Fides and Bellona. This source of divine powers,
inexhaustible in its nature, still worked for a time stimulating the
religious imagination, which was otherwise already completely
devoid of a specific power to create.

It remains an open question whether this kind of creation of new
state gods through the splitting of older divinities or through adoption of new personifications was treated legally like the reception of
foreign cults, or whether a particular resolution of the Senate was
required for the foundation of an altar for an already-recognized
divinity under new cult epithets or likewise for a new divine abstraction. That the Roman sacral law distinguished both categories
emerges from the fact that Cicero in his work *De Legibus* separates
di novi and *advenae* (or *alienigenae*) ["new," "immigrant" and
"foreign-born gods"] from one another twice (2.19 and 25) in opposition to the state divinities already recognized. Furthermore "to
sacrifice by a new or foreign rite" (Livy 25.1.12: *novo aut externo
ritu sacrificare*) in institutions is contrasted with the *patrius ritus*.
["ancestral rite"].[41] The creation of new epithets or personifications
is probably valid only as the continuation of existing service to the
gods, so that it does not require special authorization. The religious
freedom of the individual citizen is limited by religious officials only
in so far as he may not sacrifice either *in loco publico sacrove* ["in a
public or consecrated place"] to gods other than those recognized by
the state or in other rites; in the service of the gods at home, the *di
sive novi sive advenae* ["gods, whether new or foreign"] undoubtedly
often occupied a more important place than the gods of the state.
How far, particularly in private cult, the division of divinities through
specialized epithets and the increase of personifications went, the
countless dedicatory inscriptions of a later time allow one to see.
Before the Punic Wars, for which such direct evidence is not at our
disposal, we certainly must rely on inferences and suppositions.

For the state cult, we can follow clearly the continual intrusion of
new and foreign cults in the foundations of new temples listed in the
chronicles of the city, whose catalogue may be restored in its approximate entirety from the beginning of Republican chronology. This not
only allows us to discern at least partially the influences that shaped

---

[41] Also, the definition given by Verrius Flaccus (above p. 339, n. 39) of the *peregrina sacra*
(Festus s.v. *peregrina sacra* (268L)) includes only the second of the two types. Cf. Claudian
Gild. 131–132: "The *indigetes* mourn, and all those gods whom Rome received or herself
endowed" (*indigetes et si quos Roma recepit aut dedit ipsa deos*).

the religious politics of the Roman state at different times, but it also demonstrates clearly how the death of the old accompanies the continual influx of new gods. As the Romans constructed new places for the worship of the gods, only some of the divinities first worshiped received a real temple in place of their original open shrines (*sacella*). Others, like Carna, Angerona, Furrina, Larenta, etc., had to be satisfied as before with their groves and small shrines. The ignorance that later prevailed concerning the significance of these gods shows how early in antiquity they must have come into being .

Bibliography

Marquardt, *Staatsverwaltung*, 3:30ff. E. Aust, *De aedibus sacris populi Romani inde a primis liberae reipublicae temporibus usque ad Augusti imperatoris aetatem Romae conditis, Diss. Marpurgi* 1889. O. Gilbert, *Geschichte und Topographie der Stadt Rom im Altertum* (Leipzig: Teubner, 1883–1890), vol. 3, pp. 57ff. Wissowa, *Abhandlungen*, 184ff.

THIRD SECTION: TO THE FALL OF THE REPUBLIC

14 Decline of the state religion

Scaevola the *pontifex* and Varro were completely in their rights, if, not only from a philosophical point of view, but also from the statesman's, they rejected the stories of the poets for contradicting the being and dignity of divinity. The transfer of Greek myths to the Roman gods, which through the agency of the theater became familiar to the broader masses of the people, must have had an increasingly destructive effect on belief the more such narratives of the lives and deeds of the gods stood in contradiction to the impersonal and abstract character of the old Roman religion.[42]

The influence of philosophical ways of thinking was also always a destructive one. Even if this did not directly affect the masses, but was restricted to the circles of the literati, precisely these circles were, of course, whence qualified practitioners of the state cult originated. He who looked upon the entire state religion only as a system relying on expediency but actually far removed from reality, who, in accordance with the Stoic point of view, rejected as meaningless or harmful the whole outward practice of religion and above all sacrifices and the worship of images, surely did not bring to the duties of

[42] Cf. the explanations in Dionysius *Ant. Rom.* 2.18–19. [See also above p. 101.]

his priestly office the sort of personal interest that they demanded.

In fact, for the approximate period from the Gracchi to Caesar, we encounter a rapid decline in the Roman priesthood. The three most important colleges, whose membership increased to fifteen under Sulla, the *pontifices* (along with the board of *Epulones*, whose number was likewise probably raised by Sulla from three to seven), augurs and guardians of the oracles, became purely political authorities and involved in the struggles of the day, with the result that after the year 651 [*A(b) U(rbe) C(ondite)*, "from the foundation of the city"] = 103 BC, the appointment of new members occurred no longer through the colleges themselves, but through a special kind of popular election.[43] If the colleges also retained the right to call an assembly, this did not suffice to ensure the continuity of earlier tradition, on which had depended the expert knowledge of the priesthoods in their extensive and varied spheres of activity. Complaints about the decline of priestly knowledge increased. Intercalation, for example, which belonged to the most important duties of the *pontifices*, fell into disorder through ignorance and political bias in such a way that an unbearable state of affairs prevailed until Caesar's reform of the calendar.[44] Even the explanation for the existing formulae for sacrifices was troubled, while the performance of yearly, individual acts on the appropriate days became impossible through the discrepancy between the civil calendar and the progress of the seasons (Cic. *Leg.* 2.29). The announcement and procuration of prodigies were similarly neglected (Livy 43.13.1). In the college of augurs, the knowledge of the complicated instructions for auspices not used in daily politics was completely lost,[45] so that even augurs who were occupied in their discipline in a scholarly way could arrive at diametrically opposite views about their goals and methods.[46]

The remaining priesthoods, moreover, which were removed from political activities, fell no less into decline for different reasons. The authority bound up with the venerable positions of the *rex sacrorum*, of the important *flamines*, of the Salii, etc. were able to offer the ever-shrinking circle of candidates – very often only patricians were eligible[47] – no sufficient compensation for the restrictions on comfort

---

[43] Mommsen, *Staatsrecht*, 2:23ff.

[44] Marquardt, *Staatsverwaltung*, 3:286ff.

[45] Cicero *Div.* 1.25: "the auspices, of which Roman augurs even today are ignorant" (*auspicia, quae quidem nunc a Romanis auguribus ignorantur*); cf. *Nat. Deor.* 2.9 among others.

[46] Concerning the polemic between the augurs Ap. Claudius Pulcher and C. Claudius Marcellus, cf. Cicero *Leg.* 2.32ff.; *Div.* 1.105, 2.75 [see also pp. 309–12].

[47] See provisionally Mommsen, *Röm. Forsch.*, 1:78ff.

and personal freedom they imposed: even beyond formal ceremony and countless rules of conduct, in many cases these priesthoods demanded the complete or partial renunciation of public offices. The instances of this increase so that a person called upon to accept such a priesthood refused to take it up or hardly submitted himself to the regulations he found uncomfortable,[48] until finally in many cases positions that had become open went unclaimed. The office of *flamen Dialis*, heavily burdened by painstaking regulations, remained unoccupied a full seventy-five years after the death of L. Cornelius Merula (667 = 87), until Augustus managed to replace him in the year 743 = 11.[49] The positions of the twelve lesser *flamines* must have been vacant at the end of the Republic, at least in part, because it would otherwise be incomprehensible that a man like Varro was in absolutely no position to learn the meaning of divinities like Falacer and Furrina, worshiped by such priests.[50] The Arval Brethren and the *Sodales Titii* had been completely forgotten until they were revived by Augustus.

Nothing can be more significant than that Varro, who in his *Antiquitates Divinae* pursued the declared aim of saving the nearly forgotten indigenous gods from oblivion,[51] finds for his description of the gods of the state cult no classification more suitable than those about whom one still knows something definite (*di certi*), and those for whom this is not the case (*di incerti*).[52] Cicero's books *On the nature of the gods* lack any understanding of the history and individuality of the gods of his own people,[53] while Nigidius Figulus agglomerates the religious traditions of the Greeks, Romans, Etruscans, and Orientals into a disorderly mixture and finds in mantic arts and prodigies the basis for theological-philosophical speculation that seeks to approach divinity.[54] Moreover, the Augustan

---

[48] See Marquardt, *Staatsverwaltung*, 3:64ff.

[49] Cassius Dio 54.36.1. Tacitus *Ann.* 3.58. Suet. *Aug.* 31.

[50] Varro *Ling.* 5.84, 6.19: "today even the name is known only to a few" (*nunc vix nomen notum paucis*); 7.45: "which are obscure" (*quae obscura sunt*).

[51] Augustine *Civ.* 6.2: *Varro dicit, se timere ne pereant (di), non incursu hostili sed civium neglegentia, de qua illos velut ruina liberari a se dicit et in memoria bonorum per eiusmodi libros recondi atque servari utiliore cura, quam Metellus de incendio sacra Vestalia et Aeneas de Troiano excidio penates liberasse praedicatur* [translated on p. 323]; cf. 4.31.

[52] About the meaning of this decline, see Augustine *Civ.* 7.17 and Wissowa's comments about this in Marquardt, *Staatsverwaltung*, 3:9 n. 4, and Wissowa, *Abhandlungen*, 308ff. R. Peter in Roscher, *Lex.* 2:150f. R. Agahd, *M. Terenti Varronis Antiquitatum rerum divinarum libri I, XIV, XV, XVI* (Leipzig: Teubner, 1898) 126ff. Domaszewski is wrong in *Abhandlungen*, 155 ff.

[53] Significant is the superficial way in which Cicero *Leg.* 2.19; *Nat. Deor.* 2.61 describes Roman divinities without any internal or external order.

[54] The fragments of his books *de dis* are full of the most arbitrary explanations, e.g. he equates Apollo and Janus (Macrobius *Sat.* 1.9.8) or declares the Roman Penates as the gods

reorganization, which will be discussed in the next section,† not only shows priesthoods unoccupied, temples in decay, and festivals forgotten, but also reveals that often the old was buried to such an extent that the reforms of the emperor constituted a reconstruction more than a restoration.

What the situation was with regard to the religious interests of the masses, no testimony survives. Even if the old worship of the gods lasted longer in the countryside and in the smaller cities, we will still have very little basis on which to estimate the religious devotions of the populace of Rome. Only in one kind of cult observance was there always an extraordinarily active interest: the games not only experienced a huge increase in number (the number of days when games were held had, from the end of the Hannibalic War up to Caesar's death, approximately quintupled), but also actually lost any intrinsic connection with the worship of the gods, even if in theory the sacred character of these events was still occasionally emphasized.[55] An especially sad indication of the drop in religious feeling is provided by the often attested decline in *sacra privata* ["private rites"; cf. p. 231 on gentilician rites], whose lasting preservation in the family and transmission from one generation to the next the old religious order had greatly esteemed. Now, the old religious order – in spite of the proper, still steadfast supervision of the *pontifices* – was avoided through sly, legal quibbling as an inconvenient burden to those obligated to take it over, and was abandoned to ruin.[56] That one proverbially called a stroke of luck lacking any bitter aftertaste "a legacy without rites" (*sine sacris hereditas*[57]) reveals clearly the mood of the society at large.

---

who built the walls of Troy, Apollo and Poseidon (Macrobius *Sat.* 3.4.6; Arnobius 3.40; Servius *Aen.* 1.378). Concerning Nigidius as Goëten (Jerome calls him "a follower of Pythagoras and a magician" (*Pythagoricus et magus*) [*Chron.* s.a. 1972]), see R. Reitzenstein, *Werden und Wesen der Humanität im Altertum* (Strassburg: J.H.E. Heitz, 1907), 80.

† Fourth Section, "The Religion of the Empire," part 15: "The religious reforms of Augustus" [Wissowa, *Religion und Kultus*, 73–78)]. On the "Augustan restoration" see esp. Nock 1972: 16–25.

[55] See, e.g. Cicero *Verr.* 5.36.

[56] Cf., e.g. Cicero *Mur.* 27 and especially *Leg.* 2.46 ff.

[57] Evidence in A. Otto, *Die Sprichwörter und sprichwörtlichen Redensarten der Römer* (Leipzig: Teubner, 1890), no. 806.

FOURTH SECTION:
THE RELIGION OF THE EMPIRE

*16 The religious conditions in the first two
centuries of the Empire*

The reforms of Augustus create the basis for such development of religious conditions in the Roman Empire as occurred up to the time of the Antonines, even if the seeds sown by the founder of the monarchy did not develop uniformly. This entire period was dominated by the prevalence of a dynastic point of view in all areas of cult. Although the state religion was transformed with great speed into a court religion, it did not, as Caesar had had in mind, assume the forms of Hellenistic ruler cult. Here, as in external politics, Augustus assigned himself a much narrower goal than his great predecessor, and it was thanks to his careful and deliberative action that the influence of Hellenistic ruler cult made such narrow inroads in the territory of Roman belief.[58]

In the public observance of state cult, two Augustan innovations were particularly momentous: the establishment of the worship of the *Genius Augusti* and of the cult of the *Divi imperatores*, which Augustus introduced through the building of the temple of *Divus Iulius*. Caesar never actually numbered among the *Divi*: this was true because he had never really ruled, and it was in accordance with sacral law. In his own lifetime, Augustus had already declared a certain expectation of his own later rise to divinity through his use of the denomination *Divi filius* ["son of the god"]. After his death, Augustus himself then received a temple and priests and thus initiated the ranks of deified emperors, which increased more and more in the course of time. Henceforth, the *Genius* of the ruling emperor and current *Divi imperatores* together created a tightly-knit group of new gods, which, standing next to and even above the old divinities of the state religion in importance,[59] claimed a dis-

---

[58] The connection of the Roman cult of the emperor with the worship of Alexander the Great and the Diadochoi as gods and with Hellenism's world of ideas has often been stated (see namely Kornemann, "Herrscherkulte"; P. Wendland, "Σωτήρ," *Zeitschrift fur die neutestamentliche Wissenschaft und die Kunde des Urchristentums* 5 (1904), 335–353; cf. idem, *Kultur*, 73 ff., 91 ff.); A. Elter, *Donarem Pateras* (Bonn: C. Georgi, 1907), 40, 41ff., rightfully stresses that this level of analysis alone is not sufficient, even if I cannot consider his own solution (the model of the cult of the emperor is the apotheosis of Romulus, supposedly established by Ennius) correct.

[59] Valerius Maximus 1 *praef.*: "For if ancient orators rightly began from Jupiter best and greatest ..., my humility will run all the more justly to your goodwill, insofar as that other divinity is inferred by opinion, while yours is seen by present certainty equal to the star of your father and grandfather, by whose outstanding light much famed radiance has been added to

tinguished place in all public performances of cult. This stands out most clearly in the formulae of the oaths of office. Between Juppiter Optimus Maximus and the *Di penates*, the gods concerned during the Republic (see p. 330, n. 1), was now inserted this group of divinities, so that in the time of Domitian, for example, one swore "by Juppiter and the divine Augustus and the divine Claudius and the divine Vespasian Augustus and the divine Titus Augustus and the *genius* of Imperator Caesar Domitian Augustus and the *dei Penates*" (*per Iovem et divom Augustum et divom Claudium et divom Vespasianum Augustum et divom Titum Augustum et genium imperatoris Caesaris Domitiani Augusti deosque penates*).[60] The same grouping also appears more than once in the sacrifices of the Arval Brethren.[61]

The loyalty of private persons, not only of individuals and groups, but of communities and provinces, was inclined to go considerably further. It was not enough to offer the *genius* of the emperor the same kind of devotion shown within the house to the *genius* of the *paterfamilias* by the members of the family and the servants. The figure of the ruling sovereign was made into the object of direct adoration without the intercession of the *genius*.[62] Augustus was already

---

our rites: for we have received the other gods, but we have bestowed the Caesars" (*nam si prisci oratores ab Iove optimo maximo bene orsi sunt ..., mea parvitas eo iustius ad favorem tuum decucurrerit, quo cetera divinitas opinione colligitur, tua praesenti fide paterno avitoque sideri par videtur, quorum eximio fulgore multum caerimoniis nostris inclitae claritatis accessit: reliquos enim deos accepimus, Caesares dedimus*); cf. Prop. 3.11.66 ("Rome need hardly fear Jupiter while Caesar lives" [*vix timeat salvo Caesare Roma Iovem*]) and Ovid *Pont.* 1.1.63 ("Though the gods should favor me, and he who is more present than they ..." [*ut mihi di faveant, quibus est manifestior ipse*]).

[60] Report of Salpensa and Malacca: *ILS* 6088 clause XXV. Abbreviated at *CIL* 2.172: *Iuppiter optimus maximus ac Divus Augustus ceteriq(ue) omnes di imortales CIL* 2.172. See also *SIG* 364.19: "By Zeus the Savior and the god Caesar Augustus" (Δία Σωτῆρα καὶ θεὸν Καίσαρα Σεβαστόν); *ILS* 8781; and, in addition, V. Gardthausen, *Neue Jahrbücher für das klassische Altertum* 13 (1904), 249.

[61] At the celebration of the anniversary of Nero's ascension to the throne in 58, the Arval Brethren sacrificed to Juppiter Optimus Maximus, Juno, Minerva, Felicitas, Genius ipsius, Divus Augustus, Diva Augusta, and Divus Claudius (*CFA* 27, 10–12; cf. *CFA* 28a–c, 13–14, among others). At their *lustrum missum* [namely, at their *lustratio*], the report of AD 224 records, at the end of the series of gods deriving from ancient ritual, the performance of a sacrifice to "the Genius of our Lord Severus Alexander Augustus ... and, likewise, to the deified emperors, 20 in number" (*CFA* 105b, 12–13; only the Divi: *CFA* 94, col. II l. 14). Naturally, according to the occasion of the sacrifice one could also call upon the *genius* of the emperor (e.g. on his birthday: *CFA* 24, 6–9) or the *Divi imperatores* (e.g. on the *Augustalia*: *CFA* 32, col. IIcef, 31–34) alone.

[62] Augustan poetry went very far in that direction, since it not only recognized the expectation of the emperor's future divinity (Verg. *Georg.* 1.24 ff.; Hor. *C.* 3.3.11 ["Reclining among them, Augustus will drink nectar with crimson lips" (*quos inter Augustus recumbens purpureo bibet ore nectar*)]; Ovid *Ars* 1.203 ff. ["Father Mars and Father Caesar, grant him your divinity as he goes, for one of you is a god, the other will be" (*Marsque pater Caesarque pater date numen eunti, nam deus e vobis alter es, alter eris*)]), but gives him also (Philo *Leg.* 23) the designation *deus*, which he chose to refer to himself (Verg. *Ecl.* 1.6 ff., 42 ff, where the model

honored as a god in his own lifetime, in the east of the Empire as often as in the west, and even in Italy itself. Private persons and communities, who could establish such a cult on their own and may have been convinced that an overzealousness in devotion would not cause them harm, established temples and shrines to the emperor, created priests for him and founded *collegia* for his cult without further ado.[63] However, we also find sporadic attempts to disguise these actions, insofar as the imperial cult appears above all in subordination to the worship of another divinity of the communities in question and seems bound up with these, until the former gradually pushes the latter into the background and becomes the focus.[64] In those cases where imperial approval was necessary, especially for the founding of an imperial cult for entire provinces, Augustus gave his assent only on the condition that the temple and cult were simultaneously offered to the goddess Roma.[65] Nevertheless, the worship of the living emperor in its different forms and modifications spread widely throughout the entire Empire during the reign of Augustus, with two exceptions: at Rome and in the state cult.

This state of affairs evolved not insignificantly after Augustus died and was deified. In the cults dedicated to him in the communities and provinces, his successors did not immediately step into his place, but worship was by this time primarily dedicated to Augustus with whom, on the one hand, the remaining *Divi imperatores* and, on the other, the actual ruling emperor could be connected.[66] In prac-

---

of Caesar's apotheosis clearly remains in his mind. Prop. 3.4.1., 4.11.60. Ovid *Pont.* 2.8; the remaining passages from Ovid in F. Koepp, *De gigantomachiae in poeseos artisque monumentis usu* (Bonn: Univers, 1883), 57 ff., ibid. 16 ff. equate the emperor with Juppiter).

[63] Tacitus *Ann.* 1.73: "The worshipers of Augustus, who existed in every house after the fashion of a priestly college" (*Cultores Augusti, qui per omnes domos in modum collegiorum habebantur*). Concerning Italian cults of the living Augustus of private or municipal foundation, see Hirschfeld, "Kaisercult," 838 (cf. H. Nissen, *Pompeianische Studien zur Städtekunde des Altertums* [Leipzig: Breitkopf und Härtel, 1877], 182 ff.). Beurlier, *Culte*, 17. Heinen, "Kaiserkult," 175.

[64] Thus, we find in the lifetime of the emperor a *magister Mercurialis et Augustalis* in Nola (*CIL* 10.1272), *Herculanei Augustales* in Tibur (see *CIL* 14, p. 367), similarly in Grumentum (*CIL* 10.230), *Augustales aeditui Castoris et Pollucis* in Tusculum (*CIL* XIV.2620, cf. 2637), *Augustales Concordiales* in Patavium (*CIL* 5.2525, 2872); the alleged *ministri Augusti Mercurii Maiae* in Pompeii (*CIL* 10, p. 1149) are, according to E. Bormann, "Aus Pompeji," *Wiener Eranos* (Vienna: Alfred Hölder, 1909), 309–316 at 314ff., to be discounted.

[65] Suetonius *Aug.* 52: "He permitted temples in no province unless they were dedicated to him and Rome in common" (*Templa ... in nulla ... provincia nisi communi suo Romaeque nomine recepit*). About the provincial imperial cult, see Hirschfeld, "Kaisercult," 847ff. (also M. Krascheninnikoff, "Ueber die Einführung der provinzialen Kaisercultus im römischen Westen," *Philologus* 53 (1894), 147–189). Beurlier, *Culte*, 99 ff. C. G. Brandis, *RE* 3 (1895) s.v. ἀρχιερεύς, cols. 471–483 at 473ff. Kornemann, "Herrscherkulte," 98ff. Toutain, *Cultes*, 1:77–97.

[66] This is expressed in priestly designations like *flamen Romae Divorum et Augustorum provinciae Hispaniae citerioris* (*CIL* 2.4205 among others), ἀρχιερεὺς τῶν Σεβαστῶν καὶ

tice, the living ruler may often have stood in the foreground,[67] so his worship lost that personal aspect, so to speak, which it derived from his connection to the founder of the monarchy,[68] and counted more for government authority in the abstract. In any case, never afterwards did an individual living emperor enjoy a special esteem in the Empire like Augustus.[69]

The very different position that individual rulers personally took toward imperial cult did not significantly displace the general foundations of the institution as these were established in their initial development. The great circumspection practiced by Tiberius[70] and Trajan, for example, was unable substantially to harm the dominant position of the imperial cult in provincial and municipal worship of the gods; nor did the heightened demands that Caligula, Nero, and Domitian put on public adulation have the power to overturn the principle that the *princeps* could only become the object of worship in the state cult after he was separated from the ranks of the living and then deified.[71] This principle was maintained steadfastly until Diocletian. The state cult recognized only the *Divi imperatores* and the *genius* of the ruling emperor. The religious observance of the emperor's image, the *imago principis*, was also based on the latter,[72] which clearly resulted from the worship of the *genius Augusti* between the images of the Lares (cf. the *collegia Larum et imaginum Augusti*, "the colleges (for the worship) of the Lares and the portraits of Augustus," *CIL* 6.307 among others), while the addition of an

Νέρωνος Κλαυδίου Καίσαρος Σεβαστοῦ (*IG* 7.2713); the provincial cult was probably reserved for the ruling sovereign, while the worship of the *Divi* fell to individual communities (Hirschfeld, "Kaisercult," 849).

[67] Expressions such as *sacerdos arae Aug(usti) n(ostri) p(rovinciae) P(annoniae) infer(ioris)* CIL 3.10,496 (cf. 1433) and *sacerdos ad templum Romae et Augustorum* (*CIL* 13.1706) or also *Romae et Augg.* (*CIL* 13.1691) under the common administration of more emperors point to this, Toutain, *Cultes*, 1:43–54.

[68] Cf. especially Mommsen, *Staatsrecht*, 2:734ff.

[69] Active priests with names of designated emperors are completely absent in the west (Hirschfeld, "Kaisercult," 843 n. 48, who declares *CIL* 2.49 suspicious; cf. ibid. 842 n. 45), in the east they are also not very numerous (examples in Brandis, *loc. cit.*, 479 ff.).

[70] Suet. *Tib.* 26: "He forbade temples, flamens and priests to be decreed to him, and even the setting up of statues and portraits without his permission; he allowed them only on this condition, that they were placed not among the images of the gods but among the decorations of the temples" (*Templa, flamines, sacerdotes decerni sibi prohibuit, etiam statuas atque imagines nisi permittente se poni, permisitque ea sola condicione, ne inter simulacra deorum, sed inter ornamenta aedium ponerentur*). See also Mommsen, *Ges. Schr.*, 4:269.

[71] Tacitus *Ann.* 15.74: "For divine honor is not paid to a *princeps* before he has ceased to live among humans" (*Nam deum honor principi non ante habetur, quam agere inter homines desierit*). Concerning the demands of the named emperors see Suet. *Calig.* 22; Tacitus *loc. cit.*; Pliny *Paneg.* 52.

[72] Cf. Friedländer, *Sittengeschichte*, 3:252ff., and about the statues of emperors in camps, see Domaszewski, *Religion*, 68ff.

emperor's name in the song of the Salii, through which Augustus[73] and other emperors were honored in their lifetimes, did not necessrily need to imply their numbering among the gods.[74] If such was intended, one has to think here of the *genius* of the emperor.

How, in spite of this limitation on the imperial cult, the entire state worship became directed more and more toward the glorification of the imperial house, the record of the Arval Brethren reveals with full clarity. While already in the year AUC 724 = 30 BC it had been arranged that the Roman state priests and priestesses should always be mindful of the emperor at all prayers and votive offerings performed on behalf of the Senate and people,[75] the leadership of the Arval Brethren shows how deeply this measure took hold in the whole operation of state cult. Apart from the announcement and celebration of the annually recurring festival of *Dea Dia* and from the propitiatory sacrifices occasioned by extraordinary causes, the activity of the priesthood focused almost exclusively on sacral manifestations of loyalty. Beside the general *vota* for the good of the imperial house on 3 January, we encounter similar, regular, annual *vota* for every regnal year of the emperor, as well as additional one-off sacrifices and offerings of entreaty and thanks in special circumstances: at the illness of the emperor or the empress' giving birth, at the departure of the sovereign on campaign or upon his victorious return, and among others – until the Flavians removed these celebrations from the procedures of the Arval Brethren – sacrifices on all personal anniversaries of the ruling sovereign and his family. The strangeness of grafting this entire genre of holy acts onto the sacred duties of the Arval Brethren one sees best from the fact that the divinities called upon in these rituals are completely different than those that appear at the old annual festivals and propitiatory sacrifices. Even *Dea Dia*, to whom the entire worship of the priesthood is dedicated, appears only very early on – behind the Capitoline Triad – in the *vota* for the new year, after which the acts-of-loyalty take place without the actual proprietress of the cult being mentioned

---

[73] Augustus *Res Gestae* 10.1; Cassius Dio 51.20.1; others in Marquardt, *Staatsverwaltung*, 3:438.

[74] A true apotheosis of a living man depends on the installation of his image in the temple of a god next to the cult statue; this happened under Caesar ("co-resident in a temple with Qurinus" (σύνναος Quirini), Cassius Dio 43.45.3; Cicero *Att.* 12.45.3 and 13.28.3), Augustus refused it (Cassius Dio 53.27.3), and since this installation occurred only for dead and deified individuals (Caesar: Cassius Dio 45.7.1; Augustus: Cassius Dio 56.46.4; Drusilla: Cassius Dio 59.11.2) with the sole exception of Nero, for whom the Senate resolved to install a statue as large as that of the cult image in the temple of Mars Ultor (Tacitus *Ann.* 13.8).

[75] Cassius Dio 51.19.7 and in addition Heinen, "Kaiserkult," 143ff.

in even one word. The bond between old and new sacred duty is broken.

The service of all state priesthoods experienced similar upheavals. For example, the deferential introduction of the names of the emperor and the imperial princes into the ritual songs of the Salii, alongside ancient formulae that had long since become incomprehensible to the priests themselves, must have seemed very odd. The ranks of the gods called upon in the offerings of entreaty, thanks, and remembrance by the Arval Brethren and other priests belong in their entirety to none of the old state cults, but are brought together individually for the performance of cult. The gods of the Capitol, Juppiter Optimus Maximus, Juno Regina, and Minerva, create a base to which *Salus publica p. R. Q.* ("Communal Health of the Roman People, the Quirites") enters as a fourth. This group, called upon in the *vota* of the new year, is then expanded mostly in symbolic meaning through the addition of other gods, according to the reason for the festival.†

Imperial subjects initially revealed their loyalty by sacrificing to the state gods for the well-being and the health of the emperor and the prosperity of his house and endowing those gods with special epithets (*Conservator, Custos, Protector, Redux,* etc.) ["Preserver," "Guardian", "Protector," "Returning"] identifying them as protectors of the *princeps*. They soon went further, placing the success and advantages of the imperial government itself among the gods.[76] The prayer *pro salute, victoria,* and *concordia* ["for the health, victory, and concord"] of the emperor changed into the worship of *Salus, Victoria,* and *Concordia Augusta* ["Augustan Health, Victory, and Concord"]. Already under Augustus, the Senate had celebrated the return of the emperor from the east in AUC 735 = 19 BC and from the Spanish-Gallic campaigns in AUC 741 = 13 BC through the founding of altars to *Fortuna Redux* ["Fortune Returned"] and *Pax Augusta* ["Augustan Peace"], respectively, and in AUC 744 = 10 BC Augustus himself erected altars and statues of *Concordia, Salus Publica,* and *Pax* from donations delivered to him by the Senate and the people.[77] These personifications, on the one hand of the blessings brought about by the emperor (*Felicitas, Pax*), and on the other of the divine powers protecting the emperor (*Victoria, Fortuna*), assume an always larger place at the performances of *sacra*; and they do

---

† Cf. above pp. 171–74.

[76] Cf. Usener, *Götternamen,* 300 ff., where the division between real divinities of cult and mere named personifications remains to be drawn more precisely.

[77] Cassius Dio 54.35.2. Ovid *Fast.* 3.881 ff.

so at the expense of the older gods of the state. They also become indirect representatives of imperial cult, since they serve the glorification of the *princeps*. This stands out still more clearly, if the real or supposed virtues or character attributes of the emperor become the subject of public and private veneration. When Augustus brags that the Senate and people of Rome hung a golden shield in the Curia Julia to honor him, with the inscription "for the sake of his virtue, clemency, justice and piety" (*Res Gestae* 34.2: *virtutis clementiae iustitiae pietatis causa*),[78] this is the immediate preliminary stage to the cults, later so widely spread, of goddesses like *Virtus Augusta*, *Clementia Augusta*, *Iustitia Augusta*, and *Pietas Augusta*, among others. In this way, the importance of the old gods is limited on all sides and diminished.

The Capitoline Triad alone affirms its place at the head of the Roman state cult and wins a decisive victory against its competition, which had arisen for a time in the Augustan private cult of Apollo Palatinus and Mars Ultor. The magnificence and importance of its sanctuary was particularly enhanced by the Flavian emperors, among whom Domitian instituted the glorious *Agon Capitolinus* ["Capitoline Games"], and then significantly by Trajan.[79] The union of Juppiter Optimus Maximus, Juno Regina, and Minerva Augusta appears not only in the introduction of all invocations of the gods at official sacrifices and prayers, but also in countless dedicatory inscriptions from all parts of the Empire. Above all, the dedications of the different corps of the Roman army[80] show that Juppiter Optimus Maximus, together with his divine companions, was considered as before the actual divine patron of the Roman state and army. The remaining gods of the Republic, however, lose their importance more and more. The better emperors certainly put a value on participating publicly in state cult, not only as holders of the chief pontificate and as members of the great priestly colleges, but also, like Augustus, as restorers of the temples and defenders of the old ceremonial law.[81] But it is now only a question of the superficial

---

[78] Cf. Mommsen, *Res gestae divi Augusti* (2nd ed., Berlin: Weidmann, 1883), 152 ff. The citation for the fact mentioned elsewhere in the text in § 54.

[79] Evidence in E. Aust in Roscher, *Lex.* 2:749 ff. Toutain, *Cultes*, 1:181–193.

[80] See Domaszewski, *Religion*, 22 ff.

[81] Restoration of temples by Tiberius: Tacitus *Ann.* 2.49; Vespasian "the preserver of public rites and restorer of sacred building": *CIL* 6.934; Trajan "restored the places where the sacred objects of the gods were stored, when they had collapsed from old age": *CIL* 6.962; Hadrian "paid most diligent attention to Roman rites": *Historia Augusta Hadrian* 22.10 (ibid. 19.10: "At Rome he restored ... many sacred buildings"); Antoninus Pius is honored by the Senate and the people "because of his outstanding concern and religious zeal for public rites": *CIL*

preservation of cult, from which the inner life disappears more and more. The best evidence for this is the fact that – apart from Domitian's whimsically extravagant cult of Minerva – new temples and cults in this period were established only for those divine personifications of abstract ideas in which the religious imagination was still productive.[82] The exceptions, naturally, are those cults established for the deified emperor and the foreign divinities of the east. Vespasian's *Templum Pacis* and Hadrian's Temple of Venus and Rome offer significant examples.[83]

For the literati in society, the gods became empty shadows. The sharpening of religious anxiety, which reveals itself clearly in Seneca and Epictetus, and later in Fronto and Marcus Aurelius, does not bring about a return to the old gods; rather, individuals turn in prayer to a vague, universal, abstract, and highly impersonal divinity. In the place of positive belief came a colorless, moral law detached from all historical and national assumptions. To be sure, the old gods survived longer in the private practice of religion by the middle and lower social classes. This was particularly true of Silvanus, Liber, Diana, Hercules, Minerva, Mercurius, and the Lares. These were intimately bound up with domestic and rustic life or were respected as the protectors of certain vocations and activities,[84] but even their worship did not remain untouched by the devotion to the ruler that now permeated everything.

Augustus' inspiration, that of commending the gods of his house to universal worship, now bears fruit: proceeding from the cult of the *Lares Augusti* and of *Vesta Augusta*, i.e. of the hearth-gods of the emperor, people gradually added the epithet *Augustus* without exception to all the names of the gods,[85] to express thereby that they worshiped the respective divinities in the same sense as the emperor did in his own household cult.

The Roman gods experience a still greater alienation from their old individuality through the diffusion of their cult in every part of

---

6.1001 (Cf. *Historia Augusta Antoninus Pius* 13.4 and, concerning his image on coins, Eckhel, *D. N.* 7, 29 ff.).

[82] Annona, to whom Friedländer, *Sittengeschichte*, 4:159, calls special attention, also belongs in this circle.

[83] Cf. E. Aust, *Die stadtrömischen Tempelgründungen der Kaiserzeit*, Jahresbericht des königlichen Kaiser-Friedrichs-Gymnasiums zu Frankfurt am Main, Easter 1898 (Frankfurt: Enz and Rudolf, 1898), where, however, the *aedes publicae* and private shrines are not distinguished, and appendix 2 [Wissowa, *Religion und Kultus*, 594–597].

[84] Concerning the divinities of the *collegia*, cf. W. Liebenam, *Zur Geschichte und Organisation des römischen Vereinswesens* (Leipzig: Teubner, 1890), 288 ff.

[85] Collection of material in E. de Ruggiero, *Dizionario epigrafico di antichità romana* (1886), 1, 925 ff. and in *TLL* vol. 2, col. 1393ff.

the Empire, whereby they assimilate to the gods of the barbarians and cloak the foreign cults of the provinces with Roman names. The governance of the Empire allowed the inhabitants of the provinces their native beliefs and encroached on their activity only insofar as these offended the laws of the Empire.[86] Roman officials and soldiers took the state cult of Rome into all parts of the Empire[87] and brought about an approximation and equivalence between these and the religious ideas they encountered. In the conviction that the divinities of foreign religions differed only in name from the Roman, but were intrinsically either identical or related, the Roman applied the *interpretatio Romana* (Tac. *Germ.* 43) everywhere abroad. That is to say, he recognized his own gods in foreign *numina*, with greater or lesser correctness with respect to individual similarities of religious observance or belief, and so endowed those foreign *numina* with names that the provincials, too, adopted in the same degree as they remained receptive to the higher culture of the Romans.[88] Whether the indigenous name of the god remained next to the Roman one, was preserved as an epithet, or disappeared made no significant difference in this matter. If, for example, a British god appeared now as *deus Cocidius*, now as *deus Mars Cocidius*, now in the end simply as Mars,[89] we encounter the same divinity in three different stages of Romanization. If, among the Roman gods who became the transmitters of foreign religious ideas, Mars and Mercury[90] stood next to the greatest god Juppiter Optimus Maximus at the top – especially in the Celtic and German provinces – this is simply an expression of the reality that the Roman soldier and Roman merchant entered new territory as the first cultural pioneers and naturally were inclined to identify the gods of their profession with the most respected divinities of the foreign land. Other Roman divinities also find translation

[86] Such grounds of a police-like kind were forbidding the Gallic religion druids (Suet. *Claud.* 25; Aur. Vict. *Caes.* 4.2; cf. Pliny *Nat.* 30.13) and intervening against human sacrifice in the African worship of Saturn (Tertullian *Apol.* 9: "In Africa, babies were openly sacrificed to Saturn, up to the proconsulate of Tiberius, who hung the priests [who performed those sacrifices] on the very trees of the temples, in whose shade their crimes had been committed; the soldiers of my native city were witnesses to those, as they executed this punishment on behalf of that proconsul"). Cf. also Lactantius *Inst.* 1.21.1: "Among the Cypriots, Teucer gave a human victim to Zeus and handed down that sacrifice to posterity; it was recently abolished under the emperor Hadrian."

[87] Dionysius *Ant. Rom.* 7.70.5: "and they have established it as good for all the peoples whom they rule, that they should honor the gods in Roman fashion."

[88] F. Richter, *De deorum barbarorum interpretatione Romana quaestiones selectae* (Halis Saxonum: C.A. Kaemmerer, 1906).

[89] The evidence in Richter, *loc. cit.*, 13; that the same god was also called *deus Silvanus Cocidius* once (*CIL* 7.642) reveals how such an equivalence met with approval first after certain divergent attempts.

[90] Evidence in Roscher, *Lex.* 2:2397ff. and Steudig, ibid. 2: 2828 ff.

into foreign gods, although we cannot always ascertain the conclusive factors for whatever equivalence was established, for example, Saturnus for the Punic Ba'alchammân, Minerva for the Britannic goddess of the hot springs of Bath (*Aquae Sulis*), Neptune for Bindus of the Iapygians, Silvanus for a Dalmatian god, etc. Often, it is only the conflation of a foreign divinity that allows us to recognize a barbarian god under a well-known Roman name: for example, the pairing of Mercury and Rosmerta among the Treverii, which changes before our eyes, so to speak, into Mercury and Maia, and thus cloaks one of its constituent members in Roman dress.[91]

This is by no means a question of the one-sided transmission of Roman ideas into the provinces, but of a real exchange of religious points of view, in which the Romans are as much the takers as the givers. The acquaintance of the Romans with foreign gods was accomplished on the one hand by commercial traffic and the presence of Roman merchants abroad,[92] and on the other by the army, whose corps of foreign troops, in preserving their national composition, maintained their native tutelary divinities.[93] By this process, for example, the Celtic stable- and horse-goddess Epona achieved veneration also among the bodies of Roman citizen troops (*CIL* 3.3420) and even in Rome itself. Extremely instructive regarding this kind of infiltration of foreign divinities are the votive stones discovered in the Roman barracks of the *Equites singulares* [select cavalry serving in the imperial bodyguard], who were recruited primarily from the Germans and Celts. The different veterans from these companies set up these stones in the years 132–141. The dedications, apart from random deviations, always appeal to the same group of gods, namely Juppiter Optimus Maximus, Juno, Minerva, Mars, Victoria, Hercules, Fortuna, Mercury, Salus, Felicitas, Fata, Campestres, Silvanus, Apollo, Diana, Epona, Suleviae, and Genius individually. They involve therefore (a) the triad of Capitoline divinities; (b) a trio of chief German gods, Tiu, Donar, and Wodan, romanized as Mars, Hercules, Mercury; (c) the personifications Victoria, Fortuna, Salus, Felicitas, the first two corresponding to the luck of

---

[91] F. Richter, *loc. cit.*, 43 ff.

[92] V. Pârvan, *Die Nationalität der Kaufleute im römischen Kaiserreiche* (Breslau: H. Fleischmann, 1909), 37 ff., 107 ff. This establishing of trade was particularly important for the importation of eastern cults, but also, for example, the marble base disovered in the Forum Romanum with the dedication *Numini deae Viennae* (Ch. Hülsen, "Neue Inschriften vom Forum Romanum," *Beiträge zur alten Geschichte* 2 (1902) 227–283 at 238) obviously belongs to a *statio* of *municipes* ["municipal staging-post"] from Vienna (cf. also the small bronze with the dedication *Arausioni CIL* 6.30,850 and in addition E. Caetani Lovatelli, "Di una tabelleta in bronzo con epigrafe sacra al genio di Arausio," *Bulletino* 19 (1891), 245–251.

[93] Cf. the excellent and fruitful research of Domaszewski, *Religion*, 45 ff.

the unit in war, the other two, as with the Arval Brethren, to the welfare of the Empire; (d) the native local gods of the unit, namely Fata, Campestres, Epona, Suleviae for the Celts and Germans; Silvanus, Apollo, Diana for the Illyrians and Dacians; and, finally, (e) according to the Roman point of view, the *genius* as the divine embodiment of the unit.[94] A similar interweaving of old and new, of Roman and barbarian views, is also exhibited in different ways by countless other sacral monuments from the provinces.[95] There is no imperial religion, but the transparent wrapping of Roman names covers an inexhaustible multiplicity of conceptions of different kinds of religion,[96] which were connected with the whole only casually through the worship of Juppiter Optimus Maximus and the imperial cult in its different forms and nuances, while the actual state religion remained bound to the soil of the city of Rome and so for that reason could not have developed into an imperial religion.

Bibliography

G. Boissier, *La religion Romaine d'Auguste aux Antonins* (Paris, 1874). Friedländer, *Sittengeschichte*, 4:119ff. V. Duruy, "La formation d'une religion officielle dans l'empire Romain," *Revue de l'histoire des religions* 1 (1880), 161-174. Toutain, *Cultes*, vol. 1, "*Les provinces latines*," treats fully the imperial cult of the western provinces and the worship of the Roman state gods, above all of Juppiter Optimus Maximus. An indispensable preliminary work for the history of religion of the empire, a *geographia sacra imperii Romani* remains to be done. Wendland, *Kultur*, pp. 92ff. T. Glover, *The Conflict of Religions in the Early Roman Empire*, 3rd edition (London: Methuen, 1909), 33 ff.

---

[94] The inscriptions *CIL* 6 3,138–31,187; in addition, for the German triad, cf. C. Zangermeister, *Neue Heidelberger Jahrbücher* 5 (1895), 46 ff. (Supplements of G. Sixt, ibid. 6 (1896), 59 ff.; see also Domaszewski, *Religion*, 46 ff.); for Salus and Felicitas, see Wissowa, *Gesamm. Abhandlungen*, 299 ff.; about Fata, Campestres, Suleviae, M. Siebourg, *De Sulevis Campestribus Fatis* (Bonn: Georgi, 1886). M. Ihm, "Der Mütter- oder Matronenkultus und seine Denkmäler," *Bonner Jahrbücher* 83 (1887), 1–200, and in Roscher, *Lex.* 2:2464ff., for Silvanus, Apollo, Diana as Illyrian-Thracian gods, see Domaszewski, *Religion*, 52 ff. A similar group of gods (Juppiter Optimus Maximus, Victoria Victrix, Diana, Apollo, Genius Terrae Britannicae, Mars, Minerva, Campestres, Hercules, Epona, Victoria) are shown on the altars on the Antonine Wall dedicated by a Roman centurion (*ILS* 4831; cf. also *ILS* 3091).

[95] Particularly instructive for the mixing of Gallic and Roman ideas are the two monuments in Mainz, which Domaszewski, *Abhandlungen*, 129 ff., 139 ff. already explains.

[96] For the Gallic-German part of the empire, cf. F. Hettner, *WZ* 2 (1883), 8 ff. (*Belgica and Germania inferior*); O. Hirschfeld, ibid. 8 (1889), 135 ff. (*Narbonensis*); Hirschfeld, "Aquitanien," 44ff. (*Aquitania*); A. Riese, *WZ* 17 (1898), 1 ff. J. B. Keune, *Metz in römischer Zeit* (Metz 1900), 10 ff. (*German superior*); for Dalmatia, C. Patsch, "Archäologisch-epigraphische Untersuchungen zur Geschichte der römischen Provinz Dalmatien," *Wissenschaftliche Mitteilungen aus Bosnien und der Hercegovina* 5 (1897), 177–241; for the African provinces, J. Toutain, *Les cités Romaines de la Tunisie* (Paris: Thorin, 1896), 206 ff. A. Schulten, *Das römische Africa* (Leipzig: Dieterich, 1899), 20 ff.

Works cited by short title

Beurlier, *Culte* = E. Beurlier, *Le culte impérial. Son histoire et son organisation depuis Auguste jusqu'à Justinien.* Paris: Thorin, 1891.

Domaszewski, *Abhandlungen* = A. von Domaszewski, *Abhandlungen zur römischen Religion.* Leipzig and Berlin: Teubner, 1909.

Domaszewski, *Religion* = A. von Domaszewski, *Die Religion des römischen Heeres*, Westdeutsche Zeitschrift für Geschichte und Kunst 14. Trier: 1895.

Friedländer, *Sittengeschichte* = L. Friedländer, *Darstellungen aus der Sittengeschichte Roms in der Zeit von August bis zum Ausgang der Antonine.* Eighth edition. Leipzig: S. Hirzel, 1910.

Heinen, "Kaiserkult" = H. Heinen, "Zur Begründung des römischen Kaiserkultus. Chronologische Uebersicht von 48 v. bis 14 14 n. Chr." *Klio* 11 (1911) 129–177.

Hirschfeld, "Aquitanien" = O. Hirschfeld, "Aquitanien in der Römerzeit," *Sitzungsberichte der königlich preussischen Akademie der Wissenschaften zu Berlin, Gesammtsitzung,* 1896 no. 20 (16 April 1896), 429–456.

Hirschfeld, "Kaisercult" = O. Hirschfeld, "Zur Geschichte des römischen Kaisercultus," *Sitzungsberichte der königlich preussischen Akademie der Wissenschaften zu Berlin, Sitzung der philosophisch-historischen Classe,* 188 no. 35 (19 July 1888), 833–862.

Jordan, *Topographie* = H. Jordan, *Topographie der Stadt Rom im Alterthum.* Berlin: Weidmann, 1871–1907. 2 volumes in four parts. Part 3 of volume 1 completed by Ch. Hülsen.

Kornemann, "Herrscherkulte" = E. Kornemann, "Zur Geschichte der antiken Herrscherkulte," *Beiträge zur alten Geschichte* 1 (1901) 51–146.

Laqueur, "Triumph" = R. Laqueur, "Über das Wesen des römischen Triumphs," *Hermes* 44 (1909) 215–236.

Marquardt, *Staatsverwaltung* = J. Marquardt, *Römische Staatsverwaltung.* Vol. 2 of the second edition completed by H. Dessau and A. von Domaszewski; vol. 3 of the second edition completed by G. Wissowa. Leipzig: S. Hirzel, 1881–1885. Reprint New York: Arno, 1975.

Mommsen, *Röm. Forsch.* = T. Mommsen, *Römische Forschungen.* Berlin: Weidmann, 1864–1879.

Mommsen, *Ges. Schr.* = T. Mommsen, *Gesammelte Schriften.* Berlin: Weidmann, 1905–1913.

Mommsen, *Staatsrecht* = T. Mommsen, *Römisches Staatsrecht.* Lepzig: S. Hirzel, 1887.

Nissen, *Landeskunde* = H. Nissen, *Italische Landeskunde.* Berlin: Weidmann, 1883–1902. Reprint Amsterdam: Hakkert, 1967.

Pernice, "Sakralrechte I" = A. Pernice, "Zum römischen Sakralrechte. I." *Sitzungsberichte der königlich preussischen Akademie der Wissenschaften zu Berlin, Sitzung der philosophisch-historischen Classe,* 1885 no. 51 (10 December 1885), 1143–1169.

Pernice, "Sakralrechte II" = A. Pernice, "Zum römischen Sakralrechte. II." *Sitzungsberichte der königlich preussischen Akademie der Wissenschaften zu Berlin, Gesammtsitzung,* 1886 no. 51 (9 Dec. 1886), 1169–1203.

Richter, *Topographie* = O. Richter, *Topographie der Stadt Rom.* 2nd edition. Munich: C. H. Beck, 1901.

Schwegler, *Römische Geschichte* = A. Schwegler, *Römische Geschichte.* Freiburg and Tübingen: Mohr, 1884.

Toutain, *Cultes* = J. Toutain, *Les cultes païens dans l'empire Romain.* Paris: E. Leroux, 1907–1917.

Usener, *Götternamen* = H. Usener, *Götternamen: Versuch einer Lehre von der religiösen Begriffsbildung.* Bonn: F. Cohen, 1896.

Wendland, *Kultur* = P. Wendland, *Die hellenistisch-römische Kultur in ihren Beziehungen zu Judentum und Christentum.* Tübingen: Mohr, 1912.

Wissowa, *Abhandlungen* = G. Wissowa, *Gesammelte Abhandlungen zur romischen Religions- und Stadtgeschichte.* Munich: C. H. Beck, 1904.

Chronology

BC

753	Legendary date for the foundation of Rome.
753–509	Regal period: Rome ruled by kings.
509–27	The Republic.
13 Sep. 509	Traditional date of the dedication of the temple of Capitoline Jupiter.
451–450	The laws of the Twelve Tables.
390	Sack of Rome by the Gauls. Foundation of a temple to Aius Locutius.
367	The Licinian Laws open the consulate to the plebs; plebeians also become *decemviri sacris faciundis*.
348	Traditional date for the first Secular Games.
340	Devotion of the consul Decius Mus.
312	Censorship of Appius Claudius. Care of the cult of Hercules of the *ara maxima* is taken away from the Potitii and assigned to public slaves.
304	The scribe Gnaeus Flavius marks days *fasti* or *nefasti* on the calendar.
300	The Ogulnian Law allows plebeians to enter the pontifical and augural colleges.
295	Devotion of Decius Mus, son of the consul of 340.
293	Introduction of the cult of Aesculapius on the recommendation of the Sibylline books.
264–241	First Punic War.
249	Secular Games.
218–202	Second Punic War.
217–216	Many prodigies: the Sibylline books are consulted, and expiatory ceremonies are performed. The Roman vow a *ver sacrum*, a sacred spring, in which all produce of one season is surrendered to the gods. In 216, two couples, male and female, one of Gauls and one of Greeks, are sacrificed.
213	Measures taken again superstition; new texts added to the Sibylline books.

359

212	*Pontifex maximus* becomes an elected office.
205	The Sibylline books recommend the introduction of Cybele, the Great Mother.
4 Apr. 204	Cybele is welcomed to Rome and installed in the temple of Victory. Creation of the *ludi Megalenses* (the games of the Great Mother).
202	Roman victory at Zama.
200–197	Macedonian War.
195	The *ver sacrum* vowed in 217 is carried out. Because of a formal irregularity, the sacrifice is repeated in 194.
186	The suppression of the Bacchanalia.
154	The Aelian and Fufian laws rule that magistrates have the right to challenge legislative assemblies by announcing an unfavorable sign.
149–146	Third Punic War.
146	Destruction of Carthage; expulsion of Chaldaean philosophers from Rome. Secular Games.
139	Chaldaen philosophers and Jews expelled from Rome.
114	Two couples, male and female, one of Gauls and one of Greeks, are sacrificed.
104–103	The Domitian Law assigns the election of priests of all four major colleges to the people.
87	Suicide of the *flamen Dialis*; the office remains vacant until 11 BC.
83	A fire on the Capitol burns the Sibylline books.
76	Reconstitution of the Sibylline books.
63	Consulate of Cicero. Julius Caesar is elected *pontifex maximus*.
59	Consulate of Julius Caesar; altars of Isis and Serapis on the Capitol are destroyed.
50–48	Civil war between Caesar and Pompey.
47	Varro completes his *Human and Divine Antiquities* and dedicates the latter portion (in sixteen books) to the *pontifex maximus*, Julius Caesar. (The dating is deeply insecure, and a date in the mid-50s is not unlikely.)
46	Caesar reforms the calendar.
45	Cicero writes *On the Nature of the Gods*.
44	Caesar assassinated; the name of the month Quintilis changed to Iulius. Cicero finishes *On Divination*.
42	The Rufrenan law deifies Caesar.
32	Octavian (the future Augustus) declares war on Egypt following the ritual of the fetials.
31	Octavian victorious over Antony at Actium.
18 Aug. 29	Dedication of the temple of Divius Julius (the deified Julius).

27 BC–AD 476	The Empire.
27 BC–AD 68	The Julio-Claudian dynasty.
13 Jan. 27	Octavian is named Augustus.
27–25	Construction of the Pantheon.
17	Secular Games.
6 Mar. 12	Augustus elected *pontifex maximus*.
28 Apr. 12	Dedication of an altar to Vesta in Augustus' house on the Palatine.
30 Jan. 9	Dedication of the Ara Pacis Augustae.
8	Month Sextilis renamed Augustus.
2	Augustus is named *pater patriae*, 'father of his country.' Dedication of a temple to Mars Ultor in the Forum of Augustus.
AD	
14	Augustus dies and is deified. Tiberius becomes emperor. The *sodales Augustales* and a *flamen Augustalis* are created to celebrate the cult of Augustus.
14–37	Tiberius is emperor.
19	Tiberius has a temple to Isis destroyed and her statue thrown into the Tiber.
37–41	Caligula is emperor.
38	Caligula has a temple to Isis built on the Campus Martius.
41–54	Claudius is emperor.
42	Deification of Livia, wife of Augustus.
47	Secular Games, celebrated at the eighth centenary of the foundation of the city.
54–68	Nero is emperor; Claudius is deified.
64	Great fire at Rome; persecution of the Christians at Rome.
68–9	Nero's assassination is followed by a civil war.
70–96	Flavian dynasty.
70	Jerusalem sacked and the Temple destroyed by Titus.
87	Secular Games.
96–192	Antonine dynasty.
147	Secular Games.
197	Tertullian's *Apology*.
202	Edict prohibiting Jewish and Christian proselytism.
204	Secular Games.
212	Caracalla extends citizenship to all free aliens residing in the empire.
248	Secular Games celebrating the millennium of the foundation of the city.
250	Decius orders the citizens of the Empire to sacrifice to the gods.
257	Valerian bans the Christian cult.

311	Galerius issues an edict of tolerance with respect to the Christian cult.
313	Christians granted freedom of worship; property restored to Christian churches.
330	Foundation of Constantinople.
342	Sacrifice banned.
361–3	Julian the Apostate is emperor.
378–95	Theodosius is emperor and issues increasingly strident legislation against traditional cult.
379	Gratian refuses the office of *pontifex maximus*.
391	Theodosius definitively bans pagan cult, initiating an even more virulent period of temple-burning.
*c.*400	Stilicho burns the Sibylline books.
410	Alaric sacks Rome.
413–26	Augustine writes *The City of God*.
1776	Edward Gibbon publishes the first volume of *The History of the Decline and Fall of the Roman Empire*, containing a famous and influential Englightenment view of Roman polytheism as inherently tolerant.
1858	W. Henzen and G. B. de Rossi begin publication of the acts of the Arval Brethren.
1891	Publication of first major scholarly edition of the *commentarii* recording the Secular Games under Augustus.
1911	W. Warde Fowler, *The Religious Experience of the Roman People*.
1912	G. Wissowa, *Religion und Kultus* (2nd edn).
1949	L. R. Taylor, *Party Politics in the Age of Caesar*.
1960	K. Latte, *Römische Religionsgeschichte*.
1970	G. Dumézil, *Archaic Roman Religion*.
1990	J. Scheid, *Romulus et ses frères*; J. Z. Smith, *Drudgery Divine*.
1998	M. Beard, J. North, and S. Price, *Religions of Rome*.

Biographical Dictionary

Augustine (AD 354–430): Bishop of Hippo, Church Father. His *City of God* (written 413–26) is a very important source for the history of Roman religion.

Augustus (63 BC–AD 14): Caesar's adopted son. After defeating Mark Antony, he became the first Roman emperor.

Caligula (AD 12–41): Third Roman emperor.

Cato (234–149 BC): Roman senator. The author of, among other works, a treatise *On Agriculture*.

Cicero (106–43 BC): Roman senator. His literary oeuvre is one of the most important to have been preserved. It includes private correspondence and philosophical treatises, among many other kinds of writing.

Decii: A family two or three of whose members won fame by "devoting" themselves to the gods of the underworld in battles in the fourth and third centuries BC.

Dionysius of Halicarnassus (late first century BC): Greek critic and historian. In the reign of Augustus he wrote a history of Rome in Greek (the surviving part covers the origins of the city down to the mid-fifth century BC).

Festus (second century AD): Roman grammarian who summarized the dictionary of Verrius Flaccus entitled *On the Meaning of Words*, composed during the reign of Augustus.

Fulvius Nobilior (late third/early second century BC): consul in 189 BC, and victor over the Aetolians. A cultivated man, associated with the poet Ennius. With the booty from his campaign, he built the temple of Hercules and the Muses in the Circus Flaminius.

Gaius (second century AD): Legal writer.

Germanicus (15 BC–AD 19): Adopted son of Emperor Tiberius, and his designated successor.

Gracchi: Roman senators, the brothers Tiberius (died 133 BC) and Gaius (died 121 BC). Both introduced radical "popular" legislation and were killed in the political conflicts that followed.

The following list is adapted from that published in J. Scheid, *An Introduction to Roman Religion* (Edinburgh: Edinburgh University Press, 2003), with thanks to Prof. Scheid and the Press for their permission.

Julian (331–63): Roman emperor and strong supporter of pagan religion.

Julius Caesar (100–44 BC): Roman senator who, as "dictator," effectively established one-man rule at Rome in the mid-first century BC. He was *pontifex maximus* from 63 BC until his assassination in 44.

Livy (59 BC–AD 17): Author of a Roman history in 142 books, covering the origins of Rome down to the Principate of Augustus. Only 35 books and a summary have survived.

Macrobius (early fifth century AD): Author of the *Saturnalia*, an encyclopedia written in the form of a literary banquet, which contains much information about religion.

Ovid (43 BC–AD 17): Roman poet whose works include a poem on the Roman calendar (*Fasti*) and many versions of Graeco-Roman myth.

Pliny the Elder (AD 23/4–79): Roman polymath and author of a multivolume encyclopedia, the *Natural History*.

Pliny the Younger (*c.*AD 61–112): Roman senator and nephew of the elder Pliny. Author of a published collection of *Letters*.

Plutarch (late first/early second century AD): Greek writer and priest at the sanctuary of Apollo at Delphi. A large number of his biographical, philosophical, and antiquarian works survive.

Seneca (AD 1–65): Toman senator, consul (in 56) and Stoic philosopher. The tutor of Nero; very influential during the early years of Nero's Principate. Author of philosophical treatises and letters, and also tragedies.

Servius (late fourth century AD): Grammarian and the author of a large commentary on the works of Vergil, which contains much information on religion.

Suetonius (late first/early second century AD): Roman *eques* who filled various posts in the imperial administration. Author of a surviving series of biographies of emperors.

Tacitus (*c.*AD 56–*c.*120): Roman senator (consul in 97) who wrote histories of the early empire (*Annals* and *Histories*).

Tertullian (*c.*AD 160–after 220): Carthaginian Christian, author of an *Apology* (a defence of Christianity) and numerous other works.

Tiberius (42 BC–AD 37): Adopted son of Augustus, second Roman emperor.

Valerius Maximus (first century AD): Author of a book of *Memorable Deeds and Sayings*, recording many anecdotes from the history of the Republic.

Varro (116–27 BC): Roman senator who, after a political career alongside Pompey, devoted himself to research and literary activities. In 47 he dedicated his *Divine Antiquities* to the *pontifex maximus*, Julius Caesar. Between 46 and his death, he published numerous works on literary and linguistic subjects.

Verrius Flaccus (*c.*55 BC–*c.*AD 20): Roman freedman and leading scholar of Latin and of Roman institutions. His lost work, *On the Meaning of Words*, is partly preserved in the summary of Festus.

Glossary

Arval Brethren	The *fratres Arvales* were the twelve priests who oversaw the cult of Dea Dia.
augur, pl. *augures*	"Augur(s)"; Roman priest(s); as a collective, one of the four great colleges. They possessed special expertise in *auspicium*, whence Cicero called them the "interpreters of Jupiter Optimus Maximus" (*Leg.* 2.20). As a college, they were consulted by the Senate, primarily about cases of ritual error (*vitium*) by magistrates. As individuals, they celebrated special rites (known as *auguria*) and inaugurated priests and temples.
Augustalis, pl. *Augustales*	An adjective sometimes used as a substantive, sometimes modifying *sevir* (pl. *seviri*). A *sevir* was one of a college of six men, often a former slave, with an official role in the local institution of the imperial cult, as well as other public duties. *Augustales* who were not *seviri* could number in the hundreds in larger towns.
auspicium	Literally, "the watching of birds." Romans came to apply the term to various forms of divination, the interpreting of signs either casually observed (*oblativa*) or specially sought out (*impetrativa*). Such signs could include thunder and lightning, the flight of birds, the behavior of particular sacred chickens, the behavior or condition of four-footed animals, or unusual and threatening events. The signs could be interpreted as expressions of divine approval or disapproval of particular courses of action, but were held to be valid for only one day. Hence they were applied almost exclusively to the timing of a particular action, and not to its soundness *per se*.

Caesareum	A temple devoted to the imperial cult.
collegium	In general, a guild, society or confraternity. In public law or religion, a board of magistrates or priests, normally of equal rank and hence subject to mutual control. In matters of religion, the priestly colleges served as advisory boards to the Senate and in that capacity acted as collectives. Priests acted as individuals apart from their colleagues in assisting individual magistrates.
decemviri	See *quindecimviri*.
dii manes	The dead of a community as a collective – the singular does not occur – to whom the living entrusted their dead.
divus, fem. *diva*, pl. *divi*	A title applied to deified Roman emperors or deified members of the imperial family.
duoviri (*sacris faciundis*)	See *quindecimviri*.
eques, pl. *equites*	Literally, a cavalryman; in classical Rome, an "equestrian" was a member of the *ordo equester*, the "equestrian order," a juridical class of similar economic background to senators. Under the Republic, senators and equestrians were juridically and ideologically distinct and were held to pursue different interests, in politics and commerce, respectively. The Principate saw the rise of a very substantial hierarchy of equestrian offices in the imperial army and administration.
evocatio	Literally, the "calling-forth." A ritual by which the Romans invited the tutelary deity of an enemy city to come to Rome and be worshipped there.
feriae	Holidays.
fetialis, pl. *fetiales*	"Fetial(s)"; Priest(s) concerned with foreign relations, especially declarations of war and treaties.
flamen, pl. *flamines*	Roman priest(s) assigned to the cult of a single god. There were three major *flamines*, of Jupiter (the *flamen Dialis*), of Mars (*Martialis*), and of Quirinus (*Quirinalis*), and twelve minor ones. The title was also used for priests of the imperial cult. Certain wives of *flamines* were entitled *flaminicae* (sing. *flaminica*) and had religious duties specific to themselves.
genius	Originally, the double of a mortal in the divine sphere. It was not itself immortal, nor is a *genius* ever depicted acting as an autonomous agent.

The *genius* might be described as a deified abstraction of the idiosyncratic traits of an individual man. The corresponding figure for Roman women was the *Juno*, a concept that may have developed later, on analogy with the *genius*. At some unknown date the Romans began identifying a *genius* for collectives (most notably, for cities and legions), born at the moment of their constitution.

haruspex, pl. *haruspices* Etruscan diviner(s) consulted by Roman magistrates or the Senate on the interpretation of signs of particular kinds, especially lightning (*fulgura* – above all when it struck a public building), unusual events (*ostenta*), and entrails (*exta* – above all, the liver).

homonoia Literally, "oneness of mind." A political ideal, it became a catchword in classical and Hellenistic Greek politics, referring to unanimity either within a particular city or throughout the Hellenic community.

imperium The power of command held by legitimately elected Roman magistrates.

instauratio The repetition from the beginning of a religious rite interrupted during its performance or held to be incorrectly performed.

ludi Games held in conjunction with a religious festival, commonly theatrical (*ludi scaenici*) or involving chariot racing (*ludi circenses*).

ludi saeculares "Secular Games." With these, the Romans celebrated the end of one *saeculum* and the start of another. A *saeculum* was fixed in the Republic at 100 years. Republican historians assigned the first games to 348 BC; they were certainly celebrated in 249 and 146. Political turmoil prevented their celebration in the 40s BC; Augustus therefore made their celebration in 17 BC an important fixture in his claim to have renewed Rome. Claudius fixed a new cycle in AD 47, the 800th birthday of Rome.

lustratio To perform a *lustrum*, a ritual of purification. The ritual commonly including a circumambulation around the persons or place being purified. The procession included the animals to be sacrificed at the ritual's close. The ceremony could expel or exclude evil, but it was also performed

	to mark new beginnings, for the Roman people after the performance of a census or for an army that was for whatever reason held to be newly constituted.
lustrum	See *lustratio*.
numen, pl. *numina*	Divine power(s); like a mortal's *genius*, a god's *numen* was conceived of as a kind of double, without autonomous identity or capacity for action.
pater patratus	A member of the college *of fetiales*. The origin and meaning of the name are obscure. *Fetiales* seem always to have operated in pairs: a *verbenarius* carrying herbs, the *paterpatratus* speaking (e.g., the words of a treaty or declaration of war, or the deed of sale of an individual Roman to a hostile state).
paterfamilias	The head of a Roman household and extended family (a *familia*), who exercised "paternal power" (*patria potestas*) over his own children and those descended from his male children (provided that these resulted from legitimate marriages and that the female descendants did not marry into another family). Romans thought their conception of paternal power to be distinctly their own. The *paterfamilias* had specific religious duties associated with his unique position.
patrician/plebeian	Patricians were members of particular *gentes*, extended families, each of which derived – if only in legend – from a single, noble progenitor who had been a member of the Senate as it was constituted by Romulus. Tradition also allowed that some immigrant aristocratic families obtained patrician status during the regal period. Certain priesthoods remained open exclusively to patricians, even into the imperial period. Plebeians (members of the *plebs)* were defined negatively as all those who were not patrician.
piaculum, pl. *piacula*	A victim offered, or rite performed, by way of atonement.
plebs	See patrician/plebian.
pomerium	The religious boundary of the city of Rome. Established by augural action, it was the point beyond which the *auspicia urbana*, the "urban auspices," could not be taken.

pontifex, pl. *pontifices*	Roman priest(s) with a wide range of duties both public (they supervised the calendar) and private (they administered the laws regarding tombs). The pontifical college included the *pontifices*, the *rex sacrorum*, and the three major *flamines*. The head of the college was *pontifex maximus*. The college, and in particular its head, exercised supervisory roles over the minor *flamines* and the Vestal Virgins.
postliminium	The right of return 'beyond the threshold.' Roman citizens captured by the enemy were regarded by Roman law as slaves, whose citizen rights were held in suspense. A captive who returned recovered all his rights, though relationships having some physical aspect, such as possession as opposed to ownership of movable goods, were not automatically restored.
princeps, pl. *principes*	A title for the emperor, it connoted "first in authority among equals," and so was used in the Republican period for, e.g., those senators who had once been consuls, or for the individual recognized by the censors as the senior senator (the *princeps senatus*). Its derivative, *principatus*, "principate," describes both a form of constitution (governance by a *princeps*), and a period (the Principate, as opposed to the Republic).
quindecimviri (*sacris faciundis*)	"The fifteen men for the performance of rites." Originally two in number (*duoviri*), the college was increased first to ten (*decemviri*), then to fifteen. Their principal responsibility was to read and interpret the Sibylline books, and through that function they long served as the main advisors to the Senate on relations between the Roman state and foreign religions.
rex sacrorum	A priest of the Roman state who, in the classical period, was held to continue the religious duties of kings from Rome's regal period (see chronology). It is important to observe that the Romans traced the origins of many priesthoods back to the regal period; hence, even on their understanding, the Roman kings had never held a monopoly of priestly authority.
sacra	A substantive of *sacer*, meaning things reserved for a god. It commonly refers both to sacred objects and to religious rites.

Salii
An ancient *sodalitas*, an archaic analog for the *collegium*, attested at Rome and elsewhere in central Italy. At Rome, they performed a set of ritual dances for Mars and sang an archaic song whose lyrics Romans of the late Republic four.d unintelligible.

Sebasteion
A temple devoted to the imperial cult, from *Sebastos*, the Greek translation for *Augustus*.

septemviri epulonum
"Seven men in charge of feasts" for the gods, in particular the *epulum Iovis*, a feast for Jupiter.

sodalis, pl. *sodales*
Member(s) of a *sodalitas*, an archaic analog for the *collegium*. These fraternities often took institutional form in the late Republic and early empire and dedicated themselves to the worship of particular deities, most particularly members of the imperial house.

Sodales Titii
Members of a *sodalitas* associated with a specific *gens*, that of the Titii.

suovetaurilia
The sacrifice of a pig, a ram and a bull.

supplicatio
An offering of incense and wine to a god, and particularly a thanksgiving.

syncretism
The identification of gods with each other, within or between religious systems, who often remain distinct at the level of cult. The phenomenon is most familiar in the Graeco-Roman world in three forms: the formation of the traditional Graeco-Roman pantheon in the preliterary Mediterranean; the assertion of a significant identity between native divinities and Roman ones within the provinces of the Empire, often in such a way that a god's Roman identity suppressed its old one; and the trend in philosophical religion in the late Empire toward henotheism, at least in theology and the language of prayer.

syngeneia
Kinship between peoples. In the Hellenistic world such ties were formally researched, negotiated, and recognized, and served as the basis for political actions of many kinds.

triumphator
A Roman general who had won a major victory might be permitted by the Senate or the people to hold a triumph: a religious procession ending at the temple of Jupiter on the Capitol. The general presided as *triumphator*, and wore a costume variously described as that of the Roman kings

	or based upon the iconography of Jupiter's cult statue on the Capitol.
Vestal Virgins	Six priestesses of Vesta, the Roman goddess of the hearth. Vesta was worshipped both privately, as goddess of the hearths of private dwellings, and publicly, in a building considered by Romans to be shaped like a primitive house. The Vestals occupied a unique position within the Roman community: they served for a minimum of thirty years and were required to remain chaste (the punishment was burial alive), and yet they wore a matron's cloak; they were freed from the paternal power of their fathers (see *paterfamilias*).
VIIviri epulonum	See *septemviri epulonum*.
votum, pl. *vota*	Vow(s) made to a deity.
Xviri (sacris faciundis)	See *quindecimviri*.
XVviri (sacris faciundis)	See *quindecimviri*.

Guide to Further Reading

In keeping with the aims of the series in which this volume appears, I refer in this guide principally to works in English. Except for references to translations in the next two paragraphs, I cite publications by author, short title, and date; more information about works thus cited may be found in the bibliography. The notes to the editorial matter also refer to much valuable material, which I have not discussed again here.

Almost all major literary sources for the study of Roman religion are happily available in translation, with the caveat that translations are perhaps never less reliable than in matters of religion. The Penguin's Classics, Oxford World's Classics, and Harvard Loeb Classical Library provide convenient access to almost all relevant material. Alas, no one person has translated the fragments of Varro's *Divine Antiquities*. On the other hand, most of the major fragments of that work are preserved in Augustine's *City of God*, and it may well be that the fragments are best read within the context of Augustine's polemic. Among widely available translations of that work, that by Henry Bettenson for Penguin provides the fullest annotation. The only English translation of Macrobius' *Saturnalia* – that by Percival Vaughan Davies (New York: Columbia University Press, 1969) – is unfortunately out of print, while the late fourth-century commentary on Vergil's *Aeneid* by Servius has received no translation at all.

Much important evidence is, of course, non-literary, whether epigraphical or archaeological. L. Richardson's *New Topographical Dictionary of Ancient Rome* (Baltimore: Johns Hopkins University Press, 1992) provides convenient access to a great deal of information; R. Turcan, *Religion Romaine* (1988), consists of two volumes of images of artistic and material remains relevant to Roman religious practice. Among sourcebooks, pride of place in this context belongs to the second volume of Beard, North, and Price, *Religions of Rome* (1998). Honorable mention accrues to N. Lewis and M. Reinhold, *Roman Civilization* (New York: Columbia University Press, 1990, 3rd edn), and R. K. Sherk, *Rome and the Greek East to the Death of Augustus* and *The Roman Empire: Augustus to Hadrian* (Cambridge: Cambridge University Press, 1984 and 1988, respectively).

Several good and very different introductions to Roman religion are now in print. In ascending order of length, these include David Potter's "Roman religion" (1999), John North's *Roman Religion* (2000), John Scheid's *Roman Religion* (Edinburgh: Edinburgh University Press, 2003, a translation with revisions of Scheid 1998a), and Mary Beard, John North, and Simon Price's *Religions of Rome* (1998). Also valuable and highly idiosyncratic are R. M. Ogilvie, *The Romans and their Gods* (1969) and R. MacMullen, *Paganism* (1981). English-language readers will also soon have access to the work of Jörg Rüpke, among the most prominent of modern students of Roman religion: his *Die Religion der Römer: eine Einführung* is now being translated for Polity.

Finally, for those restricted to English, no one author's body of work offers greater rewards than Arthur Darby Nock's *Essays on Religion and the Ancient World* (1972). Unfortunately, quotations from Greek and Latin remain there untranslated.

Part I: Among recent methodological and historiographic essays, the reviews of Beard, North, and Price, *Religions of Rome*, occupy a special niche: three in English are J. Rives (1998), J. Linderski (2000), and A. Bendlin (2001), the last providing a particularly trenchant overview of the tradition within which Beard, North, and Price are situated. Bendlin provides a kindred, critical look at the historical tradition in "Looking beyond the civic compromise" (2000). W. J. Tatum, "Roman religion," though not a review *per se*, is consonant with Bendlin and Linderski (and Woolf, Chapter 2, above) in his hesitation regarding the implicitly totalizing view of state cult to which most textbooks subscribe.

J. Bremmer's "'Religion,' 'ritual'" (1998) provides an excellent intellectual-historical perspective on the history of some key terms in scholarship on religion. Similarly lexicographical in focus are Roloff on "Ritus" (1954) and Sachot on "Religio/supersitio" (1991), though these are not in English. J. Scheid, "Polytheism impossible" (1987), takes a similar look at the latent incomprehension with which nineteenth- and twentieth-century historians treated the gods of Rome. H. J. Rose, "Roman religion 1910–1960" (1960), provides an extremely idiosyncratic overview of a half-century's scholarship; for recent work, consult Bendlin, Haase, and Rüpke, "Forschungsbericht" (2000). But the sharpest pen writing on the history of histories of ancient religion is that of Jonathan Z. Smith, whose *Drudgery Divine* (1990) is a marvel of research and composition.

Part II: To consider properly the problem of power and authority in Roman religion and society, one would have to study in depth the instiutions through which social power was organized at Rome, among which law would have have its place. Alas, there is nothing in English to compare with A. Magdelain, "*Ius* archaïque" (1986, reprinted in Magdelain 1990), or Y. Thomas, "Sanctio" (1988). On priesthood, Beard, "Priesthood" (1990), and Rüpke, "Controllers and professionals" (1996b), begin with priests and move out, as it were; Gordon, "The veil of power" (1990c), starts from a more panoptic, more explicitly theorized view of power and then focuses on priesthood as a special case.

Among specialized histories of religion and politics, very broadly construed, Rawson, "Scipio" (1973) and "Religion and politics" (1974), focus on the second century BC (both are reprinted in Rawson 1991), while Taylor, *Party Politics* (1949), concentrates on the first. S. Weinstock, *Divus Julius* (1971), was perhaps the most important work on Roman religion since Wissowa's *Religion und Kultus* (1912). Long, insistent in its consideration of detail, it provides a unique view of the late Republic and of the capacity of Roman religious beliefs and institutions both to shape, and be shaped by, changing political, social, and economic realities.

The place of religious institutions in Roman foreign policy, at the level of both ideology and practice, merits special consideration. N. Rosenstein, *Imperatores Victi* (1990), studies the careers of generals who suffered defeats and assesses the role of religion in exculpating them – in other words, in shoring up the legitimacy of an aristocracy whose twin claims to authority were military and religious expertise. More sweeping in scope is Scheid (1981). Religion and war is a topic to which Jörg Rüpke has returned several times; I cite several of his works on the topic in the bibliography. But he has also written penetrating analyses of religion and social power in ancient city-states: see especially "Antike Großstadtreligion" (1999) and "Religiöse Kommunikation" (2001b).

Part III: T. P. Wiseman, *Remus* (1995), is more than a superb book on Roman myth; it is a thrilling read. Many of his further essays on the transmission and invention of Roman myths and historical legends are available in *Historiography and Imagination* (1994) and *Roman Drama and Roman History* (1998). His recent essays on "Liber" (2000) and "History, poetry, and *Annales*" (2002) carry further his project of tracing the origins and transmission of Roman myths, and the elucidation of the intellectual and political contexts in which they were told and retold.

Outside her essay on the Parilia (Chapter 12 in this volume), Mary Beard, "Looking (harder) for Roman myth" (1993), engages with the problem of myth in Roman culture and seeks a specifically Roman, non-Greek form of mythography. In French, P. Borgeaud, "À propos de Denys d'Halicarnasse" (1993), studies the passage that started it all, as it were: the claim by the Augustan historian Dionysius of Halicarnassus that the Romans had no myths but those that they (selectively) borrowed from Greece. It is, of course, scarcely obvious why anyone should have believed Dionysius.

On ritual and orthopraxy, Catherine Bell's *Ritual Theory* (1992) and *Ritual* (1997) provide important overviews of scholarship outside classical studies. Tangentially related to the problem of orthopraxy is that of innovation, a problem rarely studied: see Rüpke, "Innovationsmechanismen" (1996c), which concentrates on sacral law. Among works focused specifically on Rome, nothing in English can compare with three essays that John Scheid has written with three different collaborators: with J.-L. Durand, "'Rites' et "religion" (1994), with M. Linder, "Quand croire c'est faire" (1993), and with J. Svenbro, "Carmen, speech act, rituel" (1989–90). Their conclusions receive some consideration and elaboration in this volume's editorial material; I urge those who can to study those essays with care.

Part IV: Although Varro himself has not received the extended study in English that his work deserves, religion as a topic of intellectual discourse in late Republican and early imperial Rome has not been neglected. Beard, "Cicero and divination" (1986), is a wonderful meditation on how Cicero – and by extension, Roman thinkers in general – came to treat religion discursively at all; on that topic, in French, see Moatti, *Raison de Rome* (1997). Among essays seeking to rehabilitate Latin theology in particular, and upper-class religiosity in general, Jocelyn, "The Roman nobility" (1966) and "Varro's *Antiquitates*" (1982), and Linderski, "Cicero and divination" (1982), deserve mention. Indeed, Jocelyn's article on Varro is without rival in English and, in point of fact, provides a powerful and polemical survey of late Republican religious life.

Reliable, traditional treatments of the antagonism between "religion" and "philosophy" include Brunt, "Philosophy and religion" (1989), and Attridge, "Philosophical critique" (1978). Neither of those essays treats Polybius, who wrote a deeply problematic and highly influential assessment of religion's place in the Roman state of the mid-second century BC. On him, see Vaahtera, "Roman religion" (2000).

On the theological presuppositions actualized and reified in cult and religious art, see Gordon, "Production and religion" (1979), one section of which treats the ancient tendency to refer to statues of Athena, for example, as "Athena" rather than "an image of Athena." Two recent essays that take up Gordon's work are Elsner, "Image and ritual" (1996), and Woolf, "Representation as cult" (2001). Cancik, "Grösse and Kolossalität" (1990), discusses the theological implications of size in portraiture. Gladigow's "Präsenz der Bilder" (1985/6) and "Epiphanie" (1990) concentrate on Greece, but they make valuable progress in framing questions and gathering evidence.

Duncan Fishwick has devoted his career to the study of the imperial cult in the western provinces of the empire. Among many topics, he has written superbly on the import of the theological vocabulary used in worshipping the emperor. These essays constitute more than salutary interventions in the study of ruler cult; they provide valuable clarity to a topic almost entirely neglected. In addition to the publications collected in *Imperial Cult in the Latin West* (1987), see "Numen Augusti" (1989), "Votive offerings" (1990), and "Numinibus Aug(ustorum)" (1994).

Earlier work in this field concentrated on two specific problems, namely, the association of emperors and gods in cult and the attribution to the emperor of a divine "companion." On those topics see Kantorowicz, "ΣΥΝΘΡΟΝΟΣ ΔΙΚΗΙ" (1965: 1–6), Nock, "ΣΥΝΝΑΟΣ ΘΕΟΣ" (1972: 202–51) and "The emperor's divine *comes*" (1972: 653–75).

Part V: Beard, North, and Price, *Religions of Rome* (1998), devotes much of its critical energy to the issue of "Roman and alien," and deserves careful and extended study. The cult of Cybele is perhaps the most famous of the foreign cults naturalized at Rome under the Republic. For its status, and the disquiet that its peculiar priests and practices aroused, see Beard, "The Roman and the foreign" (1994b), as well as Wiseman, "Cybele" (1984). Cancik, "The reception of Greek cults" (1999), remarks suggestively on the religious landscape of late Republican Rome, a period when many Greek cults made important inroads at Rome itself; that essay should be read alongside Cancik, "Rome as sacred landscape" (1985/6). On immigrant populations at Rome under the empire and the religions they brought with them, see MacMullen, "The unromanized in Rome" (1993), and Cracco Ruggini, "Nuclei immigrati" (1980), two delightfully detailed and suggestive articles.

Ancient and modern constructions of "Roman religion" both work in part by excluding "magic." Richard Gordon has supplied by far the two best introductions to magic in the Roman world: "Aelian's peony" (1987) and "Imagining Greek and Roman magic" (1999). Jonathan Z. Smith, "Trading places" (1995), provides a similar, more compressed examination of the historiographic tradition and the world it has studied. On religious figures outside of traditional priesthoods and their relations with persons of power at Rome, see MacMullen, *Enemies of the Roman Order* (1966), and especially Potter, *Prophets and Emperors* (1994).

Among modern attempts to construct models of religious life at Rome that do not adhere to the same polarities that animated Roman conceptions of "religion," the most influential has perhaps been John North, "Development of religious pluralism" (1992), to which Andreas Bendlin has provided a major challenge in two recent essays, "Peripheral centres-central peripheries" (1997) and "Looking beyond the civic compromise" (2000). On the general problem of polytheism as somehow inherently tolerant (and, therefore, on the Enlightenment view that Romans as polytheists must have *been* tolerant) see Rüpke, "Polytheismus und Pluralismus" (2001a).

The spread of Roman cults outside the city of Rome, and the extension of authority by Roman priests beyond the *pomerium*, are topics that have received less study than they deserve, particularly in English. Olivier de Cazanove, "Religious Romanization" (2000a), an important exception, concentrates on the middle Republic. Otherwise, consult Scheid, "Aspects religieux de la municipalisation" (1999a), Frateantonio, "Autonomie" (1997), Rüpke, "Religiöse Kommunikation" (2001b), and Wissowa's classic essay on "Interpretatio Romana" (1916/19).

Part VI: Work in English on religion and space at Rome remains fairly limited. By far the most approachable and most wide-ranging study is Gargola, *Lands, Laws and Gods* (1995). Linderski, "The augural law" (1986), is relentlessly detailed but inaccessible to the non-specialist. And while the place of religious structures in the urban transformation of mid-Republican Rome has received considerable attention – see Ziolkowski,

Temples (1992), and Orlin, *Temples* (1997) – scholars have shied away from attempting a comprehensive analysis of the Augustan restoration as an intervention in the urban fabric. Readers might consult Boyle, *Ovid and the Monuments* (2003), an idiosyncratic study of the monuments mentioned by Ovid. Essays on single temples, however, abound: see, for example, Kellum, "The city adorned" (1990). On Roman temples, Stambaugh, "The functions of Roman temples" (1978), is a useful starting point. But for sheer brilliance (and quality of images), readers who can should consult Gros, *Aurea Templa* (1976) and *L'Architecture Romaine* (1996).

Michels, *The Calendar of the Roman Republic* (1967), provides a detailed overview of the Republican calendar and its evolution. Far more approachable, and far more exciting, is the chapter devoted to the calendar in the second volume of Beard, North, and Price, *Religions of Rome* (1998). Scullard, *Festivals and Ceremonies* (1981), provides a convenient guide to the festivals of the Roman religious year in the classical period. Nothing attests to the malleability and importance of the Roman calendar quite like Ovid's *Fasti*, in which explication of the calendar and its holidays becomes a vehicle for political, religious, and literary reflection of a very idiosyncratic kind. On that work, readers may consult two very different studies: Herbert-Brown, *Ovid and the Fasti* (1994), and Newlands, *Playing with Time* (1995). In German, readers should consult Rüpke, *Kalendar* (1995).

Part VII: The periodization and analysis of religious change at Rome presents a number of challenges. In a polytheistic system, does the mere accretion of new gods constitute historical change? Is imperial cult genuinely new? Roman religion must have changed, insofar as Rome grew, but how are we to name and study the religions of the empire? Are they Roman by virtue of having been practiced within the borders of the empire? By Roman citizens? Apart from works already mentioned in the introductions or above, let me simply recommend here four works, one essay and three books. Rives, "The decree of Decius" (1999), attempts to isolate in the so-called "Decian persecution" a genuinely new aspect of religion and religious politics. Liebeschuetz, *Continuity and Change* (1979), has had lasting influence, largely because of its isolation in English-language scholarship. Finally, Lane Fox, *Pagans and Christians* (1987), and Chadwick, *The Church in Ancient Society* (2001), both narrate the rise of Christianity, the former distinguished by its powerful evocation of the vitality of pagan religions in the high empire, the latter by its extraordinary scope and enormous learning.

Bibliography

Ando, C. 2000. *Imperial Ideology and Provincial Loyalty in the Roman Empire*. Berkeley: University of California Press.

Ando, C. 2002. "The Palladium and the Pentateuch: towards a sacred topography of the later Roman empire." *Phoenix* 55, 369–410.

Ando, C. forthcoming. "Idols and their critics." In James Boyd White, ed., *How to Talk about Religion*. Notre Dame, IN: University of Notre Dame Press.

Ankarloo, B. and S. Clark, eds. 1999. *Witchcraft and Magic in Europe: Ancient Greece and Rome*. Philadelphia: University of Pennsylvania Press.

Asad, T. 1993. *Genealogies of Religion: Discipline and Reasons of Power in Christianity and Islam*. Baltimore: Johns Hopkins University Press.

Attridge, H. W. 1978. "The philosophical critique of religion under the early empire." *ANRW* 2.16.1.45–78.

Bailey, C. 1932. *Phases in the Religion of Ancient Rome*. Berkeley: University of California Press.

Batsch, C., U. Egelhaaf-Gaiser, and R. Stepper, eds. 1999. *Zwischen Krise und Alltag: Antike Religionen im Mittelmeerraum*. Stuttgart: Steiner.

Beard, M. 1985. "Writing and ritual: a study of diversity and expansion in the Arval Acta." *PBSR* 53, 114–62.

Beard, M. 1986. "Cicero and divination: the formation of a Latin discourse." *JRS* 76, 33–46.

Beard, M. 1987. "A complex of times: no more sheep on Romulus' birthday." *PCPhS* 33, 1–15.

Beard, M. 1989. "Acca Larentia gains a son: myths and priesthood at Rome." In M. M. Mackenzie and C. Roueché, eds, *Images of Authority*. Cambridge: Cambridge Philological Society, 41–61.

Beard, M. 1990. "Priesthood in the Roman Republic." In Beard and North 1990: 19–48.

Beard, M. 1991. "Writing and religion: ancient literacy and the function of the written word in Roman religion." *Literacy in the Ancient World*. JRA Supplement 3. Ann Arbor, MI: Journal of Roman Archaeology, 35–58.

Beard, M. 1993. "Looking (harder) for Roman myth: Dumézil, declamation and the probems of definition." In Graf 1993a: 44–64.

Beard, M. 1994a. "Religion in Republican Rome." *CAH* IX², 573–624.

Beard, M. 1994b. "The Roman and the foreign: the cult of the 'Great Mother' in imperial Rome." In N. Thomas and C. Humphrey, eds, *Shamanism, History and the State*. Ann Arbor, MI: University of Michigan Press, 164–90.

Beard, M. 1998. "Documenting Roman religion." In Moatti 1998: 75–101.

Beard, M. and J. North, eds. 1990. *Pagan Priests: Religion and Power in the Ancient World*. Ithaca, NY: Cornell University Press.

Beard, M., J. North, and S. Price. 1998. *Religions of Rome*. Cambridge: Cambridge University Press. 2 volumes.

Belayche, N. 2001. *Iudaea-Palaestina: The Pagan Cults in Roman Palestine (Second to Fourth Century)*. Tübingen: Mohr Siebeck.

Bell, C. 1992. *Ritual Theory, Ritual Practice*. New York: Oxford University Press.

Bell, C. 1997. *Ritual: Perspectives and Dimensions*. New York: Oxford University Press.

Bendlin, A. 1997. "Peripheral centres-central peripheries: religious communication in the Roman empire." In Cancik and Rüpke 1997: 35–68.

Bendlin, A. 2000. "Looking beyond the civic compromise: religious pluralism in late republican Rome." In Bispham and Smith 2000: 115–35.

Bendlin, A. 2001. "Rituals or beliefs? 'Religion' and the religious life of Rome." *Scripta Classica Israelica* 20, 191–208.

Bendlin, A., M. Haase, and J. Rüpke, eds. 2000. "Forschungsbericht, Römische Religion (1990–1999)." *ARG* 2, 283–345.

Berger, A. 1953. *Encyclopedic Dictionary of Roman Law*. Transactions of the American Philosophical Society, 43.2. Philadelphia: American Philosophical Society.

Bispham, E. and C. Smith, eds. 2000. *Religion in Archaic and Republican Rome and Italy*. Edinburgh: Edinburgh University Press.

Black, M. 1962. *Models and Metaphors*. Ithaca, NY: Cornell University Press.

Boëls-Janssen, N. 1993. *La Vie Religieuse des Matrones dans la Rome Archaïque*. Rome: École Française de Rome.

Borgeaud, P. 1993. "Quelques remarques sur la mythologie divine à Rome, à propos de Denys d'Halicarnasse (ant. Rom. 2, 18–20)." In Graf 1993a: 175–87.

Boyancé, P. 1972. *Études sur la Religion Romaine*. Rome: École Française de Rome.

Boyer, P. 1994. *The Naturalness of Religious Ideas: A Cognitive Theory of Religion*. Berkeley: University of California Press.

Boyle, A. J. 2003. *Ovid and the Monuments*. Leiden: Brill.

Bradley, K. 1998. "Contending with conversion: reflections on the reformation of Lucius the Ass." *Phoenix* 52, 315–34.

Bremmer, J. N. 1991. "'Christianus sum': the early Christian martyrs and Christ." In G. J. M. Bartelink, A. Hilhorst, and C. H. Kneepkens, eds,

Eulogia: Mélanges Offerts à Antoon A. R. Bastiaensen à l'Occasion de son Soixante-Cinquième Anniversaire. Steenbrugis: In Abbatia S. Petri, 11–20.

Bremmer, J. N. 1998. "'Religion,' 'ritual' and the opposition 'sacred vs. profane': notes towards a terminological 'genealogy.'" F. Graf, ed., *Ansichten griechischer Rituale.* Stuttgart: Teubner, 9–32.

Brunt, P. A. 1989. "Philosophy and religion in the late Republic." In Griffin and Barnes 1989: 174–98.

Bruun, C., ed. 2000. *The Roman Middle Republic: Politics, Religion and Historiography c.400–133 BC.* Rome: Institutum Romanum Finlandiae.

Burkert, W. 1993. "Mythos: Begriff, Struktur, Funktionen." In Graf 1993a: 9–24.

Cancik, H. 1985/6. "Rome as sacred landscape: Varro and the end of Republican religion at Rome." *Visible Religion* 4/5, 250–65.

Cancik, H. 1990. "Grösse und Kolossalität als religiöse und aesthetische Kategorien. Versuch einer Begriffsbestimmung am Beispiel von Satius, Silve I 1: Ecus Maximus Domitiani Imperatoris." *Visible Religion* 7, 51–68.

Cancik, H. 1999. "The reception of Greek cults in Rome." *ARG* 1.2, 161–73.

Cancik, H. and J. Rüpke, eds. 1997. *Römische Reichsreligion and Provinzialreligion.* Tübingen: Mohr Siebeck.

Cancik, H., H. Lichtenberger, and P. Schäfer, eds. 1996. *Geschichte – Tradition – Reflexion. Festschrift für Martin Hengel zum 70. Geburtstag.* Bd. II: *Griechische und Römische Religion.* Tübingen: Mohr Siebeck.

Cancik-Lindemaier, H. 1996. "Der Diskurs Religion im Senatsbeschluß über die Bacchanalia von 186 v. Chr. und bei Livius (B. XXXIX)." In Cancik, Lichtenberger, and Schäfer 1996: 77–96.

Cardauns, B. 1976. *M. Terentius Varro, Antiquitates Rerum Divinarum.* Mainz: Akademie der Wissenschaften und der Literatur. 2 volumes.

Cardauns, B. 1978. "Varro und die römische Religion: zur Theologie, Wirkungsgeschichte und Leistung der 'Antiquitates Rerum Divinarum.'" *ANRW* 2.16.1.80–103.

de Cazanove, O. 2000a. "Some thoughts on the 'religious Romanization' of Italy before the Social War." In Bispham and Smith 2000: 71–6.

de Cazanove, O. 2000b. "I destinatari dell'iscrizione di Tiriolo e la questione del campo d'applicazione del senatoconsulto de bacchanalibus." *Athenaeum* 88, 59–68.

Chadwick, H. 2001. *The Church in Ancient Society: From Galilee to Gregory the Great.* Oxford: Oxford University Press.

Cracco Ruggini, L. 1980. "Nuclei immigrati e forze indigene in tre grandi centri commerciali dell'impero." In J. D'Arms and E. C. Kopf, eds, *The Seaborne Commerce of Ancient Rome.* Memoirs of the American Academy in Rome, 36. Rome: American Academy at Rome, 55–76.

Curran, J. 1994. "Moving statues in late antique Rome: problems of perspective." *Art History* 17, 46–58.

Degrassi, A. 1963. *Inscriptiones Italiae.* Vol. 13, pt 2: *Fasti anni Numani et Iuliani.* Rome: Libreria dello stato.

Demougin, S., ed. 1994. *La Mémoire Perdue: À la Recherche des Archives Oubliées, Publiques et Privées, de la Rome Antique.* CNRS – Série Histoire Ancienne et Médiévale, 30. Paris: Sorbonne.

Demougin, S., H. Devijver, and M.-Th. Raepsaet-Charlier, eds. 1999. *L'Ordre Équestre: Histoire d'une Aristocratie (IIe siècle av. J.-C.–IIIe Siècle ap. J.-C.).* Rome: École Française de Rome.

Derks, T. 1998. *Gods, Temples, and Ritual Practices: The Transformation of Religious Ideas and Values in Roman Gaul.* Amsterdam: Amsterdam University Press.

Dihle, A. 1996. "Die Theologia tripertita bei Augustin." In Cancik, Lichtenberger, and Schäfer 1996: 183–202.

Dirven, L. 1999. *The Palmyrenes of Dura-Europas: A Study of Religious Interaction in Roman Syria.* Leiden: Brill.

Dubourdieu, A. and J. Scheid. 2000. "Lieux de culte, lieux sacrés: les usage de la langue. L'Italie romaine." In A. Vauchez, ed., *Lieux Sacrés, Lieux de Culte, Sanctuaires: Approches Terminologiques, Méthodologiques, Historiques et Monographiques.* CÉFR, 273. Rome: École Française de Rome, 59–80.

Durand, J.-L. and J. Scheid. 1994. "'Rites' et 'religion': remarques sur certains préjugés des historiens de la religion des grecs et des romains." *Archives de Sciences Sociales des Religions* 85, 23–43.

Dyck, A. R. 1996. *A Commentary on Cicero, De Officiis.* Ann Arbor, MI: University of Michigan Press.

Dyck, A. R. 2003. *A Commentary on Cicero, De Legibus.* Ann Arbor, MI: University of Michigan Press.

Elsner, J. 1996. "Image and ritual: reflections on the religious appreciation of classical art." *CQ* 46, 513–31.

Estienne, S. 1997. "Statues de dieux 'isolées' et lieux de culte: l'exemple de Rome." *Cahiers Glotz* 8, 81–96.

Feeney, D. 1998. *Literature and Religion at Rome.* Cambridge: Cambridge University Press.

Fink, R. O., A. S. Hoey, and W. F. Snyder. 1940. "The Feriale Duranum." *Yale Classical Studies,* 7. New Haven, CT: Yale University Press.

Fishwick, D. 1987. *The Imperial Cult in the Latin West: Studies in the Ruler Cult of the Western Provinces of the Roman Empire.* 4 volumes in 2. Leiden: Brill.

Fishwick, D. 1989. "Numen Augusti." *Britannia* 20, 231–4.

Fishwick, D. 1990. "Votive offerings to the Emperor?" *ZPE* 80, 121–30.

Fishwick, D. 1994. "Numinibus Aug(ustorum)." *Britannia* 25, 127–41.

Frankfurter, D. 1998. *Religion in Roman Egypt: Assimilation and Resistance.* Princeton: Princeton University Press.

Frateantonio, C. 1997. "Autonomie in der Kaiserzeit und Spätantike." In

Cancik and Rüpke 1997: 85–97.

Frederiksen, P. 1986. "Paul and Augustine: conversion narratives, orthodox traditions, and the retrospective self." *JThS* 37, 3–34.

Gabba, E. 1984. "Dionigi, Varrone e la religione senza miti." *Rivista Storica Italiana* 96, 855–70.

Gargola, D. J. 1995. *Lands, Laws and Gods: Magistrates and Ceremony in the Regulation of Public Lands in Republican Rome.* Chapel Hill, NC: University of North Carolina Press.

Gladigow, B. 1985/6. "Präsenz der Bilder – Präsenz der Götter: Kultbilder und Bilder der Götter in der griechischen Religion." *Visible Religion* 4/5, 114–33.

Gladigow, B. 1990. "Epiphanie, Statuette, Kultbild: Griechische Gottesvorstellungen im Wechsel von Kontext und Medium." *Visible Religion* 7, 98–121.

Gladigow, B. 1994. "Zur Ikonographie und Pragmatik römischer Kultbilder." In H. Keller and N. Staubach, eds, *Iconologia Sacra: Mythos, Bildkunst und Dichtung in der Religions- und Sozialgeschichte Alteuropas. Festschrift für Karl Hauck.* Berlin: de Gruyter, 9–24.

Gordon, R. 1979. "Production and religion in the Graeco-Roman world." *Art History* 2, 5–34.

Gordon, R. 1987. "Aelian's peony: the location of magic in Graeco-Roman tradition." *Comparative Criticism* 9, 59–95.

Gordon, R. 1990a. "From Republic to Principate: priesthood, religion and ideology." In Beard and North, 1990: 179–98.

Gordon, R. 1990b. "Religion in the Roman empire: the civic compromise and its limits." In Beard and North 1990: 235–55.

Gordon, R. 1990c. "The veil of power: emperors, sacrificers and benefactors." In Beard and North 1990: 201–31.

Gordon, R. 1999. "Imagining Greek and Roman magic." In Ankarloo and Clark 1999: 159–275.

Graf, F., ed. 1993a. *Mythos in mythenloser Gesellschaft: Das Paradigma Roms.* Stuttgart: Teubner.

Graf, F. 1993b. "Der Mythos bei den Römern: Forschungs- und Problemgeschichte." In Graf 1993a: 25–43.

Griffin, M. and J. Barnes, eds. 1989. *Philosophia Togata.* Oxford: Clarendon Press.

Gros, P. 1976. *Aurea Templa: Recherches sur l'Architecture Religieuse de Rome à l'Epoque d'Auguste.* Rome: École Française de Rome.

Gros, P. 1996. *L'Architecture Romaine. 1: Les Monuments Publics.* Paris: Picard.

Habinek, T. 1998. *The Politics of Latin Literature.* Princeton, NJ: Princeton University Press.

Herbert-Brown, G. 1994. *Ovid and the Fasti: An Historical Study.* Oxford: Clarendon Press.

Hoffman, Lewis, M. W. 1955. *The Official Priests of Rome under the Julio-*

Claudians. Papers and Monographs of the American Academy in Rome, 16. Rome: American Academy in Rome.

Horsfall, N. 2000. *Virgil, Aeneid 7: A Commentary*. Leiden: Brill.

Horsfall, N. and J. Bremmer. 1987. *Roman Myth and Mythography*. London: Institute of Classical Studies.

Husson, G. 1997. "Les questions oraculaires chrétiennes d'Égypte: continuités et changements." In B. Kramer, W. Luppe, and H. Maehler, eds, *Akten des 21. internationalen Papyrologenkongresses, Berlin 1995*. Archiv für Papyrusforschung, 3. Leipzig: Teubner, 482–9.

Jocelyn, H. D. 1966. "The Roman nobility and the religion of the Republican state." *Journal of Religious History* 4, 89–106.

Jocelyn, H. D. 1982. "Varro's *Antiquitates Rerum Divinarum* and religious affairs in the late Roman republic." *Bulletin of the John Rylands University Library of Manchester* 65, 148–205.

Kallet-Marx, R. M. 1995. *From Hegemony to Empire: The Development of the Roman Imperium in the East from 148 to 62 BC*. Berkeley: University of California Press.

Kantorowicz, E. 1965. *Selected Studies*. Locust Valley, NY: Augustin.

Kellum, B. A. 1990. "The city adorned: programmatic display at the *Aedes Concordiae Augustae*." In K. A. Raaflaub and M. Toher, eds, *Between Republic and Empire*. Berkeley: University of California Press, 276–96.

Koch, C. 1960. *Religio: Studien zu Kult und Glauben der Römer*. Nürnberg: Verlag Hans Carl.

Krause, J.-W., J. Mylonopoulos, and R. Cengia. 1998. *Schichten, Konflikte, religiöse Gruppen, materielle Kultur*. G. Alföldy, *Bibliographie zur römischen Sozialgeschichte*, 2. Stuttgart: Steiner.

Lane Fox, R. 1987. *Pagans and Christians*. New York: Knopf.

Latte, K. 1960. *Römische Religionsgeschichte*. Munich: C. H. Beck.

Lenel, O. 1889. *Palingenesia Iuris Civilis*. Leipzig: Tauchnitz.

Lieberg, G. 1973. "Die Theologia Tripartita in Forschung und Bezeugnung." *ANRW* 1.4.63–115.

Lieberg, G. 1982. "Die Theologia tripertita als Formprinzip antiken Denkens." *RhM* 126, 25–53.

Liebeschuetz, J. H. W. G. 1979. *Continuity and Change in Roman Religion*. Oxford: Clarendon Press.

Lincoln, B. 1999. *Theorizing Myth: Narrative, Ideology, and Scholarship*. Chicago: University of Chicago Press.

Linder, M. and J. Scheid. 1993. "Quand croire c'est faire: le problème de la croyance dans la Rome ancienne." *Archives de sciences sociales des religions* 81, 47–62.

Linderski, J. 1982. "Cicero and divination." *Parola del Passato* 202, 12–38.

Linderski, J. 1986. "The augural law." *ANRW* 2.16.3.2146–2312.

Linderski, J. 2000. "Religio et cultus deorum." Review of Beard, North, and Price 1998. *JRA* 13, 453–63.

MacCormack, S. 1981. *Art and Ceremony in Late Antiquity*. Berkeley:

University of California Press.

MacCormack, S. 1998. *The Shadows of Poetry: Vergil in the Mind of Augustine*. Berkeley: University of California Press.

MacMullen, R. 1966. *Enemies of the Roman Order: Treason, Unrest, and Alienation in the Empire*. Cambridge, MA: Harvard University Press.

MacMullen, R. 1981. *Paganism in the Roman Empire*. New Haven, CT: Yale University Press.

MacMullen, R. 1990. *Changes in the Roman Empire: Essays in the Ordinary*. Princeton, NJ: Princeton University Press.

MacMullen, R. 1993. "The unromanized in Rome." In S. J. D. Cohen and E. S. Frerichs, eds, *Diasporas in Antiquity*. Brown Judaic Studies, 288. Atlanta: Scholars Press, 47–64.

Magdelain, A. 1968. *Recherches sur l'"Imperium": La Loi Curiate et les Auspices d'Investiture*. Paris: Presses Universitaires de France.

Magdelain, A. 1986. "Le *ius* archaïque." *MÉFRA* 98.1, 265–358.

Magdelain, A. 1990. *Jus Imperium Auctoritas: Études de Droit Romain*. CÉFR, 133. Rome: École Française de Rome.

Mandouze, A. 1958. "Saint Augustin et la religion romaine." *Recherches Augustiniennes* 1, 187–223.

Michels, A. K. 1962. Review of Latte 1960. *AJPh* 83, 434–44.

Michels, A. K. 1967. *The Calendar of the Roman Republic*. Princeton, NJ: Princeton University Press.

Michels, A. K. 1976. "The versatility of *religio*." In *The Mediterranean World: Papers Presented in Honour of Gilbert Bagnani, April 26, 1975*. Peterborough, Ont.: Trent University.

Mikalson, J. 1998. *Religion in Hellenistic Athens*. Berkeley: University of California Press.

Millar, F. 2002. *Rome, the Greek World, and the East*. Vol. 1: *The Roman Republic and the Augustan Revolution*. Chapel Hill, NC: University of North Carolina Press.

Mitchell, S. 1993. *Anatolia: Land, Men, and Gods in Asia Minor*. Oxford: Clarendon Press, 2 volumes.

Moatti, C. 1997. *La Raison de Rome: Naissance de l'Esprit Critique à la Fin de la République*. Paris: Seuil.

Moatti, C., ed. 1998. *La Mémoire Perdue: Recherches sur l'Administration Romaine*. CÉFR 243. Rome: École Française de Rome.

Momigliano, A. 1987. *On Pagans, Jews, and Christians*. Middletown, CT: Wesleyan University Press.

Mommsen, T. 1887. *Römisches Staatsrecht*. Leipzig: S. Hirzel. 3rd edn. 3 volumes in 5.

Muth, R. 1978. "Von Wesen römischer 'religio.'" *ANRW* 2.16.1.290–354.

Muth, R. 1988. *Einführung in die griechische und römische Religion*. Darmstadt: Wissenschaftliche Buchgesellschaft.

Newlands, C. 1995. *Playing with Time: Ovid and the Fasti*. Ithaca, NY: Cornell University Press.

Nisbet, R. G. 1939. *M. Tulli Ciceronis De Domo sua ad Pontifices Oratio*. Oxford: Clarendon Press.

Nock, A. D. 1933. *Conversion: The Old and the New in Religion from Alexander the Great to Augustine of Hippo*. Oxford: Clarendon Press.

Nock, A. D. 1972. *Essays on Religion and the Ancient World*. Ed. Z. Stewart. Oxford: Clarendon Press.

Norden, E. 1939. *Aus altrömischen Priesterbüchern*. Lund: Gleerup.

North, J. 1992. "The development of religious pluralism." In J. Lieu, J. North, and T. Rajak., eds, *The Jews among Pagans and Christians in the Roman Empire*. London: Routledge, 174–93.

North, J. 1998. "The books of the *pontifices*." In Moatti 1998: 45–63.

North, J. 2000. *Roman Religion*. Greece and Rome, 30. Oxford: Oxford University Press.

O'Daly, G. 1999. *Augustine's City of God: A Reader's Guide*. Oxford: Clarendon Press.

Ogilvie, R. M. 1965. *A Commentary on Livy Books 1–5*. Oxford: Clarendon Press.

Ogilvie, R. M. 1969. *The Romans and their Gods in the Age of Augustus*. London: Chatto and Windus.

Orlin, E. M. 1997. *Temples, Religion and Politics in the Roman Republic*. Leiden: Brill.

Parke, H. W. 1988. *Sibyls and Sibylline Prophecy in Classical Antiquity*. New York: Routledge.

Parker, R. 1996. *Athenian Religion: A History*. Oxford: Clarendon Press.

Pease, A. S. 1955. *Marcus Tullius Cicero, De Natura Deorum*. Cambridge, MA: Harvard University, 1955. 2 volumes.

Pease, A. S. 1963. *M. Tulli Ciceronis De Divinatione Libri Duo*. Darmstadt: Wissenschaftliche Buchgesellschaft. Repr. New York: Arno, 1979.

Pépin, J. 1956. "La théologie tripartite de Varron." *Rev. Ét Aug.* 2, 265–94.

Pighi, G. B. 1965. *De Ludis Saecularibus Populi Romani Quiritium Libri Sex*. Amsterdam: Schippers.

Potter, D. S. 1990. *Prophecy and History in the Crisis of the Roman Empire*. Oxford: Clarendon Press.

Potter, D. S. 1994. *Prophets and Emperors: Human and Divine Authority from Augustus to Theodosius*. Cambridge, MA: Harvard University Press.

Potter, D. S. 1999. "Roman religion: ideas and actions." In D. S. Potter and D. J. Mattingly, eds, *Life, Death, and Entertainment in the Roman Empire*. Ann Arbor, MI: University of Michigan Press, 113–67.

Price, S. 1984. *Rituals and Power: The Roman Imperial Cult in Asia Minor*. Cambridge: Cambridge University Press.

Rawson, E. 1973. "Scipio, Laelius, Furius, and the ancestral religion." *JRS* 63, 161–74.

Rawson, E. 1974. "Religion and politics in the late second century BC at Rome." *Phoenix* 28, 193–212.

Rawson, E. 1991. *Roman Culture and Society.* Oxford: Clarendon Press.

Richlin, A. 1997. "Carrying water in a sieve: class and the body in Roman women's religion." In K. King, ed., *Women and Goddess Traditions in Antiquity and Today.* Minneapolis: Fortress, 330–74.

Rives, J. B. 1995. *Religion and Authority in Roman Carthage.* Oxford: Clarendon Press.

Rives, J. B. 1998. "Roman religion revived." *Phoenix* 52.3–4, 345–65.

Rives, J. B. 1999. "The decree of Decius and the religion of the empire." *JRS* 89, 135–54.

Rohde, G. 1936. *Die Kultsatzungen der römischen Pontifices.* Berlin: Töpelmann.

Roller, M. B. 2001. *Constructing autocracy: Aristocrats and Emperors in Julio-Claudian Rome.* Princeton, NJ: Princeton University Press.

Roloff, K.-H. 1954. "Ritus." *Glotta* 33, 36–65.

Rose, H. J. 1960. "Roman religion 1910–1960." *JRS* 50, 161–72.

Rosenstein, N. 1990. *Imperatores Victi: Military Defeat and Aristocratic Competition in the Middle and Late Republic.* Berkeley: University of California Press.

Rüpke, J. 1990. *Domi Militiae: Die Religiöse Konstruktion des Krieges in Rom.* Stuttgart: Steiner.

Rüpke, J. 1995. *Kalendar und Öffentlichkeit: Die Geschichte der Repräsentation und religiösen Qualifikation von Zeit in Rom.* Berlin: de Gruyter.

Rüpke, J. 1996a. "Nundinae: Kalendarische Koordination im republikanischen Rom." In G. Binder and K. Ehrlich, eds, *Kommunikation in politischen und kultischen Gemeinschaften.* Stätten und Formen der Kommunikation im Altertum, 5. Trier: Wissenschaftliche Verlag Trier, 75–98.

Rüpke, J. 1996b. "Controllers and professionals: analyzing religious specialists." *Numen* 43, 241–61.

Rüpke, J. 1996c. "Innovationsmechanismen kultischer Religionen: Sakralrecht im Rom der Republik." In Cancik, Lichtenberger, and Schäfer 1996: 265–85.

Rüpke, J. 1997. "Religion und Krieg: Zur Verhältnisbestimmung religiöser und politischer Systeme einer Gesellschaft." In R. Faber, ed., *Politische Religion – religiöse Politik.* Würzburg: Königshausen und Neumann, 309–28.

Rüpke, J. 1999. "Antike Großstadtreligion." In Batsch, Egelhaaf-Gaiser, and Stepper 1999: 13–30.

Rüpke, J. 2001a. "Polytheismus und Pluralismus." In A. Gotzmann, V. N. Makrides, J. Malik, and J. Rüpke, eds, *Pluralismus in der europäischen Religionsgeschichte.* Marburg: Diagonal, 17–34.

Rüpke, J. 2001b. "Religiöse Kommunikation im provinzialen Raum." In W. Spickermann, ed., *Religion in der germanischen Provinzen Roms.*

Tübingen: Mohr Siebeck, 71–88.

Sachot, M. 1991. "'Religio/superstitio': historique d'une subversion et d'un retournement." *RHR* 208, 355–94.

Scheid, J. 1978. "Les prêtres officiels sous les empereurs julio-claudiens." *ANRW* 2.16.1.610–54.

Scheid, J. 1981. "Le délit religieux dans la Rome tardo-républicaine." *Le Délit Religieux dans la Cité Antique*. CÉFR, 48. Rome: École Française de Rome, 117–69.

Scheid, J. 1984. "Le prêtre et le magistrat: réflexions sur les sacerdoces et le droit public à la fin de la République." In C. Nicolet, ed., *Des ordres à Rome*. Paris: Publications de la Sorbonne, 243–80.

Scheid, J. 1985a. *Religion et Piété à Rome*. Paris: Decouverte.

Scheid, J. 1985b. "Numa et Jupiter ou les dieux citoyens de Rome." *Archives de Sciences Sociales des Religions* 59.1, 41–53.

Scheid, J. 1987. "Polytheism impossible; or, the empty gods: reasons behind a void in the history of Roman religions." *History and anthropology* 3, 303–25.

Scheid, J. 1987/9. "La parole des dieux: l'originalité du dialogue des romains avec leurs dieux." *Opus* 6–8, 125–36.

Scheid, J. 1988. "L'impossible polytheisme: les raisons d'un vide dans l'histoire de la religion romaine." In F. Schmidt, ed., *L'Impensable Polythéisme. Études d'Historiographie Religieuse*. Paris: Éditions des Archives Contemporaines, 425–57.

Scheid, J. 1989/90. "'Hoc anno immolatum non est': les aléas de la *voti sponsio*." *Scienze dell'Antichità. Storia Archeologia Antropologia* 3–4, 773–83.

Scheid, J. 1990a. *Romulus et ses Frères: Le Collège des Frères Arvales, Modèle du Culte Public dans la Rome des Empereurs*. BÉFAR, 275. Rome: École Française de Rome.

Scheid, J. 1990b. "Rituel et écriture à Rome." In A.-M. Blondeau and K. Schipper, eds, *Essais sur le Rituel II*. Bibliothèque de l'École des Hautes Études, Section des Sciences Religieuses, 95. Paris and Louvain: Peeters, 1–15.

Scheid, J. 1993a. "Cultes, mythes et politique au début de l'Empire." In Graf 1993a: 109–27.

Scheid, J. 1993b. "The priest." In A. Giardina, ed., *The Romans*. Trans. L. G. Cochrane. Chicago: University of Chicago Press, 55–84.

Scheid, J. 1994. "Les archives de la piété." In Demougin 1994: 173–85.

Scheid, J. 1995a. "Les espaces cultuels et leur interprétation." *Klio* 77, 424–32.

Scheid, J. 1995b. "*Graeco ritu*: a typically Roman way of honoring the gods." *HSCP* 97, 15–31.

Scheid, J. 1996. "Pline le jeune et les sanctuaires d'Italie: observations sur les lettres IV, 1, VII, 8 et IX, 39." In A. Chastagnol, S. Demougin, and

C. Lepelley, eds, *Splendidissima Civitas: Études d'Histoire Romaine en Hommage à François Jacques*. Paris: Publications de la Sorbonne, 241–58.

Scheid, J. 1998a. *La Religion des Romains*. Paris: Armand Colin.

Scheid, J. 1998b. "Les livres Sibyllins et les archives des quindécemvirs." In Moatti 1998: 11–26.

Scheid, J. 1998c. "Nouveau rite et nouvelle piété: réflexions sur le ritus Graecus." In F. Graf, ed., *Ansichten griechischer Rituale*. Stuttgart: Teubner, 168–82.

Scheid, J. 1998d. *Commentarii Fratrum Arvalium qui Supersunt: Les Copies Épigraphiques des Protocoles Annuels de la Confrérie Arvale, 21 av.–304 ap. J.-C.* Rome: École Française de Rome.

Scheid, J. 1999a. "Aspects religieux de la municipalisation: quelques réflexions générales." In M. Dondin-Payre and M.-T. Raepsaet-Charlier, eds, *Cités, Municipes, Colonies: Les Processus de Municipalisation en Gaule et en Germanie sous le Haut Empire Romain*. Paris: Publications de la Sorbonne, 381–423.

Scheid, J. 1999b. "Hiérarchie et structure dans le polythéisme romain: façons romaines de penser l'action." *Archiv für Religionsgeschichte* 1.2, 184–203.

Scheid, J. 1999c. "'Livres' sacerdotaux et érudition: l'exemple des chapelles des Argées." In Batsch, Egelhaaf-Gaiser, and Stepper 1999: 161–70.

Scheid, J. and M. G. Granino Cecere. 1999. "Les sacerdoces publics équestres." In Demougin, Devijver, and Raepsaet-Charlier 1999: 79–189.

Scheid, J. and J. Svenbro. 1989–90. "Carmen, speech act, rituel." *Annuaire de l'École Pratique des Hautes Études, Section Sciences Religieuses* 98, 327–33.

Scheid, J. and J. Svenbro. 1997. "Le comparatisme, point de départ ou point d'arrivée?" F. Boespflug and F. Dunant, eds, *Le Comparatisme en Histoire des Religions*. Paris: Cerfs, 295–312.

Schilling, R. 1979. *Rites, Cultes, Dieux de Rome*. Paris: Klincksieck.

Scullard, H. H. 1981. *Festivals and Ceremonies of the Roman Republic*. Ithaca, NY: Cornell University Press.

Sedley, D. 1989. "Philosophical allegiance in the Greco-Roman world." In Griffin and Barnes 1989: 97–119.

Sherk, R. K. 1984. *Rome and the Greek East to the Death of Augustus*. Cambridge: Cambridge University Press.

Smith, J. Z. 1978a. *Map is Not Territory: Studies in the History of Religions*. Studies in Judaism in Late Antiquity, 23. Leiden: Brill.

Smith, J. Z. 1978b. "Towards interpreting demonic powers in Hellenistic and Roman antiquity." *ANRW* 2.16.1.425–39.

Smith, J. Z. 1990. *Drudgery Divine: On the Comparison of Early Christianities and the Religions of Late Antiquity*. Chicago: University of Chicago Press.

Smith, J. Z. 1995. "Trading places." In M. Meyer and P. Mirecki, eds, *Ancient Magic and Ritual Power*. Leiden: Brill, 13–27.

Stambaugh, J. E. 1978. "The functions of Roman temples." *ANRW* 2.16.1.554–608.

Tatum, W. J. 1999. "Roman religion: fragments and further questions." In S. N. Byrne and E. P. Cueva, eds, *Veritatis Amicitiaeque Causa: Essays in Honor of Anna Lydia Motto and John R. Clark*. Wauconda, IL: Bolchazy-Carducci, 273–91.

Taylor, L. R. 1949. *Party Politics in the Age of Caesar*. Berkeley: University of California Press.

Thomas, Y. 1988. "Sanctio: les défenses de la loi." *Écrit du Temps* 19, 61–84.

Toynbee, A. J. 1965. *Hannibal's Legacy*. Oxford: Oxford University Press. 2 volumes.

Turcan, R. 1988. *Religion Romaine*. Iconography of Religions, Section XVII: Greece and Rome. Fasc. 1. Part 1: Les dieux. Part 2: Le Culte. Leiden: Brill.

von Ungern-Sternberg, J. 1993. "Romulus-Bilder: Die Begründung der Republik im Mythos." In Graf 1993a: 88–108.

Vaahtera, J. E. 2000. "Roman religion and the Polybian *politeia*." In Bruun 2000: 251–64.

Vaahtera, J. 2002. "Livy and the priestly records: à propos *ILS* 9338." *Hermes* 130, 100–8.

Versnel, H. S. 1990, 1993. *Inconsistencies in Greek and Roman Religion*. Leiden: Brill. 2 volumes.

Warde Fowler, W. 1911. *The Religious Experience of the Roman People, from the Earliest Times to the Age of Augustus*. London: Macmillan.

Waszink, J. H. and J. C. M. van Winden. 1987. *Tertullianus De Idololatria*. Leiden: Brill.

Weinstock, S. 1961. Review of Latte 1960. *JRS* 51, 206–15.

Weinstock, S. 1971. *Divus Julius*. Oxford: Clarendon Press.

Wiseman, T. P. 1984. "Cybele, Virgil and Augustus." In A. J. Woodman and D. West, eds, *Poetry and Politics in the Age of Augustus*. Cambridge: Cambridge University Press, 117–28.

Wiseman, T. P. 1994. *Historiography and Imagination: Eight Essays on Roman Culture*. Exeter: University of Exeter Press.

Wiseman, T. P. 1995. *Remus: A Roman Myth*. Cambridge: Cambridge University Press.

Wiseman, T. P. 1998. *Roman Drama and Roman History*. Exeter: University of Exeter Press.

Wiseman, T. P. 2000. "Liber: myth, drama and ideology in Republican Rome." In Bruun 2000: 265–99.

Wiseman, T. P. 2002. "History, poetry, and *Annales*." In D. S. Levene and D. P. Nelis, eds, *Clio and the Poets: Augustan Poetry and the Traditions of Ancient Historiography*. Leiden: Brill, 331–61.

Wissowa, G. 1904. *Gesammelte Abhandlungen zur romischen Religions- und Stadtgeschichte*. Munich: Beck.

Wissowa, G. 1912. *Religion und Kultus der Römer*. Munich: C. H. Beck. 2nd edition.

Wissowa, G. 1916/19. "Interpretatio Romana: Römische Götter im Barbarenlande." *Archiv für Religionswissenschaft* 19, 1–49.

Woolf, G. 1997. "Polis-religion and its alternatives in the Roman provinces." In Cancik and Rüpke 1997: 71–84.

Woolf, G. 1998. *Becoming Roman: The Origins of Provincial Civilization in Gaul*. Cambridge: Cambridge University Press.

Woolf, G. 2000. "The religious history of the northwest provinces." Review of Derks 1998. *JRA* 13, 615–30.

Woolf, G. 2001. "Representation as cult: the case of the Jupiter columns." In W. Spickermann, ed., *Religion in der germanischen Provinzen Roms*. Tübingen: Mohr Siebeck, 117–34.

Ziolkowski, A. 1992. *The Temples of Mid-Republican Rome and their Historical and Topographical Context*. Rome: "L'Erma" di Bret- schneider.

de Zulueta, F. 1946, 1953. *The Institutes of Gaius*. Oxford: Clarendon Press. 2 volumes.

Index